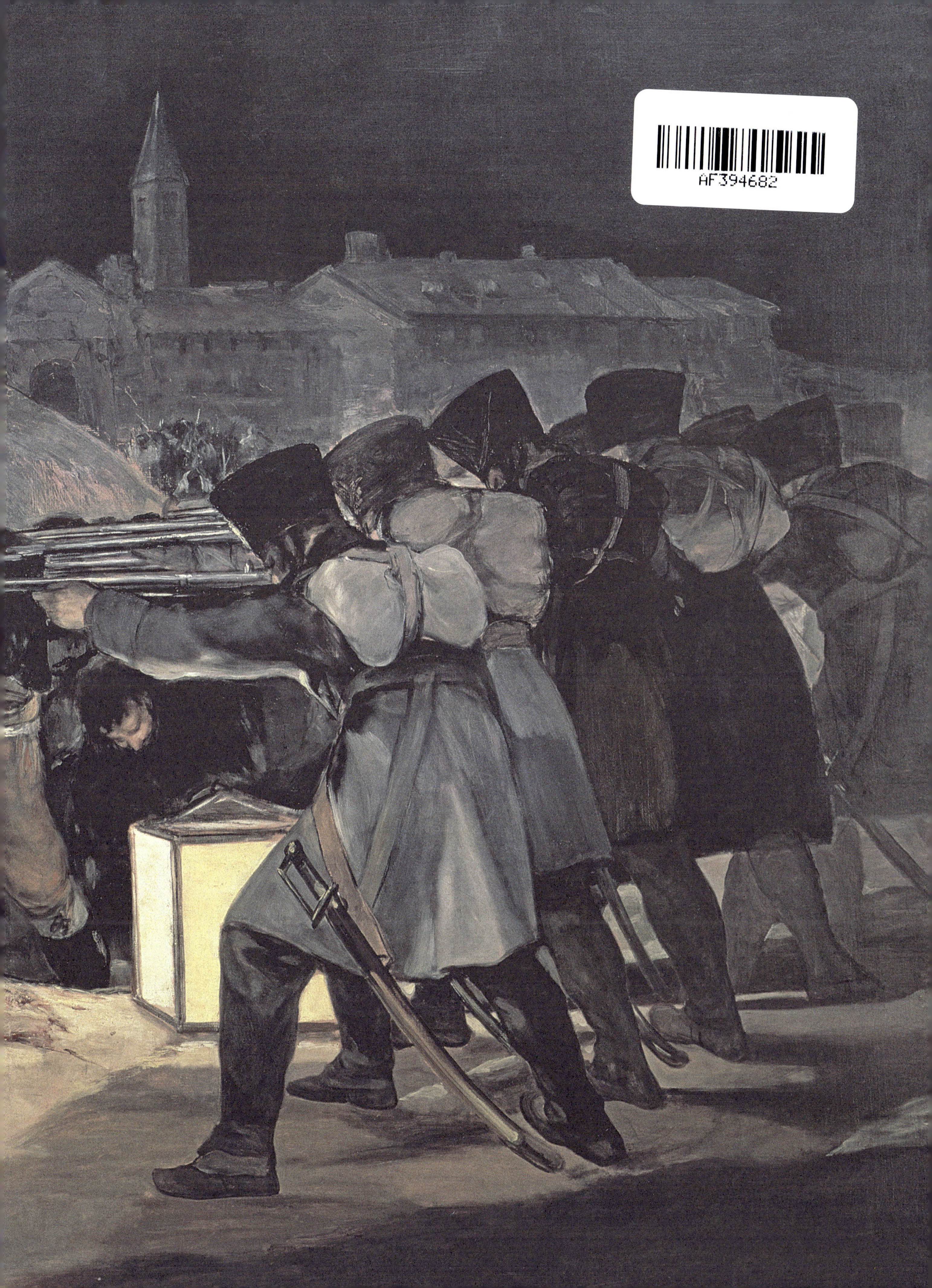

GOYA

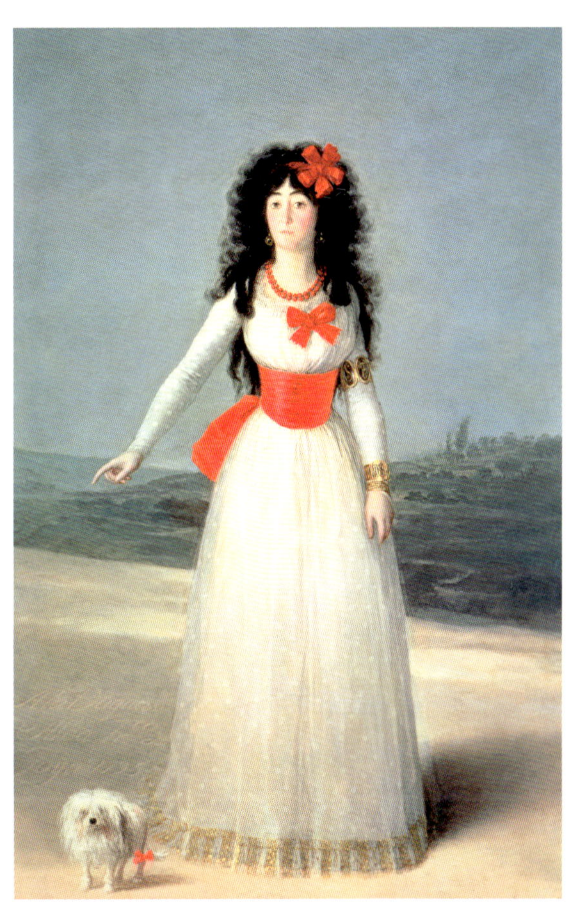

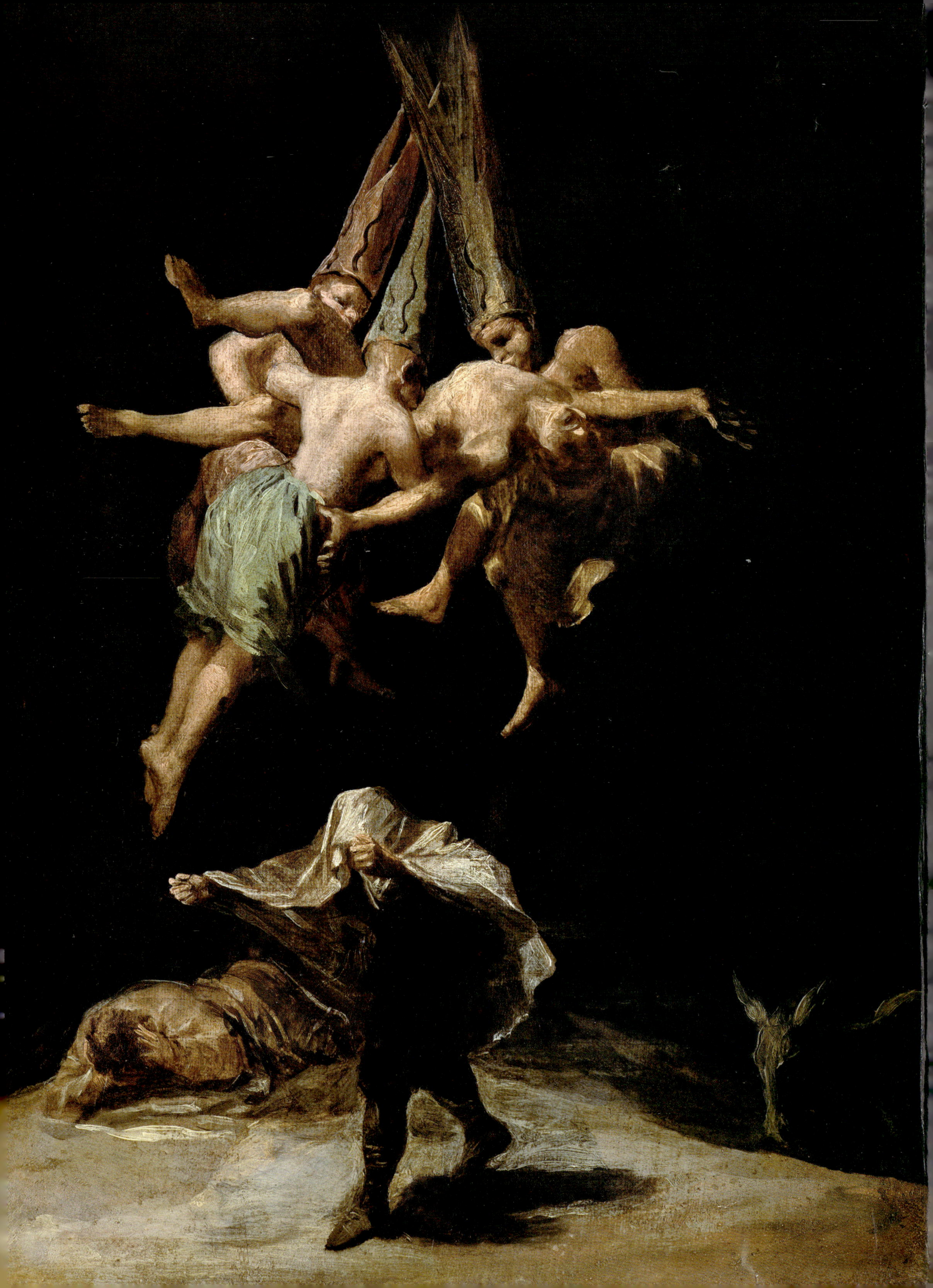

GOYA

HIS LIFE AND WORKS IN 500 IMAGES

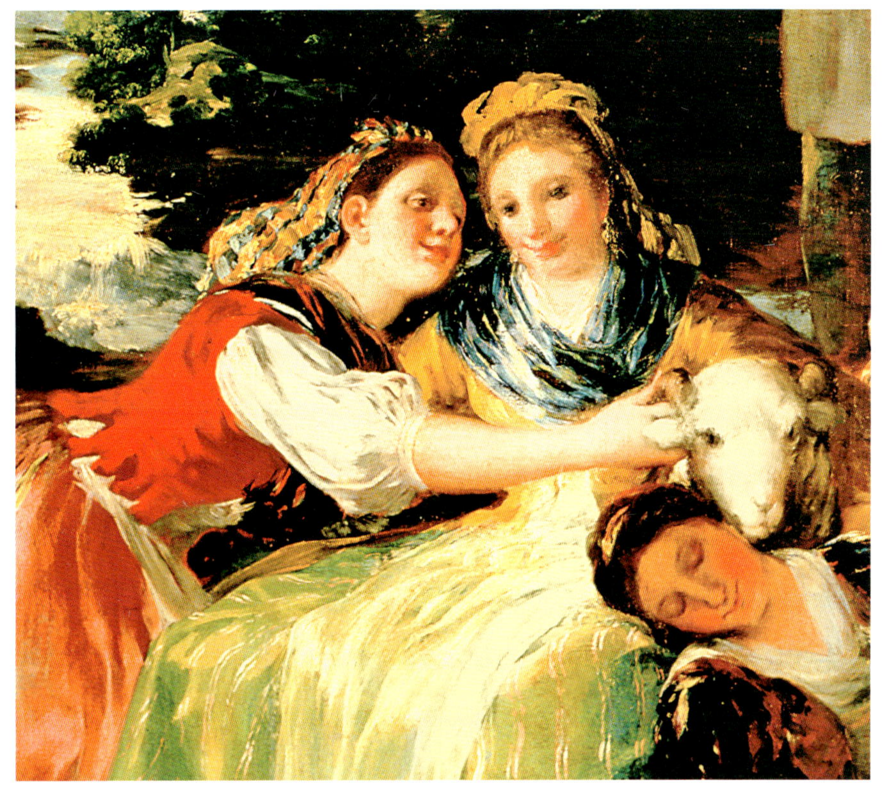

AN ILLUSTRATED ACCOUNT OF THE ARTIST, HIS LIFE AND
CONTEXT, WITH A GALLERY OF 300 PAINTINGS AND DRAWINGS

SUSIE HODGE

LORENZ BOOKS

This edition is published by Lorenz Books
an imprint of Anness Publishing Ltd
info@anness.com
www.lorenzbooks.com
www.annesspublishing.com

Publisher: Joanna Lorenz
Project Editor: Joy Wotton
Designer: Nigel Partridge
Production: Ben Worley

Page 1: *The Duchess of Alba,* 1795.
Page 2: *The Witches' Flight,* 1797–8.
Page 3: *Washerwomen,* 1779–80.
Below: *Self-portrait in the Studio, c.*1790–5.
Opposite (left): *Charles IV,* 1789.
Opposite (middle): *Autumn* or *The Grape Harvest,* 1786.
Opposite (right): *The Second of May 1808,* 1814.

PUBLISHER'S NOTE

Although the information in this book is believed
to be accurate and true at the time of going to press,
neither the authors nor the publisher can accept
any legal responsibility or liability for any errors or
omissions that may have been made.

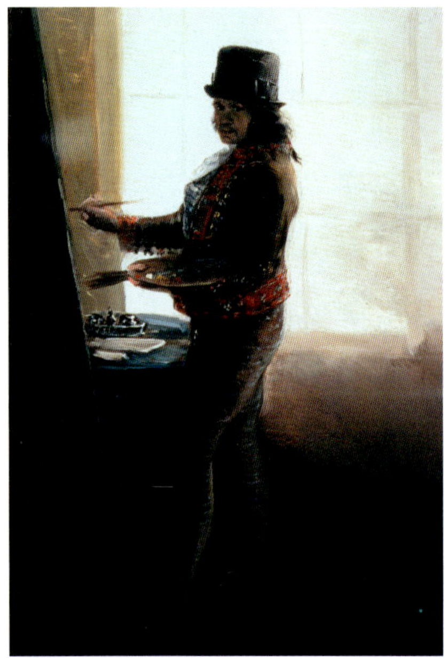

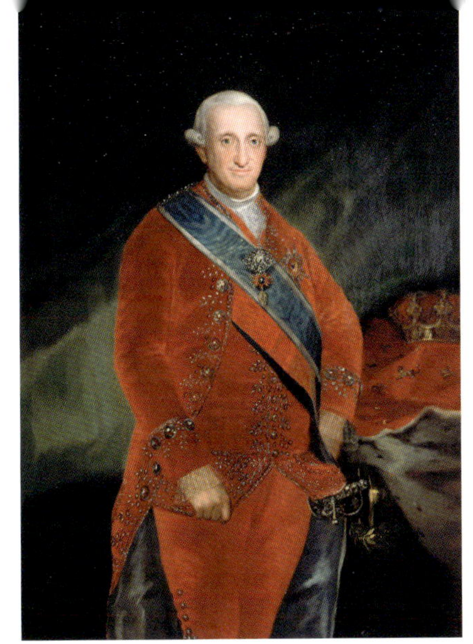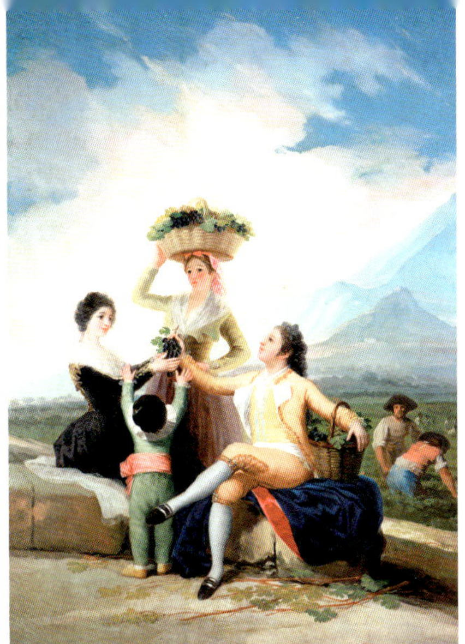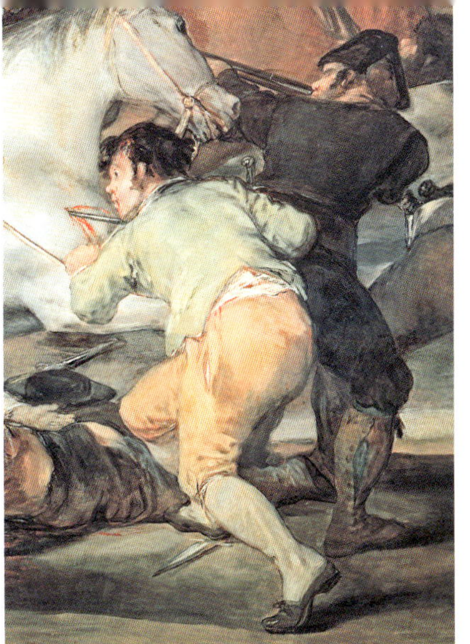

CONTENTS

INTRODUCTION

Through art that encapsulated the turbulence of late 18th- and early 19th-century Spain, Goya became known as the last Old Master and the first of the great moderns. From royal portraits to bizarre, grotesque illustrations, his legacy shows a tortured genius, generating some of the most compelling art ever seen.

When Francisco de Goya was born in 1746, Spain's Golden Age had been over for almost 100 years. Goya lived through a time of revolution and dramatic changes in thought, knowledge and behaviour, and his insightful gaze sought new ways of portraying human experience, both as he observed it, and as his astute imagination and skill interpreted it.

TURMOIL AND DISORDER

The Spanish king Philip V (1683–1746) was French by birth, and so naturally affiliated with France in diplomatic relations. After the War of Spanish Succession, in 1715, Philip changed much of Spain's constitution by unifying most of the traditionally held rights and privileges of the different kingdoms that formed the country. Philip was succeeded by one son, Ferdinand VI (r.1746–59) and then another, Charles III (r.1759–88), who both continued making reforms, and Spain began to

Below: Juan Bautista Martínez del Mazo (c.1612–67), View of Saragossa, *1647 – painted just over 100 years before Goya grew up there.*

experience prosperity and confidence once more. However, Charles III's son, Charles IV, who ruled from 1788 to 1808, brought this progress to an uncomfortable halt and reversed many of the reforms instigated by his forbears. Believed to be mentally handicapped, Charles IV was dominated by his wife's favourite, Manuel de Godoy (1767–1851). His vacillating actions eventually led to his enforced abdication and his son Ferdinand VII took the throne.

Taking advantage of the dissensions within the Spanish court, the French emperor Napoleon I invaded in the spring of 1808, and within months he had deposed the Bourbon kings and established his eldest brother Joseph as King of Spain. The citizens of Madrid rose up in rebellion against French occupation, and across the country insurrections broke out, initiating the Peninsular War.

Eventually in 1813, Ferdinand VII was restored as king, but severe damage had been wrought on the country's economy and Spain and its colonies continued to suffer in the political turbulence that followed.

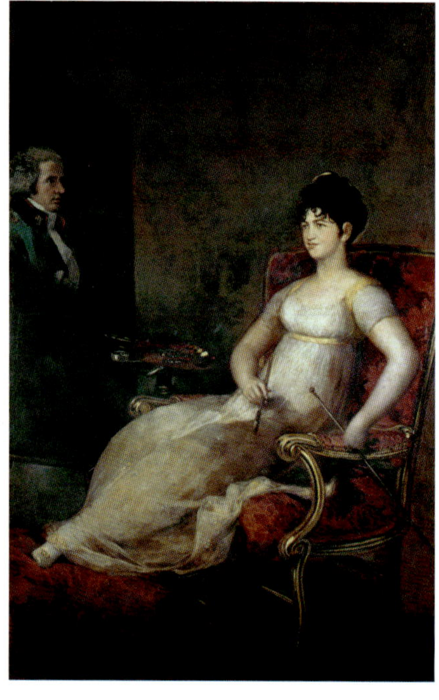

Above: Painted in 1805 by Goya, The Marchioness of Villafranca *was also an artist as well as his patron and friend.*

CROSSING BOUNDARIES

Amid all these disturbances, Goya grew up, became Court Painter to several of the kings and established himself as

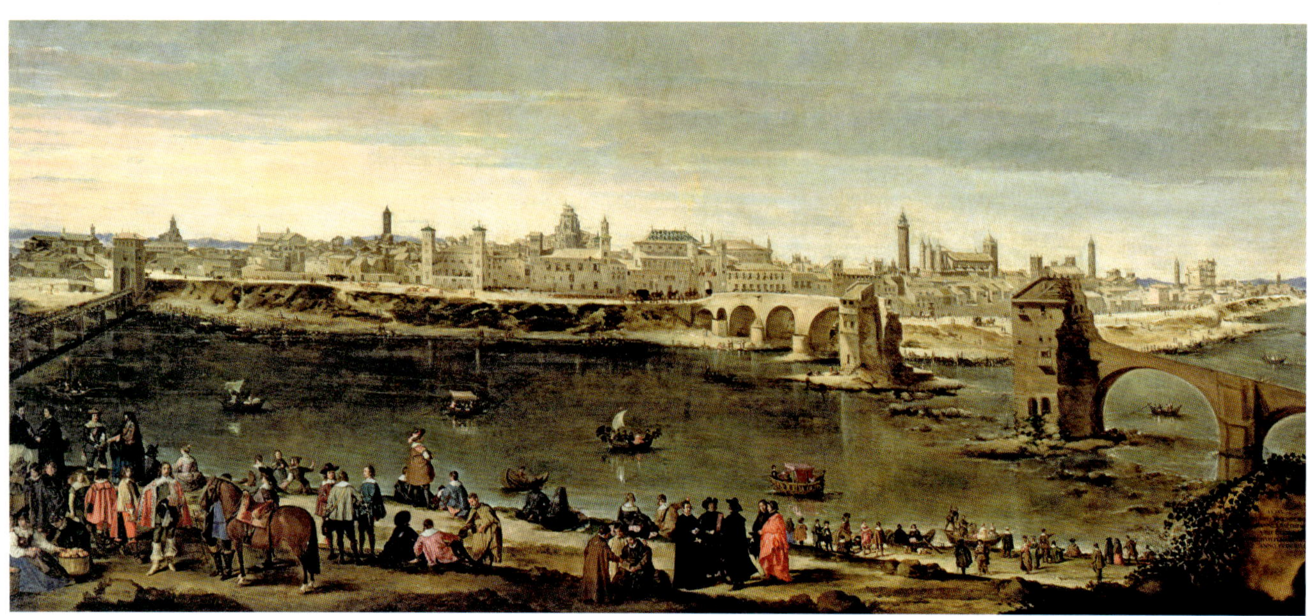

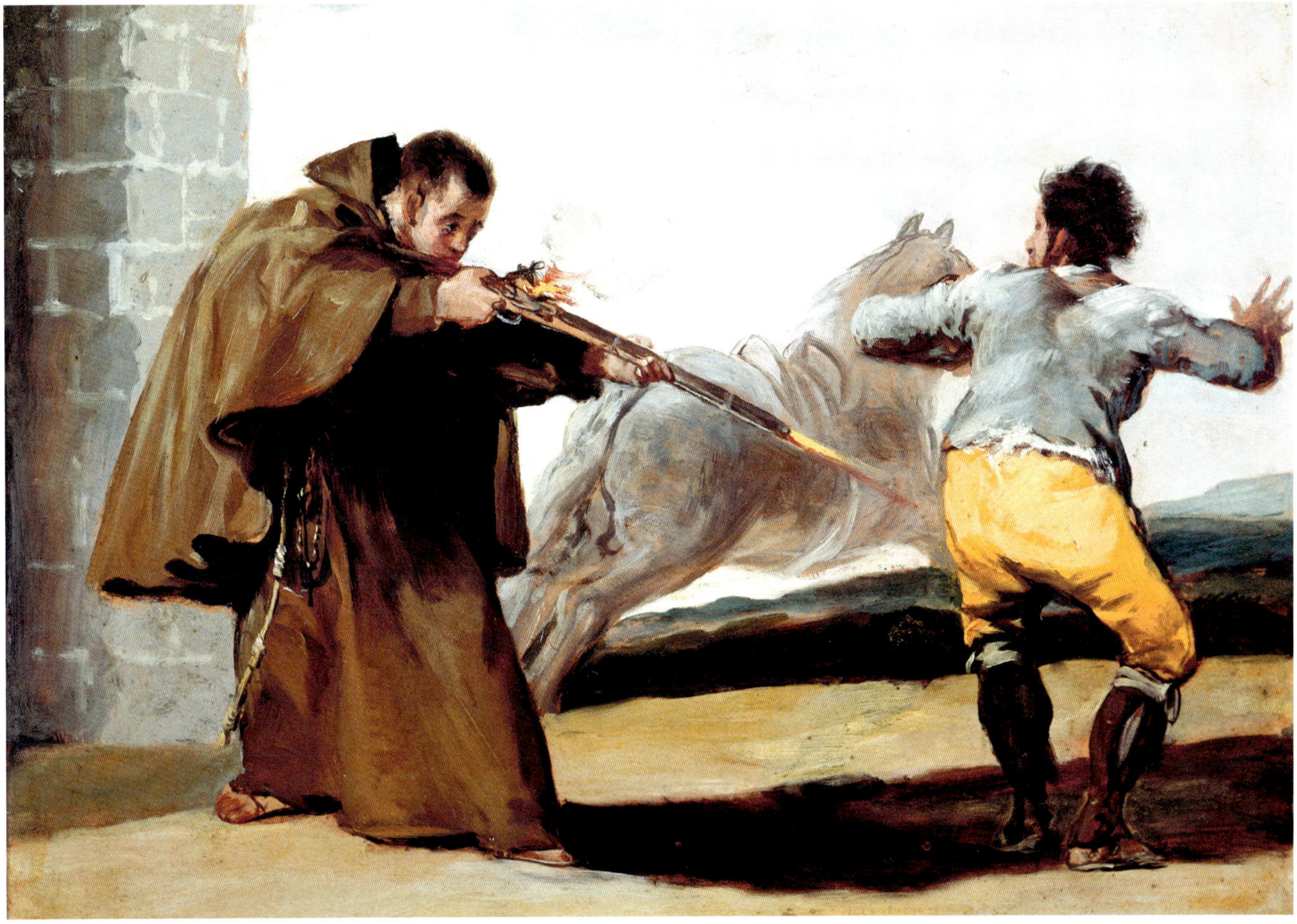

Above: Friar Pedro Shoots El Maragato as His Horse Runs Off, *1806–7 – Goya records the true-life event of a monk capturing a bandit (see also pages 212–13).*

the greatest artist in the land. From fairly humble beginnings, he became exceptionally wealthy, influential and highly valued, and his artistic innovations brought Spanish art to the notice of the world. Always ahead of his time, he is classed as one of the first Romantic artists, and over his long career, he produced hundreds of paintings, etchings and drawings, for tapestries, churches, private houses and palaces. He crossed previously accepted boundaries, being religious painter, printmaker, portraitist, contemporary chronicler and a respected member of the royal court.

Yet a mysterious illness at the age of 47 left him completely deaf and seemed to change his outlook. On the surface he remained politically neutral, but his art shows his horror and disgust at the events that surrounded him. He continued to create dynamic religious works,

naturalistic figure paintings, bucolic tapestry designs and insightful portraits, but he also produced some of the most repulsive and scandalous images that had ever been seen.

It is not clear why Goya chose to depict such raw, scathing and disconcerting imagery. He was not born in the Middle Ages and so he did not share the moral and religious beliefs of the medieval artist Hieronymus Bosch (c.1450–1516) for example. But his work is similarly satirical, moralistic and damning, portraying the savagery, stupidity and moral degradation of his contemporaries.

Many of his prints and paintings are difficult to look at, shocking even now, centuries after they were made, and yet he was working against the background of the formidable Spanish Inquisition, absolutist kings, wars and political

Right: Etching of 1797–8, Of What Ill Will He Die? *Goya illustrates poor medical practices in Spain by depicting a doctor as a donkey.*

turmoil. Bravely, or perhaps recklessly, he applied his innovative, distinctive style and perceptive observations to all his images – including brutally honest portraits of royalty and the nobility, street urchins, bandits, señoritas and demons – and through them, he changed art forever.

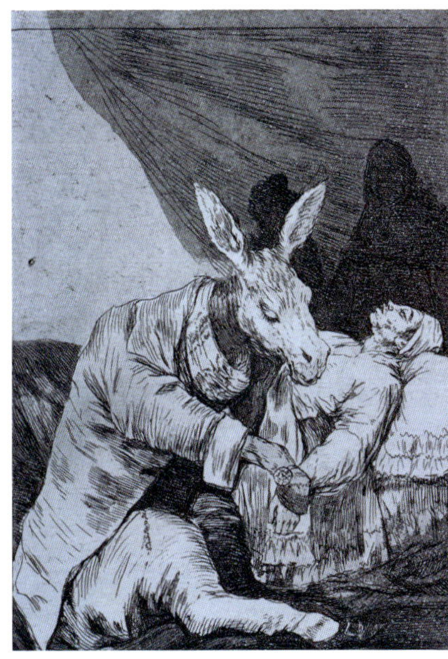

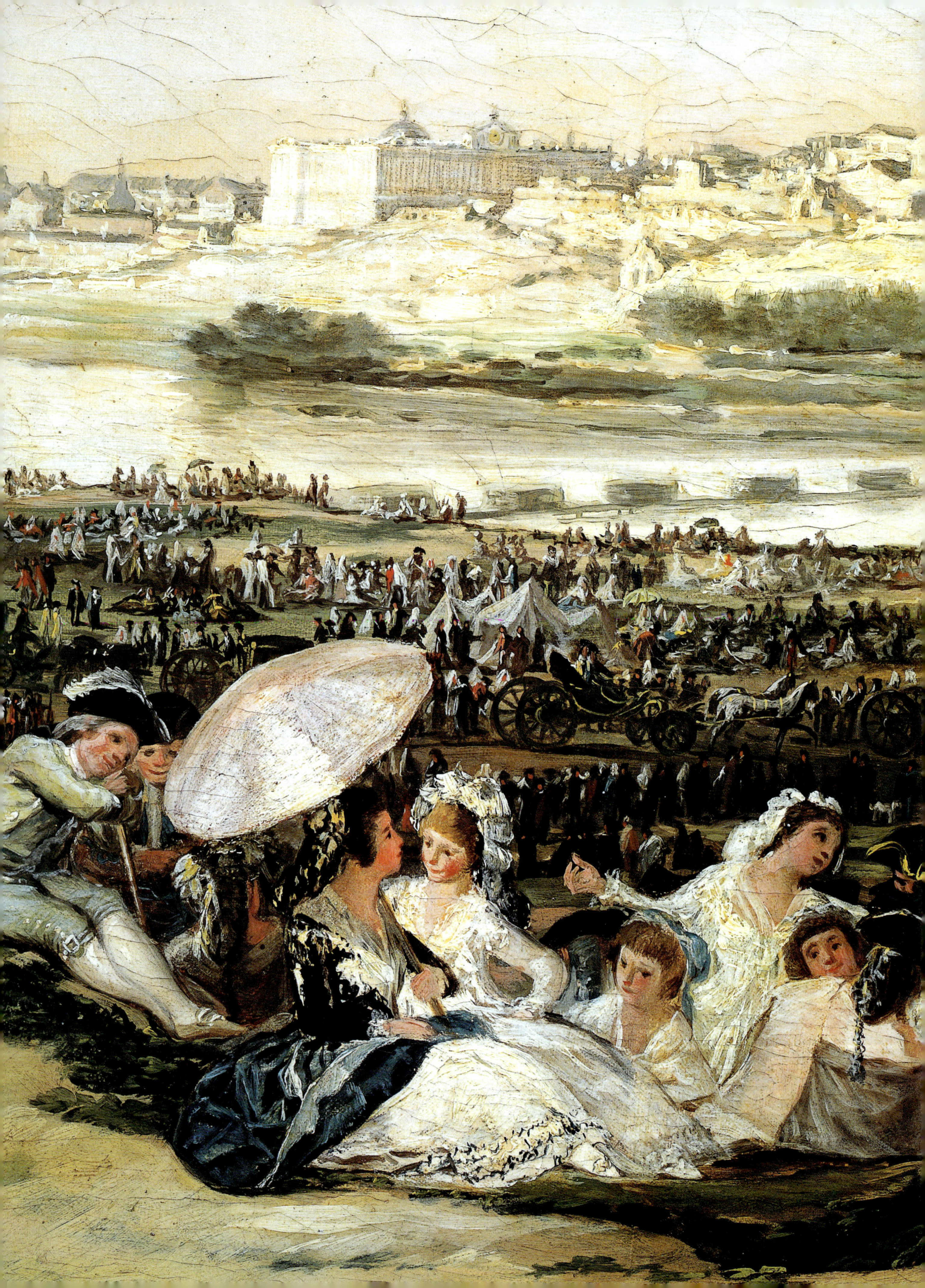

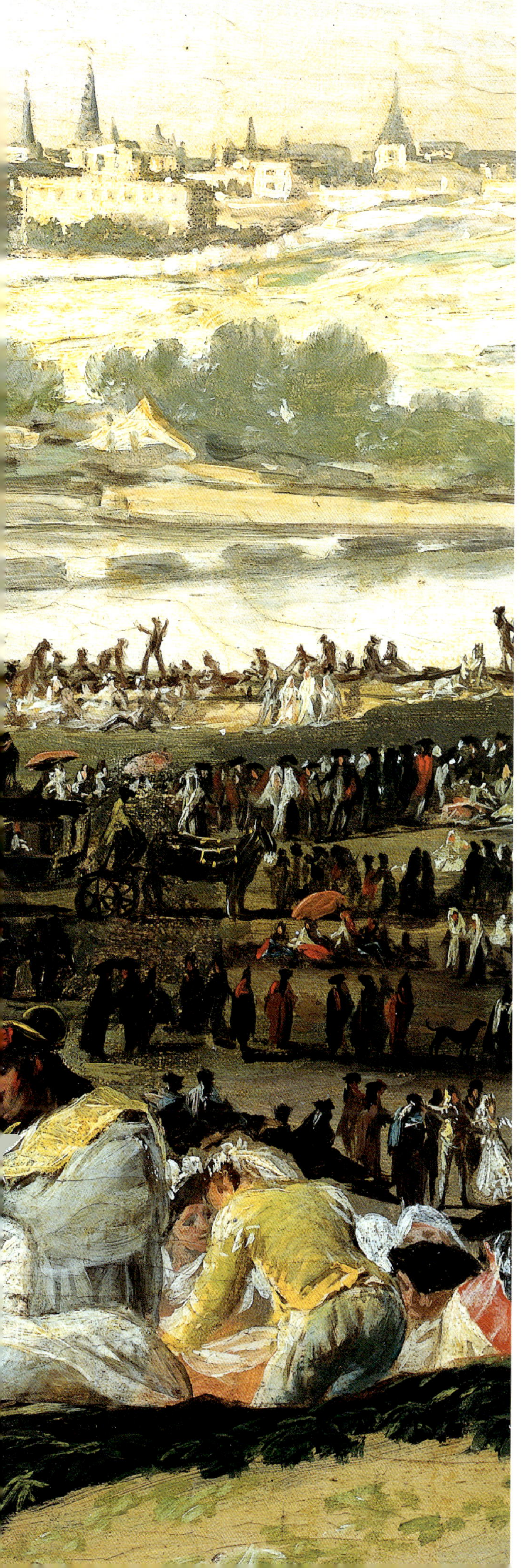

DRAMA AND PASSION

Francisco de Goya (1746–1828) lived for 82 years and worked as an artist for more than 60 of them, at a time when the average life expectancy was less than 50 years. Sensitive to moral and social issues, as both commentator and chronicler of his era, he influenced generations of artists who followed him. His enigmatic images capture a vivid picture of 18th- and 19th-century Spain's undulating fortunes, of the experiences of the aristocracy and ordinary citizens alike, and of his own sympathies and passions. In satirizing many contemporary attitudes and events, he put himself in danger. To criticize both Spain and the Church at the time of the Inquisition was a high-risk activity, yet Goya continued to assert his belief in the need for freedom from tyranny and superstition. By the early 19th century, he had moved on from his sumptuous court paintings of his early career, and was producing moralizing images, dramatic illustrations of the human condition and bizarre, fantastical scenes.

Left: Detail of The Meadow of San Isidro on His Feast Day, *1788, commissioned for a bedroom in the El Pardo Palace, Goya portrayed crowds gathering to celebrate the feast day of San Isidro, the patron saint of Madrid.*

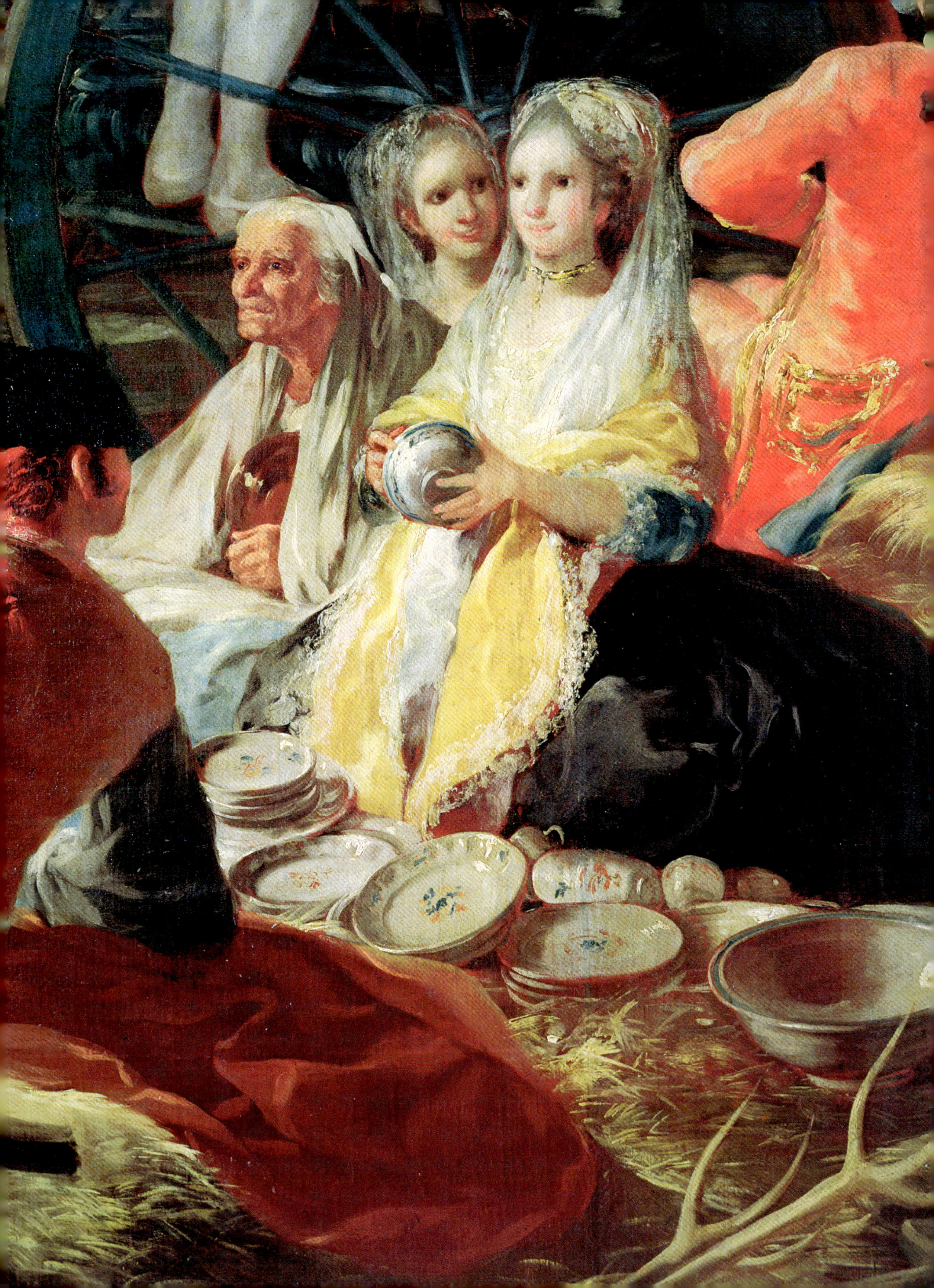

CELEBRATED COURT PAINTER

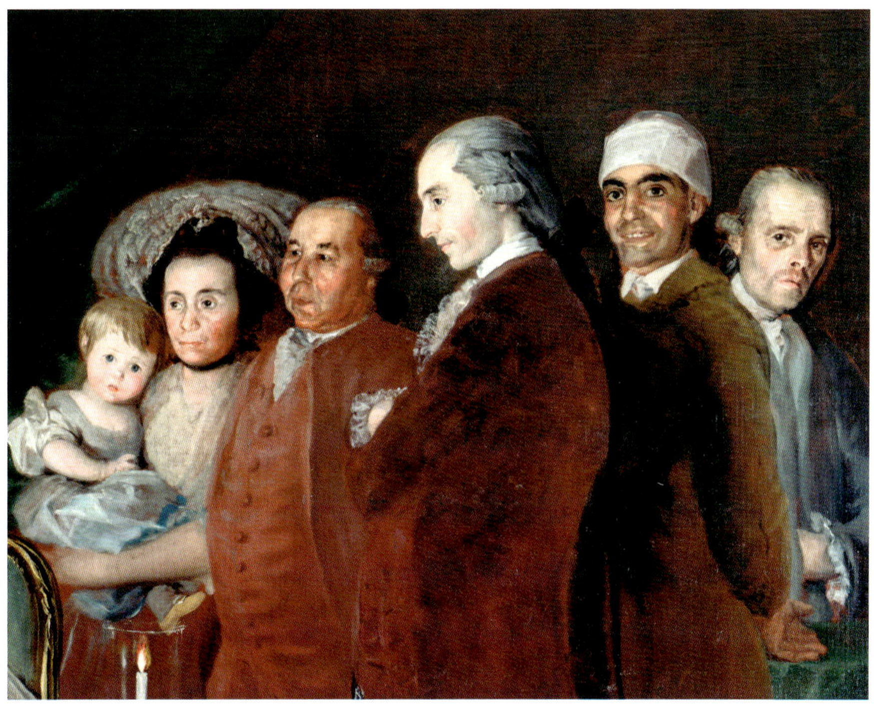

No one really knows how precocious were Goya's talents as a child.
Numerous stories were related by those who knew him as a boy, or
those who wished they had after his fame had spread. However he began,
Goya was noticed by royalty by the time he was 30 and a decade later,
was appointed painter to King Charles III. In 1789, at the age of 43, he was
promoted to Court Painter under the newly crowned Charles IV. At this
time, his work was refreshingly natural. He captured aristocrats and courtiers
in relaxed situations, using rich colours and fluid brushwork.

Above: Detail of The Family of the Infante Don Luis de Bourbon, *1784;
Goya described Don Luis, the younger brother of King Charles III, and his wife
Maria Teresa de Vallabrigay Rosas, as 'angels.'*

Left: Detail of Ladies Buying Pottery at a Stall in Madrid, *1799; a design for
a tapestry for a bedroom in the El Pardo Palace.*

BIRTH AND EARLY LIFE

Francisco José de Goya y Lucientes was born on 30 March 1746 to Gracia Lucientes and José Goya, in the remote village of Fuendetodos, some 40 miles (64km) from Saragossa, the capital city of Aragón. Surrounded by hills and crumbling Roman and Moorish ruins, Fuendetodos was a small and quite inaccessible hamlet.

With its rocky, unmade roads, few travellers passed through Fuendetodos, and with barely 100 inhabitants, it had little to offer a growing family, so it has often been speculated why the Goyas lived there. Previously, they had lived in Saragossa, and it was to this city that they soon returned.

SOCIAL STANDING

Goya was born in his mother's relatives' house in Fuendetodos, a simple building made of stones to protect its inhabitants from the harsh summer heat and the bitter winter cold. It also displayed his maternal family's coat-of-arms.

His mother, Gracia Lucientes, was a minor 'hidalgo', or member of the lesser nobility. The word 'hidalgo' derived from the phrase 'hijo de algo', which means literally, 'the son of somebody'. In 18th-century Spain, hidalgos constituted almost five per cent of the population, but apart from the prestige of having their own

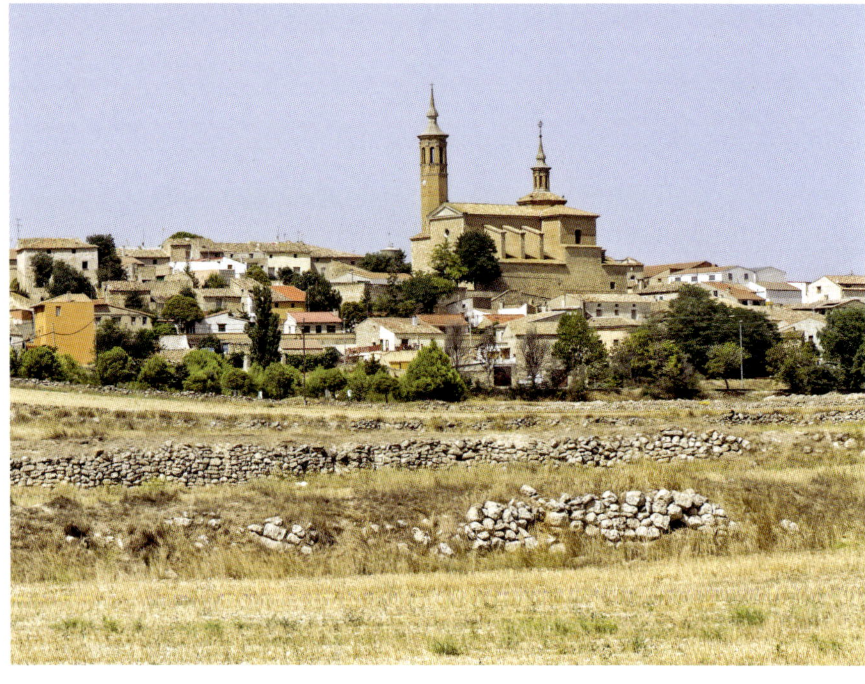

Above: A photograph of the village of Fuendetodos, the quiet birthplace of Francisco de Goya.

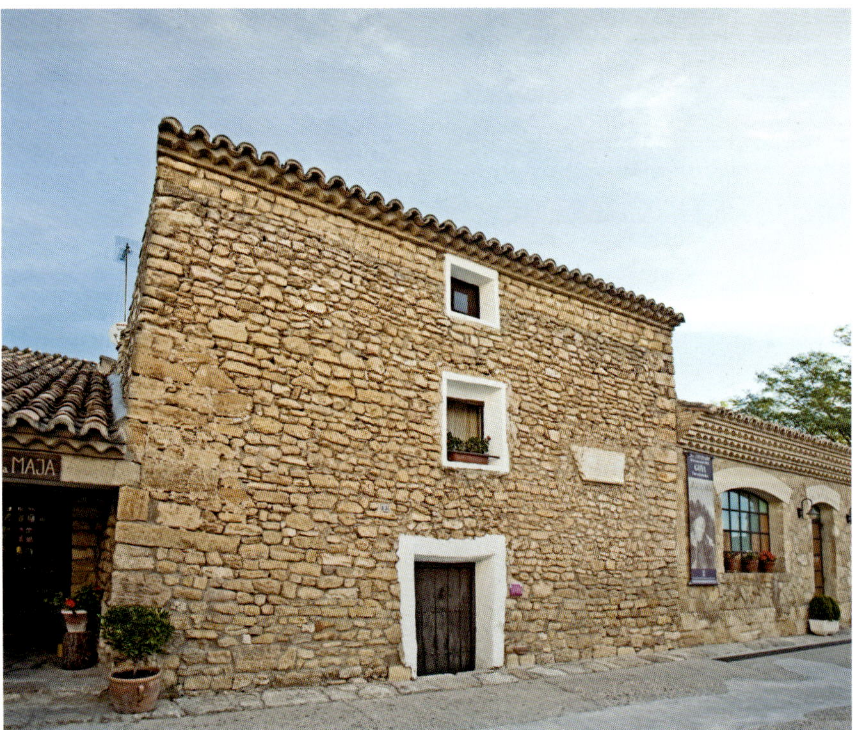

Below: Goya's birthplace, a tiny house of stones, three rooms up and three down, with few windows to protect against the harsh weather.

coat-of-arms and the privilege of being addressed respectfully as 'Don' or 'Doña', little else distinguished them.

José Goya was a master gilder, a profitable occupation during a time when gilded objects were greatly in demand for public buildings, churches and private homes. José's father, Francisco's grandfather, had been a respected notary, which entitled his family to be considered members of the lower middle class. This combination of backgrounds meant that Francisco's family were regarded as middle class. In later life, he attempted to document what he believed was his noble ancestry and to reconstruct his mother's coat-of-arms.

THE GOYA FAMILY

Francisco was baptized in the church of Fuendetodos. The local priest, Father Joseph Ximeno wrote:

'On the 31st day of March, 1746, I the subscribing priest, baptized a child born on the day immediately preceding, the legitimate son of Joséph Goya and of Gracia Lucientes, legally married, inhabitants of the parish, in the district of Saragossa. He was named Francisco Joséph Goya, his godmother being Francisa de Grasa, of this parish.'

Francisco was Gracia and José's fourth child. Their first was a daughter, Rita, born in 1737. Their second was Tomás, born in 1739, and their third was another daughter, Jacinta, born in 1743. After Francisco, in 1750 the couple had a third son, Mariano, and Camilo, their sixth child, was born in 1753.

EDUCATION

At some point during Goya's childhood, the family moved back to Saragossa and it was there that he first developed his artistic talents. History has been obscured by varied accounts of this. One tale relates that a passing priest saw him drawing a pig on a rock with a burnt stick and was so taken by the child's skill that he convinced Francisco's parents to let him attend drawing classes. Another story describes how the Count of Fuentes saw his drawings and immediately arranged for him to study art. Yet another report tells of his own father recognizing the potential of his son's drawings at an early age. Whatever the truth, Goya first attended the Escuelas Pías de San Antón, a church school offering free education to gifted children of the poor. There he became friends with Martín Zapater (1747–1803);

a friendship that lasted their entire lives. At the time, Spain's education system fell behind the rest of Europe, but Escuelas Pías was better than many Spanish schools, and Francisco was given a fairly good grounding in reading, writing, mathematics, theology, art and Latin.

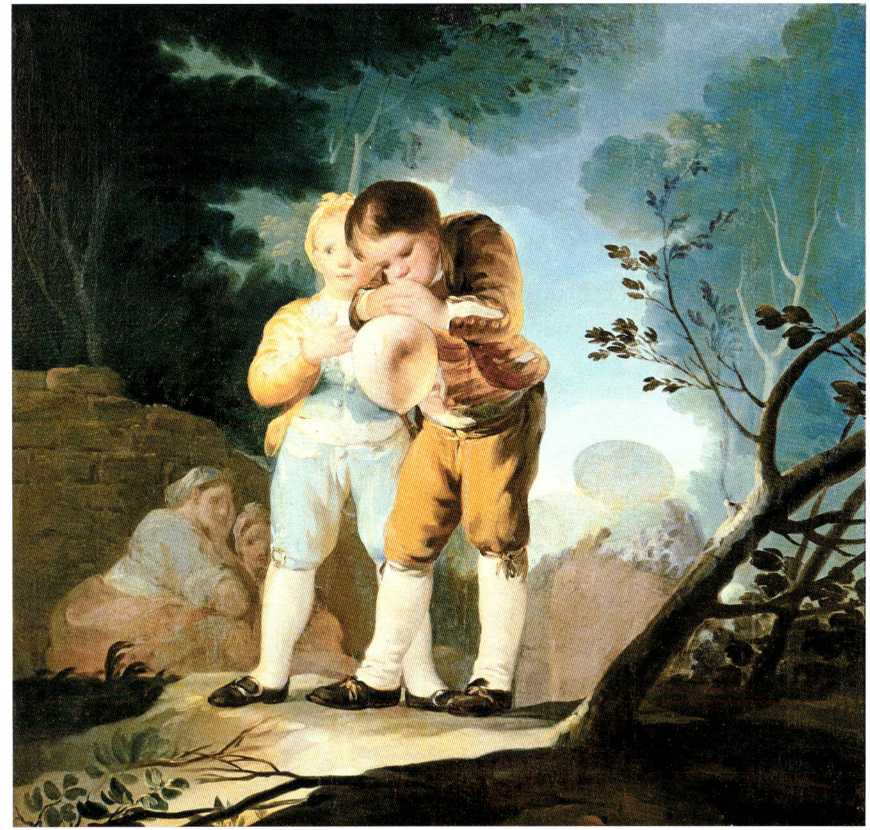

Above: Goya painted Boys Inflating a Bladder *in 1778, perhaps recalling his own childhood, growing up with his brothers.*

Below: Painting Studio, *c.1700, Thomas Gerard (1663–1721). This is the kind of studio to which the young Goya aspired.*

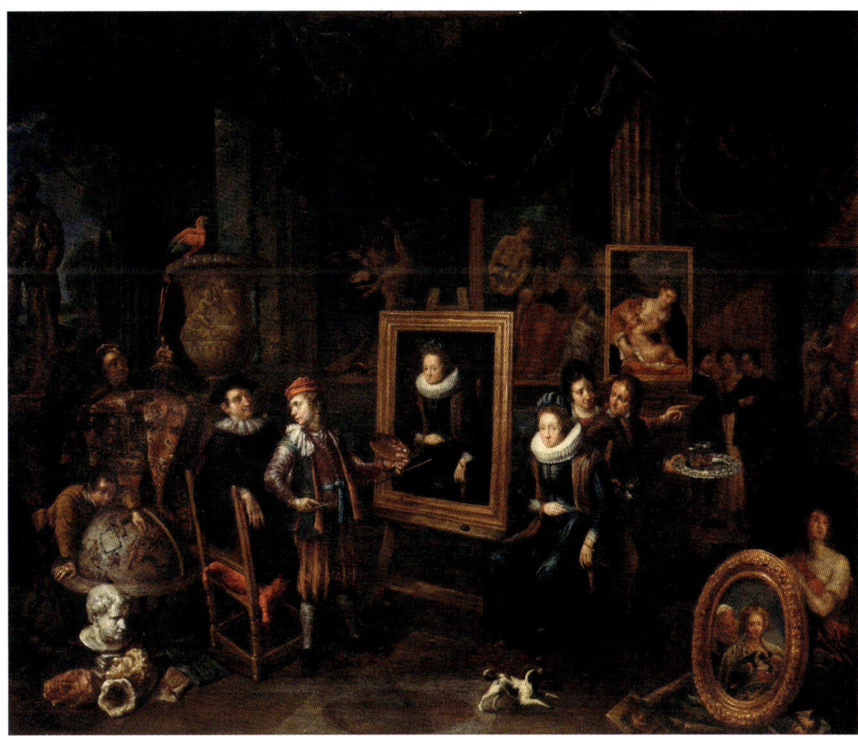

A SPECIAL FRIENDSHIP

The friendship between Martín Zapater and Goya was unique. Spanning some 50 years, the two wrote almost 150 letters to each other, and it is through these letters that we know so much about Goya's life and career. Zapater remained single all his life, had a broad range of cultural interests and amassed a considerable fortune through shrewd business deals. Goya painted his portrait twice (see page 191).

EUROPE IN THE 18TH CENTURY

Before Goya's birth, the first half of the 18th century was dominated by conflict over royal successions. The second half saw the Seven Years' War, improvements in farming, the start of the Industrial Revolution and an abundance of new ideas, discoveries and developments that became known as the Age of Enlightenment.

Despite several wars involving most of the great powers of the time, in general, as Goya grew up, life was less turbulent than in previous centuries. Fewer epidemics occurred as the result of better sanitation, and developments in farming generated greater agricultural cultivation, which led to an improvement in overall nutrition. The Industrial Revolution, from about 1760 to 1840, saw the development of machine production, chemical manufacturing and greater efficiency of water and steam power. One result of all this was an unprecedented rise in Europe's population.

THREE WARS

The century began with the death of the sickly, insane Habsburg King Charles II of Spain, who left no direct heir. Consequently, war broke out across Europe over the Spanish succession.

Just six years before Goya's birth, once again, controversies arose over European crowns. The War of the

Below: Venetian-born Baroque composer Antonio Vivaldi was also a violinist and priest, famed for his concertos, sacred choral works and over 40 operas. He died six years before Goya was born.

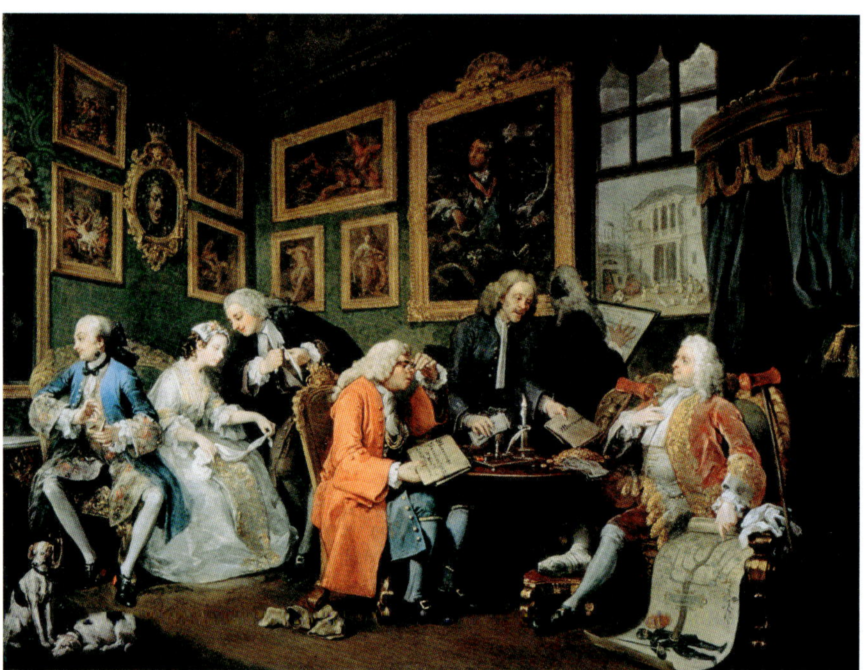

Above: Marriage à la Mode, *c.1743. William Hogarth's sardonic paintings and engravings of 'modern moral subjects' predated Goya's later satirical work.*

Austrian Succession lasted from 1740 to 1748 over the question of the Habsburg Maria Theresa's succession as Queen of Hungary, Croatia and Bohemia, and Archduchess of Austria and Duchess of Parma.

The Seven Years' War began when Goya was a child in 1754/56, driven by antagonism between European dynasties and conflicts of interests in colonial and trade empires. This unrest involved Europe, most of America, the West African coast, India and the Philippines.

THE STRUCTURE OF SOCIETY

Across Europe, class hierarchy dominated society, which was why Goya was so keen to use his mother's coat-of-arms. At the pinnacle of society was royalty, followed by the nobility who controlled the political system and were patrons of the arts. Next were the bourgeoisie or middle classes, comprising merchants and international traders, shopkeepers, financiers and industrialists. The bourgeoisie bought expensive goods, many of them became patrons of the arts and many pushed for political and social change. Meanwhile, poverty was more prevalent than ever, and the lower classes made up the bulk of society.

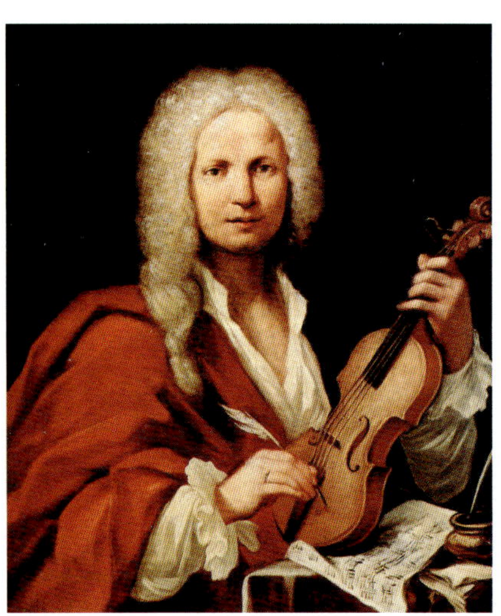

ANCIENT ROME

The ancient Roman cities of Pompeii and Herculaneum were mostly buried under ash and pumice in the eruption of Mount Vesuvius in 79 CE. In 1738, Herculaneum was rediscovered by workmen. Ten years later, Pompeii was rediscovered through planned excavations. The incredible archaeological discoveries of the almost intact cities fuelled a Europe-wide passion for ancient Roman art and artefacts.

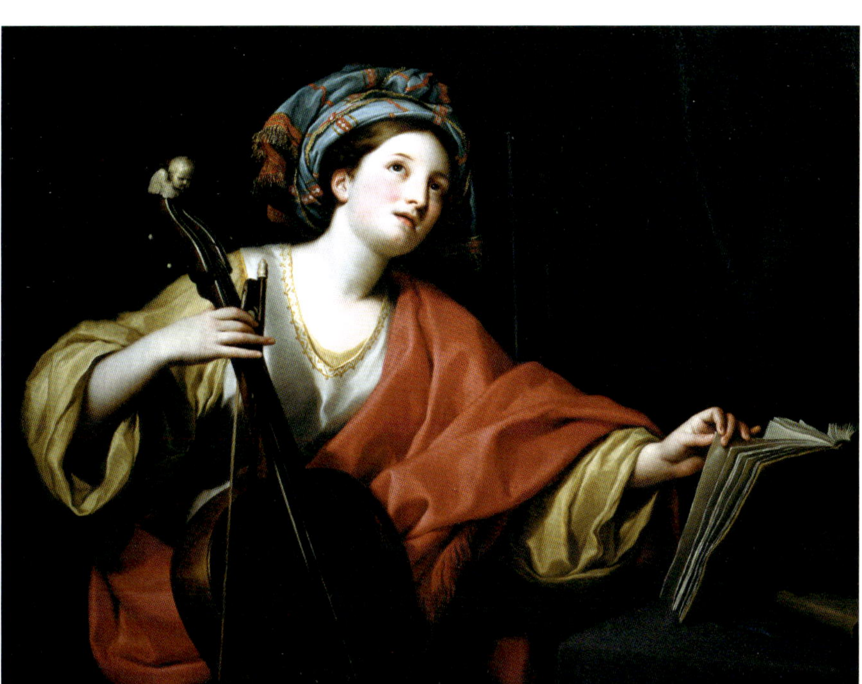

Left: Mengs, often called 'the Father of Neoclassicism', was a strong influence on Goya. Saint Cecilia, 1760–1, shows a range of emotion Goya later included in his work.

GOYA'S CONTEMPORARIES

From the time Goya was 13 until he reached artistic maturity, Spain was ruled by Charles III, who was sympathetic to change and reform, echoing most of Europe at the time. Alongside many of the developments and inventions, new ideas proliferated through books, newspapers, coffee-houses and literary salons, as this period of optimism was expressed in many ways by some of the greatest names in science and the arts, all contemporaries of Goya's, including:

Composers: Vivaldi, Mozart and Beethoven

Writers and philosophers: Jonathan Swift, Samuel Johnson, John Locke, Voltaire, Rousseau, Kant and Goethe

Scientists: Isaac Newton, Benito Feijóo and Edward Jenner

Architect: Robert Adam

Painters: Antoine Watteau, Jean-Baptiste-Simeon Chardin, William Hogarth, Canaletto, Giovanni Battista (Giambattista) Tiepolo and Anton Raphael Mengs

INSPIRATION

Added to the discoveries in Pompeii and Herculaneum, increasing patronage from the aristocracy and middle classes inspired a flourishing of the arts. Wealthy young aristocrats took the Grand Tour, visiting parts of Europe to experience the art, architecture and culture. Musicians found new forms of expression through opera, orchestras and chamber music. As education improved, literacy increased and there was an increase in cheaply printed books, newspapers and magazines. After the death of the French 'Sun King', Louis XIV in 1715, many tried to emulate the lavish architecture of the Palace of Versailles. In painting and sculpture, a burgeoning number of artists appealed to popular tastes, developing the prevailing styles in unique ways.

Below: Canaletto's Ducal Palace, Venice, c.1755, shows the increasing sophistication of society and architectural style during Goya's lifetime.

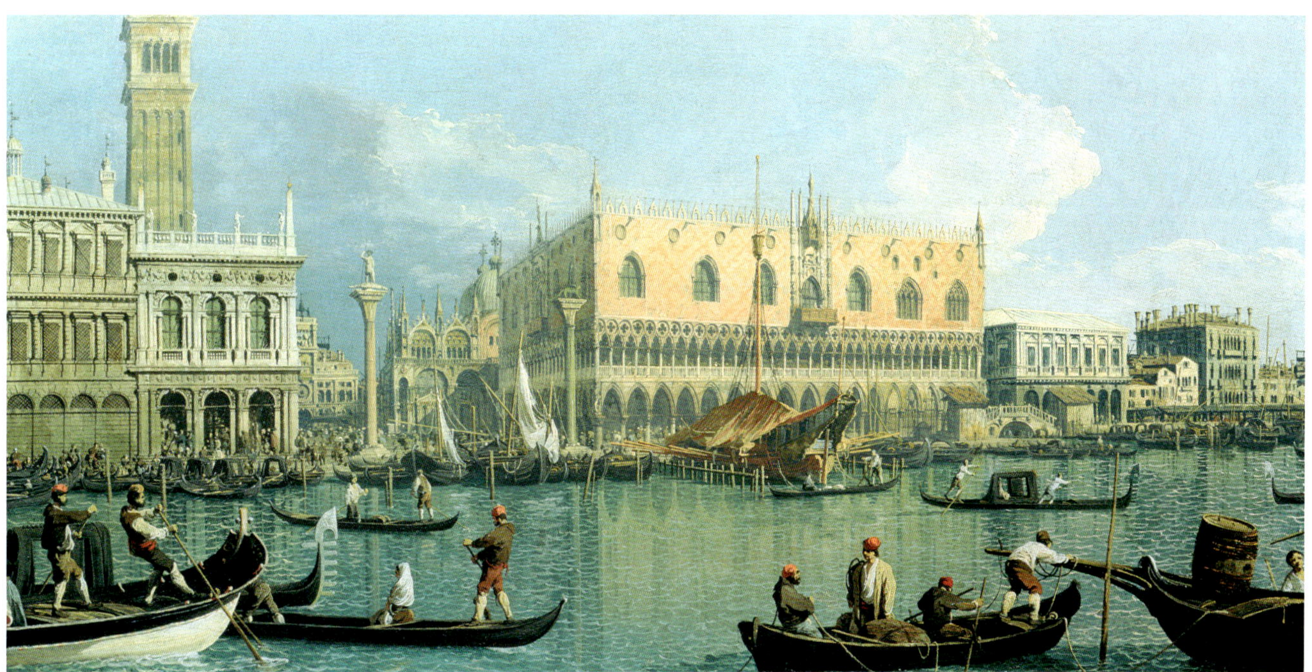

LEARNING HIS ART

In 1759 at the age of 13, Goya was apprenticed to José Luzán y Martinez (1710–85), Saragossa's master painter. Luzán had travelled to Italy in his youth and had adopted the ornate and extravagant styles of the Italian Baroque. Even so, he was a mediocre artist and an uninspiring teacher.

There were no public art galleries or museums in Spain at that time and in Saragossa, it was fairly prestigious to have been accepted as an apprentice by Luzán. Goya's father had befriended Luzán's brother Juan who was a fellow gilder, and Luzán accepted Goya who was already showing some precocious talents. Keen to study art, Goya nonetheless found the regime fairly monotonous. Day after day, he and his fellow students were instructed to copy Italian, French and Flemish engravings, before being allowed to move on to draw plaster casts, and finally after months, they were permitted to draw from life, but with no tradition of the nude in puritanical Spain, their models were always fully dressed. Although this was established art teaching for the time, years later, Goya declared that he learned nothing from those lessons. Luzán's skills and piety however, had gained him the respect of the Spanish Inquisition, as they employed him as an auditor, to censor and alter artists' paintings that might have otherwise corrupted public morals.

MASTERING A STYLE

While at Luzán's, Goya was trained to work in the prevailing late Baroque and Rococo styles. He also learned the craft of grinding colours, preparing canvases and painting in oils, but the only way any apprentice could develop individual expression was by close observation of the styles of great masters through the engravings they copied. It is probable that the engravings they worked from included examples by their fellow countryman, Diego Velázquez (1599–1666), the leading artist of the Court of King Philip IV of Spain, whose treatment of light and space inspired Goya throughout his career, and of the prolific and innovative Dutch artist Rembrandt van Rijn (1606–69).

During his four-year apprenticeship with Luzán, Goya befriended two other students; Ramón Bayeu (1746–93) and his older brother Francisco Bayeu (1734–95), whom Goya later described as his teacher. In 1762, Francisco Bayeu was called to Madrid to work with Anton Raphael Mengs on the decoration of the royal palace. A few years later, Bayeu was established as a Court Painter.

FIRST COMMISSION

While still an apprentice, in 1762, when he was 16 years old, Goya received his first commission to decorate a reliquary

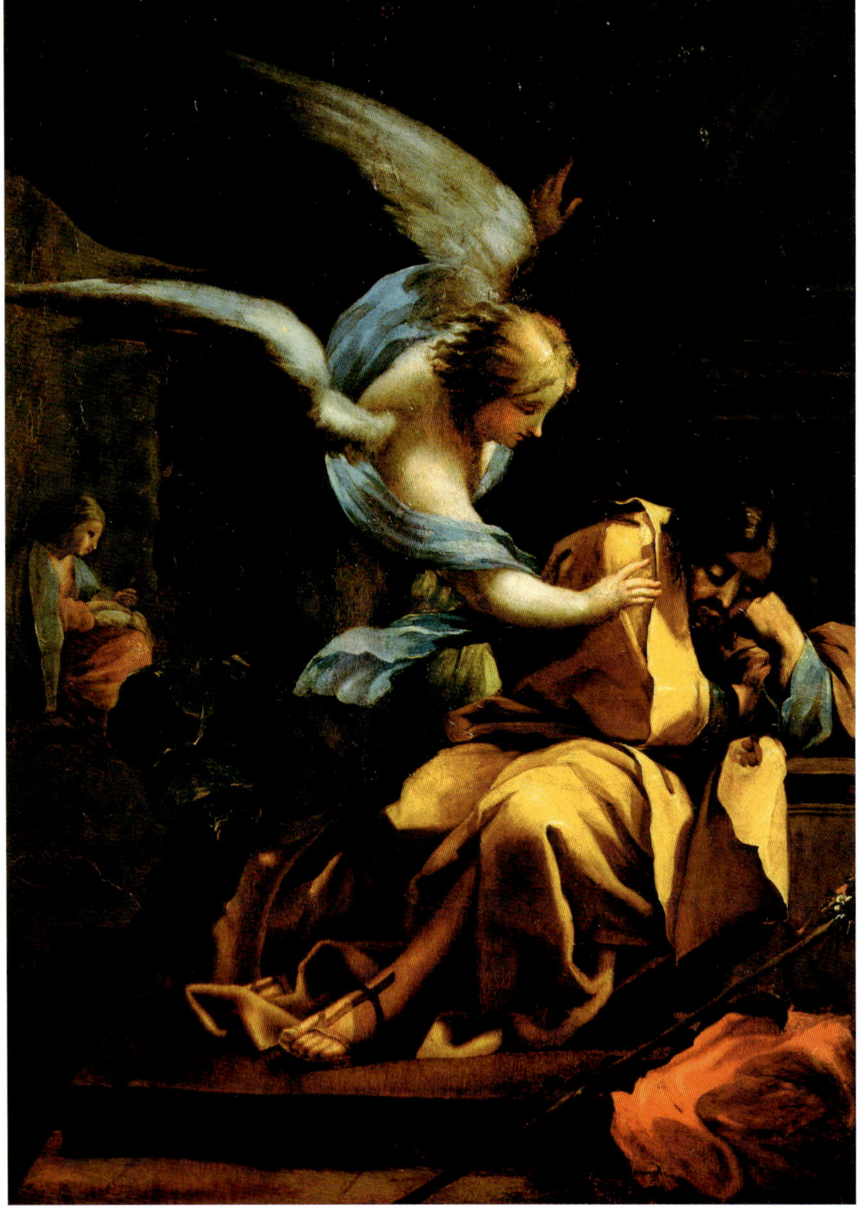

Left: The Dream of Saint Joseph, c.1770–1. One of a series of paintings by Goya for the chapel of the palace of Sobradiel in Saragossa.

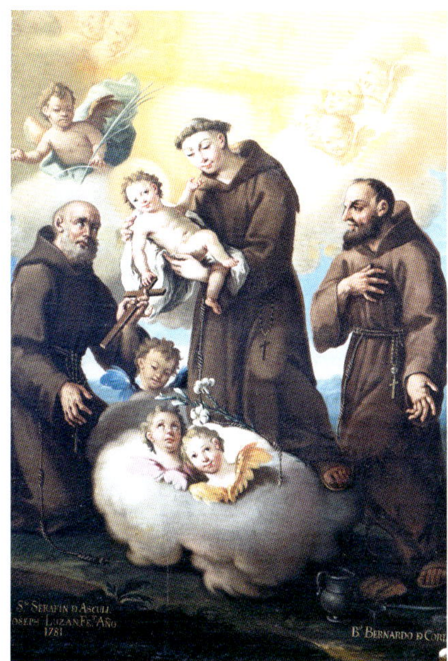

Above: An altarpiece from Saragossa showing Saint Anthony of Padua painted by Luzán in 1781. Although respected by the Inquisition, Goya found Luzán an uninspiring teacher.

cabinet in the church of his baptism in Fuendetodos. The paintings (destroyed with the church in 1936 during the Spanish Civil War), of a canopy, the Virgin Mary and Saint Francis, show the influence of Luzán and the flowing exuberance of the late Baroque and Rococo styles.

THE PLEASURES OF LIFE

Although Goya grew up to be one of the most imaginative and innovative artists of his day, he always maintained that to him, painting was merely a profession rather than a passion. He once wrote to Zapater that he considered hunting to be a far more pleasurable pastime than painting, and it was known that he liked nothing better than to sit and drink chocolate or shoot partridges. A lively, intuitive and intelligent observer of life, he was no theoretician and said he had little interest in the new ideas that fostered and sustained the Age of Enlightenment,

Right: Detail of Self-portrait *from* Las Meninas, *1656. Velázquez was the leading artist of the Spanish Golden Age, and one of Goya's greatest influences.*

yet his acutely perceptive observations of human characteristics and failings, showed that Goya was far shrewder than he believed.

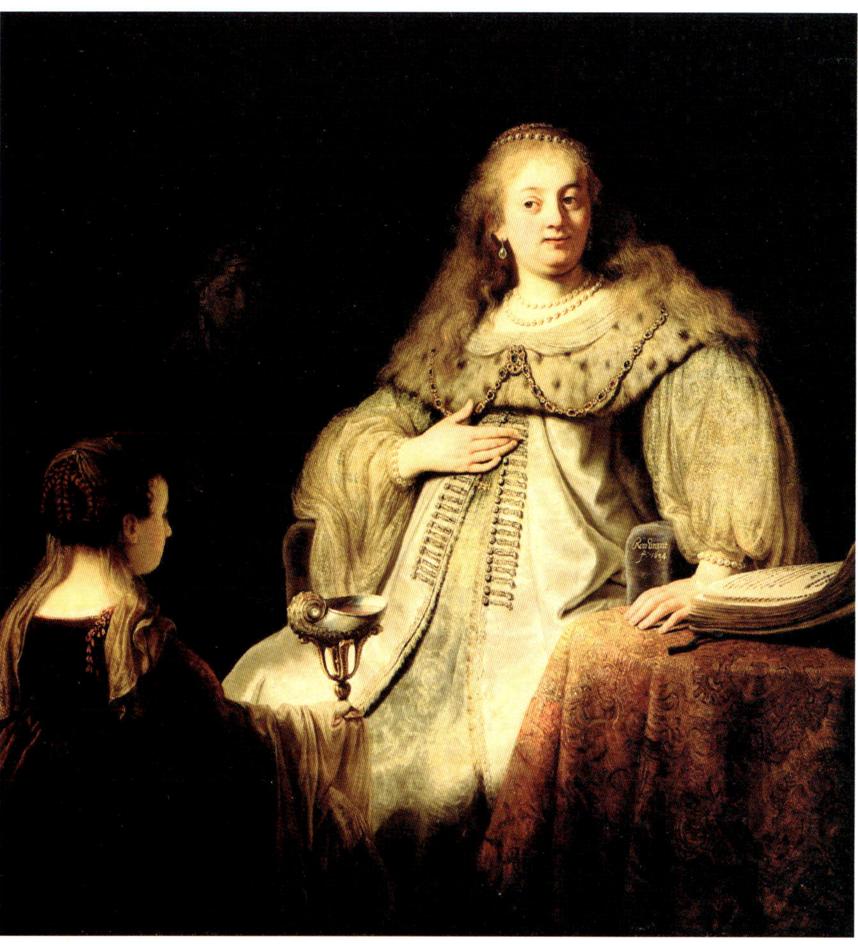

Above: Artemisia, *Rembrandt, 1634. In later life, Goya described himself as 'a pupil of Velázquez, Rembrandt and nature.'*

THE BAROQUE

From the Portuguese *barocco*, Spanish *barroco* or French *baroque*, meaning 'rough or imperfect pearl', the Baroque was a style of art that began in Italy in about 1600, and spread across Europe, lasting until about 1760.

The Baroque movement was one that developed in response to the Protestant Reformation, when the Roman Catholic Church asked artists and architects to communicate religious themes boldly and to encourage emotional involvement. The main characteristics of Baroque art include dramatic effects of light, space and expression, dynamic compositions and an emphasis on intense emotions.

ROCOCO AND NEOCLASSICISM

When Goya began painting, Spanish art was languishing. Since Spain's Golden Age had been led by artists such as Velázquez, Zurbarán (1598–1664) and Murillo (1617–82), artistic endeavour had lost its impetus. In an attempt to rekindle Spanish art, Charles III called two of Europe's leading artists to his Court.

In October 1761, Mengs arrived from Rome in response to Charles III's summons. Early the following year, Mengs was joined by the Venetian painter Giovanni Battista Tiepolo (1696–1770). The King asked the artists to decorate the rooms in his new palace in Madrid. At the age of 66, the celebrated Tiepolo worked in the now largely outmoded style of Rococo painting, while Mengs at 34 worked in the new Neoclassical style.

APPEAL AND PROMINENCE

As the more experienced artist with an international reputation as a leading fresco painter, Tiepolo decorated the most important rooms of the Spanish palace with his son Giovanni Domenico (1727–1804). Famed for his Rococo frescoes in Venetian palaces and churches, Tiepolo created his last great

Below: The Music Party, *Watteau, c.1718. Goya was aware of the skills of artists like Watteau, and borrowed several of Watteau's ideas in his early paintings.*

masterpieces in Madrid's Palacio Real and won many honours and awards there. The large ceiling paintings in the throne and audience rooms feature allegories glorifying the Spanish king, but Tiepolo's style of art, although technically impressive, skilfully painted and glowing with radiant colour, was seen by many as outmoded.

Mengs meanwhile, became extremely prominent in artistic circles in Madrid. Highly respected and admired for his new style of classically inspired paintings, his opinions were respected and within a short time, he reformed the Academy of Art, became director of the Royal Tapestry factory, and encouraged many younger Spanish artists in their work. When he was given painting commissions, he invited some of these young, promising painters to work with him as his assistants, and generally helped to promote their careers. This was why he invited Francisco Bayeu (1734–95) to join him in 1762. A few years later, he asked Goya to do the same.

ROCKS AND SHELLS

The word Rococo probably comes from the French word *rocaille*, which means rock and shell formations and describes the typically shaped motifs used in many of the designs. The Rococo style was used in design, painting, literature, architecture, music and sculpture, from about 1720 to 1770. It had developed as a reaction against the grandeur, symmetry and strict regulations of the Baroque, and art became more light-hearted, flamboyant and graceful, featuring asymmetry, elaborate curves, scrolls often in the shapes of the letters S and C, soft colours and shapes taken from the natural world, such as acanthus leaves. By the end of the 18th century however, people were tiring of it, and Neoclassicism gained greater regard. Successful Rococo painters include

Below: Adoration of the Shepherds, *Mengs, 1770. Impressed by Mengs, Goya emulated his powerful chiaroscuro effects and solid-looking compositions.*

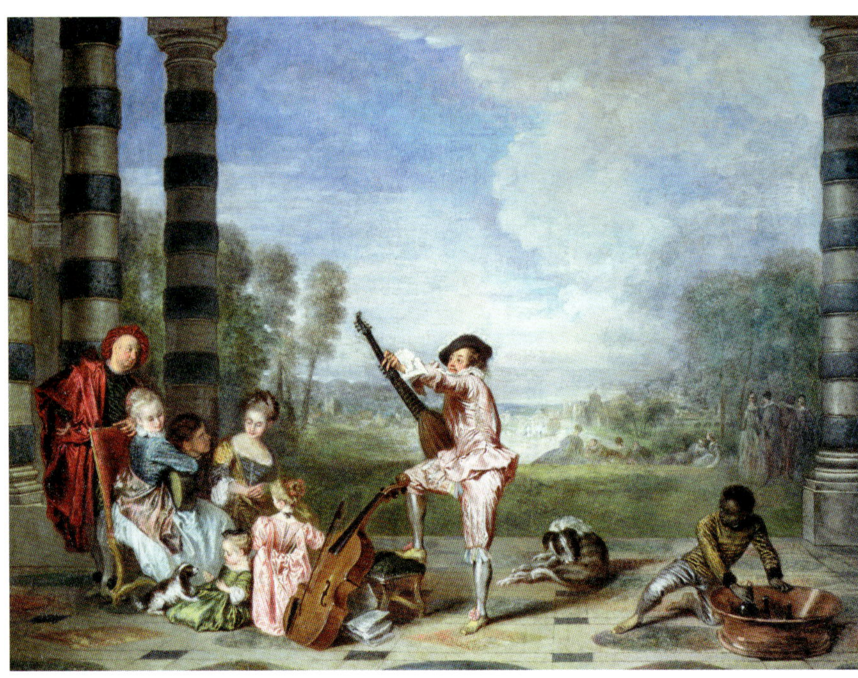

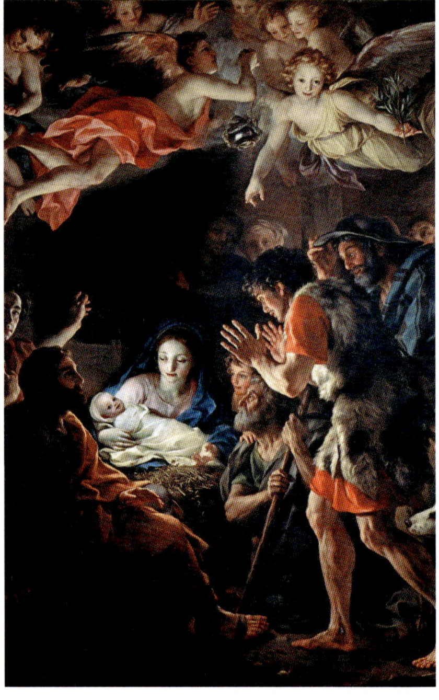

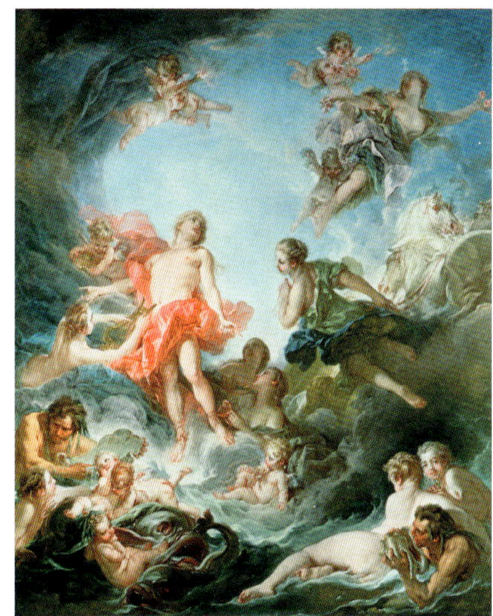

Above: The Rising of the Sun, *Boucher, 1753. Although he never felt comfortable with the sweet, playful style of the Rococo, Goya developed his own style through studying works such as this.*

Tiepolo, Jean-Antoine Watteau (1684–1721), François Boucher (1703–70) and Jean-Honoré Fragonard (1732–1806).

REDISCOVERY AND RENEWAL

Mengs was born in Bohemia, but spent most of his life in Rome where he befriended Johann Joachim Winckelmann (1717–68), a German art historian and archaeologist. After the discoveries at Pompeii and Herculaneum, Winckelmann began promoting the revival in interest in ancient Greek and Roman art. He believed that perfect art should be a blend of classical Greek and Roman art and the art of the Italian High Renaissance. He once said: 'The only way for us to become great...is the imitation of the Greeks.' Mengs followed Winckelmann's ideals closely, particularly emulating the styles of Raphael (1483–1520) and Titian (c.1488/90–1576) whom he admired above all.

So Neoclassicism evolved, partly as a reaction against the frivolity of the Rococo and partly from the resurgence of interest in the arts of antiquity. Following on from the Baroque and Rococo styles, it seemed both radical and exciting, with its clean lines, sinuous but firm contours, accurate perspective, pure or sensitive colours,

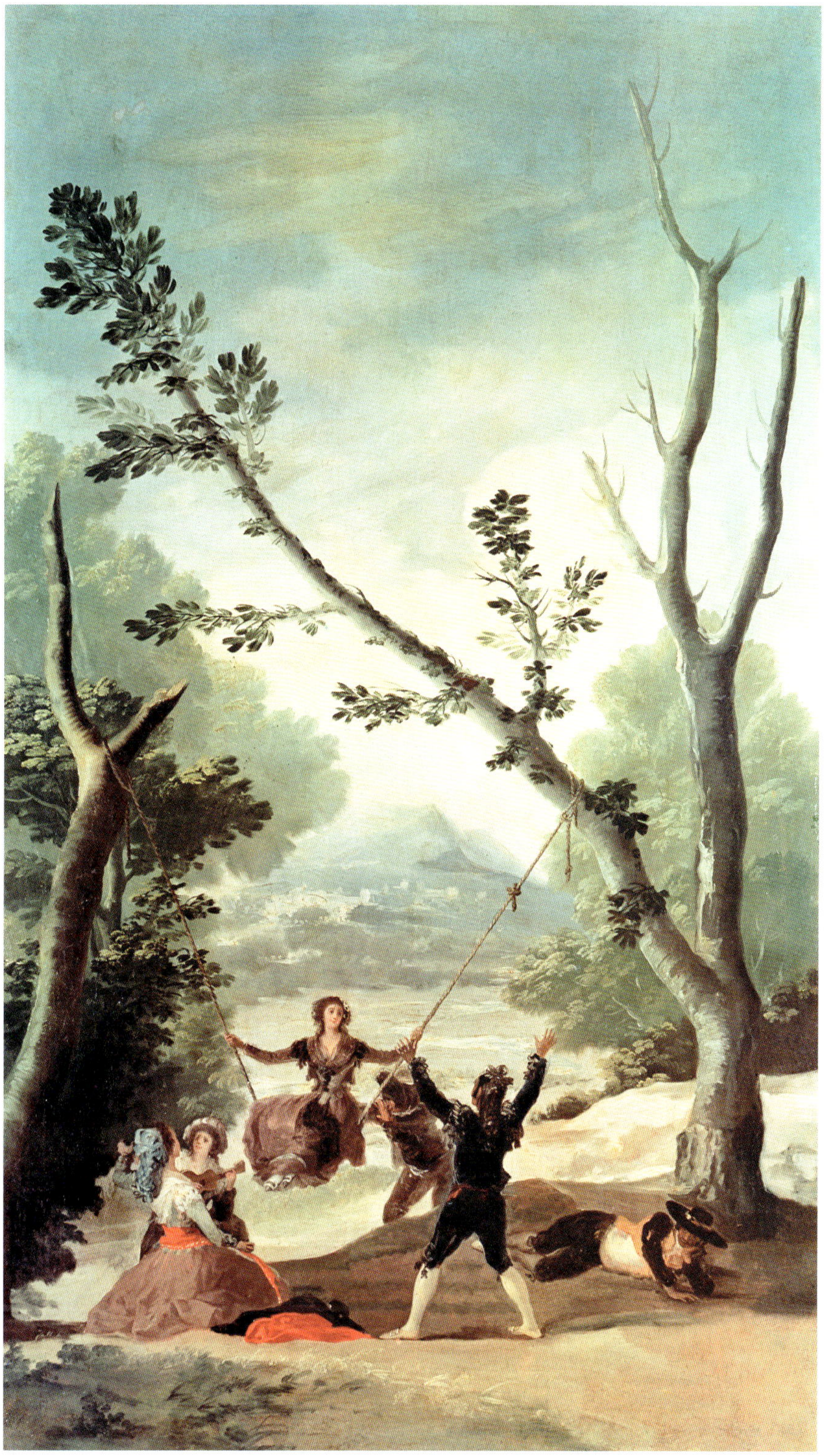

Above: The Swing, *1786–7, shows how Goya could assimilate both the Rococo and Neoclassical styles, without adhering to either.*

balanced proportions and often serious or dramatic messages. Renowned Neoclassical artists included Jacques-Louis David (1748–1825), Jean-Auguste-Dominique Ingres (1780–1867), Angelica Kauffmann (1741–1807), Antonio Canova (1757–1822) and Antoine-Jean Gros (1771–1835).

Throughout his career, Goya demonstrated a clear understanding of all styles, including Rococo and Neoclassical, but although he was influenced at first by those around him, he generally distanced himself from all current trends.

RELIGIOUS PAINTING

Devoutly Roman Catholic Spain prized religious painting above all subjects and, after the Court, the Church was the most important source of commissions. The Spanish Inquisition, although declining by this period, encouraged imagery that inspired prayer. Goya was aware religious commissions could establish his reputation.

At that time, a successful career as an artist was difficult to achieve without academic recognition. The Royal Academy of Fine Arts of San Fernando in Madrid held a three-yearly competition for a scholarship to study there, so in 1763, Goya travelled from Saragossa to enter the competition. Each applicant was required to submit one painting in oil on canvas, 6 × 4½ft (1.8 × 1.4m), on a theme that had been set for them. Next, the candidate had to paint spontaneously while there for two-and-a-half hours on a previously undisclosed subject. Goya did not win. Three years later, he returned to Madrid and entered

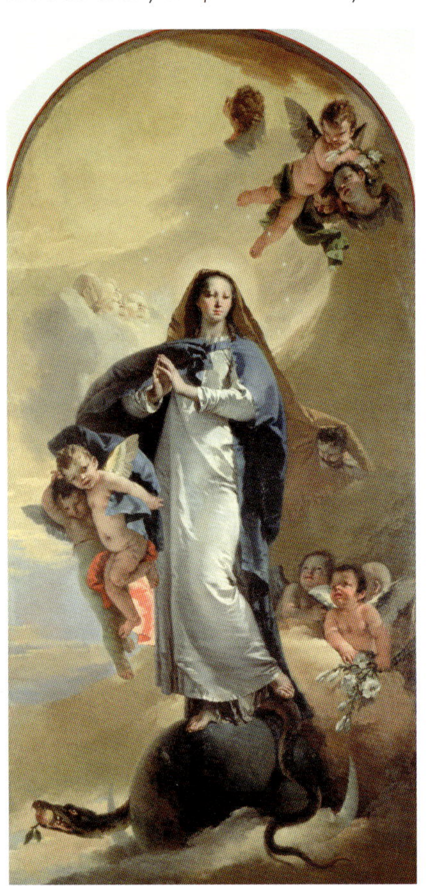

Below: The Immaculate Conception, *Tiepolo, 1766–8. To attain success, Goya sought to follow Tiepolo's characteristically sumptuous Italian style.*

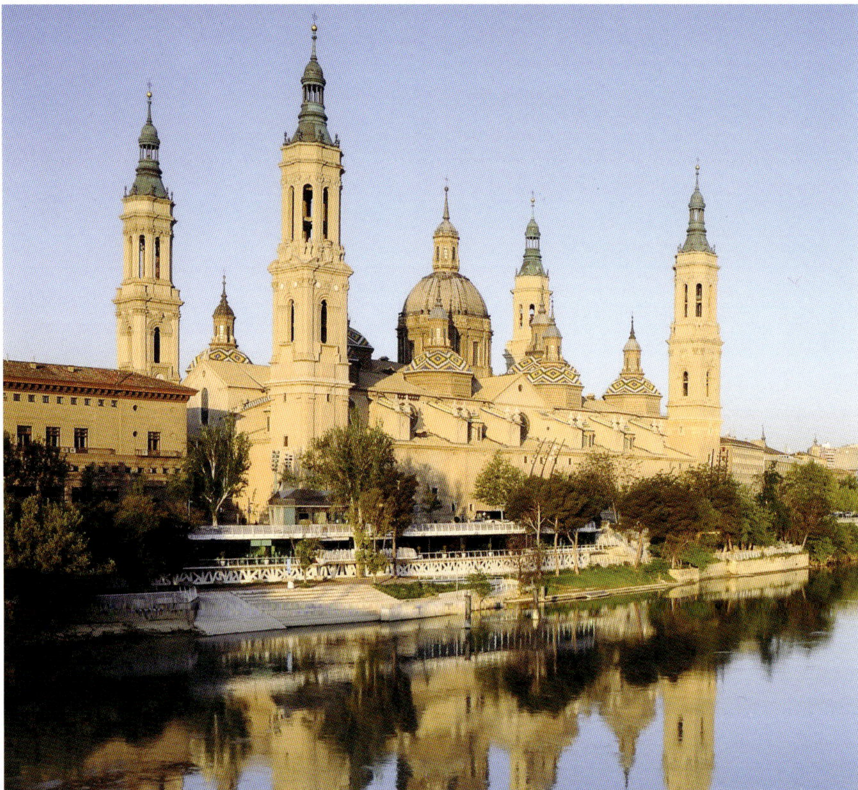

Above: The Basilica of Our Lady of El Pilar, Saragossa, where Goya produced some of his first and most important religious works.

the competition again. One of the judges was Francisco Bayeu and one of the entrants was his younger brother Ramón. Goya received no votes from any of the judges and Ramón was awarded the scholarship. Although probably feeling somewhat bitter, Goya apprenticed himself to Francisco Bayeu.

VISIT TO ITALY

Goya was 20 years old in 1766. After the disappointment of not winning, he set his sights on travelling to Italy instead to continue his education there, studying the masterpieces of antiquity, the Renaissance and the Baroque. Italy was the centre of the art world at that time and Goya believed he could learn how to paint in the Neoclassical style there.

By 1770, he had raised the money to make the trip.

He lived in Italy for two years, staying in Rome for one of them with a friend of Mengs's, a Polish artist named Taddeo Kuntz (1727–93). As he had planned, he studied the works of the great masters and made contact with other contemporary artists. Little is documented of his Italian travels, but he studied the technique of fresco painting following the Baroque and Rococo examples of such artists as Tiepolo and Correggio (1489–1534), and he found that Neoclassicism was not to his taste after all. In 1771, he entered an open painting competition provided by the Academy of Parma in northern Italy. Although not verified, it has been suggested that he won second prize and earned commendation from at least one of the judges. The successful painting was *The Victorious Hannibal,* and

THE TECHNIQUE OF FRESCO

The expression fresco derives from the Italian 'buon fresco', meaning 'true fresco'. It is a technique of painting on to fresh, wet lime plaster with water-soluble paint. (Fresco secco is paint applied to dry plaster.) In the buon fresco method, the paint bonds with the wall as the plaster dries, forming a durable image. As soon as the colour is applied, it becomes part of the wall, so that application requires a confident hand.

the judge praised his light brushstrokes and 'warmth of expression', but also told that his composition was a little eccentric and his colours not realistic enough. Still, it was the greatest success he had achieved so far.

RETURN TO SARAGOSSA

Soon after the competition in Parma, Goya returned to Saragossa. Arriving there in the late summer or early autumn of 1771, almost immediately, he was commissioned to complete a series

Below: Goya was highly respectful of Francisco Bayeu's work. In this unusual Visitation, 1774, Goya demonstrates Bayeu's skilful use of composition and light. Another detail is shown on page 109.

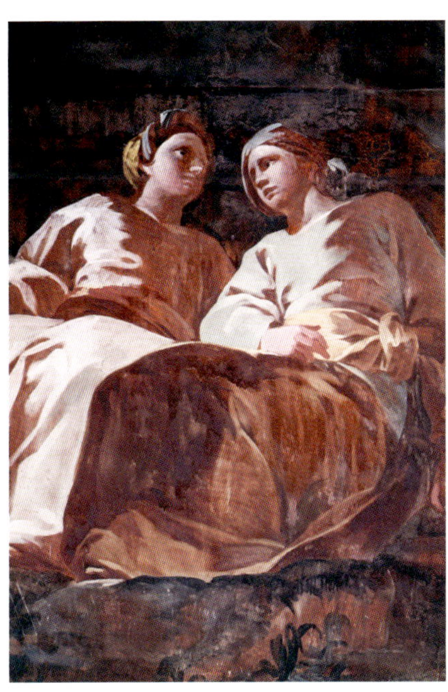

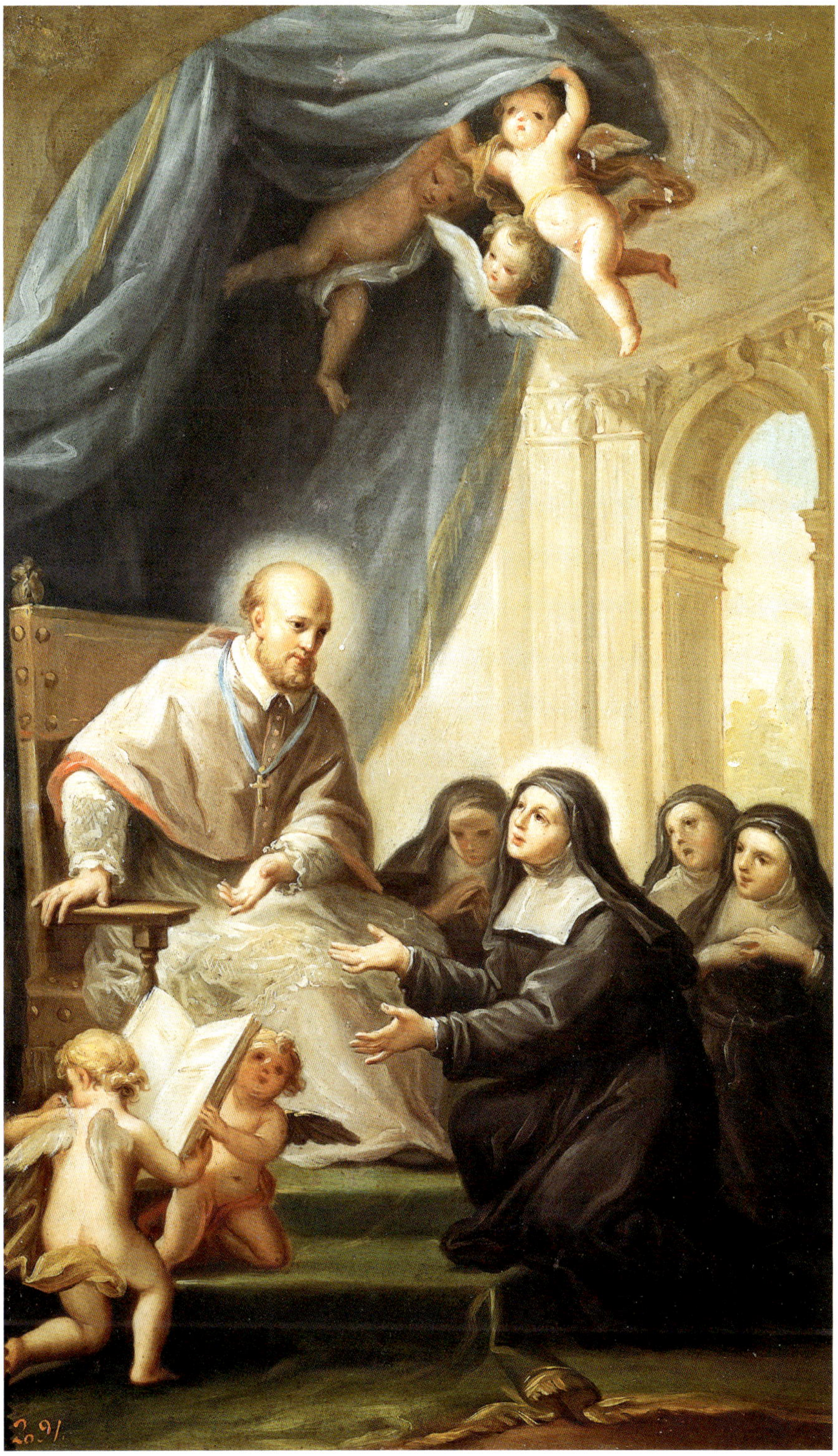

of frescoes in the Sobradiel Palace, owned by the Counts of Gabarda, and another series of paintings for the monks of the Aula Dei monastery. These were all religious works and in October, he was asked to submit sketches for a fresco in the Basilica del Pilar in Saragossa. He completed the sketches in three weeks and undercut all the other artists in line for the work

Above: Saint Francis de Sales Gives Jeanne Francoise de Chantal the Constitution of the Order of the Visitation, *by Francisco Bayeu (1734–95).*

by offering to do it for 10,000 reales less than anyone else. He got the job, completed the work in six months, and his religious paintings were extremely well-received.

MADRID

Establishing his position as a painter of religious frescoes in Saragossa, Goya's career seemed to be pursuing a promising path. Despite a lack of academic training, at 27 he was earning more than his old teacher Luzán. Then, in 1774, his career took an unexpected turn. Mengs called him to Madrid.

Within two years of his return to Spain, Goya had visited Francisco Bayeu, who after the death of his parents was head of the family. Goya asked Bayeu for his sister's hand in marriage. Bayeu must have believed in the younger man's promising future and his sister must have been willing, as on 25 July 1773, Goya and Josefa Bayeu (1747–1812) were married.

Below: Elegant Couple from Madrid by Lorenzo Baldissera Tiepolo. This 1770 work by Tiepolo's (other) son conveys a strong sense of personalty; something Goya became particularly skilled at.

MARRIED LIFE

By 1774, Goya had become Saragossa's most prosperous artist (not that this was especially impressive in comparison with other European artists; Saragossa was not known for its great artists). He and Josefa settled down to domesticity. It has been reported that Josefa had 20 pregnancies, but this is possibly an exaggeration. No records exist for this, as miscarriages and deaths of children under seven were not recorded, but she did have multiple pregnancies with at least seven of their children being baptized. Yet only one of their children survived; a son, Francisco Javier Goya, born in 1784. Little else is

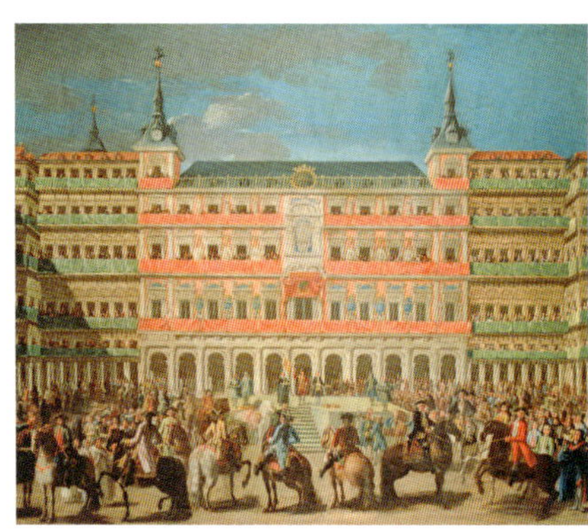

Above: Created for Charles III in 1760, this Neoclassical façade of the Plaza Mayor in Madrid would have looked sophisticated and modern to Goya and his contemporaries.

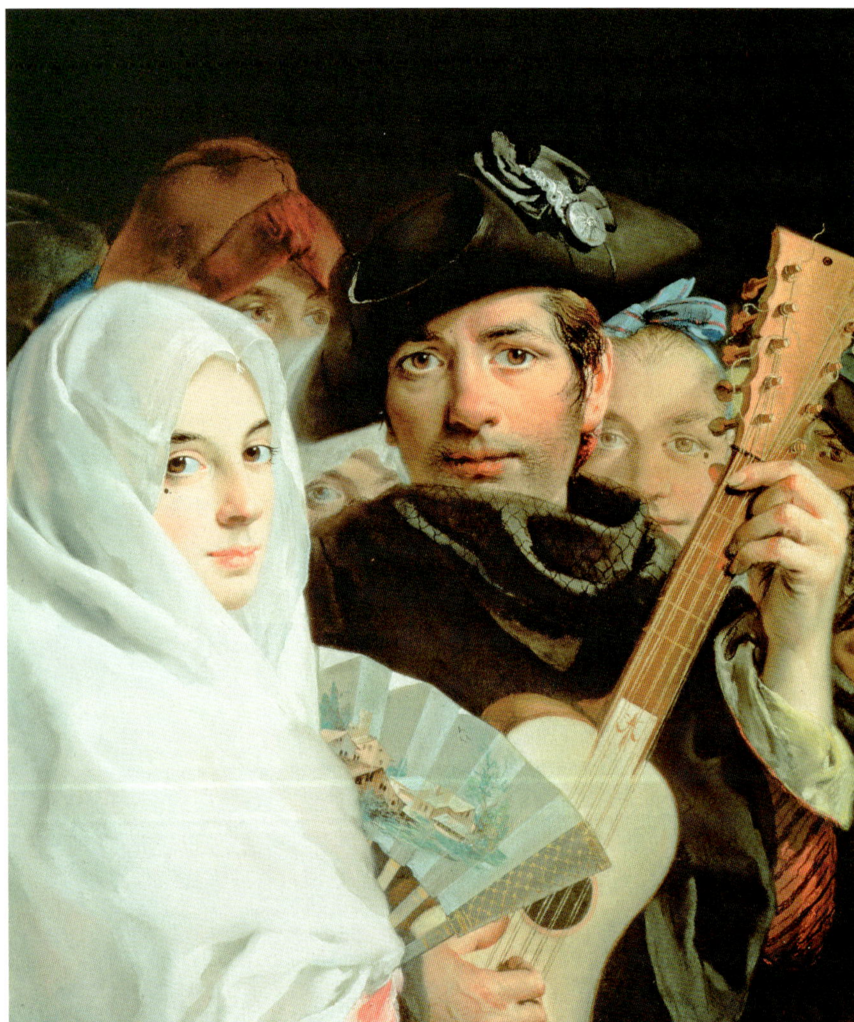

CAPITAL CITY

During the mid-16th century, after the kingdoms of Castile and Aragon had been united, the Habsburg King Philip II sought a permanent residence for his Court and somewhere healthy for his fragile young wife Elisabeth. He chose to establish his Court in Madrid, as it was geographically in the centre of Spain and was favoured with clean, dry air. The monarchs who followed him continued to maintain Madrid as the Spanish capital, but it was not built on historical foundations, and when Goya and Josefa moved there, it was still not one of the great capital cities of Europe. The palaces were relatively new and it lacked amenities and character. But King Charles III and his immediate predecessors, Philip V and Ferdinand VI, were determined to make it as attractive as the other European capitals and had added fountains, public baths, trees and paving stones, while contemporary architects were building in the new Neoclassical styles.

Right: The Count of Miranda, c.1774, *originally believed to have been by Goya, the authenticity of this painting has now been called into question.*

known about Josefa, whom Goya called La Pepa, which roughly translated means 'the pip' and refers fondly to her diminutive size. She was quiet, loved clothes, and she must have suffered greatly with so many miscarriages, stillbirths and early deaths of a number of her children.

THE DRAWINGS

Francisco Bayeu had a great influence on Mengs's decision to invite Goya to Madrid. Although not Spanish, Mengs had been made First Painter to the King, and Bayeu was a Court Painter alongside him. Mengs had recently reorganized the Royal Tapestry factory in Madrid with a view to rejuvenate it and bring it up to the high standards of the French Gobelins tapestry factory in Paris. To do this, many more tapestries needed to be made and Mengs's idea was to bring some of the best artists of Spain to Madrid to design images for the weavers, who would translate them into tapestries. But Goya had so far only worked as a religious painter, not as a designer of tapestries, and the tapestry cartoons were to be pictures of everyday scenes.

FACE TO FACE WITH VELÁZQUEZ

As soon as he moved to Madrid and began working on the tapestry designs, Goya took advantage of his connections with Mengs and Bayeu, and went to see the vast collection of paintings in the royal palaces, the El Pardo, El Escorial and the Palacio Real. Previous kings had amassed works by great Spanish and Italian painters and it was in the palaces that Goya saw paintings by Diego Velázquez at first hand. Until then, he had probably seen some of Velázquez's images in engravings at Luzán's studio, but he was unprepared for the effect the paintings would have over him.

Right: The Glory of Spain I, *Tiepolo, 1764, ceiling of the Throne Room in the Palacio Real. Goya later interpreted similar drama in his own images to be seen from below.*

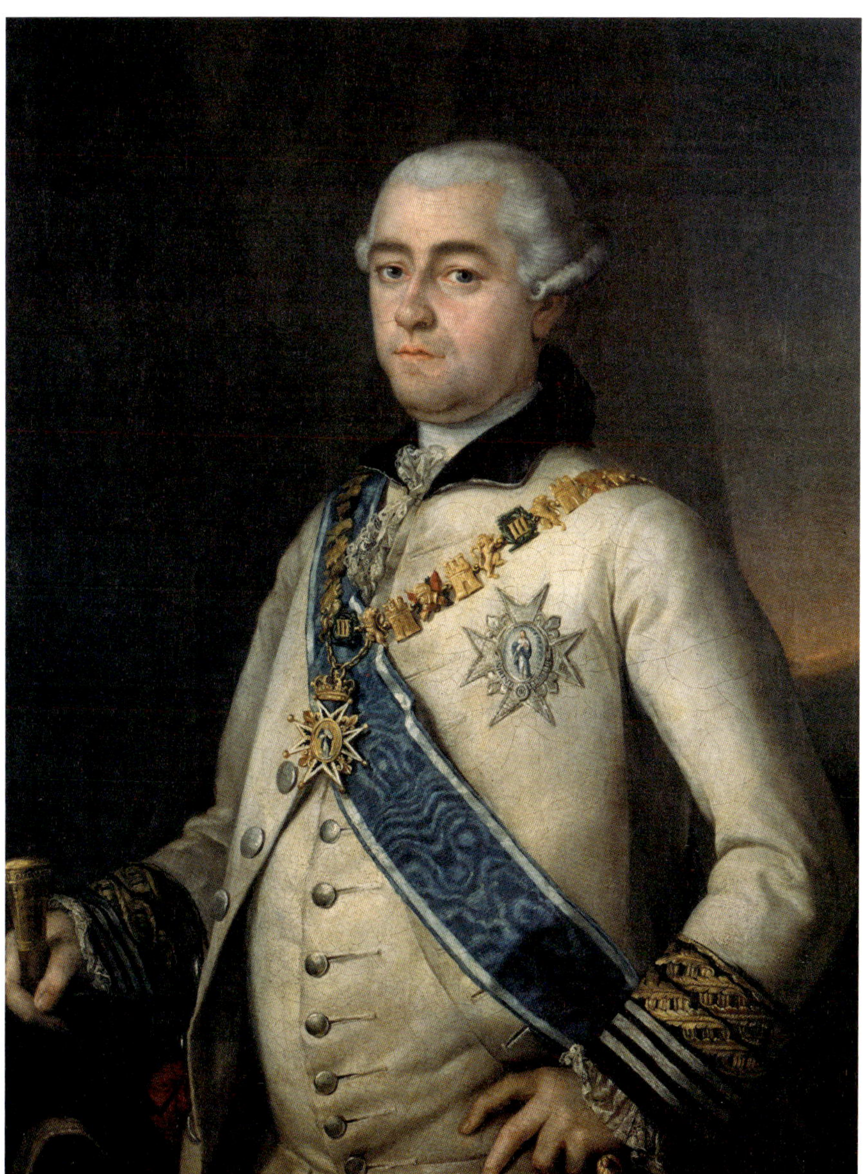

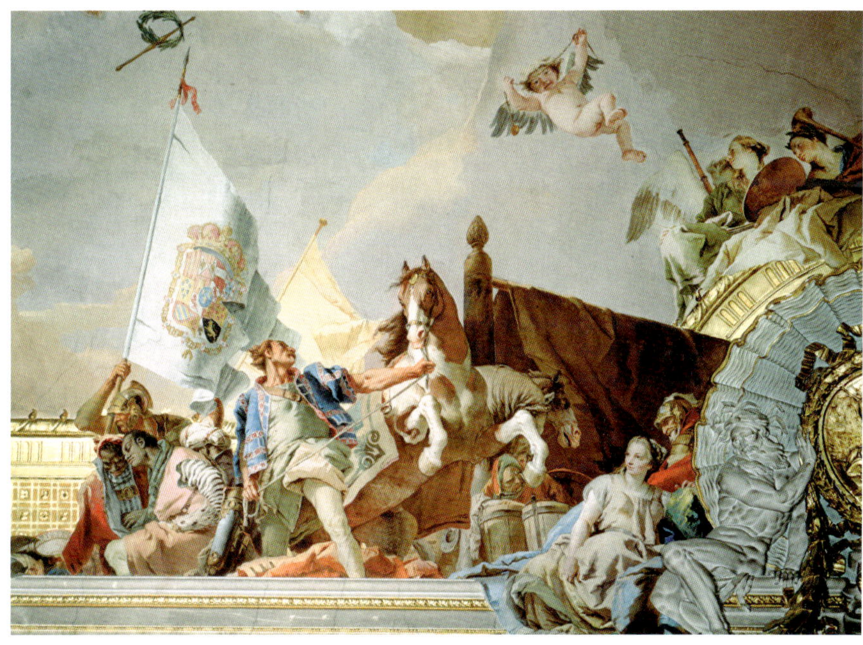

THE ROYAL TAPESTRIES

Despite Mengs's Neoclassical ideals, he decided to create tapestries of images to please the King, featuring scenes of country life, such as picnics and excursions, following French Rococo ideas. Mengs's primary aim was to retain royal favour, so Goya's first assignment was a series of hunting and fishing scenes.

While the new tapestry designs neither projected the fashionable Neoclassical style, nor featured the more conventional biblical or mythological subjects of the period, the painter Anton Raphael Mengs was right; the King loved the bucolic, light-hearted subjects. But Goya's first paintings for these tapestries were not outstanding. Instead, they were rather dull, and showed a close and self-conscious compliance to Bayeu's style.

POSITIVE MESSAGES

The Spanish Royal Tapestry factory had been founded in 1720 and immediately placed under the management of a tapestry specialist from Antwerp. Until Mengs took control, all the tapestries made there had been designed following engravings of Dutch paintings. Mengs's idea to bring in young, promising Spanish painters was masterful. It emitted positive messages outside Madrid that King Charles III was progressive and was investing in the Spanish creative industries, and it gave the young artists a chance to prove themselves worthy of working

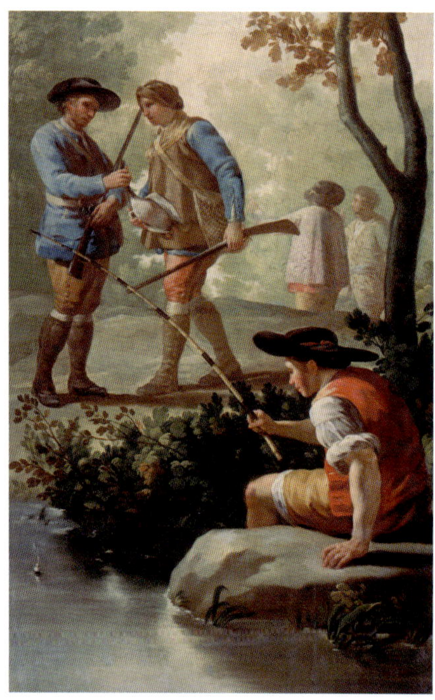

Above: Fishermen with Rods *(detail), 1775; Goya's dependence on Bayeu's style is clear, with only his treatment of natural light showing originality.*

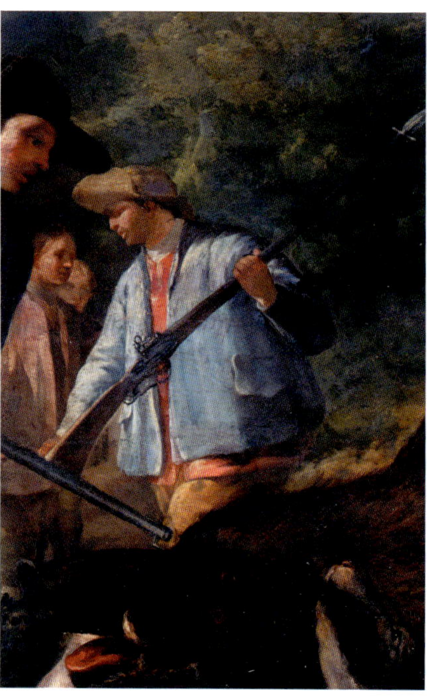

Above: Wild Boar Hunt, *1775; a detail of one of Goya's first cartoons on the theme of hunting.*

for the King and of producing art that compared favourably with the art of other countries. Consequently, it meant that Spanish tapestries would become original and modern.

DECORATION AND INSULATION

The tapestries were to be richly coloured wall decorations that would enliven the royal palaces, while also serving the practical purpose of blocking out bitter winter drafts. Many of them are unusually shaped, as they were made to cover specific areas on the palace walls. It is clear from their style that Goya's first cartoons were designed under Bayeu's close supervision, but this was to be expected; Bayeu had been his teacher, was the elder and more successful and experienced artist, and Goya had never designed tapestry cartoons before. It is natural that Bayeu

taught him the specific techniques required for the job.

SPANISH FOLK SCENES

The first series of cartoons were made for the King at the El Escorial palace in Madrid. Consisting of eight hunting scenes and one fishing scene, they were delivered in two lots, on 24 May and 30 October 1775. Goya was commissioned to produce a second series, which he painted between 1776 and 1778. These were to decorate the dining room of the Prince and Princess of the Asturias (the future Charles IV and Queen María Luisa) in the El Pardo palace. This second series included 19 cartoons, which Goya painted in a far more original, dynamic and colourful style than his first cartoons. The Crown Prince and his wife had requested typical Spanish folk scenes, and Goya duly designed cheerful,

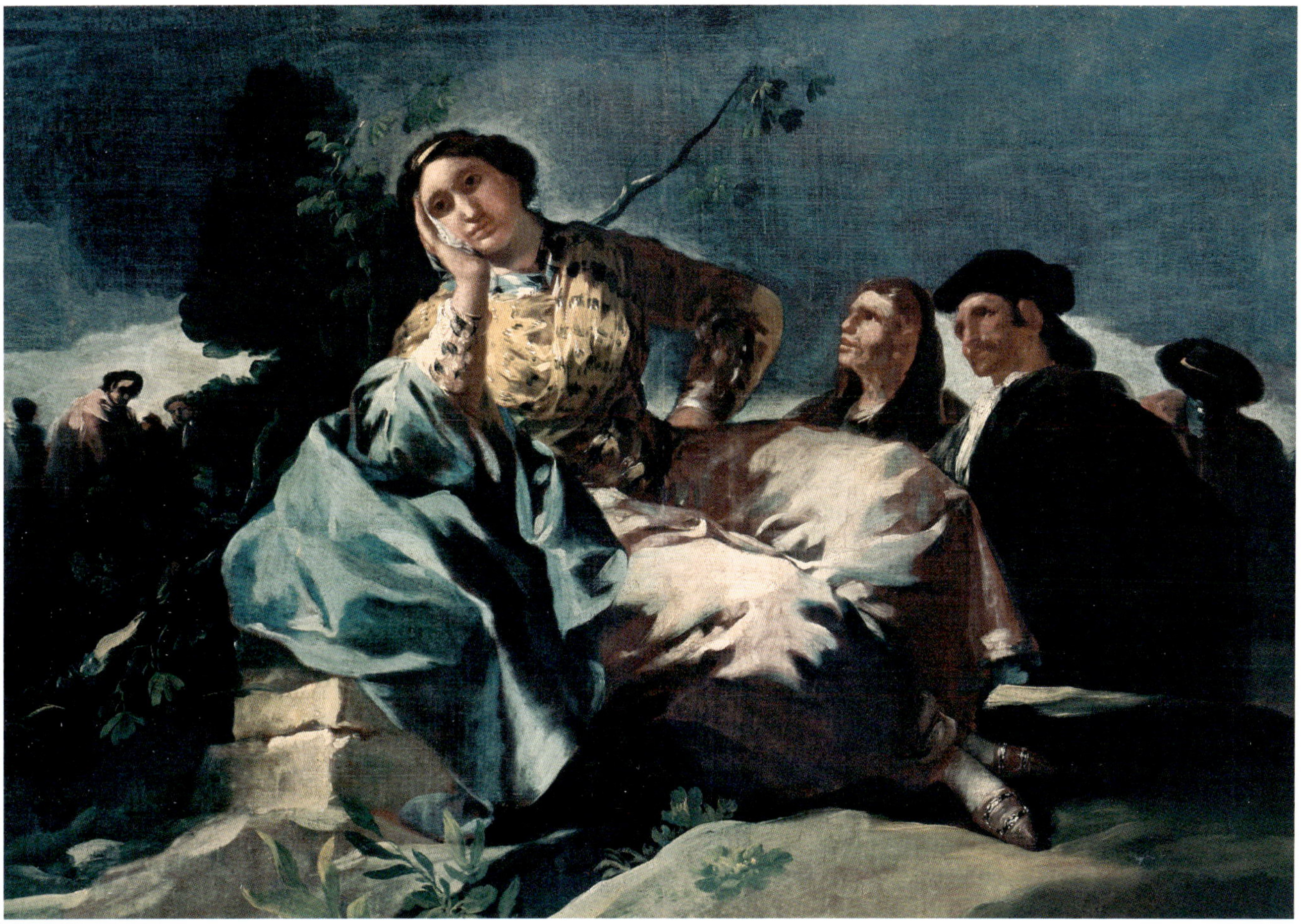

Above: The Rendezvous, *1779–80; for a tapestry located above a window in the El Pardo palace (see page 38), Goya earned 1000 reales for this design.*

vibrant compositions, featuring dancers, woodcutters, washerwomen, children playing, bullfights, travelling pedlars and other typically charming characters and events, all set in the Spanish countryside. Several featured majas and majos; streetwise and colourful Spanish women and men, instantly recognizable by their elaborate dress based on traditional Spanish costume and their provocative and flirtatious behaviour. During the 18th century, the lifestyle, attire and conduct of the majas greatly appealed to fashionable society women.

For many years, Goya's first cartoons were attributed to one or other of the Bayeu brothers. Without any individual recognition or obvious personal style, his work did not stand out, and as an illustration of his lack of significance, a document of the time called him Ramón Goya. But his second series of tapestry designs brought him notice.

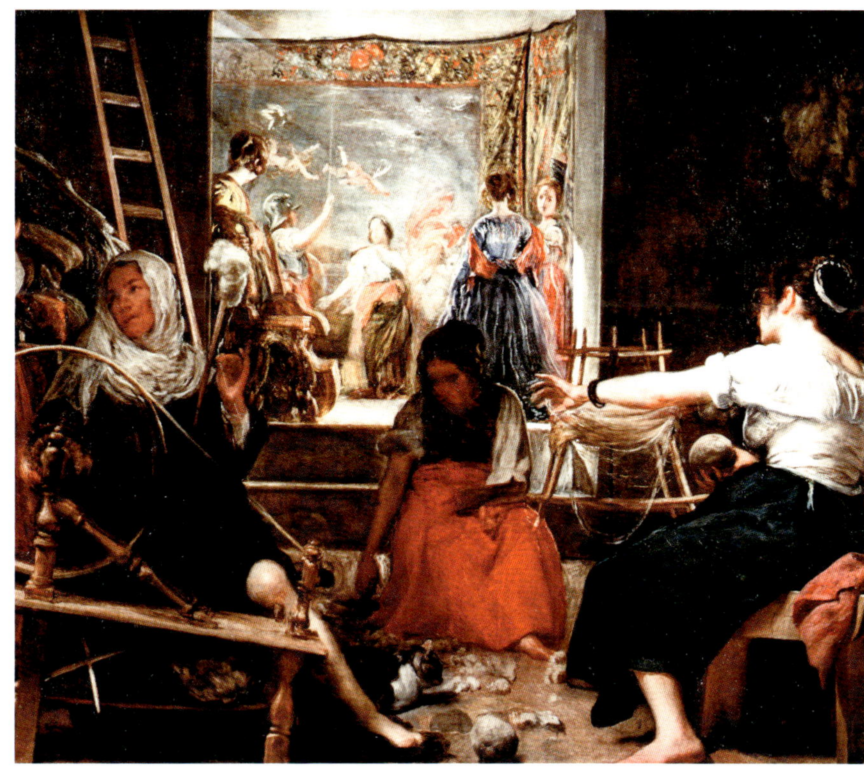

Right: Detail from The Fable of Arachne, *1657; Velázquez's depiction of an ancient Greek myth, featuring weavers from the earlier royal tapestry factory in Madrid.*

THE ROYAL ACADEMY

Goya's cartoons made for the Prince and Princess of the Asturias were bright, lively and original. Soon, word about his abilities began to spread. So when in 1779, Mengs died in Rome leaving an opening for a member at the Spanish San Fernando Royal Academy, Goya put himself forward.

Mengs had been a generous supporter of younger artists and a great help to Goya. While the first cartoon series was being completed, he had been consulted about the new tapestries for the El Pardo palace. He had written a testimonial: 'Don Francisco Goya has also worked for the Royal Tapestry Factory, he is a person of talent and intelligence who is capable of making great progress in his art, supported by the royal munificence and at the present time, he is already proving himself useful in the service of the King.' Mengs proposed that Goya should receive 8,000 reales a year for the work. (At the time, Bayeu was earning 30,000 reales as Court Painter.) Goya was given the commission.

Below: Detail from Picnic on the Banks of the Manzanares, *1776. In lavishly painted detail, Goya shows how this colourful orange seller touts her wares.*

VELÁZQUEZ ENGRAVINGS

Before the invention of photography in 1839, prints were the only means of reproducing paintings. On 29 July 1778, an advertisement in the newspaper *Gaceta de Madrid* advertised nine etchings after paintings by Velázquez, 'engraved by Don Francisco Goya' (see page 120). This was Goya's first close encounter with his hero's work. Goya originally made precise drawings of the paintings, which he then etched on copper plates to produce as prints.

APPLYING FOR MEMBERSHIP

Believing that he could capitalize on the success of his latest cartoons, almost as soon as the 51-year-old Mengs had died, Goya applied for the position of Court Painter. On 24 July 1779, he wrote to the King (who was busy on other matters as Spain had just entered the American Revolutionary War as an ally of France).

Below: Picnic on the Banks of the Manzanares *(detail), 1776. This tapestry cartoon is classed as one of Goya's first great masterpieces (see also page 101).*

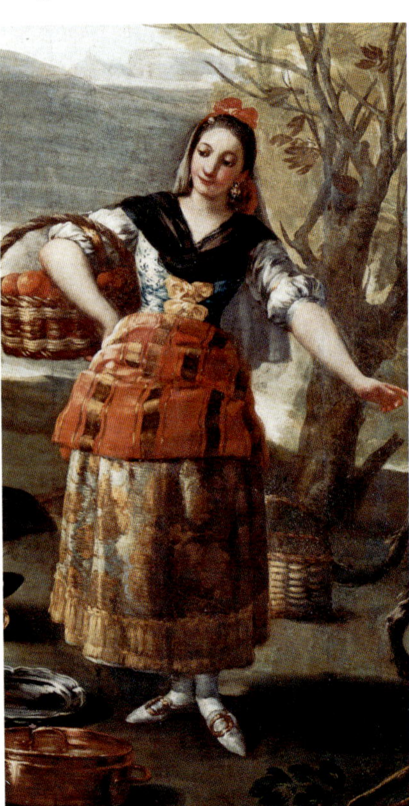

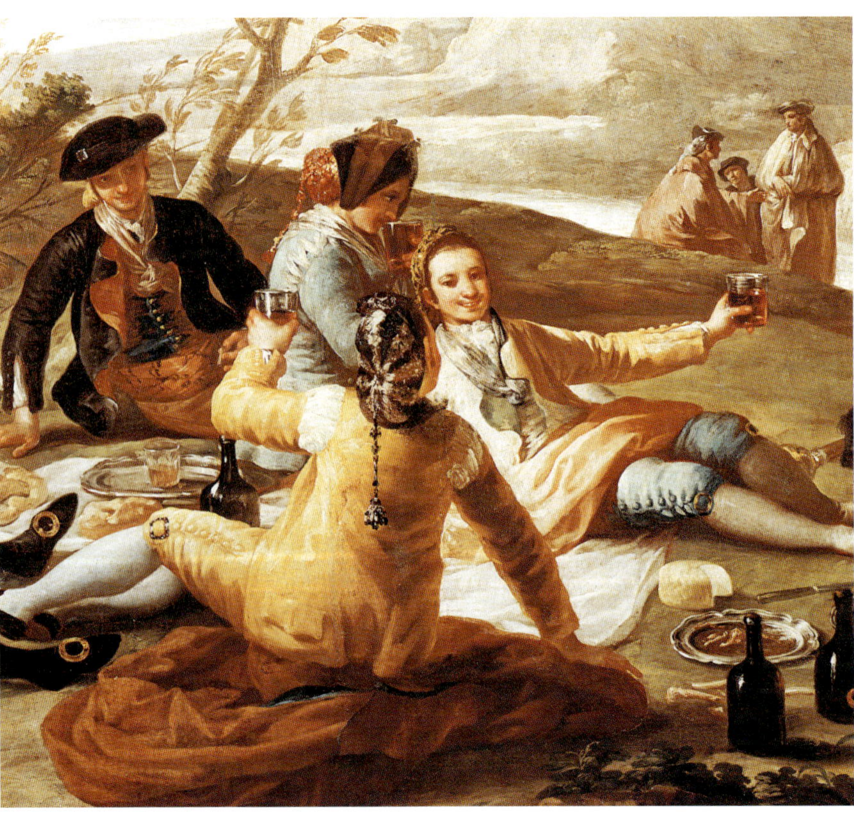

Right: The Drawing Lesson, *1788, by Domenico Fedeli or Maggiotto (1713–94). Official European art academies were powerful and Goya's acceptance to the Spanish academy was a sign of the esteem with which he was held.*

Below: One of Goya's 1778 etchings, after Velázquez's painting, Aesop, *1640; the 6th-century* BCE *Greek writer of fables.*

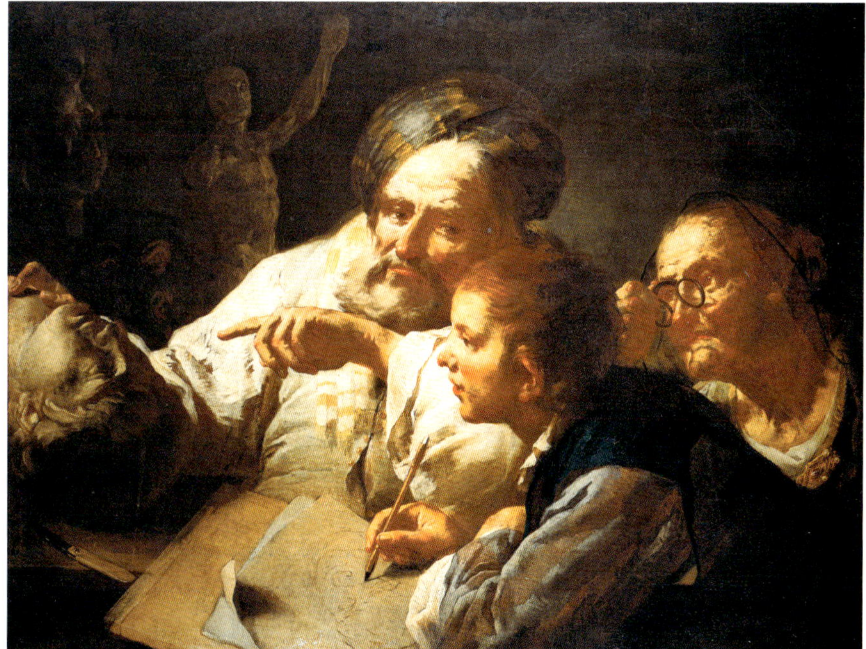

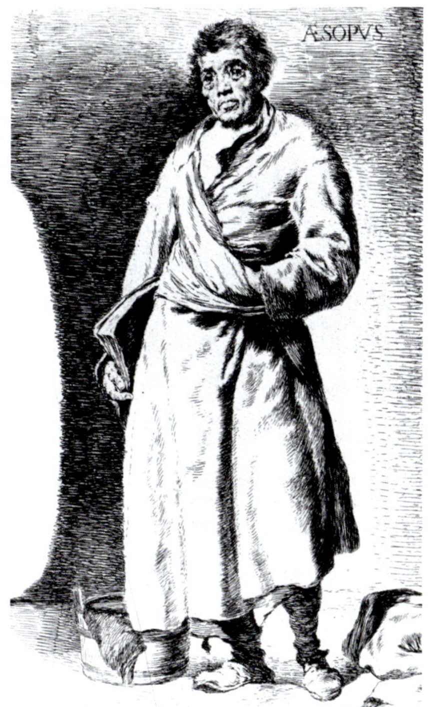

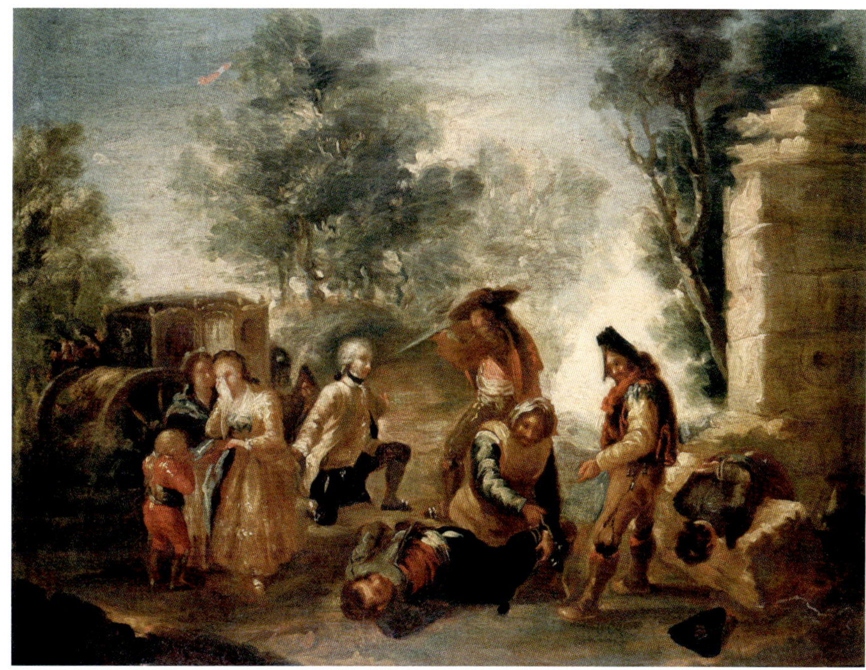

Goya's petition – in the third person – declared: '...having practised his art in his birthplace Saragossa, and in Rome whither he travelled and lived at his own expense, he was summoned by Don Antonio Rafael de Mengs to continue it in the service of Your Majesty.' However, the position of Court Painter was awarded to another artist, ten years Goya's senior. Instead, Bayeu advised him to try for the now vacant membership at the Royal Academy. With two previous rejections there, Goya was not optimistic, but Josefa was pregnant with their fourth child and all commissions at the Royal Tapestry factory had been temporarily suspended. He determined to capitalize on the success he had been building, and to continue to show his brothers-in-law that he could support their sister. Returning to the reliability of religious art, for his submission to the Academy,

Goya painted an image of *Christ Crucified* (see page 132), following the traditional images of the subject produced by Velázquez in c.1613 and Mengs in 1761–9. He adopted Velázquez's plain dark background and the pose of Christ from Mengs, making every effort to achieve the highly finished execution that was the academic ideal.

After his two disappointments in the 1760s, in May 1780 the Spanish Royal Academy elected Goya unanimously as a member of Spain's most prestigious institution of art.

Above: Bandits attacking a Coach, *c.1776–8. Bandits were a common problem in 18th- and 19th-century Spain.*

NEW HOME

That year, Goya and Bayeu quarrelled. While working together on a fresco in Saragossa's Cathedral, Bayeu asked Goya to alter some things, but Goya refused. A row ensued and inflamed, Goya returned to Madrid with Josefa. They moved into a house in the Calle del Desengaño where Goya kept a studio for nearly 20 years.

THE ENLIGHTENMENT

By the middle of the 18th century, a shift in thinking occurred that became known as the Enlightenment or the Age of Reason. Goya developed as an artist during this period of intellectual, social and political fervour. Generated by a range of influences, the Enlightenment began in France and spread across Europe and beyond.

Focusing on intellectual thought and reason, the Enlightenment embraced the advancement of scientific knowledge and supported the need for human rights, and religious tolerance, challenging the misuse of power by the Church and the State. Many of the ideas were generated by philosophers, writers, mathematicians and scientists, such as Baruch Spinoza (1632–77), Montesquieu (1689–1755), Denis Diderot (1713–84), Voltaire, Kant, Hume, Newton, Locke and Rousseau.

The Enlightenment was a period of optimism, bolstered by the belief that with science and reason – and the consequent shedding of old superstitions – people and society could be improved.

NEW PERSPECTIVES

Recent scientific discoveries had been overturning many previously accepted notions and introduced new perspectives about the world and man's place within it. Enlightenment thinkers developed new theories on nearly every aspect of life, including education, economics, law, the universe and social and political reform. Rousseau, for example, questioned the idea of the divine right of kings, pointing out that God did not choose kings; people did. Voltaire (real name François-Marie Arouet) criticized the Church, supporting compassion, acceptance and freedom of expression. A new way of understanding the universe was proposed. Called 'Deism', it accepted the existence of God, but not his continual presence and control of human life. Enlightenment theorists also condemned Rococo art for being unethical, calling for a new kind of moral art that would teach people the values of right and wrong. The philosopher and art critic Diderot wrote that writers, artists and artisans had a duty 'to make virtue attractive, vice odious, ridicule forceful. That is the aim of every honest man who takes up the pen, the brush or the chisel.' Neoclassicism had the qualities needed.

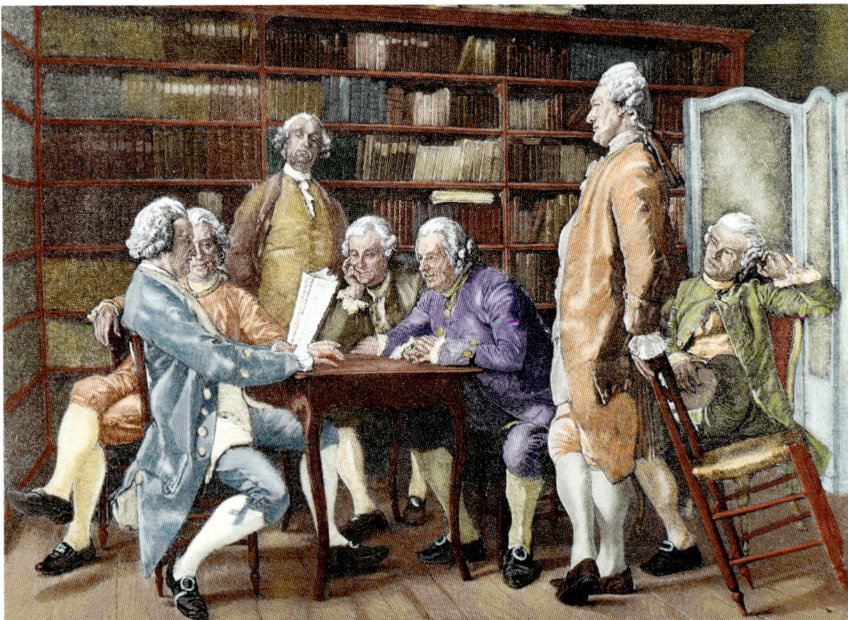

Top left: A 20th-century illustration of The Tertulia of Diderot. *There was no comparable Spanish philosopher, but Goya and his friends were fascinated by Diderot's theories.*

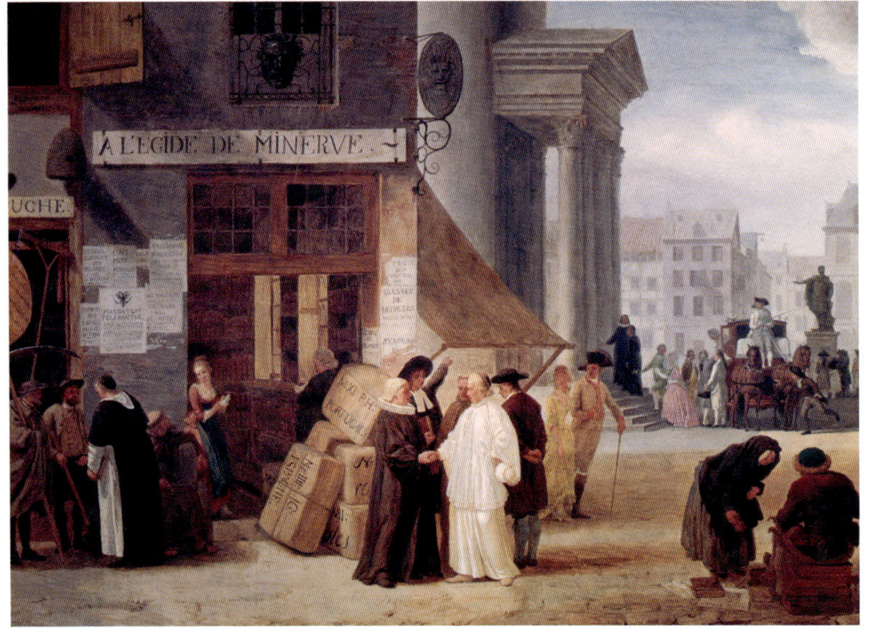

Left: At Aegis Minerva, c.1782, Léonard Defrance (1735–1805). Symbolizing Enlightenment beliefs, representatives of the main religions gather. Goya believed in religious tolerance.

L'ENCYCLOPÉDIE

In Paris in 1751, a huge work was published. Conceived as a dictionary of arts, sciences and professions, it was called *L'Encyclopédie*, edited by Diderot, and (until 1759) Jean le Rond d'Alembert (1717–83), a mathematician, physicist, philosopher and music theorist. Comprising an astounding 72,000 articles written by 300 intellectuals, *L'Encyclopédie* embodied the ideals of the Enlightenment more than any other work, but it was condemned by the Pope and many others because it used science to scorn Christianity.

SUPPRESSION IN SPAIN

Unlike France, Italy, England and Germany, Spain was behind on the new thinking. The domination of the monarchy, the Church and the Inquisition there aimed to suppress Enlightenment ideas. Concepts such as human rights and universal education were suppressed in Spain, and Goya and his friends who discussed such things were regarded with mistrust by the majority of Spanish people – the ideas seemed suspiciously French.

Below: Initially, many disapproved of Diderot's Encyclopédie, *and there was no Spanish equivalent.*

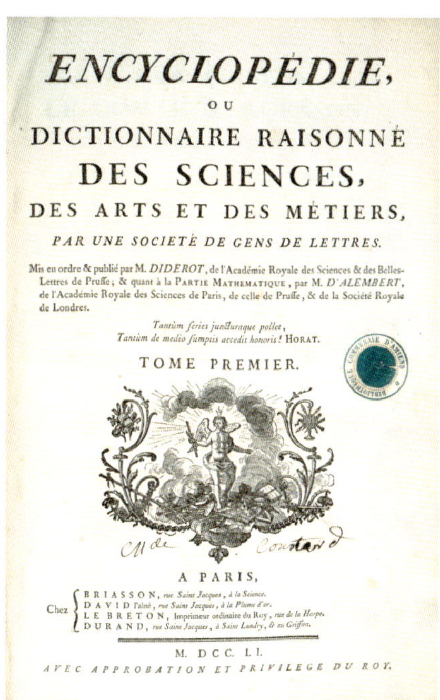

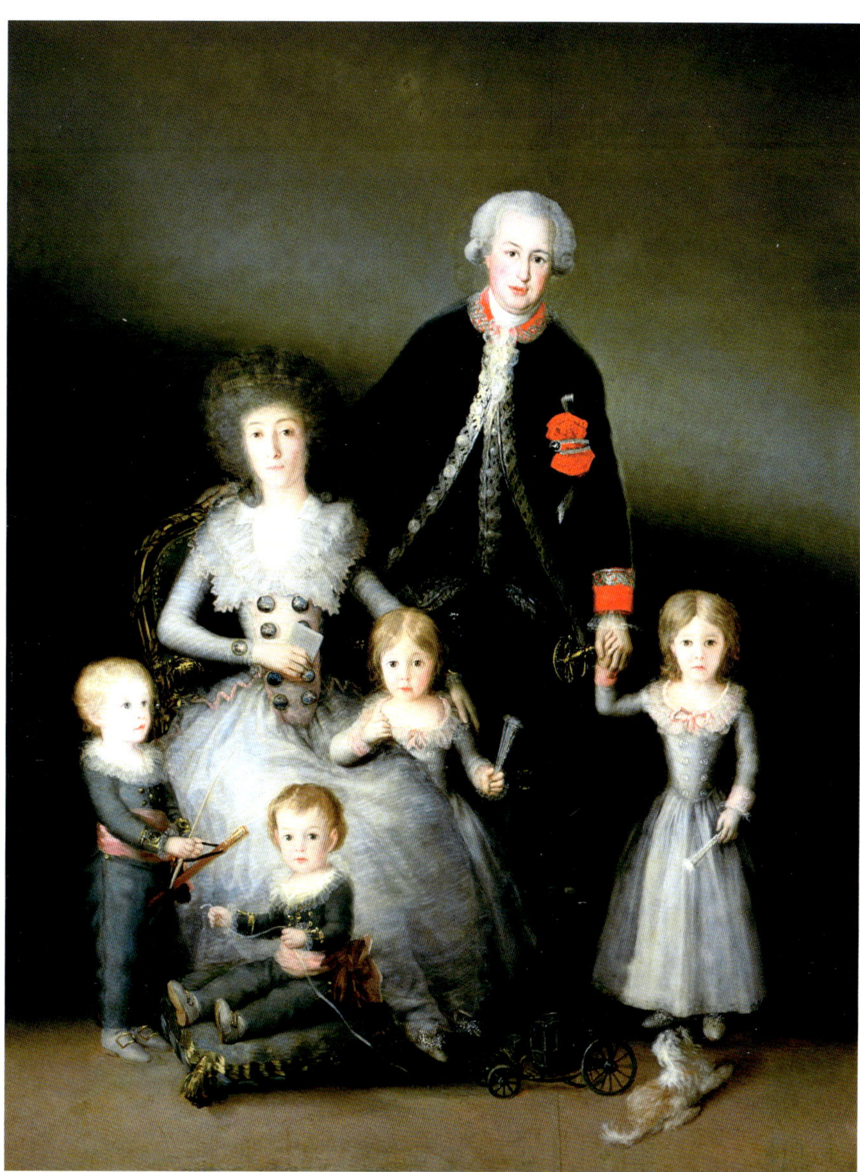

Above: The Duke of Osuna and Family, 1788. A portrait by Goya of the Spanish aristocrat who co-founded a society 'for the promotion of national cultural consciousness'.

REVOLUTION

Within a relatively short time, Enlightenment ideals, combined with a financial crisis and poor harvests left many ordinary French people both angry and hungry. In 1789, the French Revolution began as the people believed the new thinking would help them, subsequently the king and his nobles began the Counter-Revolution. In its first stage, all the revolutionaries asked for was a constitution that would limit the power of the king. Ultimately however, their demands were not met, the idea of a constitution failed, and the revolution entered a more radical stage. In 1792, Louis XVI and his wife Marie-Antoinette were beheaded along with thousands of other aristocrats believed to be loyal to the monarchy. When these new intellectual forces spread from Europe to America, they influenced Benjamin Franklin (1706–90) and Thomas Jefferson (1743–1826) among many others, and played a major role in the American Revolution.

The Enlightenment flourished until about 1800, after which a reaction occurred against the Industrial Revolution and the Enlightenment's rationalization of science, values, beliefs and traditions, and a counter-revolution gained force, giving way to Romanticism which focused on emotion, the imagination and intuition.

IMPORTANT PORTRAITS

After Goya had been made a member of the Royal Academy, he focused on attracting new patrons from among Madrid's upper classes. Until then, he had painted few portraits, but he soon began to be commissioned to paint them for distinguished members of society, including the King's First Minister.

King Charles III, the fourth son of Philip V, had ascended the throne in 1759 and since then had shown a preference for foreign politicians. His subjects were not happy about this, especially over the First Minister, the Italian Pablo Grimaldi y Pallavicini (c.1720–89) who had served since 1763 under King Ferdinand IV.

COUNT FLORIDABLANCA

In 1777, the king replaced Grimaldi with the Spanish José Moñino, Count Floridablanca (1728–1808). The Spanish nobility felt that as an ex-magistrate, Floridablanca was even less worthy of the position than a foreigner had been.

But Floridablanca became an extremely forceful Chief Minister, establishing many reforms, including in education, farming and banking and he instigated the lowering of taxes and the stimulation of economic growth. Next to the king, he became the most powerful man in Spain.

In 1783, Floridablanca asked Goya to paint his portrait. Goya painted two, both full-length. One work (see page 136) shows the Prime Minister in a red satin evening suit, holding a pair of spectacles. In the 18th century, spectacles represented intelligence or acuity. Behind him stands the architect Francisco Sabatini (1722–97) showing him plans for a canal, and in front of him, Goya holds up a painting for his approval. Floridablanca was shorter than Goya, and self-conscious of his height, so it seems rather diplomatic of Goya to have painted himself as smaller than the Prime Minister, although the composition is somewhat awkward. In the other portrait, Floridablanca is portrayed standing alone, about to deliver his report on the creation of the National Bank of San Carlos to Charles III, one of his most successful initiatives. Yet it seems that Floridablanca was not particularly pleased with either work as it was months before he paid Goya. If Goya had hoped that the First Minister would recommend him to others, he was mistaken. But during the sittings, he had become acquainted with the king's younger brother, the Infante Don Luis de Bourbon.

THE FAMILY OF THE INFANTE

The Infante Don Luis and his family lived away from Court, nearly 65 miles from Madrid. He and his wife María Teresa de Vallabriga had three children: a boy of six who later became the cardinal-archbishop of Toledo, María Teresa,

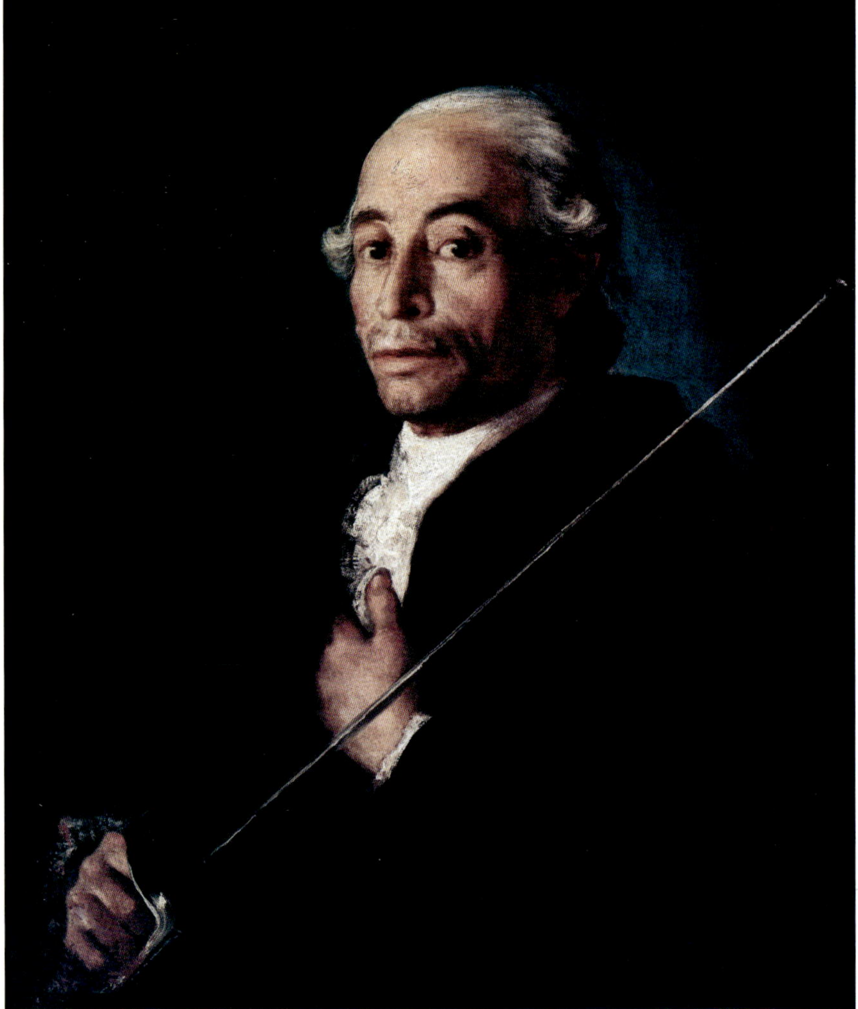

Left: Portrait of Sabatini, c.1779. This was one of Goya's earliest portraits. Francisco Sabatini (1722–97), was an Italian Neo-classical architect who worked in Spain.

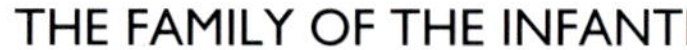

GRANDEES

In contrast with the often poor hidalgos (such as Goya's mother's family), the 'grandees' were the higher nobles of Spain who were usually outstandingly wealthy. Portraits that displayed their status and prosperity were an important part of their traditions, and it was this custom that Goya aspired to capitalize on.

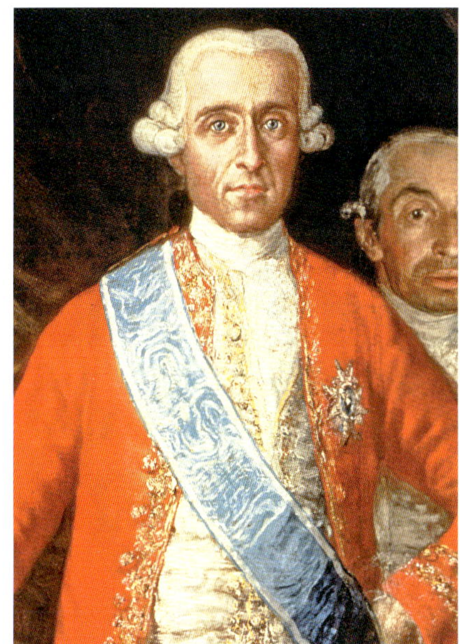

Above: Detail of Goya's 1783 portrait of the King's First Minister, Count Floridablanca, with Sabatini behind. The work helped to win Goya fame and advancement. See page 136 for the full portrait.

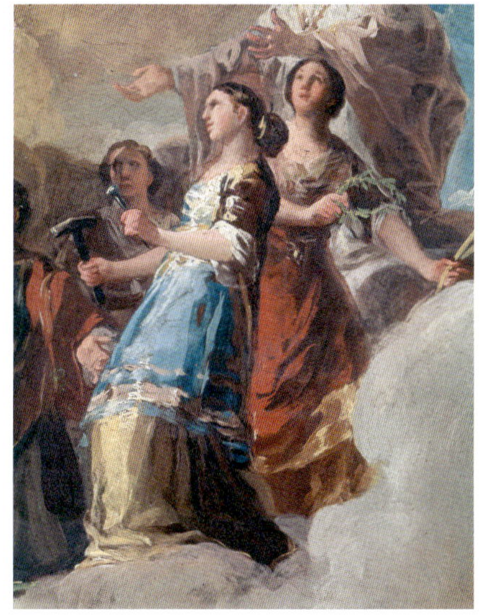

Above: A detail of Goya and Bayeu's fresco in the El Pilar in Saragossa, The Queen of the Martyrs, *1780, which gained Goya favourable recognition (see page 133).*

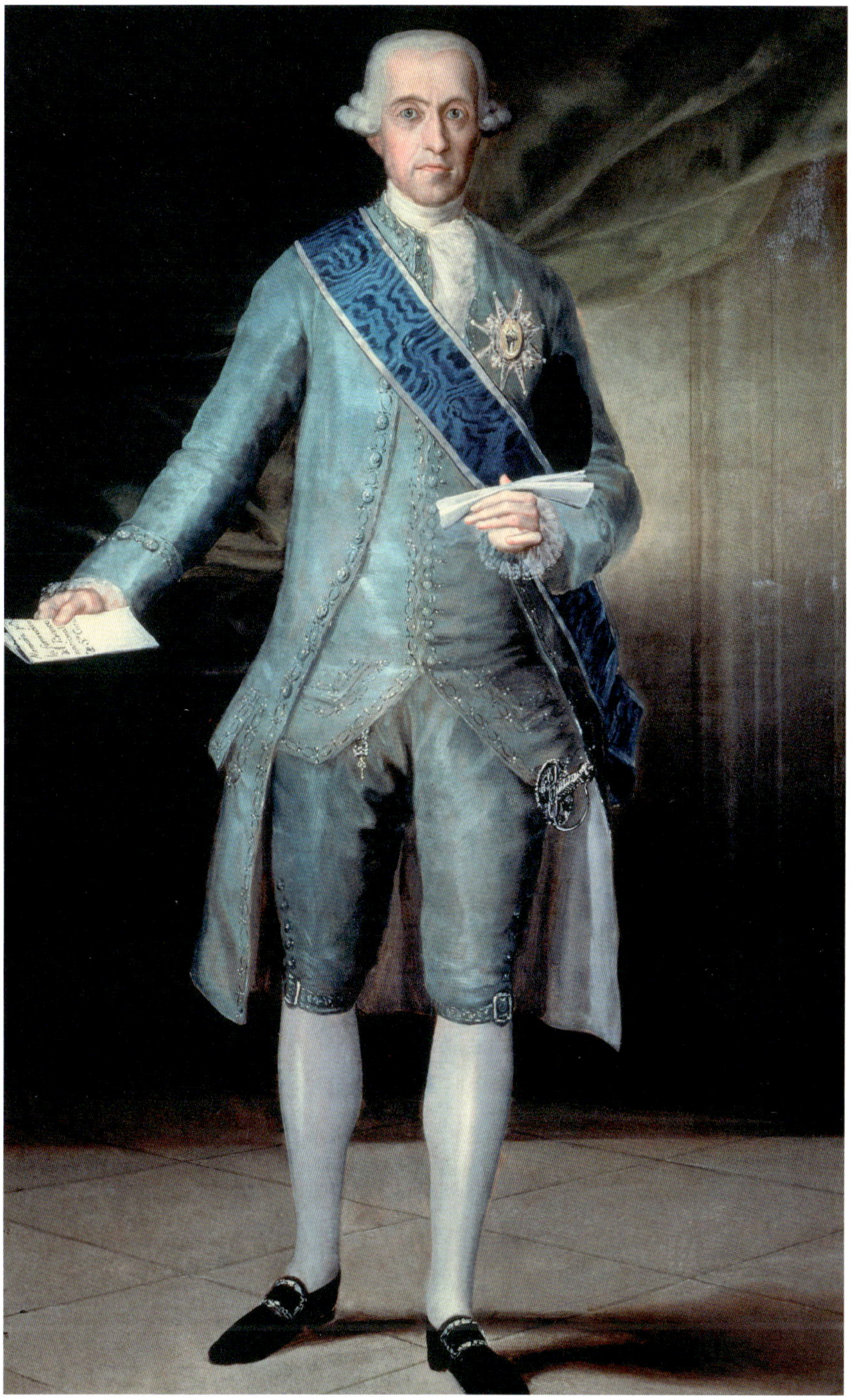

aged two years and nine months and María Josefa who was a just few months old. Don Luis invited Goya to stay with them and paint their portraits. In 1783, Goya stayed there for four weeks, painting portraits of the Infante, his wife and their two eldest children, as well as studies for a large family portrait, which he finished back at his studio in Madrid.

Above: Goya's other portrait of Count Floridablanca, c.1783, holding a report about the first National Bank of San Carlos.

The visit remained one of Goya's happiest memories and he left his hosts, paid in full and laden with gifts for himself and Josefa. He continued working for the Infante the following year, overall executing 16 works for him. He must have thought that at last he had a regular patron, but by 1785, the Infante was

seriously ill and died soon after. Goya wrote to Zapater: 'The poor Infante Don Luis...today I kissed his hand to bid him goodbye.'

A SON
Between 1775 and 1782, Josefa gave birth to five children, who all died either at birth or soon after. Then, in December 1784, a son Javier was born to them, the only one of their children who grew to adulthood.

FIRST PAINTER TO THE KING

One of Goya's skills was the ability to adapt his style, from official to personal, depending on the circumstances and commissions. Recognized for this, in 1785 he was elected Deputy Director of Painting at the Royal Academy. The following year, he and Ramón Bayeu were appointed Painters to the King.

Goya's appointment as Deputy Director of Painting at the Royal Academy was a lucrative position that gave him security and meant that he could attract further portrait commissions among the most eminent citizens, including the Infante Don Luis de Bourbon. After years of being disregarded as a relatively untrained artisan, he was suddenly propelled into new cultural and intellectual circles.

Below: Goya's imposing altarpiece of the Royal Basilica of San Francisco el Grande, 1783, shows Saint Bernardino preaching.

ROYAL CHURCH COMMISSION

Although he had been busy painting portraits, Goya had not given up on religious painting and in 1782, he was commissioned to decorate the altar of the church of San Pedro in Urrea de Gaén. The final version of *Apparition of the Virgin at Saint James of Compostela* was destroyed during the Spanish Civil War, but the sketch can be seen opposite. Also, in the year of Javier's birth, he completed a vast altarpiece for the Church of San Francisco el Grande in Madrid; the church used by the royal family. Goya was one of seven painters commissioned to paint new altarpieces there. Francisco Bayeu was another. Goya chose to paint *Saint Bernadino of Siena Preaching before Alfonso of Aragon*. In a letter, he told Zapater that he had the biggest area of all to work with. He filled a tall, vertical space with the figure of the 14th-century Italian Saint Bernadino standing on a rock bathed in holy light. Yet, despite his pride in the commission, critical opinion of the completed work was less than enthusiastic. He decided to return to portraiture.

MORE EXALTED PORTRAITS

In 1785, Goya was commissioned to paint the portraits of the directors of the newly established National Bank of San Carlos. The most important of these was the Count of Altamira, an aristocrat and a banker who was also exceptionally short. So Goya painted him sitting at a table (see page 142), perhaps in an effort to disguise his lack of height. The Count was delighted with the picture and at once commissioned Goya to paint three more portraits of his family. Further prestigious commissions followed, including a portrait of Queen María Luisa, and of the Count of Osuna and his family (see page 29), who welcomed him into their aristocratic circle.

The Osunas embodied the spirit of the Enlightenment, and surrounded themselves with philosophers, writers and musicians. Passionate about the arts and sciences, Osuna was a member of the Royal Academy; he supported the Madrid Economic Society and the Economic Societies of Friends of the Nation, and he co-founded a society 'for the promotion of national cultural consciousness.' In 1787, the Osunas commissioned Goya to decorate rooms in their beautiful villa, the Alameda Palace, known as El Capricho.

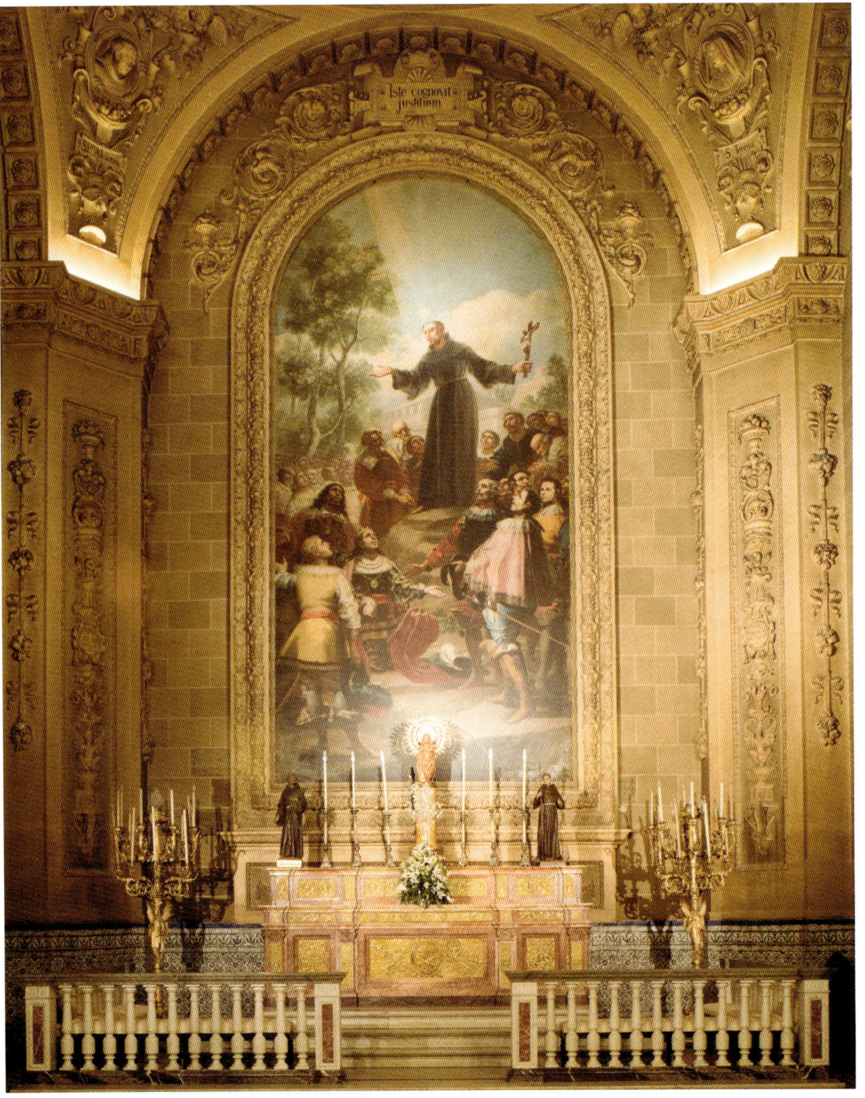

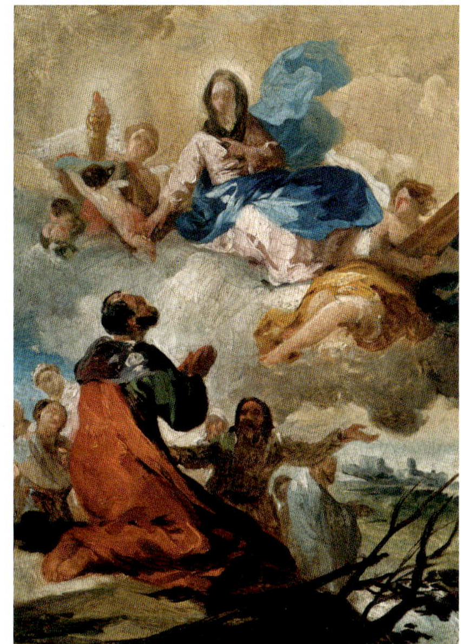

Above: Apparition of the Virgin at Saint James of Compostela, *1782. Like the Royal Basilica paintings, this shows Goya's light and expressive painting style.*

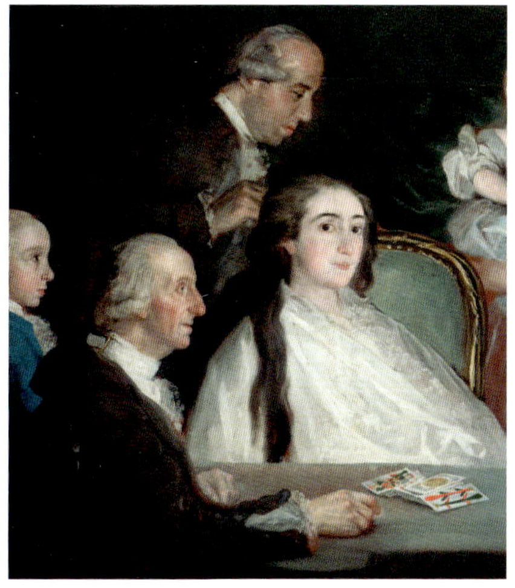

Above: Detail of The Family of the Infante Don Luis de Bourbon, *1783–4 (see page 139). Don Luis de Bourbon appreciated Goya's artistic skills as well as his friendship.*

WORKING FOR THE KING

Goya enjoyed his new-found importance; Painter to the King was a prestigious position. He had complained that his income from the bank portraits and the Academy amounted to only 12,000 or 13,000 reales a year, but by June 1786, his appointment as Painter to the King gave him an additional annual salary of 15,000 reales. He soon bought, for 7000 reales, a *birlocho*; a small English two-wheeled carriage, 'gilded and

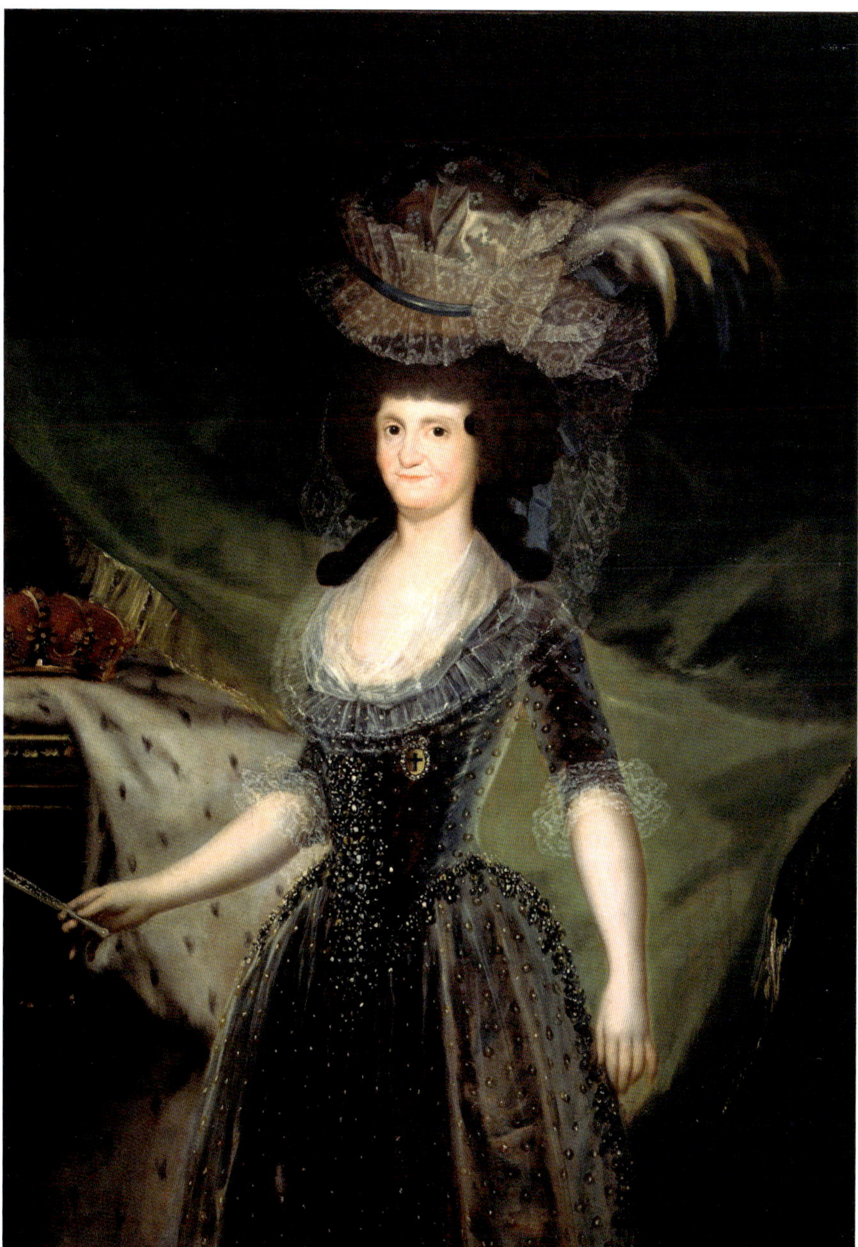

Above: Queen María Luisa of Parma, *1789; one of Goya's many paintings of the wife of Charles IV, King of Spain from 1788.*

varnished, which people stopped to look at.' It was one of only three in the whole of Madrid. He also bought an expensive house with a garden and river views, and he began to sign his name as Francisco de Goya.

It seems that the royal appointment (which Bayeu said was due to his influence) helped to reconcile Goya to his elder brother-in-law, as he painted a portrait of Francisco that year. His first tasks for the King were to paint more tapestry cartoons, and in the summer

of 1786, he designed a new series for the palace of El Pardo. The new works, which he presented to the King and the Infantes the following year, were outstanding – conventional subjects that he had invigorated with humanity, fresh perspectives, dynamism, bright colours and spontaneous gestures – a balance of fine art and lavish decoration. The paintings demonstrate his new-found confidence and more intellectual thinking, as well as his new firmer drawing style and sfumato backgrounds. That winter, he produced further portraits of the nobility and one of King Charles III (see page 144), shortly before his death.

INTO A NEW CENTURY

At the end of 1788, Charles III died. The Crown Prince and his wife ascended the throne as King Charles IV and Queen María Luisa. It was the first of many changes that heralded in the new century. Under Charles IV, Goya received the highest honours, but the new king's regime also brought decline and chaos to Spain.

Charles III had been on the throne for nearly 30 years. He had been an enlightened monarch who had tried to modernize his country, fighting against unbending traditions and the formidable power of the Church. Largely through Count Floridablanca, reforms had been made during his reign, improving the living standards of most of the populace. In Madrid, which had been smelly, with streets full of holes and no sewers, he had installed street lights and a drainage system. Charles III's death marked the end of an era. His eldest son Don Felipe was mentally retarded and epileptic, and so was passed over in favour of the younger Charles, who many considered to be good-natured but simple. He and his wife were not concerned about the same things as Charles III had been, and ignored the appalling living standards of most of their subjects.

NEW PRIME MINISTER

When he first came to the throne however, Charles IV intended to follow many of the policies of his father, and to retain Floridablanca as Prime Minister, but he preferred hunting and left affairs of state to his wife. The Queen did not care for Floridablanca and in 1792, he was ousted from office by various enemies. He was replaced with Pedro Pablo Abarca de Bolea, the Count of Aranda, but within a few months Aranda, who had been similar to Floridablanca in his intentions to raise Spain to the standards of the rest of Europe, was replaced by the 25-year-old Manuel de Godoy, the Duke of Alcudia and an intimate of the Queen. Godoy had none of his predecessors'

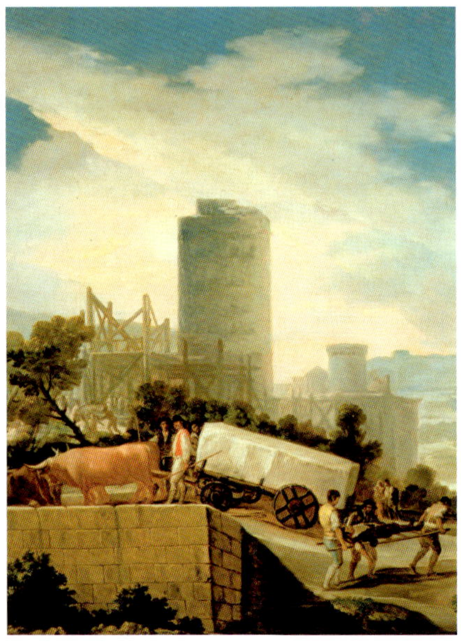

Above: Transporting a Stone Block, *1786–7; one of the seven images Goya painted for the Osunas' country residence.*

Below: The Hermitage of San Isidro, *1788; one of Goya's sketches for the Princes' bedchamber at the El Pardo.*

EVENTS IN FRANCE AND BEYOND

In France, the ideas of the Enlightenment had influenced opinions about human equality, triggering the French Revolution. Although the Spanish government kept news of the troubles from the people, all European monarchs were extremely concerned. On 14 July 1789, a group of French revolutionaries stormed the Bastille, the infamous prison of Paris. The French aristocracy lost its privileges and the Church had its possessions confiscated. King Louis XVI sent an urgent secret entreaty to his first cousin, Charles IV, asking for refuge, but fearing it would instigate similar troubles in Spain, Charles did not help. By the end of 1793, over 1000 French nobles had been sent to the guillotine, as well as Louis XVI and Marie-Antoinette.

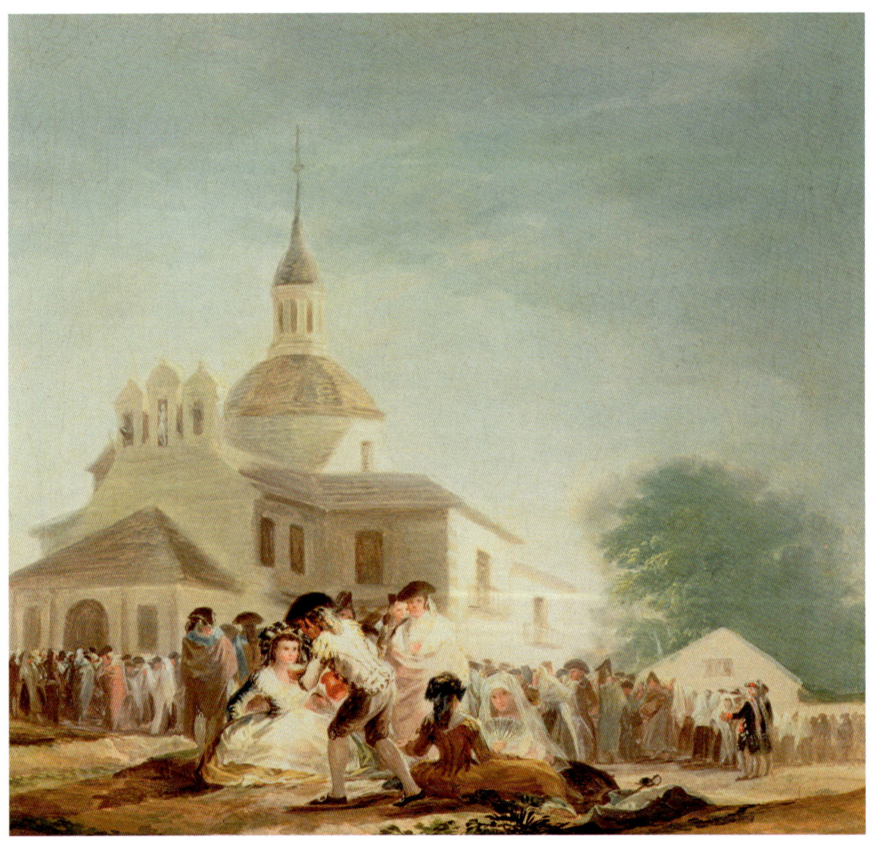

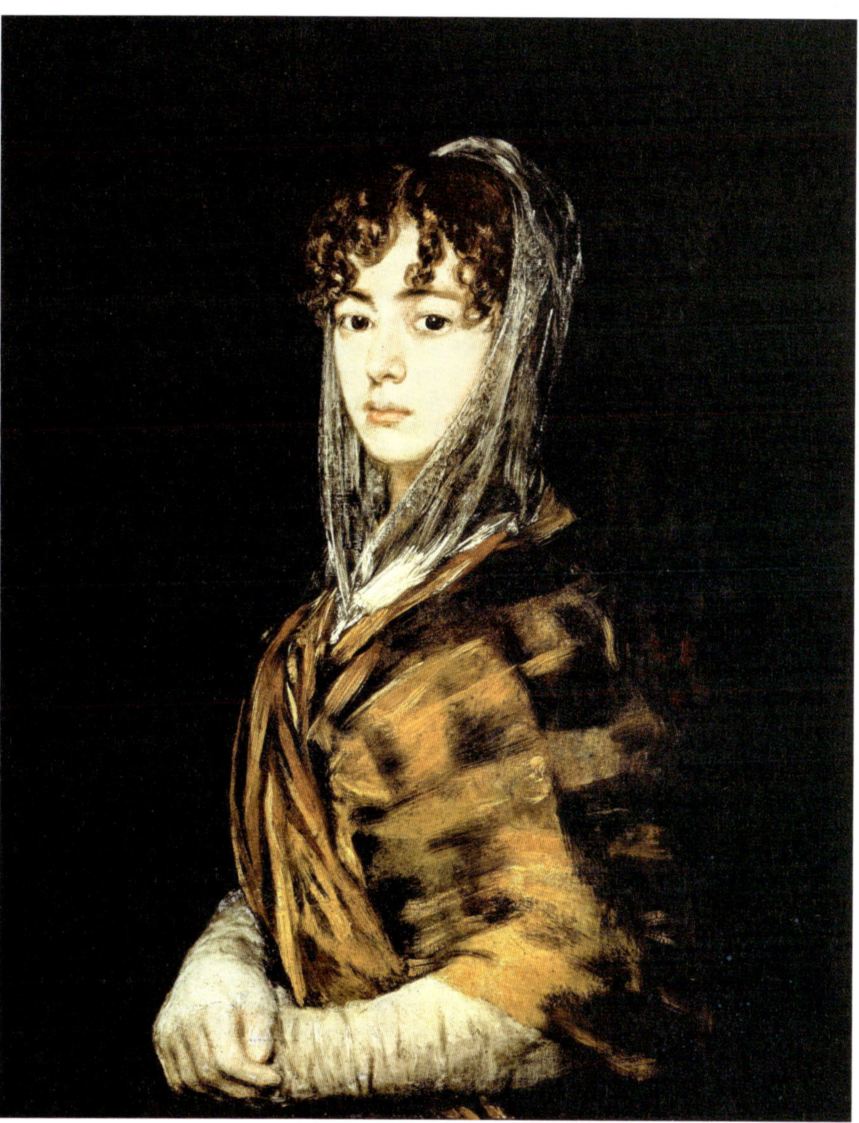

Right: Goya asked Señora Francisca Sabasa Garcia, *the niece of Spain's minister of foreign affairs, if he could paint her portrait in c.1806–11.*

vision, diplomacy and intelligence, and under his direction, along with the weak king and selfish queen, Spain began to decline once more.

COURT PAINTER

Despite the dissidence within the government and across the country, Goya's personal situation continued to improve. From the start of the new reign, as preparations were being made for the Coronation, Charles IV and María Luisa (see page 33) commissioned him to paint several official royal portraits. Numerous aristocrats followed suit, ordering their own portraits from the new artist of the moment. In 1789, the King appointed Goya Court Painter, which was superior than Painter to the King, and brought a salary increase and closer interaction with the monarch.

SPANISH STYLE

While all these shocking events were occurring on the other side of the Pyrenees, Spanish preferences in art were changing. No longer were the French and Italian styles admired above all others, instead Spanish art was beginning to be appreciated for itself, and Goya's skills, particularly as a portrait painter, were in great demand. He became known for his brutally honest images of the royal family and the nobility, and of his sensitive representations of children. In contrast with his earlier portraits, by the end of the 18th century, his portraits were more natural and relaxed, set in simpler compositions and with subtler colouring, while often also remorselessly candid.

Right: Goya's portrait of 1798–9 of Charles IV *was mercilessly unflattering, but the King was pleased with it.*

Far right: Queen María Luisa, *wearing panniers; a fashion that originated in Spain. By 1789, when Goya painted this, the style was only worn at Court. This is a companion to* Charles IV *(see page 155).*

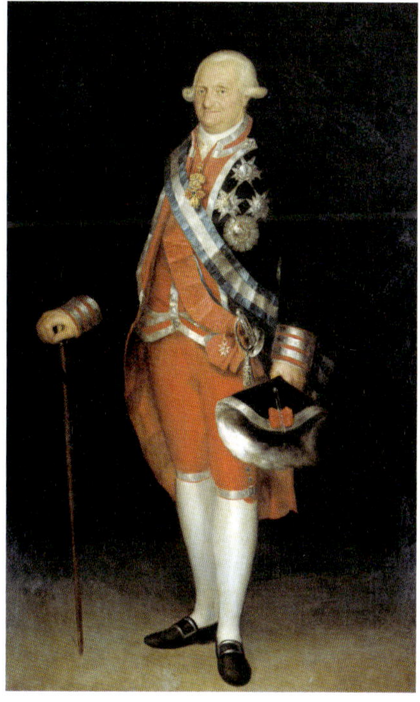

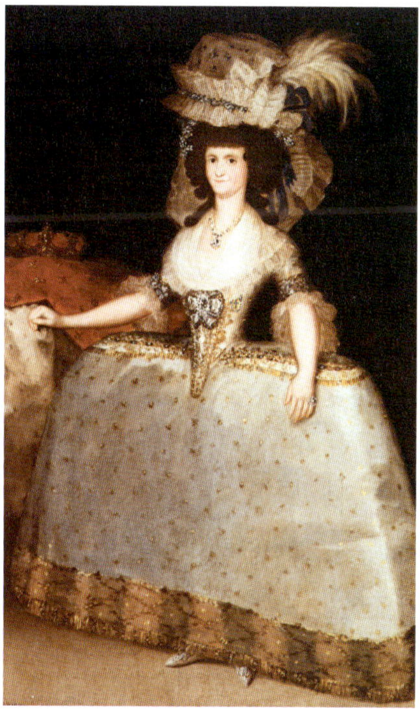

ILLNESS AND DEBILITATION

Since 1777, Goya had been experiencing some debilitating effects from an undiagnosed illness. The symptoms included pain, sickness and blackouts recurring in erratic bouts. In 1792, he left Madrid and travelled to Cádiz and Seville, but while he was away he had a relapse of the illness; the worst episode yet.

In 1792, Goya had made known his boredom with such tapestry cartoons as *Boys Climbing a Tree* and the earlier *Boys with Mastiff* and expressed his displeasure with the ideas prevalent at Court that the best painting imitated Mengs's Neoclassical style.

THE SUPERIORITY OF NATURE

In a report to the Academy on the subject of teaching art, he rejected Neoclassicism, declaring that it was 'a scandal' to deprecate nature in comparison with Greek statues: '...The smallest part of nature confounds and amazes those who know most! What statue or cast of it might there be that is not copied from divine nature? As excellent as the artist may be who copied it, can he not but proclaim that when placed at its side, one is the work of God, and the other of our own miserable hands?'

Goya's views on painting were radical for the time and not considered seriously until about 70 years later, with artists such as Édouard Manet (1832–83). Goya was clearly feeling oppressed. That November, he stopped working on the tapestry designs and, without official permission, left Madrid for Andalusia.

CÁDIZ AND SEVILLE

The rest of 1792 and beginning of 1793 is rather a mysterious time as far as Goya is concerned. The correspondence between him and Zapater that had been almost continual, virtually ceased, and he had few, if any, royal commissions.

He travelled first to Cádiz in connection with a couple of private commissions. One was to paint three large New Testament scenes for the Oratory of La Santa Cueva, a small Neoclassical chapel that was under construction. Another was to paint for his friend Sebastian Martínez (1747–1800) with whom he stayed in Cádiz.

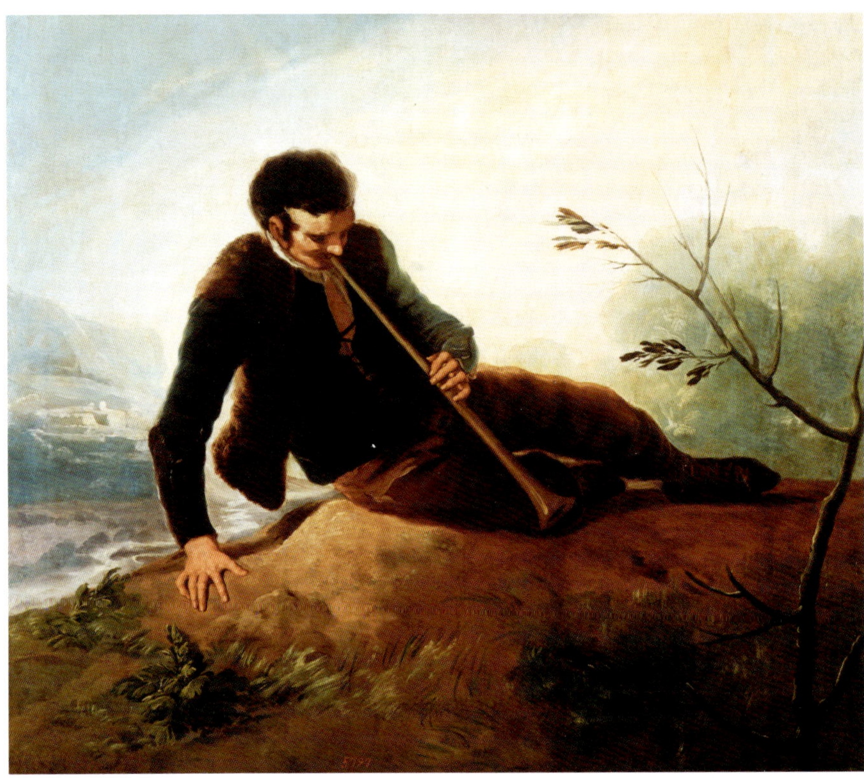

Above: Shepherd Playing a Dulzaina, *1786–7. Designed to hang over a window, this tapestry cartoon was painted between periods of sickness. A dulzaina is a traditional Spanish instrument.*

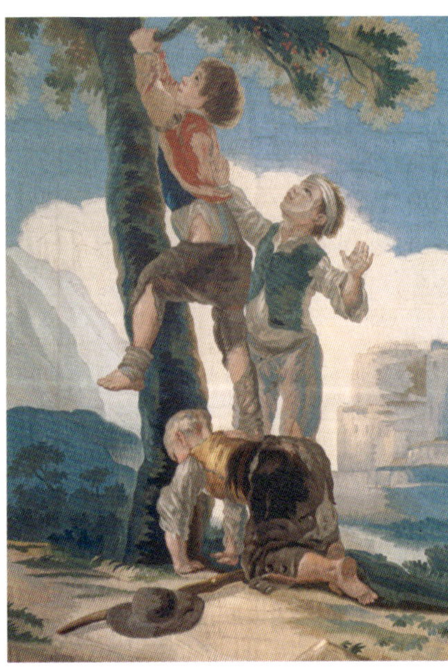

Below: Boys Climbing a Tree, *1791–2; demonstrating the empathy he had with children, this is one of Goya's last tapestry cartoons, painted when he had expressed his boredom with the designs.*

MYSTERY ILLNESS

With little evidence, no secure modern diagnosis can be made concerning Goya's illness. It has been variously attributed to Ménière's disease, botulism, polio, hepatitis, neurolabyrinthitis (an inflammation of the nerves of the inner ear), typhoid, meningitis, Vogt-Koyanagi syndrome (resulting from an eye infection), syphilis or lead poisoning. Syphilis seems unlikely as he lived for another 35 years, but lead poisoning may have been the result of the layers of white lead priming he used on all his canvases.

Like Goya, Martínez was born in a small village in northern Spain, but had risen in wealth and standing through his own abilities. A successful merchant, he was also a great collector of art, owning antique sculpture as well as paintings by artists such as Velázquez, Rubens, Titian and Mengs. He commissioned Goya to paint his portrait (see page 162) and some wooden panels in his house with images of sleeping women. Goya then travelled to the Andalusian capital Seville, to paint portraits of a friend and his wife, Juan Agustín Ceán Bermúdez (1749 –1829; see page 44) a writer on art who had founded an art academy in Seville.

DEAFNESS

While in Seville, Goya suffered a terrible relapse of his illness. He returned to Martínez, who wrote to an acquaintance: 'My friend Don Francisco de Goya... arrived at my house in a deplorable condition, in which he remains, having been unable to leave the house.' Goya's symptoms were dreadful. He heard constant loud buzzing noises in his head and his balance was badly affected. He felt dizzy and nauseous had fainting fits and periods of partial blindness. He also suffered with abdominal pains and weakness. In January that year he had received royal dispensation to remain in Andalusia for two months to convalesce and at last in March 1793, he wrote to Zapater: 'My dear soul, I can stand on my own feet, but so poorly that I don't know if my head is on my shoulders. I have no appetite or desire to do anything at all. Only your letters cheer me up.' Unfortunately, as his strength returned, he discovered that the illness had rendered him completely deaf.

Below: Boys with Mastiff, *1786–7; Goya's tapestry cartoon designed to hang over a door in the El Pardo Palace. At this time, he was beginning to suffer bouts of ill health.*

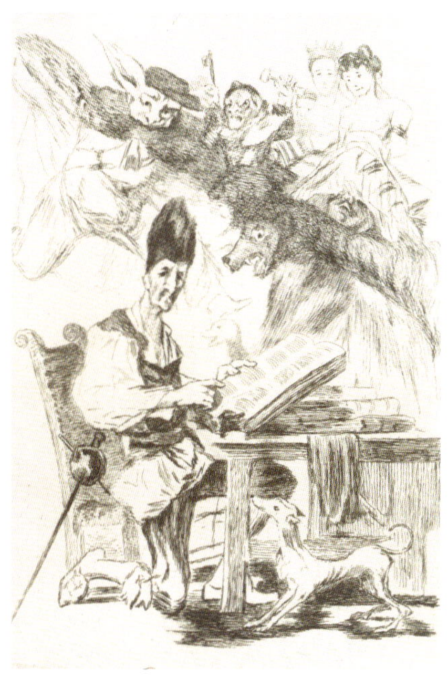

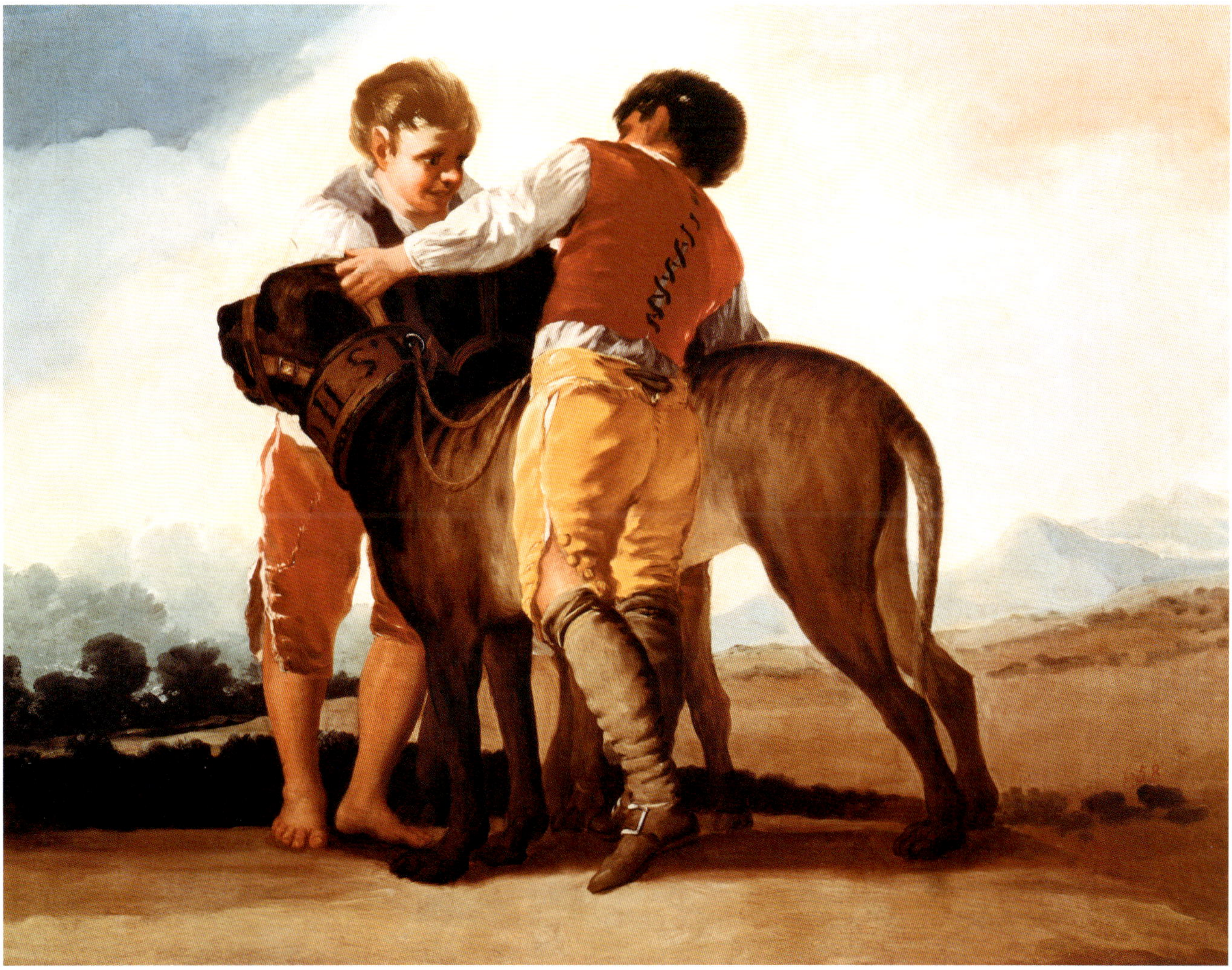

Above: Illustration for Don Quixote, *c.1812–20. After Goya's illness, his art changed as he began illustrating his inner thoughts.*

THE LAST CARTOONS

Although tired of painting tapestry cartoons, Goya had reluctantly worked on his latest commissioned series from 1791 until 1792. The King and Queen had asked for them to be 'rustic and gay', so Goya created images that were imaginative, full of light and with subtle contrasts of colour that were greatly admired.

Despite his belief that producing tapestry cartoons was now beneath his dignity, Goya made an effort to please the new monarchs. So these cartoons are fresh and bright, representing his own interpretations of traditional Spanish pastimes, activities and occupations, and helped to augment his reputation.

CHEQUERED HISTORY

The royal tapestry designs had been created intermittently since Mengs had taken responsibility for overseeing them. In March 1780, due to Spanish economic problems, execution of the cartoons had been suspended, but it was realized, that if the Royal Tapestry factory closed, the

Below: Unusually, this tapestry of Goya's design, Dance on the Banks of the Manzanares, *1777 is the same way round as the cartoon (see page 114).*

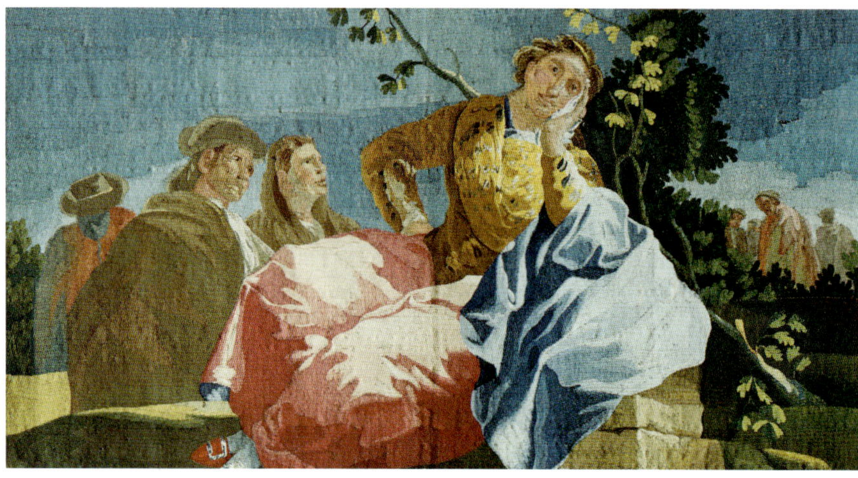

Above: Tapestry based on Goya's cartoon, The Rendezvous, *1780 (see page 25) — cartoons were almost always in reverse of the final tapestries.*

workers would have no jobs, so in 1783, work was resumed. At that time, Goya was not asked to work on them, but was commissioned again in 1786. Two years later, the death of Charles III halted things once more, but on the accession of Charles IV, Goya was appointed Court

Painter and asked to continue with the designs. He initially refused, considering the work to be incompatible with his newly elevated status. Only Bayeu's intervention and the threat of being deprived of his salary persuaded him to return once more to the task.

HINTS OF SATIRE

From 1791 to 1792, Goya painted seven cartoons with suggestions of satire that had not been apparent in his previous work. For instance in one painting, laughing young women throw a straw dummy into the air that looks like a man with no control of his own destiny; a reversal of traditional behaviour between the sexes. Another shows wedding guests laughing at the groom; a foolish old man who mistakenly thinks his pretty young bride will remain faithful to him.

The 63 tapestry cartoons that Goya painted in total were widely admired, both during his life and after his death. As they were intended merely to be patterns for weavers, he never thought they would be seen by the public, so

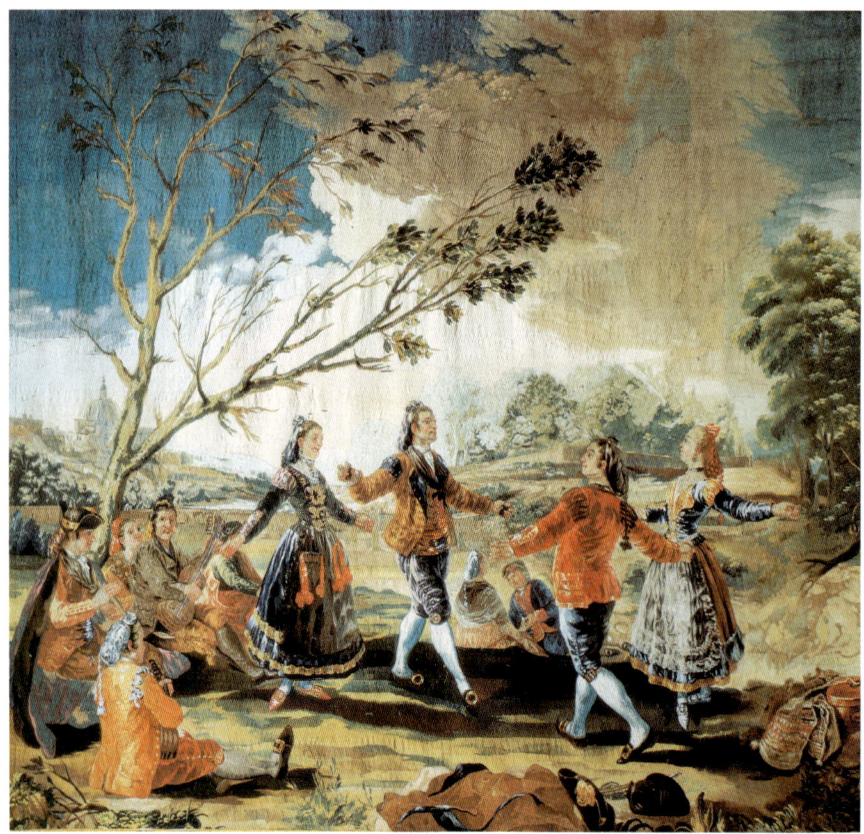

THE *ILUSTRADOS*

Since mixing with Don Luis de Bourbon and his family, Goya had made friends among the *ilustrados*: men and women of the Enlightenment who discussed issues of the moment and particularly how to overcome Spain's problems. These new friends also helped Goya to form his own intellectual ideas. Before the French Revolution, many of the *ilustrados* worked in positions of power in the Spanish government. They included Goya's close friends such as Gaspar Melchor de Jovellanos (1744–1811), an author and philosopher who was appointed Chief Justice in 1778, and Francisco de Cabarrús (1752–1810), a financier and economist who became an adviser to Charles III. However, as news of the French Revolution became more alarming, many of the *ilustrados*, with their radical views, were seen as a threat, and thrown out of office. In 1790, for no reason, Cabarrús was arrested and put in solitary confinement, and Jovellanos was banished from Spain.

they demonstrate his free expression and a lack of contrivance. An example is a large cartoon that he prepared for the young princes' chamber in the El Pardo Palace. *The Meadow of San Isidro*

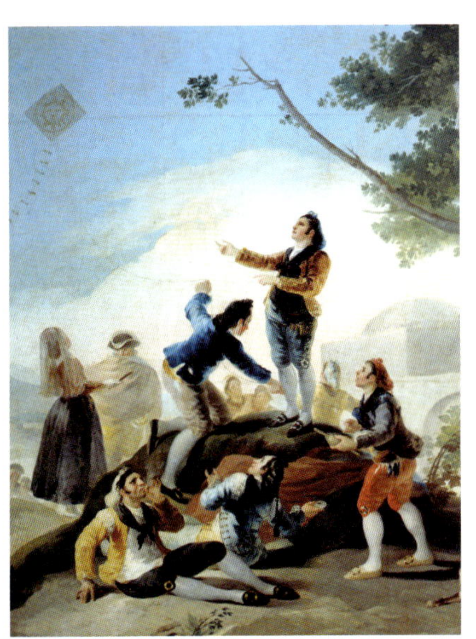

places a crowd of figures drawn from life against the distant architecture of Madrid. It is an unusual and expressive work for the time that shows a fleeting moment and Goya's understanding of human interaction. All his later cartoons display a uniqueness that was far removed from both Rococo and Neoclassicism.

Left: A tapestry based on one of Goya's early cartoons, The Kite *(see page 116), 1778, made for the future Charles IV.*

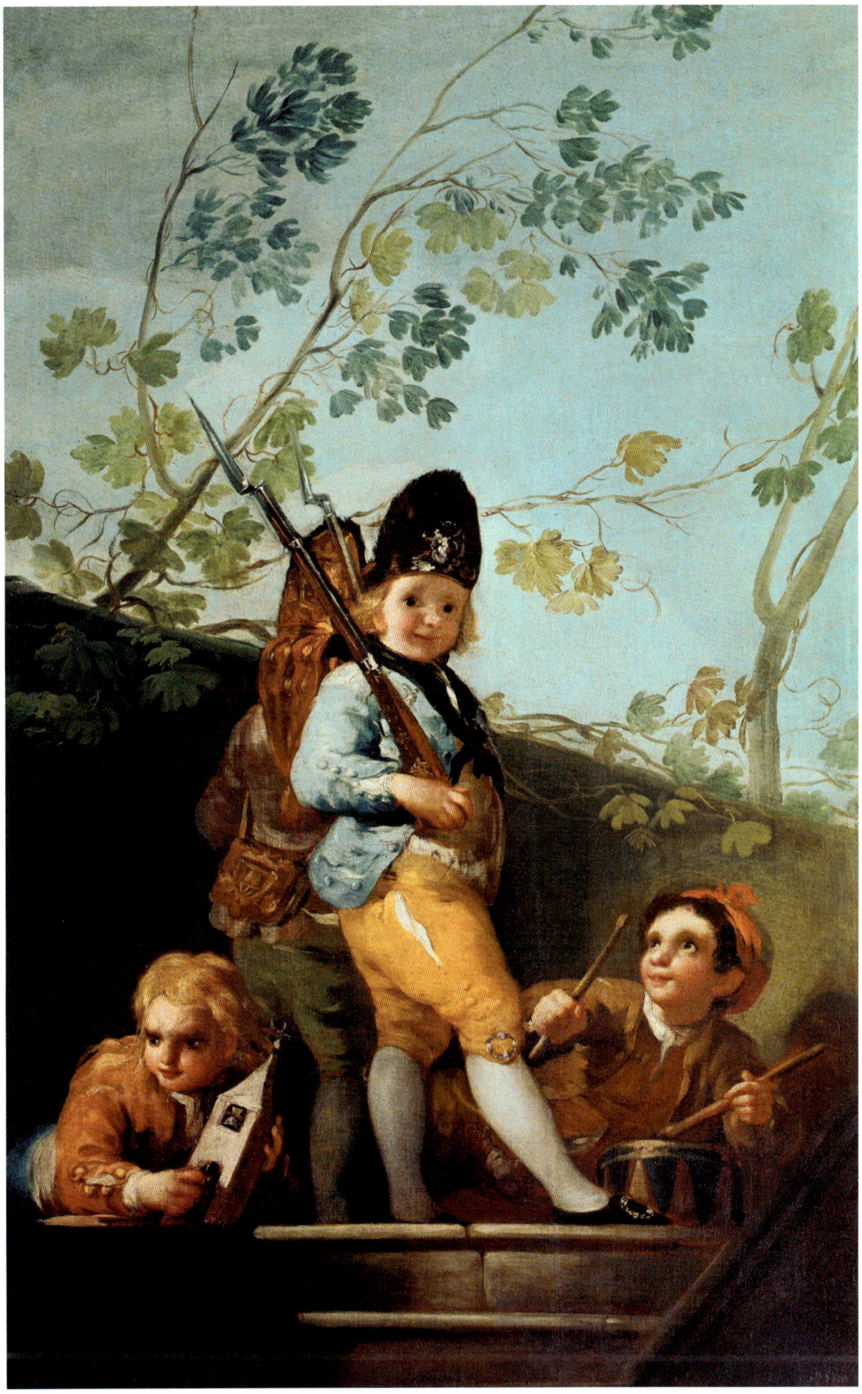

Above: Boys Playing at Soldiers, *1779 – this cartoon is one of Goya's early examples of his enchanting representations of children.*

In spite of the success of these designs, after 1792, Goya never painted a tapestry cartoon again. This was partly due to turbulent events in France. The King and Queen were disturbed by developments there and lost interest in the decoration of their palace. This was almost certainly why Goya received no further royal commissions during 1792.

TURBULENT YEARS

In January 1793, while Goya was seriously ill, Louis XVI was executed in Paris. Horrified, monarchs of Spain and Portugal joined other European rulers in an anti-French coalition. For this, France had declared war on Austria, Prussia, Great Britain and the Netherlands, and in March 1793, it also declared war on Spain.

Across Europe, other less violent changes had been occurring. By the 1790s, the Enlightenment that had been received with such excitement, anticipation and confidence just a few decades earlier, was beginning to lose potency.

The expanding middle classes, new inventions, beliefs and discoveries, and utopian ideals of society, had evolved into many lifestyle changes and attitudes, but they were not always satisfactory. Neoclassical styles still predominated much of the art and architecture that was being produced, and new types of entertainment had developed, including in literature, theatre and music. But a number of the most pivotal figures of the Enlightenment had died. Rousseau, Hume, Voltaire and Mengs for instance, had died in the 1770s, followed in the 1780s and 90s by Diderot, Samuel Johnson, Jean-Baptiste le Rond d'Alembert (1717–83), Mozart and Robert Adam.

Gradually, without these fervent champions, many of the theories of the Enlightenment began to be questioned by the more sceptical, while new ideas of Romanticism were emerging that were more appealing to less-educated members of society. Ultimately, however, the Enlightenment ended with the French Revolution, even though its discoveries and theories continued to influence Western society for centuries.

THE FRENCH REVOLUTION

Starting with the best intentions by French citizens, the Revolution had emerged from Enlightenment ideals of social and political reform and had originally been an attempt to create a fairer society for all, but it resulted in the deaths of tens of thousands of citizens. It was not just the Enlightenment however; the French Revolution was sparked by many things, including the sudden growth and prosperity of the bourgeoisie; the continued oppression

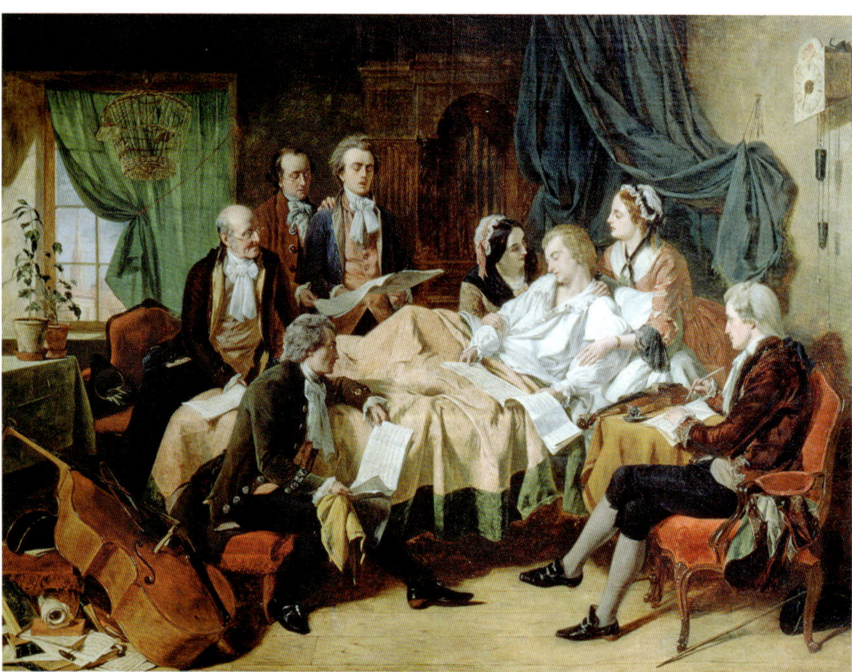

Above left: A 19th-century depiction of the Battle of San Lorenzo de la Muga, Spain in 1794, part of the French Revolutionary Wars.

Left: The Last Moments of Mozart, Mihály Munkácsy (1844–1900), 1885. Ten years Goya's junior, Mozart's brilliant life ended tragically early at a time when Goya was also suffering with poor health.

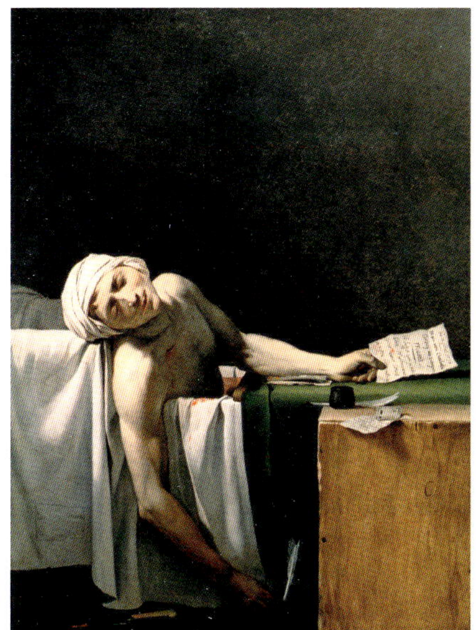

Above: Death of Marat, *1793. Almost an exact contemporary of Goya, the French revolutionary Jacques-Louis David was considered the greatest Neoclassical painter of the day.*

Right: The Shipwreck, *1793–4; an example of Goya's more expressive work after his illness (see page 42).*

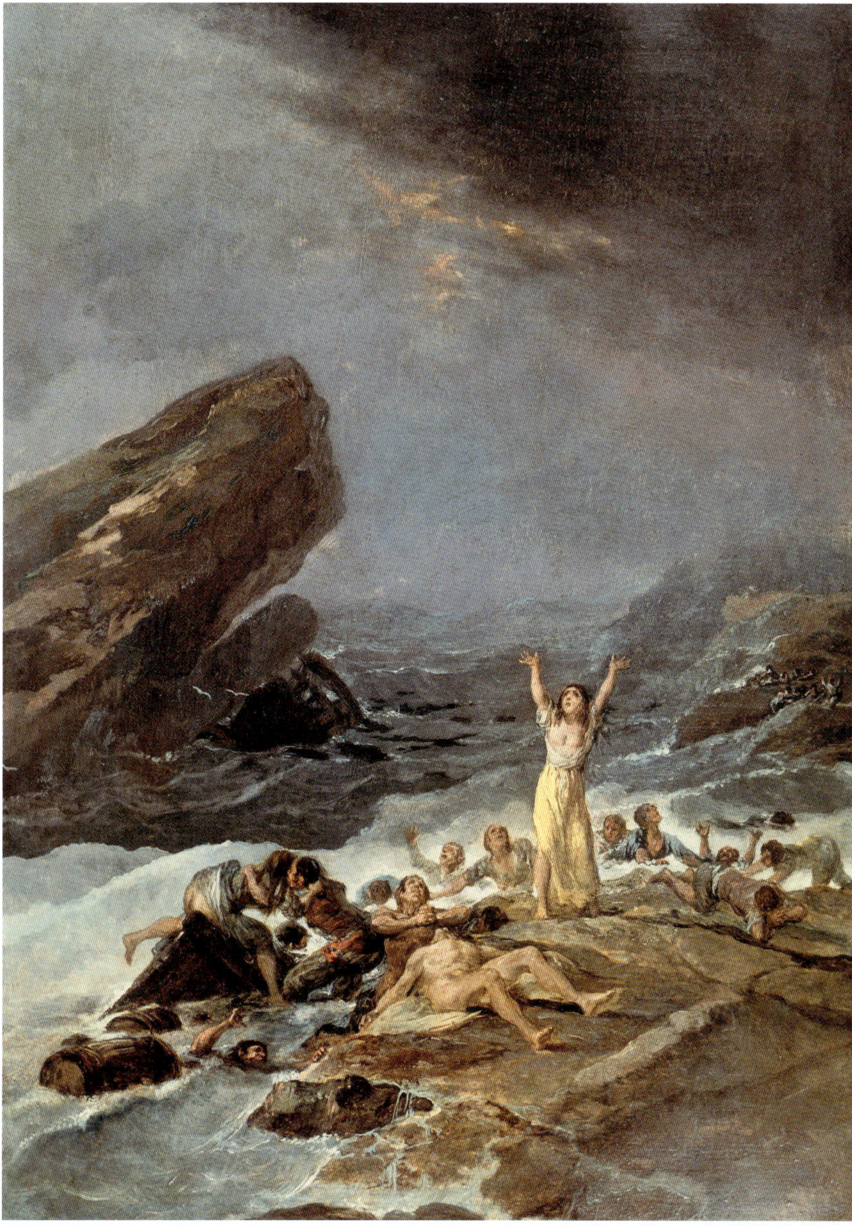

SECRET MISSION?

Although it is known that Goya was seriously ill at the beginning of 1793 and that he lay in bed for several months, half paralysed and often delirious, the exact dates of his illness have never been substantiated, and his whereabouts before returning to Cádiz have remained rather vague. On 5 January 1793, Zapater wrote to Martínez mentioning that Goya was staying with him in Cádiz. Then on 17 January 1793, Goya wrote to the treasurer of the Duke of Osuna, addressing his letter from Madrid. This could have been a mistake; confusion relating to his illness, or it has been speculated that he was actually on a secret – and ultimately unsuccessful – mission for the Spanish government to rescue Charles IV's cousin, Louis XVI. Years later, Goya's grandson related a story that Goya had told him about this, but nothing definite has ever been established.

of the peasant class; an unhealthy economy that had been aggravated by participation in the American Revolutionary War with no real gains, and crop failures that caused food prices to rise. Meanwhile, many of the policies of the weak and indecisive Bourbon King Louis XVI were disliked by those who (inspired by Enlightenment thinking), no longer believed that he ruled by divine right. Many more hated Queen Marie-Antoinette, who among many things, was falsely accused of being a spendthrift and an Austrian spy. Soon, even more critical and often false claims about the King and Queen were circulated in pamphlets across Paris, escalating opinion against them. After

three years of bloodshed, by 1792, the monarchy had collapsed, and the new principles of 'Liberté, égalité, fraternité' (liberty, equality and fraternity) were adopted.

THE INQUISITION

One of the consequences of the French Revolution was that Charles IV tightened censorship laws in Spain. Any printed material that referred to French events was sent to the Secretary of State, non-residents had to leave Madrid, and the Inquisition was reinstated. Many, including Goya, were alarmed by the sudden resurgence of the Inquisition, as it hailed a return to the old days of suspicion and terror.

FAME AND INFLUENCE

Goya's convalescence had been extremely slow and rumours spread that his professional life was over. But by July 1793, he was back in Madrid and, two years later, after the death of Francisco Bayeu, he was elected Director of Painting at the Royal Academy. Even those who doubted him were impressed by his ascendancy.

While recuperating in Cádiz, to distract himself from his illness and the accompanying pain, Goya had painted a series of cabinet pictures; small figure paintings that became popular from the 15th century among wealthy art collectors. Originally displayed in 'cabinets', or small, private rooms, these were only seen by close family and friends, but were later put in display cases, which eventually became named cabinets.

Goya's cabinet pictures are the first of his paintings to show an expressive freedom, adhering to no other person's requirements. As a result, the paintings, each no bigger than 50 x 32cm (20 x 12in), painted on tin-coated iron sheets, are energetic and daring.

PENETRATING OBSERVATIONS

Goya never completely recovered from his devastating illness; the physical and mental crisis affected him permanently, and his deafness changed the way he viewed the world. The confident Court Painter returned to Madrid a far more contemplative person. Deafness made him wary of people and penetratingly observant of life. In the summer of 1793, on his return to Madrid, he told the Royal Tapestry factory that he was 'absolutely unable to paint', which was

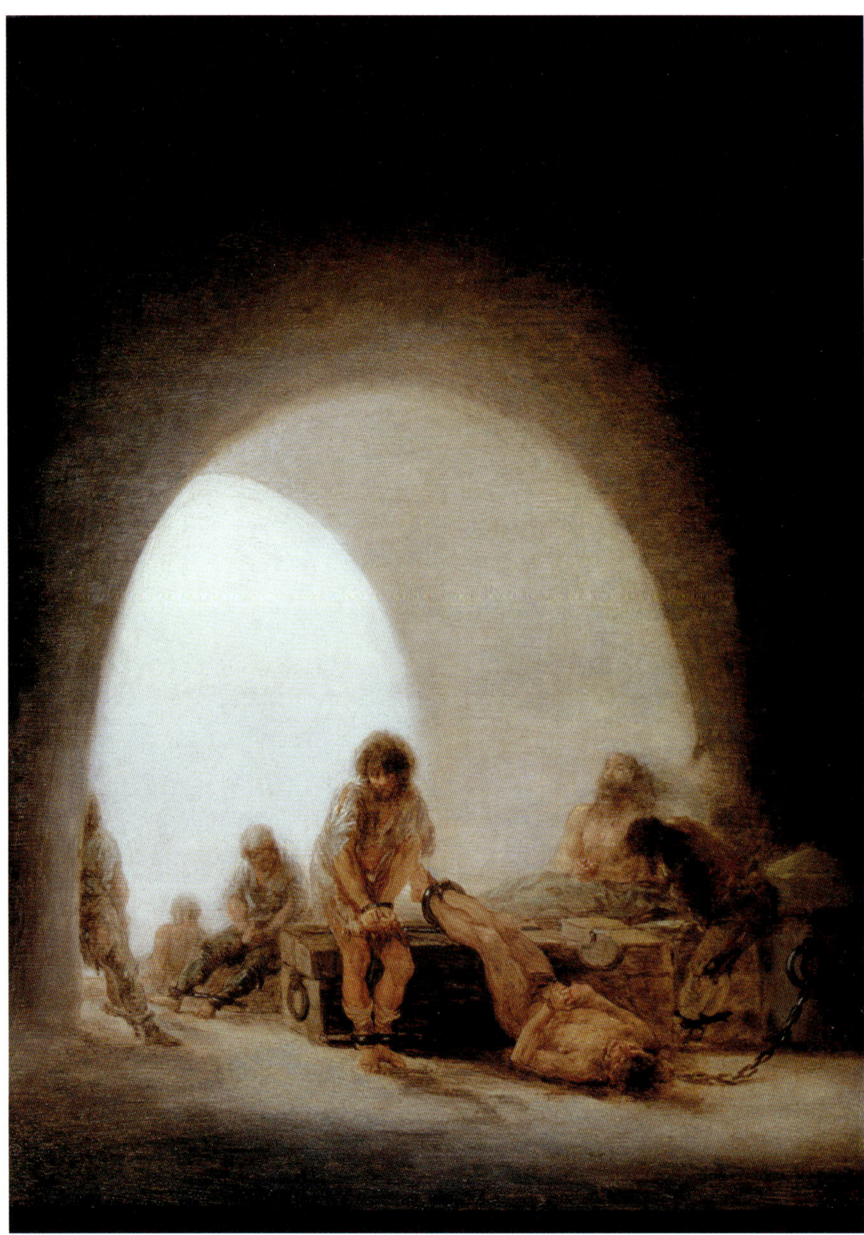

Above: Interior of a Prison, c.1793–4 – one of Goya's cabinet paintings, this depicts seven prisoners bound by chains under an archway.

untrue as he had been painting the cabinet pictures, and over the following few months he also took commissions for numerous portraits. Rumours of his alleged demise as one of the most successful artists in Spain continued, but he confounded his detractors by delivering 11 of his 15 small cabinet pictures to the Royal Academy, describing them as representing

'various scenes of national diversions' and unusually writing about them to Don Bernardo de Iriarte, the Vice-Protector of the Academy. He wrote that he had allowed himself 'to make observations that are generally not allowed in commissioned works and in which caprice and invention have free play', and that he had done them 'to occupy my imagination burdened by the contemplation of my sufferings'. Although some of the paintings are now lost, those that are known include images of adversity and circumstance, such as people fleeing from a fire at night, bullfights and street theatres, a

Below left: Girls Carrying Pitchers, 1792; this is one of Goya's sketches for a tapestry design before he fell ill.

Below right: Bulls Rounded Up, 1793 – one of Goya's cabinet paintings made during his convalescence in Cádiz.

shipwreck (see page 41), a highway robbery and a lunatic asylum (see page 162). When they saw them, the Academy members declared that they 'celebrated their merit and that of Goya'.

MILITARY PORTRAITS

With war raging across Europe, it was not surprising that Goya was asked to paint military portraits in 1793. One was of a Spanish general, Antonio Ricardos (see page 165), who was killed in battle the following year, and another was of Lieutenant Colonel Félix Colón de Larreategui (see page 164), whose family had connections with Goya's friend Cabarrús. He also painted Ramón Posado y Soto, who was distantly related to Jovellanos. Unlike his earlier,

somewhat awkward and self-conscious portraits, from this time, Goya's portraits reveal his search for psychological truth beneath the outward appearance, executed with careful brushwork and brilliant colouring.

SUBJECTIVE EXPRESSION

Although it had taken him more than 20 years to fight against the Baroque, Rococo and Neoclassical styles, by the 1790s, perhaps feeling he had little to lose after his debilitating illness, Goya was at last making his own personal and independent statements through his art. Those who had thought his career was over soon changed their opinions, and many began to look to him as the most progressive and original artist of the time.

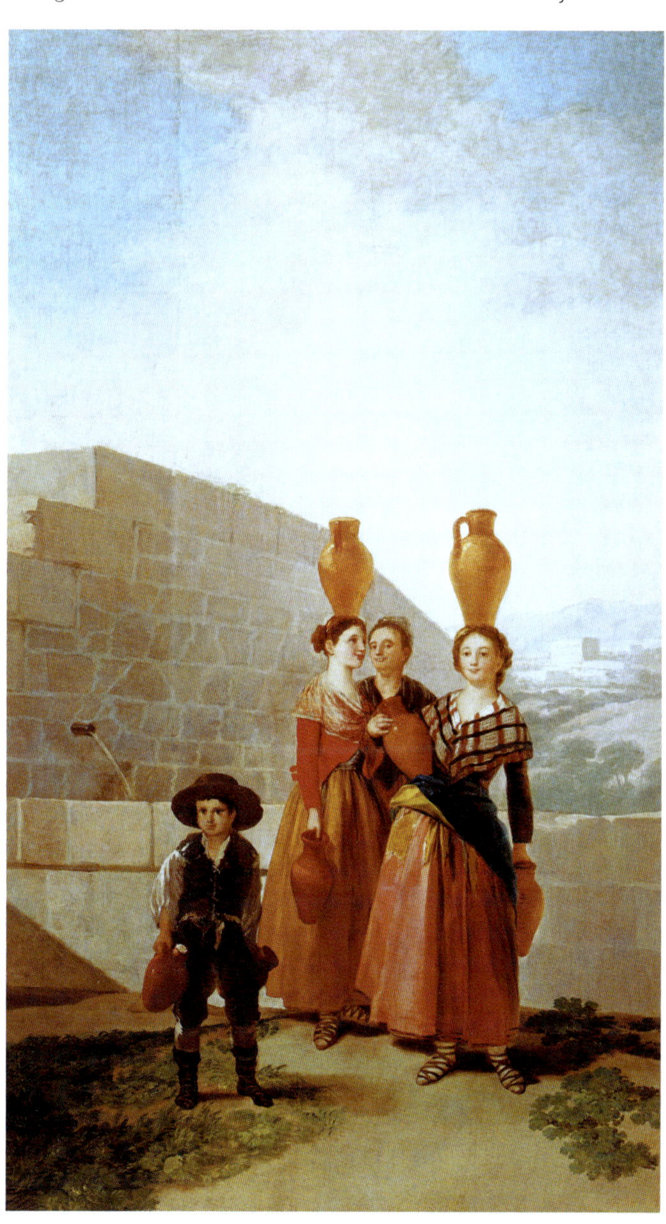

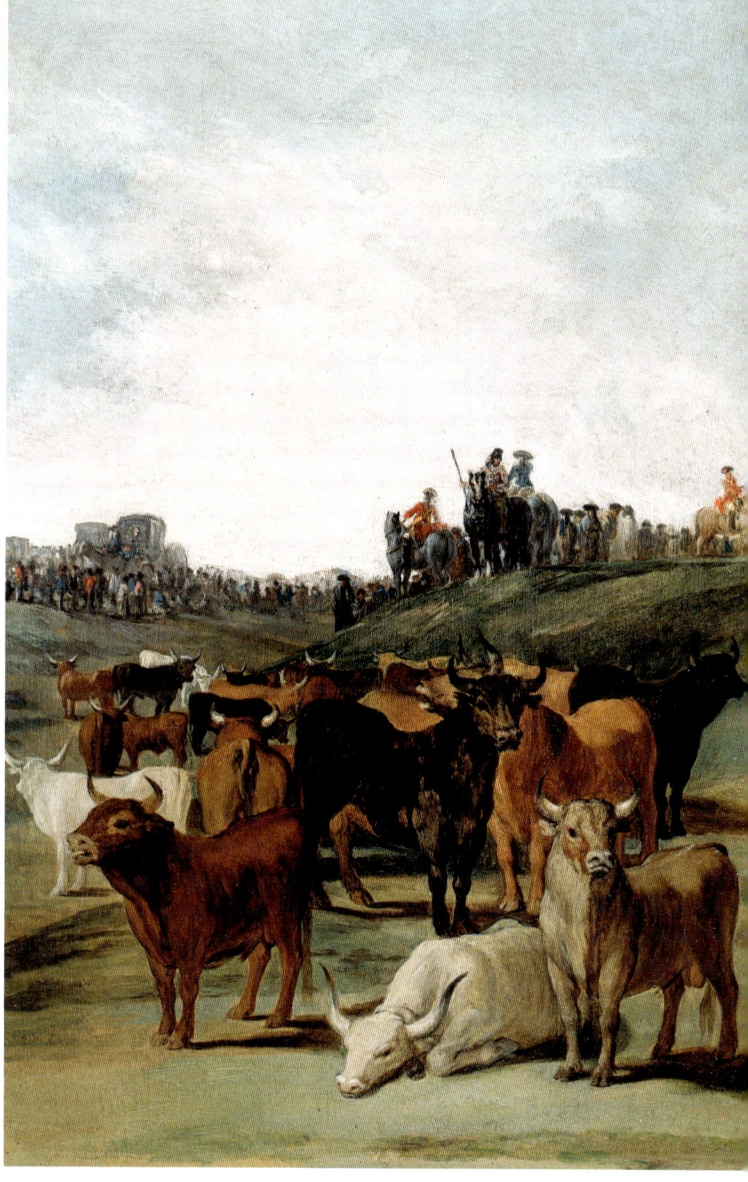

THE GENIUS OF EUROPEAN ART

During Charles IV's reign, the Queen was the most powerful figure at Court, and those she favoured progressed rapidly. Fortunately for Goya, Queen María Luisa liked him, and after he had been given his late brother-in-law Bayeu's position, his success was assured. He became the most influential artist in Spain.

Although he did not elaborate on details, in his correspondence to Zapater, Goya relayed that the Queen occasionally invited him to breakfast. How he felt about this, or his opinion of the Queen herself was not recorded, but he was not one of her numerous lovers. She genuinely seemed to admire his artistic

Below: Juan Agustín Ceán Bermúdez, c.1792–3, a portrait by Goya of his Sevillian friend and author of a biographical dictionary of the principal artists of Spain.

talents, which is perhaps surprising when viewing the candid and uncomplimentary portraits he made of her.

Many others viewed him with a similar respect, as by 1795, in spite of his still considerable health problems, he had become renowned across Spain, seen by other artists and aristocrats as the greatest artist in the whole of Europe. As well as his work for the King and Queen, he attracted many other commissions, mainly from nobles and society figures who asked him to decorate their palaces

and paint their portraits. Several of these people had become his friends, including María del Rosario Fernandez, the actress *La Tirana* (see page 167); Tadea Arias de Enríquez (see page 164); and the Marquesa de la Solana (see page 166); a playwright as well as an aristocrat. To have a portrait painted by Goya was highly prestigious and he was able to command high prices. Many younger artists wanted to learn from him and older artists applauded his new ideas and fresh, natural and independent manner of painting. The portraits he produced of his friends, even more than his official portraits, displayed a virtuosity of brushwork, a light touch and an atmosphere created by loose, confident brushwork which contrasted with conventional, more rigid painting of the time. Striving for the greatness that Velázquez and Rembrandt had achieved before him, he also practised his art through several self-portraits, such as the *Self-portrait in Glasses* shown opposite. As he declared: 'First be a magnificent artist and then you can do whatever, but the art must be first.'

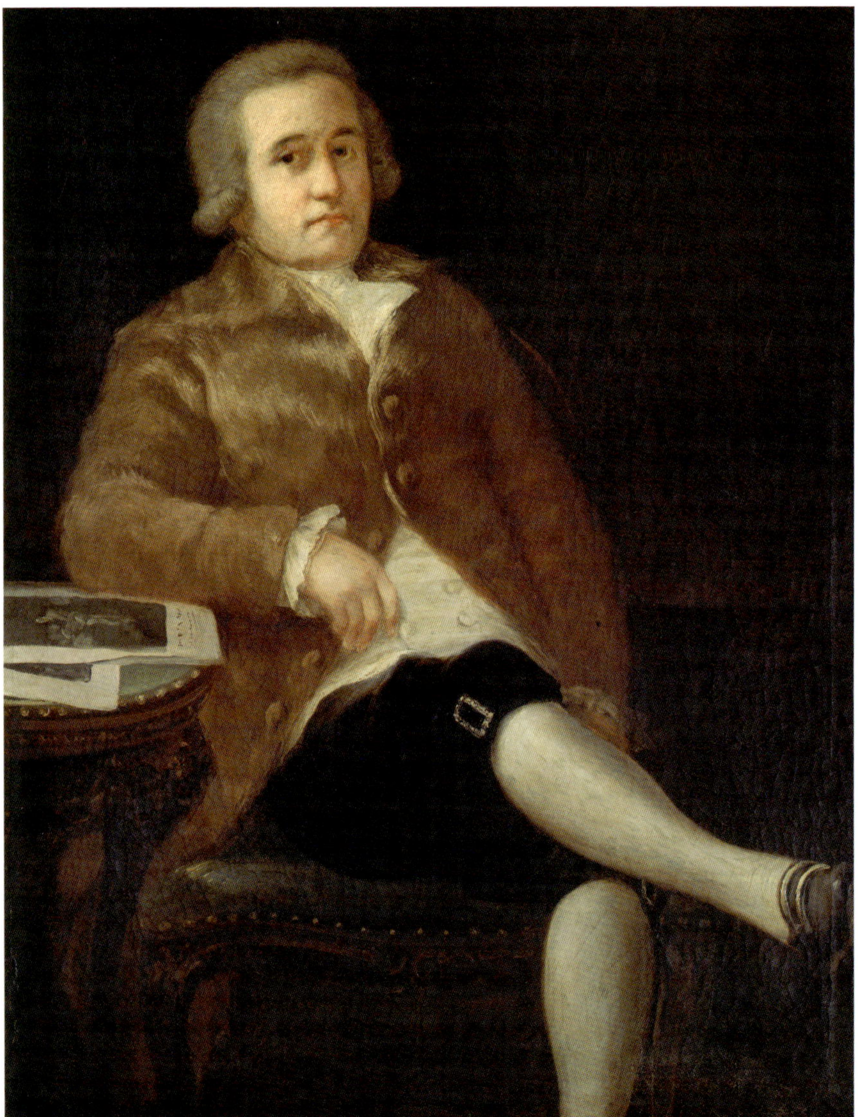

TWO STYLES

Goya was one of the first great artists to work in two different styles that were both equally admired. One was his official 'Court Painter' style, which he used for his dignified portraits and other commissioned works, and the other was his personal artistic expression, driven by his opinions and passions – and suffused with irony. Increasingly however, his second more private style began to appear in his first, with subtle and unorthodox expressions and gestures of satire that could be read clearly by some, but were missed by others.

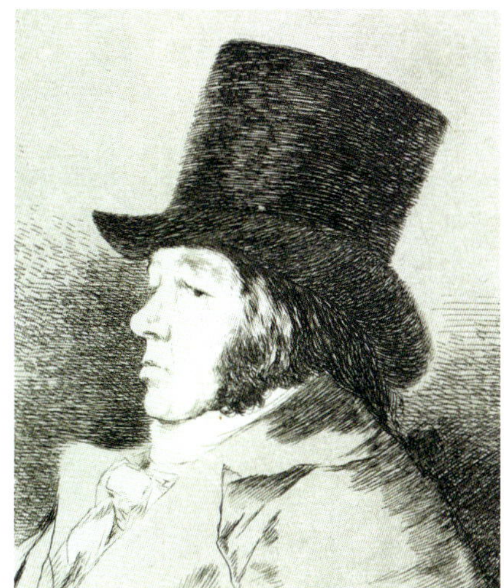

Above: Goya entitled this self-portrait etching of c.1797–8 Francisco Goya y Lucientes, I Pintor *(I, the painter).*

DUKE AND DUCHESS OF ALBA

Meanwhile, another important woman was featuring in Goya's life. María del Pilar Teresa Cayetana de Silva Álvarez de Toledo y Silva Bazán (1762–1802) was the 13th Duchess of Alba, the wealthiest woman in Spain and described by many as one of the most beautiful. Tall, slim, with dark eyes, fine bone structure and long, thick dark hair, she was vivacious, unconventional, a graceful, accomplished dancer and also admired for her sense of dress and interior design. Even strangers were compelled to write about her beauty, as one French traveller noted: 'Nothing in the world is as beautiful as she...When she passes by, everyone leans from their windows, and even children interrupt their games to look at her.'

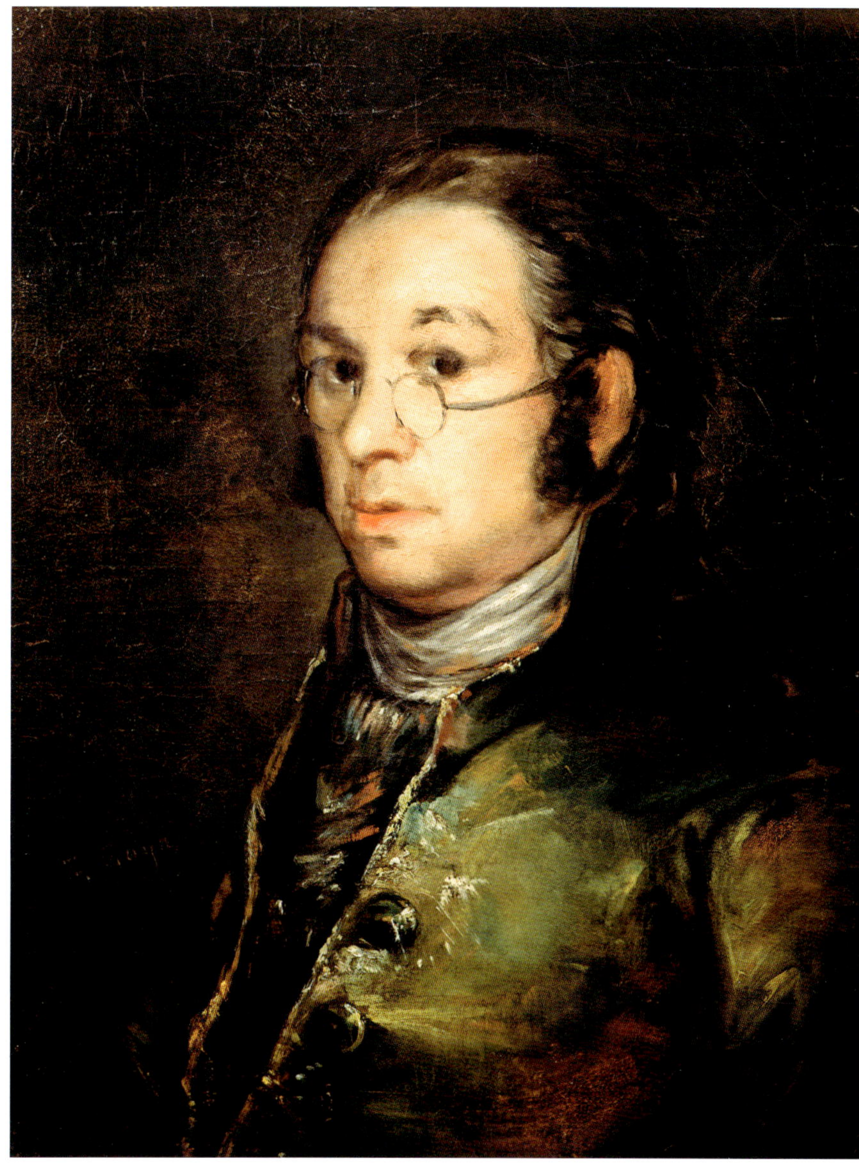

Above: Self-portrait in Glasses, *c.1797–1800; Goya depicts himself as thoughtful, well-dressed and prosperous.*

Eccentric and strong-willed, the Duchess charmed Goya from the first moment they met through her husband the Duke of Alba, who commissioned two portraits of her in 1795 (see pages 169 and 170). The Duke, Don José María Álvarez de Toledo y Gonzaga (1756–96) was an extremely important Spanish noble, who loved music and all things English. Goya had painted his portrait in 1793, wearing his riding clothes and 'his own hair' (that is, no wig). Three years later, one year after Goya had completed the commissioned portraits of the Duchess, the Duke died unexpectedly aged 40.

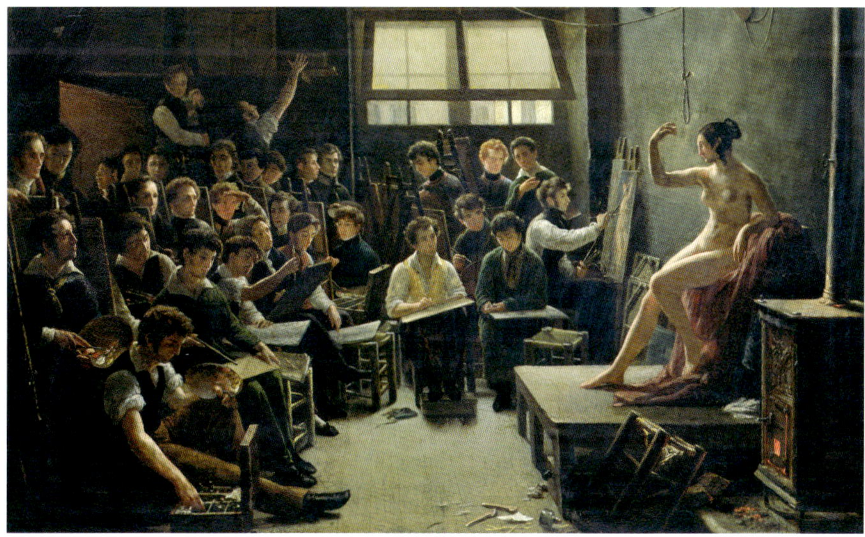

Left: The Studio of Baron Antoine Jean Gros, *Auguste Antoine Masse (1795–1836); a successful artist's studio, painted at the time Goya's own studio was flourishing.*

EXPRESSION AND INVENTION

Although Goya's first visit to Andalusia had been overshadowed by his terrible illness, he had been dazzled by the light and beauty of the place. In 1796, he made a return journey to Cádiz to install the three large paintings he had produced for the Oratory at La Santa Cueva.

Goya's circumstances had changed since he last travelled south. Now he was an illustrious painter, a friend of royalty and an accepted connoisseur of art. Although still in frail health, he was keen to see artistic treasures in southern towns and to paint for friends. As well as completing the works for the Santa Cueva, while there, he painted a portrait of Judge Altamirano of Seville and three Doctors of the Church: Saint Augustine, Saint Ambrose and Saint Gregory (see pages 106–7).

STAYING WITH THE DUCHESS

That summer, the Duke of Alba died. As custom demanded, the Duchess of Alba withdrew to her summer residence

Below: The Duchess of Alba with Her Hand Raised, *detail, 1796, one of the first sketches made by Goya at Sanlúcar.*

in Sanlúcar in Andalusia for three years. Goya had become close friends with the couple by then and unconventionally, he went to stay with the Duchess soon after her husband had died.

Conjecture about this time has been rife; much has been written on it and even a Hollywood film has been made about the relationship between Goya and the Duchess. The 50-year-old painter was clearly infatuated with the 34-year-old woman, and painted her more than any other, but whether there was any romance between them is doubtful. Much has been speculated about a portrait he painted of her during that time dressed as a maja (see page 171). He presented her wearing rings bearing the names Goya and Alba, and pointing down to an inscription *Solo Goya* (only Goya). Although this could mean that only Goya was important

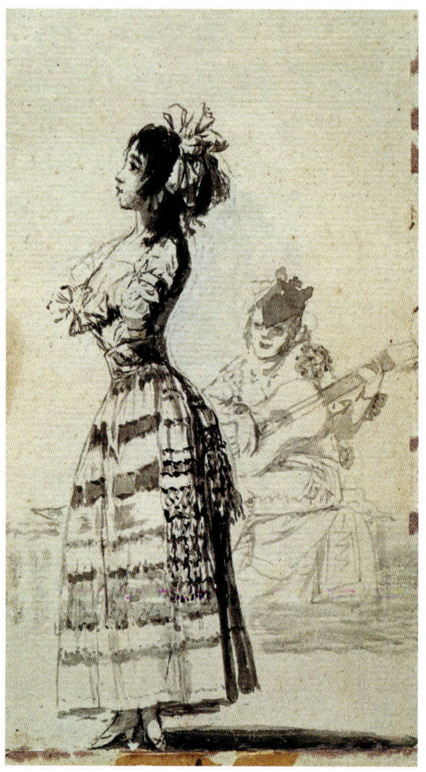

Above: Girl Dancing to a Guitar, *1796, part of Goya's series of drawings made during his stay with the Duchess.*

to her, it could also mean that this was a secret wish of Goya's, a joke between friends, or something she never knew about. As Goya kept the portrait and painted over the inscription, it seems more likely that it was simply a private hope of his own.

Three years previously, Goya was near death, now he was staying with a compelling young woman of noble birth whom he admired enormously. In Spanish hierarchy she was second to the Queen, and Goya was a fervent social climber. From the Duchess of Alba's point of view, the notion of an affair with the painter seems implausible. She had just buried her husband to whom she had been married since the age of 13. Although she had not loved him, they had nonetheless been married

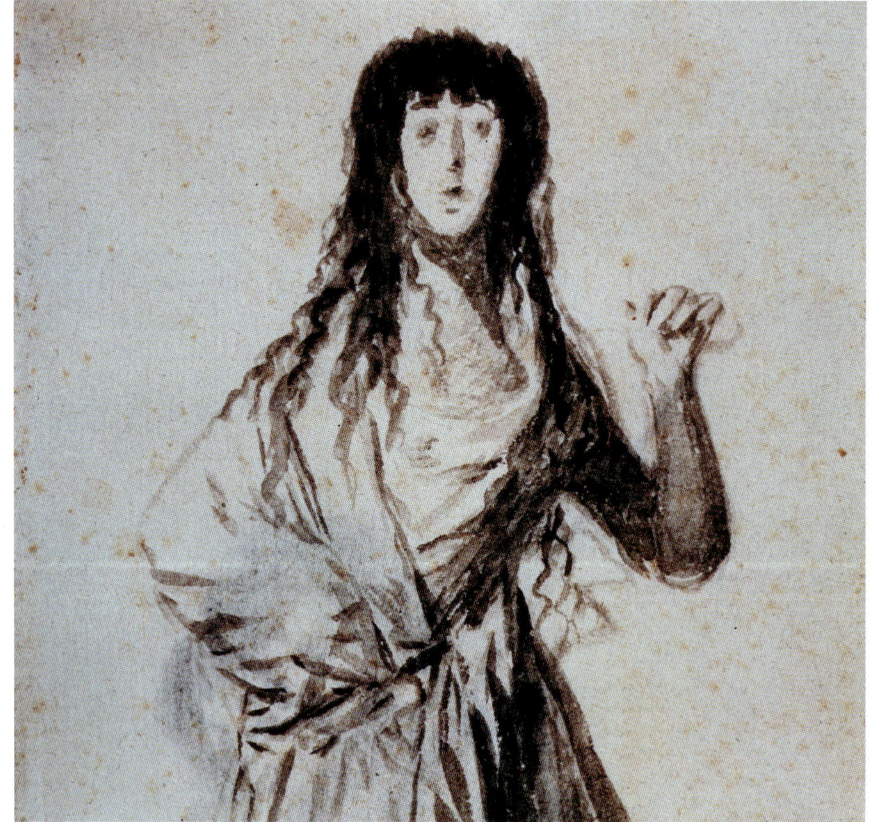

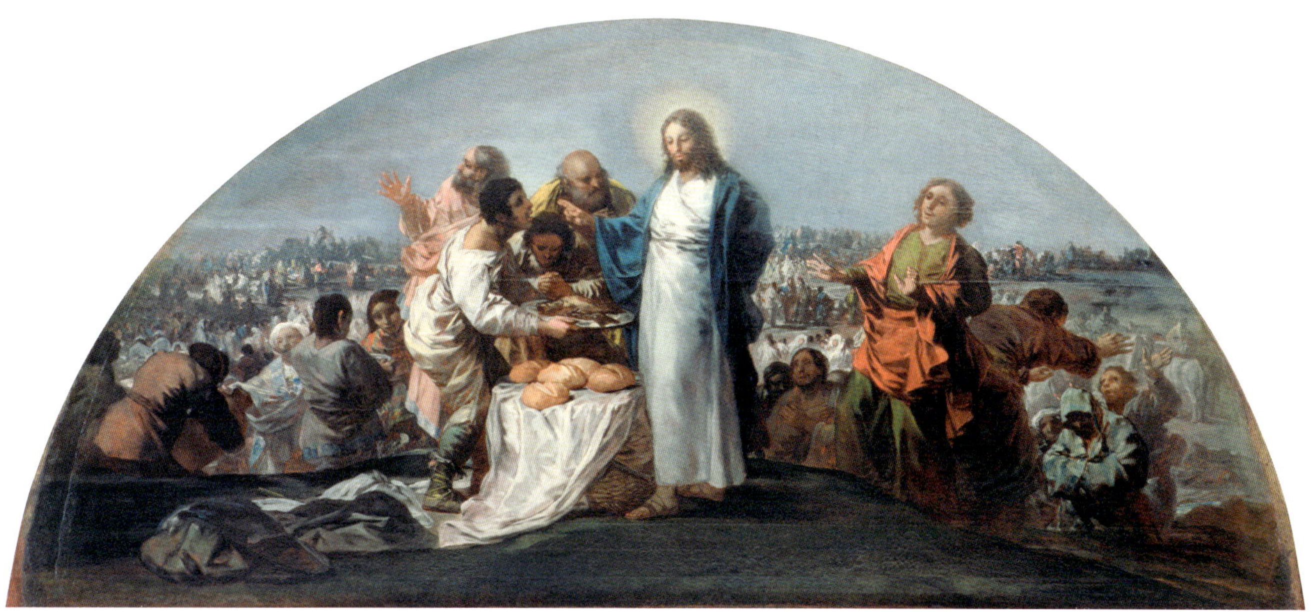

Top: Miracle of the Loaves and Fishes, *1795–6, one of the three semi-circular religious paintings Goya executed for the Santa Cueva in Cádiz.*

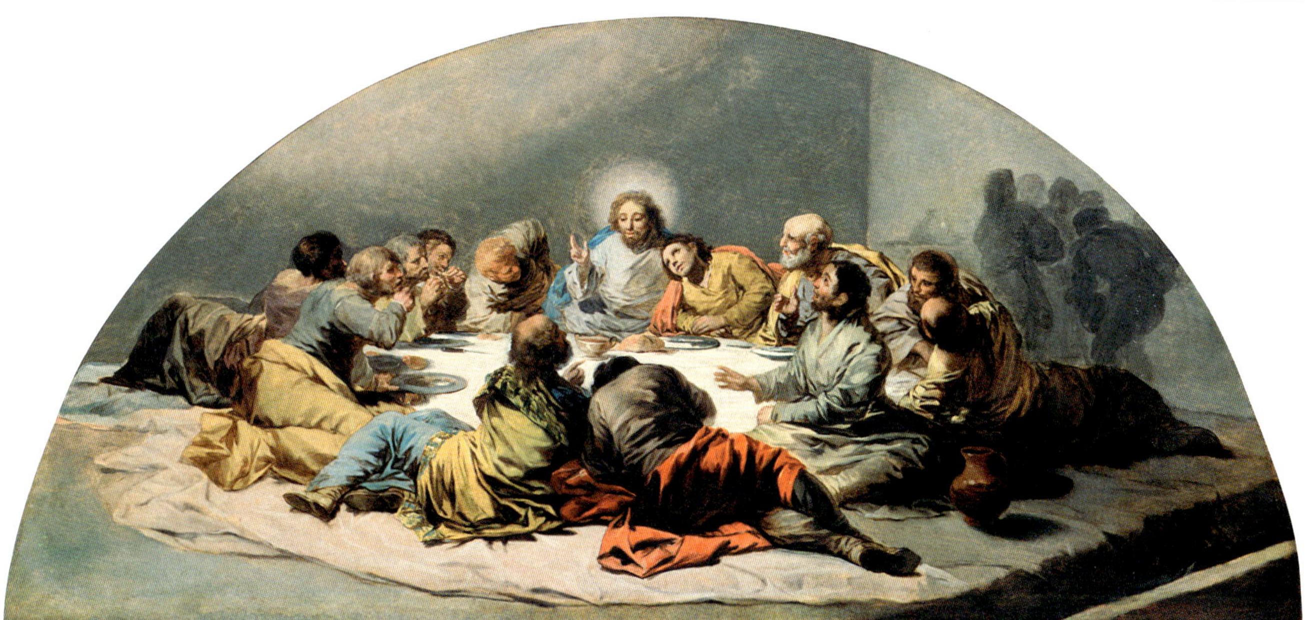

Above: The Last Supper, 1796–7. *One of Goya's three large works for the Santa Cueva.*

for over 20 years. Goya was 16 years her senior, deaf, fairly unattractive and from humble origins. For her, an affair with him could only have ever been a diversion or a provocative flouting

FACE PAINTING

The Duchess of Alba was spoilt and egocentric. One day in 1795, when Goya was painting his first portraits of her, she arrived at his studio and asked him to apply her make-up. He wrote to a friend: 'The Alba woman...asked me paint her face...I certainly enjoyed it more than painting on canvas!'

of convention (which she enjoyed). It seems most probable that Goya's strong feelings for her were not reciprocated and that she admired his work and felt sorry for him.

NEW WAYS OF CAPTURING LIFE

During that summer at Sanlúcar, Goya began filling a sketchbook with scenes and figures in unusual, often private and intimate, attitudes. Many are of the Duchess, and several are of other young women. Some are awkward, some are

explicit, many are ambiguous. They appear to be almost detached: an artist capturing natural, impromptu and personal moments, fleeting observational sketches that were not intended to be seen by the public. They also seem to have given Goya a taste for drawing as a means of expression; unselfconscious figures at their everyday tasks. Whatever happened between him and the Duchess, he soon channelled his passions back into his art, and his ensuing sketchbooks began to be more moralizing, with an increasingly barbed graphic style.

MOVING WITH THE TIMES

After his second stay in Andalusia, Goya plunged into his art with renewed purpose, expressing his inner feelings and thoughts, and completely disregarding the artistic conventions of the day. In 1797, on the grounds of ill health, he resigned from his position as Director of Painting at the Royal Academy.

How his stay with the Duchess at Sanlúcar ended has never been clarified, but by early in 1797, Goya returned to Madrid while the Duchess remained for her required period of mourning – one of the few conventions she adhered to. During that time, she wrote her will. Among many things, she bequeathed ten reales a day for the rest of his life to Goya's son Javier, whom she had never met. Legend says that during the 1790s, she also often sent Goya's wife Josefa delicacies from her own table and instructed her footmen to leave the gold dishes behind. Coincidentally, as with her first husband, the Duchess died unexpectedly at the age of 40, which fuelled suspicion of poisoning although her death has now been attributed to tuberculosis.

Right: Idealized beauty, energy and power are portrayed in this Neoclassical work of Bonaparte crossing the St Bernard Pass, May 1800, Jacques-Louis David, 1801.

NAPOLEON BONAPARTE

Meanwhile, the French Revolutionary Wars continued in Europe. In 1796, a young and relatively untried Napoleon Bonaparte had been appointed commander-in-chief of the French army and against all odds, quickly defeated a series of much larger allied armies, conquering most of northern Italy and forcing the Austrians to the negotiating table. By 1798, through Napoleon's continued leadership, France was dominant in Europe. To gain further glory, he decided to mount an expedition to Egypt. It was a nervous time for all, and Goya's dark and often sardonic representations suited the common apprehensive and sombre mood.

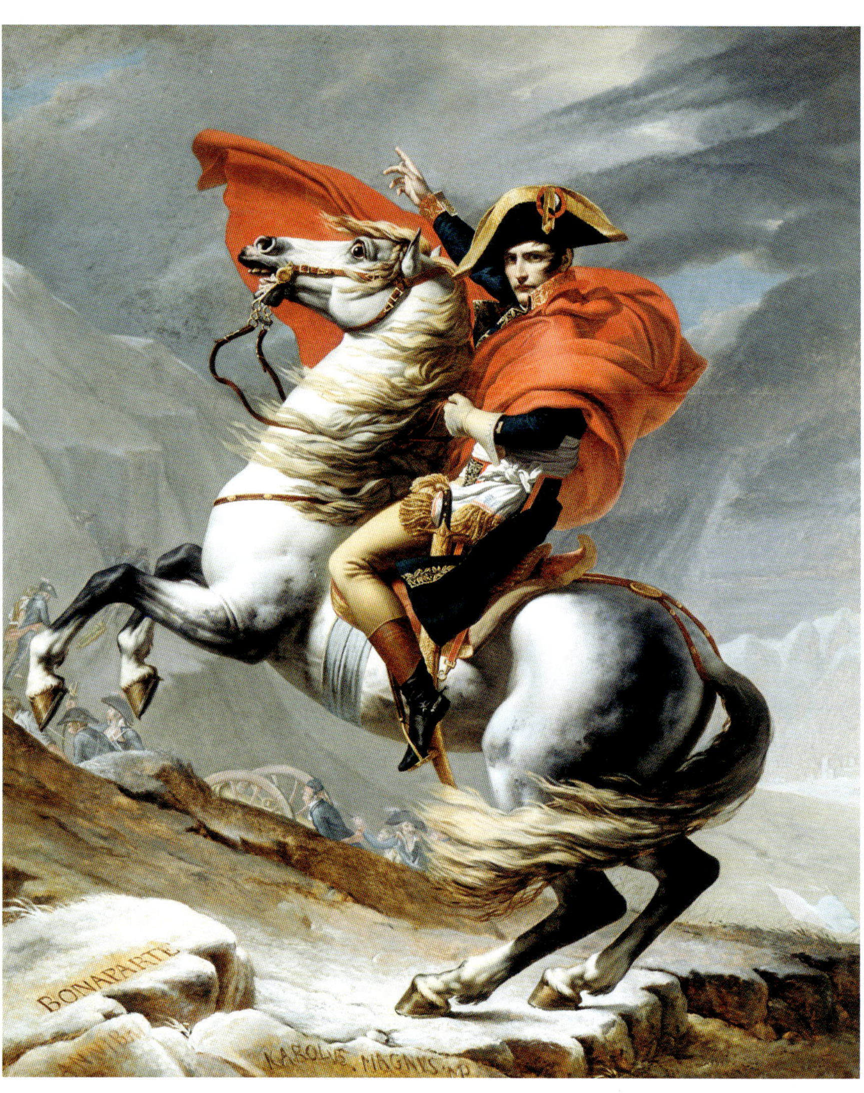

IMPORTANT COMMISSIONS

On his return journey from Andalusia, Goya stopped in Seville to study a sculpture by Pietro Torrigiano (1472–1528) and then in Saragossa to visit his friend Zapater. Back in Madrid, he retired from his teaching obligations at the Academy because of his deafness, and accepted more commissions than ever. For the Duke and Duchess of Osuna, he produced a series of cabinet paintings on the subject of witchcraft; a fashionable theme at the time. He was also commissioned by Prime Minister Godoy on his marriage to the King's niece, the Countess of Chinchón. In 1797 in celebration of this marriage – and this was not because he liked the lady in question, but because he was set to gain even greater status and wealth through it – Godoy had one of his palaces refurbished, and asked Goya to paint a series of works for it.

Now working almost solely for the Court and the aristocracy, Goya rarely painted religious works, but in 1798 he painted *The Taking of Christ* in the Sacristy of the Cathedral of Toledo, and frescoes in the chapel of San Antonio de la Florida for the King and Queen.

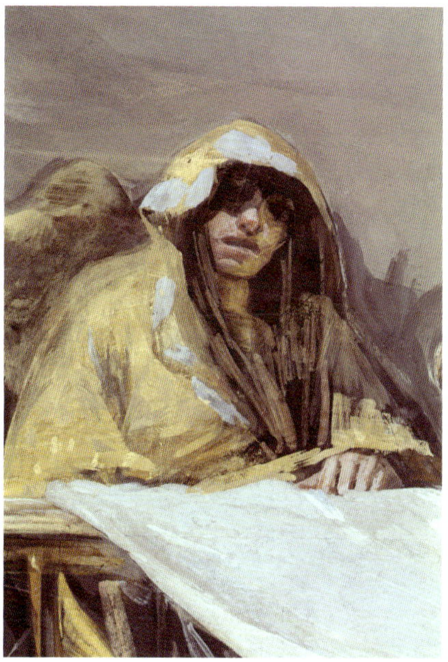

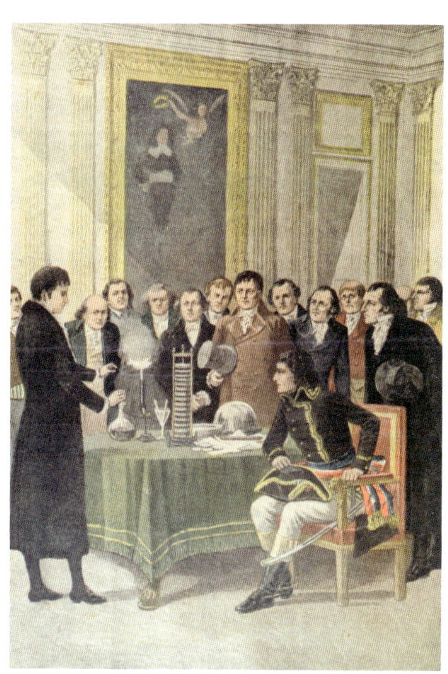

Right: Detail of a fresco by Goya in the dome of the chapel of San Antonio de la Florida; Miracle of Saint Anthony of Padua, *1798 (see page 190).*

Far right: Alessandro Volta Explains to Bonaparte the Principle of the 'Electric Column' (battery), *1801, coloured print after a painting by Bertini.*

The Queen commissioned him to decorate the newly built chapel and vault dedicated to Saint Anthony of Padua. He completed his innovative frescoes (see also page 190) there with astonishing skill in just 120 days. Everything he produced at this time was individual, progressive and inventive, and those who commissioned him had to accept his refusal to adhere to expectations.

NEOCLASSICISM VERSUS ROMANTICISM

At the time Goya lived, Neoclassicism was being eclipsed by Romanticism; a more subjective and emotional style. Artists such as Ingres, who complied with the careful and precise Neoclassical style, contrasted with other artists such as Eugène Delacroix (1798–1863) who followed the newer ideas of Romanticism, using expressive brushstrokes and optical effects of colour. Neoclassicism stood for order, reason, tradition and intellect, while Romanticism focused on emotion, passion, imagination and individuality.

The two artistic styles were commonly perceived as reason versus emotion, tradition versus innovation. Neoclassicists focused on pure lines and precise drawing, while Romanticists preferred to express themselves through colour and expansive brushstrokes. With his explorations of both reality and the imagination; the inner complexities of the human soul; and in his free and expressive technique, Goya is often described as a forerunner of Romanticism.

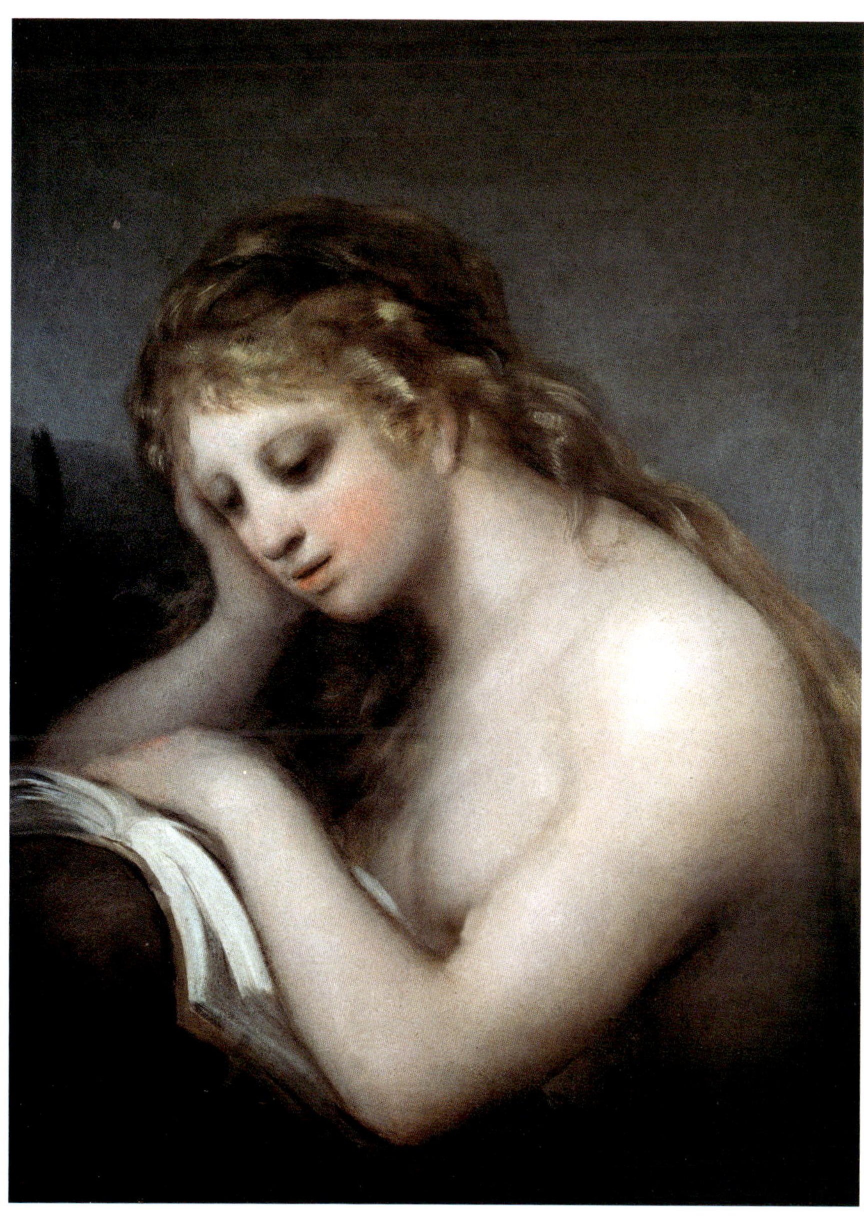

Right: Penitent Mary Magdalene, *c.1797–1800 – one of Goya's rare religious works of the period, showing his sensitivity and ability to change his style to suit the context.*

NIGHTMARISH VISIONS

Goya was 52 in 1798 and his health remained unreliable, yet his capacity for work was astounding. While completing many commissions, he also continued working on some etchings he had started in 1797. The following January they were published: a series of grotesque, satirical and enigmatic prints.

From 1797 to 1798, Goya created his series of 80 prints which he called *Los Caprichos*. An assessment of social evils and human weakness, they expressed his observations, which had been particularly acute since the onset of his deafness. The images illustrate both his personal experiences and his fantasies, and reflect many of the Enlightenment's philosophies.

THE FOLLIES OF SOCIETY

The *Caprichos* are made with extremely skilful techniques, innovatively integrating aquatints with the etchings, which enabled Goya to create fine details. This was a significant advance on what he had learned from Velázquez's example of laying etchings over aquatints. The *Caprichos* portray nightmarish visions and feature monsters, bats, owls, demons and witchcraft. In February 1799, just after the prints had been published, he made a long announcement to explain his reasoning behind them. It included the following:

'...It is as proper for a painting to criticize human error and vice as it is for poetry and prose to do, although criticism is usually taken to be exclusively the business of literature. [The author] has selected from amongst the innumerable foibles and follies to be found in any civilized society, and from the common prejudices and deceitful practices which custom, ignorance or self-interest have made usual, those subjects which he feels to be the more suitable material for satire, and which, at the same time, stimulate the artist's imagination.'

He continued:

'...The author has not copied the precedents of any other artist, nor has he been able to copy Nature herself...He who departs entirely from Nature will surely merit high esteem, since he has to put before the eyes of the public, forms and poses which have existed previously

Below: They Say Yes and Give their Hand to the First One who Comes, *1797–8, etching and aquatint.*

Below: Pretty Teacher, c.*1798, etching and aquatint. Goya wrote: 'The broom is one of the most necessary implements for witches.'*

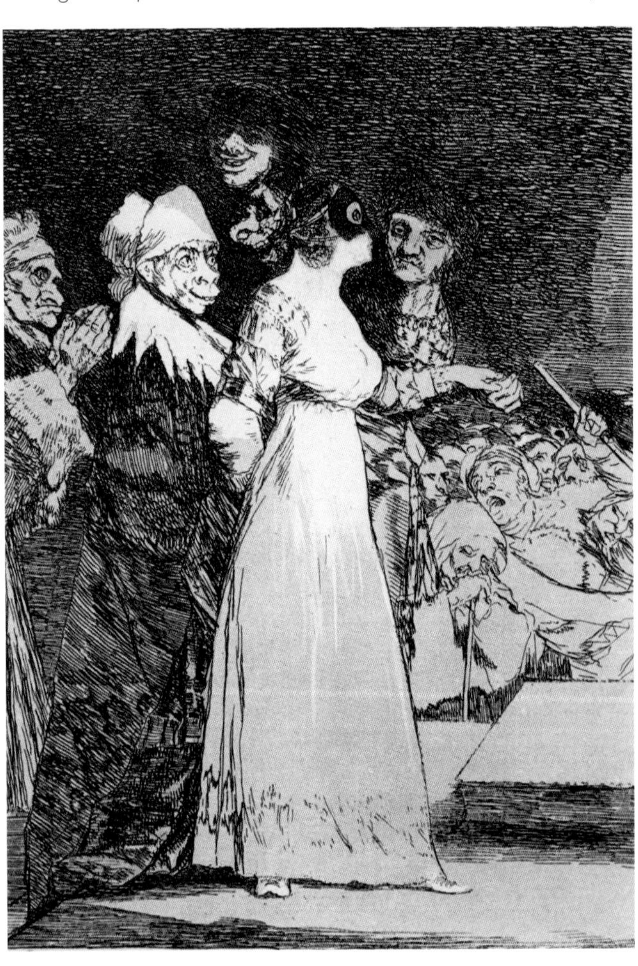

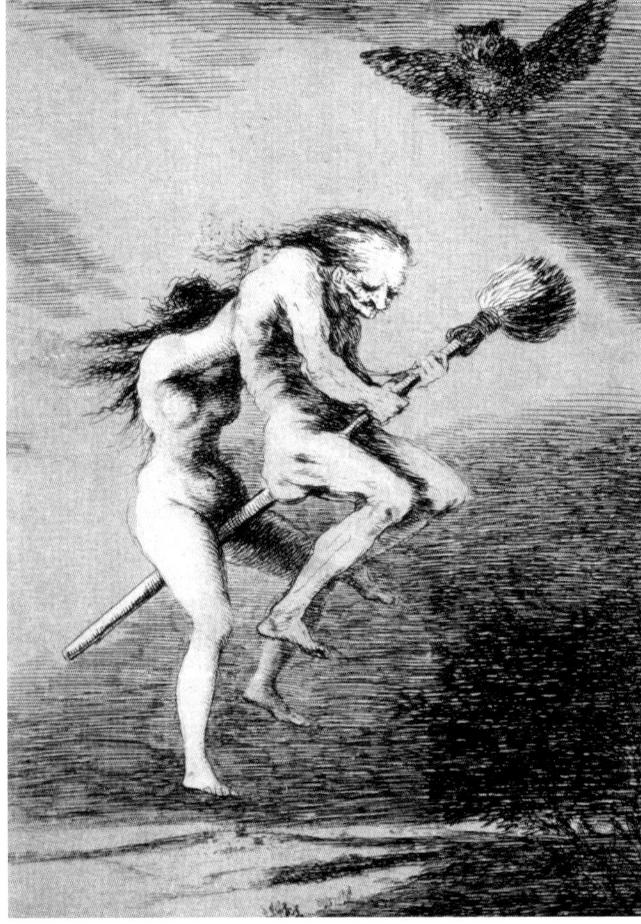

SAN ANTONIO DE LA FLORIDA

The shrine of Saint Anthony of Padua was in the grounds of La Florida, near the Royal Palace, just beyond the gates of Madrid and owned by the King and Queen. From 1792 to 1798, Charles IV and María Luisa had a new chapel built there: San Antonio de la Florida.

María Luisa commissioned Goya in 1798 to fill it with frescoes (see page 190). Instead of portraying the miracles of Saint Anthony as they happened in 13th-century Lisbon, Goya depicted them eloquently, as if in contemporary Madrid.

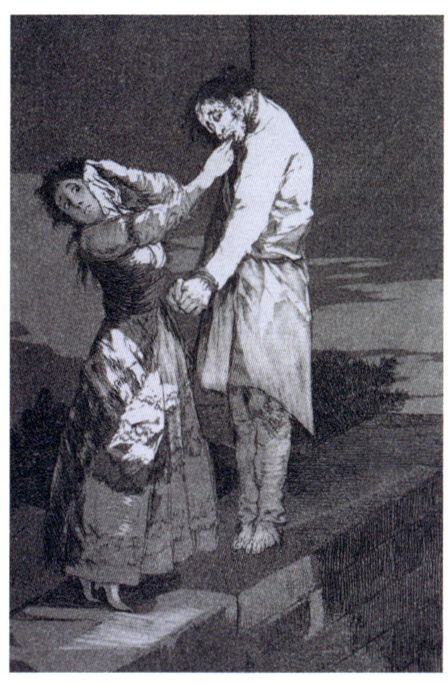

Above: Hunting for Teeth, c.1797–8, etching and aquatint. *Goya illustrates the contemporary superstitious belief in the power of a hanged man's teeth.*

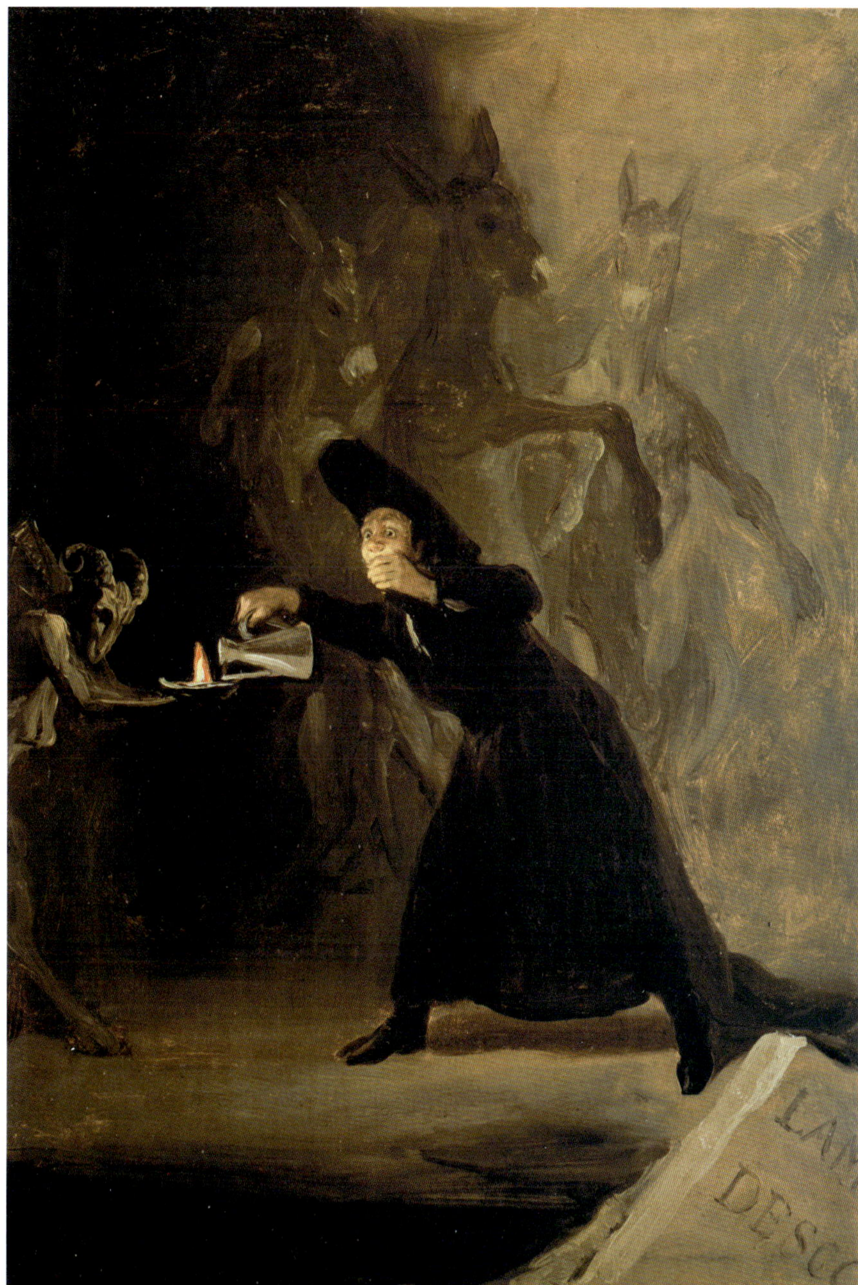

Above: The Bewitched; *one of six scenes of witchcraft Goya painted for the Duke of Osuna in 1798, this comes from a comedy first performed in 1698.*

in the darkness and confusion of an irrational mind, or one which is beset by uncontrollable passion.'

Although satire and caricature in art were fairly common in England at the time, in Spain they were not. Any who offended royalty, the aristocracy or the Church could find themselves pursued by the newly reinstated Inquisition. Goya insisted he 'intended no satire of the personal defects of any specific individual',

but it is apparent in some of the *Caprichos* that he was indeed satirizing specific figures and Court scandals. Few can now be identified individually, but his observations of the collusions between Queen María Luisa and Godoy can be detected clearly in some of them. Many of the others are more general images of corruption, jealousy, lust, superstition, hypocrisy, greed and cruelty. The prints incurred considerable criticism for their

censorious nature and out of the 300 sets he printed, only 27 sets sold. It soon became clear to him that the work was too inflammatory, and was almost certainly arousing the interest of the Inquisition, so within a short time he withdrew the prints from sale. In 1803, he gave the unsold copies as a gift to the Spanish Royal Institute of Printing, requesting that any payment for them go to his son Javier. Years later, he admitted that he withdrew them from sale because he feared the Inquisition. It was only after his death that they became admired for their imaginative content, social criticisms and technical skill.

POMP AND SATIRE

Goya's appointment as First Court Painter (as opposed to simply Court Painter) in 1799 was the culmination of his sustained efforts. Despite the criticisms of his *Caprichos*, his reputation at Court was unharmed, and in September 1799, he was asked to paint official portraits of the King and Queen.

Queen María Luísa was delighted with Goya's portraits of her; one in a mantilla (see page 196) and the other on her horse Marcial (see page 197), a gift from Prime Minister Godoy. She wrote to Godoy: 'It's said to be an even better likeness than the portrait in the mantilla.'

Concurrently, Goya also painted two portraits of the King; one in hunting dress and one on horseback (see page 197). Executed ten years after his first portraits of the royal couple, these paintings were dominated by the freedom and strength of his execution.

POLITICS AND NOBLE RELATIONSHIPS

Goya wrote to Zapater: 'The royals are mad about me.' Yet despite now mixing regularly with some of the most important figures of the realm, he prudently remained detached from political events.

Godoy had made some foolish decisions, but despite this, one of his nicknames was 'Prince of the Peace' (Principe de la Paz), and he retained enormous power at Court. In 1797, he

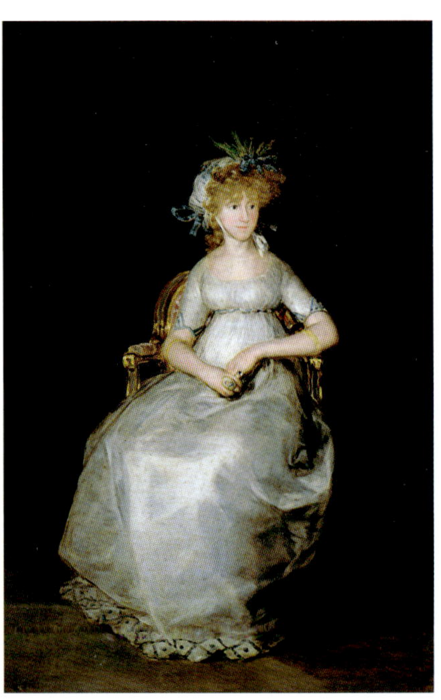

Right: The Countess of Chinchón, 1800. *She married Prime Minister Godoy when she was 18, and is pregnant with her first child in this sensitive portrait by Goya.*

Below: Detail of The Family of Charles IV, *1800–1. Goya's most important commission to date, this life-sized family portrait of the royal family portrays them as ostentatious and foolish, apparently paying a visit to his studio. See also page 200.*

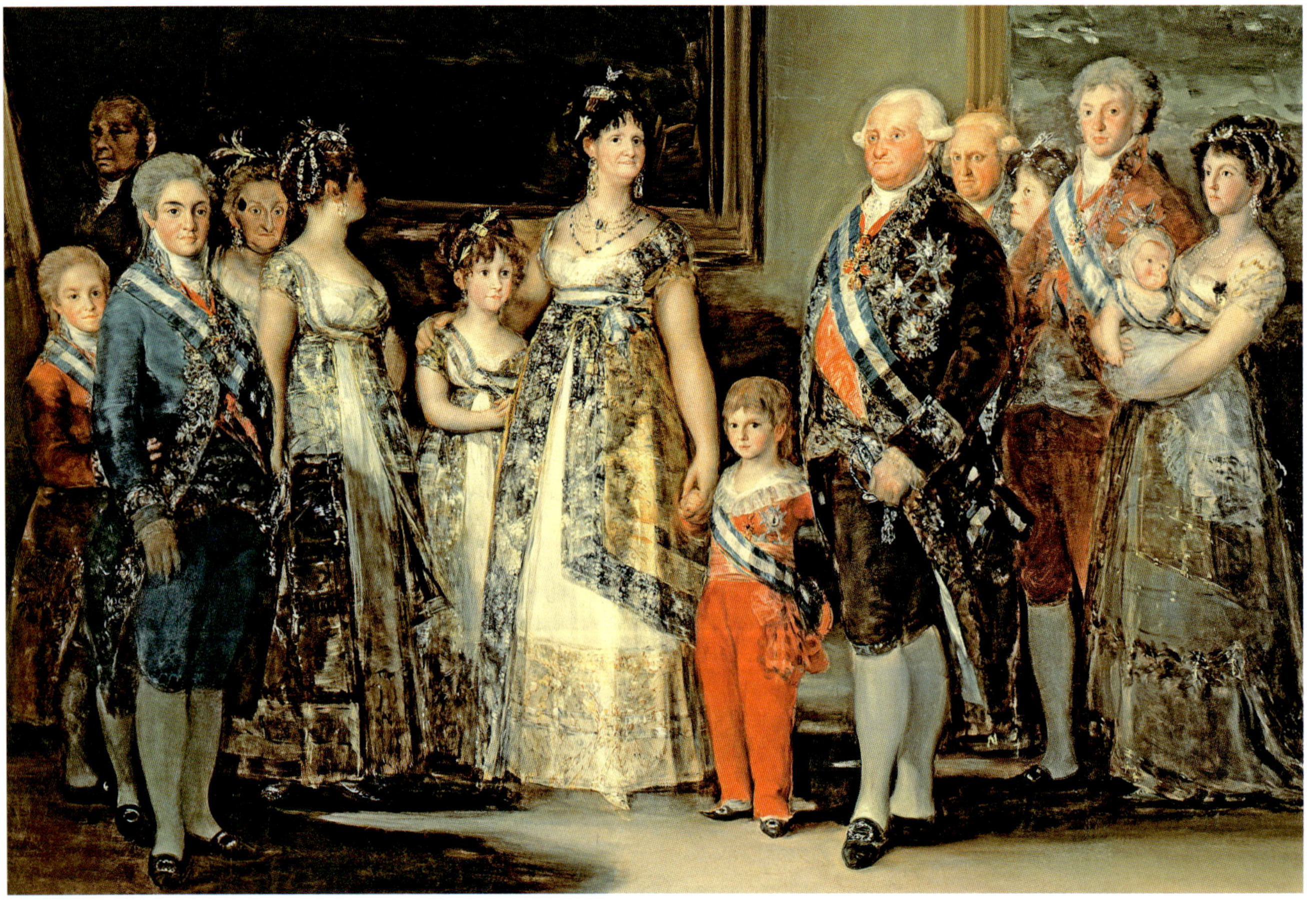

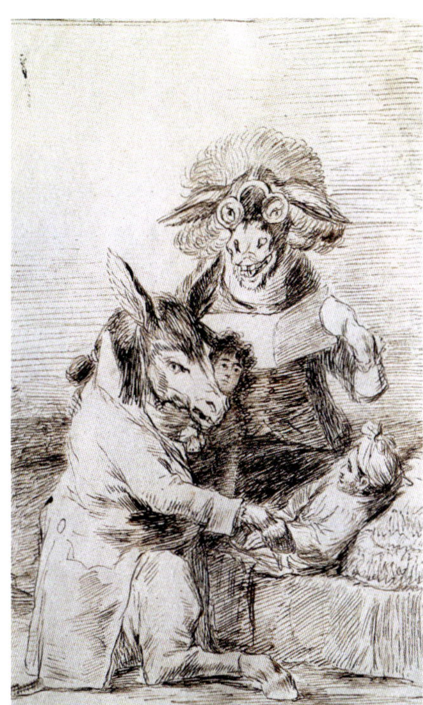

Above: A preliminary drawing for one of Goya's Caprichos *made in 1797–8, featuring donkeys to depict stupidity.*

had made the King grant noble titles on his mistress Pepita Tudó and later that year he married the King's niece, María Teresa, the Countess of Chinchón. María Teresa only agreed to the marriage as it ensured the restoration of her family's fortunes. Godoy cruelly kept Pepita Tudó, her mother and sister living in the same house as his new wife.

In the same year, Godoy was removed from the office of Prime Minister, and elevated to the position of Captain-General. In 1800, he bought the house that Goya had been living in since 1778. He commissioned Goya to paint four allegorical medallions representing Industry, Commerce, Agriculture and Science (see pages 203–4) and gave the house to Pepita. Goya bought his own house in Madrid for 234,000 reales.

That April, Goya had painted a portrait of the pregnant Countess of Chinchón. He had already painted her as a child in 1783 in *The Family of the Infante Don Luis* (see page 139). The later portrait is empathetic and sensitive; in a silvery-white muslin dress, she appears dignified and reserved, gazing into the distance, expressing disillusionment and resolve. Disgusted by Godoy's promiscuous

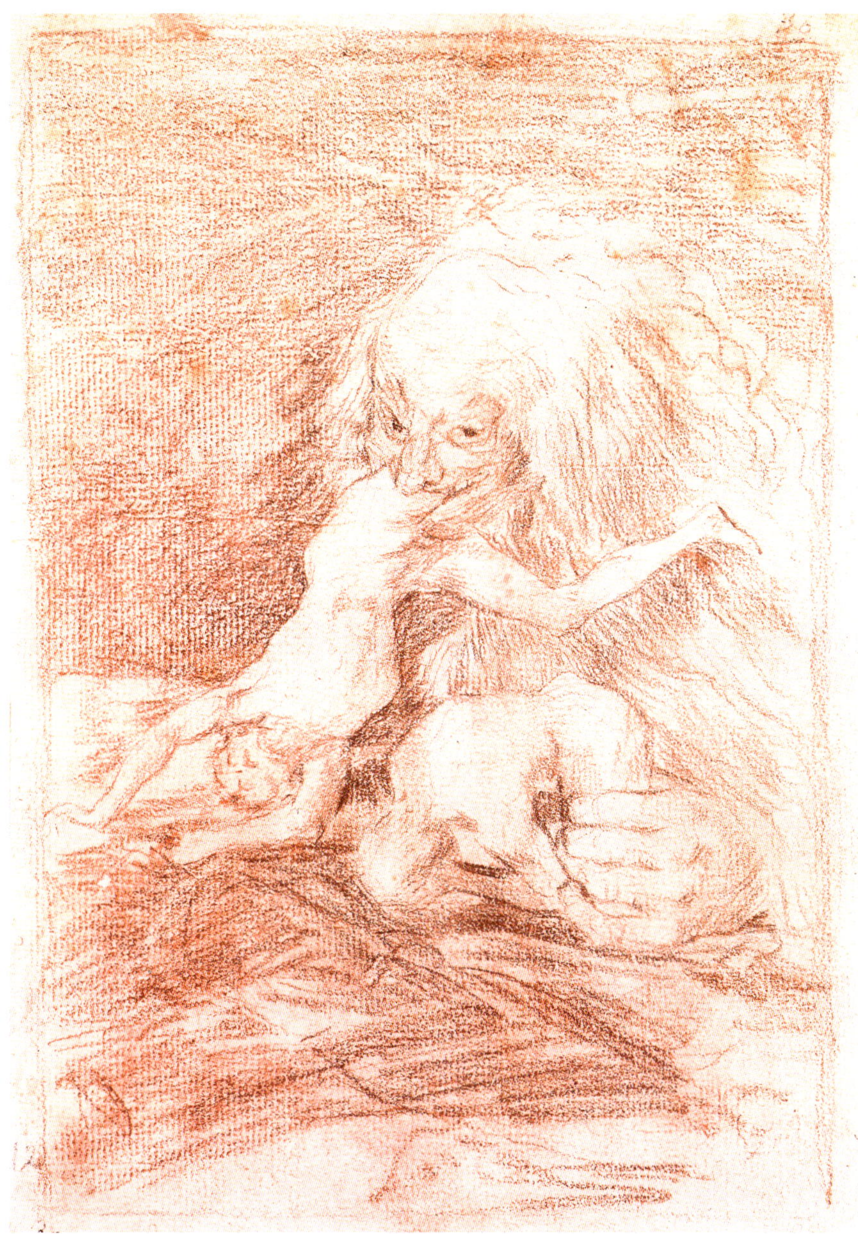

Above: In sanguine on paper, this is one of Goya's 1797–8 preparatory drawings for his later painting of Saturn Devouring One of his Children. *See page 97.*

behaviour, recently she had stopped speaking to him. The Court knew of the problems between her and her husband, and Goya was particularly sympathetic.

IMPORTANT PORTRAIT

After his individual portraits of the King and Queen, Goya was immediately commissioned to paint the entire royal family. The large *Family of Charles IV* follows Velázquez's idea of incorporating himself in *Las Meninas* of 1656. Goya painted himself at his easel in the background. All the 13 figures in the work are life-sized, standing in a room in the palace. The King and Queen are in the centre foreground surrounded by their children and other close relatives.

Despite being painted over 200 years ago, questions remain about Goya's intentions. The work seems overtly satirical. The main figures appear ugly, pompous and foolish, with no attempt at flattery, although the younger children appear ingenuous and endearing. Next to Prince Ferdinand, an unidentified young lady dressed like the Queen turns her face away. The heir's future bride was yet to be chosen. Despite Goya's apparent satire, however, the work was received with enthusiasm by the royal family.

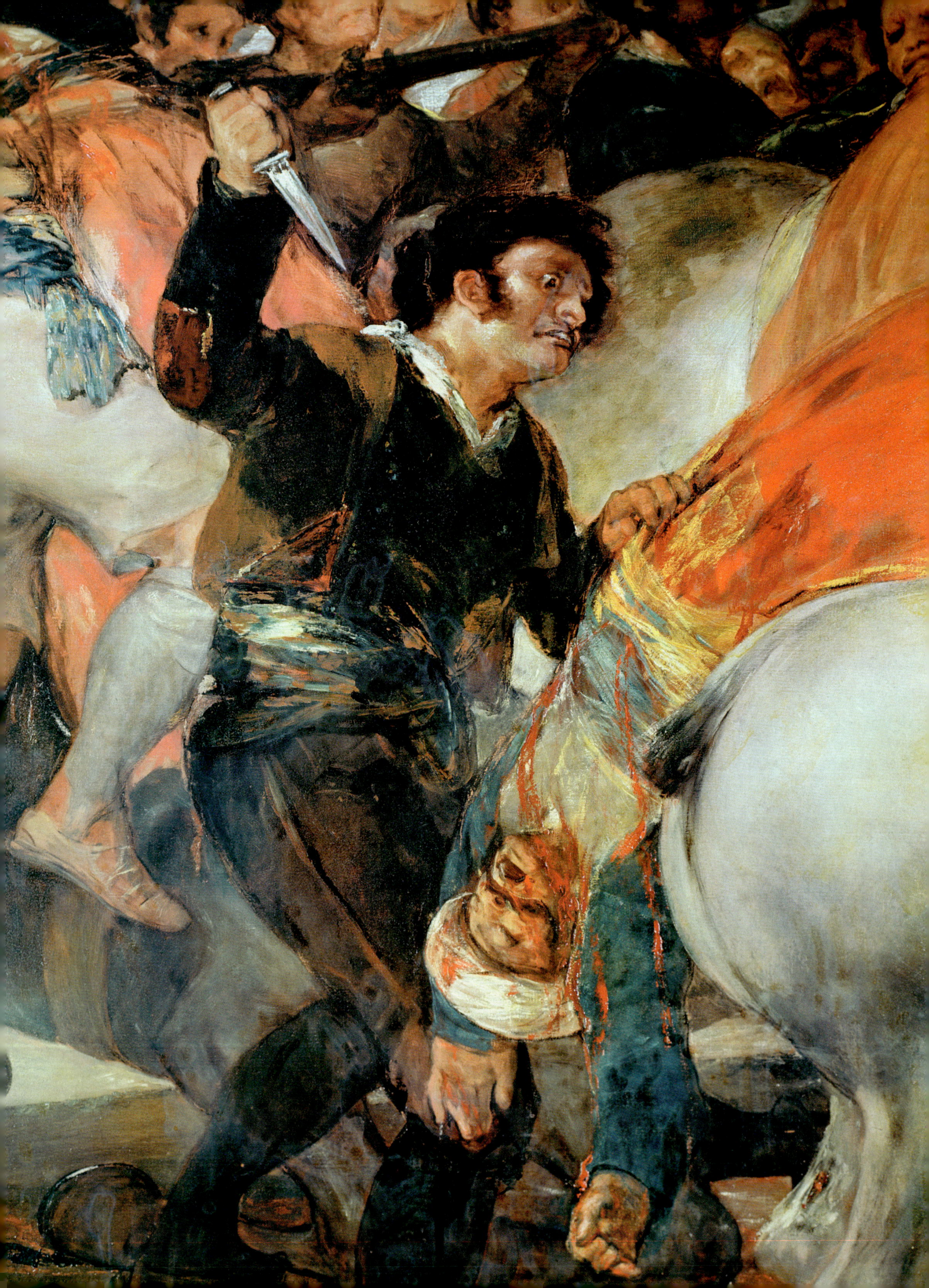

FLUCTUATING FORTUNES

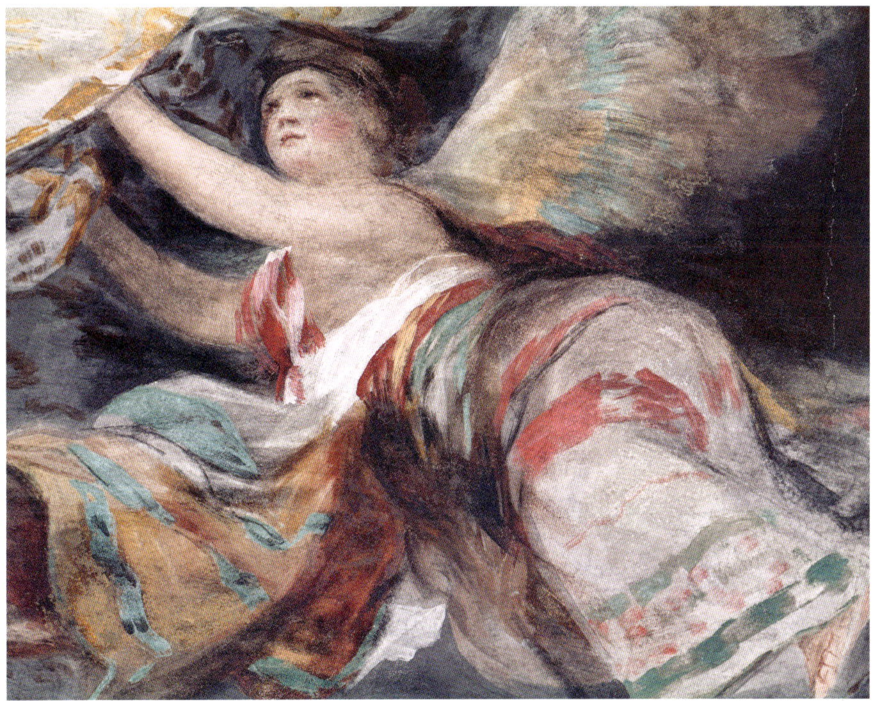

By the turn of the 19th century, Goya realized his country was heading for greater problems as Napoleon's power expanded. As his art developed, he remained the most highly esteemed artist in Spain. However, after painting *The Family of Charles IV* (see page 200), he never received another royal commission. There has been much speculation about this sudden end to his official activities, but there is no satisfactory explanation. As he retained his title and salary, it seems that he was not disgraced; he merely withdrew from Court life. He continued to be commissioned to paint numerous portraits.

Above: Detail of an angel in the fresco on the north-east vault of San Antonio de la Florida, painted by Goya in 1798.

Left: Detail from The Second of May, 1808, *also known as* The Riot against the Mamluk Mercenaries, *painted in 1814 by Goya, depicting the Spanish attacking the Mamluks who had been sent into Spain by the French (see page 233).*

PRE-EMINENCE

Although he did not paint directly for the King and Queen again, in 1801, Goya was commissioned to paint Godoy in the insouciant attitude of a victorious general, to celebrate the success of the 'War of the Oranges' against Portugal. By 1803, Goya bought a second property in Madrid.

The War of the Oranges (Guerra de las Naranjas) was a brief conflict in 1801 in which Spanish forces invaded Portugal following a request from the French government, and set the scene for the Peninsular Wars. In 1800, First Consul Bonaparte and his Spanish ally Godoy demanded that Portugal broke its long-standing alliance with Britain and instead enter into an alliance with France against Britain.

As part of the agreement, Bonaparte and Godoy (who was reappointed as Prime Minister of Spain in 1801) also insisted that Portugal surrendered the greatest part of its national territory to France. Unsurprisingly, Portugal refused, and in April 1801 the French invaded Portugal, reinforced by Spanish troops a few weeks' later under Godoy's command. When Godoy took the Portuguese town of Olivença near the Spanish frontier, he picked some fresh

Below: Executed at the same time as the similar work on page 45, c.1797–1800. Goya painted more self-portraits than any other Spanish artist of his time.

oranges and sent them to Queen María Luisa as a symbol of his success; and so the war gained its name.

TWO DEATHS
In 1802, the Duchess of Alba died after a month's illness when she was just 40 years old. It shocked all who knew her, although Goya's emotions have not been recorded, as from 1799 to 1803, he and Zapater stopped corresponding. It may be that Zapater had moved to Madrid as Goya was always urging him to do, or they may have quarrelled. Either way, in 1803, Zapater also died. Goya's feelings over the deaths of two people who had been particularly close to him have not been documented, but it can be assumed that he was exceptionally saddened.

GRAND PORTRAITIST
Despite no further direct portraits of the royal family, between 1800 and 1805, Goya produced some of his most accomplished portraits. During that time, he painted over 50 likenesses of the affluent middle and upper classes of

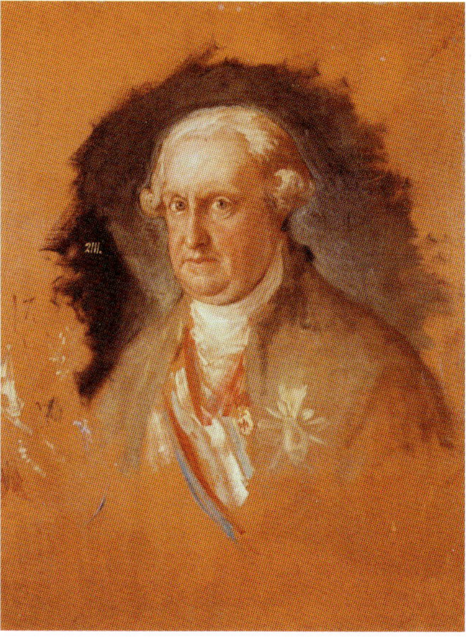

Above: Charles IV of Spain; *an animated study by Goya, 1800.*

Madrid, with whom he now mixed on a daily basis. All of these works show a remarkable sensitivity to his sitters' personalities, revealing their unique and individual features. Each portrait can be seen as a fascinating character study. His earlier, exotic, maja-type ladies were now changing to a slightly more Neoclassical style. Each image was direct, unpretentious and focused on reality. He also used the wedding of his son Javier as a reason for painting the members of his own family for the first time.

MAKING MONEY
As First Court Painter, Goya received an annual income of 50,000 reales, which was a great sum. For every portrait and sketch he painted for the King or his family, he was paid extra. He had always

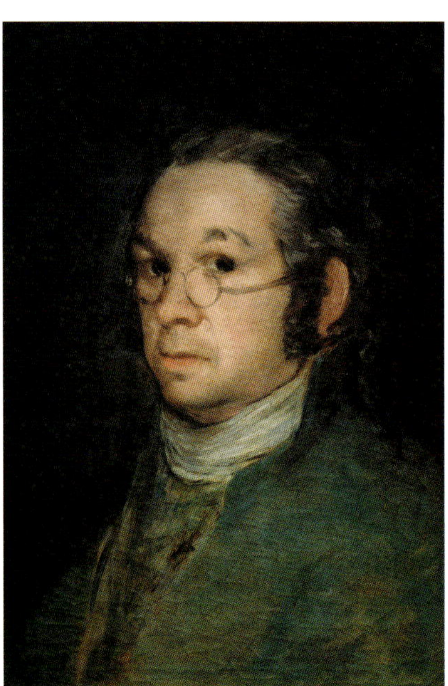

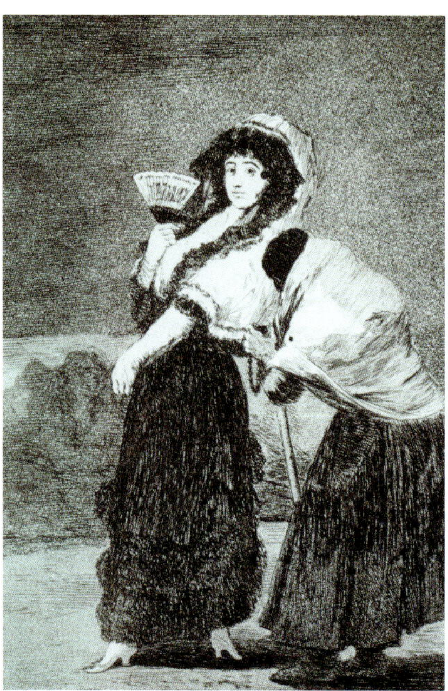

Left: Should God forgive her, she was her Mother, 1799. Goya wrote of this: 'The girl left home very young...she won a lottery prize...A dirty shrivelled hag begs for alms...the poor old woman is her mother!'

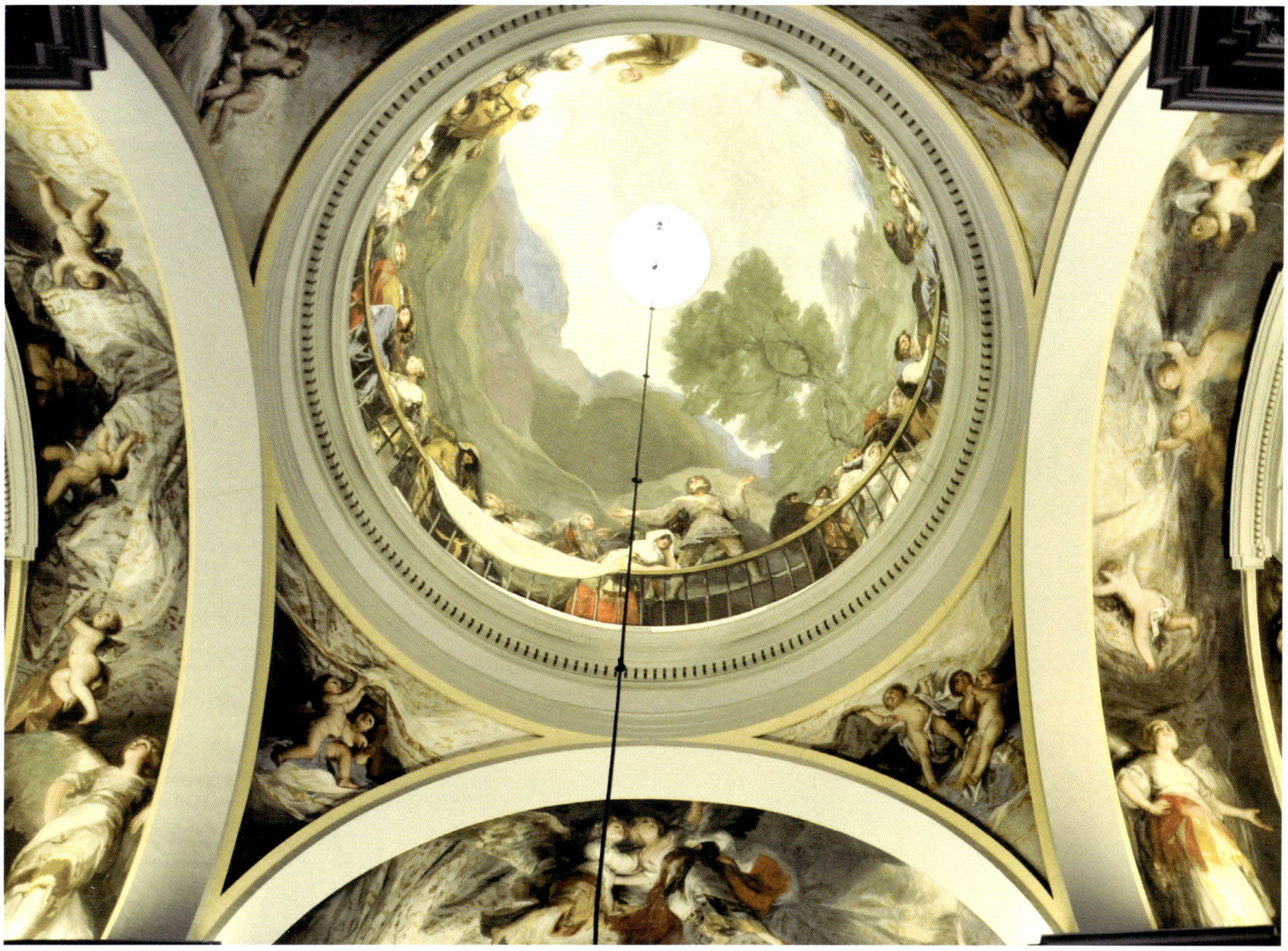

been determined to make money, and when he earned it he invested wisely in property and shares. Yet despite the fact that it might ultimately have earned him more money, he never behaved sycophantically towards his monarchs. Although he tactfully and perhaps loyally did not literally speak out, his critical observations in his art spoke volumes about his opinions of the intrigues and affairs at Court. Perhaps the greatest intrigue is that his patrons were delighted with the frank and unflattering likenesses he captured of them.

After he had completed *The Family of Charles IV* (see page 200), he gradually retreated from Court life. This could have been for many reasons, from his despair over the death of his closest friend Zapater, his continued poor health, or the uncertain politics that had seen many of his *ilustrados* friends banished or imprisoned. Or it may have been simply due to his shifting artistic interests. His salary as First Court Painter, along with his additional income

from portraits, meant that he could afford an expensive lifestyle. In 1805, he gave Javier and his new, pregnant wife Gumersinda one of his houses in Madrid and he remained in the other with Josefa.

Above: Cupola showing Saint Anthony, 1798. People marvelled at Goya's fresco skills.

Below: Children on banister, detail of the painting of the dome, Goya, 1798, showing his animated execution in a difficult space.

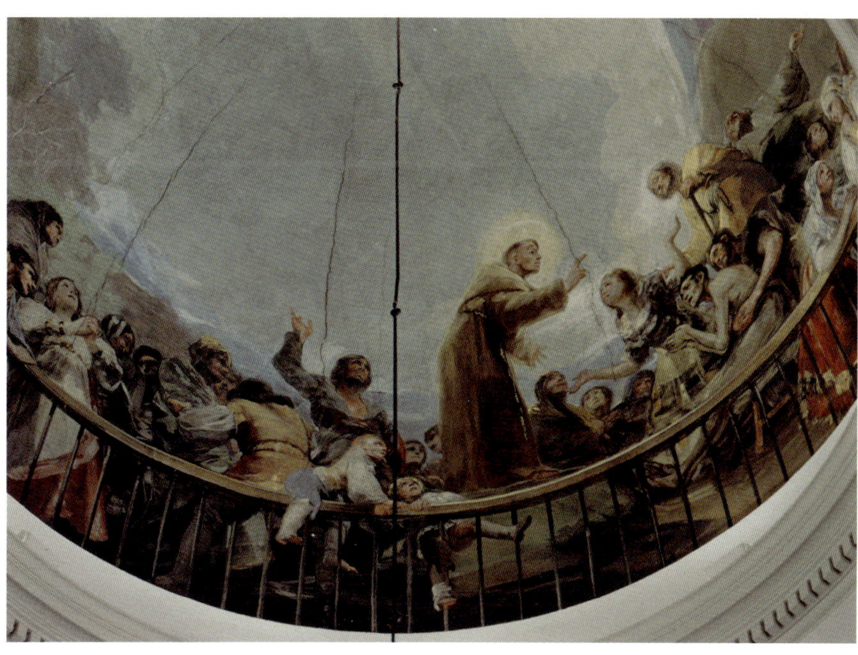

NAPOLEON AND THE ARTS

In 1804, as Goya was enjoying wealth and fame across the Pyrenees, Napoleon Bonaparte crowned himself Emperor of France. Napoleon modelled his regime on the Imperialism of ancient Rome. The Empire style reinforced the powerful Napoleonic image.

Neoclassicism communicated the new Emperor Napoleon's ideals perfectly and under his reign, it evolved into an 'Empire Style', expressed in art, design, the applied arts and architecture.

As part of Napoleon's charismatic personality, he used propaganda to manipulate public perceptions of his regime. To create and maintain his image, he commissioned leading French artists to produce works depicting an elysian, positive view of his Empire, with him as its hero. Under his patronage, designers, craftsmen and architects reinterpreted and recycled previous symbols of power, such as the eagle and the bee. Most artists working for him were inspired by the grandeur of the subjects they were being asked to represent, and created impressive, uplifting paintings and sculptures. It contrasted with the candid portraits, satirical images and expressive ceiling frescoes concurrently being produced by Goya.

Among the many artists and architects Napoleon patronized were the painters Andrea Appiani (1754–1817), Gros, David (1748–1825) and Ingres; the sculptor Antonio Canova, who became famous for his marble sculptures that appeared to render cool naked flesh,

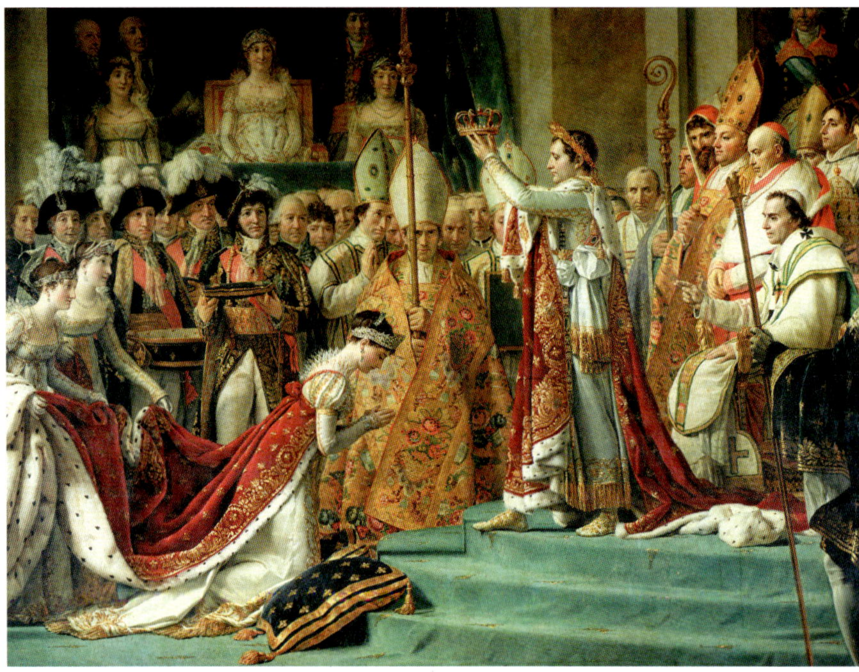

Above: The Coronation of Napoleon, *1805–7. As Napoleon's official painter, Jacques-Louis David was commissioned to produce this epic work.*

Below: View of the Projected Foro Bonaparte, Milan, *Alessandro Sanquirico, c.1800. Antolini's grand Neoclassical project was inspired by the Forum of ancient Rome, but never executed.*

and Giovanni Antonio Antolini (1756–1841). The art produced by these artists was carefully and skilfully rendered and focused on smooth contours and accurate details. Goya's art on the other hand, centred more on subjectivity and personal expression.

CONTROVERSIAL CORONATION

On 18 May, 1804, Napoleon proclaimed himself Emperor, and made his wife Josephine Empress. His coronation ceremony took place on 2 December 1804 in the Cathedral of Notre Dame in Paris, at considerable expense and with exalted pomp and ceremony. Despite paying for Pope Pius VII to travel to France, at the ceremony, Napoleon crowned himself, and then Josephine. A few months later he crowned himself again as ruler of Italy. During his regime, he created a new aristocracy, emulating the one that had been eradicated by the Revolution. In 1808, he began granting titles of nobility to those who served him especially well. His Court became a public display of grandeur and

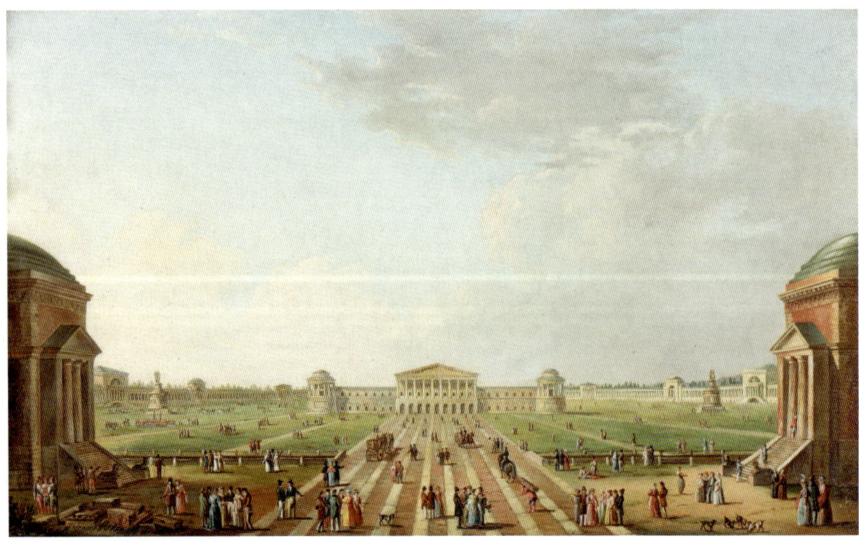

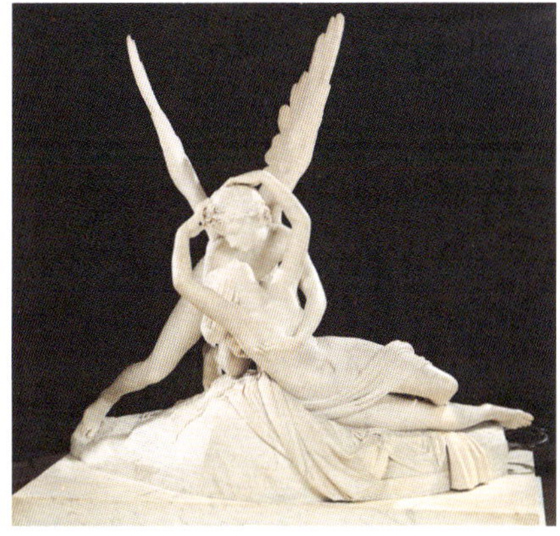

Above: Psyche Revived by the Kiss of Cupid, *1787–93. Canova combines Neoclassical and Romantic styles, depicting a moment of great emotion. For Goya's portrayal, see page 195.*

elegance, and Court protocol and rules of etiquette became strict and complex. From Spain, Goya and his compatriots had reason to be concerned.

LOOT AND PLUNDER

Napoleon and his armies plundered the countries they invaded, helping themselves to hundreds of works of art and artefacts. Back in Paris, he filled the Palace of the Louvre with these priceless treasures. In November 1802, he appointed Dominique Vivant, Baron de Denon (1747–1825), as first director of the Louvre Museum. Denon was devoted to Napoleon, and an expert at looting vast numbers of works of art across Europe. On arrival in France, many of the stolen works were publicly paraded through the streets of Paris in a procession with elephants and other wild animals, before they were placed in the Louvre, which Denon renamed the Musée Napoléon. Spain was yet to have a public art gallery.

Napoleon's newly made aristocrats began commissioning images of themselves and their experiences, including scenes from the exotic places

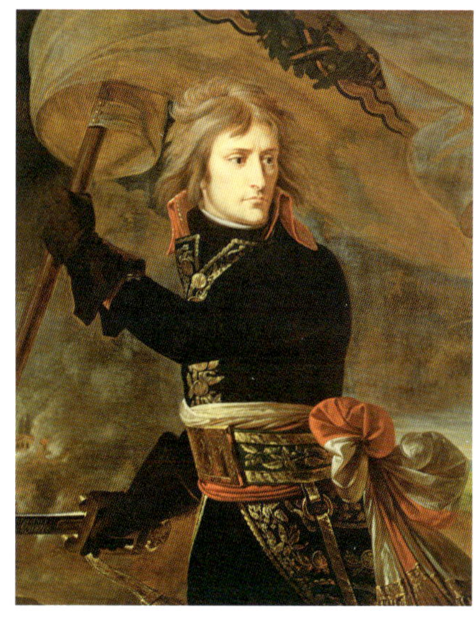

Above: Napoleon on the Bridge of Arcole, *Antoine-Jean Gros, 1801. Napoleon made a bold move here in 1796, and the ensuing French victory proved enormously significant.*

visited by the French army, which was capturing the collective imagination. As the various exploits of the French army inspired a huge wave of patriotic fervour across the nation, giant battle paintings were produced, and the appeal of various exotic themes increased.

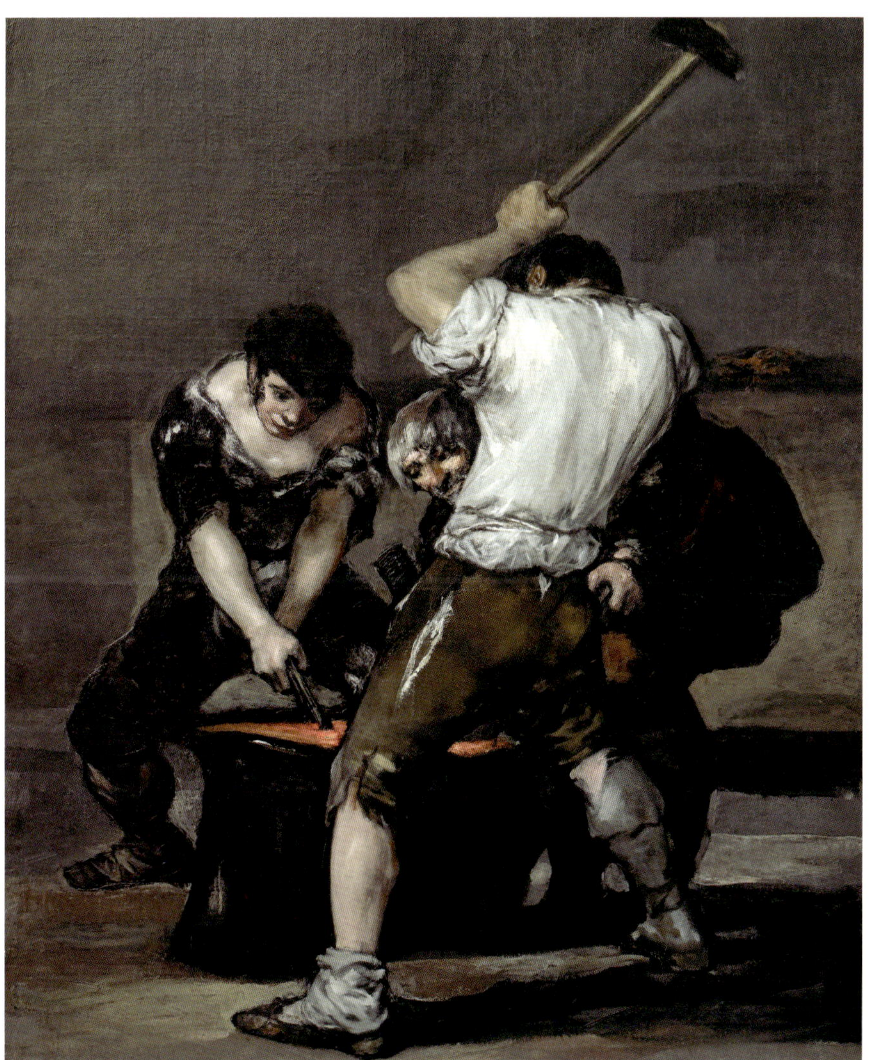

Left: The Forge, c.1815–20; *painted from life, this shows Goya as a precursor of the Realism movement, in which subjects were shown truthfully and accurately.*

INFLUENCING GOYA

As many of the ideas that were initiated by Napoleon and his regime filtered through to Spain, some influenced Goya, as can be seen for instance in his portrait of Godoy (page 203). Yet even that contrasted with portraits being produced in France. With no autocratic emperor dictating to him, Goya continued to be irreverent, flippant and often revealingly honest. Godoy, for instance, would have felt flattered by his portrait, but it was created so his enemies could smirk at it and the man's inflated sense of importance. In many ways, Goya's art anticipated Realism of the 1850s and 60s.

A SHIFT IN POWER

Goya was acutely aware of the ominous situation that was developing around his country, with Napoleon's cunning tactics, unwittingly assisted by Spain's simple-minded king, imprudent queen and the arrogant Godoy. Realizing however that he could not change anything, Goya settled into a period of relative tranquillity.

In spite of his deafness, as Spain's First Painter, Goya had achieved precisely what he had aimed for; wealth, status and admiration. For some years, the Spanish people had affectionately nicknamed him 'Don Paco el Sordo', which translates as 'Frank the Deaf'. Having worked through various artistic periods throughout his life, he continued to evolve independently. Focusing mainly on his commissioned portraits, he also experimented with new ideas, filling sketchbooks with detailed observations, producing paintings on social themes, and expressive miniatures in tempera on copper (these were for his daughter-in-law's family, the Goicoecheas).

During this period, Goya's sitters were no longer in formal poses, but depicted in ways that exposed their characters. Additionally, he portrayed light glowingly and naturally, while his brush marks were animated.

Below: A detail from The Naked Maja, *1797 –1800 (see also page 194). The Church in Spain forbade nude images, and in 1815 this painting was confiscated by the Inquisition.*

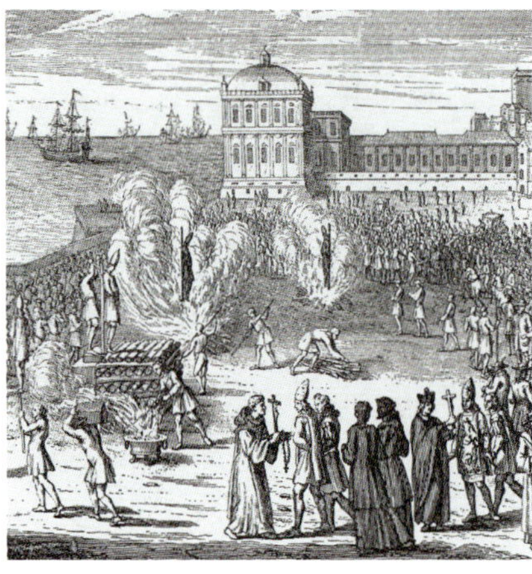

Above: Burning Suspects at the Stake *by the Spanish Inquisition, c.1800s. The Spanish Inquisition remained a menace within Spain during the early 19th century.*

Harmonious colours, luminous flesh tones and an inherent liveliness show the sophistication he had attained. As well as his long artistic career, by this time, he had come close to death, endured pain and deafness, lost his best friend, and was facing the likelihood of war in his own country. He had also recently become a grandfather.

THE SHOCK OF THE NUDE

In Spain, images of nudes were forbidden by the Church and the Inquisition. Goya greatly admired Velázquez's only nude painting *The Toilet of Venus*, now known as *The Rokeby Venus*, that in 1800 passed into Godoy's possession. However, while Velázquez's work represents a goddess with only her back and face on show, Goya subsequently painted a nude that neither pretends to be a deity nor coyly shields her modesty from viewers. Mystery surrounds the two paintings that he painted around 1800 for Godoy: *The Naked Maja* and *The Clothed Maja* (see page 194). Both he and Godoy were fully aware of the ban on nudes, yet Goya painted two pictures of the same woman (whose identity has never been verified). In both works, the woman reclines on cushions on a green velvet divan. In

Below: Charles IV of Spain Receiving the Homage of the University of Valencia, *1802, Vicente López y Portana (1772–1850).*

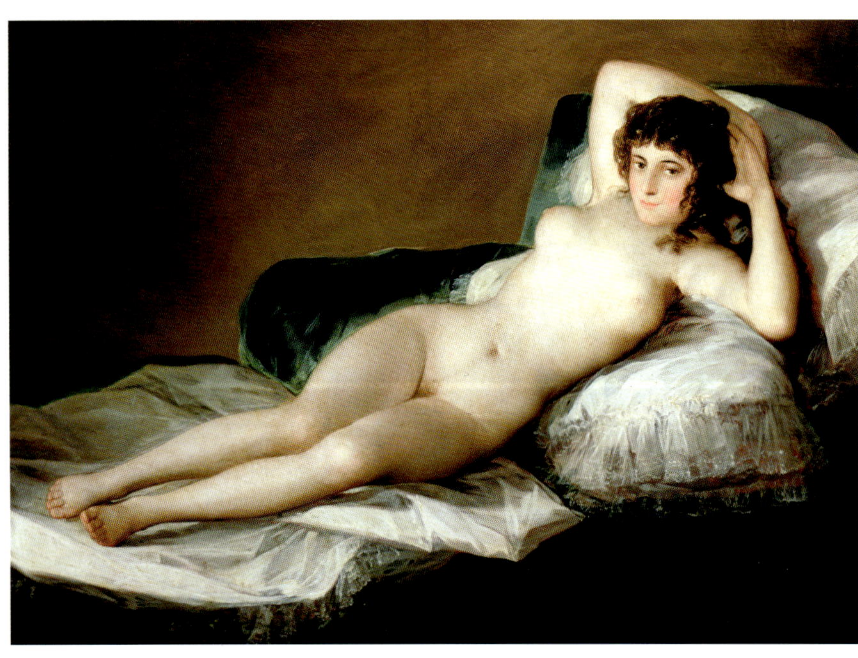

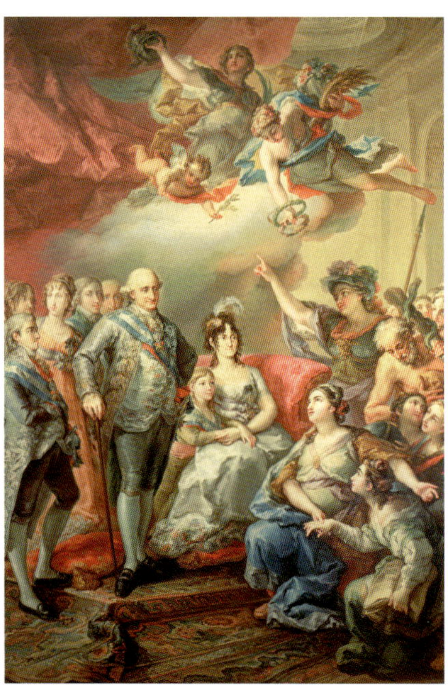

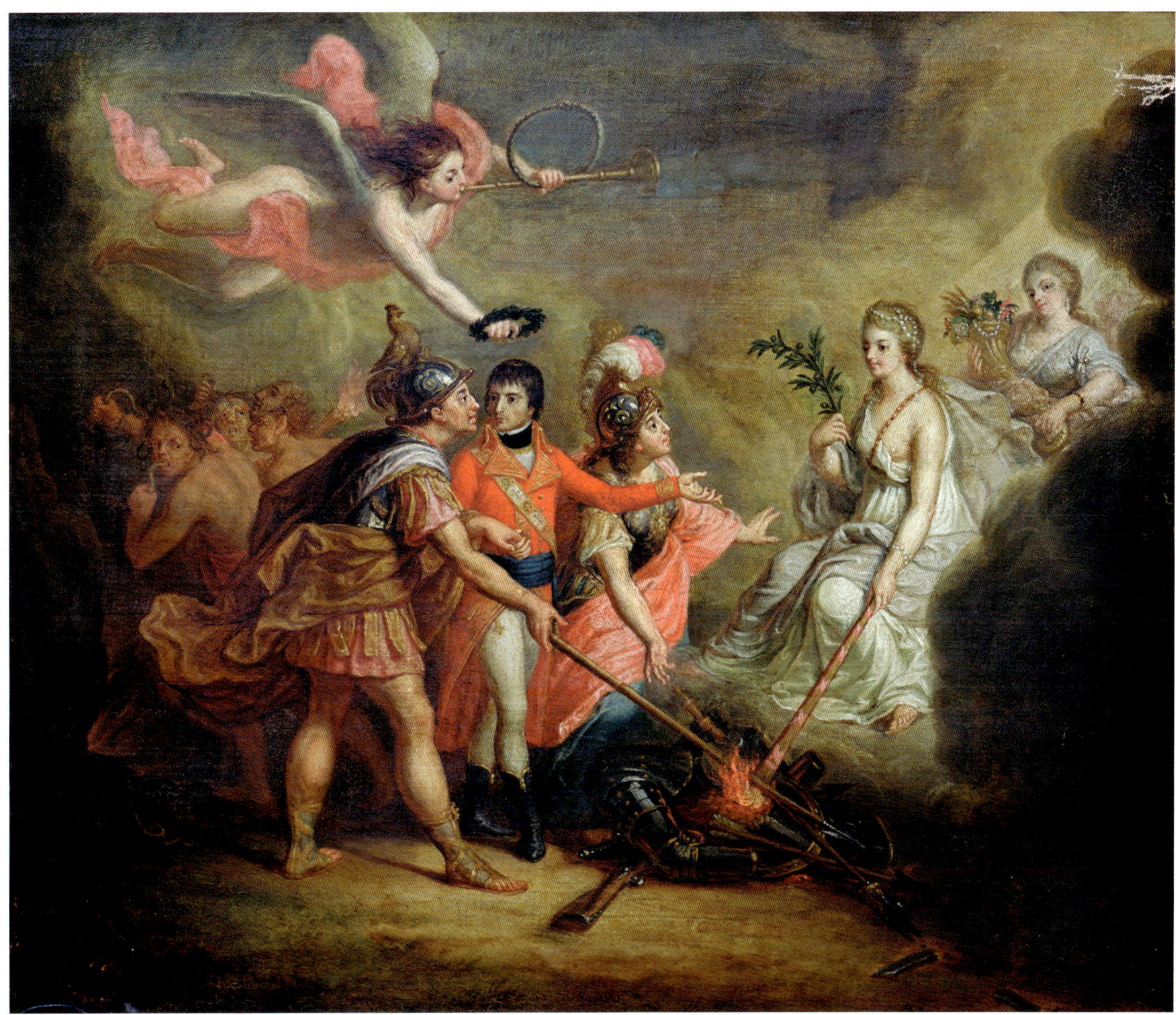

Above: The Peace of Amiens, *Dominique Doncre (1743–1820). Signed in 1802 by Britain, France, Spain and the Netherlands, this treaty gave a 14-month respite. Goya learned of the recommencement of the Napoleonic Wars with horror.*

PROBLEMS IN SPAIN

Despite French patriotism, Napoleon's conflicts continued to upset the rest of Europe. In Spain, Charles IV continued hunting rather than worry about politics while the Queen deferred matters to Godoy, whose lifestyle made him an unsatisfactory statesman. Added to this, Ferdinand, the heir-apparent, began plotting to murder Godoy and his own parents, and take the Spanish throne.

one, she brazenly gazes at viewers revealing her naked body to all. In the other, she wears a translucent dress and a jacket. The subject was considered shocking even over 60 years later when Manet followed Goya's example and also painted a bold, reclining nude. *The Naked Maja* was listed for the first time in 1800 as being in Godoy's palace. Eight years later it was listed again, along with *The Clothed Maja*. In 1815, the Inquisition confiscated it and summoned Goya to reveal who commissioned him. Goya's response was not recorded and he continued his life as before. Someone had the power to protect him.

GOSSIP AND PROPAGANDA

There is no evidence that María Luisa and Godoy were actual lovers, but their intimate behaviour and his positions

of power fuelled many rumours. Considering his low birth, his rapid promotions inspired great jealousy, and one of his greatest enemies was the Crown Prince.

As neither the King nor Queen considered book learning to be important, Prince Ferdinand received a poor education. Resenting their lack of attention, he had grown up extravagant and self-indulgent. By the time he reached his early 20s, he was desperate to take the throne and frustrated that his ineffectual father remained in robust health, while Godoy continued to control the country. Encouraged by Godoy's many other enemies, he paid cartoonists to create obscene images lampooning the relationship between his mother and her First Minister.

ROMANTICISM IN EUROPE

Often seen as the antithesis of Neoclassicism, Romanticism was colourful, dramatic and expressive.
Although he did not oppose Neoclassicism, Goya's blending of reality and the imagination, using strong
colour and dramatic light, made him retrospectively perceived as one of its most important precursors.

Romantic art developed in the last quarter of the 18th century. It was predominantly emotional, often set against a backdrop of darkness and luminous light. As Romantic art grew, strong, individual ideas in art, literature and music emerged, emphasizing links between humanity, nature and spirituality and completely contrasting with the rationality of the Enlightenment. As the ideas spread, even accepted Neoclassicists such as Canova began to produce works that displayed immediacy and expressiveness, embodying some of the Romantic ideals.

Below: The Devil's Bridge, St Gothard, *c.1803–4. Considered a forerunner of Romanticism, Turner painted breathtaking views of the European landscape.*

FREEING THE IMAGINATION

In encouraging artists' free expression, Romanticism emphasized the importance of intuition and the portrayal of the emotions, which had been suppressed in Neoclassicism. Emotions were interpreted through depictions of human activity and in untamed nature. In part, it was an escape from modern realities, so it elevated and exaggerated heroism and drama, and was interpreted broadly as Romantic artists addressed viewers directly and personally. As with most pre-20th-century art movements however, it was not recognized as such until after it was over. In hindsight, by the mid-19th century, links and similarities were recognized, and it was seen as a movement and named Romanticism, but while it was happening, the ideas seemed to be simply a fashion.

EUROPEAN ROMANTIC PAINTERS

Individually, Romanticists expressed their beliefs in spiritual freedom, invention and creativity. While Goya was working in Spain, the landscape artists J. M. W. Turner (1775–1851) and Caspar David Friedrich (1774–1840), in England and Germany respectively were painting spectacular, light-filled, dramatic landscapes. With Napoleon's patronage, the Empire period in France provoked a renewed interest in dramatic artwork, and the vibrant ideas of Romanticism came to the fore. New generations of Romantic French artists included Théodore Géricault (1791–1824), who produced

Below: Portrait of Chateaubriand, *c.1811, painted by the Romanticist Anne Louis Girodet de Roucy-Trioson (1767–1824), a pupil of Jacques-Louis David.*

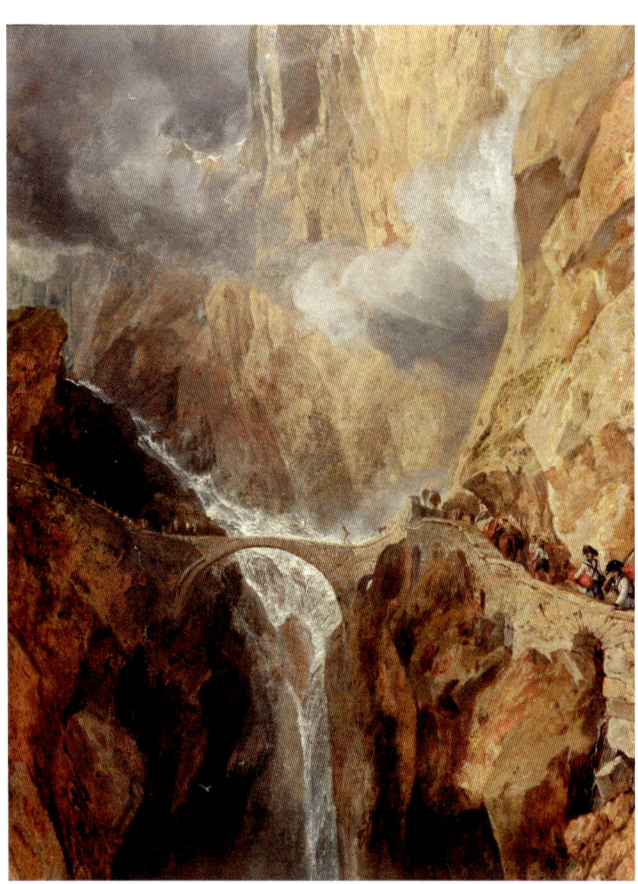

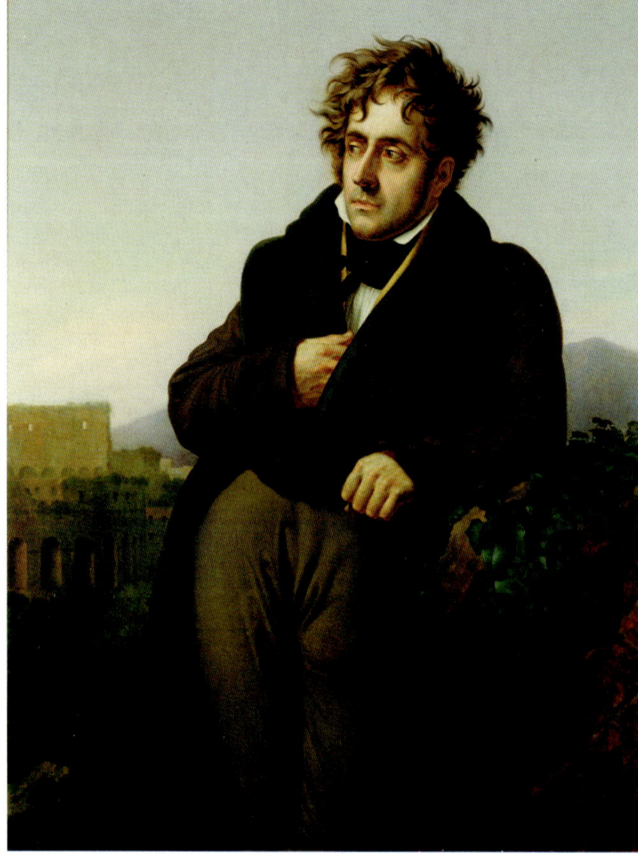

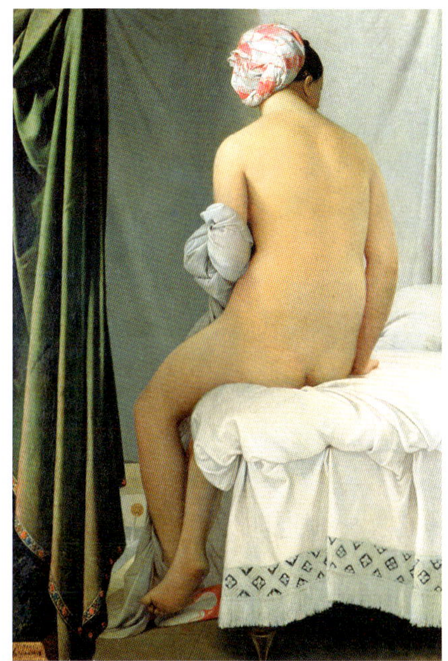

Above: Baigneuse Valpinçon, *1808, by the French Neoclassicist Ingres who opposed the ideas of Romanticism. (Nudes were permitted in Italy and France.)*

epic history paintings, and Delacroix, who created vigorous, colourful paintings, captured with sketchy brushwork, similar to Goya. Throughout his life, Ingres upheld Neoclassicist ideals and particularly abhorred Delacroix's Romantic style, even though much of

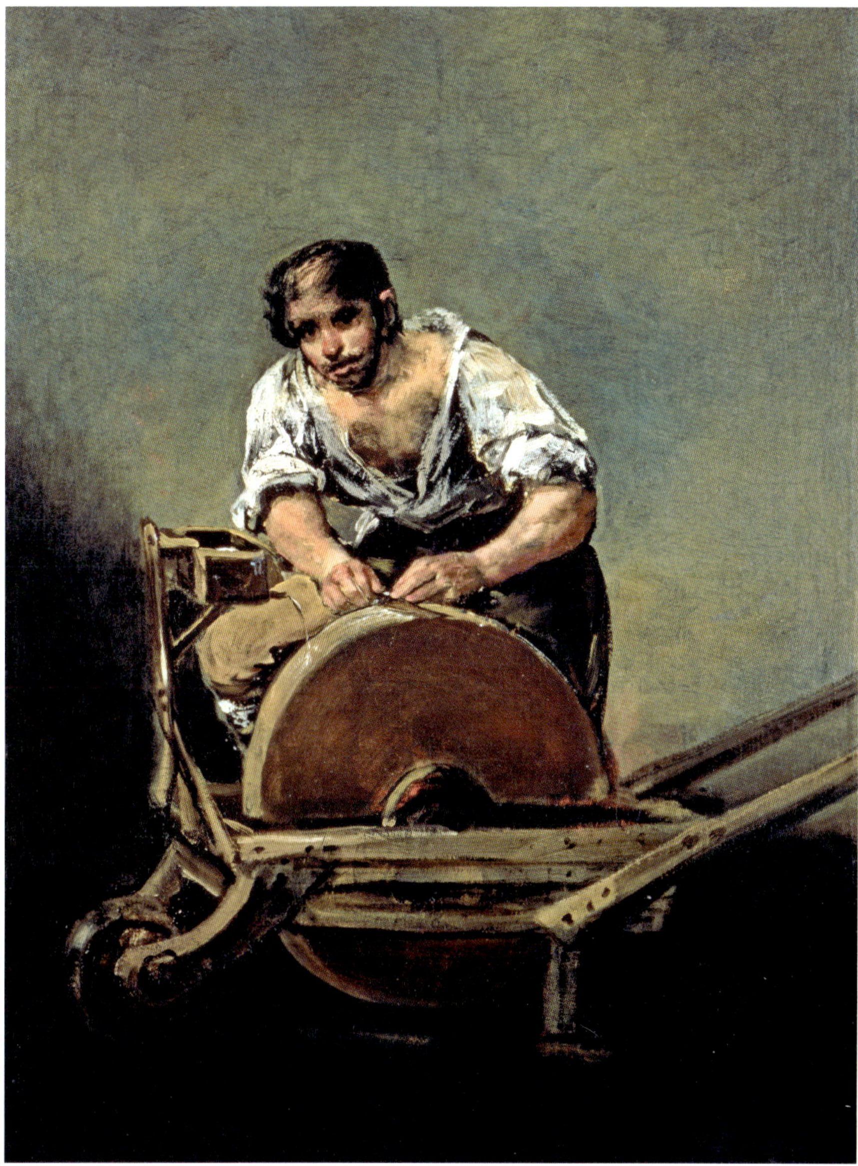

Above: Sensitive to his compatriots' feelings, Goya's The Knife Grinder, *1808–12, symbolizes ordinary working people resisting Napoleon.*

his own work can be seen to embody aspects of the Romantic spirit. He perceived the sketchy brushstrokes and bright colours of Romanticism to be undisciplined and unrefined.

GOYA AND ROMANTICISM

More than any other artist of the period, Goya exemplified the Romantic values of expressing his feelings and his imagination with a free handling of paint, visible brushstrokes and an impasto application; all contrasting with the Neoclassicists. As his work evolved, frequently expressing extreme feelings, he became a formative influence on the entire 'age of Romanticism' in Europe. His style was not really a reaction against Neoclassicism as it was with many other Romanticists however, but

it developed more from the Baroque and Rococo movements with their focus on technique that he had studied as a student. With his individual ideas and interpretations, interest in the human mind, his expressive use of colour and spirited brush marks, he helped to stimulate many of the Romantic ideas that followed. In certain ways, he continued to work with the classicism of his training, and he retained his beliefs in many theories of the Enlightenment. His natural depictions of life however also singled him out as a precursor to Realism of the later 19th century.

THE DISASTERS OF WAR

In 1804, Napoleon had crowned himself Emperor of France. In 1806, Goya's grandson Mariano was born. In October 1807, the Treaty of Fontainebleau was signed by King Charles and Napoleon. It proposed that Charles would give up Spain's Italian estates to Napoleon, in return for part of the Kingdom of Portugal.

To enable France and Spain to take Portugal, Napoleon said he would have to install his army in Spain. Not one Spaniard it seems, suspected his motives, and with weeks, tens of thousands of French troops had mobilized into Spain. In February 1808, 50,000 of Napoleon's men marched on Madrid.

Simultaneously, Prince Ferdinand was planning to depose his father. But Godoy intercepted the plot and Ferdinand was forced to apologise to the King, who against Godoy's advice, forgave his son. Napoleon was delighted; such discord could only facilitate his takeover of Spain. Unaware of this, Ferdinand was supported by both the Spanish nobles, who believed he would be a malleable pawn, and the common people, who saw him as the saviour of Spain from the incompetent ambitions of Godoy.

In March 1808, the Court travelled to Aranjuez, 30 miles from Madrid, where they traditionally spent the spring. An uprising broke out in support of Ferdinand, and King Charles was forced to dismiss Godoy and abdicate in favour of his son. Although enthusiastically acclaimed by the people, Ferdinand's future was not certain; the French were in control of Madrid and the army's leader, Napoleon's brother-in-law, Joachim Murat, refused to recognize Ferdinand as King of Spain. Both Charles IV and Ferdinand VII appealed to Napoleon to help their causes, and Napoleon summoned them both to Bayonne in France.

As soon as he reached Bayonne however, Ferdinand was compelled by Napoleon to renounce his throne once again to Charles IV, who in turn was made to resign his rights to Napoleon. Napoleon imprisoned the Spanish monarchs in France and made his elder brother Joseph the new King of Spain.

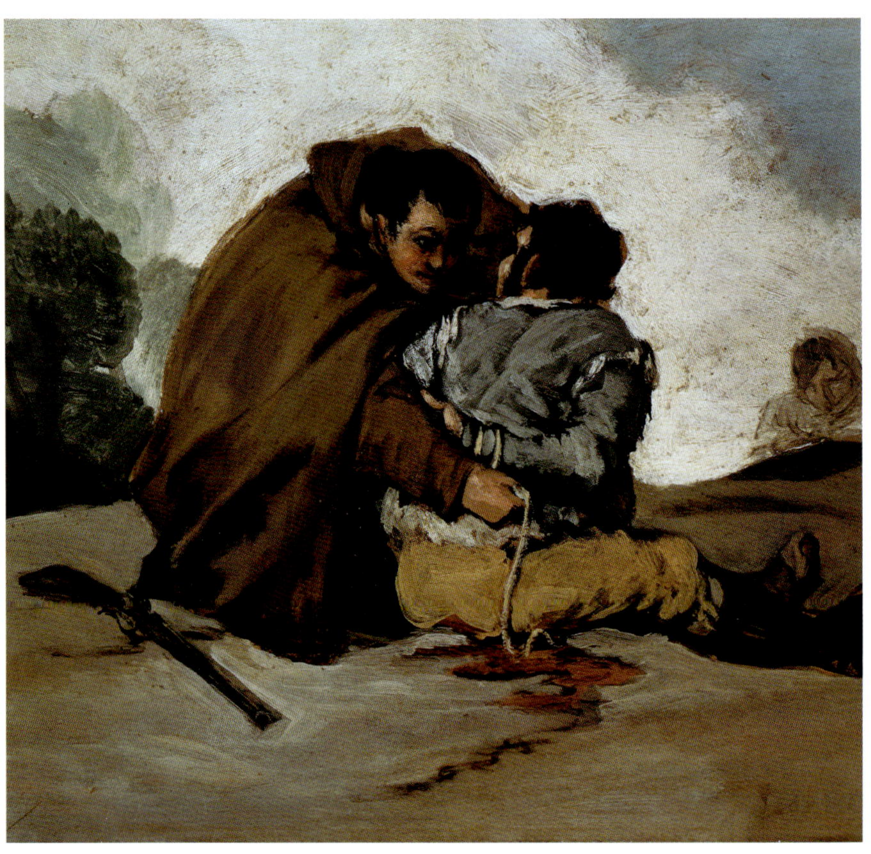

GOYA'S ACTIVITIES

Ferdinand had been king from 17 March to 6 May 1808. During that time, Goya was commissioned by the Academy of San Fernando to paint an equestrian portrait of him, but Ferdinand only managed to sit for Goya for two short sessions, on 6 and 7 April, before he left for Bayonne. Notwithstanding, Goya still managed to produce a vigorous sketch and a commanding finished painting.

Despite the alarming events taking place in his country, Goya, at 62 years old, still had a living to earn. He had always been aware that artistic freedom depended on financial independence, and he continued working unobtrusively, mainly painting portraits and small cabinet pictures. Some of these were works of realism, often violent and spirited, others were simple still lifes, generally featuring food (see page 230) or

Above: Detail from Friar Pedro and the Bandit. *In c.1806, Goya painted six works of the capture of a fearsome bandit by a friar (see pages 212–13).*

cooking implements, known in Spain as bodegóns. As usual, Goya handled these conventional subjects differently from other Spanish artists. Whereas traditional bodegóns are painted precisely and smoothly, Goya's are

BATTLE OF TRAFALGAR

On 21 October 1805 at Trafalgar, fighting alongside the French fleet, Spain lost its armada against Britain. The Spanish armada had been one of the finest in the world, and the loss ultimately resulted in the ruin of the Spanish treasury.

Right: Equestrian Portrait of Ferdinand VII, *painted by Goya in 1808 from just two brief sittings.*

expressive and dynamic with short, broken brushstrokes that anticipate the work of the Realists and the Impressionists in the second half of the 19th century.

VIOLENT PROTESTS

Napoleon had anticipated a peaceful surrender in Spain. He had known how unpopular Godoy had been and the ilustrados and Spanish government welcomed the liberal reforms he proposed. Coming after the autocratic Bourbon monarchy, the Spanish intellectuals hoped that the French regime would help to modernize Spain. But the wider population was indignant; national pride was hurt and the French occupation was vehemently opposed. As news from Bayonne filtered back, an upsurge of anger spread across Spain. On 2 May in Madrid, violent protests erupted which became the catalyst for numerous revolts throughout the country.

Below right: They Don't Know the Way, *Goya, c.1810. Another of Goya's perceptive* Disasters of War *etchings.*

Below: Charcoal sketch of a beggar, 1808–14. Goya constantly sketched the world around him, capturing life as it was.

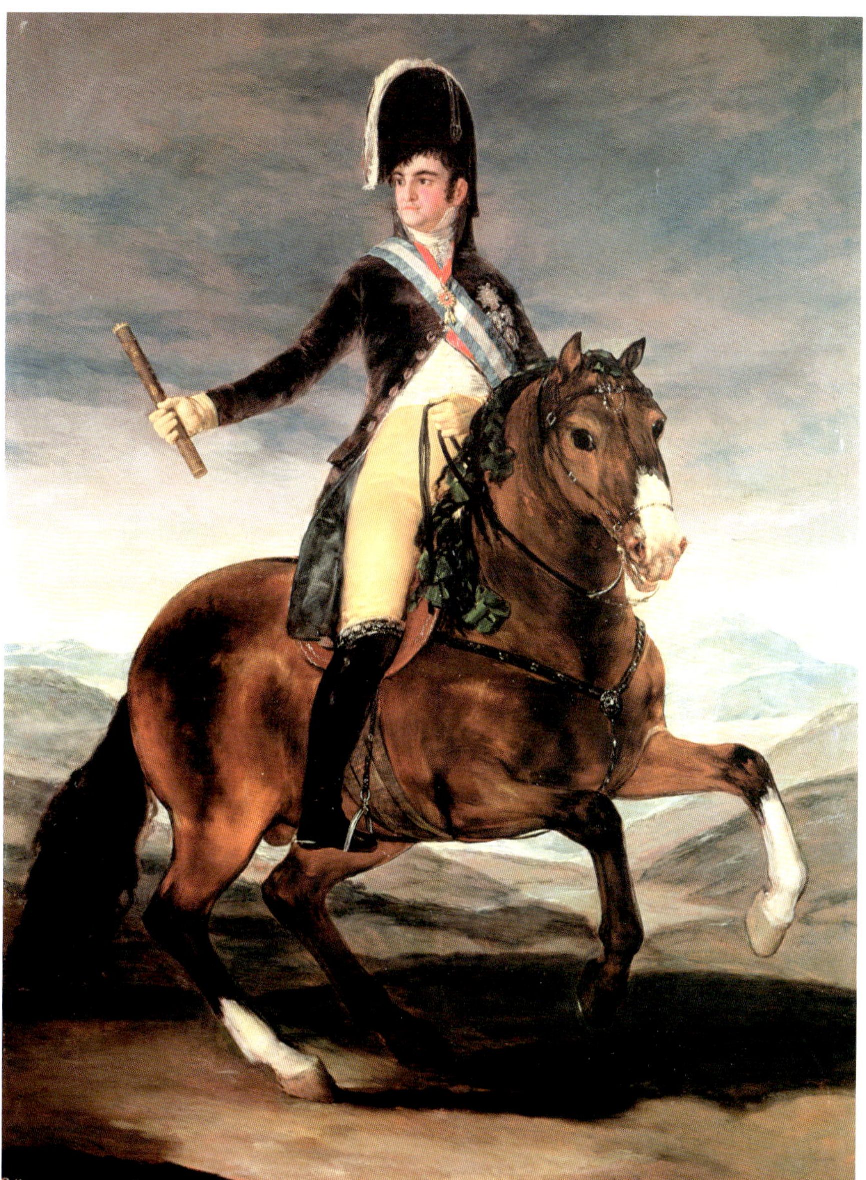

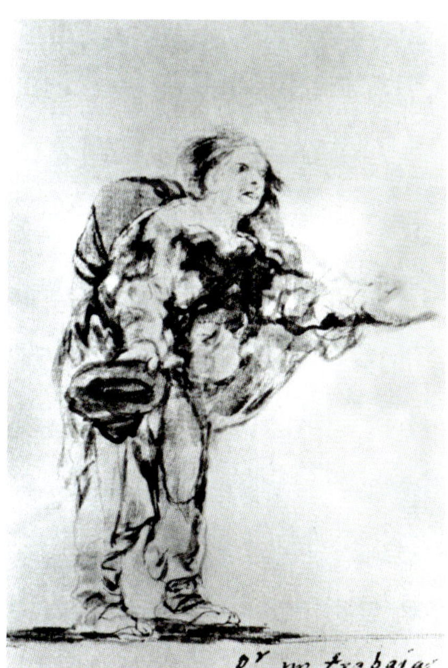

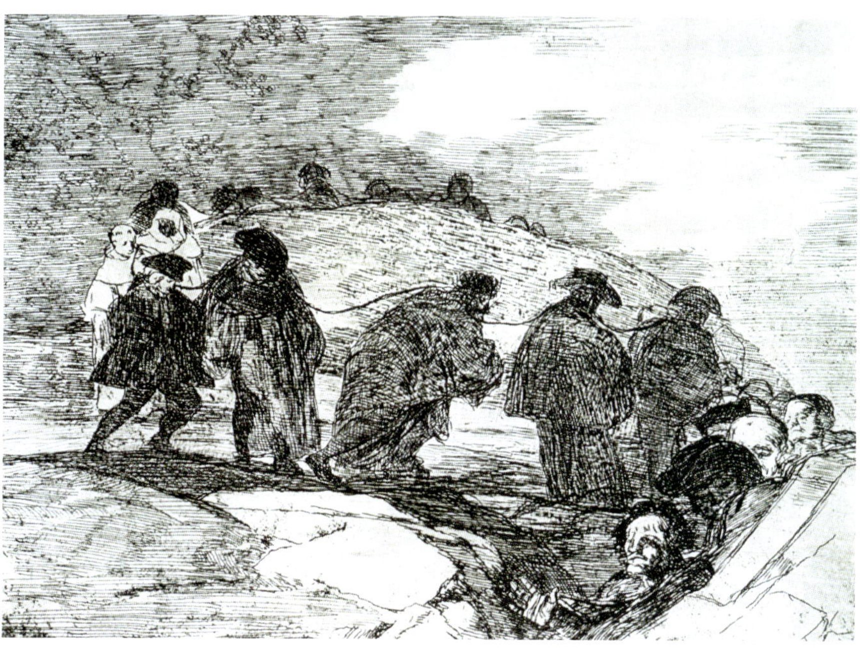

THE NEW SPAIN

Enraged with the French for leading them into disaster in the Battle of Trafalgar, and then for overrunning their country, the Spanish people felt ready to act. When the French Marshal Murat arranged to send Charles IV's children to Bayonne, an angry crowd gathered in front of the Royal Palace in Madrid.

The Dos de Mayo uprising began in the early morning of 2 May 1808, outside the Royal Palace in Madrid. The French Marshal Murat gave an order, and a procession of several carriages moved off from the palace. Someone in the crowd spotted the two young princes in one of the carriages, and a roar went up: 'They're kidnapping them!' With no plan and no order, the mob surged forward, simply attacking the French soldiers using whatever weapons they could find, including sticks, knives, cudgels and rocks. At first, the French were taken by surprise, but before long, they opened fire on the civilians. Despite heavy casualties among the ordinary people, word spread and similar uprisings occurred in other parts of the city. In one area, several Mamluks, Egyptian mercenaries who fought for the French and had no code of chivalry, attacked the Spanish civilians particularly savagely. The French troops, with greater discipline and stronger weapons, soon regained control of the city. The next day and night, French soldiers rounded up every Spaniard who might possibly have been a rebel. They were taken through the streets in open carts and shot at mass executions around the city; one not far from where Goya was living.

GOYA IN SARAGOSSA

On 15 June, the French army repeatedly tried to storm Saragossa in an attempt to suppress the uprisings occurring there. But the Napoleonic troops had not accounted for the depth of Spanish anger and patriotism, and the people's determination to rid their country of the foreign occupants. With an improvised garrison of citizens and peasants, the Spanish General José de Palafox held Saragossa for nearly three months, when at last the French withdrew. That October, Palafox invited Goya to visit his old home town to celebrate the heroic defence of the city – that became known as the Siege of Saragossa – with a painting. Although Goya remained there sketching and painting until December, the work he produced was subsequently lost or destroyed.

GOYA'S LOYALTY

While the Spanish ridiculed Joseph I by nicknaming him 'Pepe Botella', or 'Jo Bottles', for his partying and drinking,

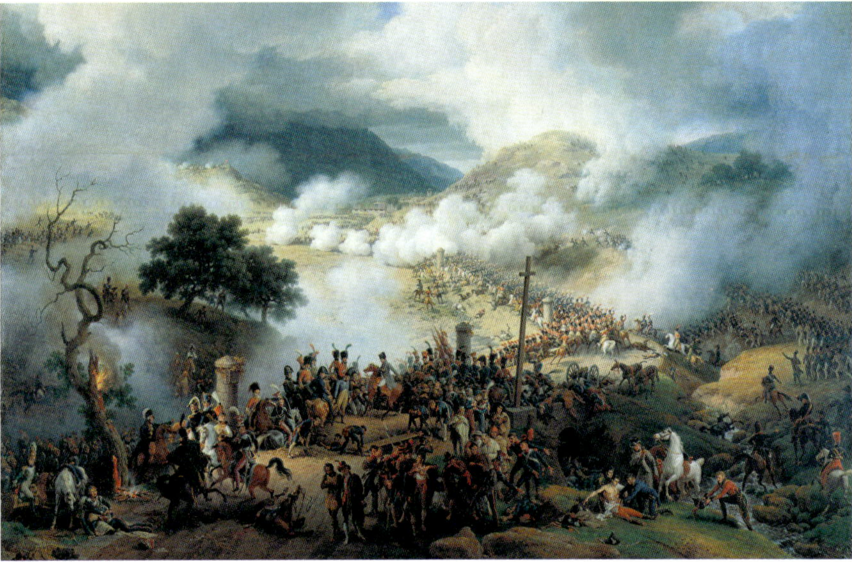

Above left: Battle of Somosierra, 30 November 1808, *Baron Lejeune, 1810. The fighting between Goya's fellow citizens and the French was relentless.*

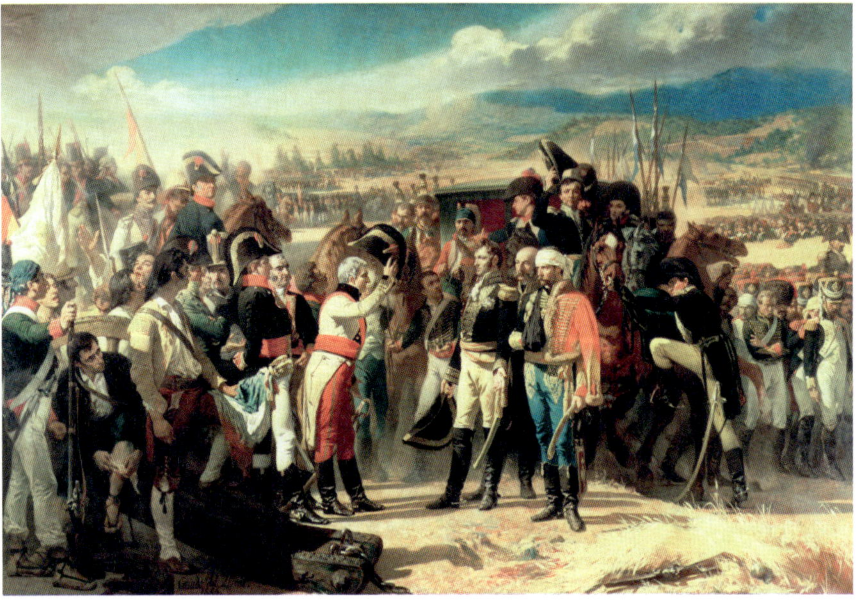

Left: The Surrender of Bailén, 23 July 1808, *Casado del Alisal, 1863. Shocking reports of battles between the French and Spanish flooded back to Goya and were depicted by artists for years.*

GUERRILLA WARFARE

Rather than staunch the rebellions, the mass executions of 3 May inflamed the fighting across the whole of Spain. The people believed that the French had stolen their king and taken control of their country. Even if Joseph had been the most reasonable ruler, to the majority of Spanish people, he had usurped Ferdinand VII and was ruling a country to which he had no right. Over the following few years, one of the most terrible slaughters Europe had ever known occurred across Spain. It was the first example of a type of combat that became known as guerrilla warfare, where small groups of untrained armed fighters attack larger traditional armies.

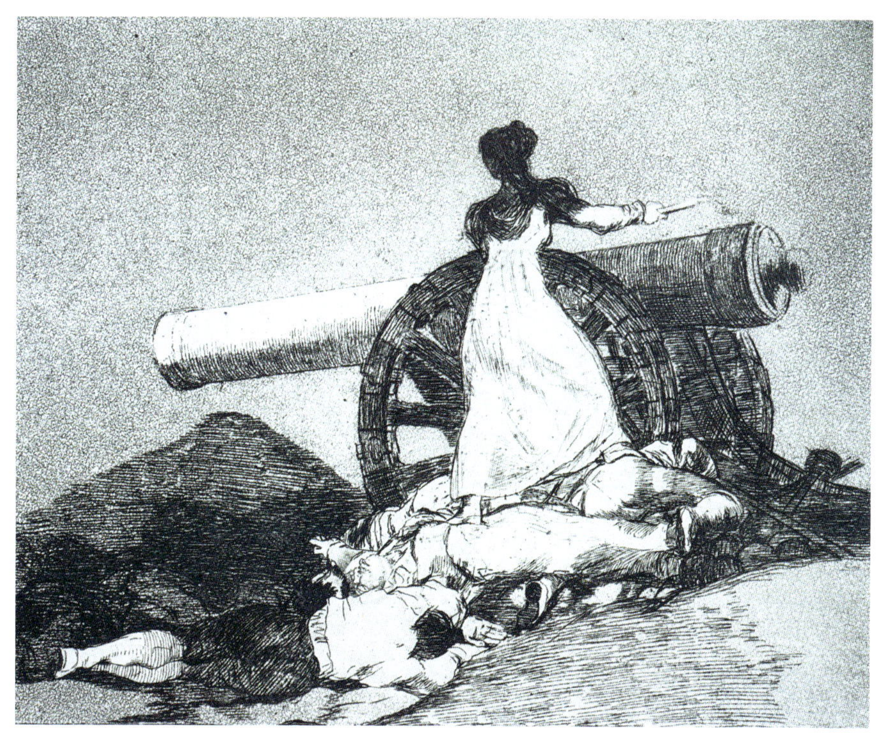

Above: What Courage! *From* The Disasters of War, *c.1809–14. During the Spanish troubles, Goya produced a series of expressive etchings.*

and most simply hated him for taking the place of their rightful king, Goya did not take sides. This may be considered contradictory, but the situation was extremely complex and Goya was caught, as were many of his friends and compatriots, in a tangle of internal conflicts. For more than 20 years, he and his friends had yearned for a better Spain, free at last from the dictatorial ruling Bourbon family. Napoleon and Joseph's reforms were actually quite liberal and loyal to Spanish traditions, including the abolition of feudal rights and privileges, and the suppression of the Inquisition. But Goya was also fiercely loyal to his fellow countrymen and women, and empathetic to the plight of the ordinary people. He also realized that the new regime would be beneficial for Spain and, always keen to earn money, he accepted several commissions from Joseph Bonaparte – which in the end were never paid for.

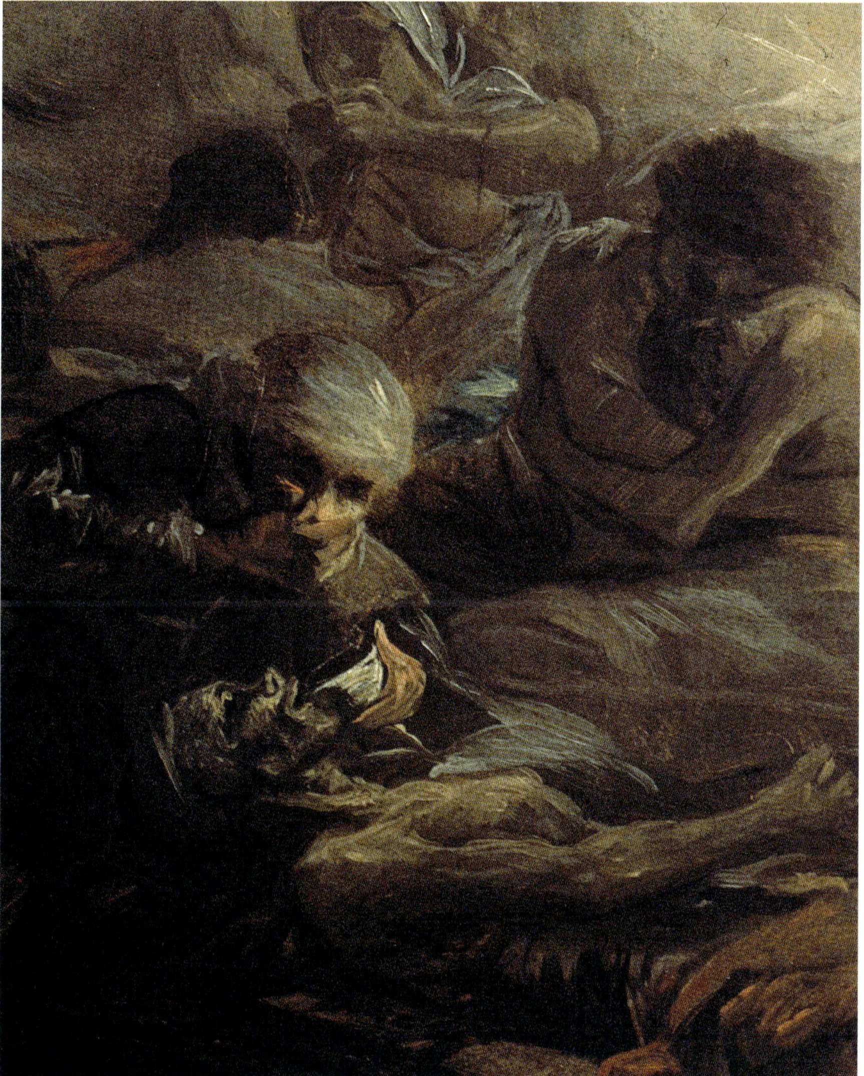

Left: Detail of The Plague Hospital, *1808 (see also page 220). To Goya, both prisons and hospitals symbolized the loss of liberty.*

A QUESTION OF LOYALTY

The years of bitterness and battles were devastating for everyone. To express what he saw and reflect events, Goya produced a series of large canvases and etchings. But when the Spanish monarchy was restored in 1814, he found himself having to explain why he had worked for the French usurpers.

No one had predicted the fortitude and determination of the Spanish people, least of all Napoleon. Guerrilla warfare continued until 1814, while the loyalties of the Spanish aristocrats, ilustrados and Goya remained confused. They were patriotic and wanted Spain for the Spanish. They also perceived the French reforms as beneficial for the country. When Napoleon installed his elder brother Joseph as king, along with all Court Painters, Goya was made to swear him an oath of allegiance, and in 1810, he painted Joseph in his *Allegory of the City of Madrid*, plus portraits of other members of the French regime. In 1811, Joseph awarded him the Royal Order of Spain.

IMAGES OF SUFFERING

On his return to Madrid from Saragossa in late 1808, Goya continued painting portraits of both Spanish and French individuals, including *Minister José Manuel Romero*, *General Nicolás Guye* and actress *Antonia Zárate* (see page 214). He continued as Court Painter while the French occupied, and he painted a large *Assumption of the Virgin* for the parish

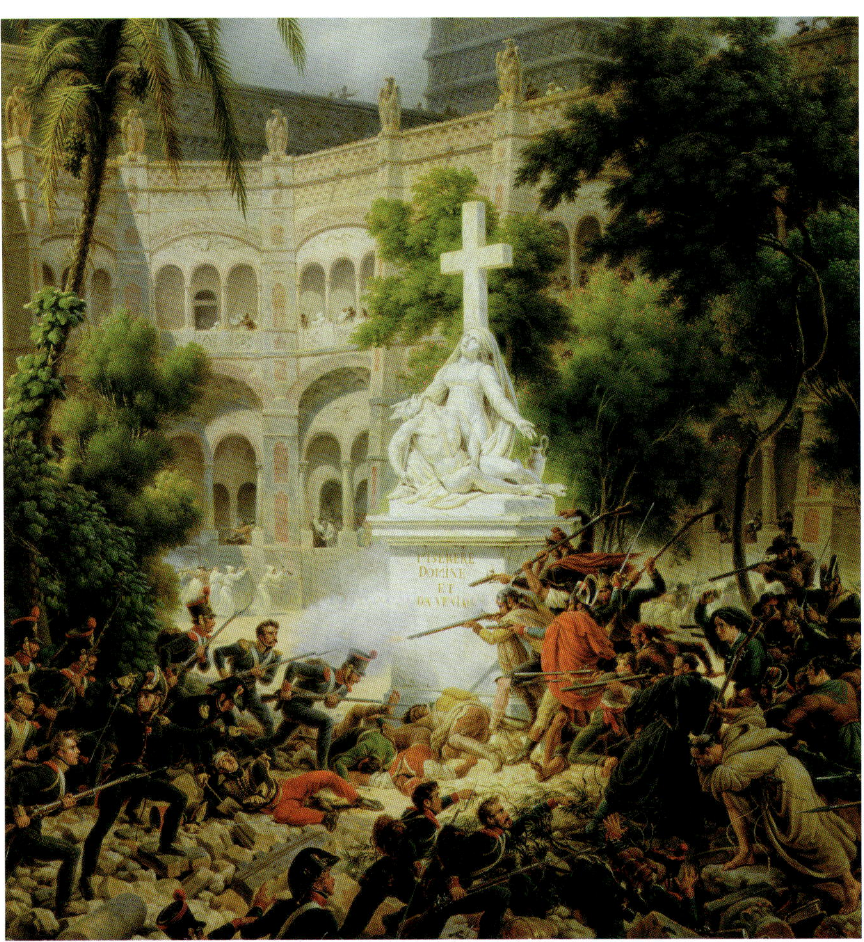

Above: Assault on the Monastery of San Engracio in Saragossa, 8 February 1809, *Baron Lejeune, 1827. A sacrilegious attack on a monastery in Goya's home town, painted by a French artist.*

DEATH OF JOSEFA

On 20 June 1812, Josefa died at the age of 65, after 39 years as Goya's wife. It is not verified whether Goya made any portraits of her, although a couple have often been cited they have proved improbable. After her death, an inventory was made of her property and divided between Goya and Javier. It included furniture, clothing, jewels, paintings by Velázquez, Tiepolo and Correggio, and 73 works by Goya. Goya received the furniture, silver, linen and some money, while Javier inherited the paintings, engravings and Josefa's many books.

church of Chinchón, to the south-east of Madrid, that was governed by his youngest brother Camilo. He also painted a series of genre scenes, including images of majas, and prints that he called *The Disasters of War*. The outpouring of hatred by many citizens of Spain during the guerrilla war was the inspiration for these prints. Goya filled pages of his sketchbooks with scenes of murder, torture, rape and death, and then translated them into a series of 80 lively etchings. They show no partisan support for either Napoleon's ideals or Spanish beliefs and no glorification of any nationality. Slaughter and cruelty is shown

Right: The Same, 1808–9, Indian ink wash: part of a series of 'visions' that Goya claimed to have seen one night.

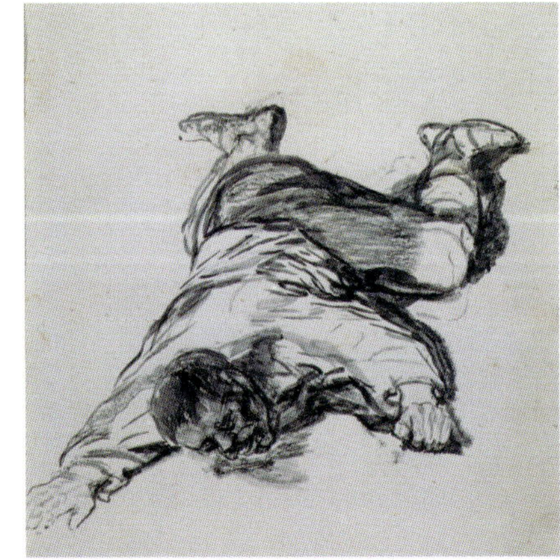

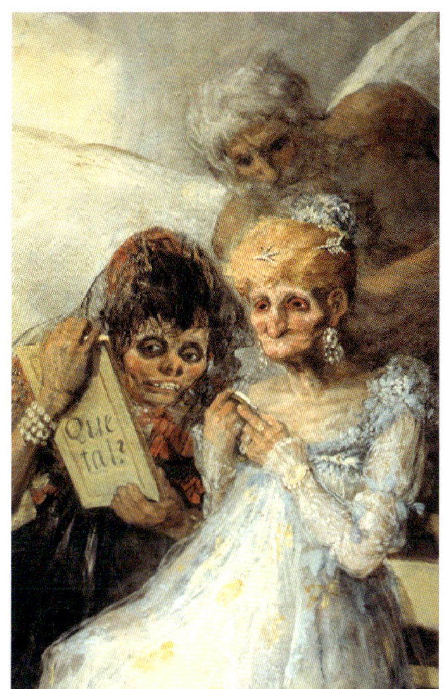

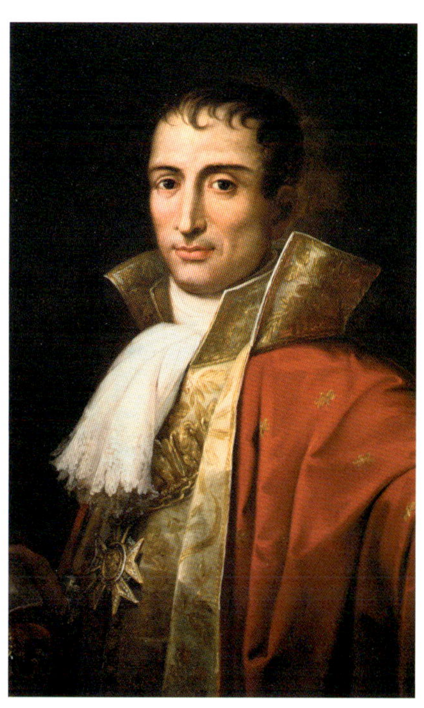

Right: Joseph Bonaparte, *Joseph Bernat Flaugier, 1809. Joseph abdicated from the Spanish throne in 1813.*

Above: Time and the Old Women *(detail, see page 226), c.1810–12 shows that disturbing events focused Goya's mind on death and mortality.*

Spain. The following year, Napoleon was defeated, Joseph abdicated and in 1814, Ferdinand was reinstated as King of Spain. But Ferdinand did not share the enlightened views of the Cortes and revoked the Constitution, re-establishing the old autocratic Bourbon regime and the Inquisition, which arrested anyone thought to have been friendly with the French during the occupation. A mass exodus ensued, as thousands fled from the country they had been defending for six years. Goya remained however, and was questioned by the Inquisition about his painting *The Naked Maja* (see page 194), and his loyalties during the occupation.

on both sides, which was completely innovatory in art – as well as the absence of both heroes and villains. The images simply illustrate universal suffering, chaos and brutality. Although they might appear to be firsthand accounts of the struggles however, it is debatable how much of the atrocities Goya actually saw. Many of his ideas must have evolved from hearsay and his imagination.

REIGN OF TERROR

In the same year as Josefa's death, 1812, Napoleon went to Russia on an ill-fated campaign, and the British army, led by the Duke of Wellington, won several victories in Europe, entering Madrid in August, expelling the French occupants and restoring Spain to the Spanish. Immediately, the Spanish parliament, the Cortes, assembled and drew up a liberal Constitution, which Goya illustrated in an enormous canvas, the *Allegory of the Constitution of 1812*. It proclaimed the hopes of many for the future of

Right: At first asked to paint a portrait of Joseph Bonaparte, Goya's Allegory of the City of Madrid, 1810, *appealed to the Bonaparte regime.*

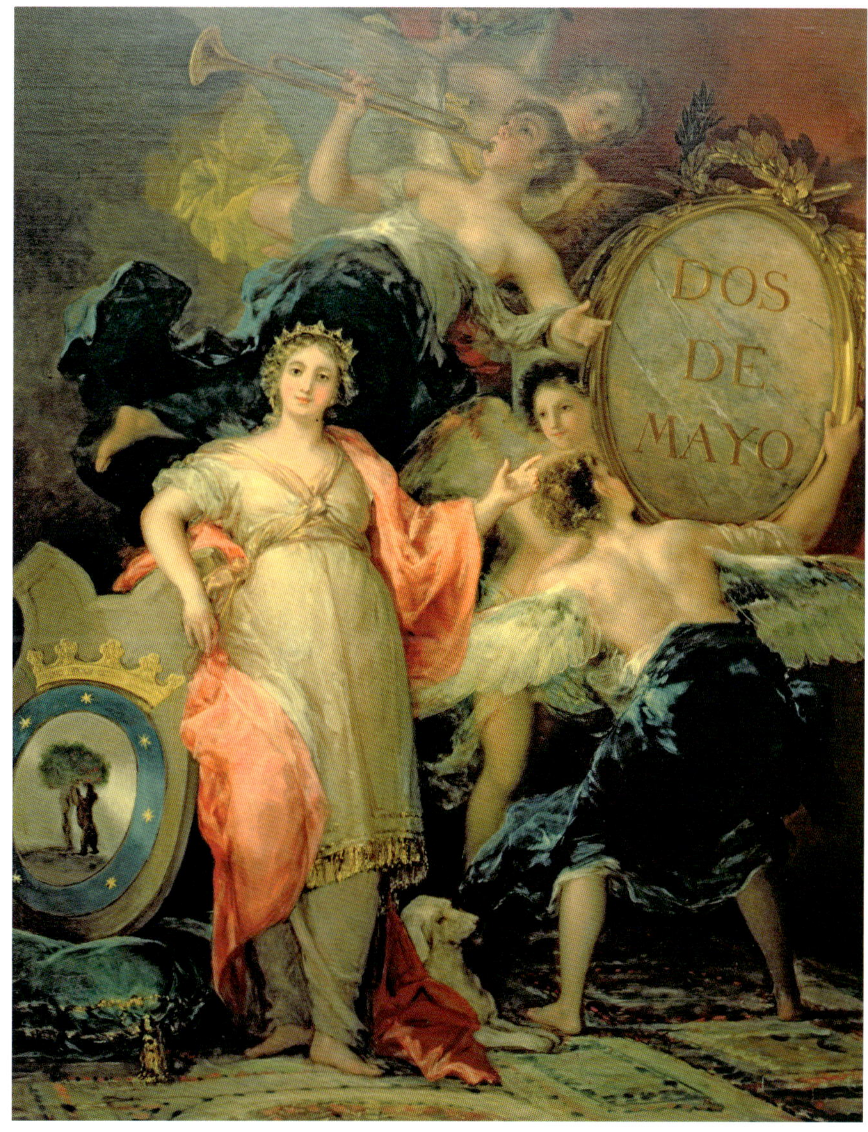

THE THIRD OF MAY

Goya was 62 years old when the Napoleonic invasion of Spain began. Six years later when it was all over, he recorded the events of the first days in 1808, when the population rose against the French and were savagely repressed by the Napoleonic army. The paintings became two of his most famous works.

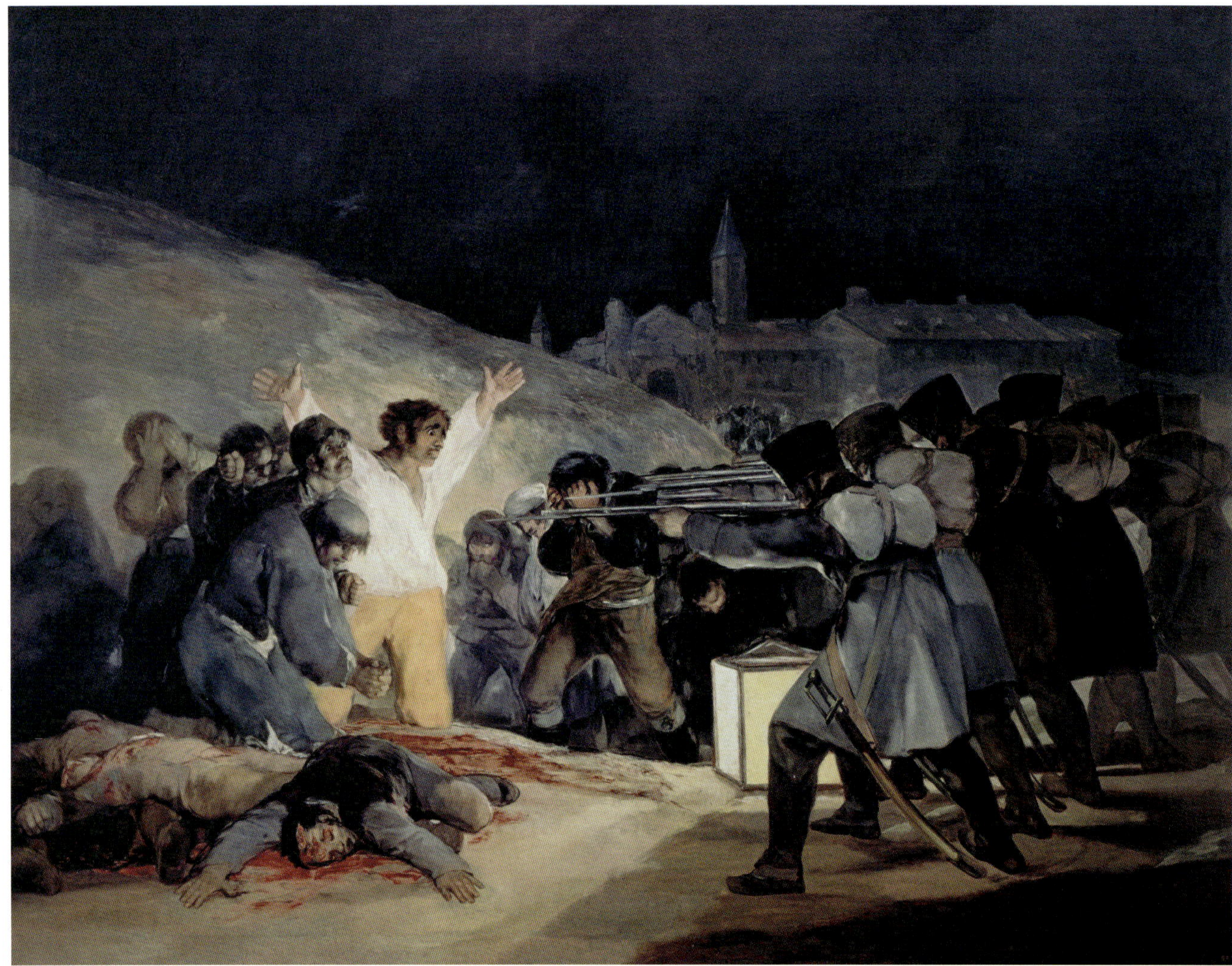

At a time when most artists deliberately suppressed their own opinions, Goya's works frequently expressed his innermost feelings, a clear break from convention. He and other Spanish liberals had anticipated the establishment of the 1812 Constitution with hope, and his large allegorical work illustrates his enthusiasm for it.

IMPORTANT WORKS

Goya's *Disasters of War* etchings were also a vivid reflection of his own feelings. None of the prints were published during his lifetime, and while none depict specific incidents, 46 show events of the guerrilla war, 18 describe aspects of the great famine that devastated Madrid between 1811 and 1812, and 15 were satirical images of the people's shattered hopes. The final print was the title page, featuring a gaunt man in rags kneeling, his arms extended and face tilted, as if pleading with God. In 1812 and 1814, Goya also painted portraits of two prominent figures: General Palafox (see page 75) and Arthur Wellesley, the First Duke of Wellington (see page 218). Both show powerful leaders, while his preparatory sketches of them are sensitive drawings showing their vulnerability, weariness and even melancholy.

Above: The Third of May, *1814. Goya makes no attempt to soften his subject's barbarity and intensity.*

THE HOSTILITY OF THE KING

Although Ferdinand VII and the Inquisition believed Goya had been a collaborator during the occupation, they did not sentence him, either for that or for his *Naked Maja* (see page 194). When interrogated, he denied any involvement with the French usurpers, and witnesses testified on his behalf that he had avoided all contact with them. The works he had produced for Joseph and his government were hidden in

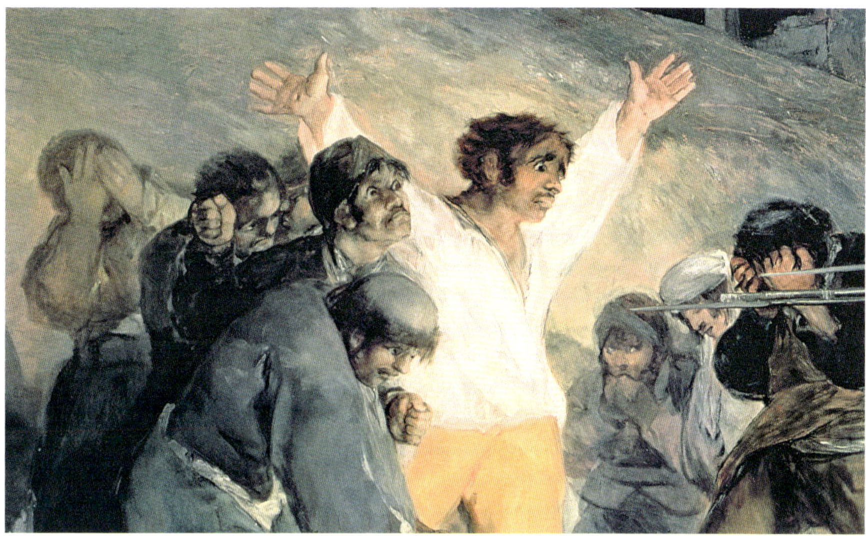

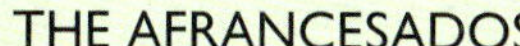

THE AFRANCESADOS

Most of Goya's friends were the Spanish liberals who had supported the initial aims of the French Revolution hoping for similar developments in Spain, known as the ilustrados (the Enlightened). Many were also called 'Afrancesados' or Francophiles. Before the war, they were simply those who followed French fashions and customs, but by 1814, they were considered conspirators and were either arrested or they escaped to France.

Above: Detail of The Third of May: *brilliantly lit by a lantern, the central prisoner flings up his arms before being shot.*

the Academy of San Fernando and not brought out again until after the King's death in 1833. As soon as Ferdinand retook the throne, Goya wrote to him that he had a 'burning desire to perpetuate by means of the brush the most notable and heroic actions and scenes of our glorious insurrections against the Tyrant of Europe.' Although Ferdinand remained hostile towards him, Goya continued to receive his official

Below: Detail of The Third of May: *Goya restricted his colours to earth tones and black with highlights of white – and the red of blood.*

Court salary, and was given money for the materials for two large paintings and an extra allowance for painting them. Goya also delivered six portraits – not commissioned – of Ferdinand, in an attempt to win his favour. The portraits, based on the sketches Goya had made before Ferdinand left for Bayonne, were accepted, but the King remained suspicious of Goya.

'NOTABLE AND HEROIC ACTIONS'
The Second of May, 1808: The Charge of Mamluks (see page 233) and *The Third of May, 1808: The Execution of the Defenders of Madrid* were the two large works Goya produced to commemorate the war. The first depicts the dramatic 'Dos de Mayo Uprising', when the Mamluks attacked the Spanish

rebels. *The Third of May 1808* was even more ground-breaking. With no distinct precedent, it is acknowledged as one of the first paintings of the modern era. Set in the early hours of the morning following the uprising, a firing squad faces captives at gunpoint across a narrow space. A lantern on the ground throws dramatic light on the scene, as other condemned figures wait to be shot, and the central figure kneels amid the bloodied corpses of those already executed, his arms flung wide in a Christ-like symbol of innocence. Most of the faces cannot be seen, and the physical proximity of the two groups adds to the brutal impact of the work.

Below: Detail of The Third of May; *the bloodied corpse of a previously shot victim.*

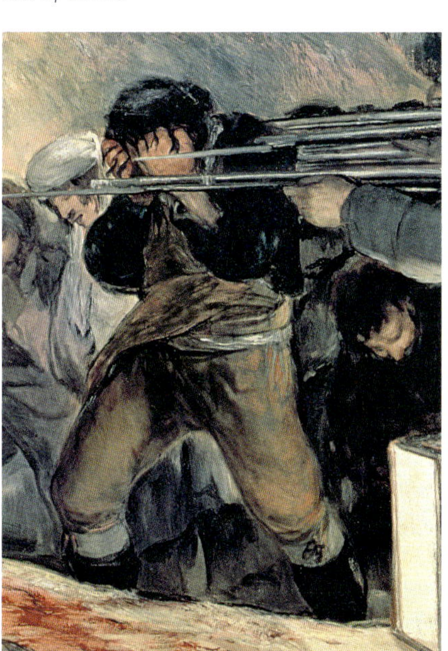

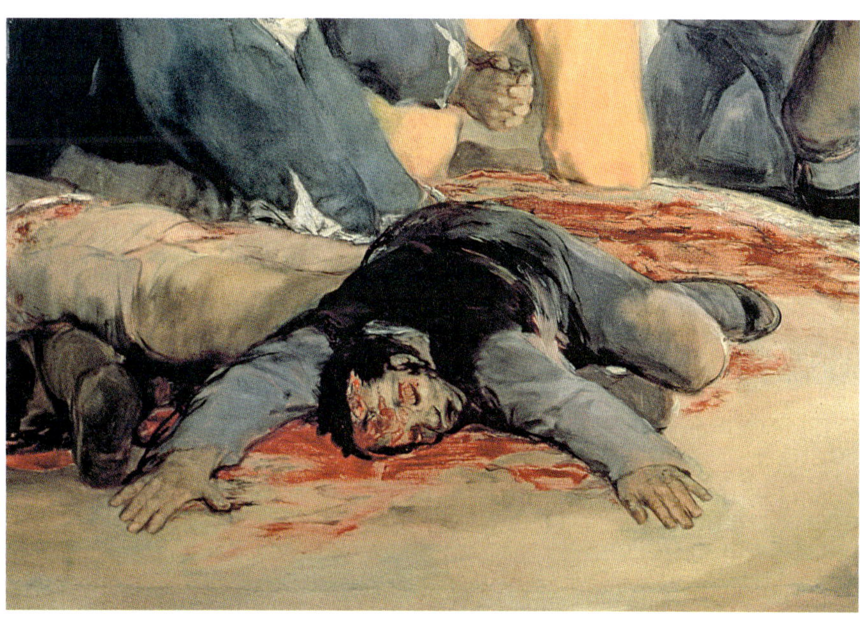

BULLFIGHTING

Goya's relationship with bullfighting was ambivalent. Throughout his life he had produced several paintings of his national sport, sometimes representing it as a noble and heroic tradition, at other times showing the cruelty of events and his abhorrence at the brutal treatment of the captive bulls.

In the year that Goya painted his images of the 1808 Dos de Mayo uprisings, Ferdinand summoned Vicente López y Portana to Court. López was a Spanish Neoclassical painter who specialized in portraits, was highly influenced by Mengs, and 26 years younger than Goya. In 1814, the King appointed him official Court Painter, and in 1817 he was made President of the Royal Academy of Fine Arts of San Fernando. It was now beyond doubt that Goya was no longer the royal favourite.

TECHNICALLY ACCOMPLISHED

From 1816 onward, Goya began accepting fewer commissions from aristocrats, instead concentrating on portraying the people around him, and bullfighting. In 1815, at 69 years old, he began producing a series of etchings depicting bullfights that he had printed the following year. Later entitled *The Tauromaquia* (*The Art of Bullfighting*), the series of 33 aquatint etchings was his third series of prints after *Los Caprichos* and *The Disasters of War*, and his largest etchings to date. Even more technically accomplished than his previous prints, they feature violent scenes that are at times infused with macabre humour.

Various motives have been suggested for Goya's production of these prints on this subject at that time, including

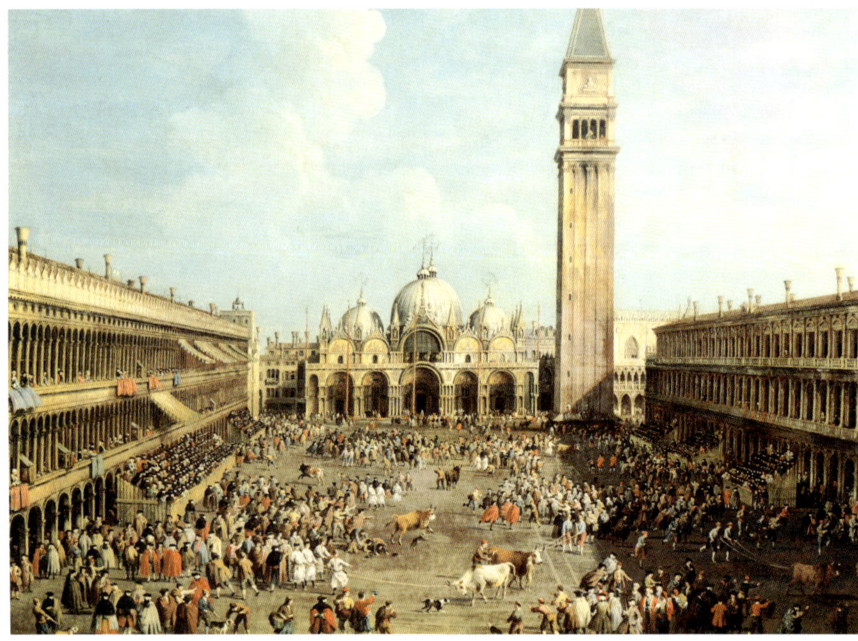

Left: Bullfighting or Bull hunting in Piazza San Marco, *Canaletto and Giovanni Battista Cimaroli, 1740: bullfighting was depicted by numerous artists before Goya.*

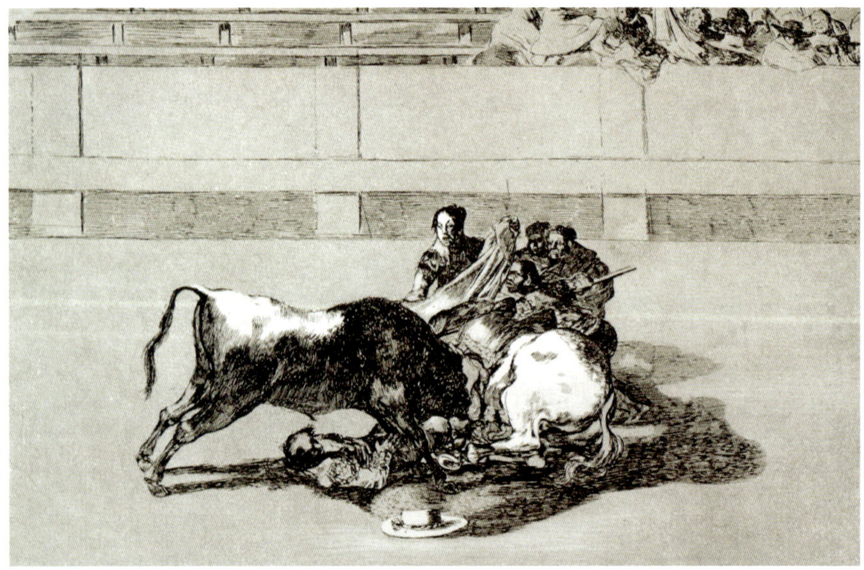

Below left: A Picador is Unhorsed and Falls Under the Bull, *1815; Goya reveals expressions of fear and anguish showing another side to the sport.*

PURGES AT THE PALACE

As part of the enquiry into loyalty during the French occupation, on 21 May 1814, the Duke of San Carlos had been made responsible for a 'purge' of the employees of the royal palace. This included Goya. It was not until April 1815 that Goya was officially listed in the first category of 'purified' employees, who had all their rights, including their salaries and pensions, restored. After his death, accounts found in Goya's papers state that not only had he not received any money from the 'intruding government' but he also had to sell his jewels in order to live during the period. In 1815, as a result of the enquiries, Goya also received a payment from the King for having refused to work for the French.

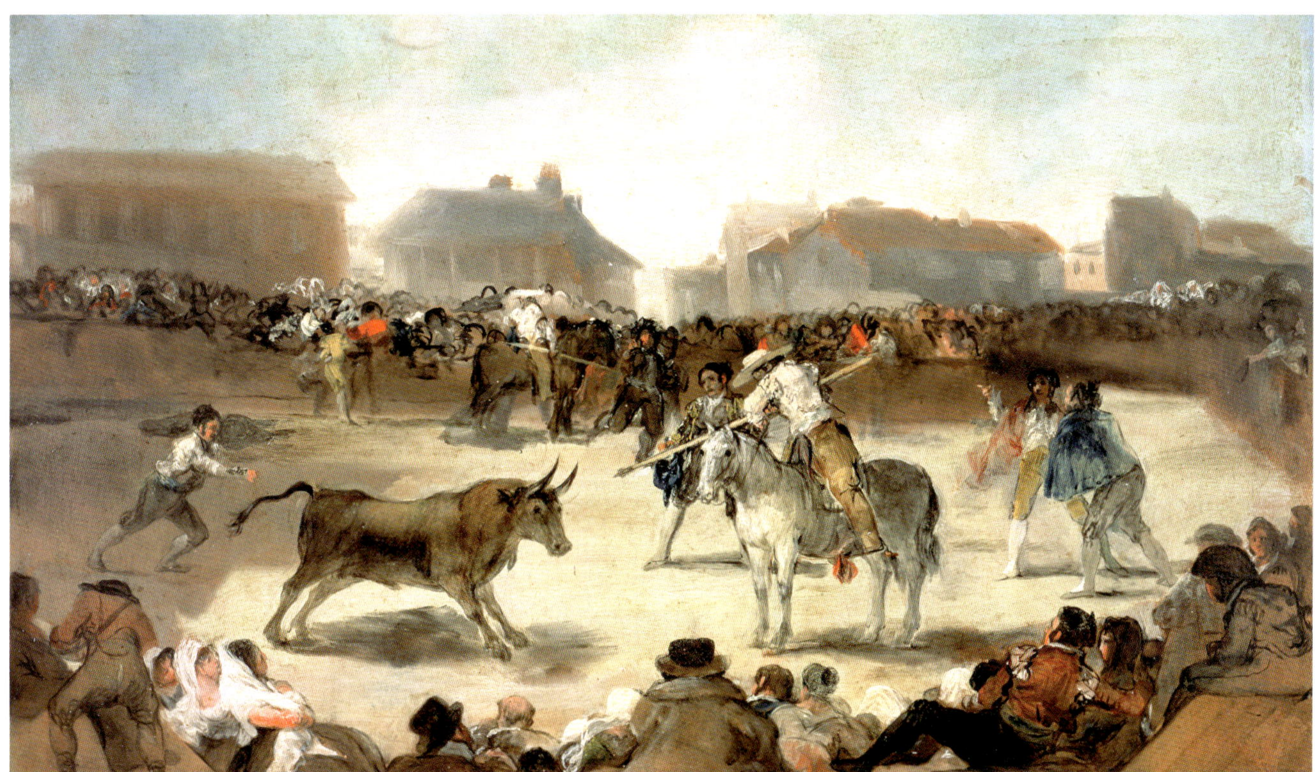

Above: Village Bullfight, *1812–4; painted before* The Tauromaquia, *Goya's sketchy style and dark tones create a vivid impression of the scene.*

his wish to move on from the war, to ignore the troubles Ferdinand was bringing to Spain, and his loneliness, as many of his friends left Spain to escape the Inquisition. Whatever his reasons, Goya invested in a large number of top-quality copper plates and proceeded to create the images, following 50 preparatory red chalk drawings, and using aquatint with etching as before to vary the lighting and to dramatize each scene. The resulting action-packed pictures are skilful, accurate, often chaotic and frequently controversial. Although a supporter of Spain's national sport, Goya's bullfight scenes are often ambiguous. Sometimes the bullfighters are portrayed as heroes, sometimes they are villains.

CRUELTY AND BARBARISM

Although it was the national identity, many of Goya's contemporaries were opposed to bullfighting, and in 1805, Charles IV abolished it. Three years later, to gain popularity with the majority, Joseph Bonaparte lifted the ban. It was

always contentious. In *The Tauromaquia*, Goya depicted some of the most renowned bullfighters of the time: Pedro Romero, Ceballos, Martincho and Pepe Illo. He also portrayed the three different stages of bullfighting: one, the two mounted picadors enter the ring with the purpose of riling the bull; two, a trio of banderilleros armed with barbed sticks weaken the animal, and finally in the third stage, the matador enters to perform his deadly ritual. In many of his bullfight paintings and prints, Goya illustrates chivalry; an equal balance

between man and beast. In many others, he reveals the barbarity of the sport, with spectators and bullfighters alike displaying excessive cruelty. Goya proves himself once again to be exceptionally accomplished at complex compositions, and an astute social observer, who questions who exactly were the beasts in the ring.

Below: The Famous Martincho Places the Banderillas Playing the Bull with the Movement of His Body, *1816: one of Goya's etchings for* The Tauromaquia.

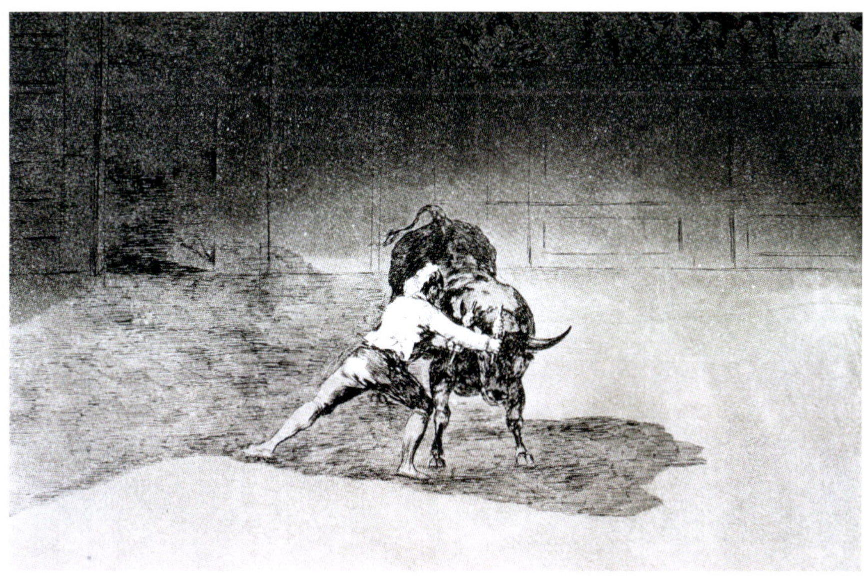

THE CLOSE OF AN ERA

Ultimately, Napoleon's plan to conquer Europe was vanquished by the various coalitions that had been formed against him. In October 1813, Great Britain, Russia, Sweden, Prussia and Austria defeated his army at Leipzig in Poland and he returned to France. The following March, the allies took Paris, forcing him to abdicate.

Yet even that was not the end of the Napoleonic era. After being exiled to the Mediterranean island of Elba, Napoleon returned to Paris on 20 March 1815, believing that he could recover power in the unstable environment that followed his abdication. Three months later, on 18 June, he was defeated once again at the Battle of Waterloo (in present-day Belgium).

Below: The French Army Crossing the Sierra de Guadarrama, Spain, December 1808, *1812. Nicolas Antoine Taunay (1755–1830) was one of several French artists chosen to portray events of the Napoleonic campaign.*

SUBJUGATION AND OPPOSITION

The years of havoc wreaked across Europe had taken their toll on almost everyone, and within most countries, unrest continued for a long time after Napoleon was defeated. Several new autocratic governments took control in different countries, which caused great problems in the wake of the wars, when most people had believed they were fighting for freedom. Spain of course was no different. When Wellington had arrived to liberate Madrid in 1812, the Spanish citizens who rejoiced his arrival had not imagined that they would be so oppressed by the King they had fought for over six long years. When Ferdinand

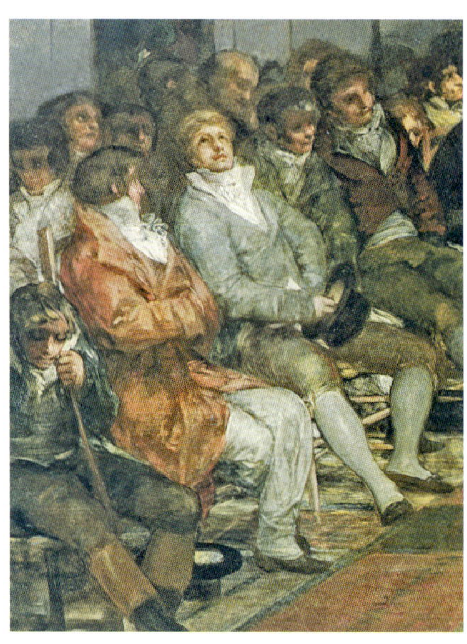

Above: Detail of The Junta of the Philippines, c.*1815 (see also page 238). Goya was officially commissioned, but he did not hide his disillusionment with the King.*

and the Inquisition took away nearly all the rights of ordinary people, this subjugation was just as bad in many ways as the guerrilla war had been, but resistance was more suppressed. People

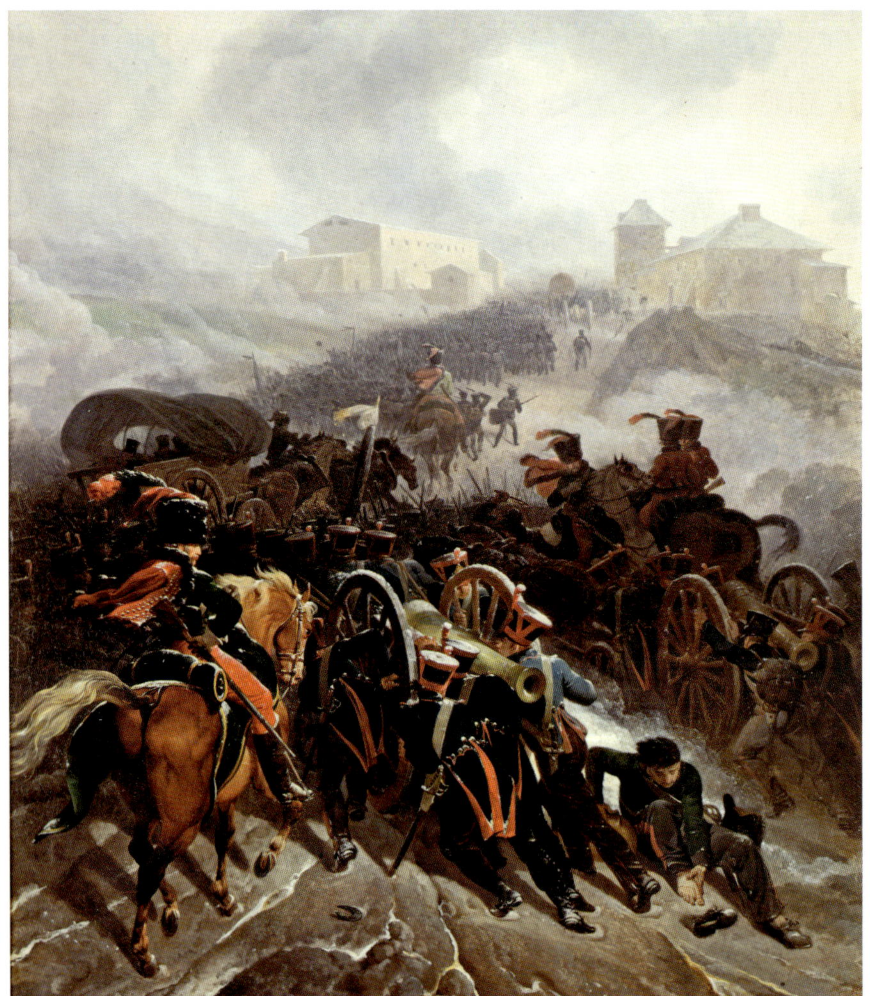

LA LEOCADIA

In 1815, Goya employed a young woman as his housekeeper. Little is known about Leocadia Zorilla de Weiss (see page 249), but it is believed she was in her early 30s and a cousin of Goya's daughter-in-law. She had two sons with her husband Isidro Weiss but he denounced her in 1811 for 'illicit conduct', and in 1814 she gave birth to a daughter, María del Rosario. It has often been assumed that Goya was Rosario's father, but although he was fond of the child and interested in her welfare, nothing has ever been verified.

were confused about what they had fought for. In the ensuing chaos, bandits and gangs roamed the countryside, swooping on innocent travellers, and beyond the towns, lawlessness abounded. Goya had been working on his *Disasters of War* series, but the desperate situation is probably why, instead of publishing the prints, he abandoned them and began working on *The Tauromaquia*.

SUCCESS AND FAILURE

While he did not publish his *Disasters of War*, Goya did print and sell his *Tauromaquia* series soon after producing them. They caught on instantly, and he made enough money from them to buy a new house. At about the same time, it is thought that his friend Ceán Bermúdez recommended him for a commission from the cathedral in Seville, even though Bermúdez preferred Neoclassicism to Goya's passionate, emotional style. Worth 23,000 reales, the commission was a painting of the saints Justa and Rufina (see page 244) for the cathedral's sacristy. When completed, the work caused a sensation in Seville; sonnets were written in praise of it and Bermúdez published a glowing critique of it.

This praise was unusual now however. As Goya reached his 70s, most of those who had admired his work and contributed to his fame and fortune from 1785 to 1808, had either

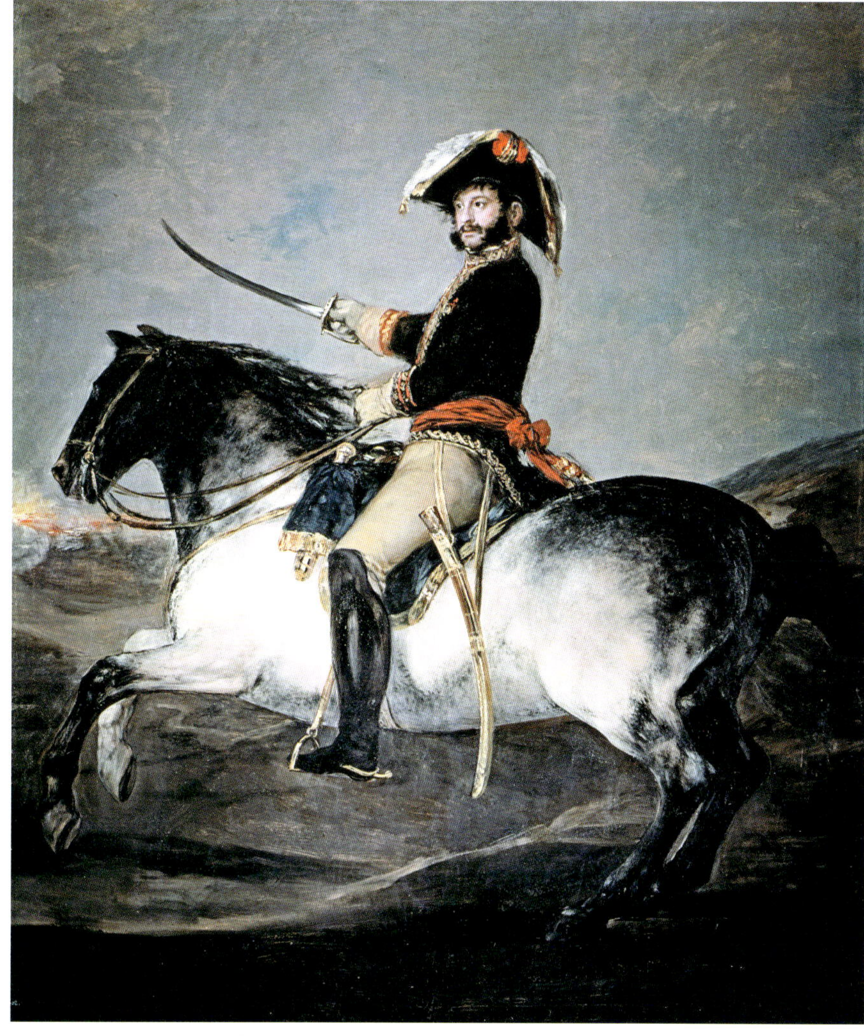

Above: Painted by Goya in 1814 (see page 70), this is the powerful Equestrian Portrait of General Palafox.

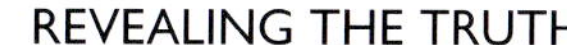

died or been scattered by the conflicts. Ferdinand's rule was establishing a preference for art that was 'safe' and unexceptional.

REVEALING THE TRUTH

At this time, Goya produced a painting of huge dimensions, called *The Junta of the Philippines*. It commemorated Ferdinand VII at a meeting of the royal company for the first time since his reinstatement. Instead of presenting a glorious image of a monarch presiding over an important meeting however, Goya made the focal point a vast empty space in the centre of the great council chamber (see page 238). The overall impression is not one of awe, but of boredom and weariness, illustrating Goya's disillusionment.

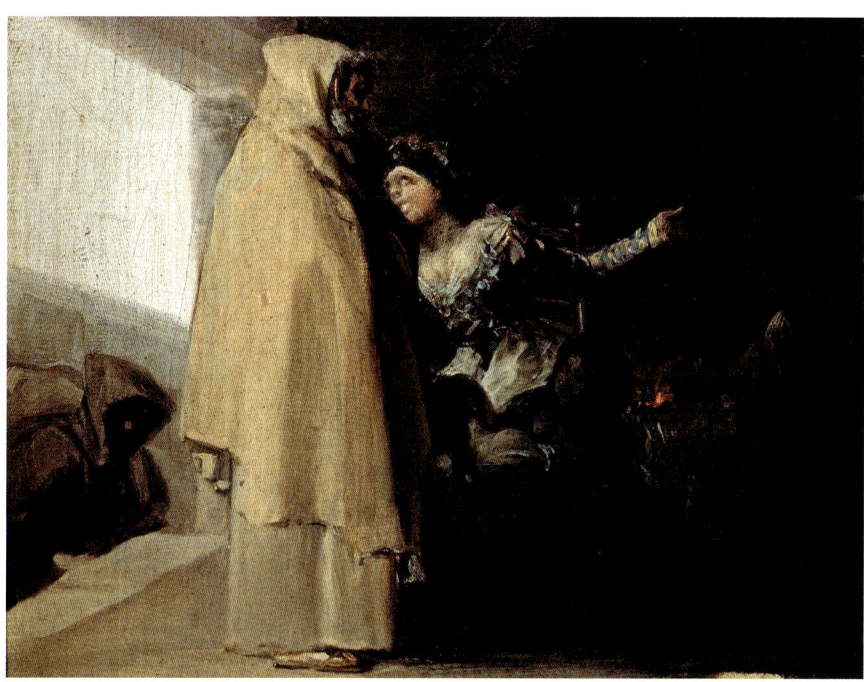

Left: The Friar's Visit *or* The Castillo Crime I, *detail. 1808–12, Goya depicts shocking, real-life events of love, deceit and murder.*

THE HOUSE OF THE DEAF MAN

Through the success of *The Tauromaquia* prints, by 1819, Goya could afford to buy another house. Tired of the intrigues, threats and unfriendliness at Court, he wanted some peace. For 60,000 reales, he bought a country house just outside Madrid, near the meadow of San Isidro that he had painted in 1788.

Goya's new house was called 'La Quinta del Sordo'. He did not name it, but by coincidence, the name means 'the house of the deaf man', after a former occupant. Its seclusion suited him as the troubles in Spain were not diminishing, and the situation at Court remained volatile.

LOSS OF THE COLONIES

The war had exhausted everyone, Spain was bankrupt, and conflicts about absolutism and liberalism continued (even the Spanish army had progressive leanings that created tensions between them and Ferdinand's despotic regime).

Below: The Procession of Monks; *this is from one of Goya's albums that he filled between 1812–1823.*

In an attempt to make Spain solvent, Ferdinand ordered the Spanish army to reconquer their former colonies in South America, with a view to exploiting their resources. Despite fierce and lengthy fighting in Venezuela, Uruguay, Paraguay, Argentina and Peru, Spain did not have enough funds to sustain prolonged conflicts and its navy was so weakened from the War of Independence that nothing could be done to regain revenues from these countries. By the 1820s, only Mexico, Puerto Rico and Cuba remained as Spanish colonies.

THE INQUISITION

Goya was the first important artist to make visual comment on the Inquisition and the corruption of the Church

while they were still powerful. He put himself in an ominous situation. At any moment, he could have been taken in for further questioning and he could have been imprisoned or even put to death for exposing his opinions. His sardonic paintings, drawings and prints of the Church, the Inquisition and their victims came from conversations, his imagination and his own experiences. He satirized penitential rituals, drew visual parallels between the barbaric practices of ancient witch-trials and interrogations by the Inquisition, and he made sinister and menacing

Below: Duel with Shields *– one of six drawings showing different duelling scenes made by Goya, c.1817–20.*

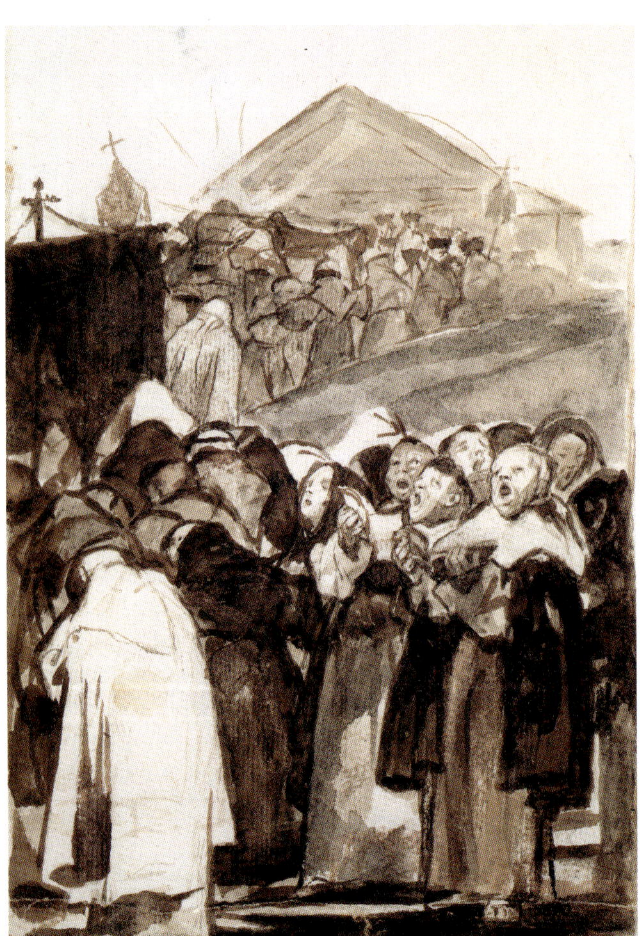

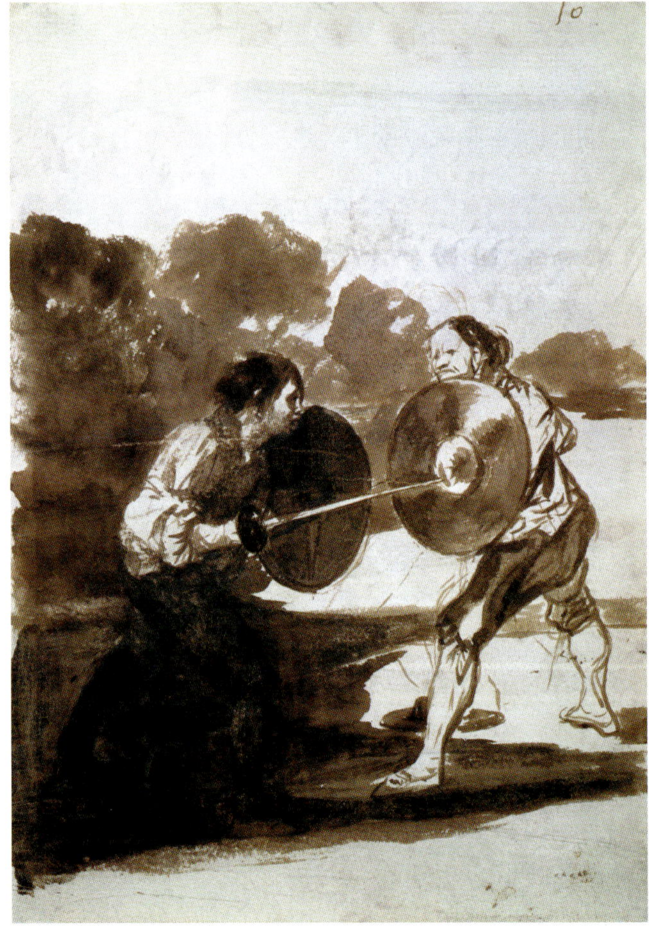

THE ILLNESS RETURNS

At the end of 1819, when Goya was 73, he suffered a relapse of his serious illness. For weeks he was close to death, but he eventually recovered. He attributed his survival to the attention and skill of his physician and friend, Dr Arrietta. In gratitude, he painted himself in his doctor's arms (see page 81).

comparisons between the enlightened King Charles III and the despotic King Ferdinand VII.

THE NEW HOUSE

Even though he officially retained his title of First Painter to the King, at the start of his illness, Goya withdrew from society, and retreated to his new house with Leocadia and her small daughter Rosario. Like Goya, Leocadia had liberal beliefs for the future of Spain, so they had a lot in common. But his family disapproved of Leocadia and of Goya's household arrangements. Javier in particular, although he had never been close to his father, was concerned about losing his inheritance to the young woman. Nonetheless, Goya lived as he chose. His new house was peacefully situated in isolation on the mountain of San Isidro, surrounded by 20 acres of land, with a view of Madrid in the distance.

As he recuperated, he was delighted to learn of the revolt that had been led by General Riego on 1 January 1820, which resulted in Ferdinand VII being forced to abide by the Constitution and to relax his tyrannical grip on Spain. On 4 April 1820, Goya attended the Royal Academy in Madrid for the last time, to swear his allegiance to the new liberal Constitution. The Inquisition was once again abolished and prisoners from the old regime were released. Although a renewed optimism spread through Spain, in actuality, things were not as promising as they had initially seemed, but on his return home, Goya, now in his 74th year, felt rejuvenated. In a burst of energy, he began to make sketches for the decoration of his two main living rooms.

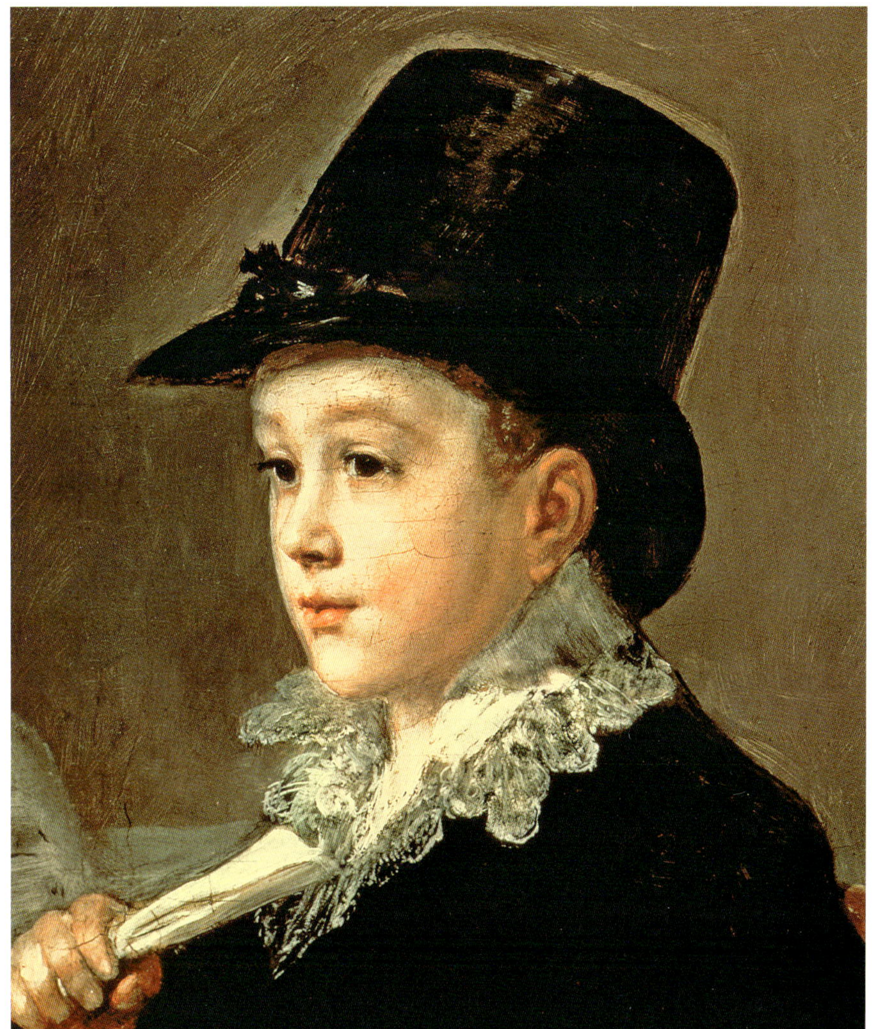

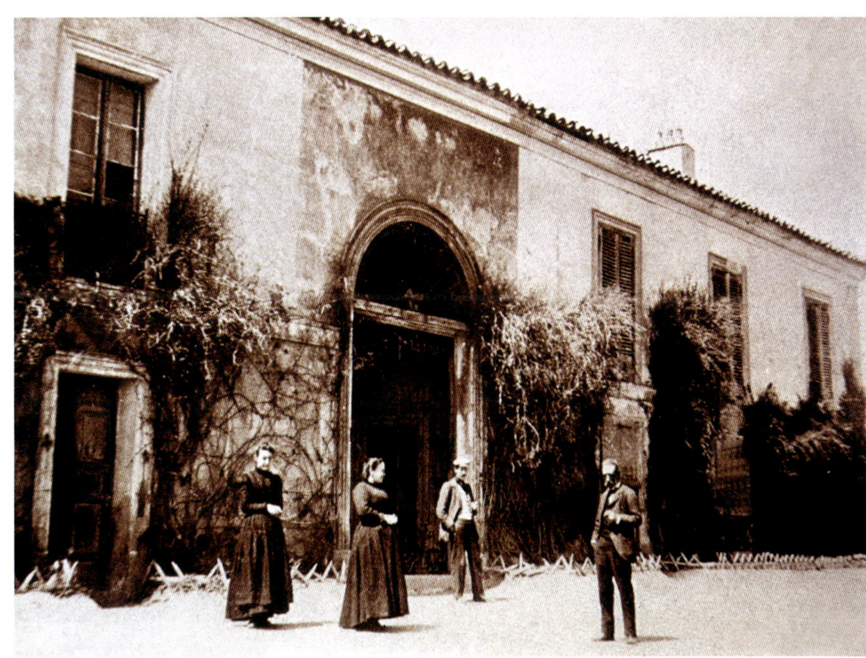

Top: Detail of Goya's portrait of his grandson, Mariano (see page 242), c.1815. In 1823, Goya gave La Quinta del Sordo to Mariano.

Above: 'La Quinta del Sordo'; Goya's 20-acre (8-hectare) property had a view of Madrid in the distance.

THE BLACK PAINTINGS

In April 1820, Goya began an extraordinary project that occupied him for the next three years. The paintings he produced in Quinta del Sordo became known as his 'Black Paintings', as they are mysterious, dark and oppressive. He originally intended to paint joyous images, but the problems in Spain affected him.

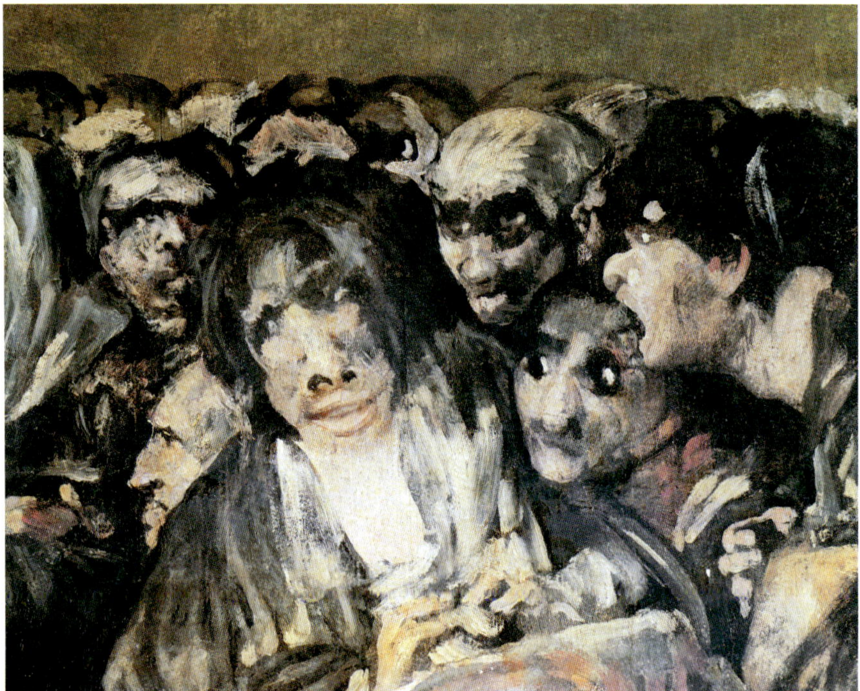

Above: Pilgrimage to San Isidro's Fountain *(detail, see page 248), 1821; contrasting with Goya's treatment of the same subject 30 years earlier in* The Meadow of San Isidro *(see page 154).*

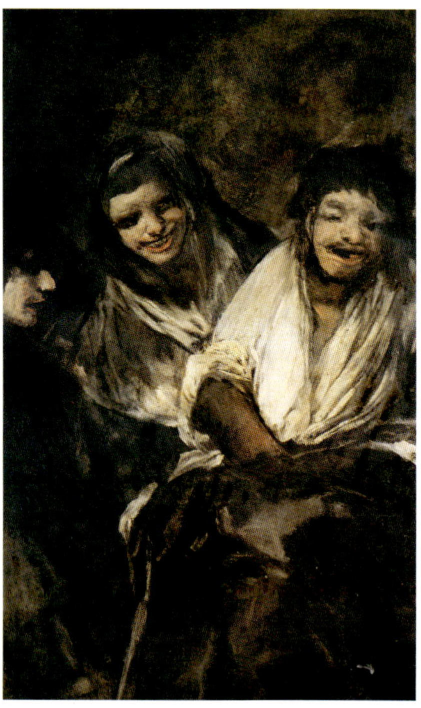

Above: Man Mocked by Two Women *or* Women Laughing, *1820–1823, in one of Goya's Black Paintings, two women laugh luridly at a simple-minded man.*

Soon after Ferdinand had sworn allegiance to the liberal Constitution, he appealed to the powers of the Holy Alliance to help him retract it. For a couple of years there was continued insecurity and unrest as most citizens realized that the King would never allow the country to follow a liberal path. Then in 1822 at the Congress of Verona, a decision was made to send a French military expedition into Spain to overthrow the constitutional regime and restore the absolute monarchy.

SYMBOLS OF STRIFE

Goya's Black Paintings consist of 14 oil paintings on the walls of the two main living rooms in his house. He used the oil-based *al secco* technique, which was quite a common method of painting frescoes on dry plaster walls. The dry wall was a firm base for the slow-drying oil paint, which meant that alterations and adjustments could be made before the oil paint dried. Goya produced preparatory drawings for each of the

paintings in his large dining room and salon, and he painted the works with a broad range of colours, although the predominant colour was black. The paintings reflect his frame of mind and symbolize the discord that Spain had experienced in recent years. His need to escape the oppression, hypocrisy and denunciations had become unbearable for him over the last five years, as he and many others wondered if the problems in their country would ever end. By then, he also knew that even if things did improve, it was unlikely that he would be alive to see it. He had already lived far longer than most – life expectancy was far shorter in the 19th century than in the 21st, and most of his contemporaries were already dead. Added to this, the Inquisition had reopened their file on him

and he was aware that at any moment they could arrest him. In the midst of all this political, economic and personal dissonance, Quinta del Sordo was a place of peace where Goya could express himself freely. Having only just recovered once again from an illness that brought him close to death for a second time, he realized that he was not likely to survive if it happened again at his time of life. As a result, the paintings show a bold lack of constraint and artistic freedom; an unrestricted expression of his innermost fears, thoughts and emotions.

CAREFUL PLANNING

It is probable that Goya painted the walls of his salon on the ground floor first. Images for this room include *La Leocadia* (see page 249), *Two Old Men*, *Aquelarre* (see page 248), *The Pilgrimage*

VISIONS OF THE AFTERWORLD

Apart from *La Leocadia* (see page 249), which appears to be of a young woman in mourning leaning on a tomb, the other 13 paintings can be understood as representing scenes from beyond the grave; probably visions seen by Goya when he was close to death. With such thoughts of his own mortality, the Black Paintings can be interpreted as images from beyond the grave, and Goya's own illness-led hallucinations.

of *San Isidro* (see page 248) and *Saturn* (see page 249). In the first-floor dining room, the paintings included *The Fates* (see page 247), *Asmodea* (see page 248), *Duel with Cudgels* (see page 247), *A Dog, Two Old People Eating* and *Men Reading* (see page 246). At first sight,

Right: Proclamation of Witches; *originally a sketch for* Los Caprichos, *Goya used some ideas for his later Black Paintings.*

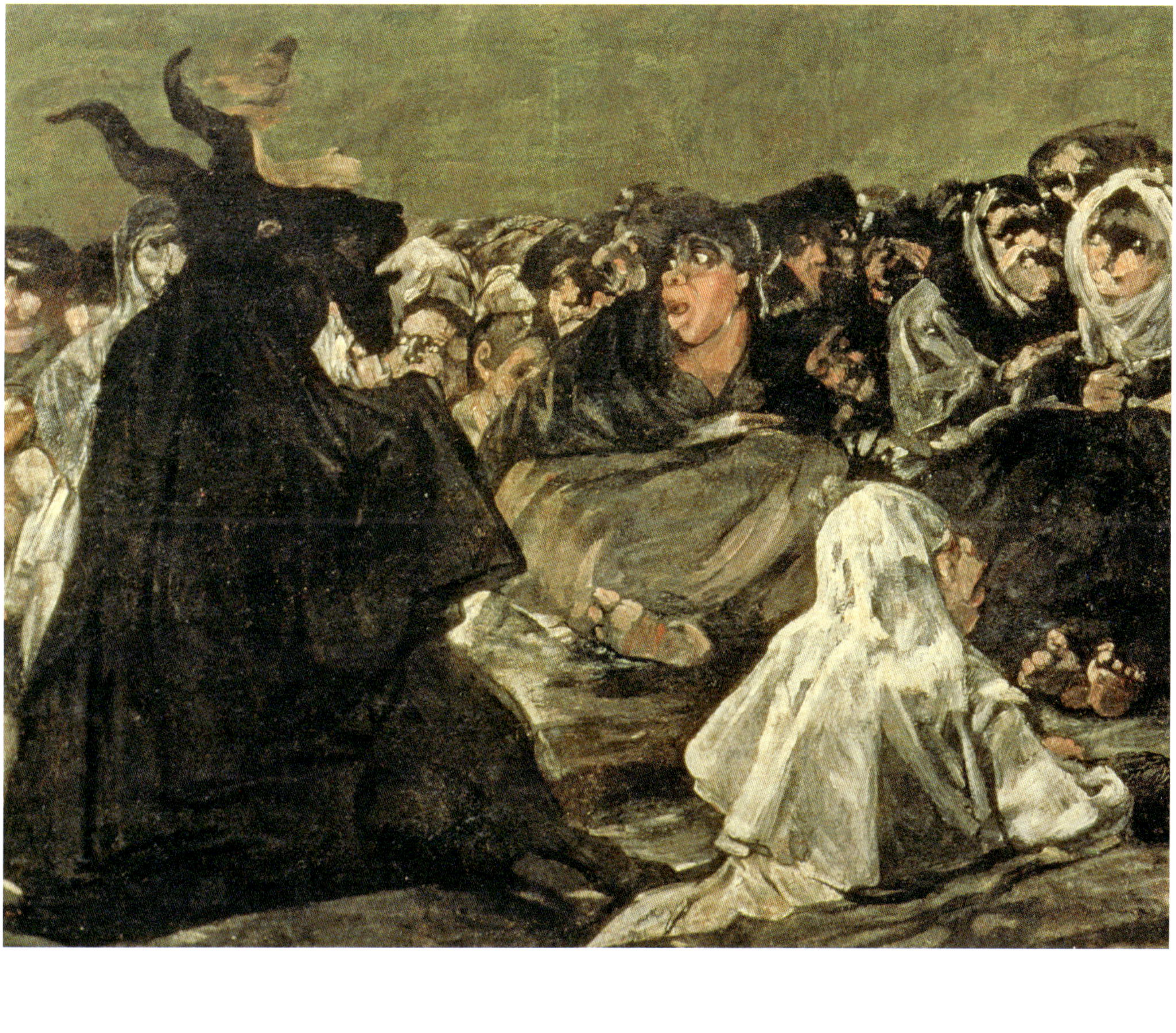

many of the works can appear to have been painted by a madman. In the light of Goya's experiences in recent years the reasons why he painted such images becomes clearer. His work was influenced not only by the horrors that had befallen his country from both external and internal forces, and the persecution, violence, famine and fighting, but also by his debilitating illnesses and deafness. Although the paintings appear to have been dashed off quickly with little thought or coherence, in reality, Goya planned every work carefully beforehand.

Below: Aquelarre (detail; see page 248), *1820–23, shows Satan as a goat, presiding over a coven of deformed, ugly witches.*

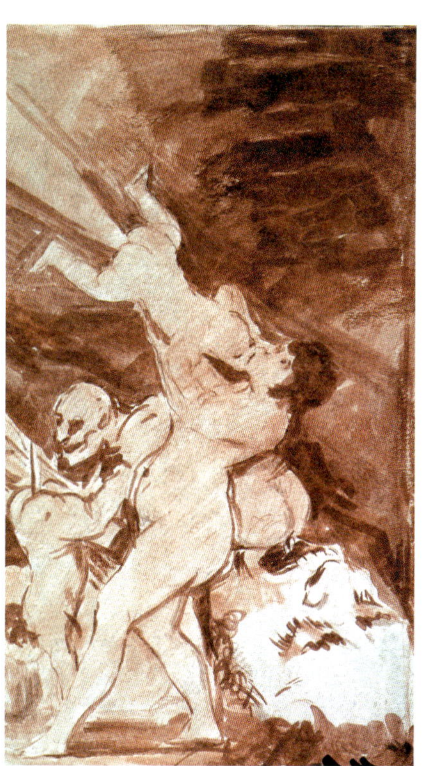

SCIENCE AND TECHNOLOGY

While Goya and his compatriots were under the control of their mercurial governments, and international unrest continued, many ground-breaking developments were being made in science and technology. With this succession of significant innovations, the world was changing enormously, transforming life for many.

Although the word 'scientist' was not used until 1833, scientific and technical discoveries and inventions were affecting the lives of most long before that. Breakthroughs ranged from steam locomotives to electric lights, an improved printing press to the stethoscope, the Jacquard loom to the tin can. The world was moving at a rapid pace, and few individuals were left untouched.

COLOUR AND LIGHT

In 1810, Goethe published his *Theory of Colour*, exploring ideas about how colours are perceived by humans. For the first time, a consideration of phenomena such as colour in shadows and refraction appeared in print, which had great repercussions on the ways that many subsequent artists used paint and interpreted what they saw. Artists such as Turner, Delacroix and Géricault began using even brighter colours than they had previously. Most painters before them had used monochromatic hues in shadows and tones, but these brighter colours enlivened their images and influenced ensuing artists.

Furthermore, gas lighting had recently been invented, which replaced oil lamps and candles. In 1809 an English chemist,

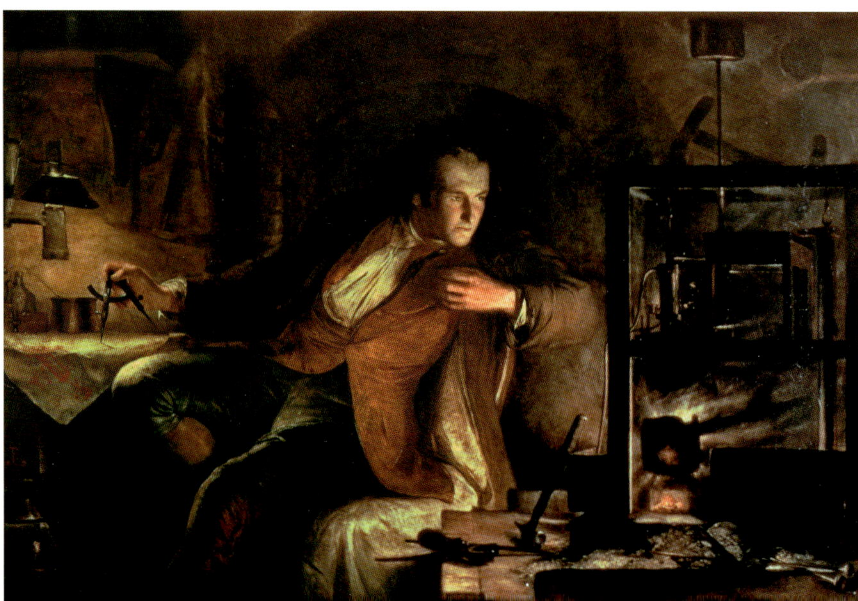

Above: James Watt and the Newcomen Engine *(detail), painted in 1855 by James Eckford Lauder (1811–69). The chiaroscuro employed by both Goya and James Wright of Derby became a prominent means of expression at the time.*

Humphry Davy (1778–1829) invented the first electric light. Brighter, more reliable illumination made artists' work easier, enabling them to work for longer hours and seeing colours and details clearly at all hours.

GOYA AND SCIENCE

Over the last few years, Goya's opinion of science had improved. In *Los Caprichos* of 1797–8, he had portrayed doctors as incompetent arrogant fools, describing them as *matasanos* (killers of the healthy). Yet in his *Self-portrait with Dr Arrieta* of 1820, he expressed respect and empathy for the doctor and therefore of medicine in general.

He was aware, through engravings, of the work of the artist Joseph Wright of Derby (1734–97), who was often referred to as 'the first professional painter to express the spirit of the Industrial Revolution'. Wright's paintings of scientific experiments illustrate the

Below: Johann Wolfgang von Goethe, *painted by Franz Gerhard von Kügelgen (1772–1820) in 1810, the year his* Theory of Colour *was published, which had a huge effect on artists everywhere.*

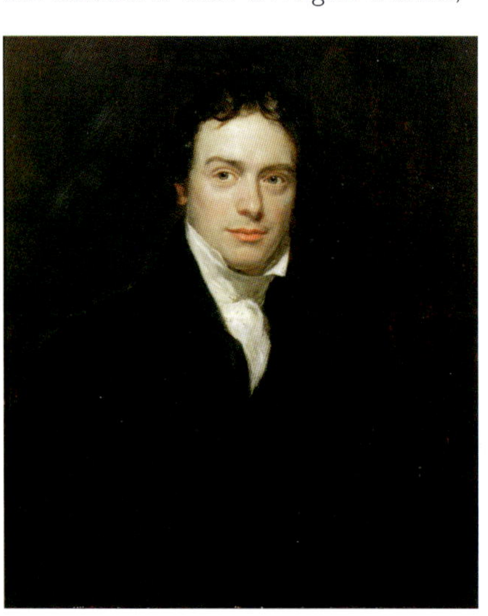

Left: Portrait of Michael Faraday, *by Henry William Pickersgill (1782–1875), 1830. Goya's influence on portraiture can be seen here.*

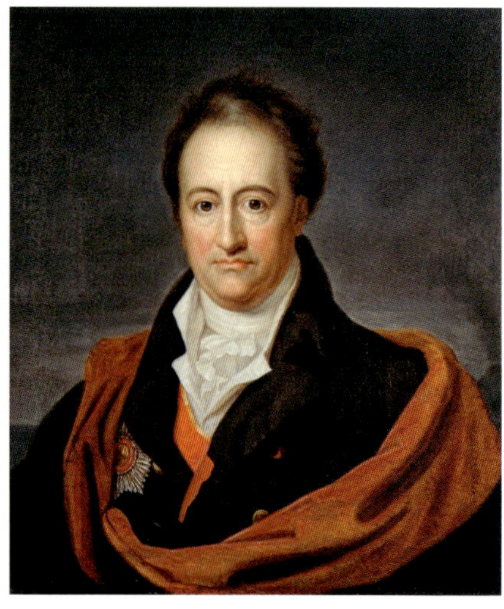

Right: Self-portrait with Dr Arrieta, *1820 (see page 250). The inscription reads: Goya thankful, to his friend Arrieta: for the skill and care with which he saved his life during his short and dangerous illness, endured at the end of 1819, at 73 years of age.*

ambivalence, astonishment and awe felt by many of the recent scientific discoveries. To enhance the drama of the moments he was portraying, Wright used strong chiaroscuro effects. In his *Self-portrait with Dr Arrieta*, Goya uses similar dramatic effects, and many of his works of the time feature comparatively striking light effects, including *The Third of May, 1808* (see page 70) and a number of his Black Paintings, such as *Pilgrimage to San Isidro* (see page 248) and *Aquelarre* (see page 248).

MAKING LIFE UNRECOGNIZABLE

The scientific and technological discoveries of the late 18th and early 19th centuries altered life quite drastically. It was not only the French Revolution and its repercussions that affected the collective outlook. This was possibly one of the reasons that Goya retreated to his house in the hills,

Below: The Astrologer, *George Lance (1802–64). Painted in 1842, the clothing and props in this painting display contemporary notions that astrology studies were fanciful and somewhat medieval. Goya was as cynical of astrology as of many other 'sciences'.*

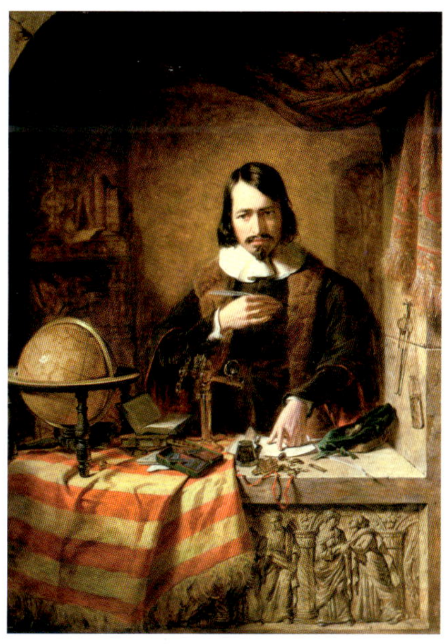

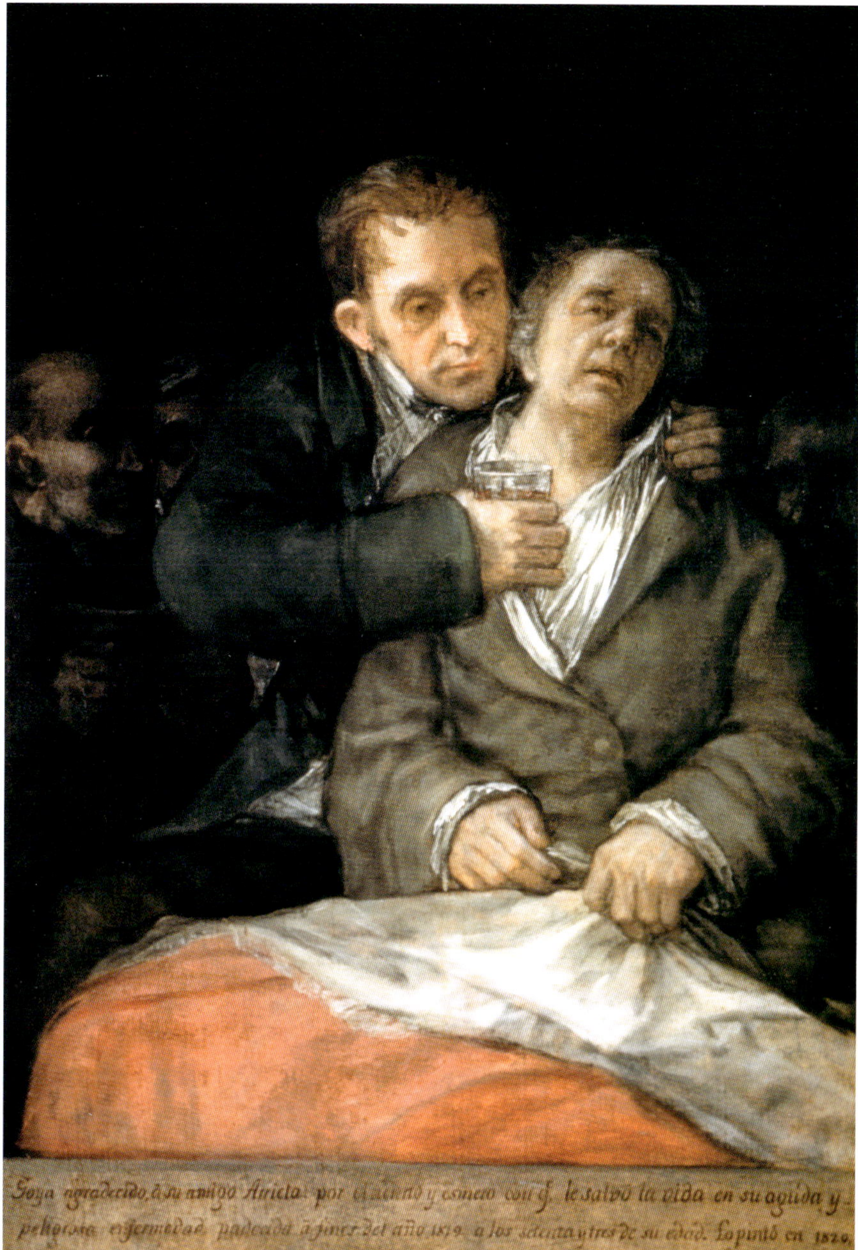

Goya agradecido, á su amigo Arrieta: por el acierto y esmero con q. le salvo la vida en su aguda y peligrosa enfermedad padecida á fines del año 1819, a los setenta y tres de su edad. Lo pintó en 1820.

as many, particularly older people, felt uncomfortable with the changes.

In 1796, the English physician Edward Jenner (1749–1823) had discovered how to vaccinate against smallpox. James Watt (1736–1819), a Scottish engineer, invented the first efficient steam engine, which fuelled the Industrial Revolution, while Italian physicist Alessandro Volta (1745–1827) invented the electric battery in 1800. In 1819, Charles Macintosh (1766–1843) found a method to make fabric waterproof and created the 'rain-coat', later nicknamed the mackintosh. In 1816, Frenchman Joseph Nicéphore Niepce (1785–1833) took a picture

with a camera obscura from his workroom window. Although it faded quickly, it was the world's first positive photographic image. In Britain, poorly educated Michael Faraday (1791–1867) attended lectures by the leading chemist Sir Humphry Davy in 1812. Faraday went on to be employed as an assistant by Davy and within a few years, became one of the most important contributors in the fields of electromagnetism and electrochemistry.

By the 1820s, when Goya was working in La Quinta del Sordo, he was aware that elsewhere, bright lights, medicines and steam-powered machines were changing the world beyond his recognition.

LITERATURE AND DESIGN

While Goya was trying to overcome his post-war problems, the Romantic literary movement was
gaining momentum. Writers emphasized emotions such as apprehension, fear, wonder, and 'melancholy'.
Internationally, design focused on the Empire and Regency styles that had evolved from France and Britain.

Romanticism was expressed by writers, designers and artists across the globe. It was especially prominent in literature, and featured in poetry, novels, plays and prose. Concerned with the individual more than with society in general, Romanticism concentrated on personal consciousness, imagination and intuition, while the primary aim was the expression of feeling.

In order to enhance their creative potential, some Romantic writers sought to attain altered states of consciousness through the use of opium. Yet although many cast aside the concepts of rationality in reaction against Enlightenment thinking, as the period continued, and particularly after the publication of Jane Austen's (1775–1817) novels from 1811 to 1818, an interest in realism began to develop. Realism gathered strength as the century continued. Although these developments occurred in various countries, the ideas spread rapidly, through the new, more efficient printing presses. In this way in Spain, Goya would have been aware of new forms and styles of writing, and of the most celebrated writers of the time.

Below: The Fire King Appears to Count Albert, *Henry Fuseli (1741–1825), c.1801–10. Fuseli and Goya painted similar expressions of nightmarish visions and savagery.*

IDEALIZING THE PAST
Due to the Industrial Revolution and the latest scientific and technological developments, many early Romantic writers began expressing themselves as a yearning for an idealized past, so poems and stories of history and mythology abounded. Romantic literature emphasized a love of nature,

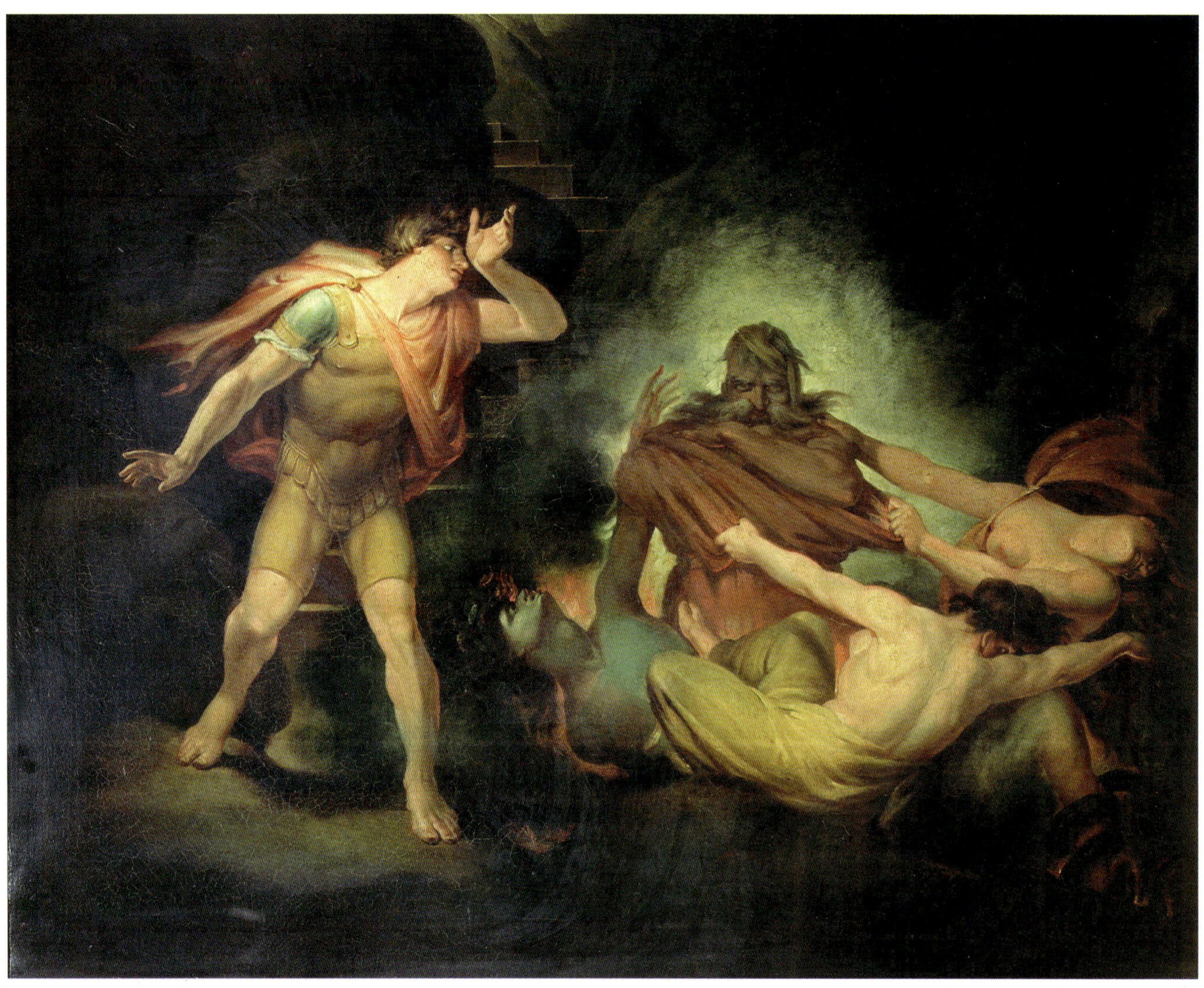

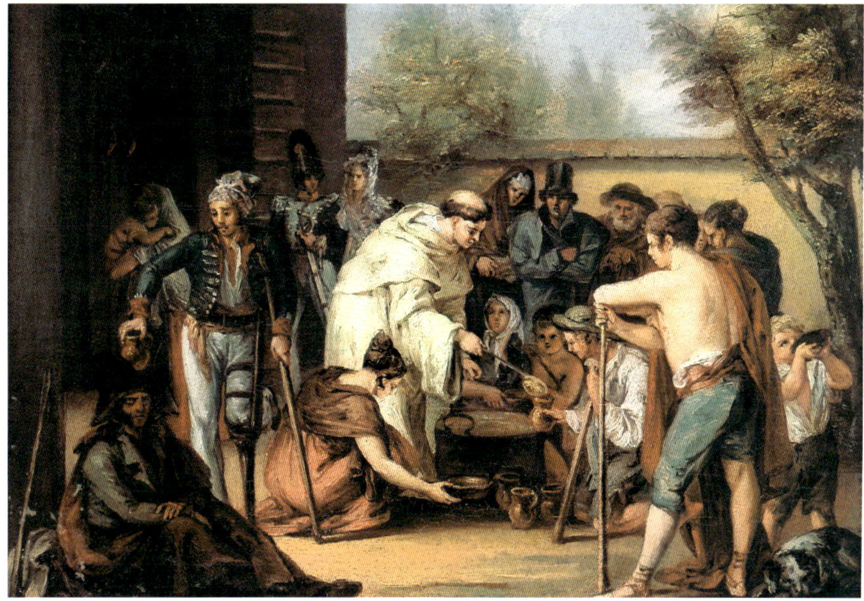

Above: Soup Distribution, *Leonardo Alenza (1807-45), c.1830. Inspired by Goya, Alenza's Spanish genre paintings reflect the developing Realist movement.*

often implying that many of the ills of society were a direct result of urbanization. Perhaps even more than in painting, literary experimentation with new styles, subjects and genres became prevalent.

INNOVATIVE WRITERS

The poet and artist William Blake (1757–1827) was one of the earliest Romanticists. As with Goya, the French Revolution and its effects informed much of his creative process. His original illustrations and poems developed from Bible stories, but many of these unique visions were misunderstood by contemporaries. William Wordsworth (1770–1850) was also one of the first writers of the Romantic period. His observant and meditative thoughts exploited the power of nature. Edgar Allen Poe (1809–49), best known for his tales of mystery and the macabre and his explorations into unusual aspects of human nature, is generally considered to be the inventor of detective fiction. Sir Walter Scott (1771–1832) instigated a fascination for historical and mystery novels, while Goethe, Chateaubriand, Samuel Taylor Coleridge (1772–1834), Nathaniel Hawthorne (1804–64) and John Keats (1792–1821) introduced further new ideas. Percy Bysshe Shelley (1792–1822) was a key member of a group of writers that included his second wife, Mary Shelley (1797–1851) author of *Frankenstein* (in 1818), and Lord Byron (1788–1824), another leading and highly influential figure of the Romantic movement. In Spain, José de Espronceda (1808–42) and José Zorrilla y Moral (1817–93) were two of the most significant Romantic poets.

DEVELOPMENTS IN DESIGN

After the structured styles of Neoclassicism, the only limit with Romantic design was the designer's imagination. Never as flamboyant however as Rococo, Romantic design ideas often featured elements of naturalism and nostalgia. With no single authoritative style, early 19th-century designers selected elements from the past and blended the old with the new. In Britain, the Gothic Revival in architecture emerged from the Romanticists' yearning for the past, in particular, the fascination for medievalism. Many designs of buildings and interiors were based on forms and patterns from the Middle Ages, usually expressing a fanciful, romantic vision of medieval chivalry and romance. Dress for men and women, in Spain as well as in the rest of Europe, followed the Empire and Regency styles that had originated in France and Britain.

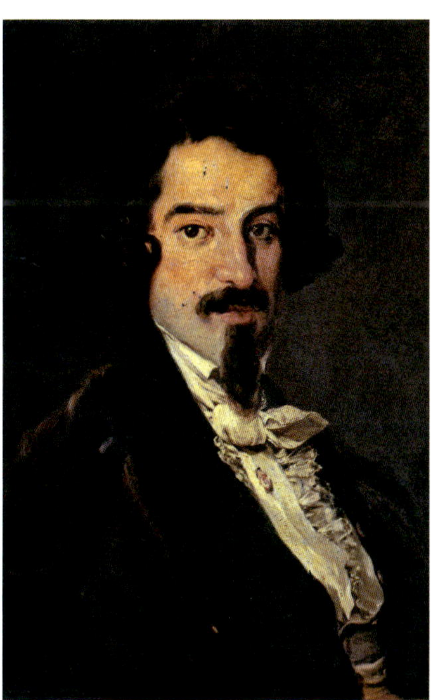

Left: José de Espronceda, *(1808-42), by Antonio Esquivel. Espronceda was a Romantic Spanish poet, exiled for conspiring against Ferdinand IV.*

ARTS AND INDUSTRY

After the Napoleonic Wars, the great changes in society, politics and industry became more apparent. It was the start of the machine age, as electricity and steam power turned industry into a mechanical process and created a new wealthy middle class. Goya was one of the first, but other artists also began 'breaking rules'.

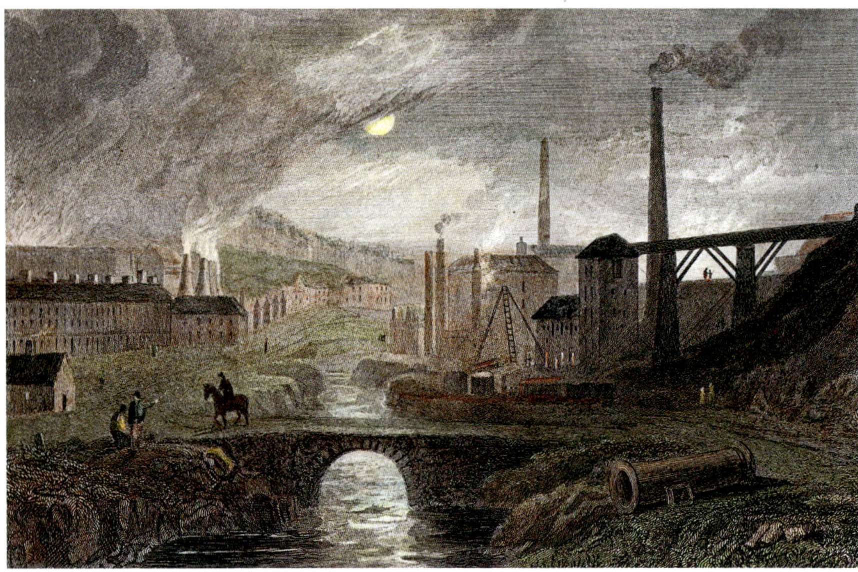

Above: Iron Works, Monmouthshire, Wales, after George Robertson. By the late 18th century, iron replaced wood as the material for making industrial machines and tools.

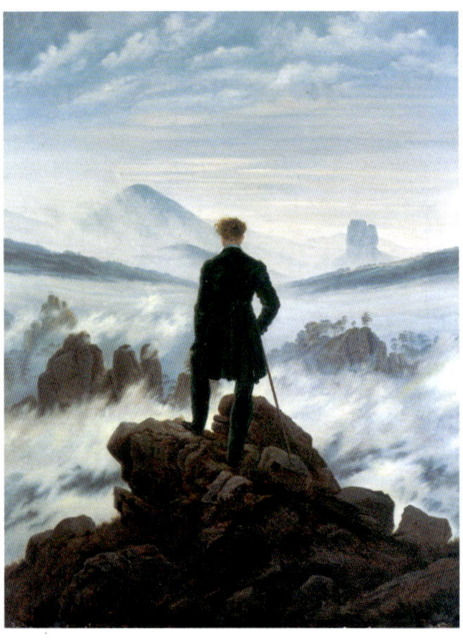

Above: Wanderer Above the Mist, *Caspar David Friedrich, 1818. Both Goya and Friedrich understood and conveyed the drama and immensity of nature.*

Because of the new, efficient steam-powered machines, rather than each worker making an entire product from start to finish, single workers performed only one stage in the manufacturing process. This was an essential element of the industrialization that advanced throughout the 19th century, making mass production possible and affecting the reorganization of workers in many ways, increasing manufacturing efficiency. In some cases, this made life more difficult as it threatened the integrity of the family; people had to work in factories away from home and in dense urban areas. It also threatened individual autonomy as workers were no longer masters of their own production, but just one part of a process, performing a limited set of functions, and not responsible for the whole. In other ways, industrialization made it possible for an increasing number of people to enjoy goods that previously only the wealthy could afford, or to buy goods that had not been available before.

Steam power aided a range of things, including printing, generating a massive expansion of newspaper and book publishing, which subsequently improved literacy.

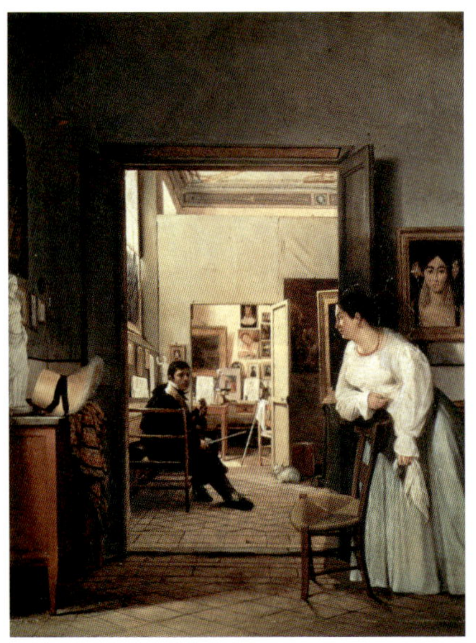

Left: The Studio of Ingres in Rome, *1818; Jean Alaux (1786–1864). Despite his independent stance, Goya was linked to many contemporary art movements, even the cool style of Neoclassicism.*

ARTISTIC REACTIONS

The growth of modern industry led to massive urbanization and the expansion of many cities across Europe and America. As well as Romantic writers, artists had nostalgic reactions and a longing for the countryside began to dominate fine art.

Romantic artists were often inspired by such writers as Dante, Shakespeare, Goethe and Byron. They also frequently depicted current events in dramatic ways, such as Delacroix's *The Massacre at Chios*, and Géricault's *Raft of the Medusa*, both heavily indebted to Goya's *Executions of the Third of May* (see pages 70–1).

Gradually, some artists began to defy accepted traditions of art and work more individually. Among many other things, they were stimulated by Goya's example (his works were known through the expansion of printing). Like Goya, other artists began to probe beneath superficial appearances, and to express penetrating observations of what was going on around them in original ways.

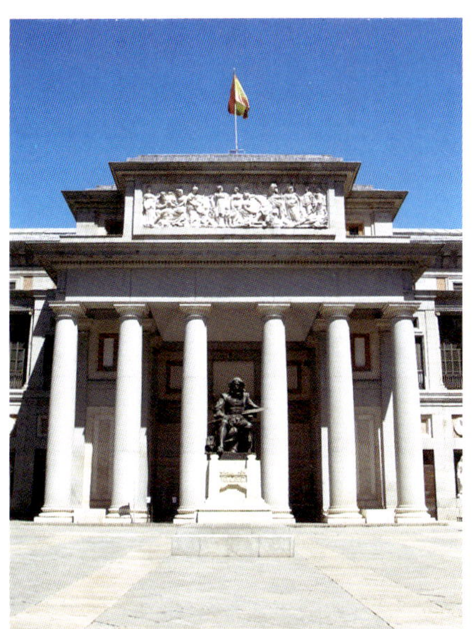

Above: The Prado Museum opened in 1819. For the first time, the public could see works from the Royal Collections. The Prado helped to bring Goya international fame.

Below: The Raft of the Medusa, *Géricault, 1818–9; this immense work was inspired by a true event, and by Goya's* Executions of the Third of May, 1808 *(see pages 70–1).*

THE PRADO MUSEUM

In Madrid, the Museo Nacional del Prado, a grand Neoclassical style building, was designed by the architect Juan de Villanueva (1739–1811) in 1785, during the reign of Charles III. Charles had been attempting to make Madrid the equal of cities such as Rome, Paris and London, and had originally planned for the building to be a Natural History Museum, but work on it stopped during the Spanish War of Independence, when the building was appropriated by the cavalry.

After the war Ferdinand VII's second wife, María Isabel, encouraged him to finish the building and to use it as a public art gallery, housing the expansive royal collections from their various palaces that had been amassed over the years by successive monarchs. In November 1819, the Royal Museum of Painting and Sculpture – the Museo Nacional del Prado – opened its doors to the public for the first time. The first catalogue was published then and featured 311 paintings, although the collection comprised over 1,510 paintings and drawings.

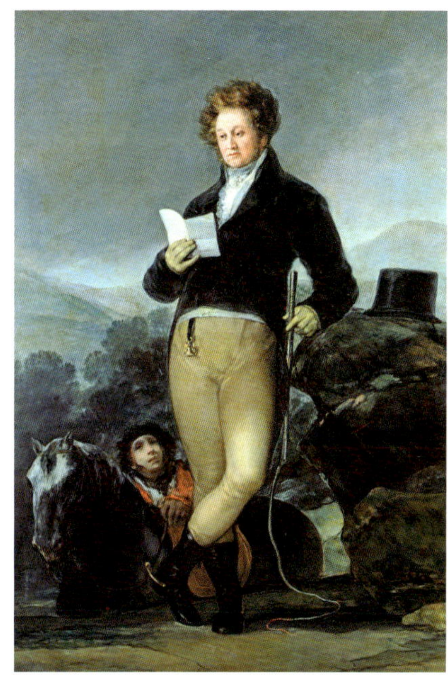

Above: Goya's portrait of his friend, the Duke of Osuna, Don Francisco de Borja Téllez Girón (1786–1851), c.1816. Supportive of industrialization, the Duke was one of the most influential figures of the Enlightenment in Spain and one of Goya's prime patrons.

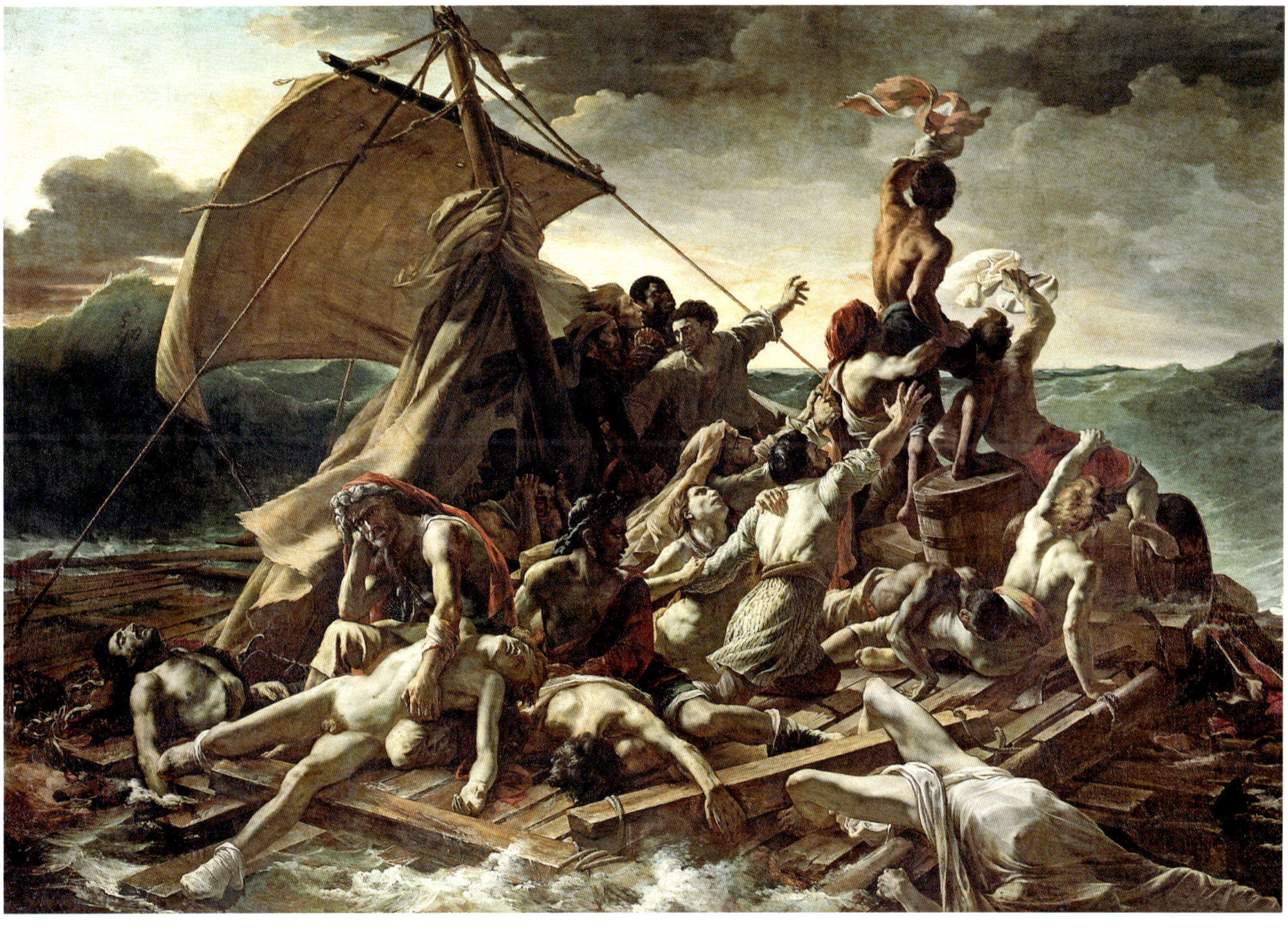

LOS CAPRICHOS AND DISPARATES

Just as the first bout of his illness in 1792 ended with Goya's production of *Los Caprichos*, his relapse in 1819 resulted in his Black Paintings (see pages 76–7). These alarming images reflect his feelings and thoughts, his despair at the continuing problems in Spain, his life in general and the uncertainties that surrounded him.

Goya had often viewed the world with pessimism, but in the past, he had been surrounded by his wife, many friends and had a successful career to keep him buoyant. Now he had few friends around him, he had lost the respect of the royal family and the Court in general, and was suffering with the after-effects of the dreadful, debilitating illness. The visions he had experienced while feverish remained vivid, and he turned them into powerful works of art. While several Romanticists were experimenting with opium to create their spectacular work, Goya's hallucinations emerged mainly through the natural symptoms of his illness.

THE FOLLIES

In 1816, Goya began making another series of prints in aquatint and etching with touches of drypoint, which are at times called *The Follies* and sometimes known as *The Proverbs* or *The Disparates*. The title of each image always includes the word 'disparate', which means

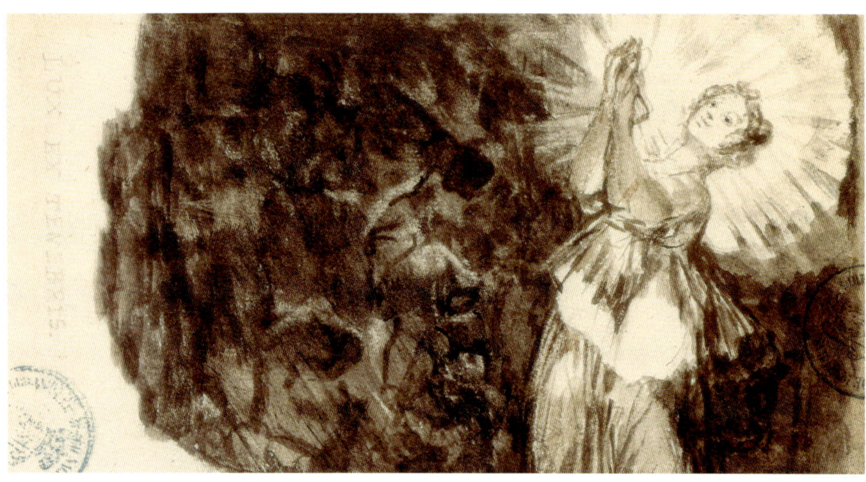

Above: Light and Darkness, *1820 – Goya made this drawing in celebration of General Riego's revolt against Ferdinand VII.*

folly or absurdity, and each is brief, such as *Feminine Folly, Flying Folly* (see page 246) or *Fool's Folly.* The pictures illustrate human weaknesses and desires, superstitions, ignorance and foolish, impractical and superficial behaviour.

Below: Fool's Folly, *1816–23; one of Goya's series* The Disparates, *this links with a traditional Spanish proverb.*

Goya's preparatory drawings for these are far more detailed than the finished prints, which he pared down to only essential elements to give the most impact. Although he completed the prints in 1823, none were published

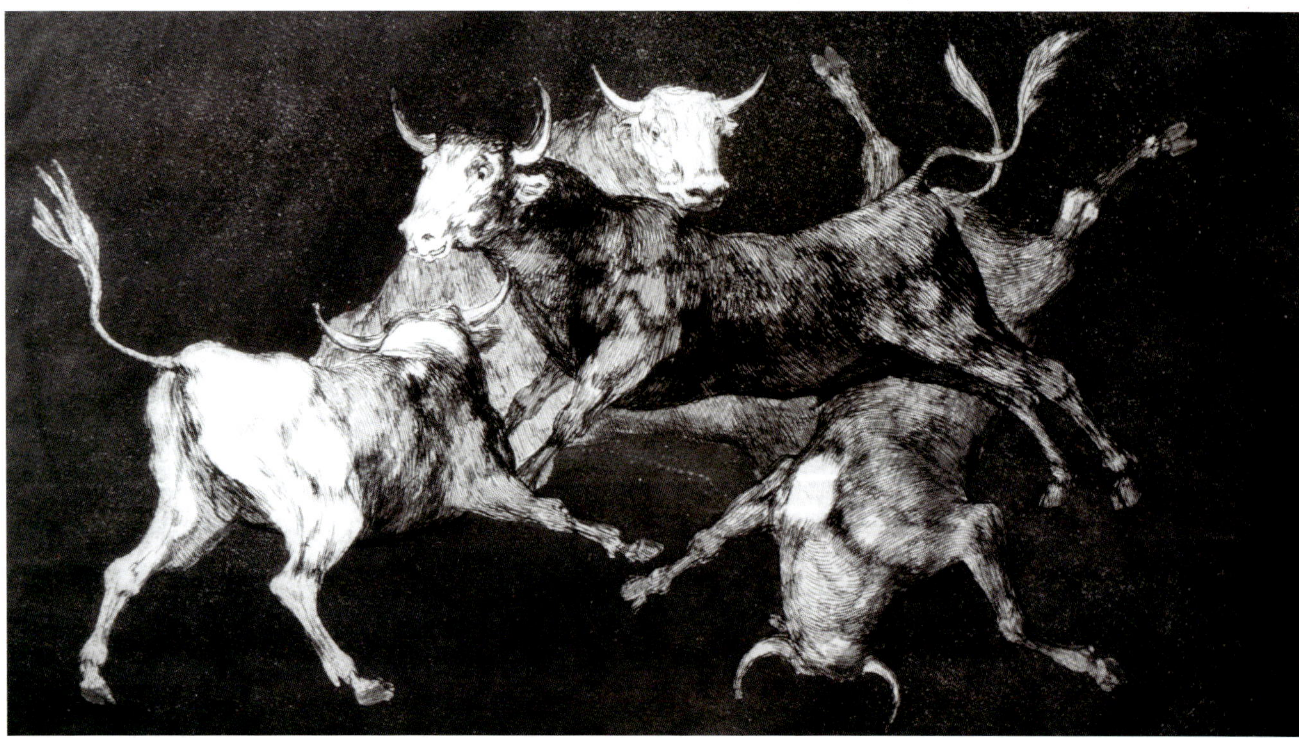

until after his death, and while 22 *Disparates* are known, it is believed that he probably planned and executed 25 in total. None are numbered, so it is not certain, and the images are difficult to understand. They include dark, dream-like scenes that relate to political issues, focusing on a condemnation of the establishment, traditional Spanish proverbs and the carnival. The Church – and by implication, the Inquisition and the King's dictatorship – are also once again criticized as being the antithesis of enlightened and progressive thought. The images emphasize the frenzied, grotesque side of the Spanish carnival festivities, linking them to the immorality, corruption and crumbling of order in Spain. In terms of mood and theme, *The Disparates* have much in common with *Los Caprichos*, but there is a striking difference in scale. In *Los Caprichos*, despite Goya's bold handling, the designs are controlled and contained within small formats, as well as being characterized by almost classical compositions in the ways in which figures are arranged. The compositions of *The Disparates* however, create a sense of limitless space, with the figures

Below: Dog Half-submerged, *1821–23; from Goya's La Quinta del Sordo, this dog's head in an undefined area focuses on the inevitability of death.*

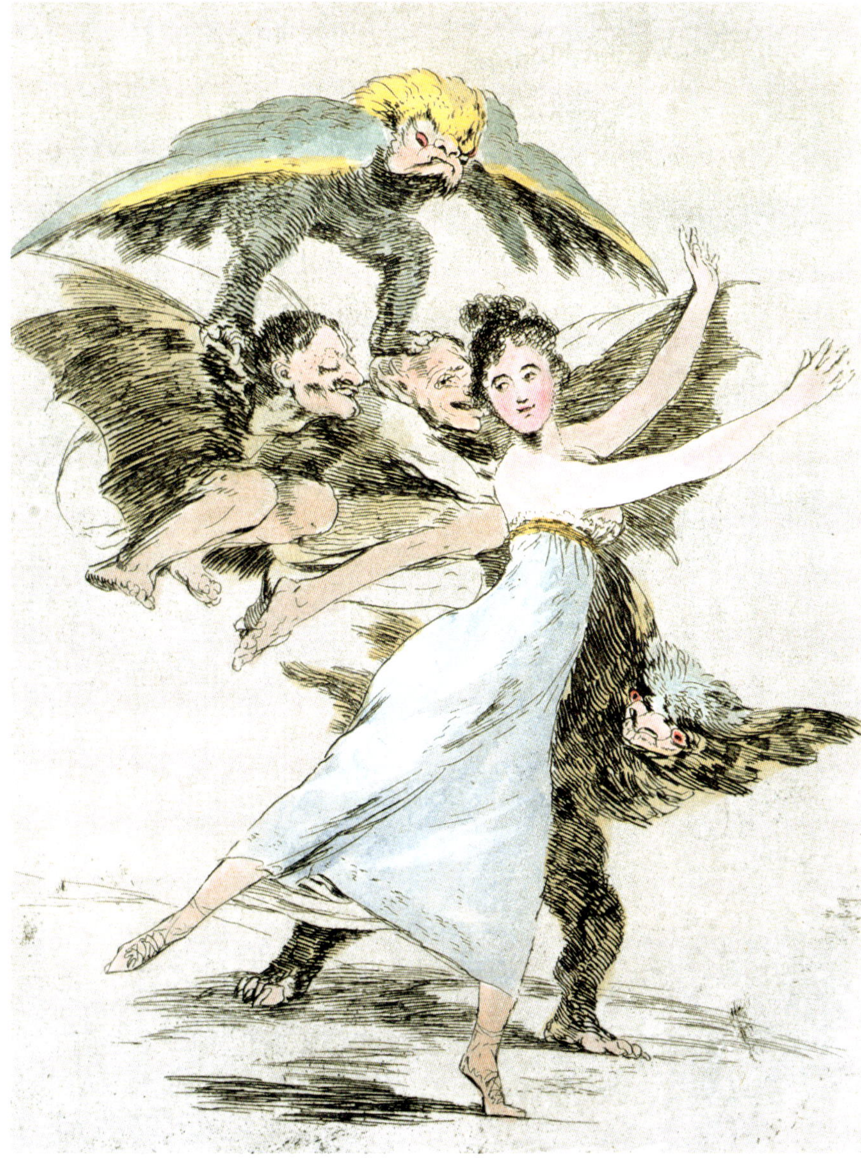

Above: Plate 72 from Los Caprichos; You Will Not Escape, 1799 – *showing the more complex compositions of Goya's earlier prints.*

looming in the foregrounds as if caught in the wide lens of a camera. All the designs feature figures that are either in asymmetrical compositions, or in circular formats, which became a characteristic feature of Goya's later work. Within the images, he crowded in memories, allusions and ideas drawn from the whole of his life, and from previous works, and as with his other prints, they all feature scathing elements of social and political satire.

FEVERISH INSPIRATION

Goya's Black Paintings and *The Disparates* all express similar macabre and uncomfortable imagery; resembling the distortions of dreams or nightmares – simultaneously strange and familiar, and drawn, not from a traditional language of

art, but from Goya's own private world. Although not amusing, he presented them as humorous; a humour that also renders a feeling of horror.

Yet while many viewers may perceive these works as the expressions of a madman, in reality, Goya was not insane. When he first moved into La Quinta del Sordo, he did not intend to decorate the rooms himself. He tended the 20-acre estate, and he enlarged and renovated the house. It was only after suffering his almost fatal illness that he began producing his visions in paint, pen and print.

FLEEING MADRID

While Goya was producing his dark, menacing visions, Spain was moving closer to civil war. In 1822, liberal politicians and army officers arrested the King. In 1823, he was freed by royalist French troops and once again, purged Spain of the liberals he hated. As in 1814, thousands fled Spain to escape persecution.

On 5 May 1821, Napoleon died on the island of St Helena, and on 13 October 1822, the sculptor Canova died in Venice. In hindsight, Neoclassicism seemed to die with them. Despite the havoc wreaked by Napoleon's desires, without him, Europe seemed to be disoriented, with various despotic rulers fighting against liberalism.

In Spain, the newly freed King Ferdinand conducted his persecution of liberals with even greater intensity than before. At 39 years old, he was likely to remain on the throne for many more years. Goya was extremely concerned. On 17 September 1823, when he was 77 years old, he gifted La Quinta del Sordo to his 17-year-old grandson Mariano, saying it was 'because of the affection I bear him', and, despite his infirmities, made plans to leave his beloved Spain.

PLANNING HIS ESCAPE

Goya's continual concern about money remained however. Formally, he was still First Painter to the King and in receipt of a salary of 50,000 reales. Any prolonged absence from Court without official leave would deprive him of this. In addition, he was a proud man and did not want to escape in secret as if in disgrace. Not so long ago he had been an influential and celebrated artist; perceived as the greatest in Spain, if not Europe, and friends with the most powerful figures in the land. The opinions he expressed through his art were either brave or foolish, but in person he had always maintained a discreet presence. Leocadia, on the other hand was not so circumspect and had become known for her outspoken, anti-absolutist political views. Her eldest son Guillermo was a member of the voluntary militia in Madrid and had to seek refuge in France, while documents from the time state that 'in 1823,

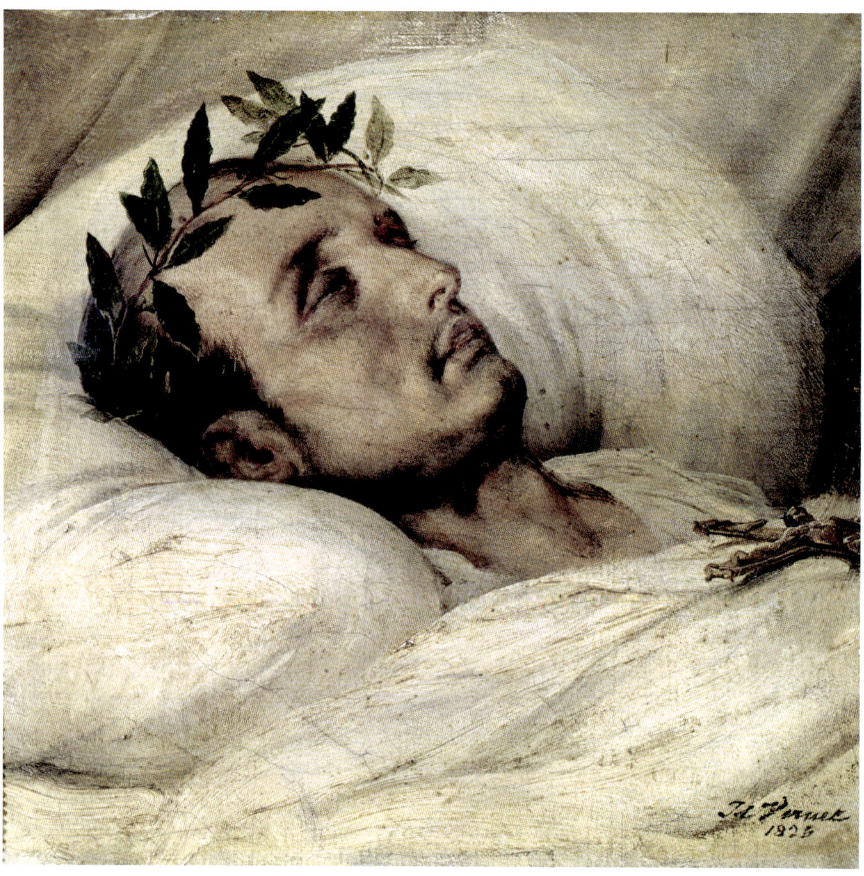

Above: Napoleon on his Deathbed, May 1821, *Horace Vernet, 1826 – as Napoleon died, Goya was busy painting in Spain and his country crept closer to civil war.*

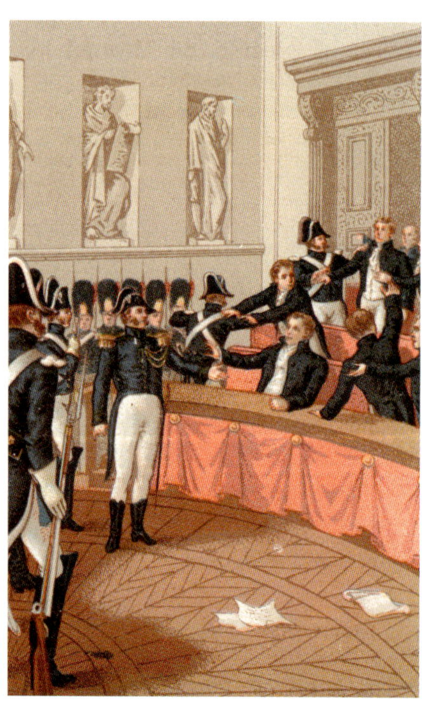

Right: The Expulsion of Manuel, March 1823. *Jacques-Antoine Manuel was a misunderstood French politician. As things became dark for him in France, Goya was executing his dark paintings in Spain.*

[Leocadia Weiss] was forced to seek asylum in France to escape the persecution to which she was subjected on account of her political opinions.'

For the first three months of 1824, Goya moved into the house of his friend José Duaso y Latre (c.1775– 1849), a Jesuit priest, who hid several liberals in his home in Madrid. Goya repaid José by painting his portrait, and

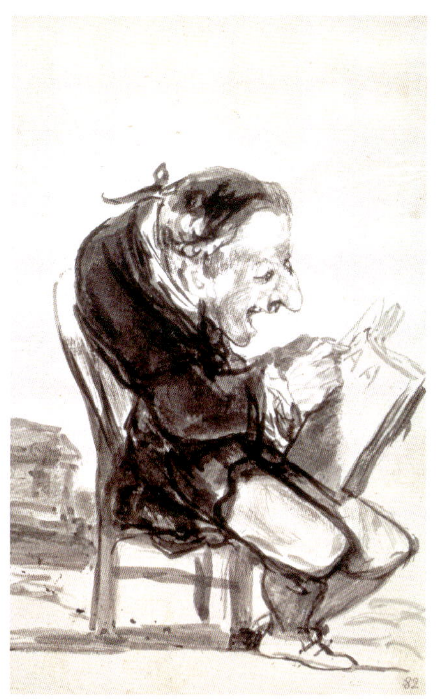

Above: One of nine drawings of comic visions by Goya, all apparently seen by him in the course of a single night.

a drawing of his nephew. In signing the works, he added his age; 78 by then. It was no time for a man of his age to be changing his life so drastically, but the situation in Spain was untenable. Many were having to escape secretly, or risk being arrested for their views. On 1 May 1824 however, negotiations between Ferdinand and the Russian ambassador meant that an amnesty was proclaimed, and anyone wanting to leave Spain could do so legally. But no one trusted the King and knew he could change his mind just as quickly.

DOCTOR'S ORDERS

So on 2 May 1824, Goya applied for six months' leave of absence, in order to 'take the mineral waters at Plombières to alleviate the sufferings and infirmities that were such a burden' to him. He said

Below: A celebration of the moment King Ferdinand returned to Madrid with his wife on 13 November 1823 by Jose Aparicio.

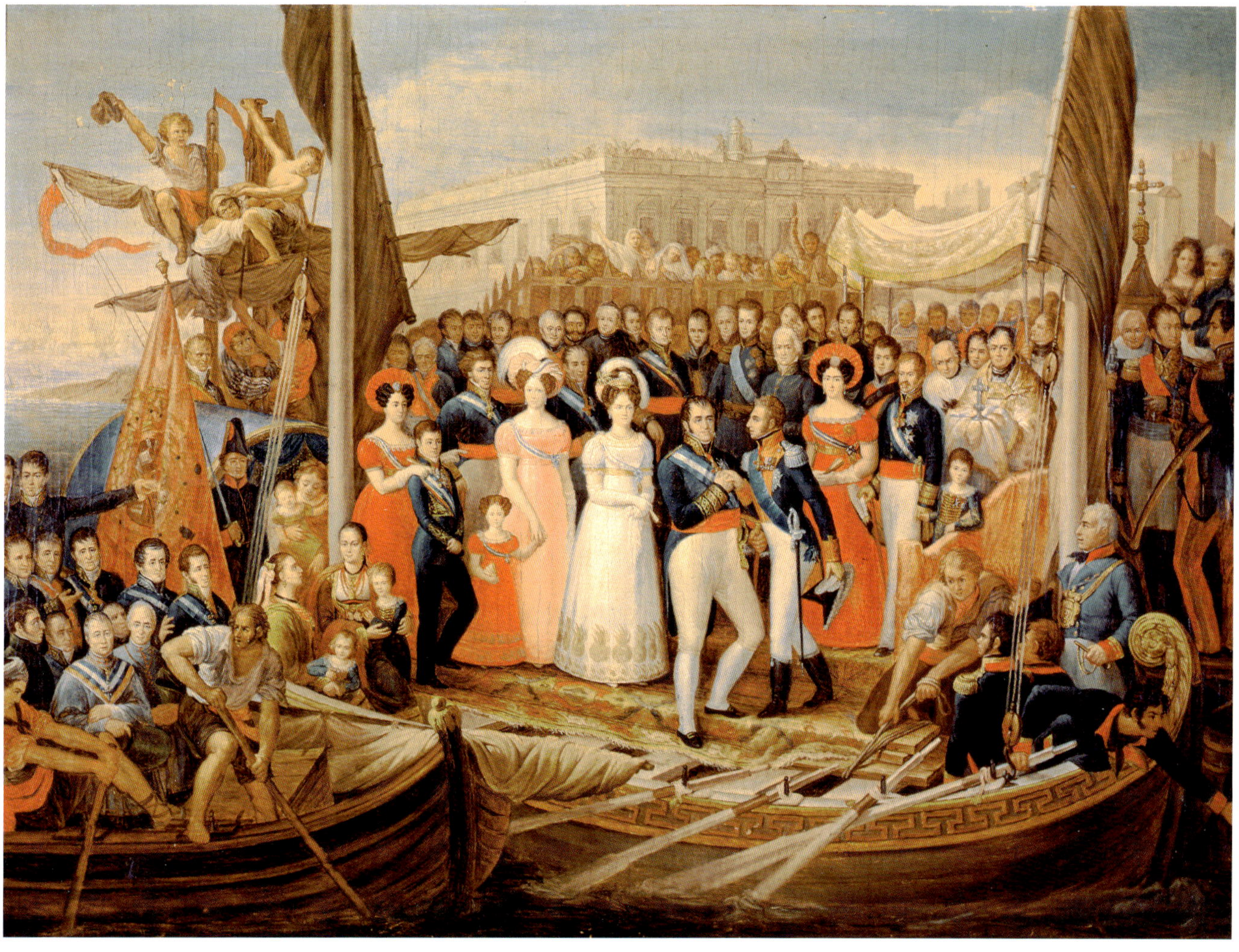

DECEIVING SERENITY

Before leaving Madrid, Goya executed one of his most remarkable portraits. During a time of great anxiety, he painted an extremely calm and serene portrait of – it is believed – Doña María Martínez de Puga, the wife of Antonio de Puga, who was witness to the power-of-attorney that ensured Goya continued to receive his Court Painter's salary when away from Spain. The portrait is strikingly modern and composed, belying the disquiet that Goya must have felt.

his request was based on his doctor's advice. The King indicated his surprise at the request, but nonetheless, on 30 May, gave his authorization. Goya never went to Plombières. Instead, he headed for Paris via Bordeaux.

BORDEAUX

On reaching France, Goya stopped for three days in Bordeaux to visit friends, particularly the dramatist Leandro Fernández de Moratín (1760–1828) and the writer and lawyer Manuel Silvela y García de Aragón (1781–1832), who were both afrancesados in exile. They affectionately nicknamed Goya the 'young traveller'.

Continuing on to Paris, Goya was welcomed by a cousin of his daughter-in-law, Jerónimo Goichoechea, with whom he stayed at 5 rue Marivaux in the Hôtel Favart.

Goya remained in Paris for two months, from June to August 1824. As he was deaf and only spoke a few words of clumsy French, the authorities reported that he posed no threat. As a well-known and respected artist, there were many French nationals and Spanish émigrés already living there who wanted to meet him. The authorities reported that he visited 'the monuments and public places'.

OTHER ARTISTS' WORK

Although he was used to seeing the work of great masters in the Spanish royal collection, Goya was probably keen to see the work of David, Vernet, Fragonard, Ingres, Delacroix and Géricault at the Louvre. Delacroix and Géricault in particular had been heavily influenced by prints of his work, but he did not meet either of them. Géricault had died just before his arrival, and he was never introduced to Delacroix. He probably never knew of Delacroix's copies of his *Los Caprichos*, that were in Paris, owned by the Guillemardet family. Delacroix had said that he 'dreamed of making caricatures in the manner of Goya.' Ferdinand Guillemardet (1769–1809) had been ambassador to Spain from 1798 to 1800 and Goya had painted his portrait (see page 185), but as he was no longer alive, Goya had no connection with his family.

While in Paris, Goya probably also saw the grand Salon exhibition featuring paintings by John Constable (1776–1837) that were creating a sensation there that summer. It is not known whether he ever met some of the French Romantic writers or artists who were creating such dark and passionate works that seem to start from a similar base as his own menacing works.

Many of the Spanish exiles in Paris either knew Goya already or were keen to meet him. After years of seclusion and loss of royal regard, it must have been extremely gratifying for him to be welcomed as a man of eminence once more. The émigrés he mixed with there included other once important Spanish individuals, such as the Duke of San Carlos, the Marquesa de Pontejos, Joaquín María Ferrer (see page 92) and González Arnao. Some commissioned him, and he also studied the relatively new technique of lithography.

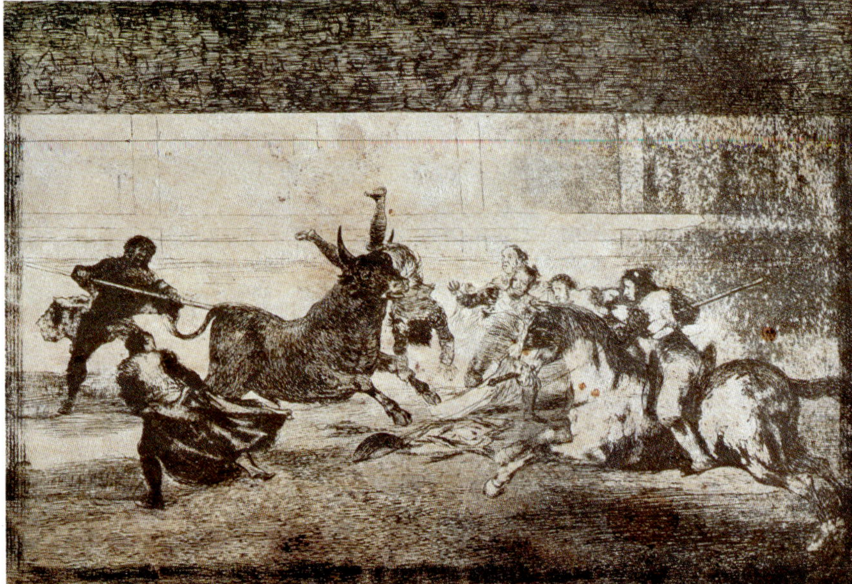

Above left: The Bulls of Bordeaux, *1825: at the age of 79, Goya mastered a new skill of lithography.*

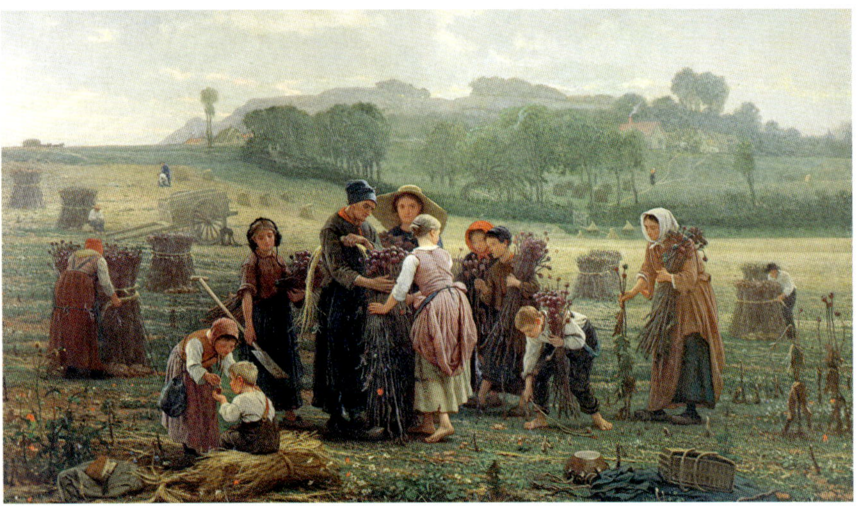

Left: Harvesting Poppies in Picardy, *Desire François Laugee (1823–96), 1860 – Goya's work in Bordeaux helped to inspire the Realism of the later 19th century.*

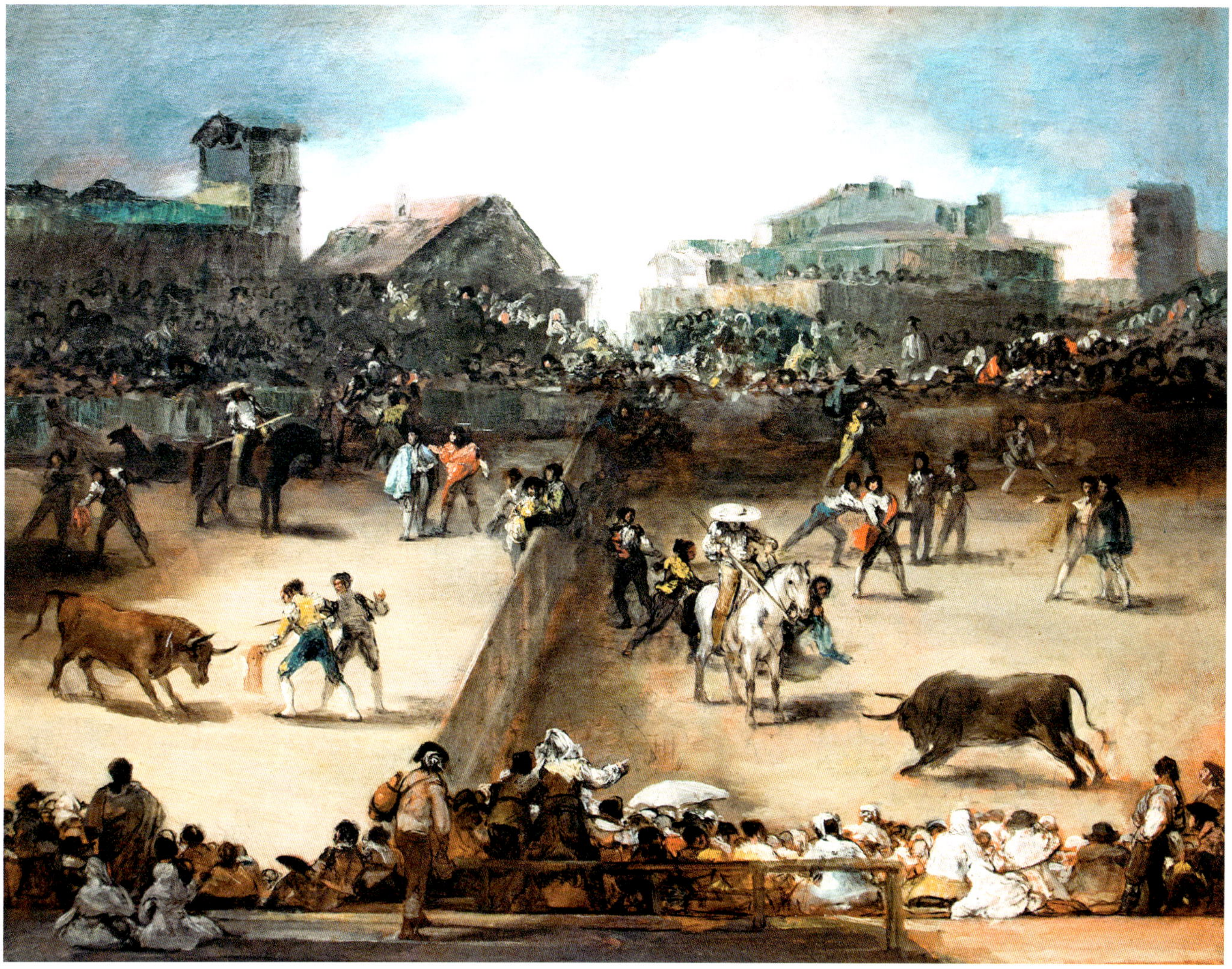

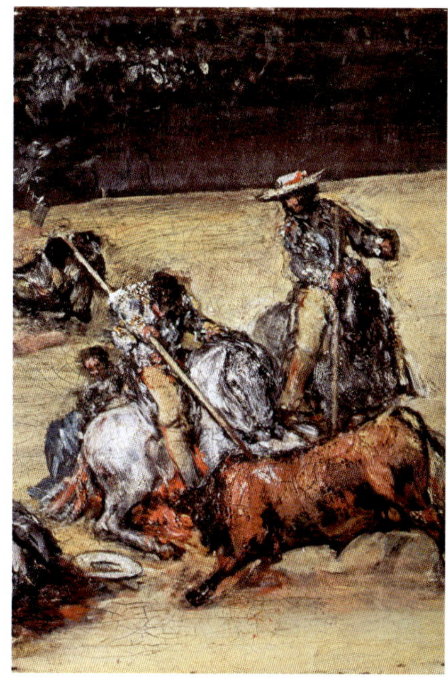

A SECOND FAMILY

In September 1824, Goya left Paris and returned to the vibrant city of Bordeaux, accompanied by his daughter-in-law's father and sister, Don Martín Miguel de Goicoechea and Manuela, and Manuela's husband José Francisco Muguiro. He moved into a pleasant house at 24 Cours de Tourny, where a few days later, Leocadia and her

WEAKENING EYESIGHT

By the 1820s, Goya's eyesight was so bad that as he worked, he wore three pairs of wire-framed spectacles, one on top of the other. Yet by the time he moved to Bordeaux in the autumn of 1824, his work became even more detailed and delicate. Once there, he began producing finely detailed prints and miniatures on ivory and marble.

Above: Bullfight in a Divided Ring, *1825 – bullfighting themes inspired Goya once more while in Bordeaux.*

daughter Rosario joined him. Her son Guillermo also moved in with them soon after that. When interrogated by the authorities in Bayonne a few days before her arrival, Leocadia had said that she was going to Bordeaux 'to join her husband'. Yet Don Isidoro Weiss was still living in Madrid at the time and never went to France. Whatever their relationship, Goya, Leocadia and her children lived together in Bordeaux ostensibly as a family.

A thriving community of Spanish refugees lived in Bordeaux, comprising bankers, lawyers, politicians, aristocrats, writers and businessmen, and their main meeting place was a chocolatier owned by Braulio Poc, a former Spanish landowner who was now a prosperous merchant.

Below: Bullfight and Picadors *(detail), Goya's workshop, after 1825. The thick impasto paint and sketchy brushwork are expressive, and follow Goya's avant-garde style.*

SELF-IMPOSED EXILE

Comfortable in Bordeaux, Goya carried on working, surrounded by many more friends than he had been in recent years in Spain. Meeting these expatriates regularly, his mood lightened. For now, the threat of the Spanish Inquisition was lifted, he had become proficient at lip-reading, and his ready humour returned.

At Poc's café on Rue de la Petite Taupe, (now Rue de la Huguerie), Goya met the other Spanish exiles practically every day. Many shared the same political creed as Goya, and similar roots. They often sat sipping Poc's mugs of thick, dark chocolate and discussed the news from Spain, along with their memories and other stories of the past. Goya had known Moratín since he used to socialize with the Duke and Duchess of Osuna, and had first painted his portrait in 1799 (see page 187). Toward the end of 1824, he made another portrait of his good friend. Other compatriots included: Silvela, Leocadia, Don Juan Bautista de Muguiro (see page 252), José Pío de Molina, Don José Miguel de Azanza, José de Carnerero, Antonio de Brugada and Marqués de San Adrián. Goya painted portraits of a number of them.

A NEW CREATIVE PHASE

When Goya's six-month permit to remain in France was about to expire, he sent a letter to King Ferdinand requesting a further six months absence, in order to take the healing waters at Bagnères in the Pyrenees. Although it was known that he had not gone to Plombières, the Spanish authorities granted him permission to remain in France for longer, which meant that he would continue to receive his Court Painter's salary. This was always an anxiety for Goya, while Javier, still in Spain, wrote to his father for further reassurance that he would not lose his inheritance to Leocadia. Goya wrote back to tell Javier that he need not worry.

Then, with astonishingly youthful energy, he began developing a new technique in lithography and in painting miniatures. At a time when most artists' production would have slowed down or ceased, Goya entered another creative phase. He mastered the difficult printing process of lithography, and he invented an original method of painting miniatures, describing his approach as being 'more like the brushwork of Velázquez than Mengs.'

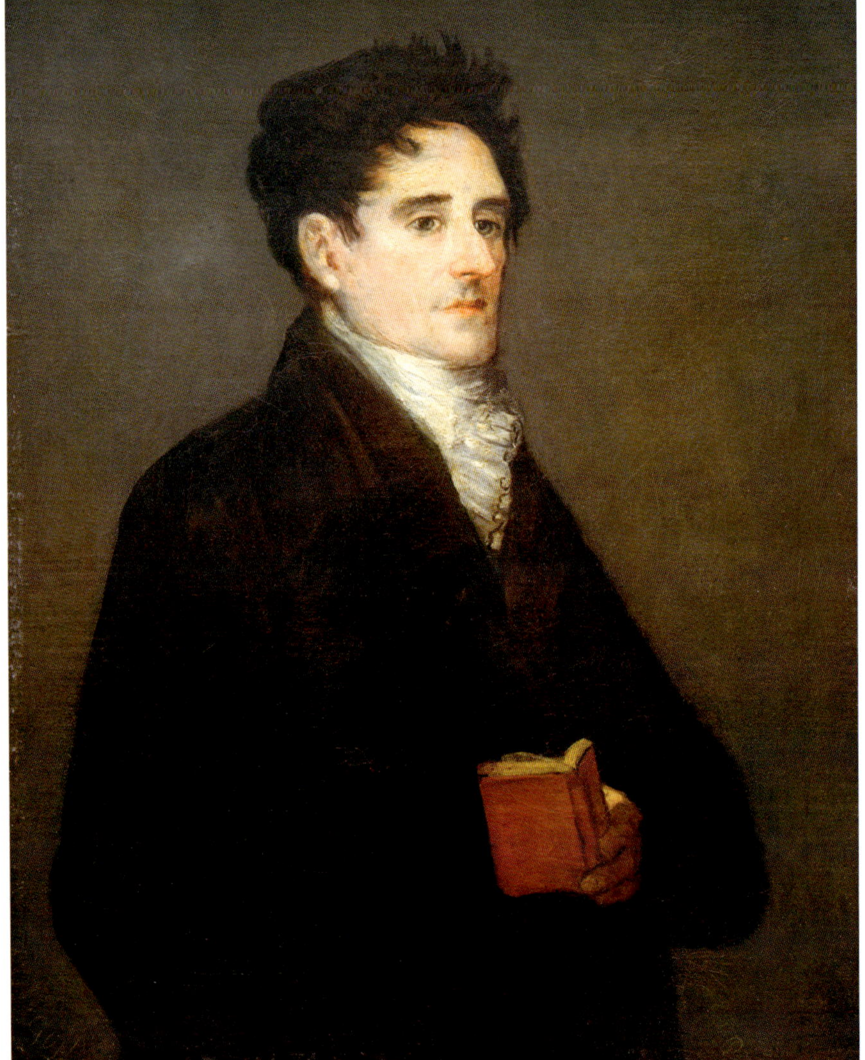

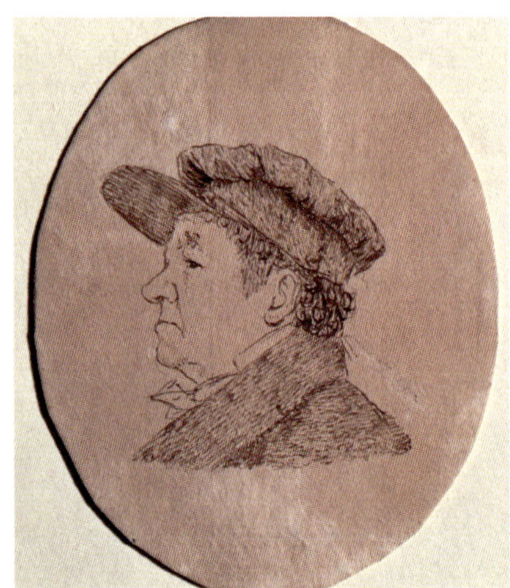

Above: Self-portrait, 1824 — in ink on paper, this small profile self-portrait lacks the bravado of some of his earlier self-portraits.

Left: Joaquín María Ferrer, Goya, 1824 — one of Goya's Spanish friends who lived in exile in Paris.

LITHOGRAPHY

There has often been speculation about the purpose of Goya's stay in Paris; many believe it was to learn the relatively new method of lithography that had been invented in 1796 by Alois Senefelder (1771–1834). Lithography uses simple chemical processes to create a printed image, although during the first years of the 19th century, mainly because of technical difficulties, it had limited scope. But during the 1820s it began to be used by artists such as Delacroix and Géricault. Goya had links with many other Paris-based artists who were beginning to work with lithography, and also in 1924 for the first time, the official Salon devoted a special section to the technique. The lithographs he subsequently produced in Bordeaux are some of the finest ever made.

EXPRESSIVE AND EXUBERANT

Goya's life with Leocadia was explosive. With her hot temper and strong opinions, their rows were often mentioned by Moratín. But Goya's relationship with Rosario was far gentler. He doted on the little girl and although he was not known for bestowing compliments on others, he boasted of her artistic precocity to his friends. Once she and her mother had moved into the house in Bordeaux, he resumed the art lessons he had been giving her in Spain, drawing countless little sketches for her to copy, which for a time after his death generated confusion when some of her poorly drawn copies were found with Goya's skilful originals.

At 80 years old, with failing eyesight, Goya's hand had become more assured than ever. He produced pages of expressive drawings, featuring real and imaginary figures; numerous perfect lithographs; several exuberant miniatures and some masterly paintings, including *The Milkmaid of Bordeaux*. Everything he did appeared to have come from the steady hand of a confident young artist, rather than from a deaf, myopic and increasingly frail elderly man.

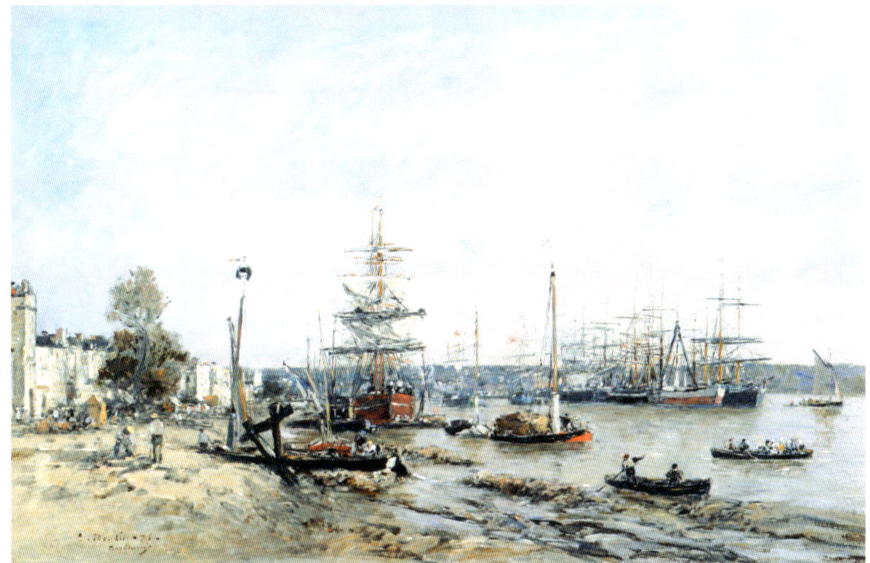

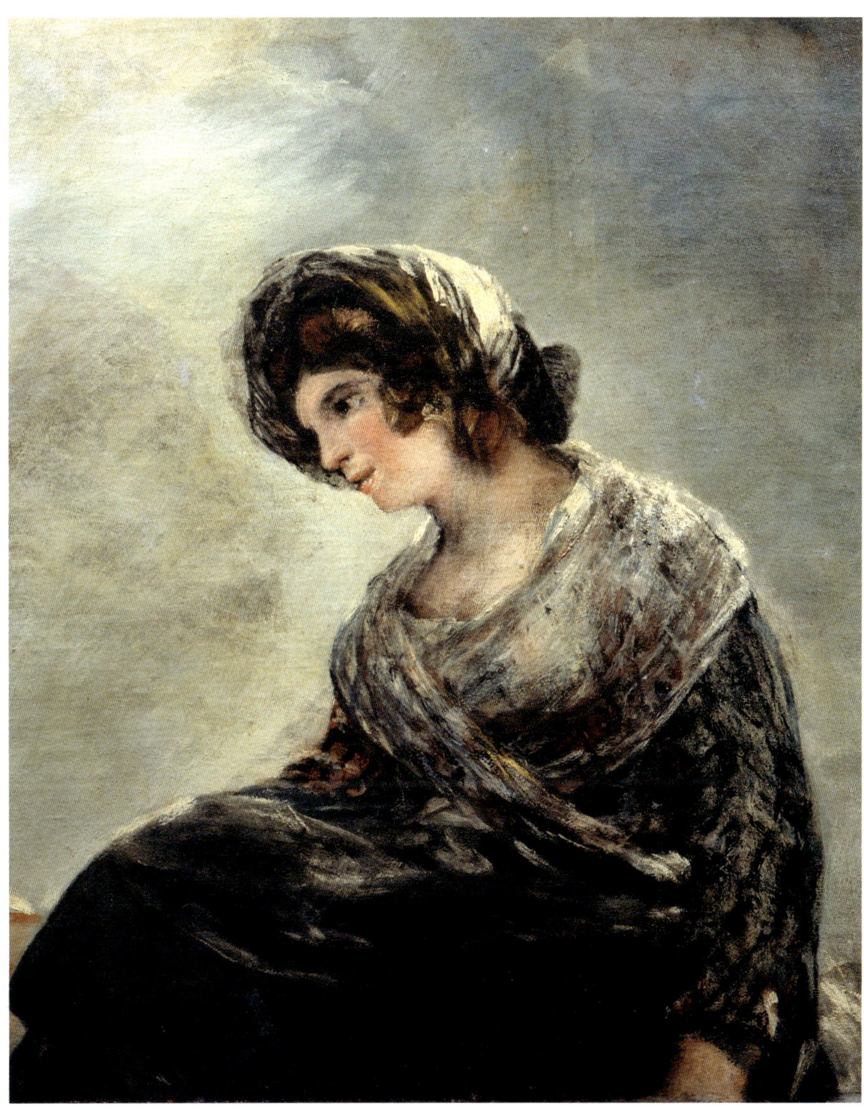

Top: A view of the bustling port of Bordeaux where Goya lived. Bordeaux; Quay and Port, Eugène Boudin (1824–98), 1874.

Above: Detail of The Milkmaid of Bordeaux *(see page 253), c.1826 – this late work demonstrates Goya's supremely confident handling, even so late in life.*

CHALLENGING TIMES

At the end of 1825, Goya wrote to his friend Joaquin María Ferrer in Paris: 'I sent you a lithographic proof that shows a fight with young bulls…I have now made three more bullfight subjects of the same size.' Earlier that year, Goya had once again been extremely ill.

This was not a recurrence of his old illness. Doctors diagnosed paralysis of the bladder and a large tumour on a bone at the top of one of his legs, which at his age was regarded as incurable. As always, he determined to carry on. On his behalf, Javier asked the Spanish authorities if his father could extend his leave of absence for another year, so he could be cared for in France. After considering a report that gave little hope for Goya's survival, on 4 July 1825, Ferdinand gave his consent.

ORIGINAL METHODS

Despite the pain he was in and the knowledge that he would not live long, Goya began working intently on his lithographs. Those he referred to in his letter to Ferrer became known collectively as *The Bulls of Bordeaux* (see page 90) and those and other lithographs he made in Bordeaux were among the first masterpieces in the medium. He mastered the techniques

Below: Portrait of Gaulon, 1824–5 – *Goya's lithographic portrait of the man who taught him his new skills.*

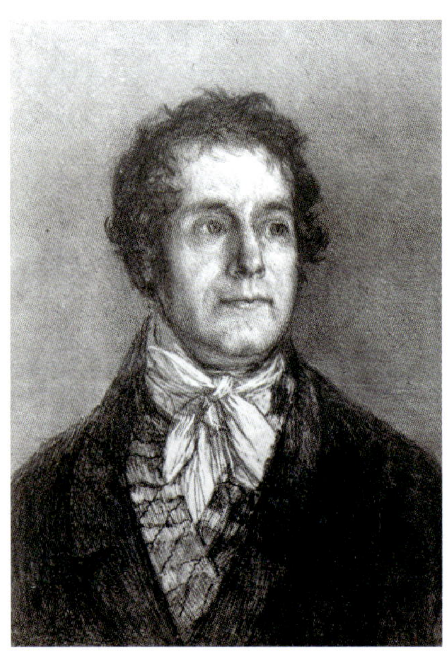

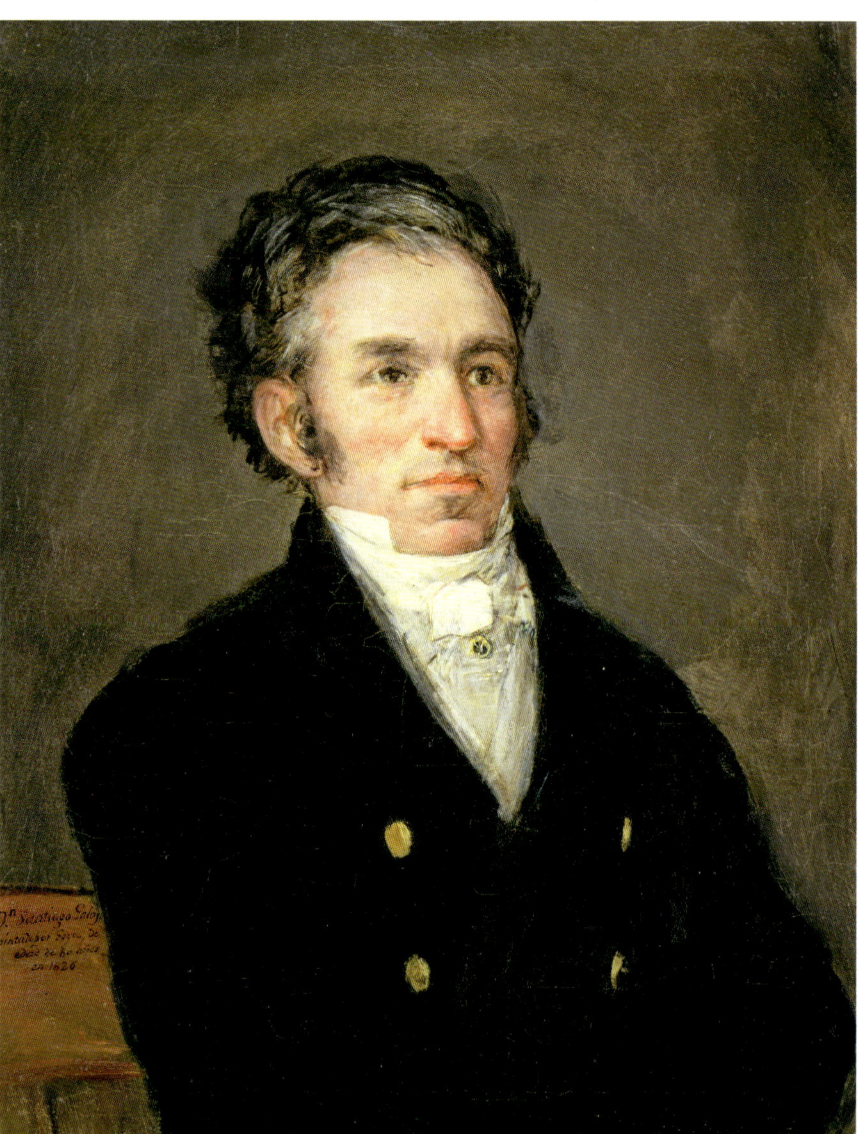

Above: Dr Galos, c.1826 – *with a limited palette and loose brushwork, Goya's hand retained its assurance in spite of his advancing years.*

rapidly and also evolved his own personal methods. Lithography is based on the principal that oil and water do not mix, and the basic tools – originally – were limestone or a metal plate, an image drawn with a greasy crayon, next treated with a mixture of acid and gum arabic, and then with water. Goya used the crayons, stone, a razor and a scraper to achieve highly original effects. One of his young admirers, the painter Antonio Brugada (1804–63) who had escaped political persecution in Spain since 1823, later described Goya's methods:

'[Goya] worked at his lithographs on the easel, the stone placed like a canvas. He manipulated his crayons like brushes and never sharpened them. He remained standing, walking backwards and forwards every other minute to judge his effects. Usually he covered the whole stone with

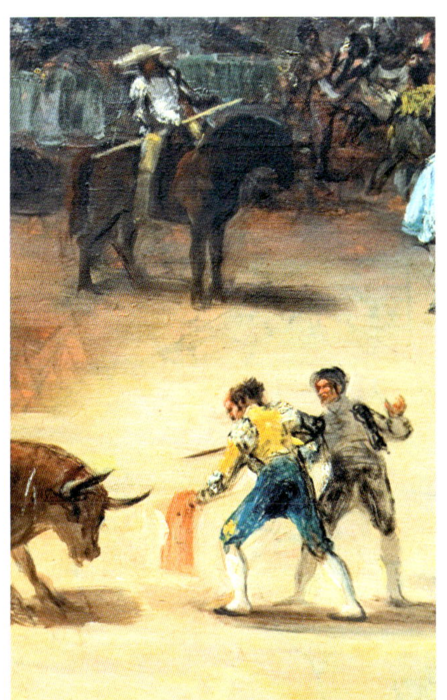

Above: Bullfight in a Divided Ring *(detail, see page 91), 1825 – the colour and energy of the scene is encapsulated in this small detail.*

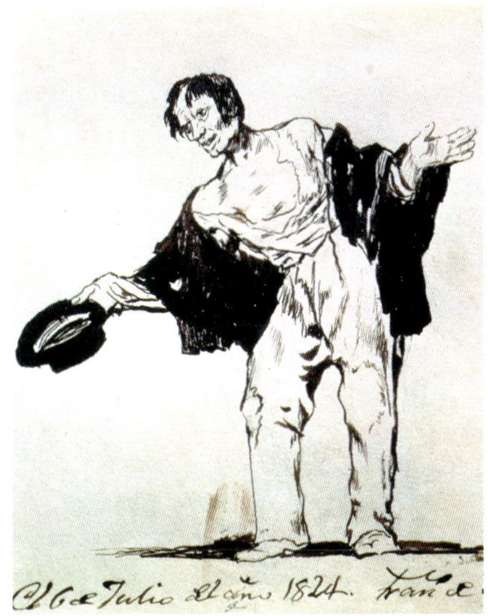

Right: Beggar Holding Out his Hat, *1824 – made in Paris, this was one of Goya's first experiments in painting on china in pen and ink.*

CONTINUING EXPERIMENTATION

Traditionally, miniatures were painted in a precise technique, but Goya painted his with more freedom. Even though he painted them with the tip of a brush, they are not detailed and can be understood better when seen from a distance. He began each picture by covering his tiny ivory plaque with a dark wash of paint and then dropped water into it, so it blotted and granulated. He then pushed the paint around with a dry brush, creating impressions of tone and texture. Although he was always concerned about money, he did not make these works specifically to sell them, so continued experimenting, trying out new methods and working in ways he

could manage. In the autumn of 1825 he rented a house on the rue de la Croix-Blanche. It had good light and a garden that Rosario loved. Early the following year, when he was 80 years old, he made up his mind to travel the 900km (559 miles) back to Madrid.

a uniform grey tone and then removed with a scraper those parts which were to appear light: here a head, a figure; there a horse, a bull. Next the crayon was again employed to strengthen the shadows, the accents, or to indicate the figures and give them movement... You would perhaps laugh if I said that all Goya's lithographs were executed under a magnifying glass. In fact, it was not in order to do very detailed work, but because his eyesight was failing.'

The man who helped Goya to achieve technical mastery in lithography and printed the first edition of *The Bulls of Bordeaux*, was the printer Cyprien Charles Marie Nicolas Gaulon. At the end of 1825, Gaulon registered an edition of 100 copies of Goya's four lithographs, which he described as *Bullfights*. Goya also made a lithographic portrait of Gaulon. Although he did not completely abandon etching, few plates are known from this time; as the etching technique was far more fiddly than lithography.

Below: Figures Climbing over a Reclining Giant, *c.1815–24 – red chalk and sanguine wash by Goya as a preparatory drawing for* The Disparates.

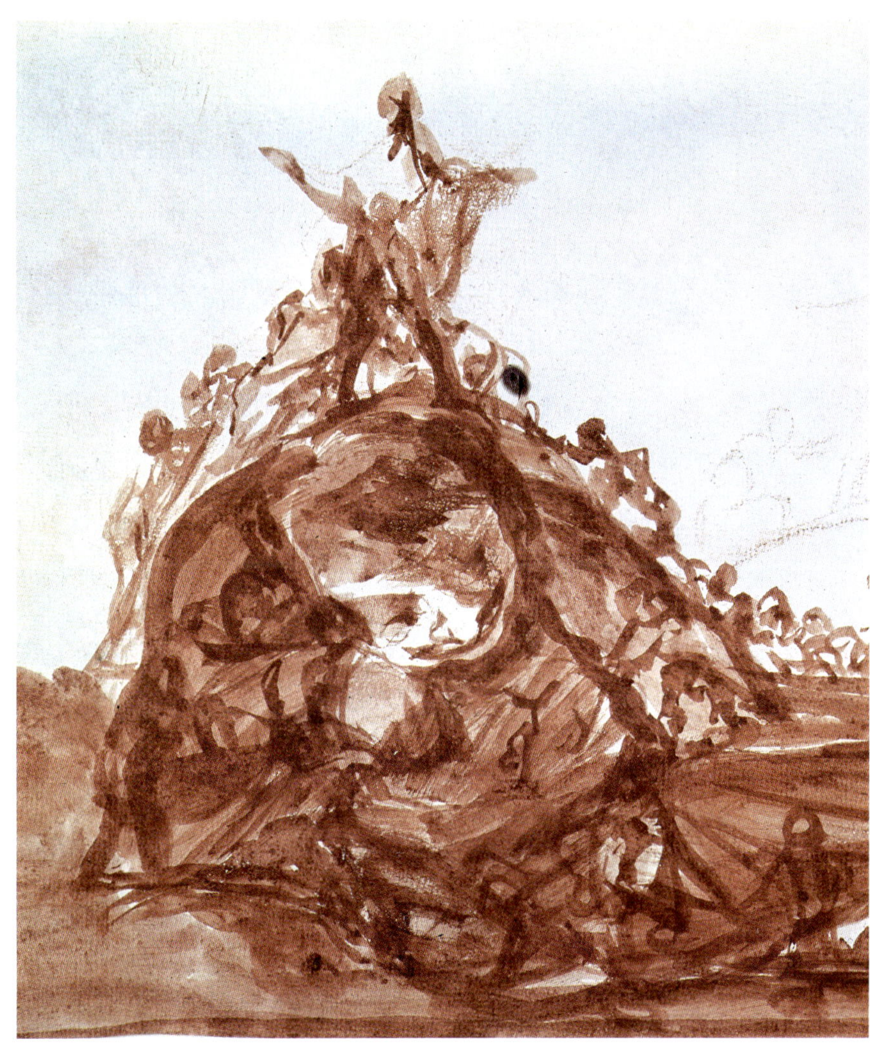

A GREAT AND TERRIFYING ARTIST

Despite his age and infirmities, Goya declared that he would cross the Pyrenees alone to reach Spain and sort out his affairs. At the end of April 1826, he left Bordeaux and reached Madrid on 30 May. It was the first time that he had entered the royal Court in six years.

At Court, Goya explained that he was now 80 years old and had worked for the Crown for 53 years, serving under three kings. He felt that he was due a retirement pension. One of Ferdinand's advisers, the Duke of Hijar, took up his cause, reminding the King that 'the artist has worked for a long time and with the utmost care, taste and intelligence on the numerous commissions he has been given. His artistic merit is so insurpassable that other artists and the general public all extol his work.' On 17 June 1826, the King agreed to give Goya a pension of 50,000 reales a year, and let him stay in France.

ENERGY AND RESOLVE

While Goya was in Madrid, Vicente López painted his portrait. Back in Bordeaux, he painted a portrait of the Spanish businessman Juan Bautista Muguiro (see page 252), a relation of his daughter-in-law who managed his affairs. Then remarkably considering his age, health and arduousness of travel, he returned to Madrid again in the summer of 1827. It is not clear why he returned again, but while there, he painted a portrait of Mariano. Back in Bordeaux, he, Leocadia, Rosario and Guillermo moved again, to a first-floor apartment, at 39 Fosses de l'Intendance, now Cours de l'Intendance, where he painted some more lively works, including *The Milkmaid of Bordeaux* (see page 93).

LAST DAYS

At the beginning of 1828, Goya transferred 45,000 francs into Mariano's name: a huge amount at the time. Then, in March, he suffered a stroke – and was found unconscious on the floor of his

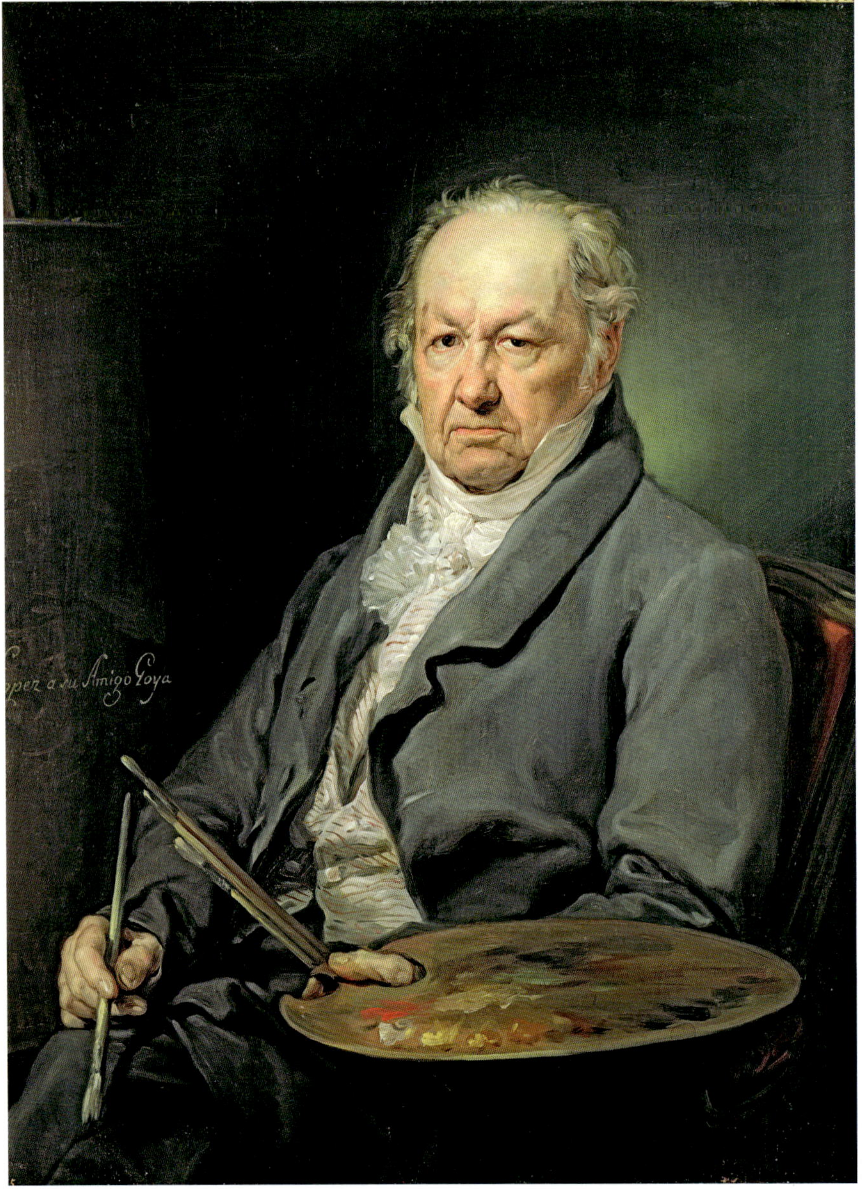

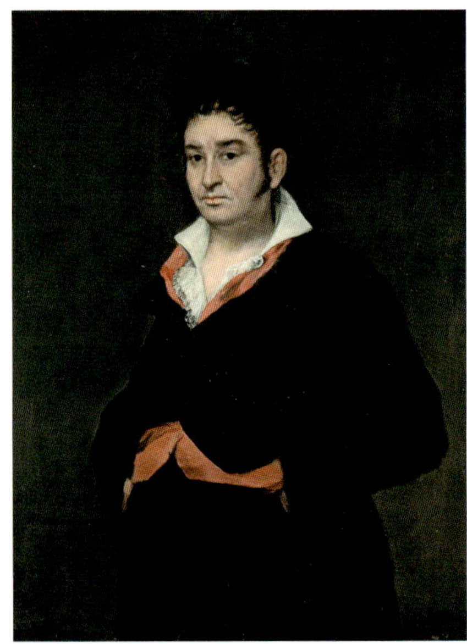

Above: Portrait of Don Ramon Satue – *painted when Goya was 77 in 1823, this is an expressive, but controlled work.*

Left: Portrait of Goya – *painted in Madrid in 1826 by the King's favourite artist Vicente López in his classical, academic style.*

GOYA'S WILL

In accordance with an irrevocable will Goya had made with Josefa in 1811, Javier inherited most of his father's estate. Mariano also received some, but Leocadia was left with nothing but some prints, drawings and *The Milkmaid of Bordeaux* (see page 253). Javier gave her just 1000 francs.

studio, still clutching his paintbrush. His daughter-in-law Gumersinda and Mariano arrived in Bordeaux on 28 March. On 1 April, he wrote to Javier: 'May God grant that I see you...then my happiness will be complete.'

But the next day he suffered another stroke, which left him paralyzed down his right side, and after 13 days, hovering between life and death, he died at 2 a.m. on 16 April 1828. Javier never came. At his bedside were Brugada and his friend and landlord José Pio de Molina. Leocadia was not with him, but later wrote: '...it was as if he just fell asleep and even the doctor was amazed at his courage and said that he did not suffer, but I am not sure about this.'

Goya was buried beside his old friend Martín Miguel de Goicoechea in Bordeaux. Among his pallbearers were Poc, Brugada and Molina. In 1901, his remains were transferred to Madrid, and finally, in 1919, they were taken to the hermitage of San Antonio de la Florida that he had decorated in 1798. When his remains were disinterred from France, his skull was missing and it has never been found.

AFTERMATH

Leocadia returned to Spain a couple of years after Goya's death, and died in poverty in 1856. Rosario worked as a professional copyist at the Museo Nacional del Prado, dying in 1843 at just 29. Javier soon sold his father's artworks and later, Mariano gambled away most of his inheritance.

Immediately after his death, Goya was recognized internationally as the 'father of modern art', and he has remained one of most influential artists ever since. He was also one of the finest printmakers in art history. In 1857, the poet Charles Baudelaire (1821–67) wrote: 'Goya often plunges into savagery or soars into comic brilliance. He is at all times a great artist and often a terrifying one.'

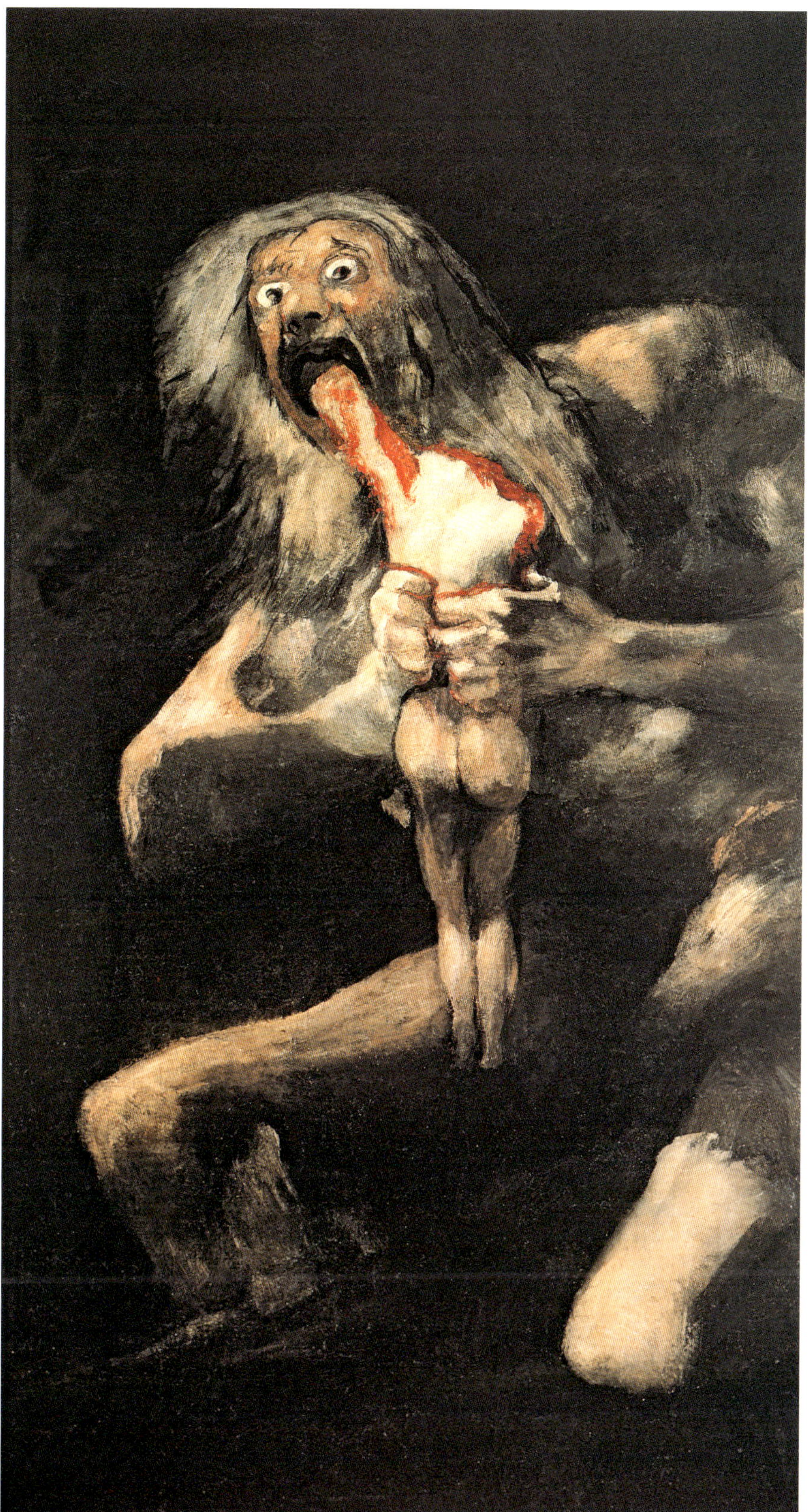

Above: Saturn Devouring One of his Children, *1820 — symbolizing Ferdinand's destruction of Spain, Goya's imagery was intentionally shocking. This depicts the myth that Saturn devoured his children, fearing he would be overthrown by them.*

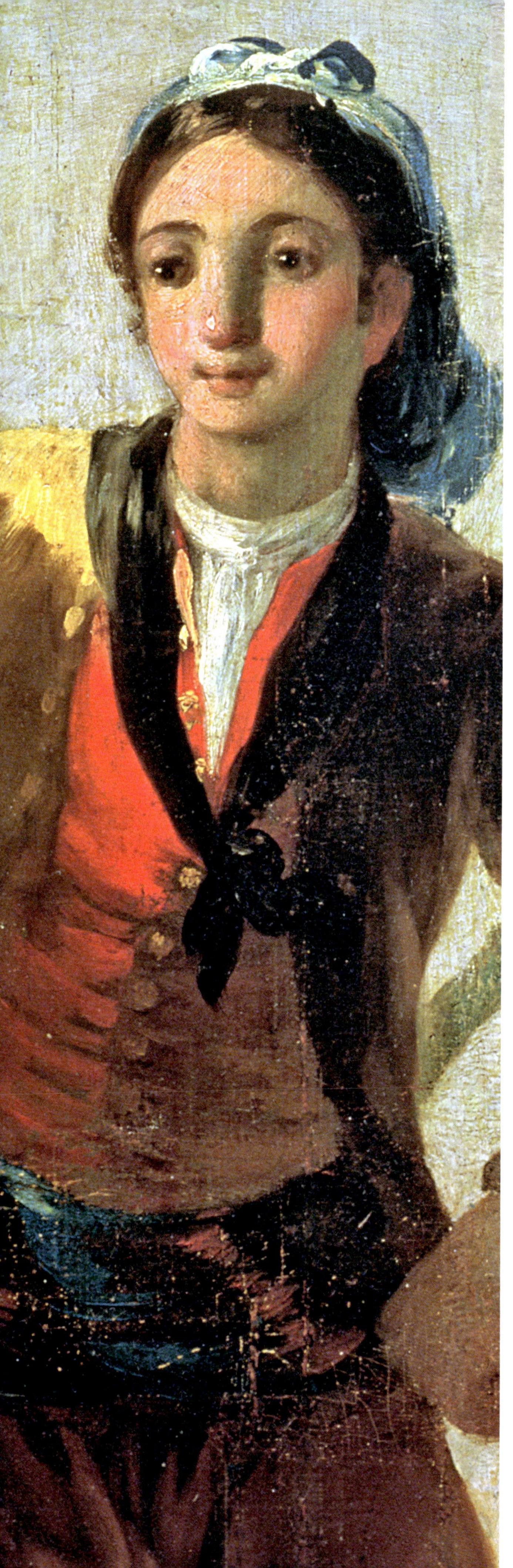

THE GALLERY

One of the most enigmatic artists in history, Francisco de Goya's lifetime spanned internal and external wars, and specifically in his own country, invasion and occupation, despotic monarchies and the Inquisition. These events were amplified by his personal sufferings, with his unexplained, almost fatal illness and subsequent deafness. As a result, his work became dramatic, often uncomfortable and scathingly satirical, while at the same time, ground-breaking and compelling. Unique and unlike any other artist before him, he was a complex figure and one of the first to express his own feelings in many of his works, that were frequently controversial and perilous to expose at that time. With no direct rival throughout his life, his work became courageous, innovative, and often difficult to comprehend. He also used many techniques and ideas that became highly influential, and subsequently, changed the landscape of art history.

Left: Detail from The Parasol *(see page 117), 1777, oil on linen, Museo Nacional del Prado, Madrid, Spain. Knowing that the tapestry that would be made from this cartoon was to hang over a door, Goya made the light and perspective extra dramatic to give it greater effect. This time was a period of intense productivity for him. He was in his late 20s and exceptionally ambitious.*

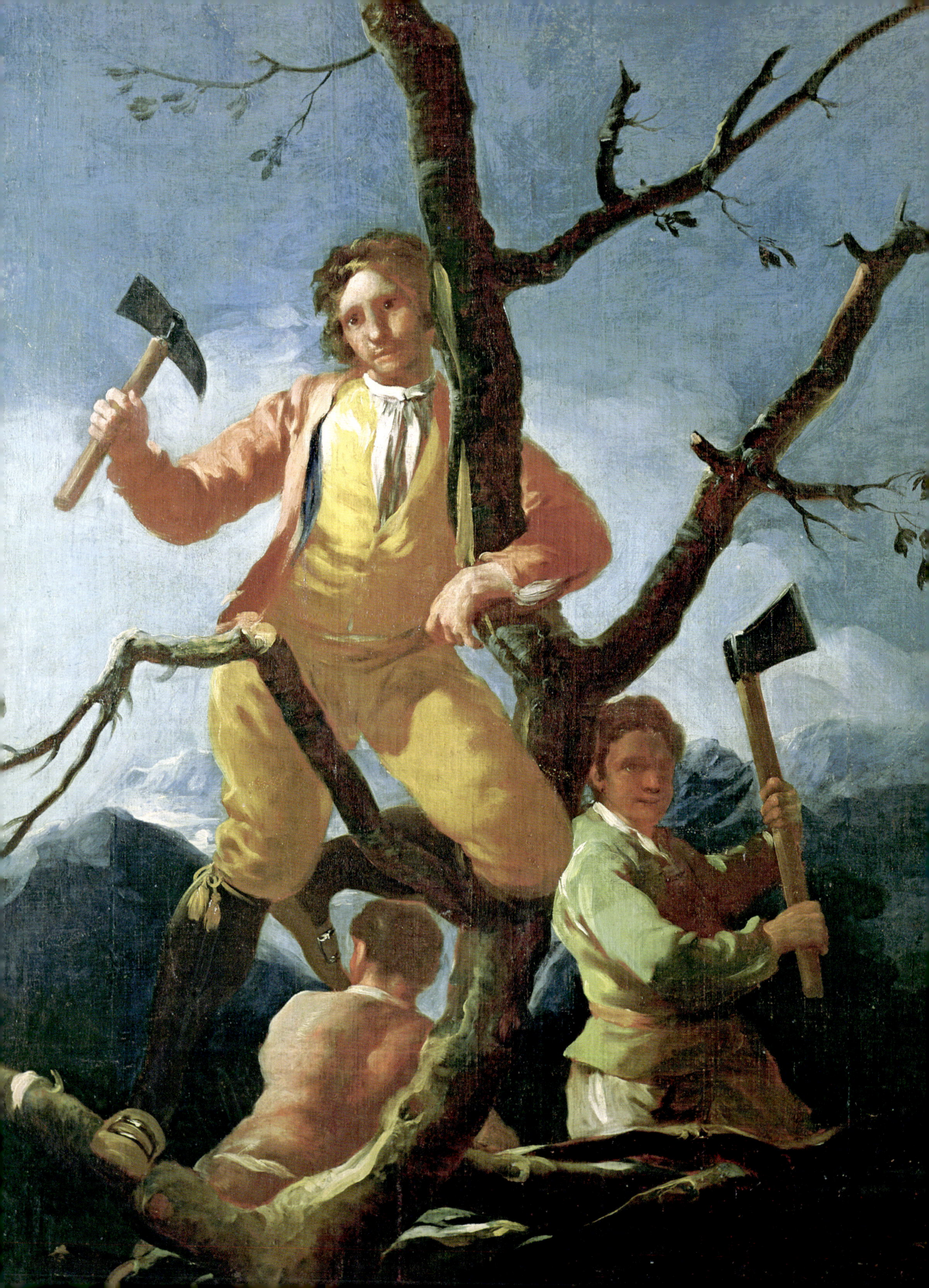

INSPIRATION AND IMITATION

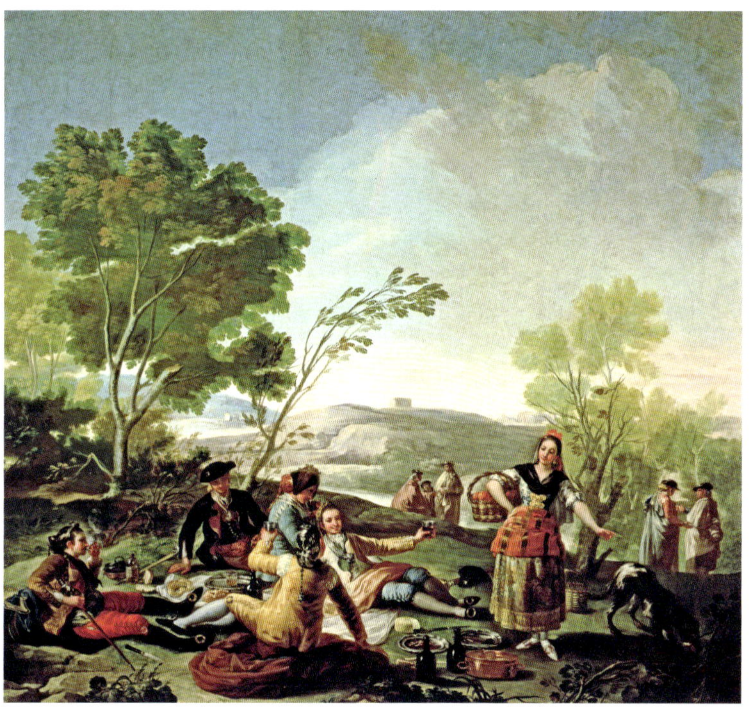

From a young age, Goya determined to rise in the Spanish hierarchy through his art. Influenced by Velázquez and Rembrandt as well as by nature, by the 1780s he had risen from humble beginnings to become Spain's leading painter. His first Courtly commissions were tapestry cartoons for the royal palaces. Knowing that his paintings were to be translated into coloured wools imposed restrictions on his designs, so most are fairly simple but full of impact. Meanwhile, his painting style was developing into complex compositions, with areas of impasto or glazing, and lively brushwork.

Above: Picnic on the Banks of the Manzanares, *1776, oil on canvas, 271 x 295cm (107 x 116in), Museo Nacional del Prado, Madrid, Spain. This cartoon was for a tapestry to hang in the Prince and Princess of the Asturias's dining room.*

Left: The Woodcutters, *1780, oil on canvas, 141 x 114cm (55½ x 45in), Museo Nacional del Prado, Madrid, Spain. This cartoon is in a spiral composition, depicting a group of three woodcutters, two holding axes to cut up a fallen tree.*

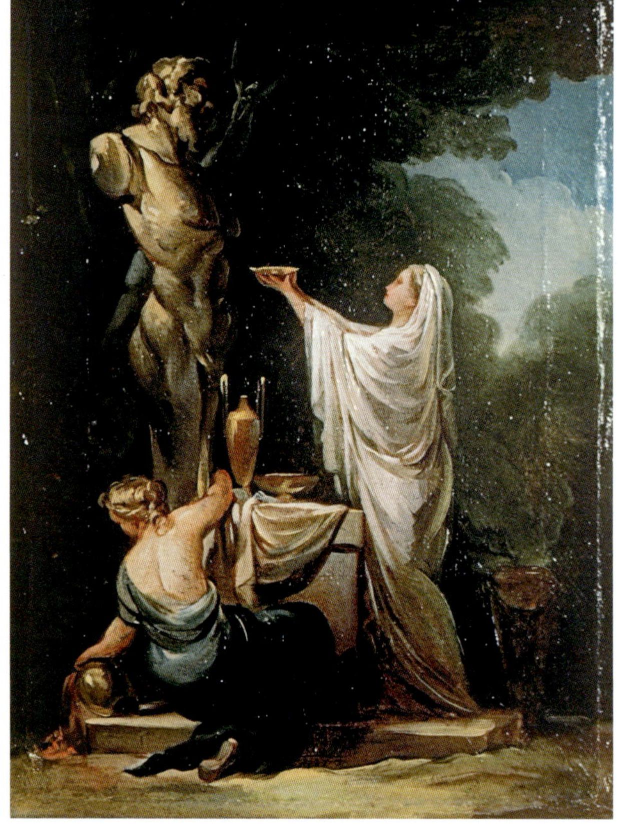

Sacrifice to Pan, c.1771,
oil on canvas, Private
Collection, 33 x 24cm
(13 x 9½in)

Goya rarely painted
mythological subjects, but
this little work and its
counterpart, *Sacrifice to Vesta*,
are believed to have been
painted by him while he was
in Rome in 1771. A young
woman in white holds up
a shallow golden bowl, its
contents taken from an urn
that has just been spilt
by another young woman.
The figures look classical
but are created with
unconventional sketchy
brushstrokes and strong
elements of chiaroscuro.

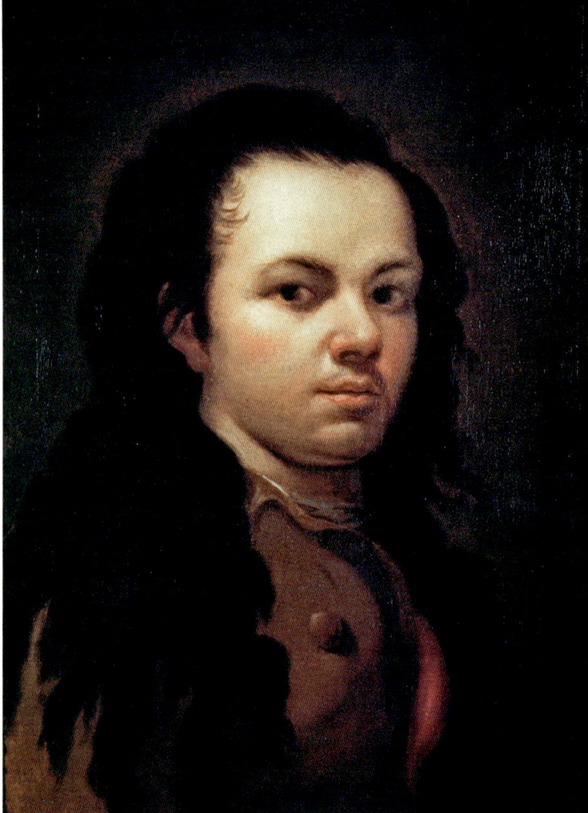

Self-portrait, c.1771–5, oil on
canvas, Marquis de Zurgena,
Madrid, Spain, 58 x 44cm
(23 x 17in)

Generally believed to be
Goya's first self-portrait, this
work was painted at around
the time of his marriage
to Josefa. The influence of
Mengs can be seen, and
Goya's personality can be
interpreted in numerous
ways: simultaneously he looks
arrogant, amicable, insecure,
serious, determined, cross
and thoughtful. It appears to
be the work of an artist on
the threshold of success.

Sacrifice to Vesta, 1771,
oil on canvas, Private
Collection, 33 x 24cm
(13 x 9½in)

Painted along with its partner,
Sacrifice to Pan, this canvas
was probably executed by
Goya while he was in Rome.
A priest and three maidens
celebrate the rite of fire
to invoke Vesta, the virgin
goddess of the hearth, home
and family in ancient Rome.
With a rather monumental,
classical composition, Goya
creates strong chiaroscuro,
clearly inspired by
Caravaggio, but his somewhat
sketchy brushstrokes and
predominantly cool palette
reveal a more contemporary,
ground-breaking approach.

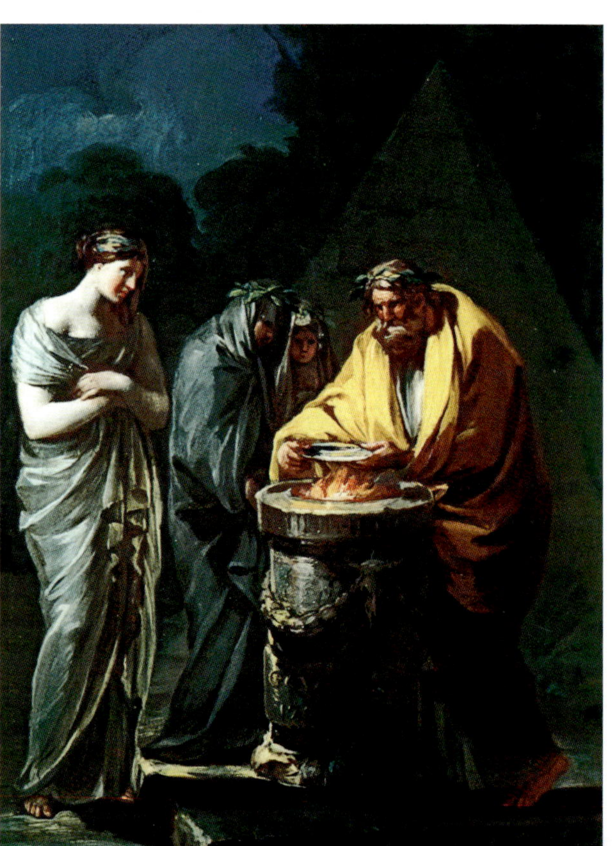

The Holy Family, c.1768–9, oil on canvas, Private Collection, Cádiz, Spain, 79 x 55cm (31 x 21½in)

In the decorative, graceful, and strongly lit Baroque style of Tiepolo, the 22-year-old Goya painted the Virgin Mary with Jesus as a toddler, surrounded by Joseph (holding his flowering staff), Saint Joachim and Saint Anne, plus angels and God himself, with the Holy Spirit above represented by a dove. The golden tones of the sky are a traditional way to symbolize the supernatural.

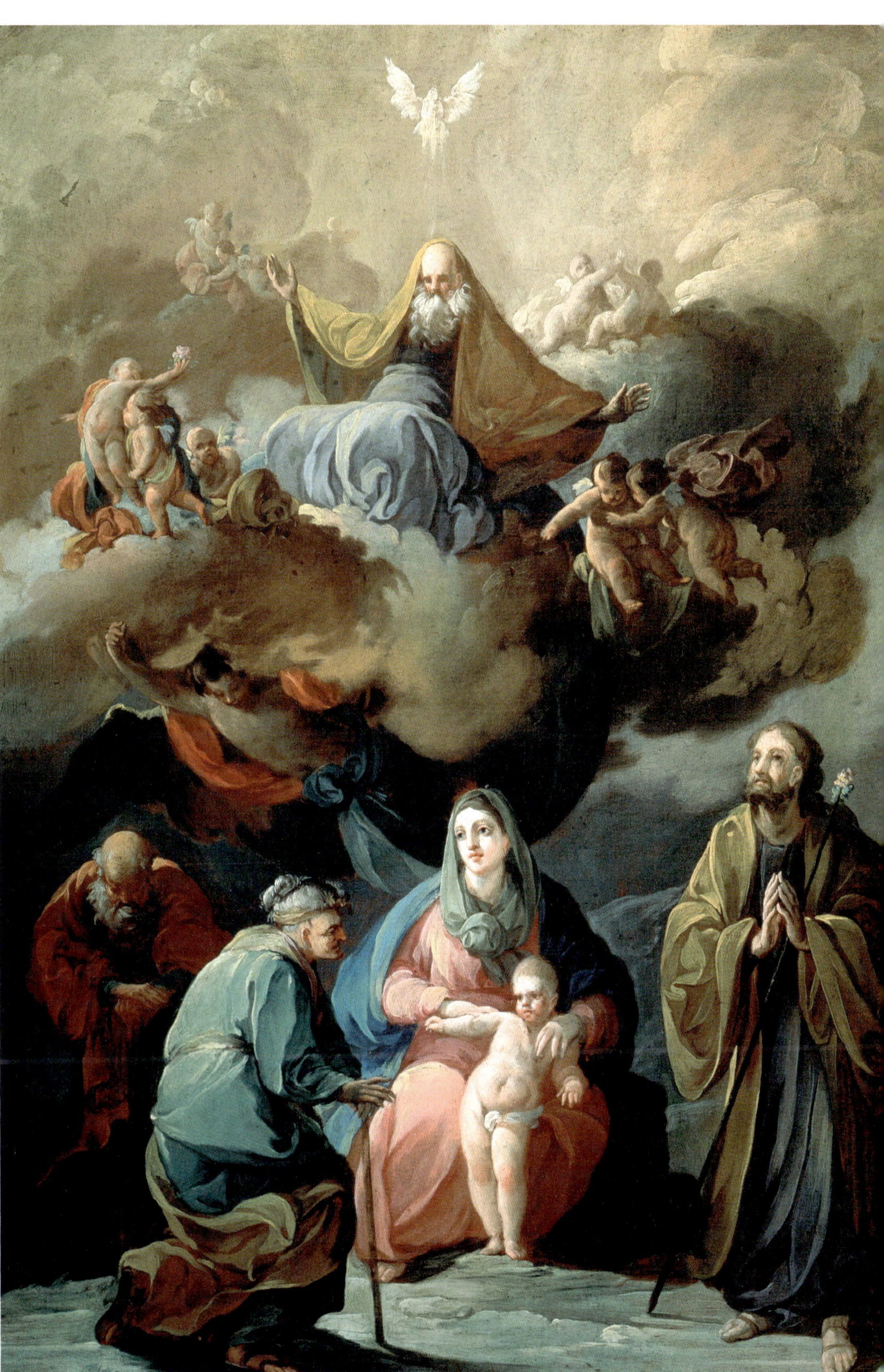

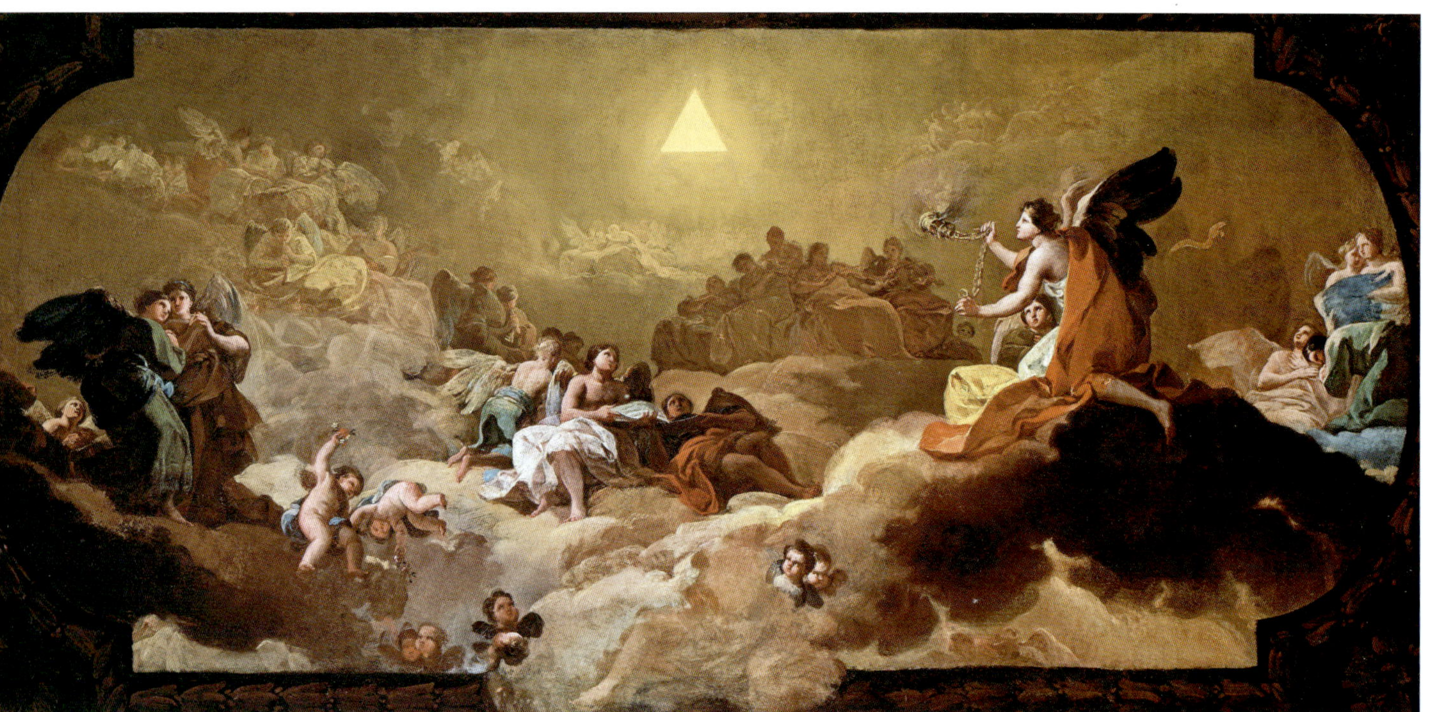

Adoration of the Name of God, 1772, ceiling fresco, Basilica del Pilar, Saragossa, Spain, 700 x 1500cm (280 x 590in)

Goya painted this fresco on the ceiling of a cupola in the cathedral of Nuestra Señora del Pilar in Saragossa in 1771. It was one of his first important commissions. With a helper to grind his pigments, he created this work to feature a strong sense of illumination and theatricality. The image conforms to the prevailing Baroque styles, although the broad brushstrokes hint of his future unique methods.

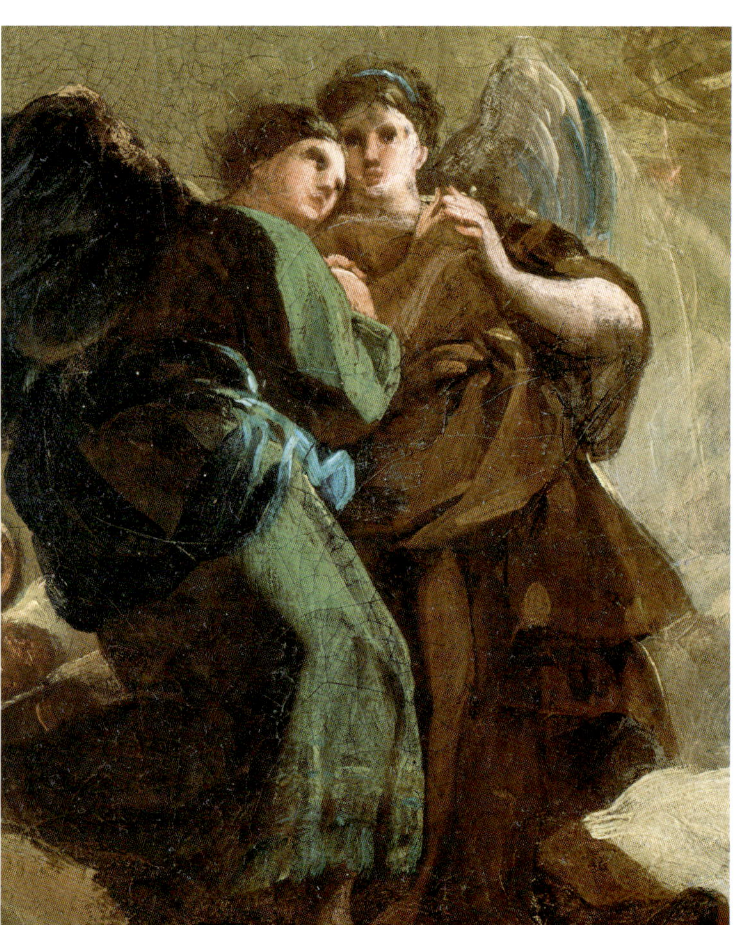

Detail from *Adoration of the Name of God* (above)

Two angels lean together on a cloud, listening to the celestial music that glorifies the Name of God. Although it has not worn well, and he did not earn as much for it as other artists were working in the same church at the time, this fresco helped to establish Goya as a painter of note, and one who could charge more for his paintings in the future.

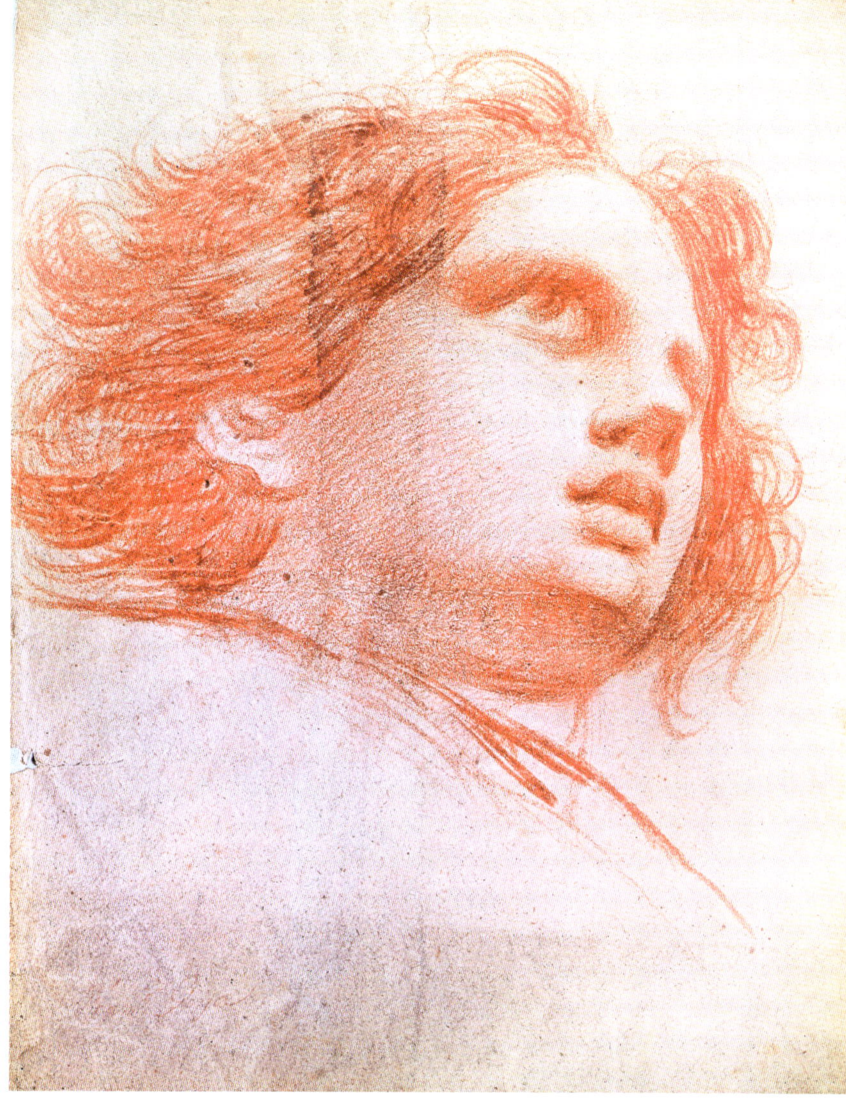

Drawing for an Angel's Head, 1772–5, red chalk on paper, Museo Nacional del Prado, Madrid, Spain, 43.5 x 34cm (17 x 13½in)

Another of Goya's studies for his ceiling fresco in the Nuestra Señora del Pilar in Saragossa, this clearly shows his attention to detail and careful planning for all his works. For this, Goya copied an engraving of an original drawing by Raphael, proving how much he made himself learn from the greatest masters of the past.

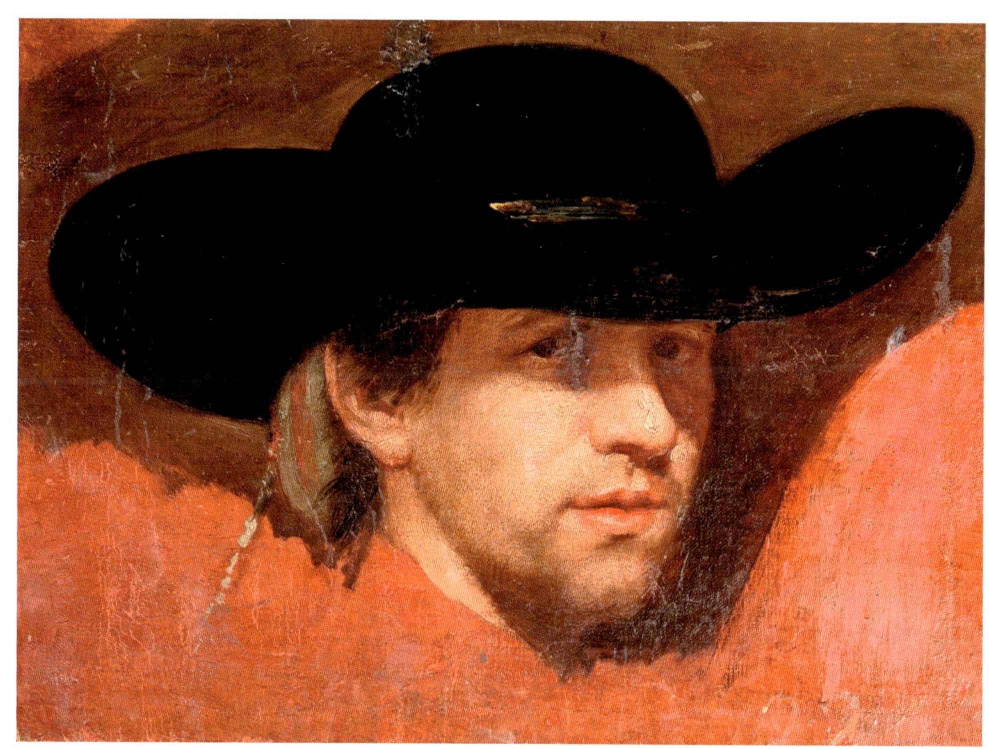

Portrait of a Man with a Hat, c.1773–5, oil on canvas, Museo de Bellas Artes, Saragossa, Spain, 37 x 53cm (14½ x 21in)

An unfinished painting of a young man in a hat, this is believed by many to be a self-portrait of Goya in his 20s. The work has also been attributed to Francisco Bayeu as verifying some works such as these of this period are particularly difficult because of Goya's ability to assume various techniques as he was developing his own style.

Interior of the Hermitage of Nuestra Señora de la Fuente in Muel, Saragossa, Spain.

Restored in 1817 and declared a National Monument in 1951, this is the interior of the church of Our Lady of the Fountain (Nuestra Señora de la Fuente in Muel) in Saragossa, showing two of the Doctors of the Church painted by Goya. On the left is Saint Jerome and on the right is Saint Gregory.

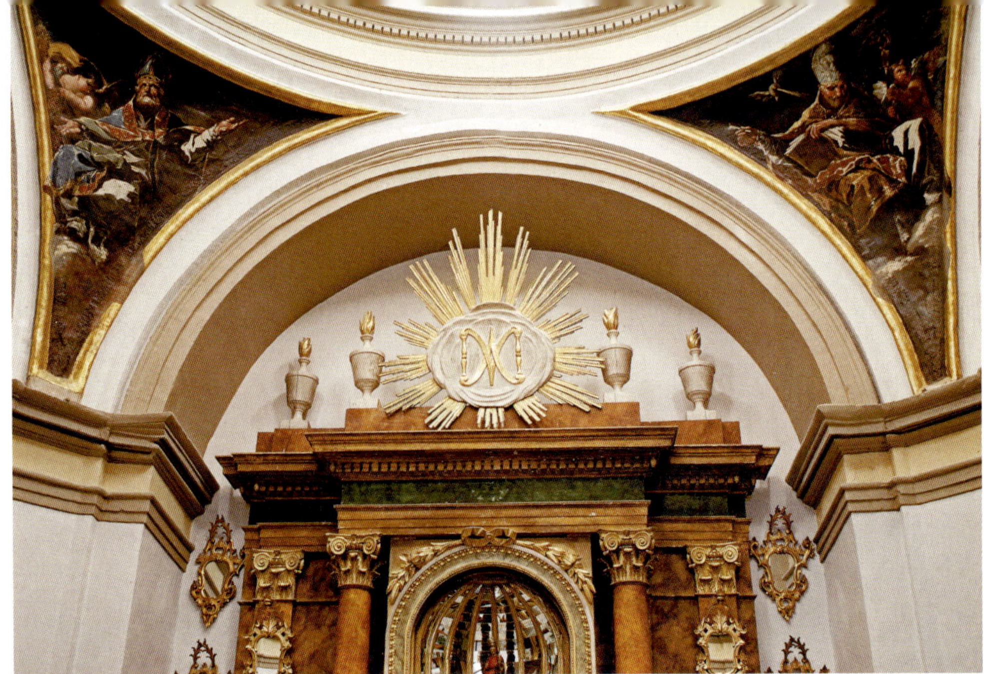

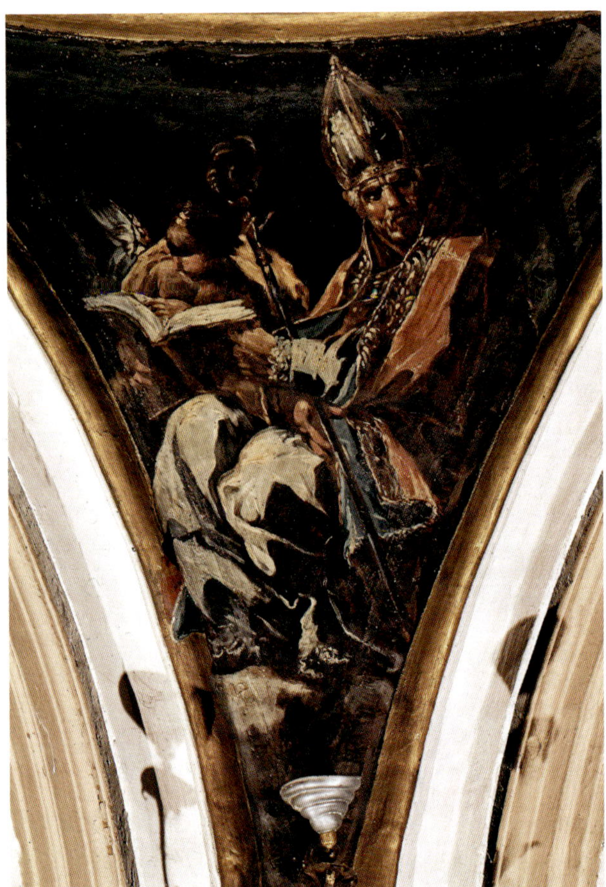

Saint Ambrose, c.1771–2, oil on plaster, Hermitage of Nuestra Señora de la Fuente in Muel, Saragossa, Spain, height: *c.*250cm (*c.*98in)

The expressive composition and palette of this painting of Saint Ambrose, one of the four Doctors of the Church, is reminiscent of Tiepolo, but also demonstrates Goya's pronounced talents. This is a mature style for such a young artist, demonstrating a superior analytical strength and richness of colour that surpassed that of Bayeu's.

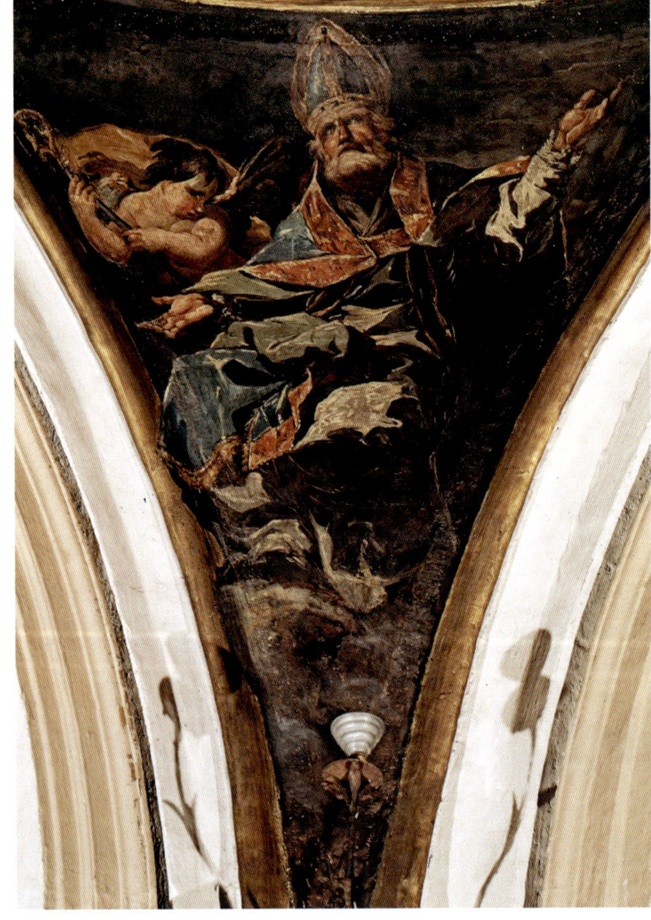

Saint Jerome, c.1771–2, oil on plaster, Hermitage of Nuestra Señora de la Fuente in Muel, Saragossa, Spain, height: *c.*250cm (*c.*98in)

One of the Doctors of the Church, Saint Jerome is best known for his extensive writings, including a translation of the Bible into Latin, and his commentaries on the Gospel of the Hebrews. As with Goya's other paintings here, he has squashed the figure in the space to create both impact and vitality.

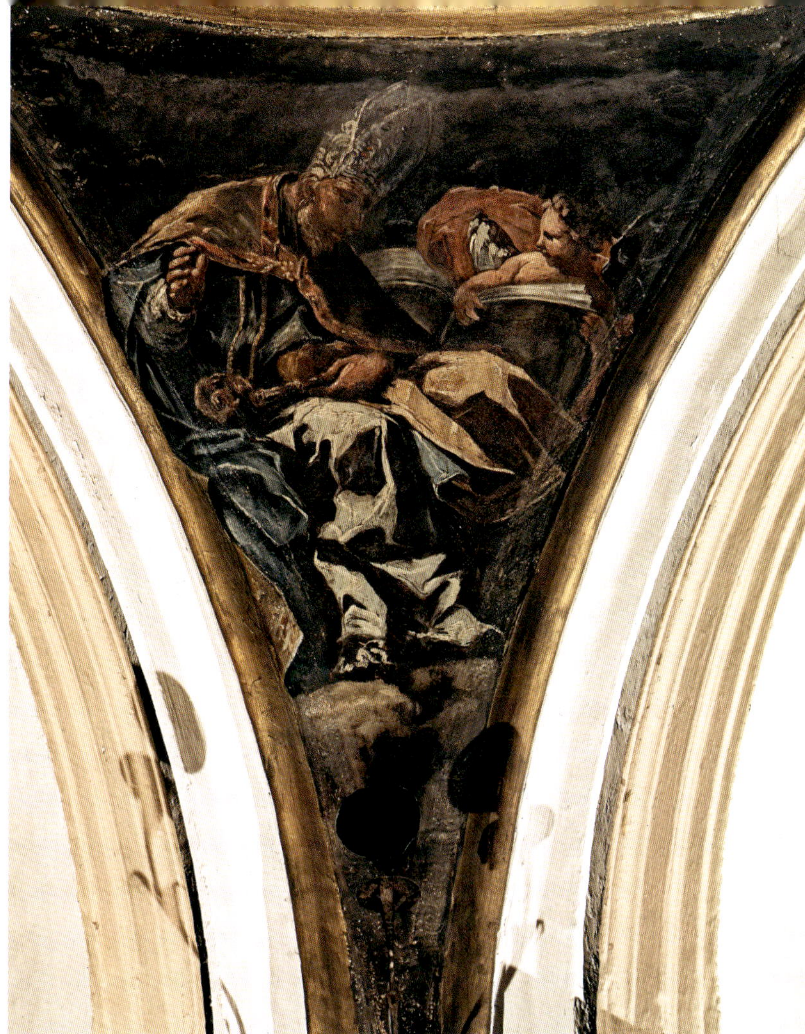

Saint Augustine, *c*.1771–2, oil on plaster, Hermitage of Nuestra Señora de la Fuente in Muel, Saragossa, Spain, height: *c*.250cm (*c*.98in)

Another of the four pendentives, or corner ceiling pieces, in the church in Saragossa where Goya painted the four doctors of the Latin Church. This is Saint Augustine. Rather than fresco, Goya painted in oils on plaster and used several of Tiepolo's ideas to accommodate the difficult shape and angle, but the work also shows evidence of his later expressionistic style.

Saint Gregory, *c*.1771–2, oil on plaster, Hermitage of Nuestra Señora de la Fuente in Muel, Saragossa, Spain, height: *c*.250cm (*c*.98in)

Goya's Saint Gregory – another of his four Doctors of the Church – is here seated on a platform in a manner that resembled Murillo's painting style. The figure is quite monumental within the triangular space, and fits in tightly, with his large book held on his lap and his papal tiara almost cut off by the top edge of the pendentive.

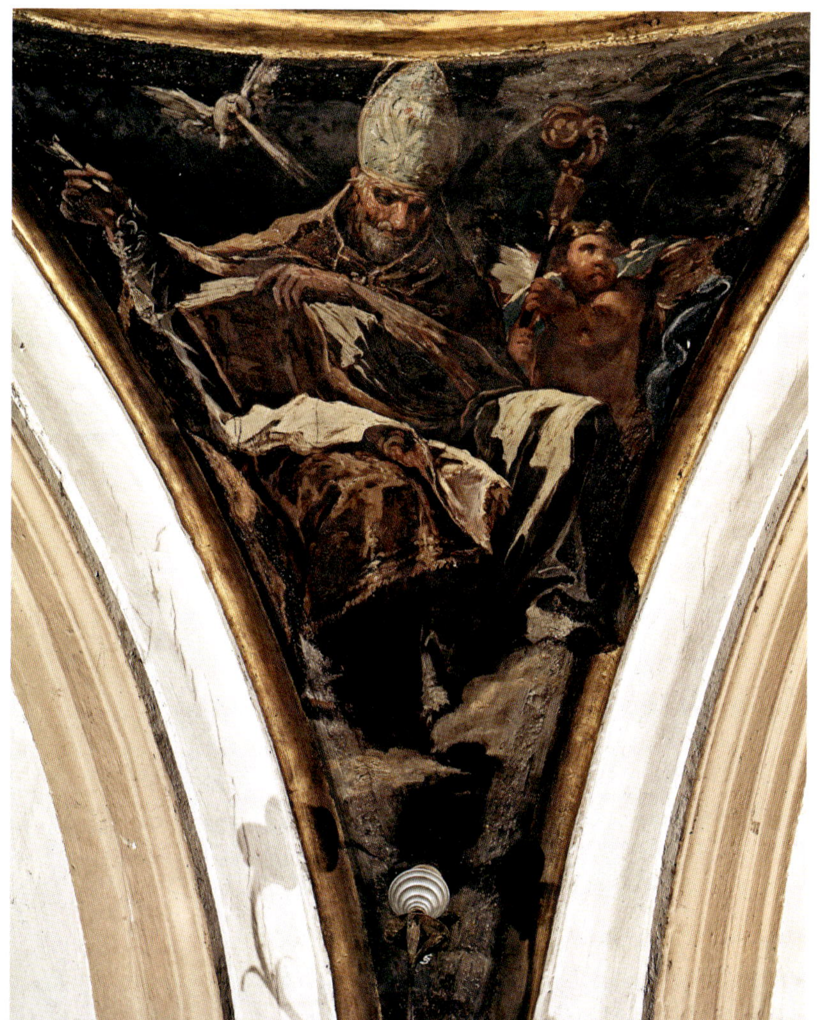

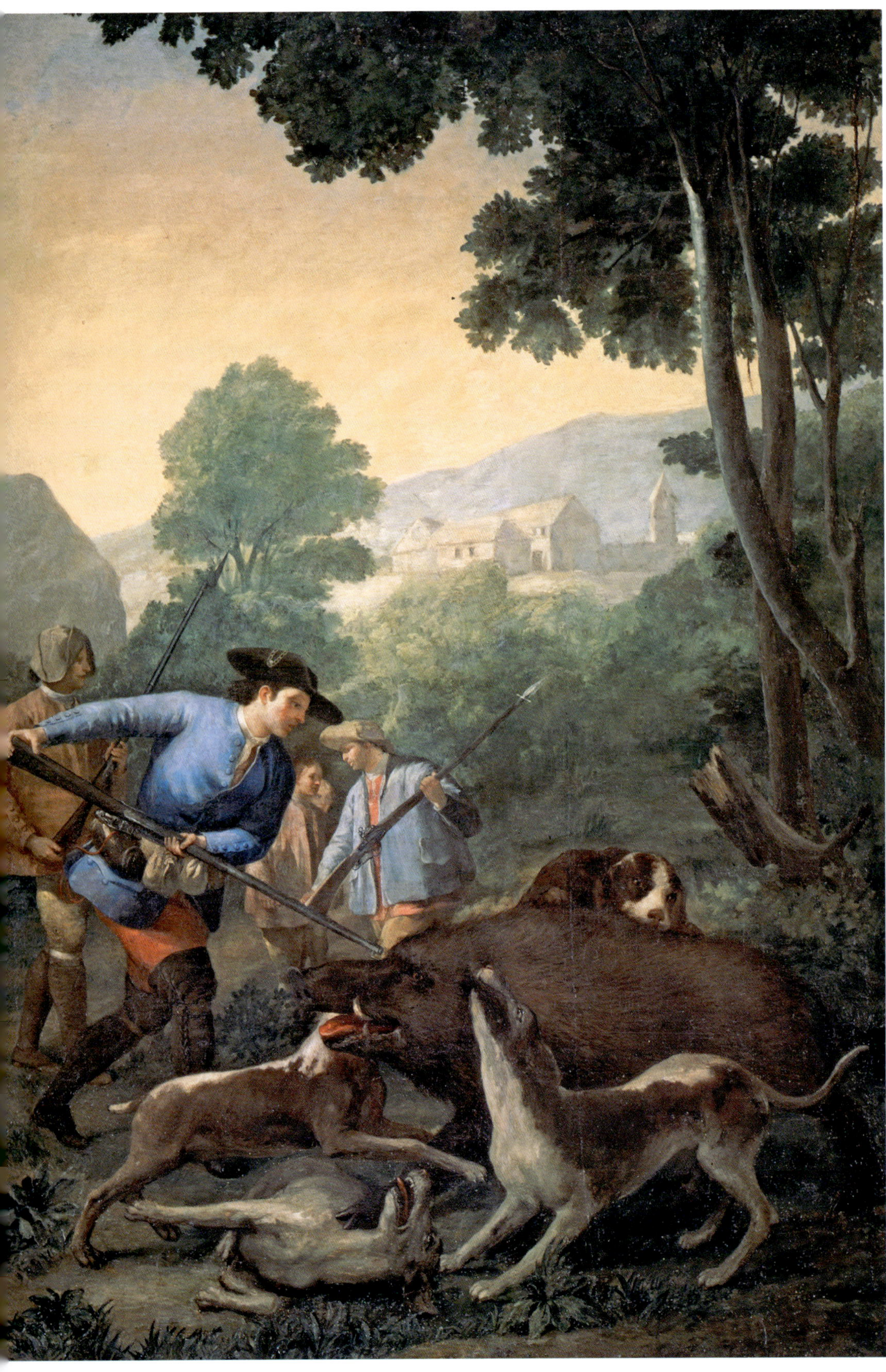

Wild Boar Hunt, 1775, oil on canvas, Patrimonio Nacional, Madrid, Spain, 249 x 173cm (98 x 68in)

In 1775, Goya was commissioned to paint nine cartoons of hunting scenes for the dining room of the Prince and Princess of the Asturias, the next in line to the throne. This is one of the first five that he painted in May. He was working under the direction of Francisco Bayeu and alongside his brother Ramón. Here, dogs have chased a boar toward the hunter.

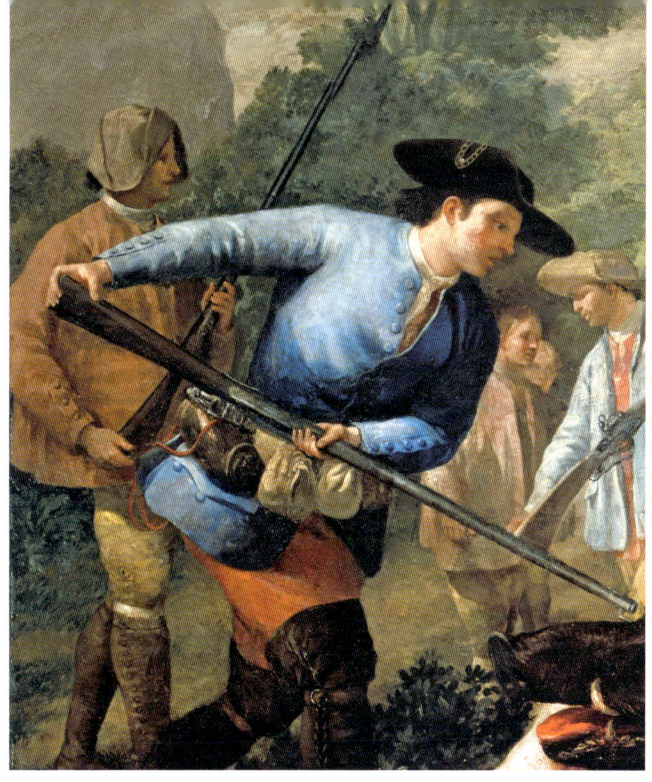

Detail from *Wild Boar Hunt* (opposite)

The future Charles IV was passionate about hunting, which is why Goya painted these scenes. The actual work however, seems somewhat impersonal and detached, probably because Goya did not enjoy painting tapestry cartoons and in his inexperience, he followed the advice of his brother-in-law Bayeu, who was particularly imperious and concerned that Goya did not offend the future king.

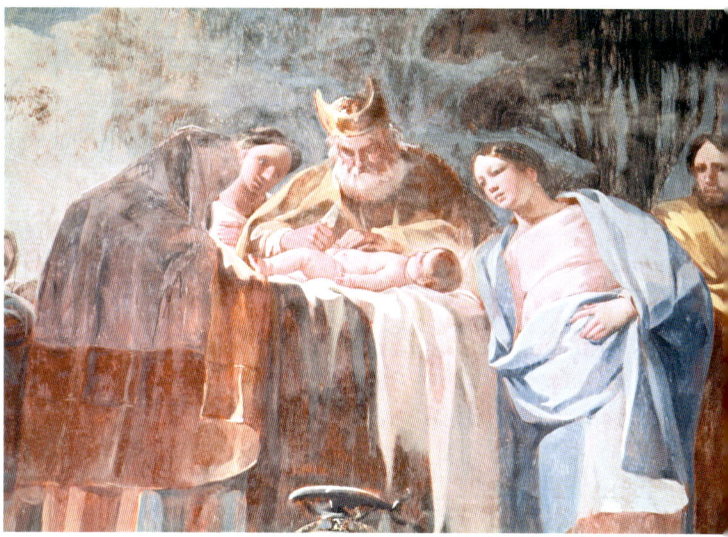

The Circumcision (detail), 1774, oil on plaster, Church of the Carthusian Monastery of Aula Dei, Saragossa, Spain

During the 18th century in Spain, the Church was the most important patron of the arts. So this commission, to decorate the chapel in the monastery of Aula Dei was of great significance in Goya's career. Here Mary, swathed in a pale blue shawl presents the infant Jesus to the priest to be circumcised. He continues at this time to follow the styles of the Renaissance.

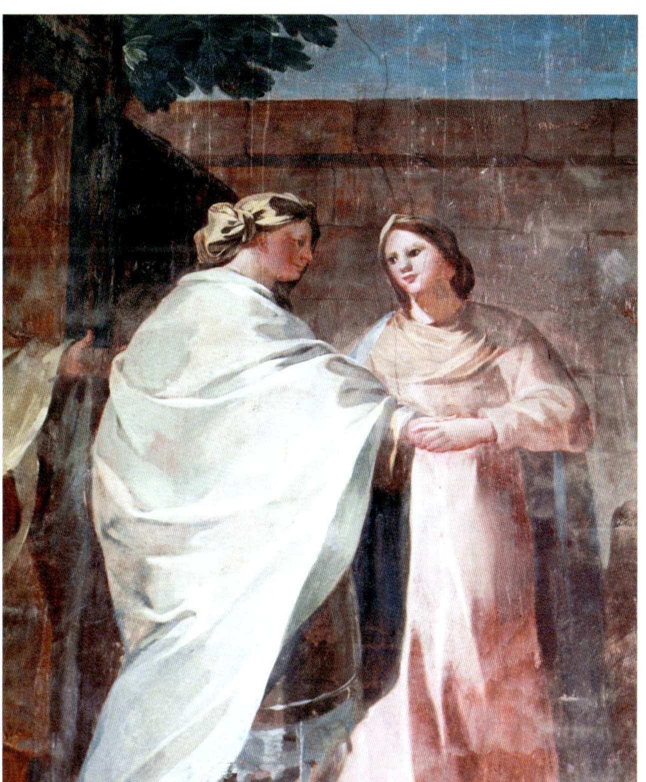

The Visitation (detail), 1774, oil on plaster, Church of the Carthusian Monastery of Aula Dei, Saragossa, Spain

Of Goya's original eleven paintings in this church that all illustrate the life of the Virgin, only seven remain. This is a detail of one of them; another detail is shown on page 21. By alternating groups of standing figures, Goya aimed to counteract the extremely horizontal format. Here, Saint Elizabeth greets the Virgin Mary as described in the New Testament Gospel of Luke. Goya adhered to Renaissance-style poses.

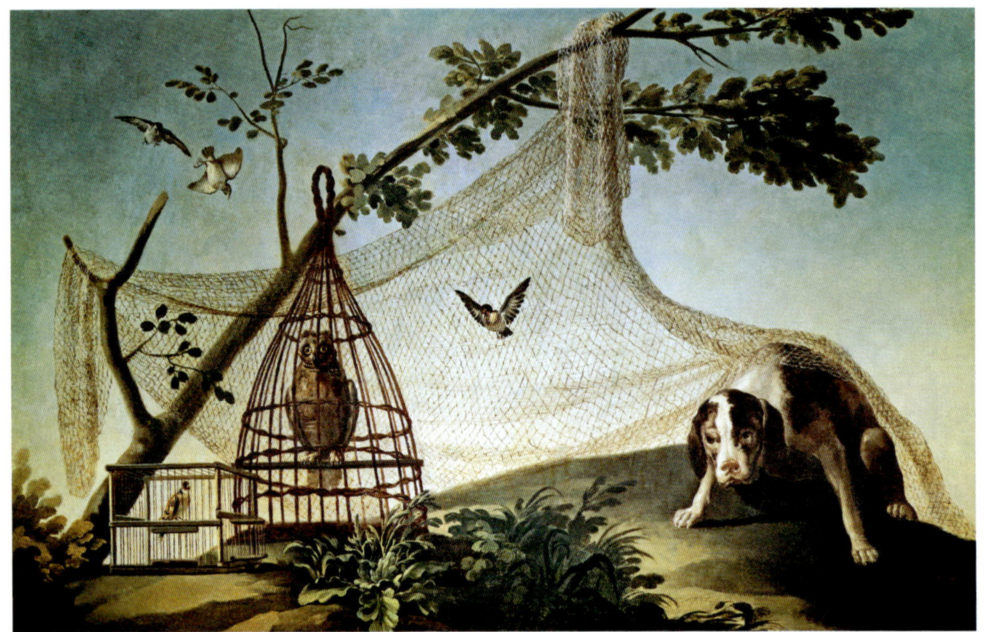

Hunting with a Decoy, 1775, oil on canvas, Museo Nacional del Prado, Madrid, Spain, 112 x 179cm (44 x 70½in)

Like its companion picture *Dogs on a Leash*, this image of a hunt with an owl and a net was designed to go over a window. The meticulous self-conscious style is not typical of Goya's work, but he was following Bayeu's instructions in order to impress the royal family and to ensure that he continued receiving commissions from the Royal Tapestry Factory.

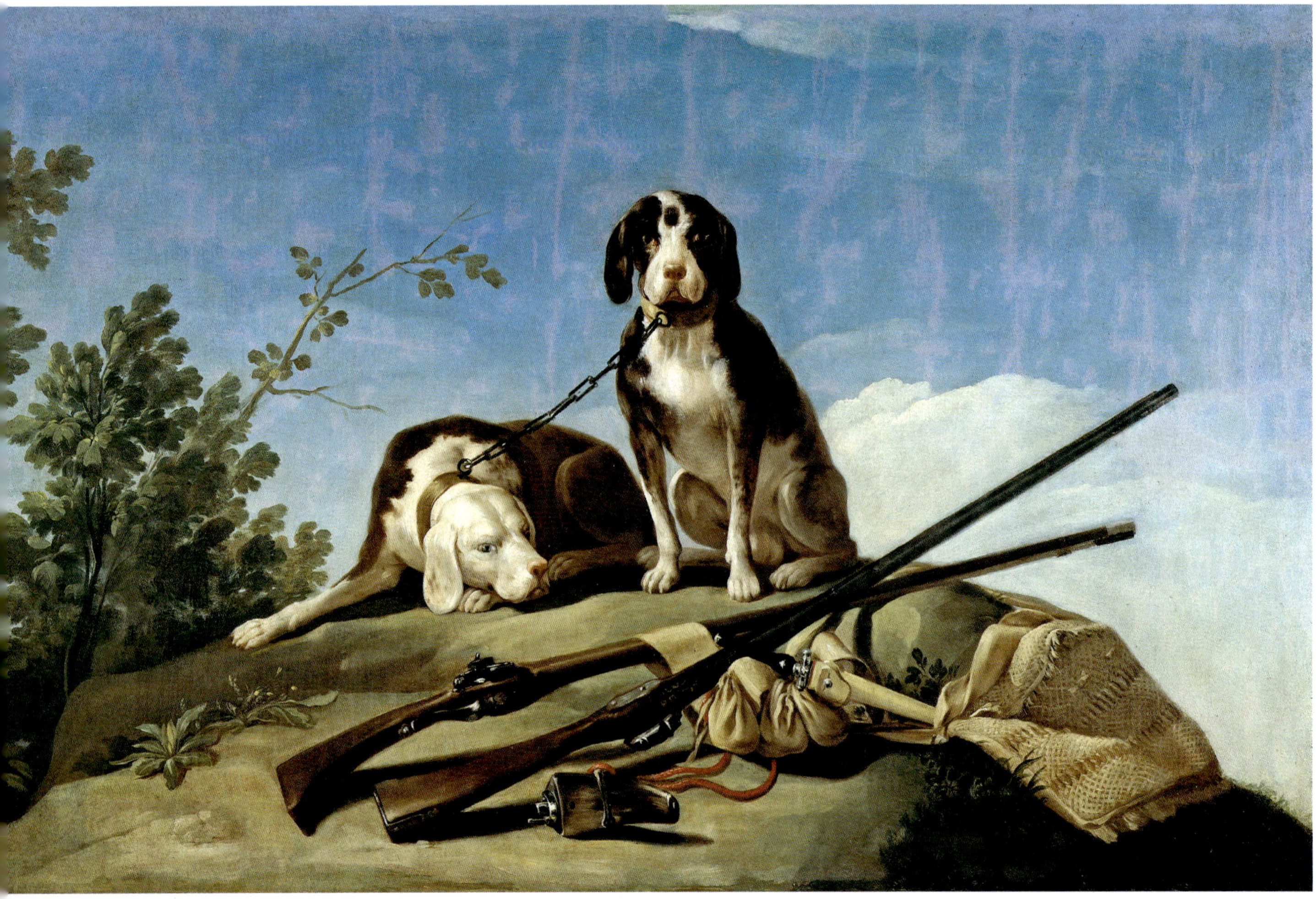

Dogs on a Leash, 1775, oil on canvas, Museo Nacional del Prado, Madrid, Spain, 112 x 174cm (44 x 68½in)

To hang in the same room as *The Wild Boar Hunt* (see page 108), this was designed by Goya concurrently. It features two dogs, two shotguns and other hunting paraphernalia on a small hill. The resulting tapestry was to hang in the Escorial Palace, and Goya made a point of designing tapestries for those locations to have dramatic perspective.

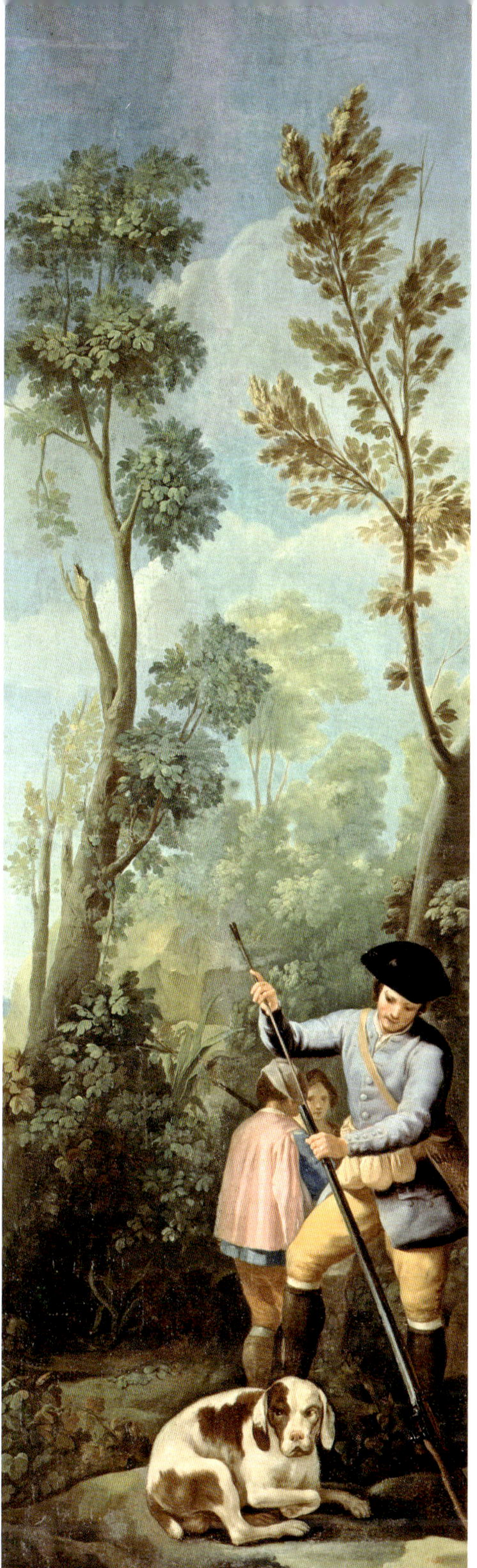

A Hunter and His Dogs, 1775, oil on canvas, Museo Nacional del Prado, Madrid, Spain, 262 x 71cm (103 x 28in)

Standing with his back to the viewer and a shotgun on his shoulder, a hunter turns to hold the leash of his two dogs in wooded surroundings. The curving composition fits in comfortably with the tall, thin shape of the canvas, which was in these dimensions because the tapestry was to hang in a narrow space in the room.

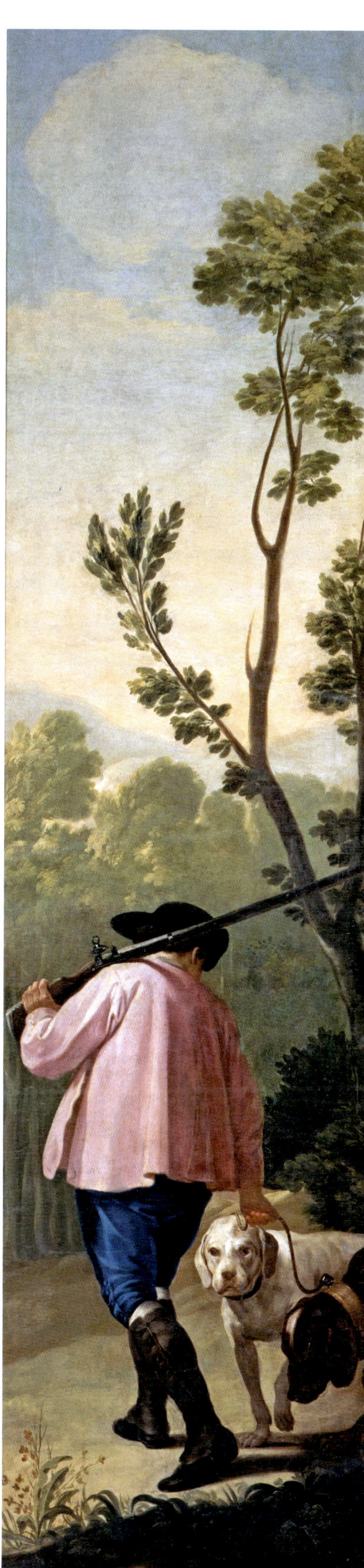

A Hunter Loading His Shotgun, 1775, oil on canvas, Museo Nacional del Prado, Madrid, Spain, 289 x 90cm (114 x 35½in)

Along with the other nine tapestry cartoons that Goya created in 1775, this was for the decoration of the dining room in the Escorial Palace. Francisco Bayeu's influence is clear in each of these works, as he kept a close eye on Goya's work. Here, the hunter loads a shotgun with a dog lying at his feet and other hunters behind him.

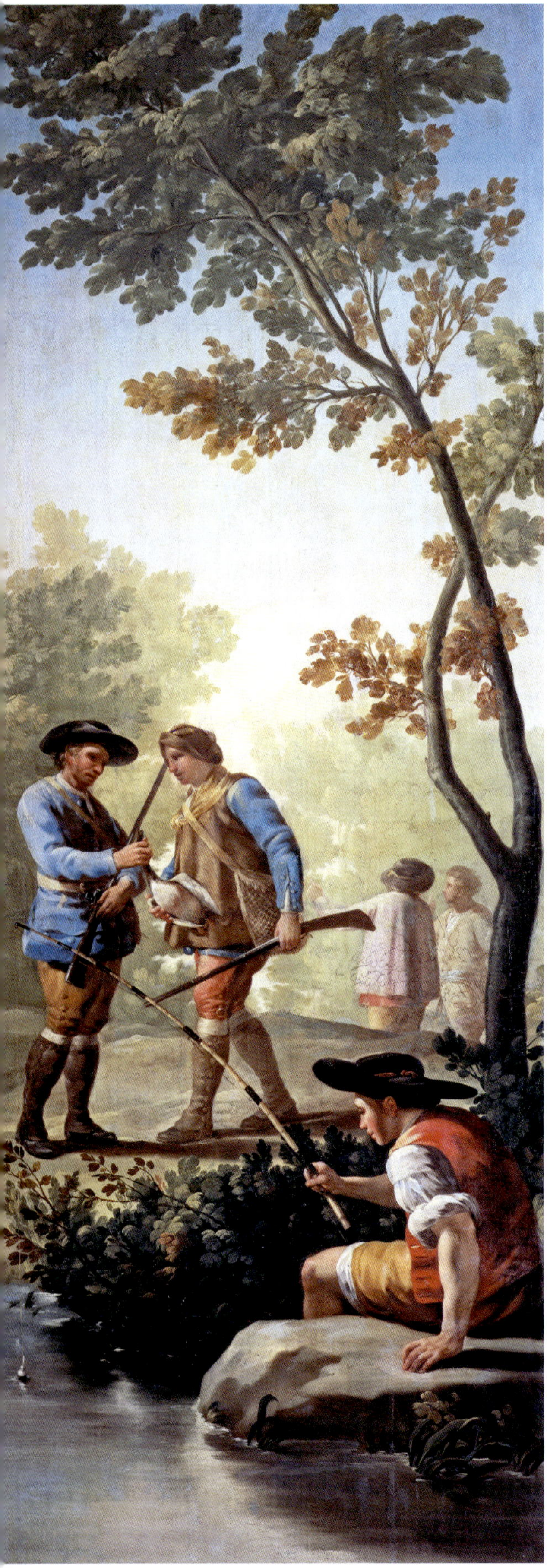

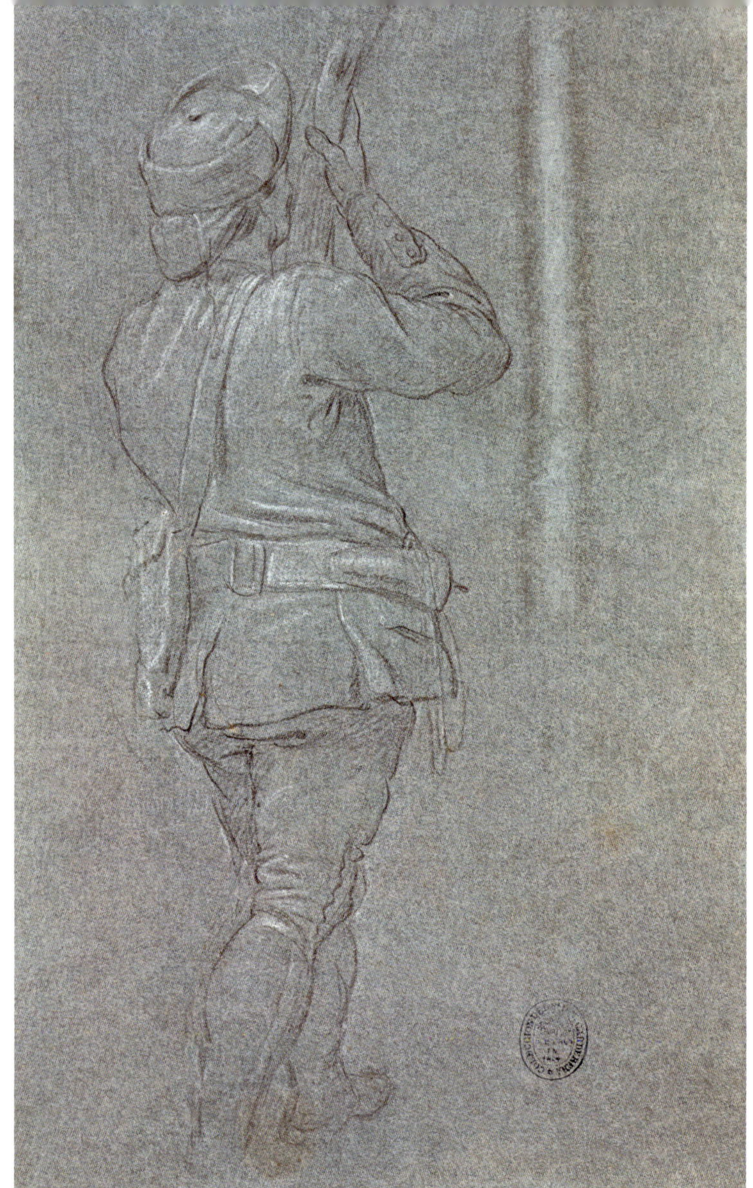

Hunter Study, 1775, black chalk heightened with white, Biblioteca Nacional de Bellas Artes, Madrid, Spain, 32.2 x 20.6cm (13 x 8in)

This is another sketch made from direct observation by Goya in preparation for his tapestry cartoon of the *Hunting Party* (opposite). He made several sketches from life of various hunters, seen from different angles before composing the painting to make sure that he would give the final work interest, vivacity and credibility.

The Fisherman with his Rod, 1775, oil on canvas, Museo Nacional del Prado, Madrid, Spain, 289 x 110cm (114 x 43in)

Painted in October 1775, Goya represented two different country activities. In the background are hunters, while in the foreground a boy is fishing. This painting is a little more relaxed than his earlier compositions of the same year. Unusually, the work also has black pencil on the leaves and branches, which might have been Goya's additions, or the weavers may have marked it.

A Hunting Party, 1775, oil on canvas, Museo Nacional del Prado, Madrid, Spain, 290 x 226cm (114 x 89in)

Two types of hunting are portrayed here; on foot and on horseback. One hunter shoots quail and another walks with his dog to find prey in the bushes. In the background, two riders hunt a hare with greyhounds. Depicting the animals and landscape with particular sensitivity the work was lifted from a mundane scene to one of interest and life.

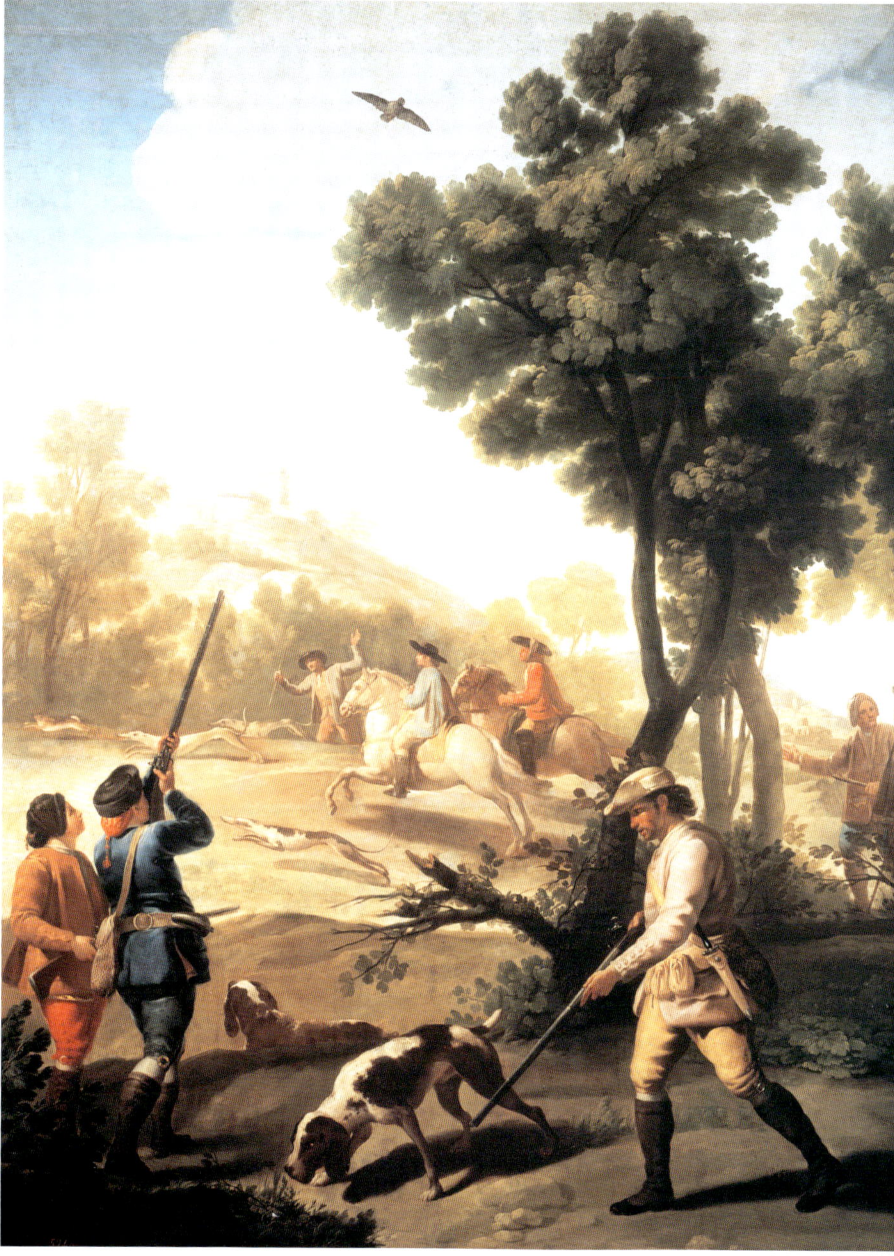

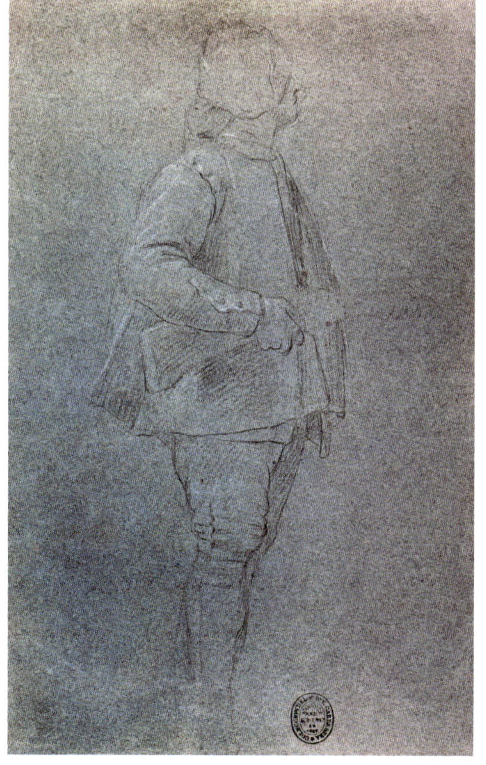

Hunter Study, 1775, black chalk heightened with white, Biblioteca Nacional de Bellas Artes, Madrid, Spain, 32.2 x 20.6cm (13 x 8in)

This provides a glimpse of Goya's working process. From early in his career he made numerous preparatory drawings before starting any painting, to be sure that he knew exactly what a finished work would look like. Often his preparatory studies were more detailed than his finished paintings, as seen here. This drawing has more subtleties of tone and details than in his tapestry cartoons.

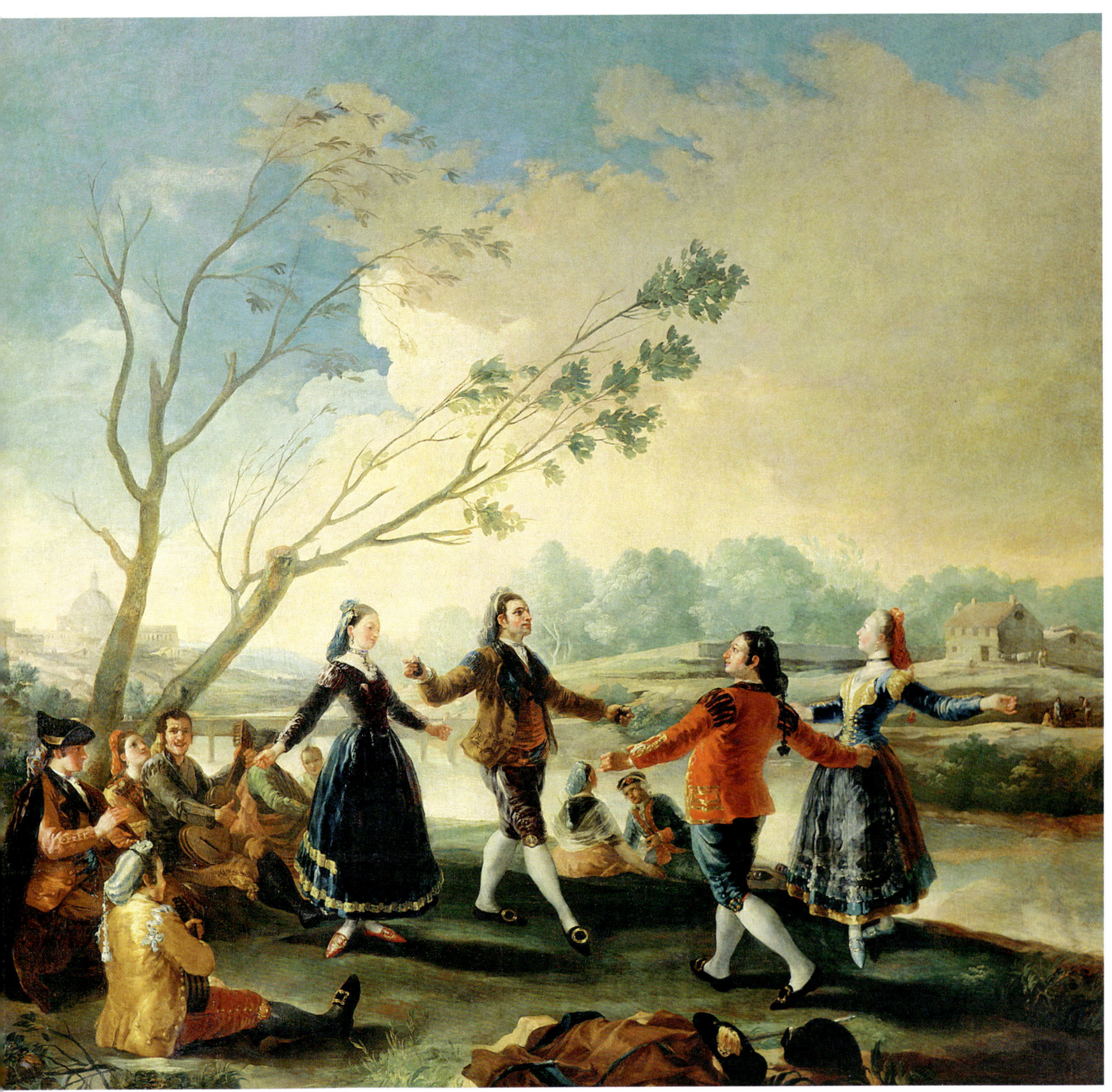

Dance on the Banks of the Manzanares, 1777, oil on canvas, Museo Nacional del Prado, Madrid, Spain, 272 x 295cm (107 x 116in)

With brilliant colouring, lively movement and forceful characterization, Goya continued to depict popular subjects such as picnics and dances (see also page 38). He also began portraying majos and majas; people from the lower classes of Spanish society who dressed in colourful traditional-style dress and displayed intentionally provocative behaviour, contrasting directly with the fashionable French styles that had been adopted by the Spanish élite.

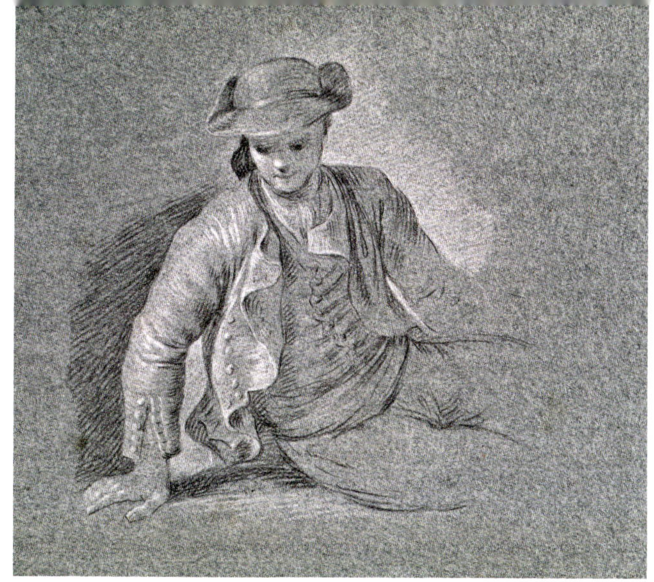

Drawing for the Picnic on the Manzanares River, 1776, black and white chalk on blue paper, Institute of Valencia of Don Juan, Madrid, Spain, 19 x 24.5cm (7½ x 10in)

As he had completed the previous nine tapestry cartoons, Goya did not feel quite so compelled to do as his brother-in-law instructed. Accordingly, he began to create more expressive, individually-inspired images. This is another drawing from life that he made in preparation for his painting of a picnic on the River Manzanares.

Drawing for the Picnic on the Manzanares River, 1776, black and white chalk on blue paper, Institute of Valencia of Don Juan, Madrid, Spain, 19.9 x 27.9cm (8 x 11in)

From 1776 to 1778, Goya produced a further ten cartoons for tapestries for the Pieza de Corner – or the dining room of the Prince and Princess of the Asturias. He was gaining confidence and beginning to work more independently as can be seen in this drawing in black chalk, heightened with white for his painting *Picnic on the Manzanares River* (see pages 26 and 101).

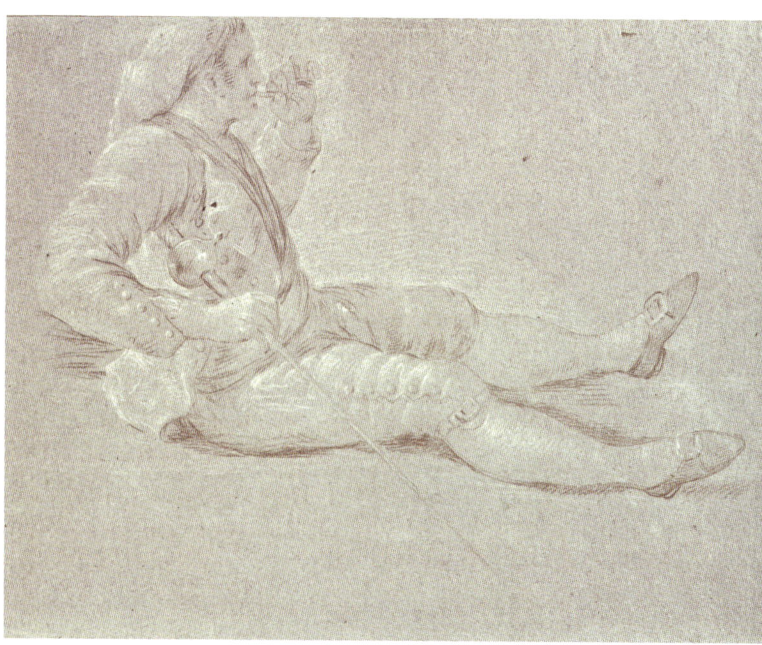

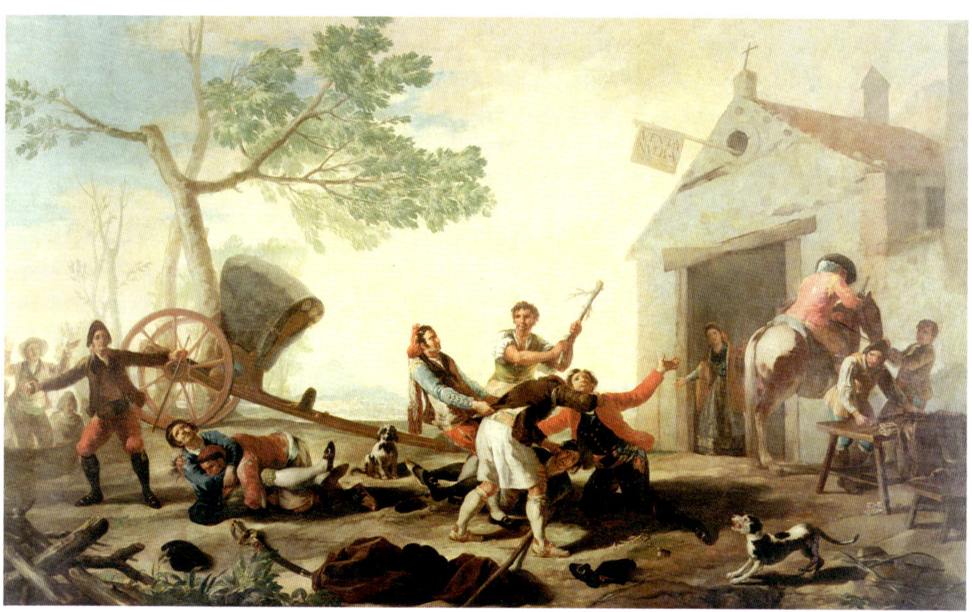

The Fight at the Venta Nueva, 1777, oil on canvas, Museo Nacional del Prado, Madrid, Spain, 275 x 414cm (108 x 163in)

A fight has arisen over a game of cards. The men punch and bite each other, and a guard arrives to break them up. The scene is painted in vivid colours and rapid brushstrokes. Other characters include rickshaw pullers and carriers, and some elegant, upper-class figures. Dogs look on in amazement at the uncivilized behaviour.

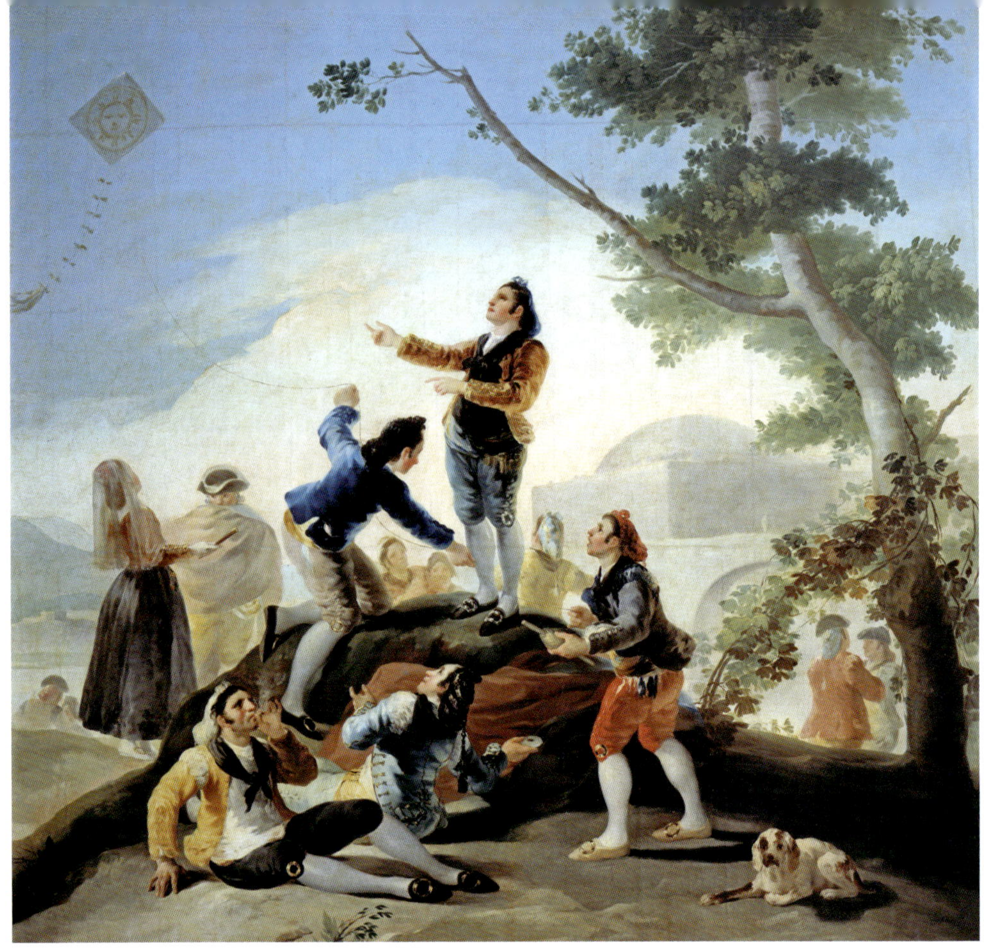

The Kite, 1777–8, oil on canvas, Museo Nacional del Prado, Madrid, Spain, 269 x 285cm (106 x 112in)

Another work for a tapestry (see page 39) that would hang in the future King and Queen's dining room in the El Pardo palace, this is an ostensibly light-hearted scene, where some young people are flying a kite in the countryside just outside Madrid. Figures behind the main group flirt coquettishly with each other. Goya has demonstrated his observations of the majas and majos of Madrid.

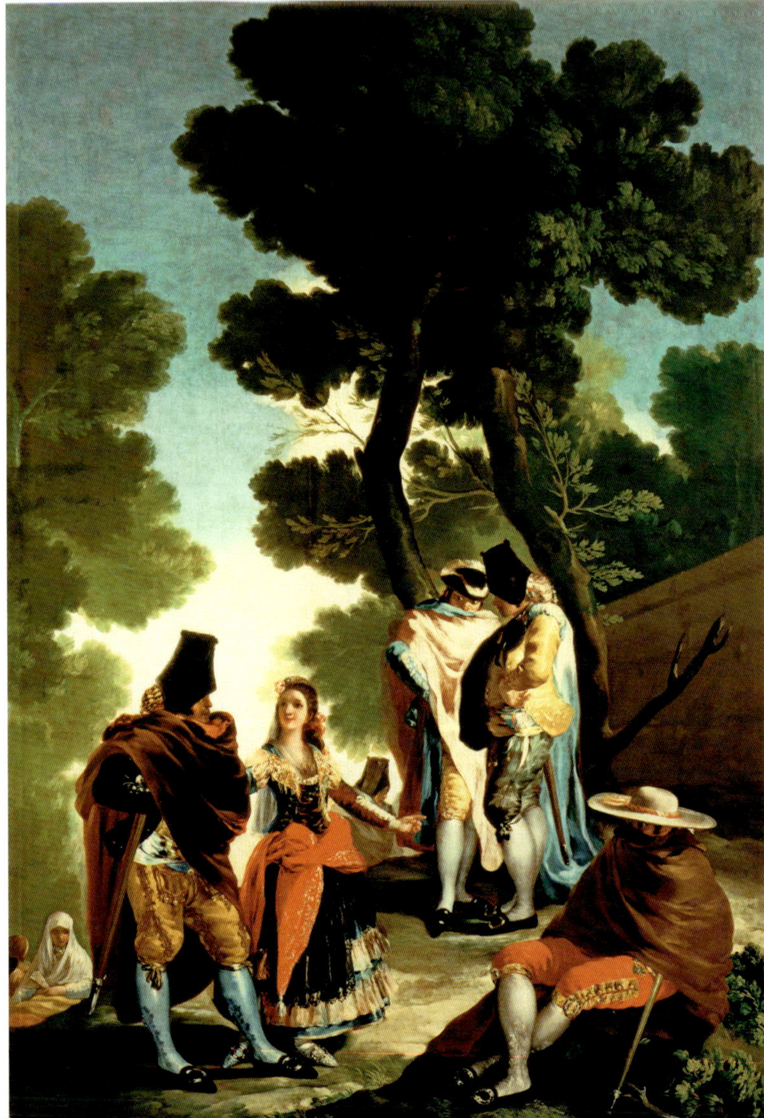

The Maja and the Cloaked Men, or *A Walk through Andalusia*, 1777, oil on canvas, Museo Nacional de Prado, Madrid, Spain, 275 x 190cm (108 x 75in)

A scene of love and jealousy representing duplicity in society, this cartoon shows a maja with some cloaked majos. The eyes reveal both admiration and envy between the characters concerned. Maja and majo dress is believed to have originated with gypsies in southern Spain and adopted in Madrid initially for May Day festivities, but it quickly gained more general popularity.

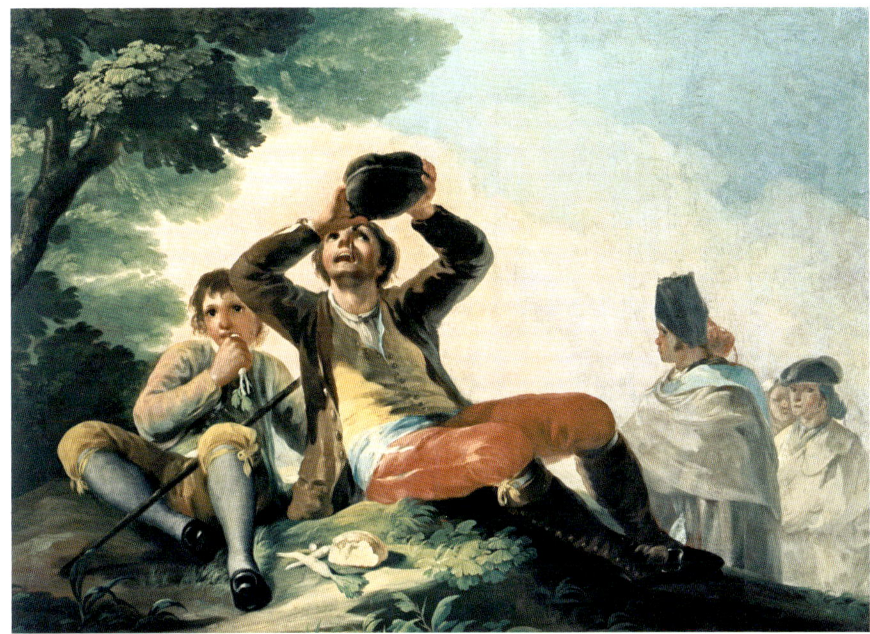

The Drinker, 1776–7, oil on canvas, Museo Nacional del Prado, Madrid, Spain, 107 x 151cm (42 x 59½in)

A young man in the foreground is drinking from a wineskin, while his companion appears to be eating an onion. Three hidalgos are walking past in the background. The resulting tapestry from this cartoon was going to hang over a window, hence the horizontal format and dynamic perspective. It was one of ten tapestry cartoons made by Goya at that time.

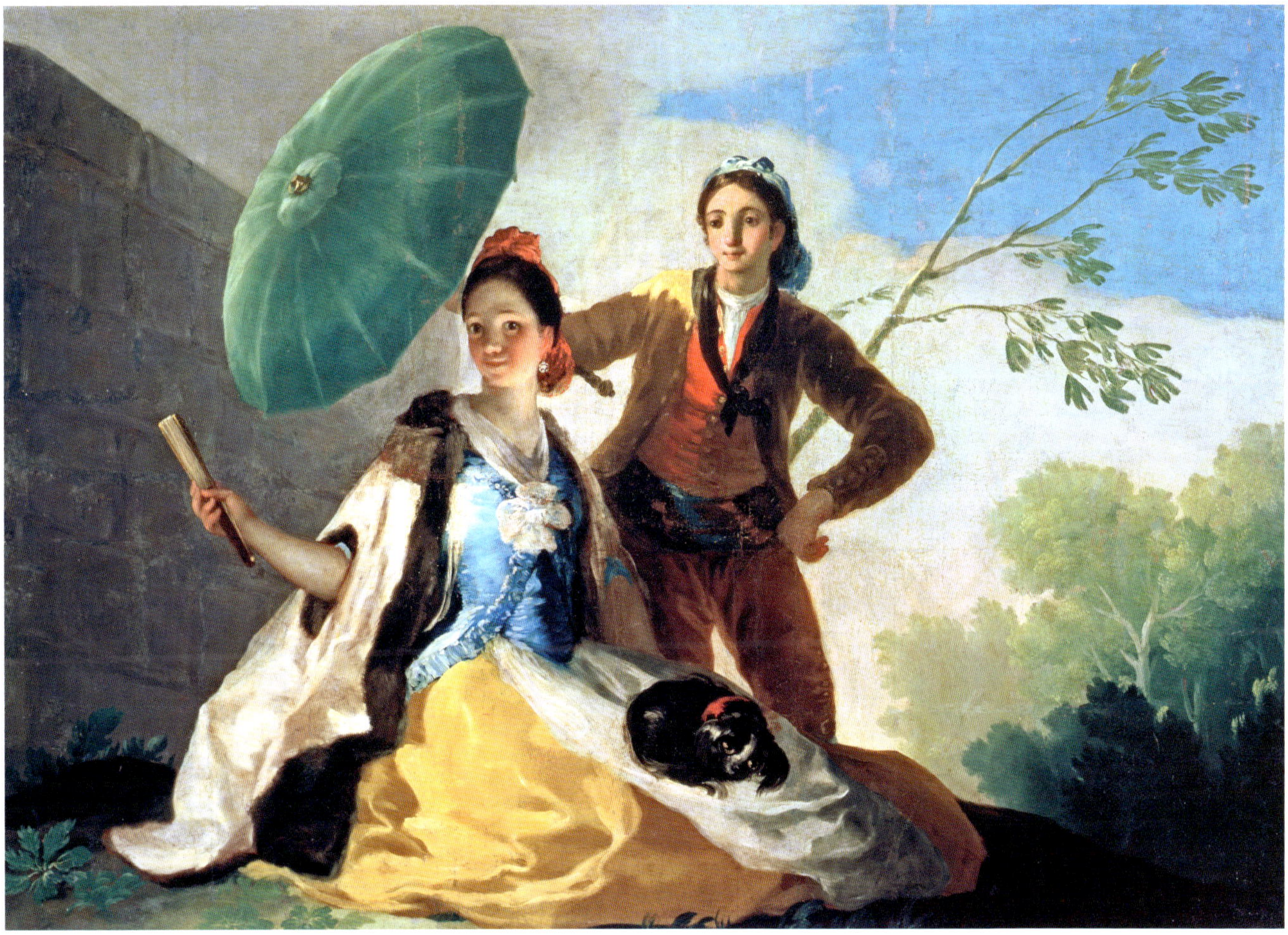

The Parasol, 1777, oil on canvas, Museo Nacional del Prado, Madrid, Spain, 104 x 152cm (41 x 60in)

A woman with a coquettish smile sits with a dog on her lap. Behind her a majo protects her from the sun with a parasol. The pyramidal composition was created to suit the tapestry's location over a window. The happy atmosphere of this work is created by the charming faces and glowing light. The green parasol works harmoniously with the brilliant colours in the woman's clothing and the background.

Card Players, 1777–8, oil on canvas, Museo Nacional del Prado, Madrid, Spain, 270 x 167cm (106 x 66in)

Card playing was an activity enjoyed by the Prince and Princess of the Asturias. Here a group of majos play cards under the shade of an awning suspended from a tree. Behind them, another majo makes signs to his companion; the two are cheating. These cartoons are Goya's first, quite gentle forays into satire.

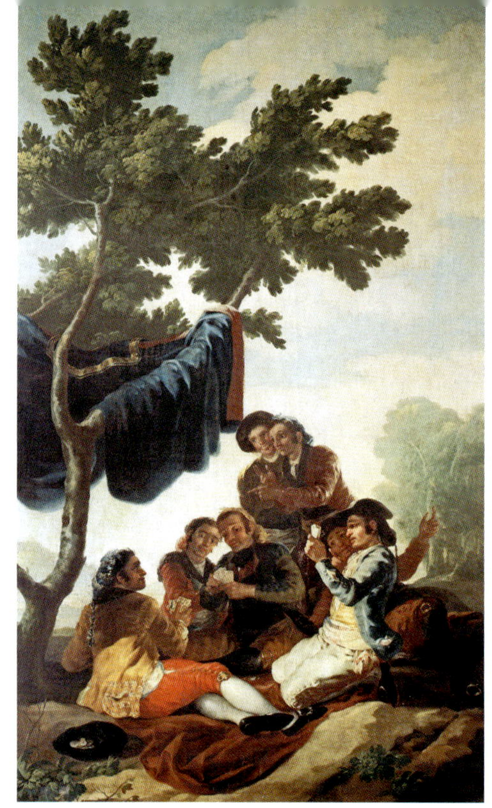

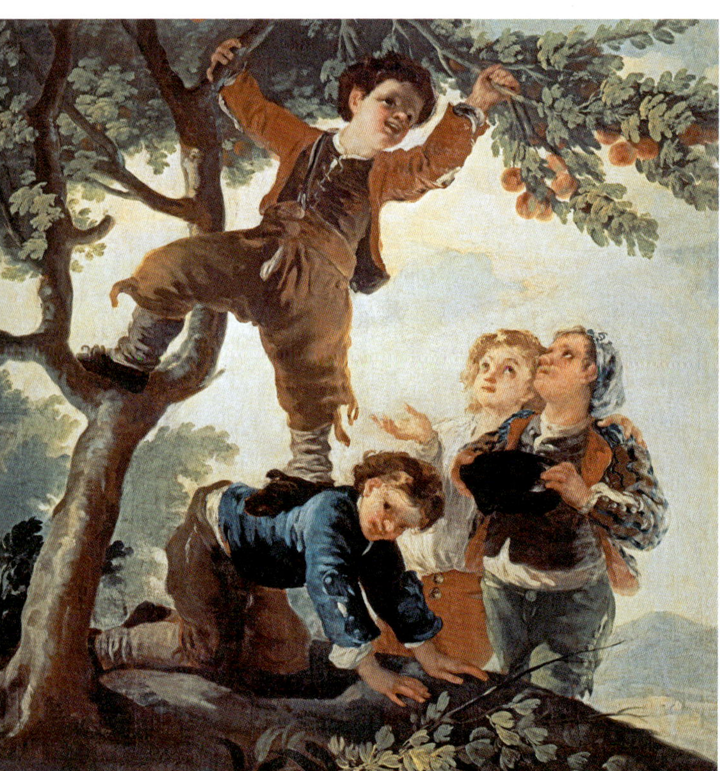

Boys Picking Fruit, 1778, oil on canvas, Museo Nacional del Prado, Madrid, Spain, 119 x 122cm (47 x 48in)

A boy stands on the back of another so he can pick some fruit from a tree. Two other boys watch him hopefully, waiting to share some of the fruit. As in many works, Goya shows his empathy with children as well as his knowledge of Murillo's paintings. He also applies a new technique, emphasizing a broad range of tonal contrasts, which was unusual in tapestry design.

The Garrotted Man, etching, 1778–80, The Metropolitan Museum of Art, New York, USA, 33 x 21cm (13 x 8¼in)

Printed in blue ink, this is a proof of Goya's etching. It was his first original etching and the earliest example of his candid, grim observations.

To die at the garrotte – or to have a screw turned through a metal collar – was considered more gentlemanly than to be hanged. This Spanish method of execution was reserved for guilty members of the upper classes.

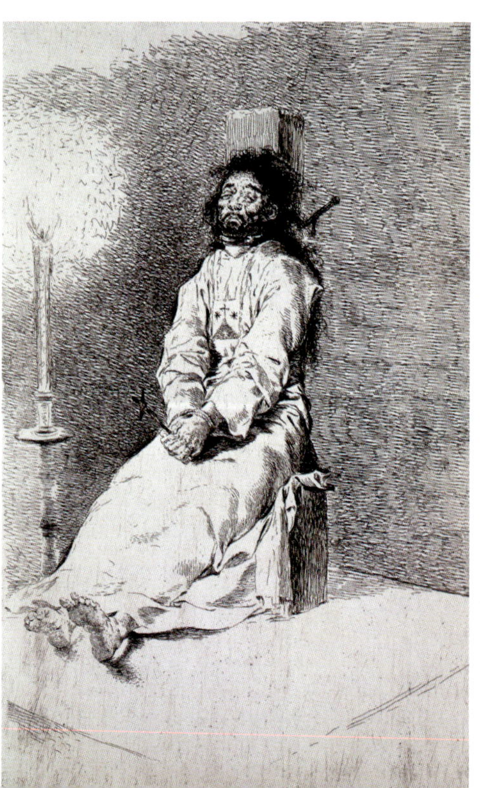

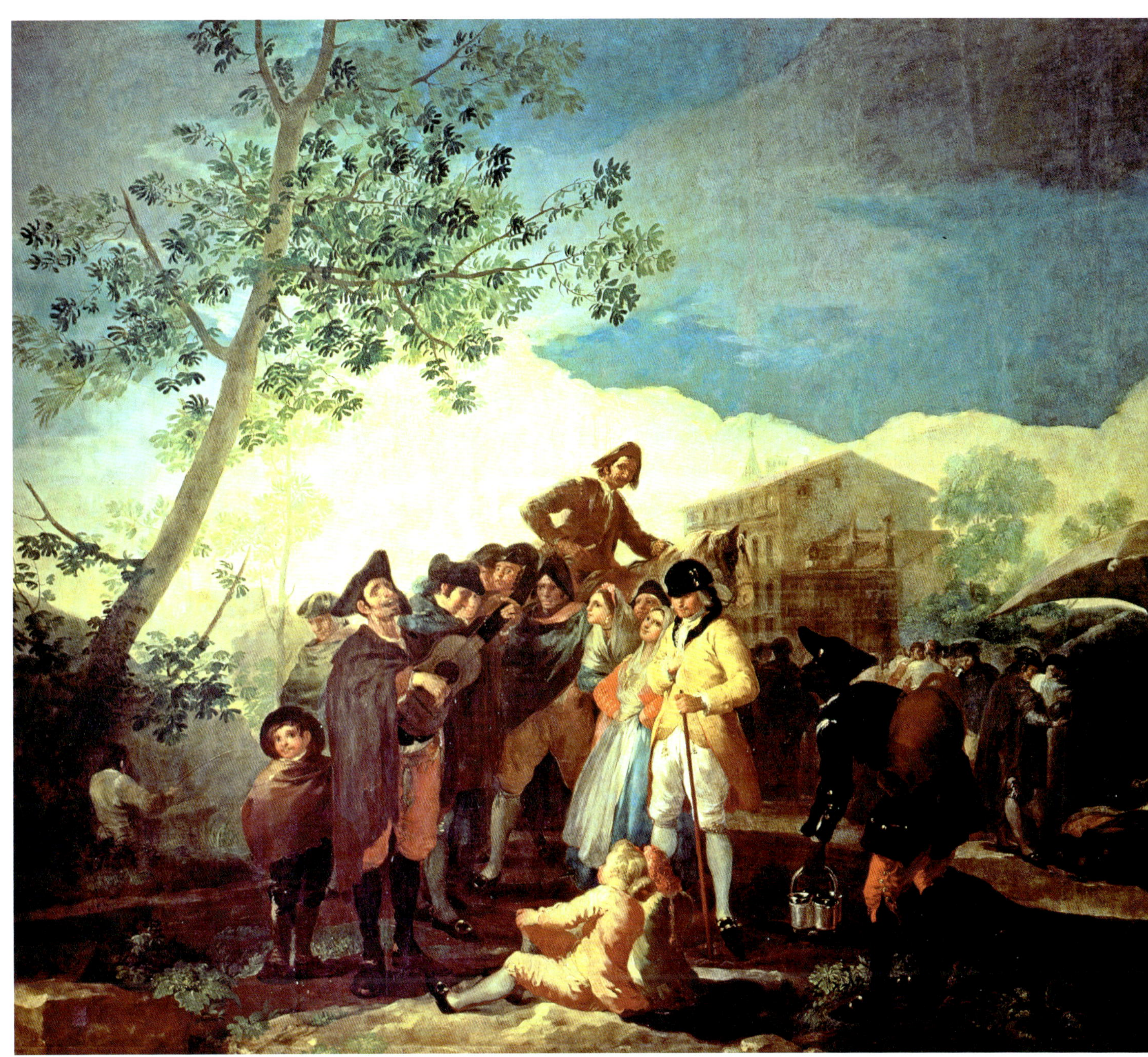

The Blind Guitarist, 1778, oil on canvas, Museo Nacional del Prado, Madrid, Spain, 260 x 311cm (102 x 122½in)

A blind travelling singer plays the guitar, surrounded by an audience made up of men, women and children. Goya has depicted their different reactions to the guitarist — fascinated, amused, unsure, curious and vaguely interested. Several of the onlookers are customary, expected figures. Others were more unusual in Madrid at the time. This was for the antechamber of the Prince and Princess of Asturias's bedroom.

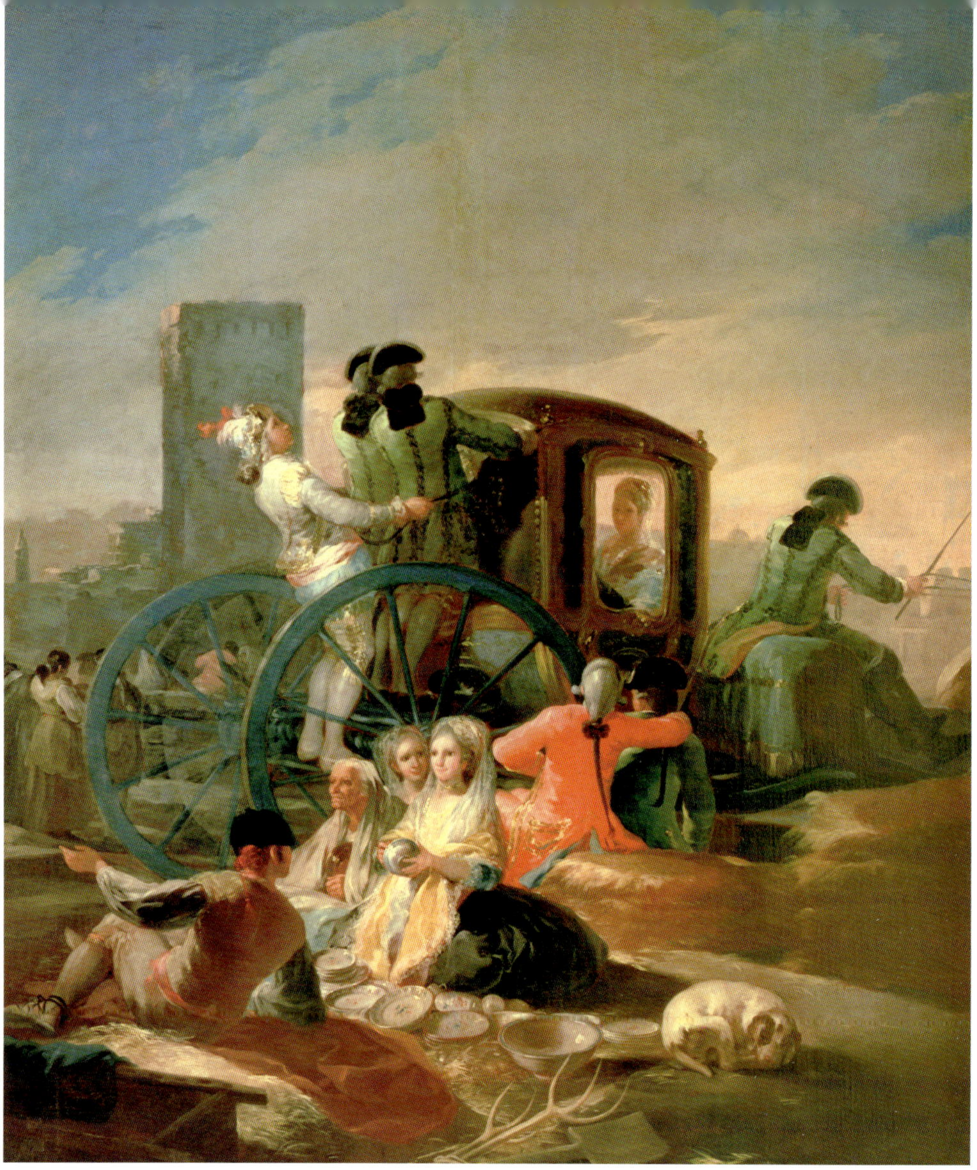

The Pottery Vendor, 1778, oil on canvas, Museo Nacional del Prado, Madrid, Spain, 259 x 220cm (102 x 86½in)

In front of a carriage, a salesman shows his crockery to two young women accompanied by an elderly one. This is all about who is showing whose wares to whom, as the young ladies display their charms to the vendor and gentlemen on the back of the carriage look at the young woman inside, while she looks directly at the viewer. The diagonal composition creates an overall dynamic image.

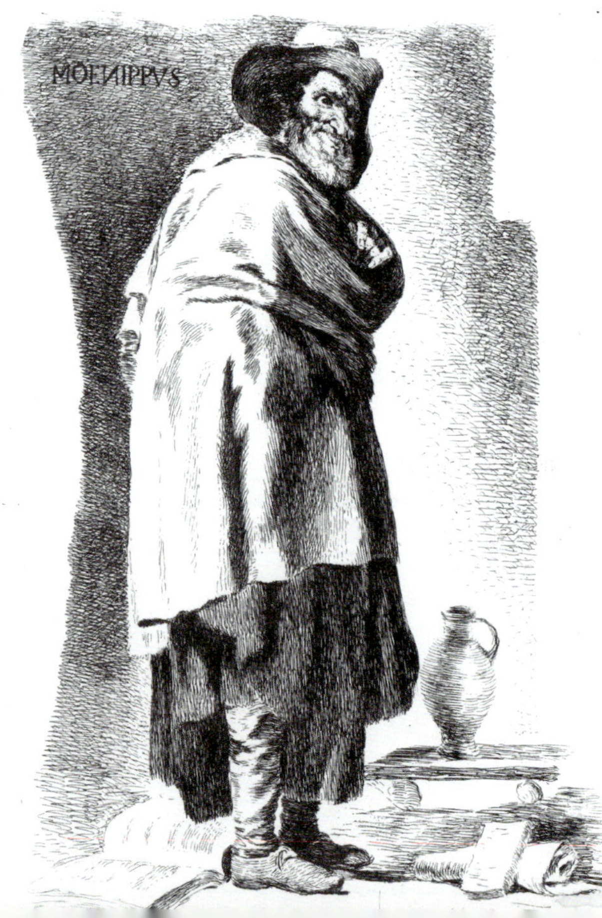

Menippus after Velázquez, etching, 1778, The Metropolitan Museum of Art, New York, USA, 30.3 x 22cm (12 x 9in)

This was one of Goya's first engravings that he made after paintings by Velázquez that he studied in the Royal Palace. In July 1778, an announcement was made in a Spanish publication that nine plates of these etchings were available for purchase. In December of that year, a further 13 plates of the etchings were published. Six preparatory drawings are known of them.

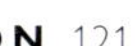

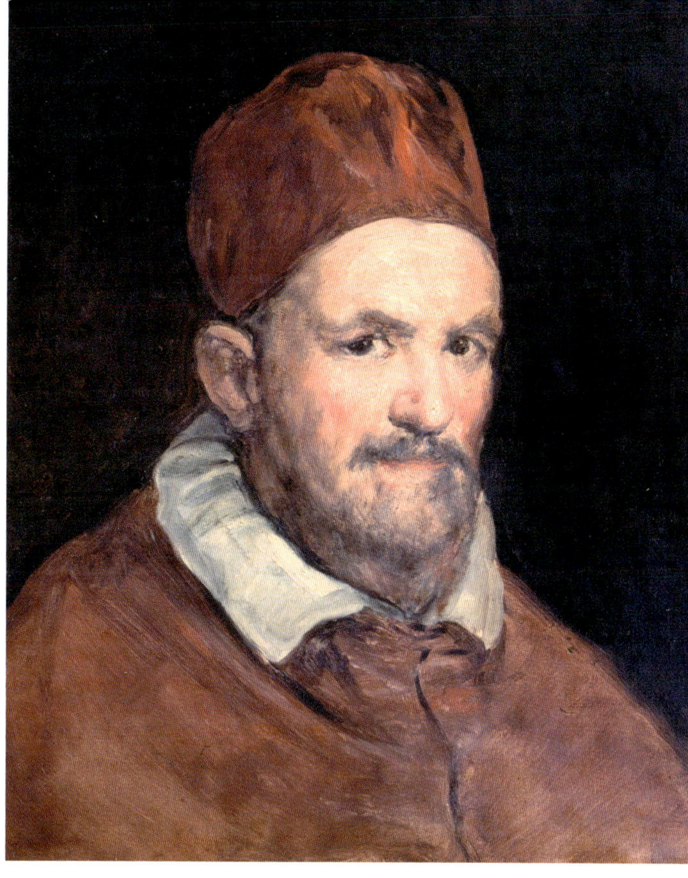

Study after Velázquez, by Goya, *c.*1778–9, oil on canvas, Private Collection, 55 x 45cm (22 x 18in)

Above all other artists, Goya admired Velázquez, and he made several etchings after paintings by the earlier artist that he saw in the Spanish royal collection. It is not certain however, exactly when he painted three copies, of which this is one. This is a fine, detailed work, displaying a sensitive observation and reproduction of the original master's palette and brushwork.

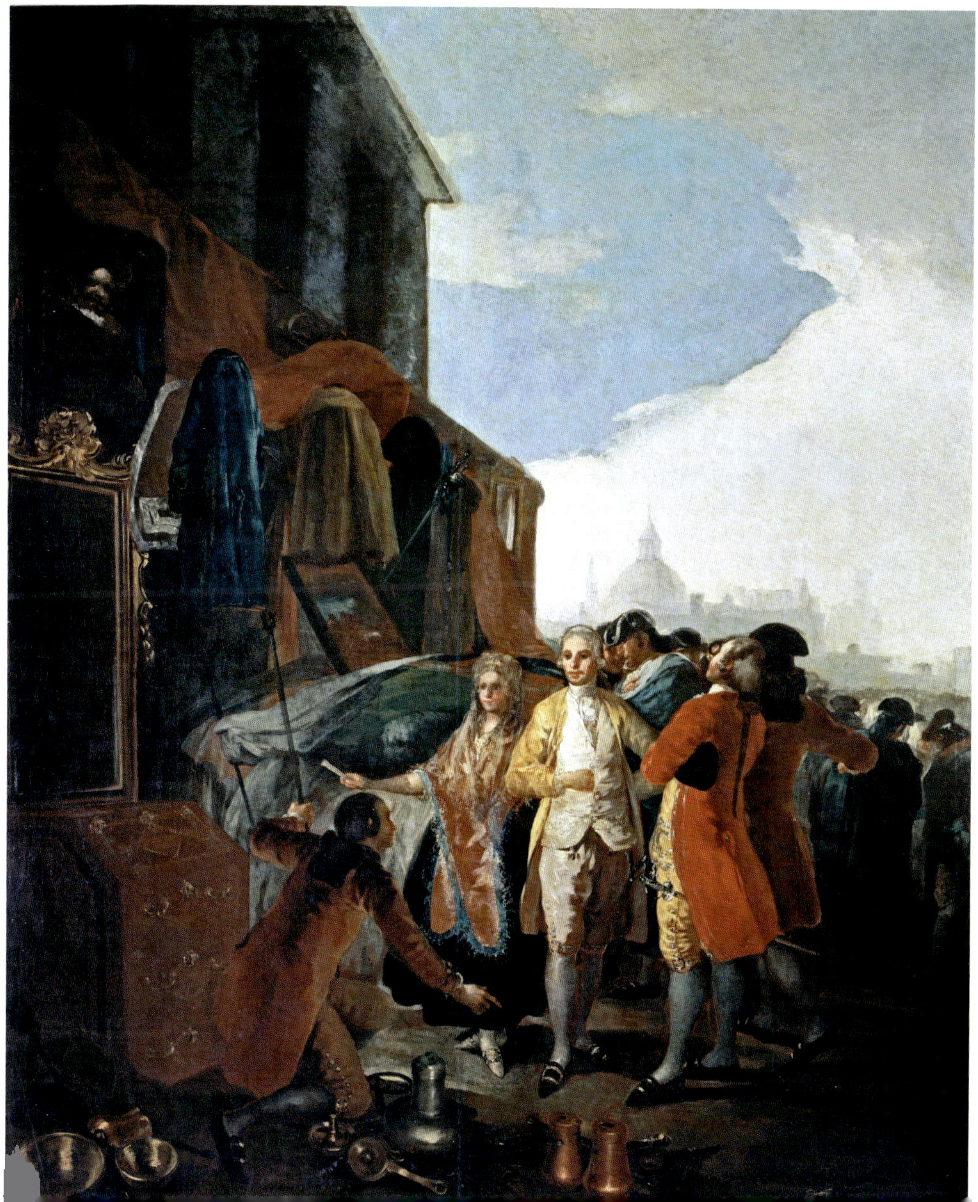

The Fair in Madrid, 1779, oil on canvas, Museo Nacional del Prado, Madrid, Spain, 258 x 218cm (101½ x 86in)

A group of people stand in front of a stall displaying vessels, furniture, second-hand clothing and paintings. The Church of San Francisco el Grande is in the background. Goya includes certain recognizable types from contemporary society in Madrid, such as the man with the monocle, the lavishly dressed woman pointing at an item with her fan, and the person bargaining with the vendor.

The Soldier and the Lady, 1779, oil on canvas, Museo Nacional del Prado, Madrid, Spain, 259 x 100cm (102 x 39in)

A lady glances up at a couple looking over a wall. Two gentleman stand near, while behind, a seated couple look back at the lady. The main woman is elaborately dressed and holds one of the gentleman's hands. She contrasts with the majas he painted in other works. The narrow format of this canvas indicates that it was designed for a space between two windows.

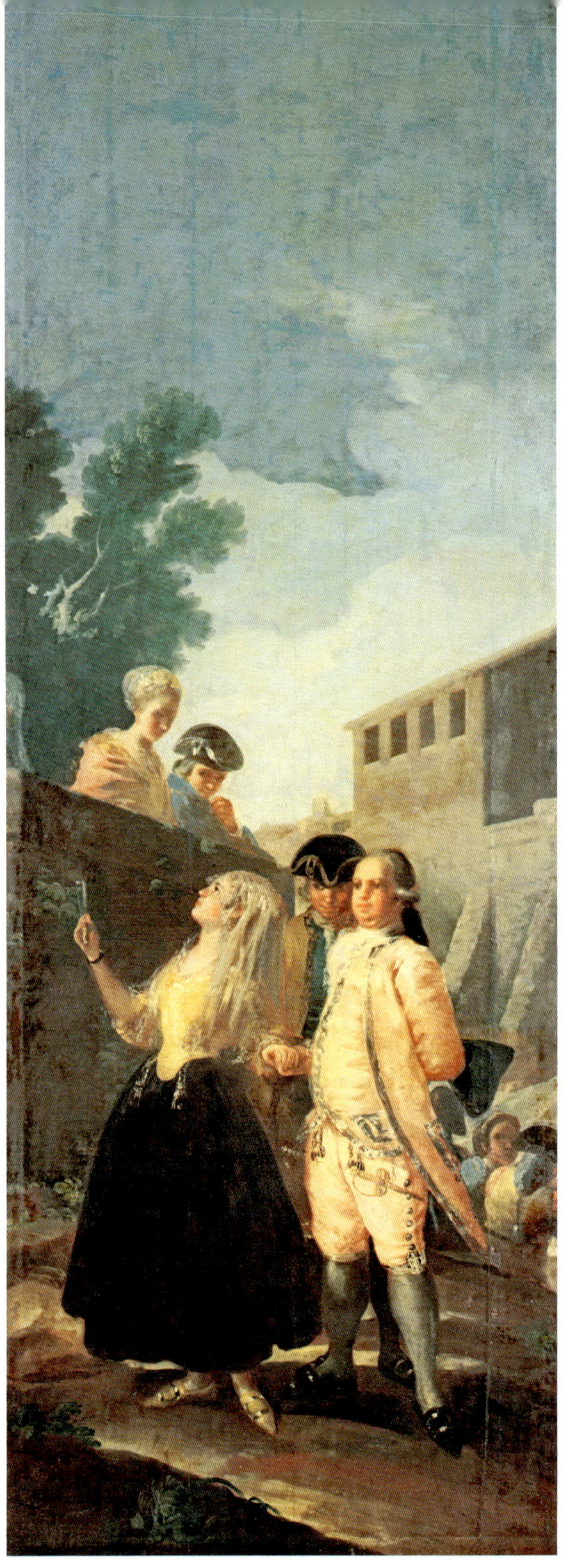

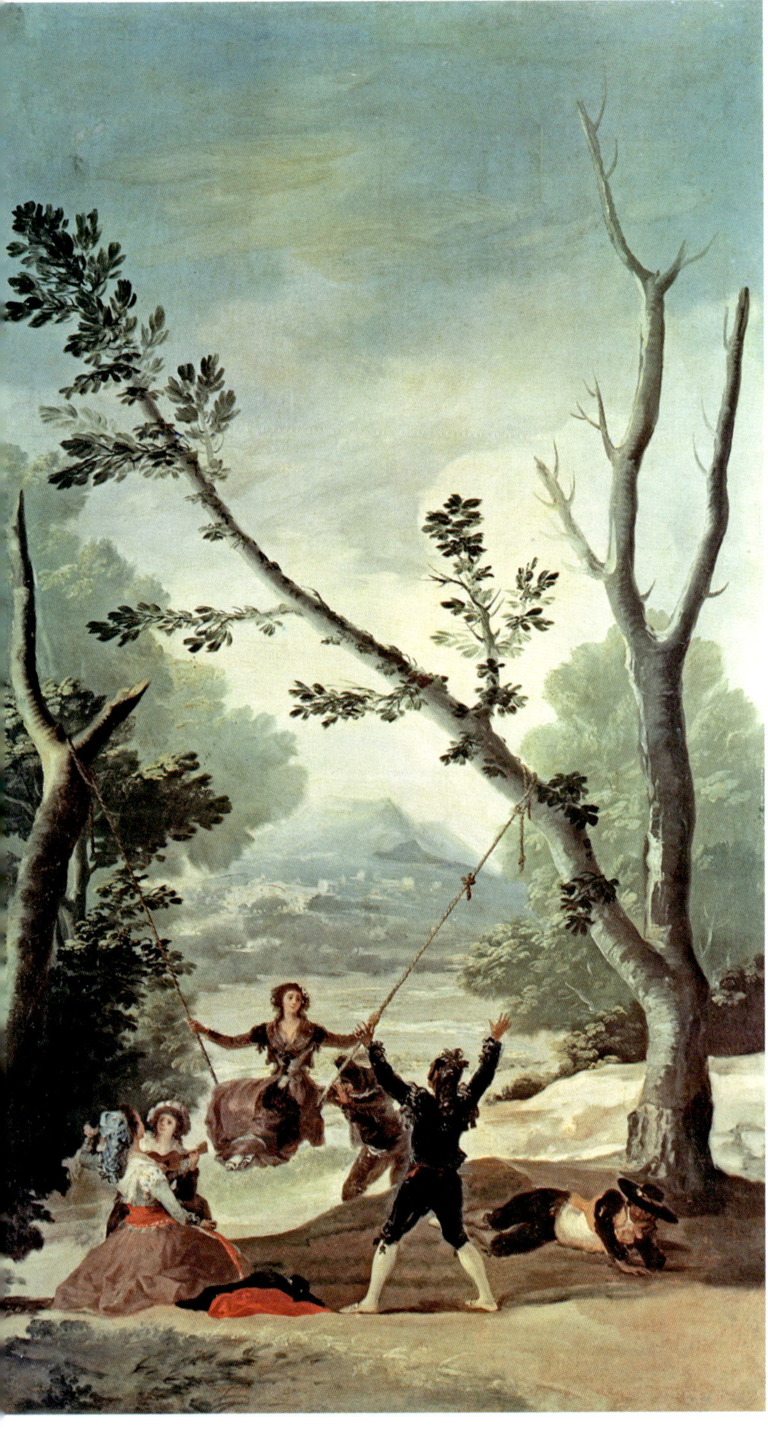

The Swing, 1779, oil on canvas, Museo Nacional del Prado, Madrid, Spain, 260 x 165cm (102 x 65in)

In this entire series, Goya displays his knowledge of the great Italian Renaissance and Baroque artists. Here, three young ladies, one on a swing attached to the branches of a tree, are looking after some children. Three farmworkers watch them from the background. Goya creates relationships between each figure, giving viewers an instant impression of alternative underlying stories. Goya revised this series of cartoons three times before their completion.

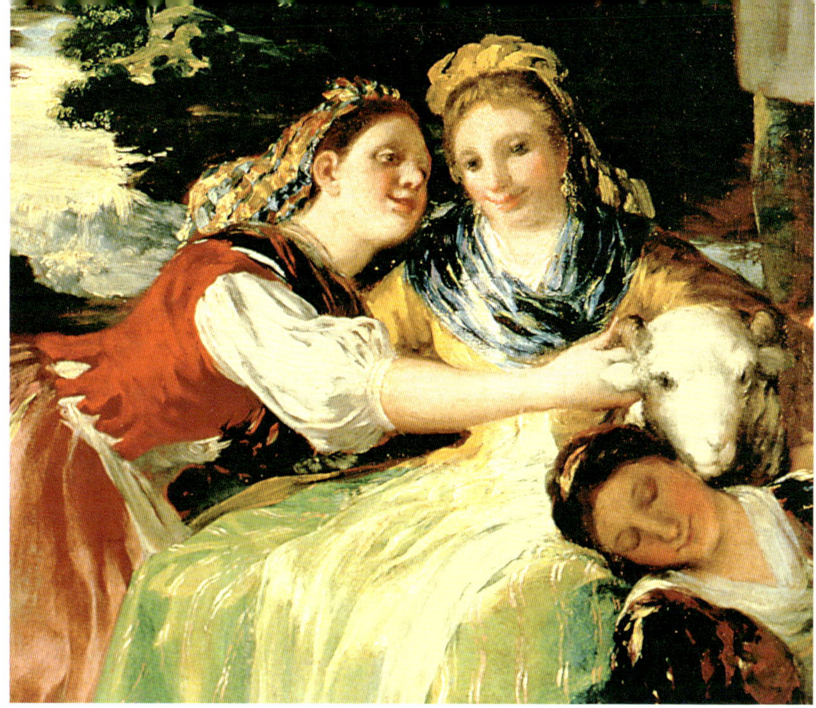

Detail from *Washerwomen* (below)

Goya masterfully creates personalities and relationships between his characters. Here, two washerwomen are about to play a practical joke on the other woman lying asleep below the ram. There is a perfect balance of colour and tonal contrast, with cool blues and greens contrasting with flashes of brighter hues. This range of contrasts was unusual for a tapestry design as it all had to be translated into wool.

Washerwomen, 1779–80, oil on canvas, Museo Nacional del Prado, Madrid, Spain, 257.5 x 166cm (101 x 65in)

A group of washerwoman are by the Manzanares River. One has fallen asleep on her friend, while another friend plays a trick on her with a ram. Two other women are busy washing behind them. Goya has built up the background behind the women, and has divided the image diagonally with the branch and drying washing. In the distance are the Guadarrama Mountains just beyond Madrid.

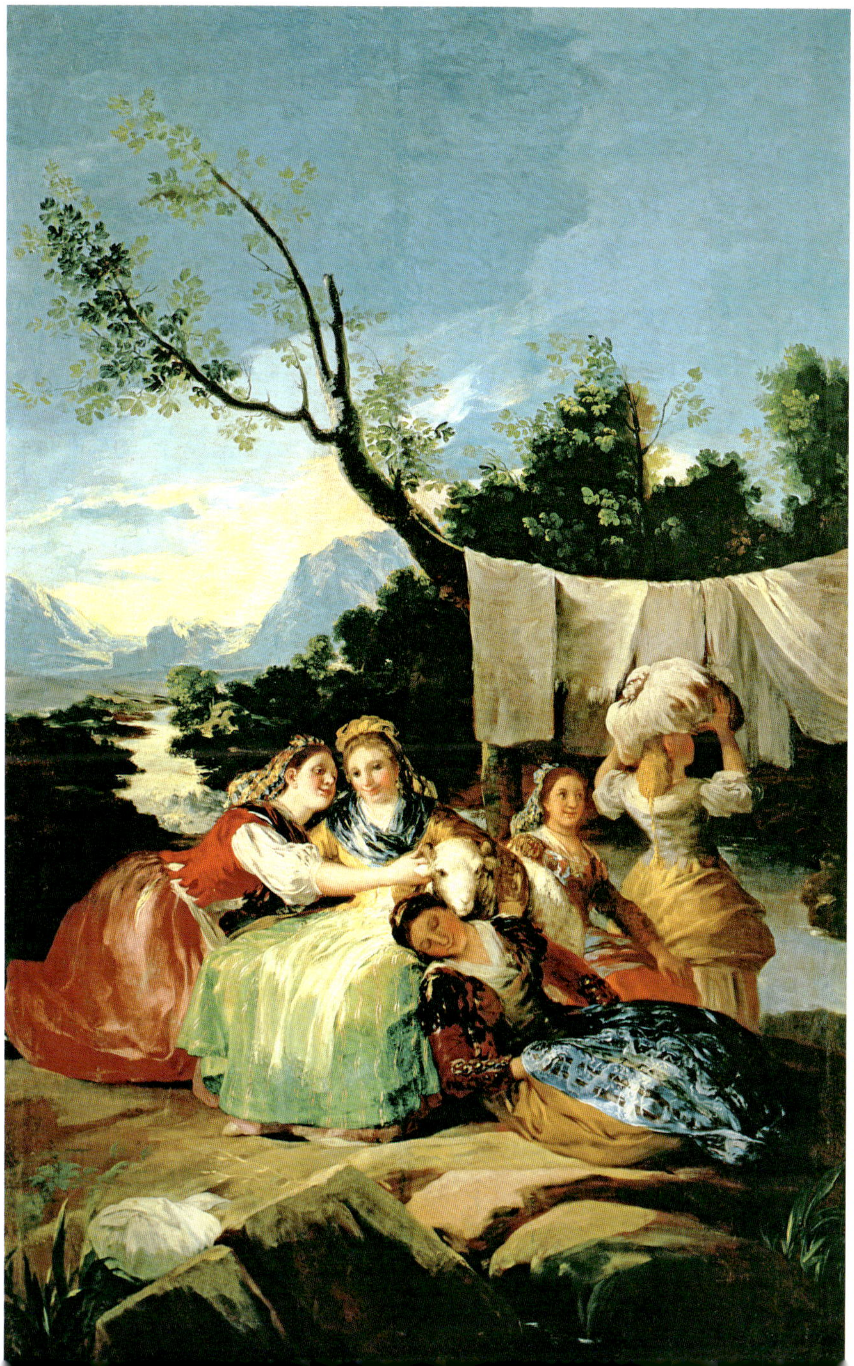

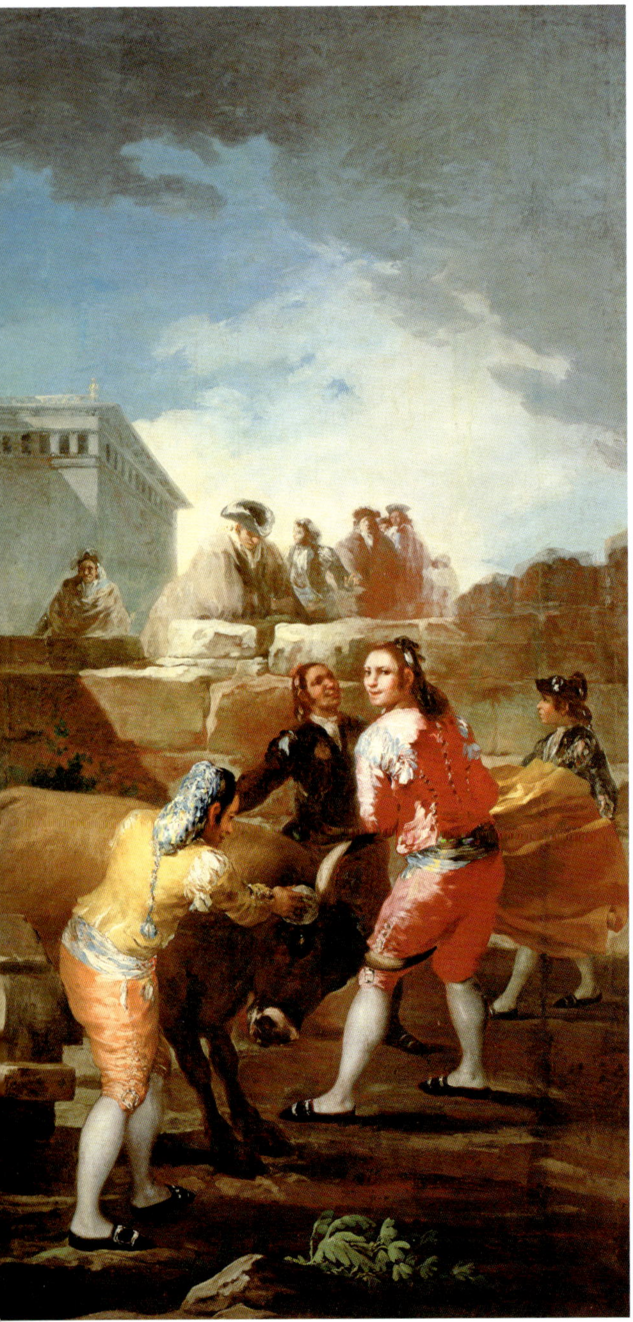

The Young Bulls, 1779–80, oil on canvas, Museo Nacional del Prado, Madrid, Spain, 259 x 136cm (102 x 53½in)

Four young men struggle to control a young bull. They are dressed as if they are about to put on an amateur bullfight. Behind the wall, a small crowd waits to watch the forthcoming spectacle. As Goya always claimed he had once taken part in a bullfight, the youth dressed in red has sometimes been thought to be his own self-portrait.

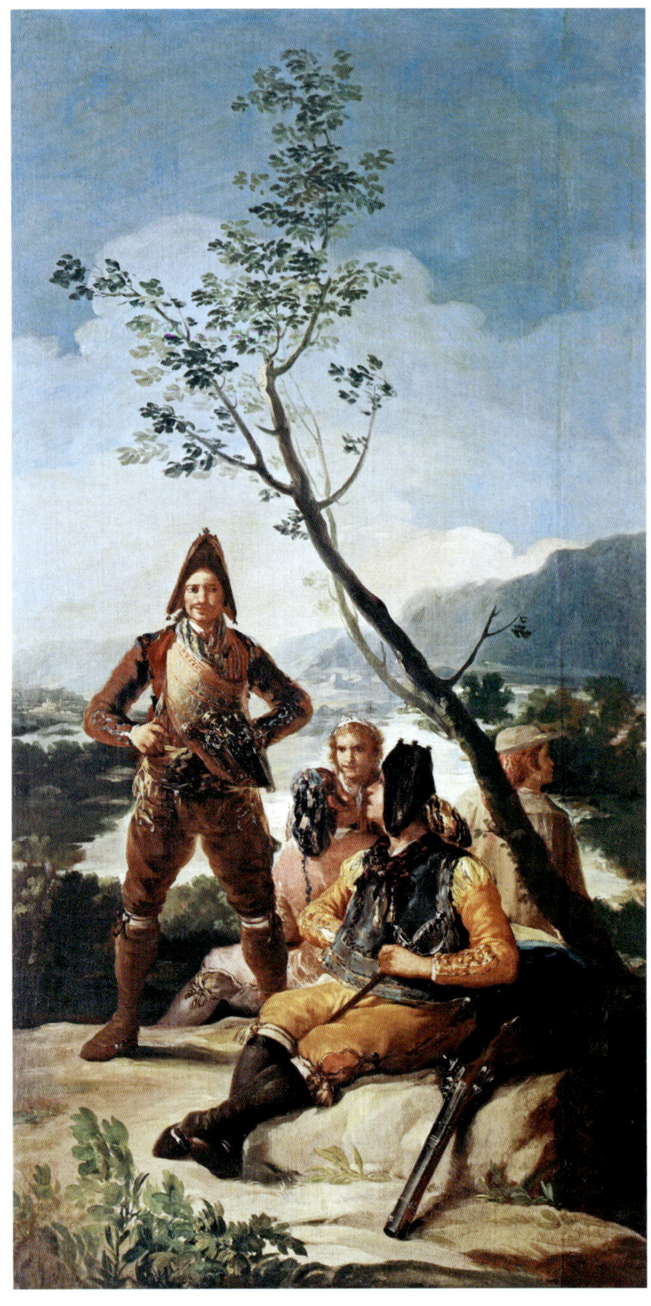

The Tobacco Guards, 1779–80, oil on canvas, Museo Nacional del Prado, Madrid, Spain, 262 x 137cm (103 x 54in)

Several guards are on patrol. One stands bombastically, legs astride. Three other figures sit nearby. The guards were there to prevent the smuggling of tobacco as it was often sold as contraband at that time. The mountains in the background are inspired by some of Velázquez's paintings of the outskirts of Madrid. Specifically male-dominated, this image contrasts with more female-orientated scenes such as *Washerwomen* (see page 123), which hung directly opposite.

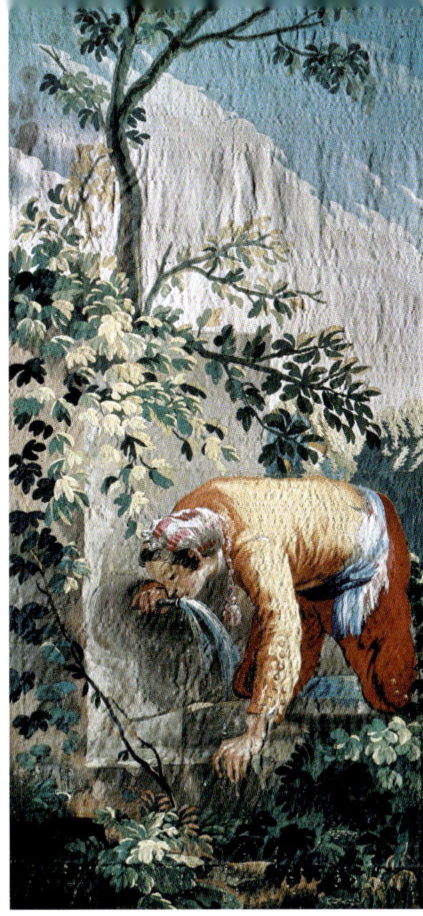

The Fountain, 1779–80, tapestry, Santiago de Compostela, Museum of the Cathedral, Galicia, Spain

This tapestry was made at the Royal Tapestry Factory from one of Goya's cartoons, along with ten others at the same time. Many of his contemporaries were surprised at the speed with which Goya created his tapestry paintings. This was made to hang in the El Pardo Palace between two windows. A man bends to drink from a fountain. Goya's tonal painting has been interpreted effectively in shimmering coloured threads.

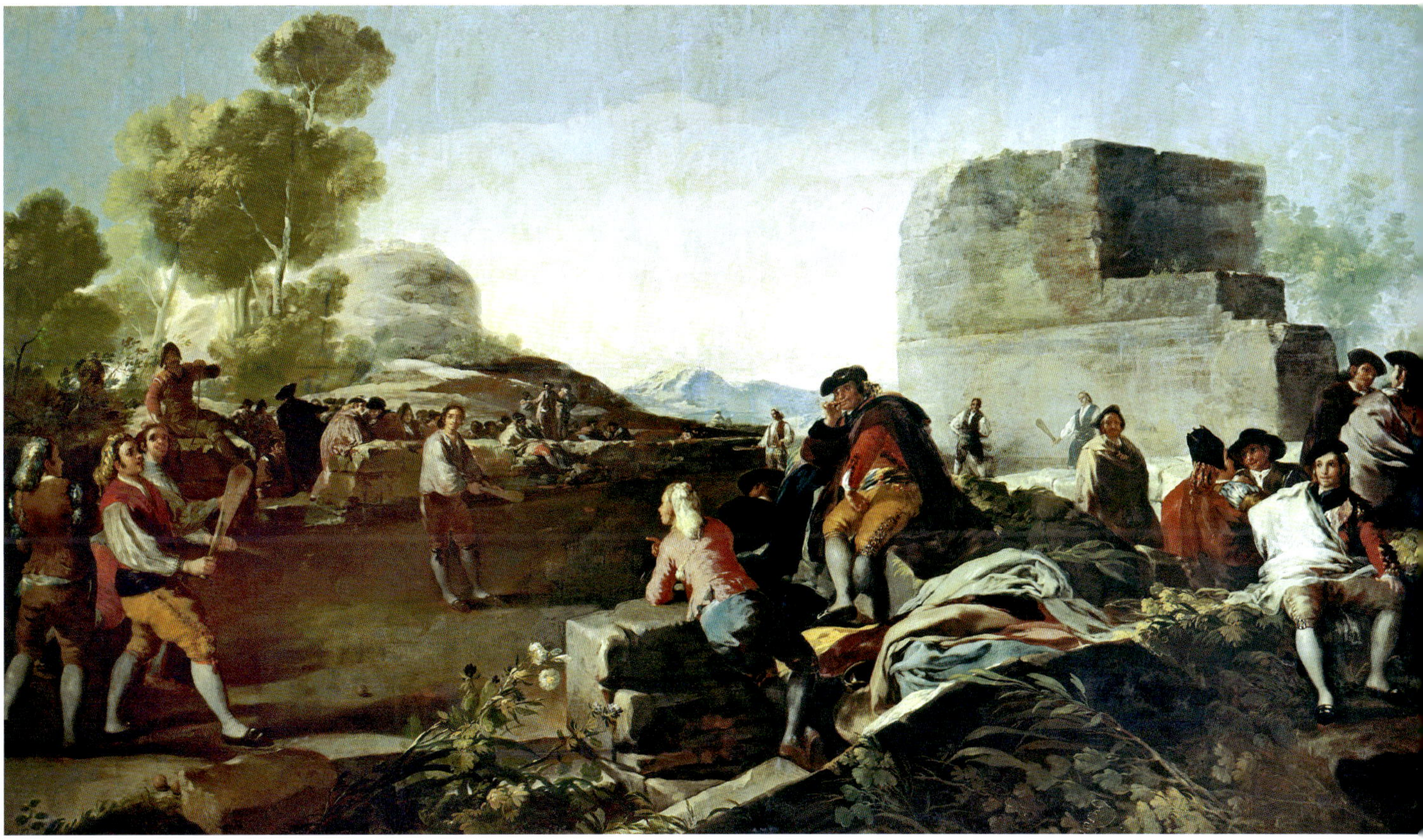

A Game of Stickball, 1779, oil on canvas, Museo Nacional del Prado, Madrid, Spain, 261 x 470cm (103 x 185in)

Painted between January 5 and July 20, 1779, this cartoon was for the main tapestry in the bedroom of the Prince and Princess of Asturias in the El Pardo Palace. Set in the outskirts of Madrid, the scene shows various figures playing in the open air. The perspective, light, colour and paint application is masterly, and shows how mature Goya's work had become in just a few years.

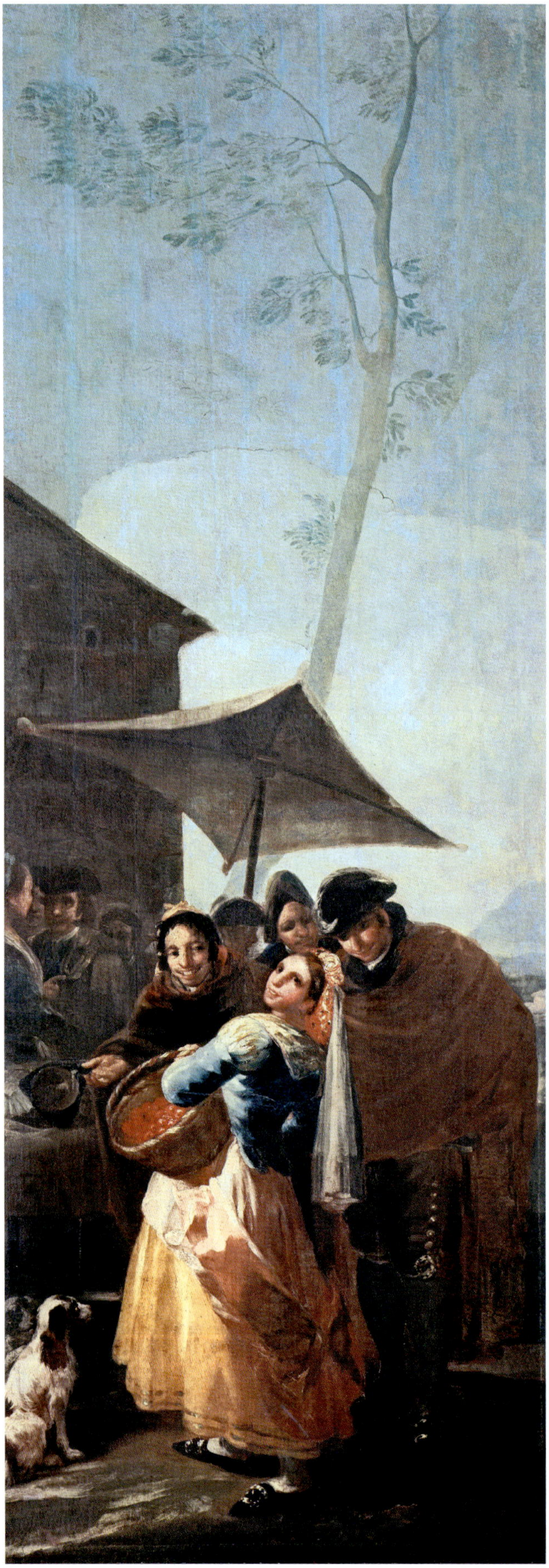

La Acerolera or *The Cherry Vendor*, 1779, oil on canvas, Museo Nacional del Prado, Madrid, Spain, 259 x 100cm (102 x 39in)

A woman dressed as a maja selling cherries turns back from a group of cloaked figures to look flirtatiously at the viewer. This represents an everyday market scene in Madrid and the men are more interested in the young woman than in her basket of fruit. Restricted by the shapes in the palace rooms where the tapestries would hang, Goya's resolutions were extremely creative.

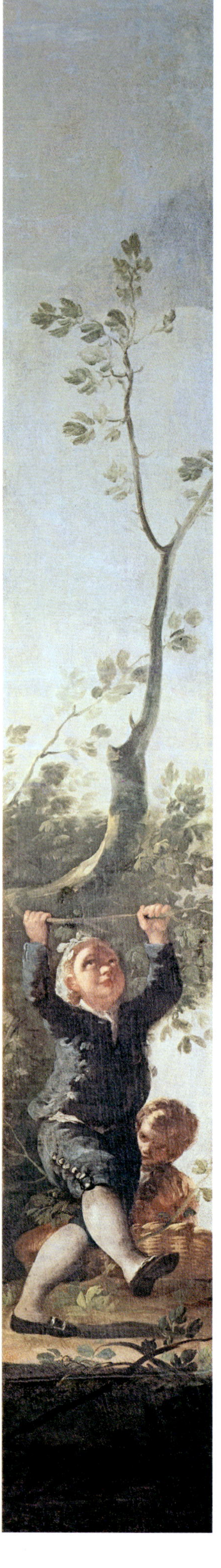

Boy and a Tree, 1779–80, oil on canvas, Museo Nacional del Prado, Madrid, Spain, 262 x 40cm (103 x 16in)

In size, format and subject, this work mirrors the painting opposite. Bold and lively, it shows two young boys playing by a tree. The main boy in the front hangs from a branch and balances his foot on another. He looks up intently, while his friend behind him holds a basket. All the signs show that they are trying to catch birds.

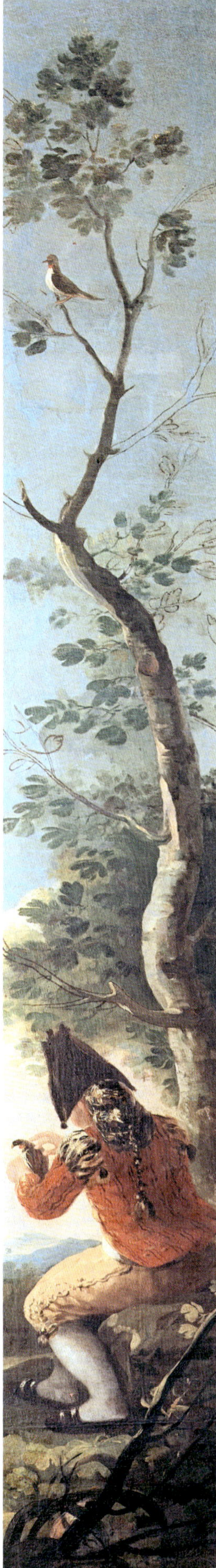

Boy with a Bird, 1779–80, oil on canvas, Museo Nacional del Prado, Madrid, Spain, 262 x 40cm (103 x 16in)

A young boy with his back to viewers strokes a goldfinch perched on his hand. At the top of a tall tree next to him is another goldfinch. This brightly coloured tapestry was intended to hang in a narrow space, which is why it is in a long, vertical format – this was one of Goya's particular challenges with the cartoons.

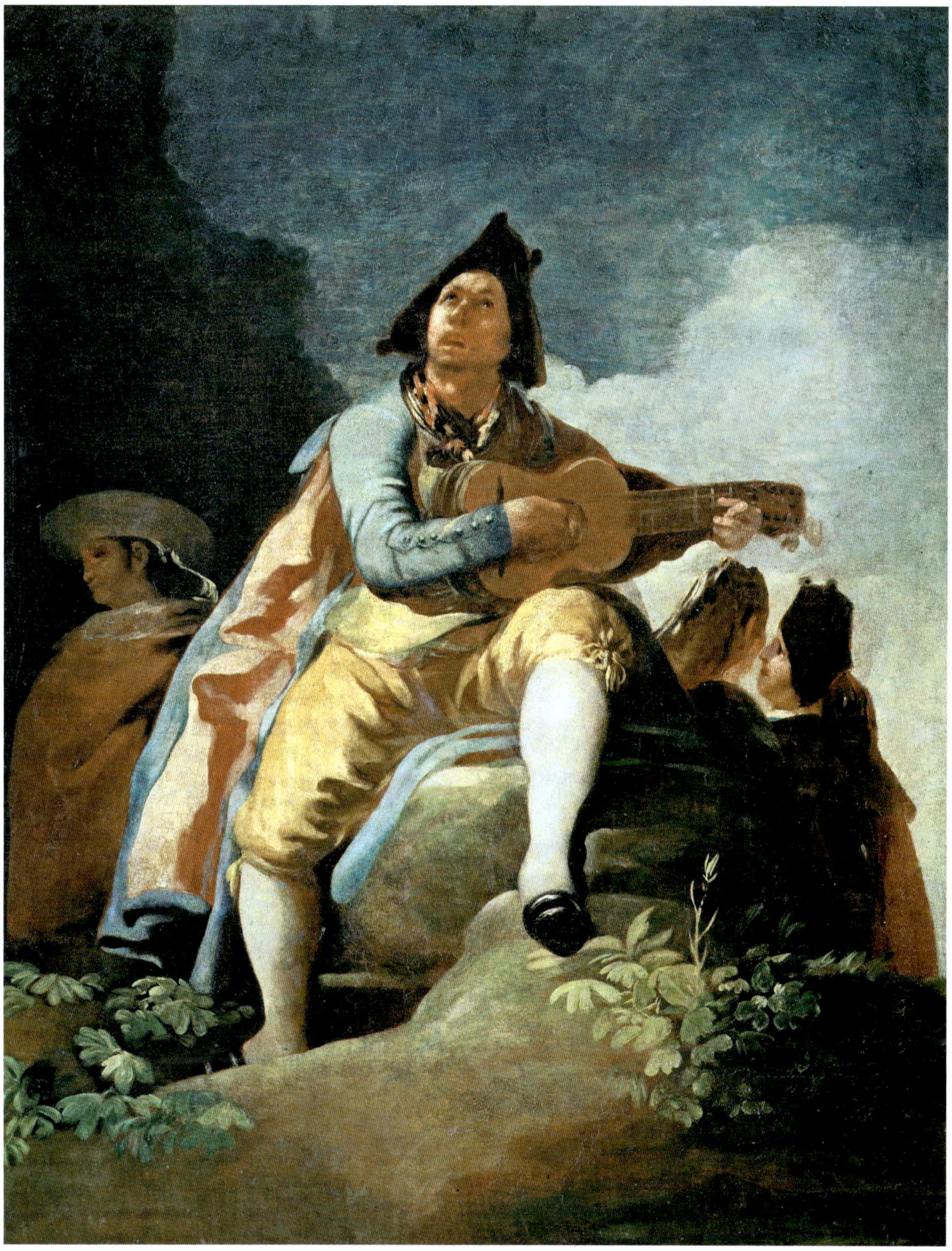

A Majo with a Guitar, 1779, oil on canvas, Museo Nacional del Prado, Madrid, Spain, 137 x 112cm (54 x 44in)

As a pendant, one of two paintings conceived as a pair, to *Washerwomen* (see page 123), this majo playing the guitar was for a tapestry intended to hang over the door of the main bedroom in the Prado Palace. When the tapestries were in this location, Goya usually put figures on a hill or rock so he could create particularly dramatic perspective. The triangular composition corresponded with emerging Neoclassical ideas.

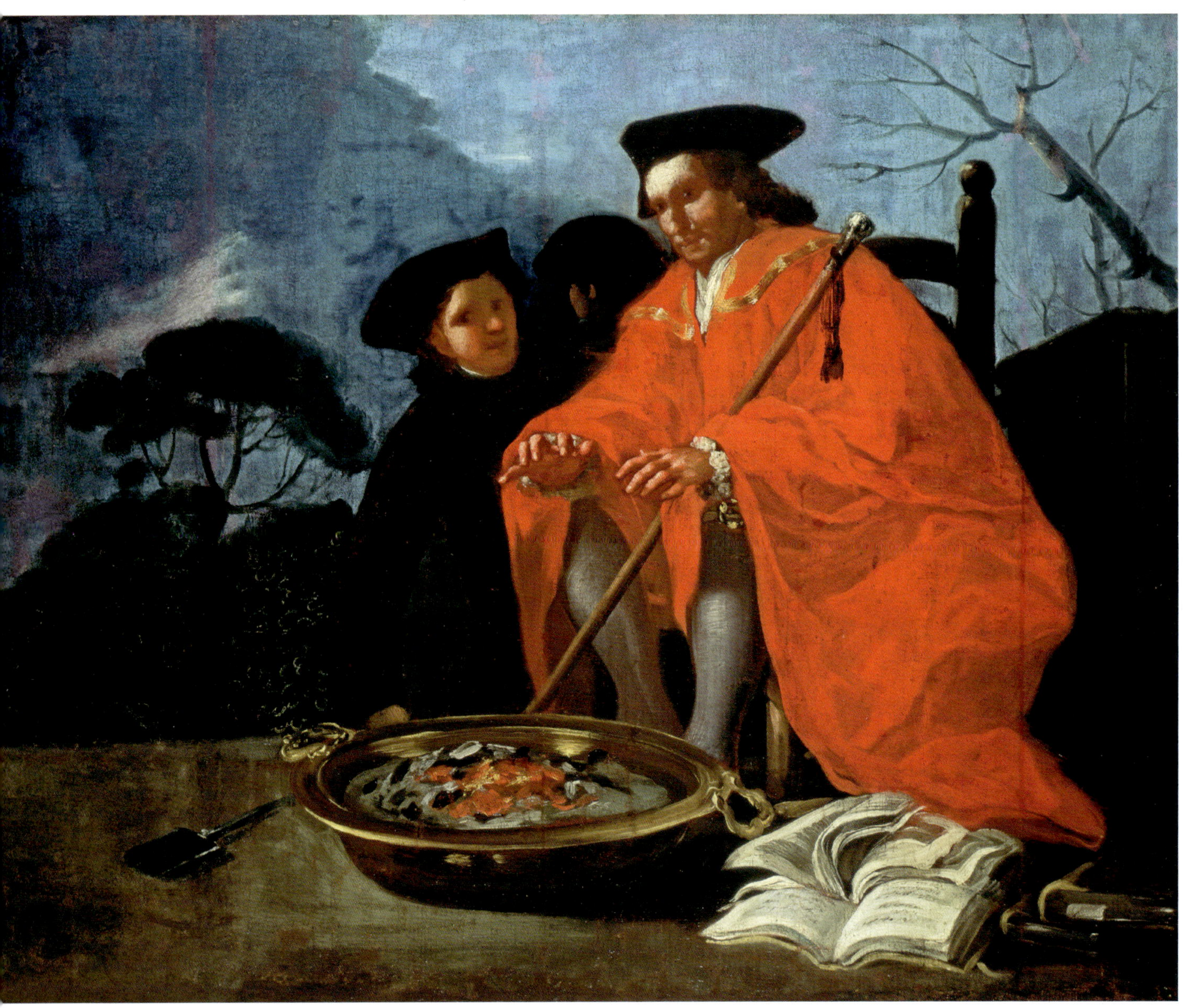

The Doctor, 1779–80, oil on canvas, Scottish National Gallery, Edinburgh, UK, 137 x 112cm (54 x 44in)

The resulting tapestry for this image was to hang over a door in the El Pardo Palace. A doctor in a red cloak accompanied by two students, warms his hands over heated coals. Combined with the leafless tree behind, it is probable that the picture's underlying theme was winter. The doctor's bright red cloak, books and the hot coals were particularly prominent in the tapestry when seen from below. Goya's mastery at composition is pronounced here: the triangular group of three figures are slightly to one side of the image, creating a sense of harmony, and their overall shape is emphasized by the vermilion of the doctor's cloak.

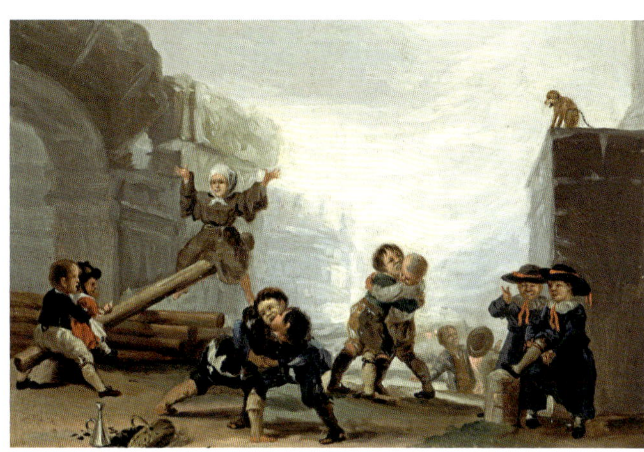

Children Playing with a See-Saw, c.1777–85, oil on canvas, Pollok House, Glasgow, UK, 29 x 42cm (11 x 16½in)

All his life, Goya was interested in children's games and toys. This small, lively painting appears spontaneous and unplanned, but Goya always prepared his compositions meticulously. In the picture, the children are all busy at various activities: four little boys are fighting, three are on the see-saw, two are chatting and a monkey looks down at them from high on a wall.

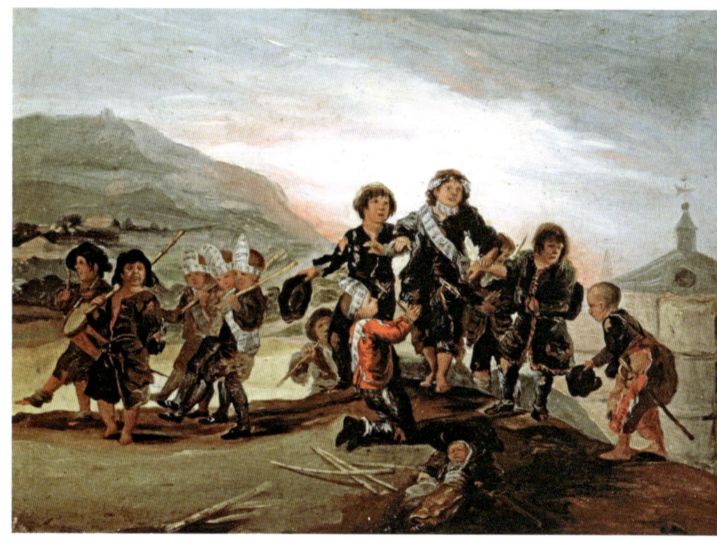

Children Playing at Soldiers, c.1777–85, oil on canvas, Pollok House, Glasgow, UK, 29 x 42cm (11 x 16½in)

Goya always maintained a strong sensitivity toward children and animals. Over approximately eight years, from about 1777 to 1785, he created six small studies of children playing. These were not for any specific commission, although they are similar in style to the tapestry cartoons he was making at the time. This little painting shows young boys playing a timeless game of pretending to be soldiers.

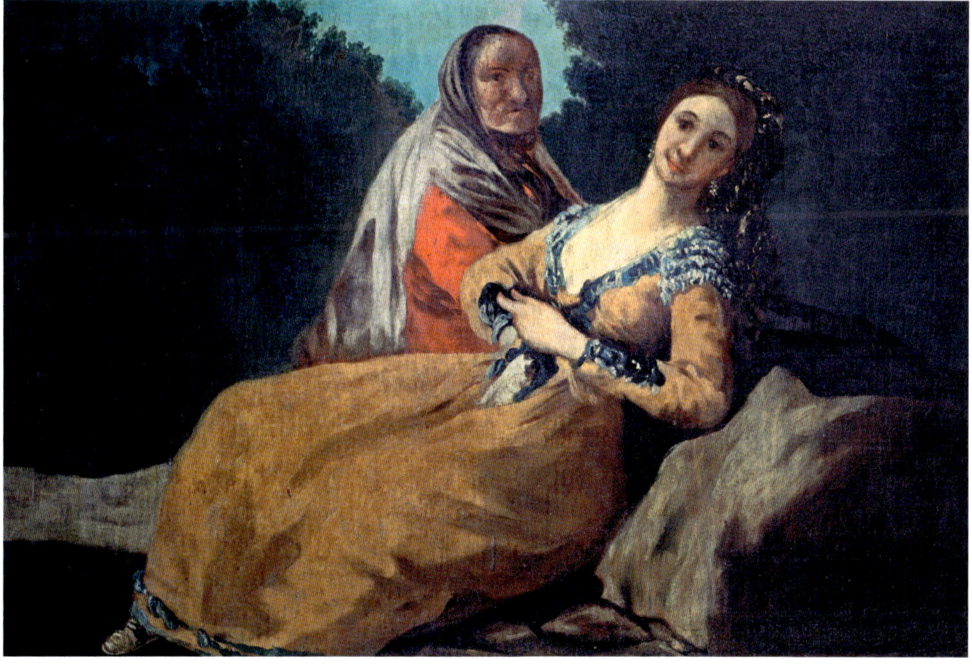

Maja and Celestina, c.1778–80, oil on canvas, Private Collection, 75 x 113cm (29½ x 44½in)

A familiar subject that Goya portrayed again in the future, was an old woman with a young one. Celestina is traditionally an old woman who was once a prostitute, while the maja is a sweet-faced young woman. Both women are wearing vivid colours, which contrast strongly with the background landscape. Goya continues to employ free brushstrokes and does not linger over details.

Children Scrambling for Chestnuts, c.1777–85, oil on canvas, Private Collection, 30.5 x 43cm (12 x 17in)

Goya had the ability to recall and represent a child's world. In this painting as in others from the same group, little ragamuffins play happily, scrambling for chestnuts. The colourful and confident treatment shows a greater naturalness than in his first tapestry cartoons when he was under the eye of Bayeu. The palette reflects the latest styles of the Rococo.

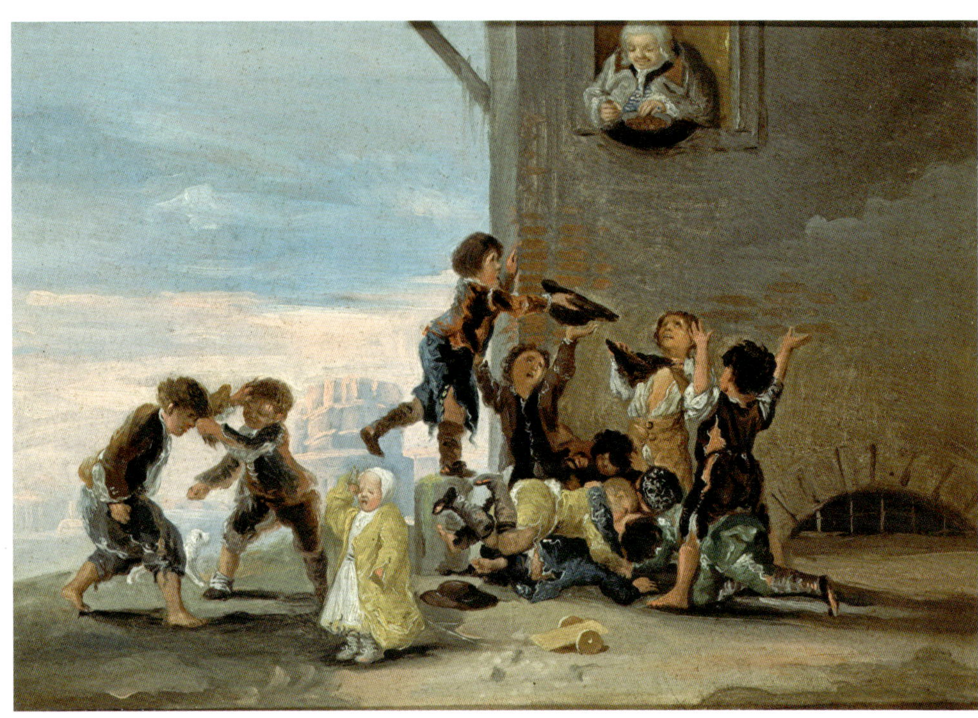

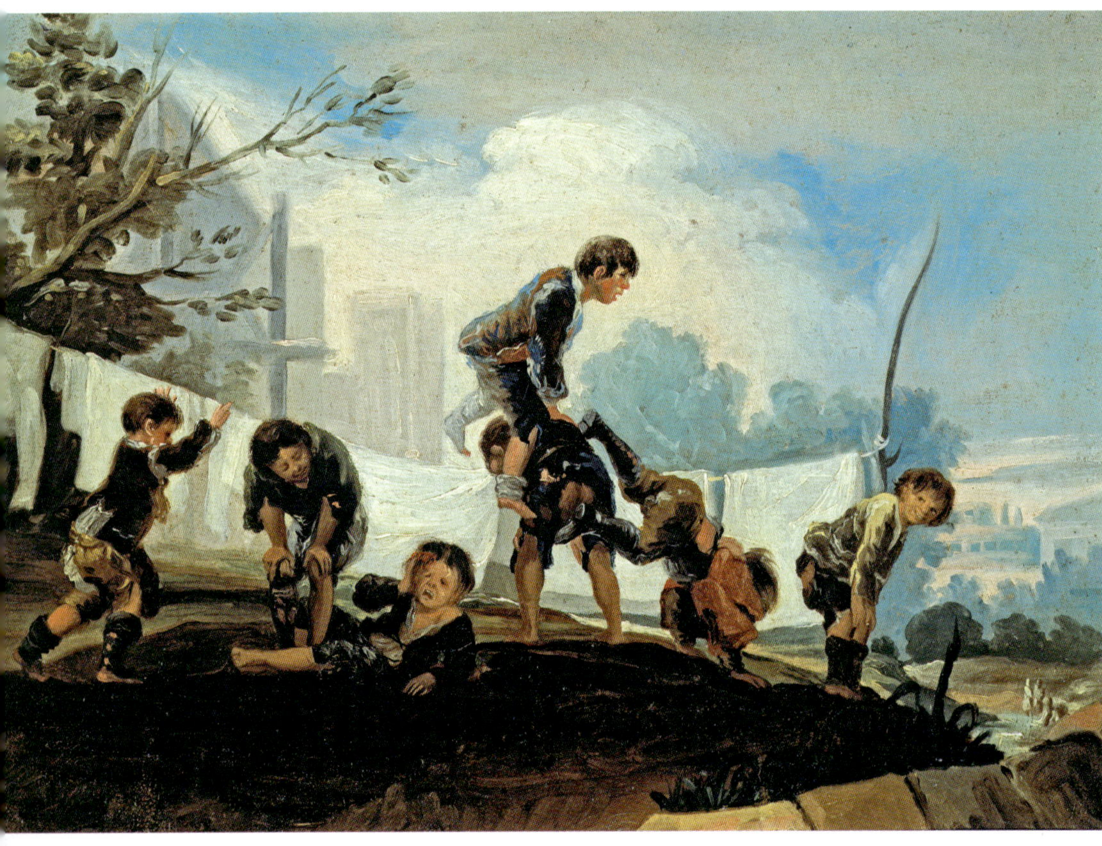

Children Playing Leapfrog, c.1777–85, oil on canvas, Academy of San Carlos, Valencia, Spain, 29 x 41cm (11 x 16in)

Another painting of children at play in the suburbs of Madrid, this pyramid-shaped composition echoes the actual game of leapfrog. The small figures play apparently naïvely, but there is always some devilment. On a late spring or early summer day, seven children play leapfrog. Some fall awkwardly, while others laugh unkindly at them. Each work in this series complements the others in terms of colour, light and composition.

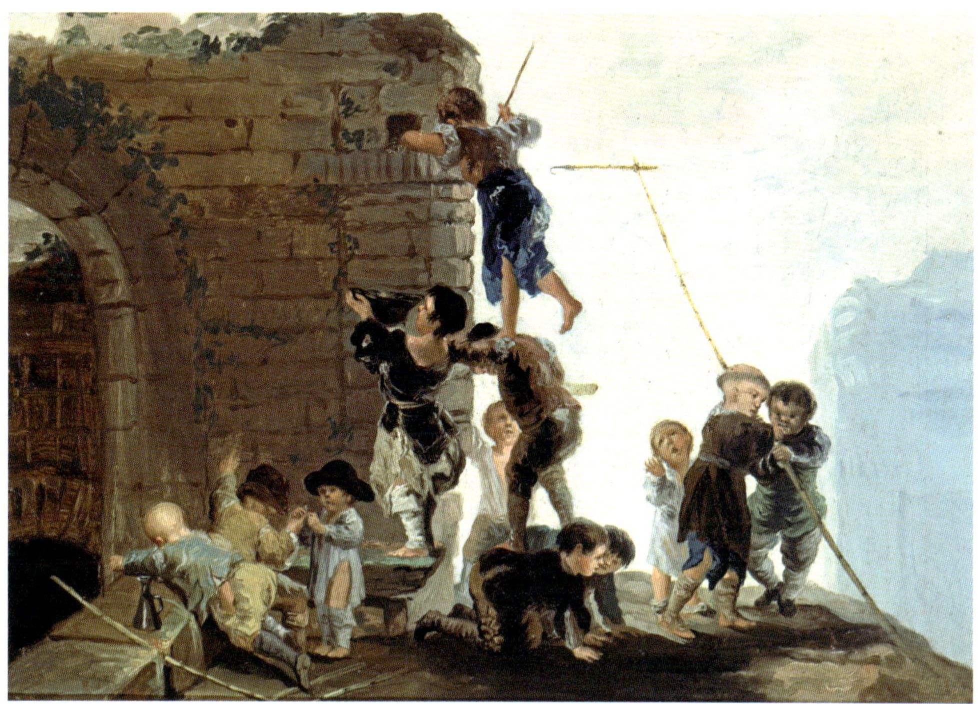

Children Birds' Nesting,
c.1777–85, oil on canvas,
Private Collection,
30.5 x 43cm (12 x 17in)

A companion painting to
Children Playing Leapfrog,
these seeming innocents are
up to mischief, stealing birds'
nests. Goya himself was a
rather naughty child and these
images suggest he retained
happy memories of that time.
The composition and colours
deliberately complement
works such as *Children
Scrambling for Chestnuts,* and
Goya has created amusing
cameos of the young children
up to all sorts of antics.

*Children Playing at
Bullfighting, c.1777–85, oil
on canvas, Fundación Santa
Marca, Madrid, Spain,
29 x 41cm (11 x 16in)*

Amid the general roguishness
and fun, some little boys are
putting on a mock bullfight.
One is under a wickerwork
'bull'. He charges at a 'picador'
who rides on the shoulders
of another boy. The children
in this painting range in age
from young babies to about
12 years old. Goya clearly
made each study directly
from life as the poses and
expressions of the children
are astutely captured.

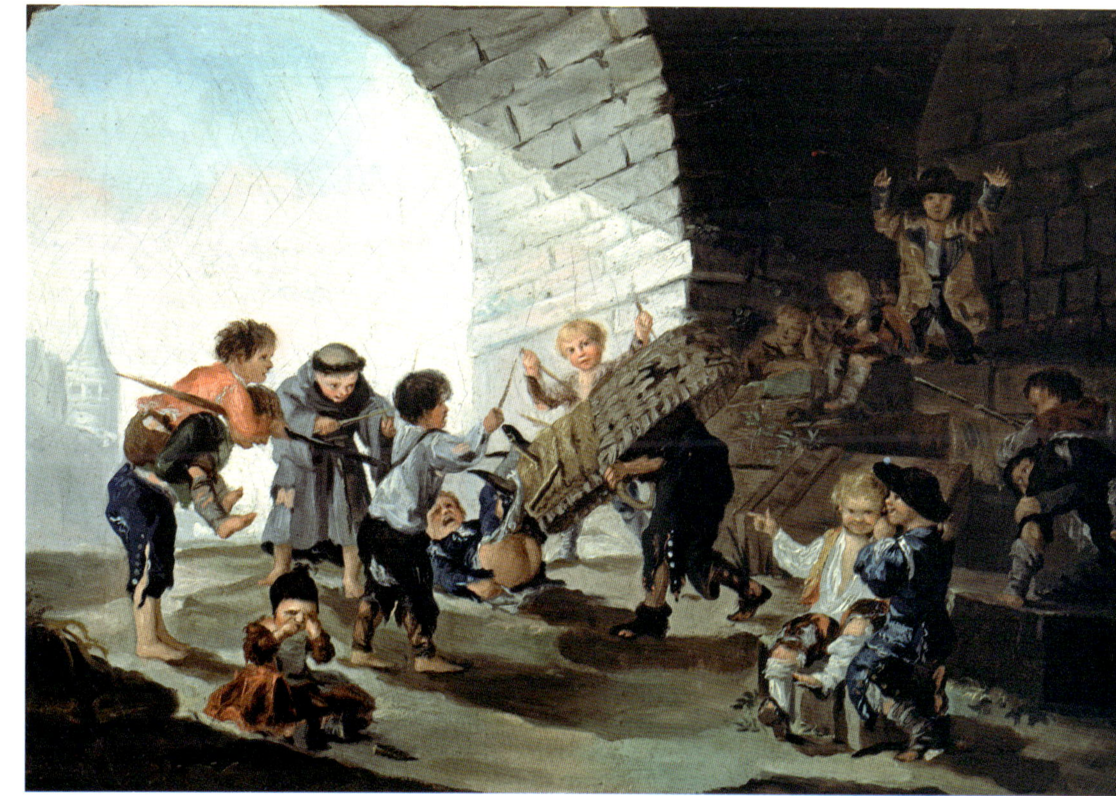

Apparition of the Virgin of the Pillar, c.1775–80, oil on canvas, Private Collection, 107 x 80cm (42 x 31½in)

According to Spanish tradition, in 40CE, James, one of Christ's original Apostles, was preaching in (then) pagan Saragossa. Disheartened at only converting a few, he prayed by the Ebro River. Mary miraculously appeared to him on top of a pillar and reassured him that the people of Saragossa would all be converted and their faith would be as strong as the pillar she was standing on.

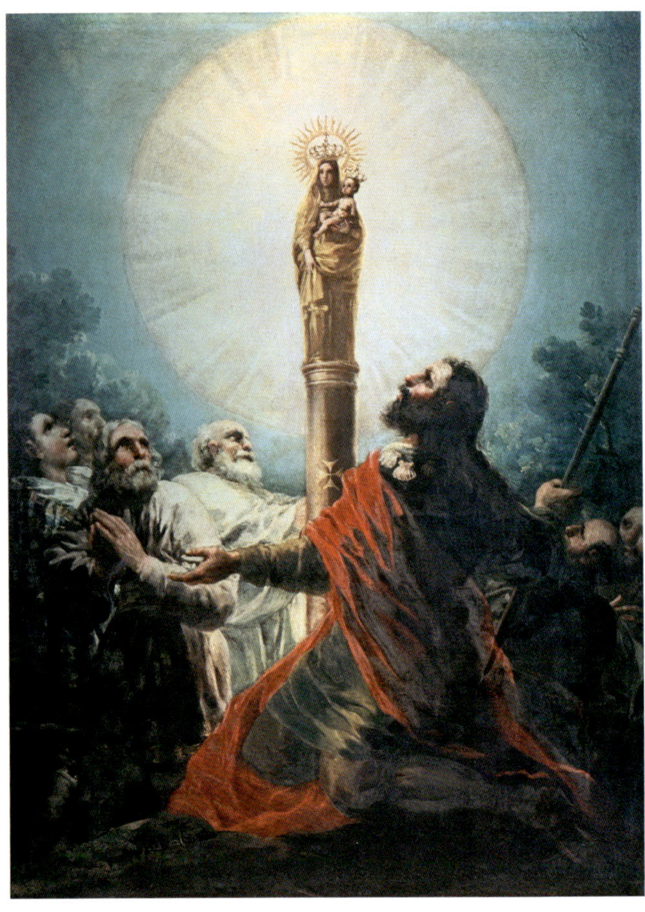

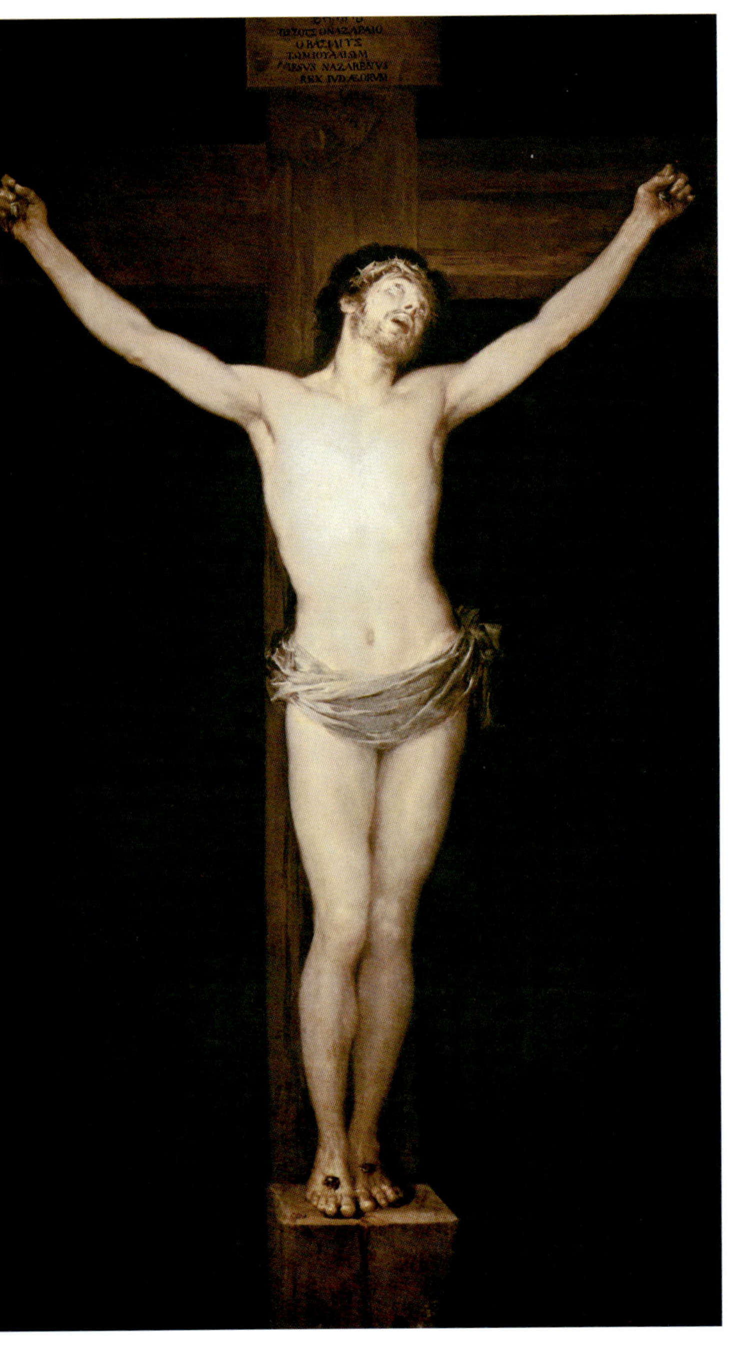
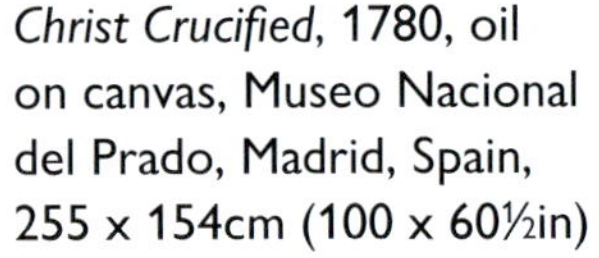

Christ Crucified, 1780, oil on canvas, Museo Nacional del Prado, Madrid, Spain, 255 x 154cm (100 x 60½in)

Goya submitted this painting to the Royal Academy in May 1780 in the hope of being accepted as a member. By his conscious following of the styles of Velázquez, Francisco de Zurbarán (1598–1664), Mengs and Bayeu, the work met the approval of the Academicians and he was awarded a Merit for it. The painting was placed on the altar of the Church of San Francisco el Grande.

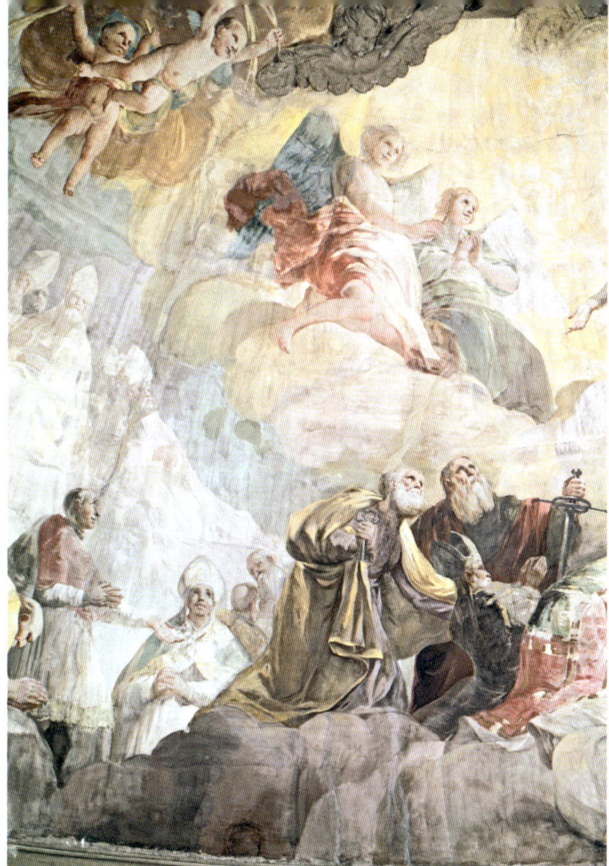

Detail from *The Queen of Martyrs* (below)

Although Goya painted this in a unique and expressive way incorporating a naturalism that had not been seen before, it also shows his early training in the rich traditions of the Baroque and Rococo styles. The figures appear animated and convincing, while still ethereal and miraculous. Seen from below, the painting of Mary and several saints seems dynamic and exciting.

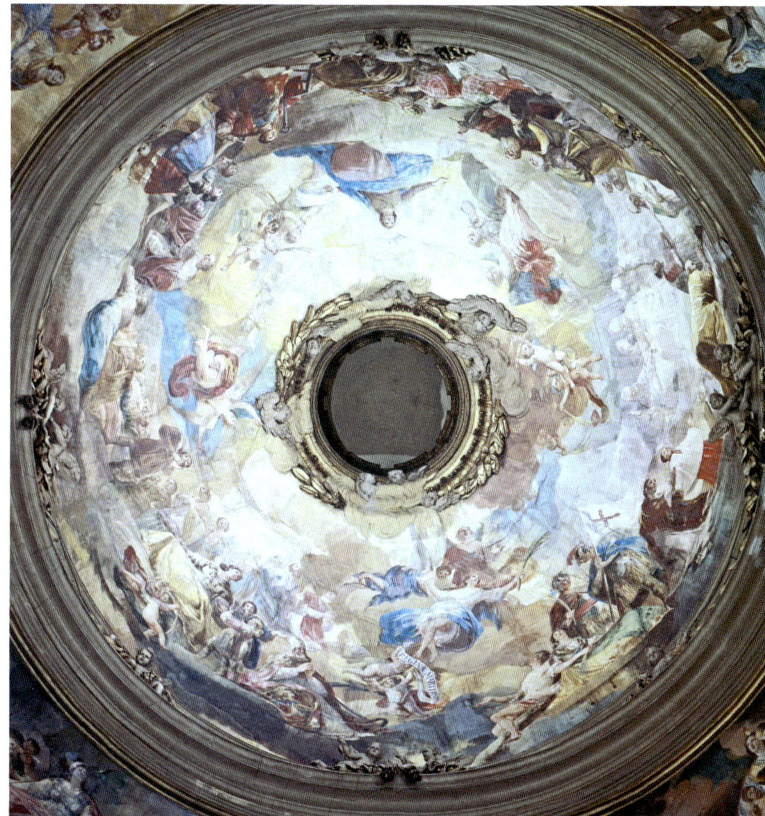

The Queen of Martyrs, 1780–81, fresco, Cathedral of Our Lady of El Pilar, Saragossa, Spain, dimensions unknown

In 1780, Goya was commissioned to decorate one of the cupolas and its pendentives in the cathedral of Our Lady of El Pilar in Saragossa. With large brushstrokes he painted rapidly, giving the image an unfinished appearance that contradicted the favoured smooth Neoclassical and Rococo styles. Although he was criticized for this approach, some commented on how the technique gave the painting freshness and immediacy.

Detail from *The Queen of Martyrs* (above)

In this detail can be seen Saint Lambert, the beheaded saint, with his head held in his hands, and the holy children Justo and Pastor next to Saint Catalina. The circular shape of the cupola has been filled cleverly with figures, that interact with each other. After initial criticism of this painting, it was soon recognized as a masterpiece, and helped to establish Goya's reputation.

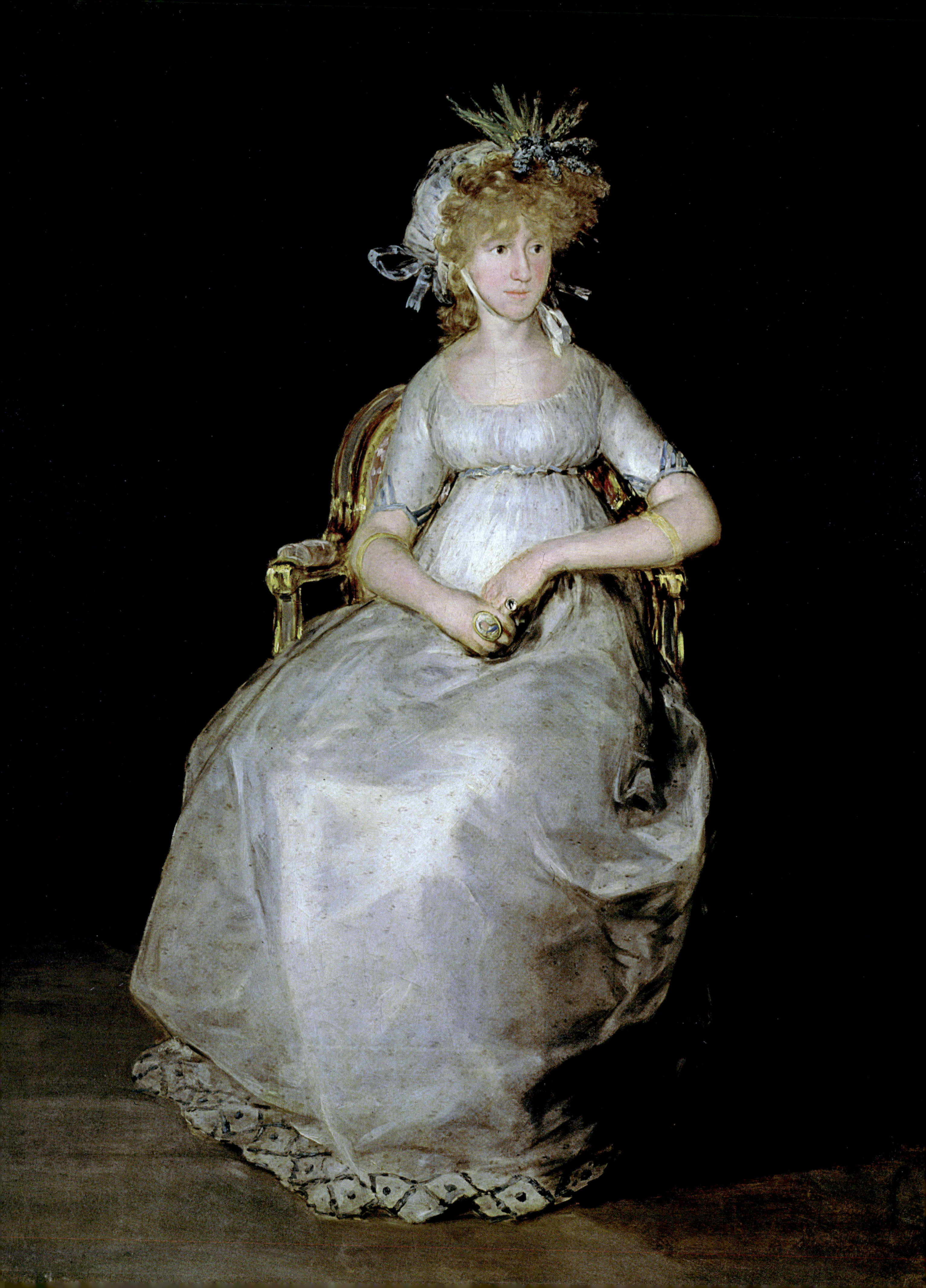

THE FIRST MODERN ARTIST

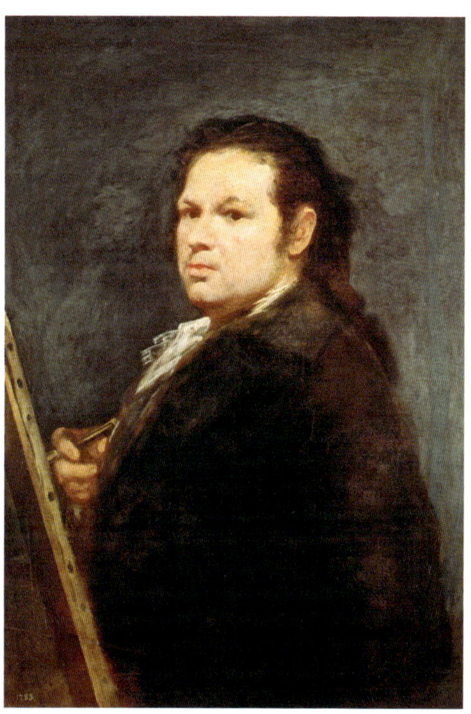

Through his own determination, by 1800, Goya had made a name for himself as both Court Painter and painter of the people. Enterprising and undefinable, he worked independently, ignoring the accepted styles of the day. He painted portraits, religious works and works of mysticism, and also created images of beauty and eroticism as well as of explicit horror. Unlike most other artists, he worked in a range of media and combined elements of the Baroque and Rococo, with Neoclassicism and Romanticism. His lively and perceptive images continued to evolve and develop throughout his life.

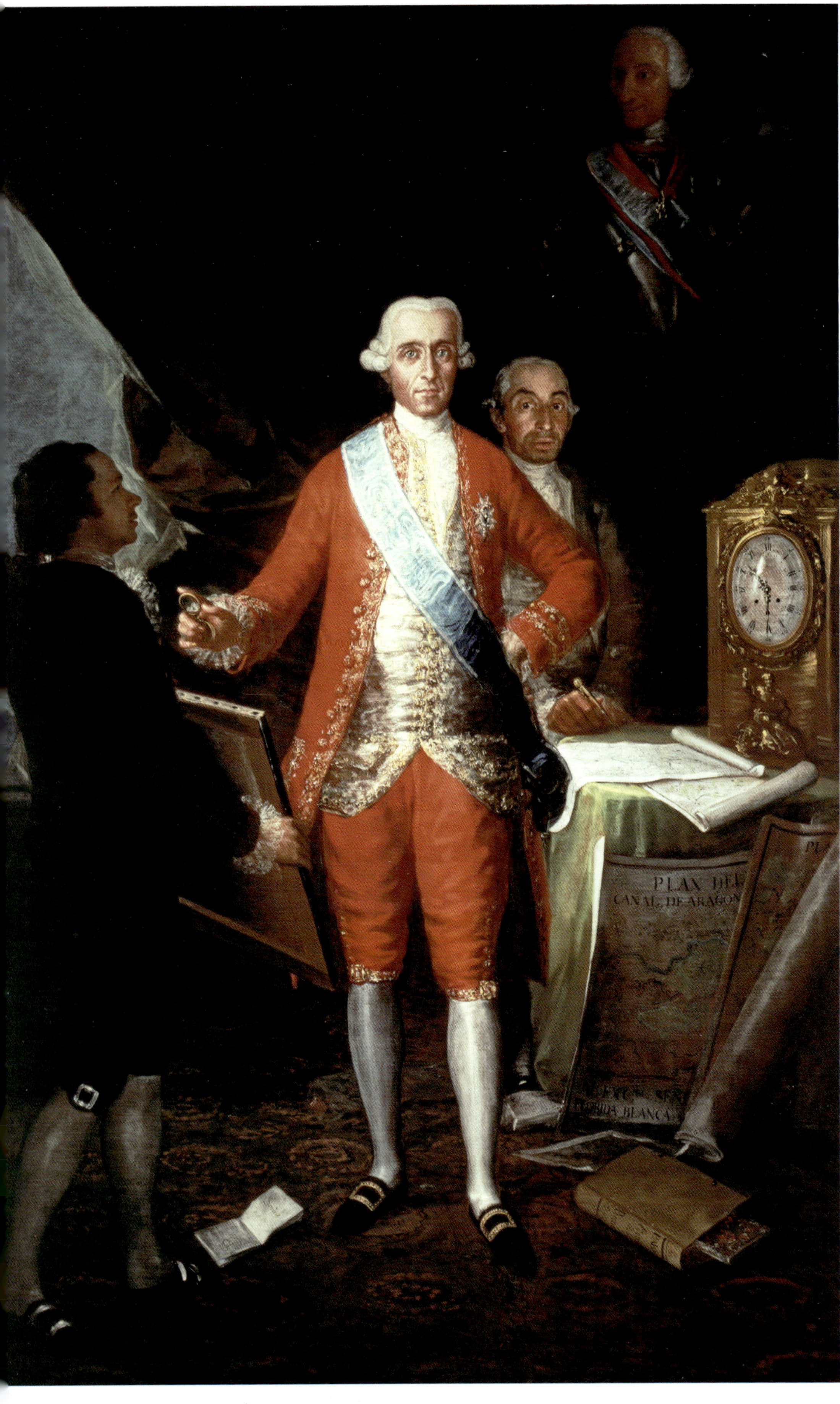

Count Floridablanca, 1783, oil on canvas, Banco de Espana, Madrid, Spain, 262 x 166cm (103¼ x 65½in)

Seen as Goya's first important portrait commission, the success of this work triggered his ascent to become the leading painter of Madrid. The time on the clock indicates that both Goya and the Count kept late working hours, while several objects around the room convey the Count's importance, intelligence and enlightenment. Yet although the light and composition are elegant, the actual portrait of the Count is somewhat static.

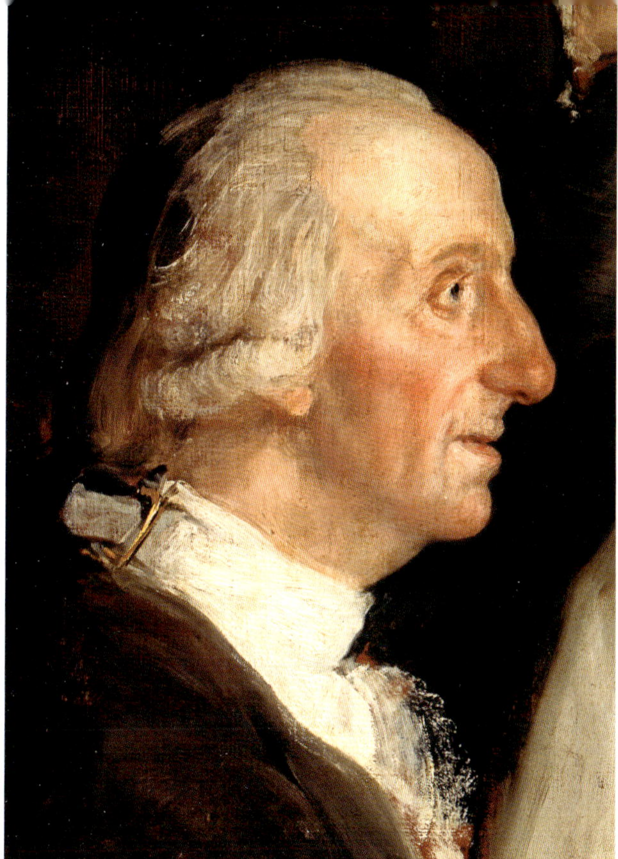

María Teresa of Vallabriga, 1783, oil on canvas, Museo Nacional del Prado, Madrid, Spain, 48 x 39.5cm (19 x 15½in)

A companion portrait to the above work, this is María Teresa Vallabriga y Rozas (1759–1820), the wife of Luis de Bourbon (1727–85), the King's brother. On the death of her husband, María's children were taken from her as they were royal but she was not. Although overall, this portrait is a little stiff, the skin is convincingly rendered and the sitter's expression is soft and natural.

Infante Don Luis de Bourbon, 1783, oil on canvas, Private Collection, 42 x 37cm (16½ x 14½in)

In 1783, Goya was invited to stay at the Court of Arenas de San Pedro, to paint portraits of Don Luis Antonio de Bourbon and his family in their own home. This informal profile of the Infante shows how relaxed Goya felt in his company. It was his first experience of being welcomed as a friend by a member of the royal family.

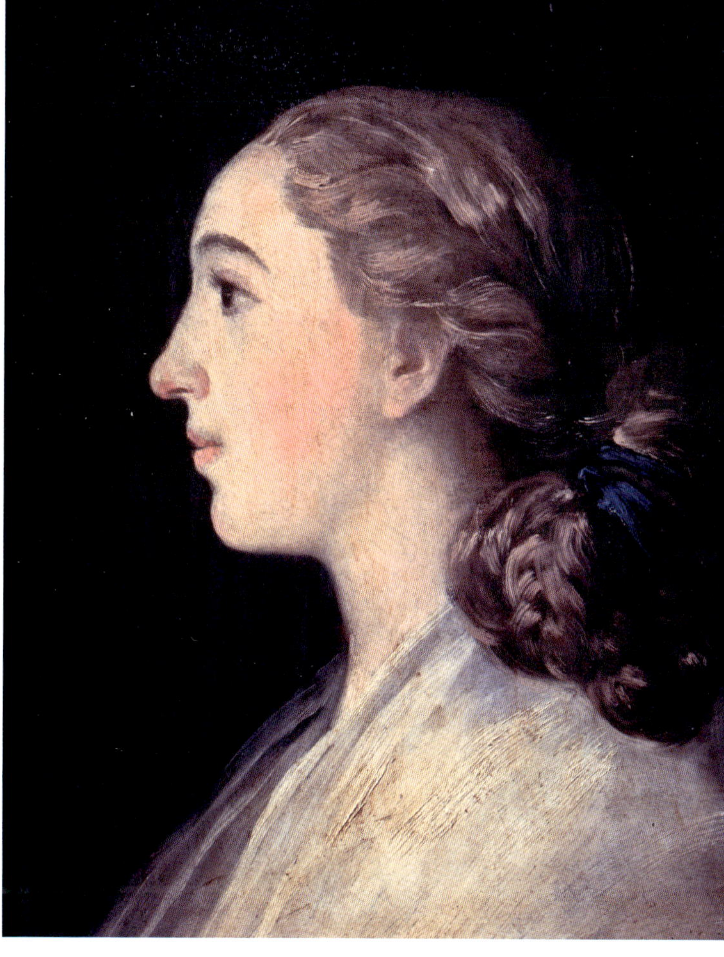

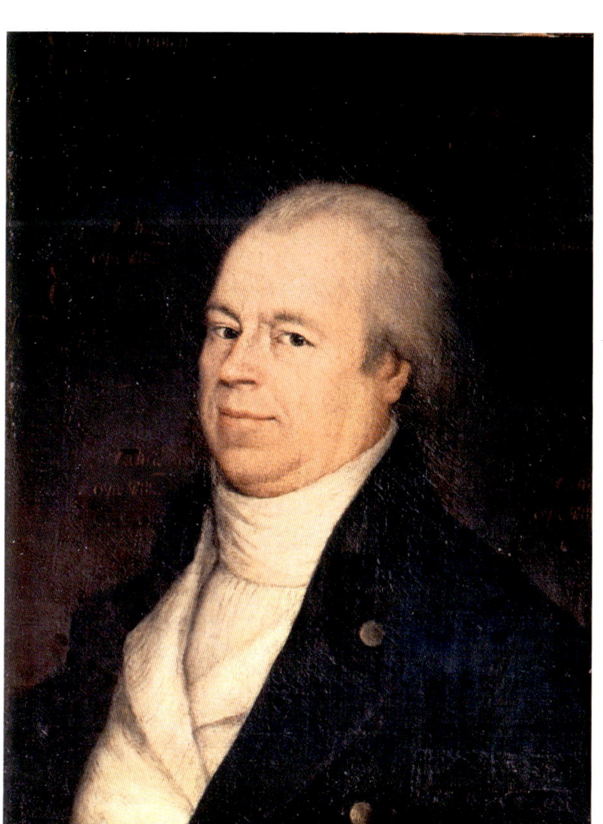

Cornelio Vandergoten, 1782, oil on canvas, Museo Nacional del Prado, Madrid, Spain, 62 x 47cm (24½ x 18½in)

This is an imposing portrait of the director of the Royal Tapestry Factory whom Goya had known since he had first created his tapestry cartoons in 1775. Silhouetted against a dark background Vandergoten's black velvet frock coat can just be seen in the soft play of light that also illuminates his face. The light additionally highlights the white of his waistcoat and collar.

Infante Don Luis de Bourbon,
1783, oil on canvas,
Cleveland Museum of Art,
Ohio, USA, 152.7 x 100cm
(60 x 39in)

An elegant portrait of the
Infante Don Luis de Bourbon,
made along with the others
while Goya was staying with
the family. As a younger son
of King Philip V of Spain,
while still a child, Luis was
forced into a religious career,
and became Archbishop
of Toledo and Seville.
His scandalous behaviour
however, meant he
renounced his ecclesiastical
offices at the age of 27.

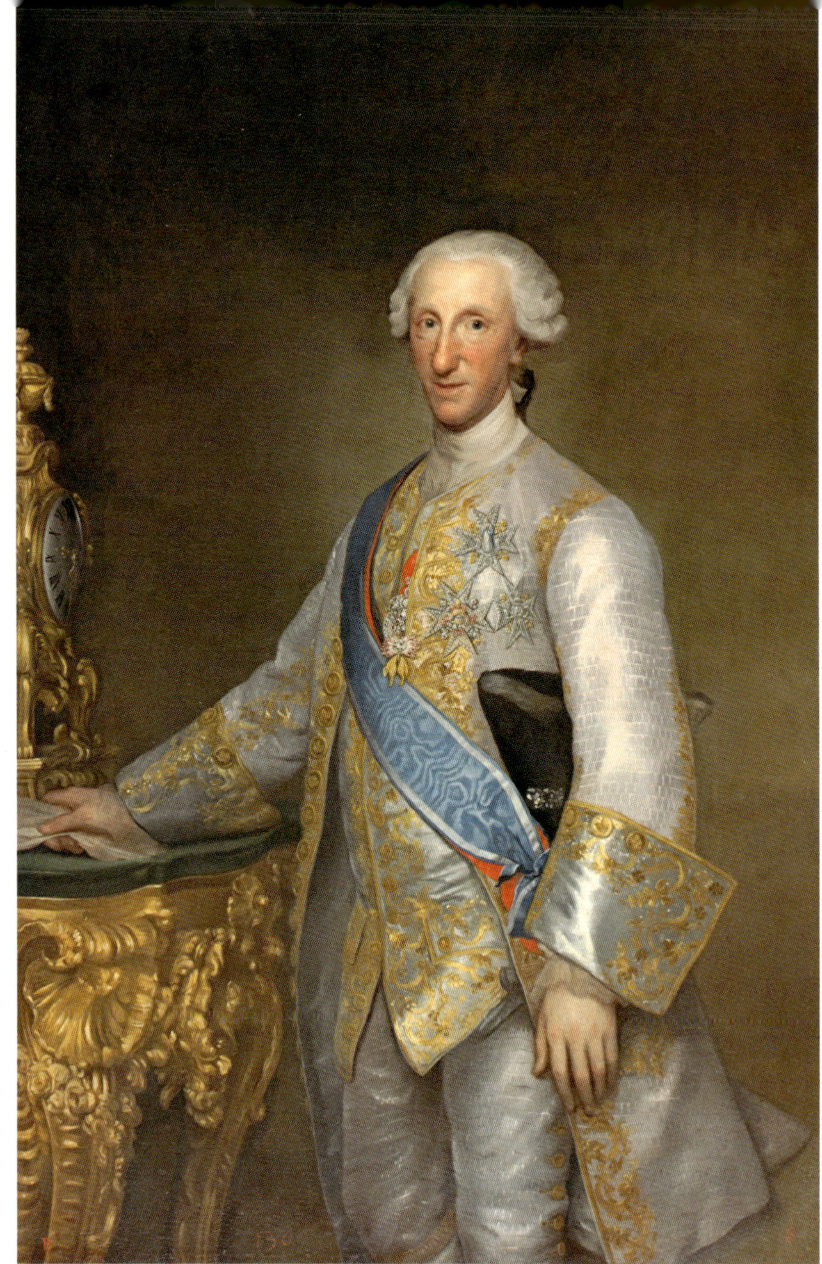

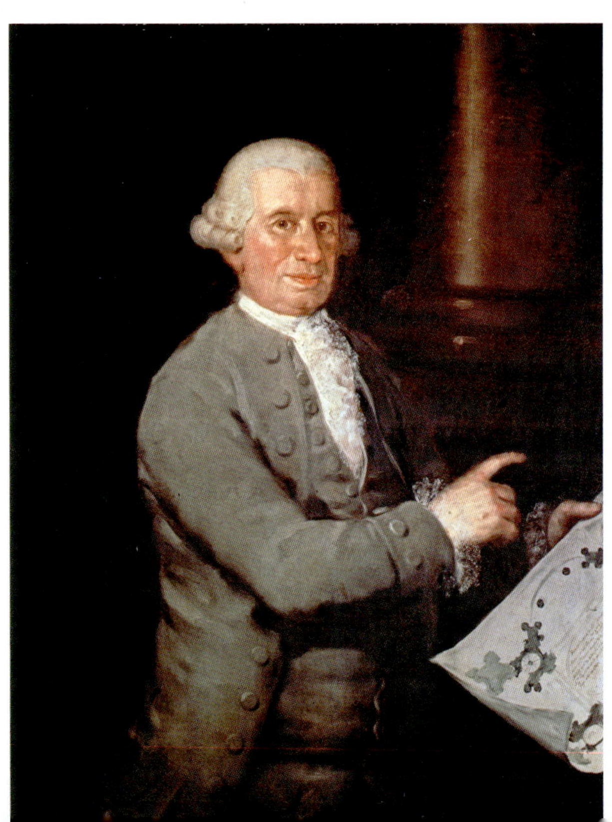

Ventura Rodriguez, 1784,
oil on canvas, National
Museum, Stockholm,
Sweden, 106 x 79cm
(42 x 31in)

Ventura Rodriguez (1717–
85) introduced Goya to the
Infante Don Luis, which was
extremely beneficial to the
artist in terms of friendship
and patronage, until Don Luis
died unexpectedly. Ventura
was Luis's favourite architect
and highly successful during
his lifetime. In this half-length
portrait, Goya shows him
as a fashionably dressed
professional, surveying his
architectural designs, while
also conveying his warm
disposition to viewers.

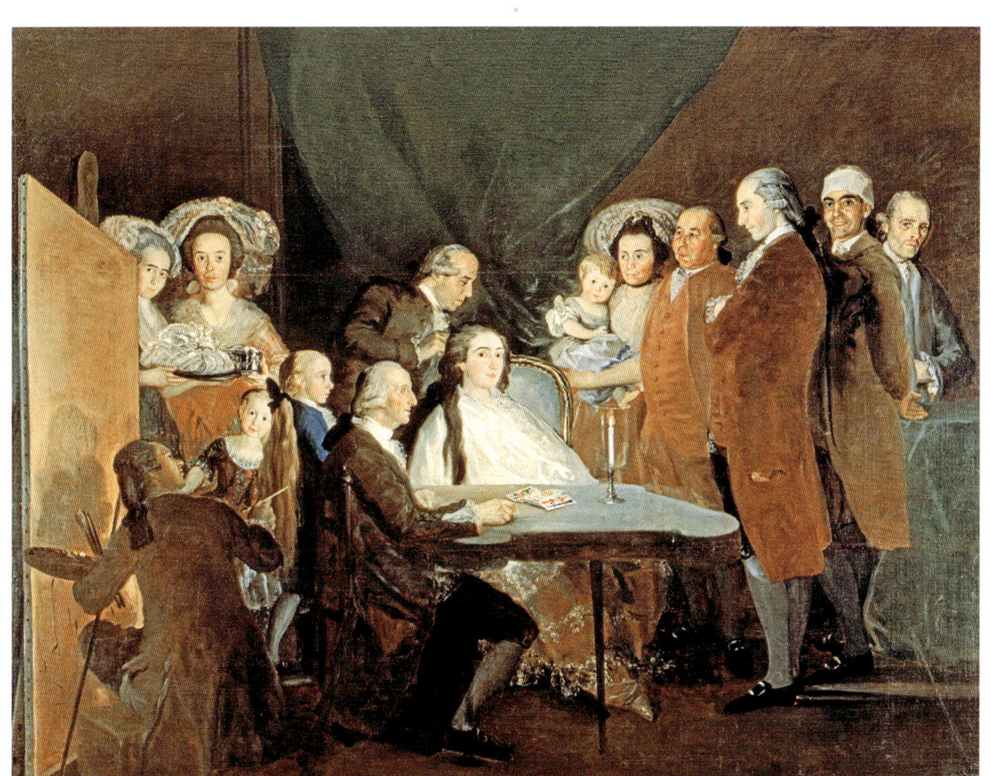

The Family of the Infante Don Luis de Bourbon, **1783**, oil on canvas, Magnani Rocca Collection, Parma, Italy, 248 x 330cm (97½ x 130in)

Among the most successful and important of Goya's early works, this shows an informal family gathering. The relaxed group of family, friends and servants fill the canvas, while the naturalness of Goya's approach creates an atmosphere of intimacy. The candle indicates that it is evening, and Goya himself can be seen in the front, holding his palette and brushes, observing his subjects.

Doña María Teresa of Vallabriga, **1783**, oil on canvas, Neue Pinakothek, München, Germany, 151.2 x 97.8cm (59½ x 38½in)

In 1776, the Infante Don Luis de Bourbon married María Teresa de Vallabriga y Rozas against his family's wishes as she was not considered noble enough for the brother of a king. So Don Luis and his family were banished from Madrid, but their marriage was happy. Doña María Teresa is dressed in the latest fashions. Her black lace mantlet covers a 'robe à la circassienne'.

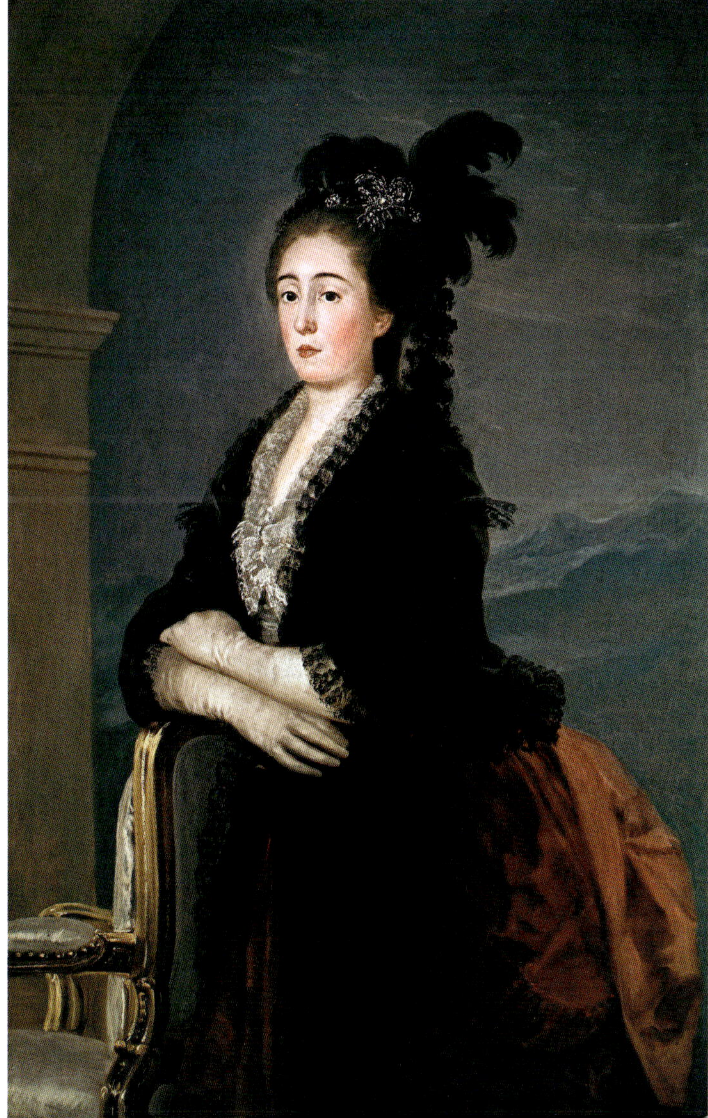

José del Toro y Zambrano, 1785, oil on canvas, Banco de España, Madrid, Spain, 113 x 68cm (44½ x 27in)

Between 1785 and 1788, Goya executed six official portraits for the Banco de San Carlos – now the Bank of Spain – of which he was a shareholder. Commissioned on the advice of his friend Ceán Bermúdez, this was the first of those portraits and is a little stiff and self-conscious, even though the overall tonality is reminiscent of Velázquez.

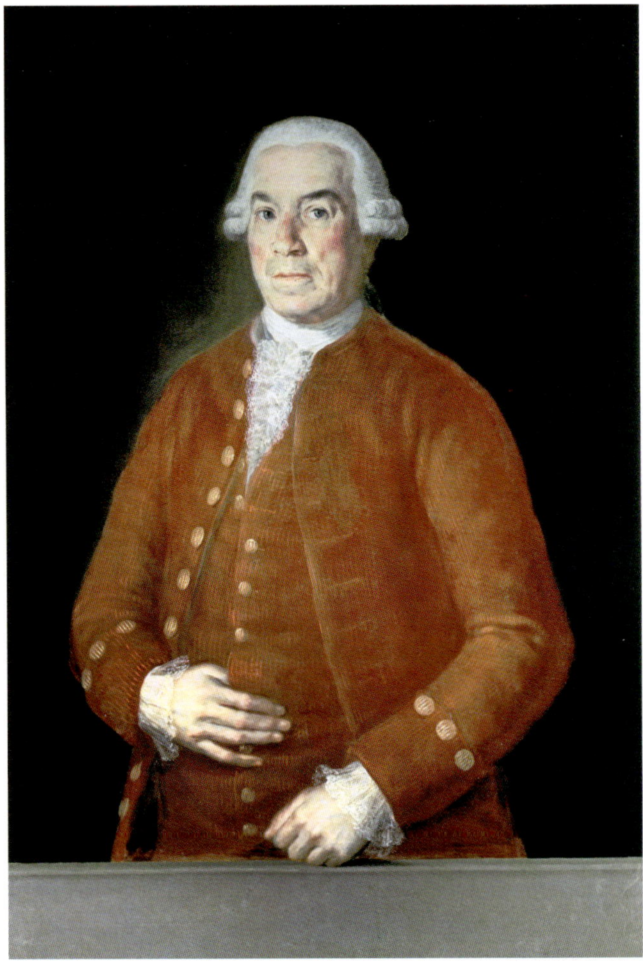

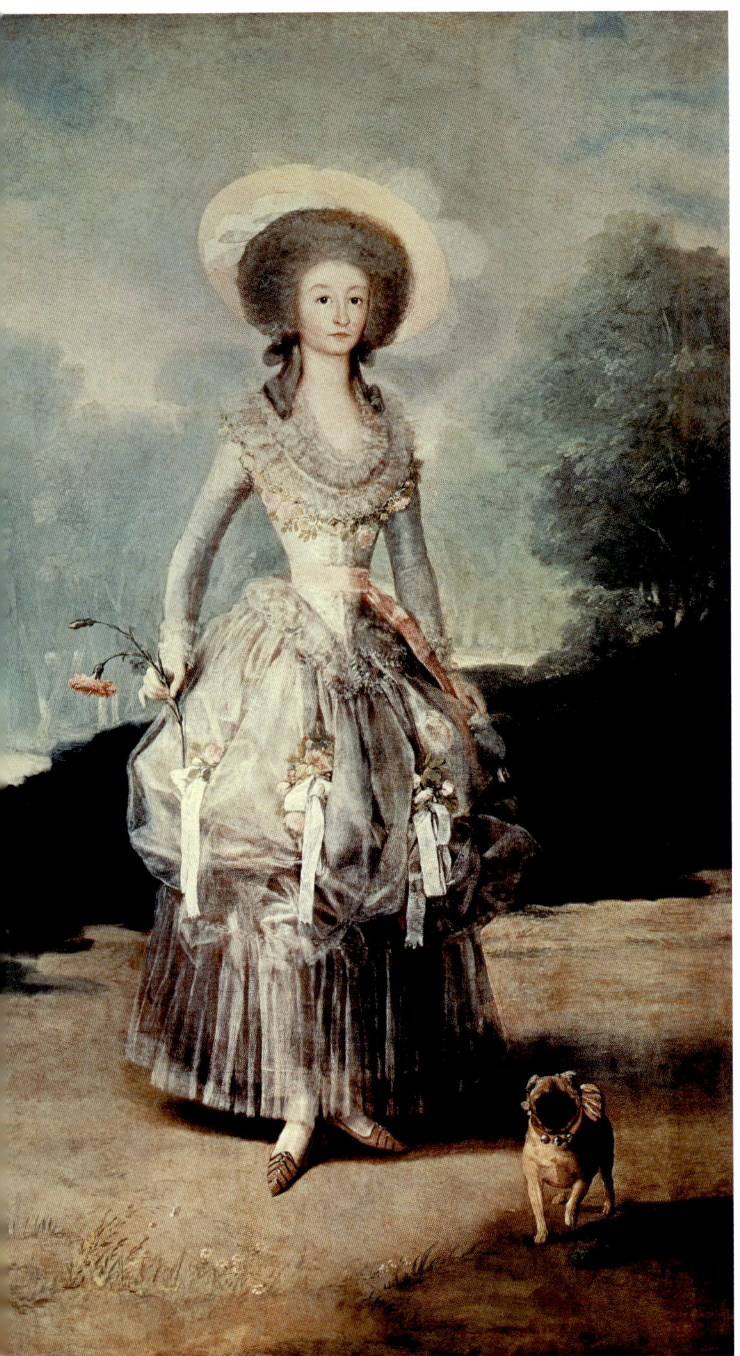

The Marquesa de Pontejos, c.1786, oil on canvas, National Gallery of Art, Washington DC, USA, 210.3 x 127cm (83 x 50in)

The Marquesa is dressed in the shepherdess-style after Marie-Antoinette, that before the French Revolution was fashionable among ladies of the Spanish aristocracy. This was probably commissioned on the occasion of the Marquesa's first marriage to Francisco de Monino y Redondo, the Count of Floridablanca's brother. Goya was clearly influenced by English portraiture, especially the work of Thomas Gainsborough (1727–88). The portrait was extremely well-received by all who saw it.

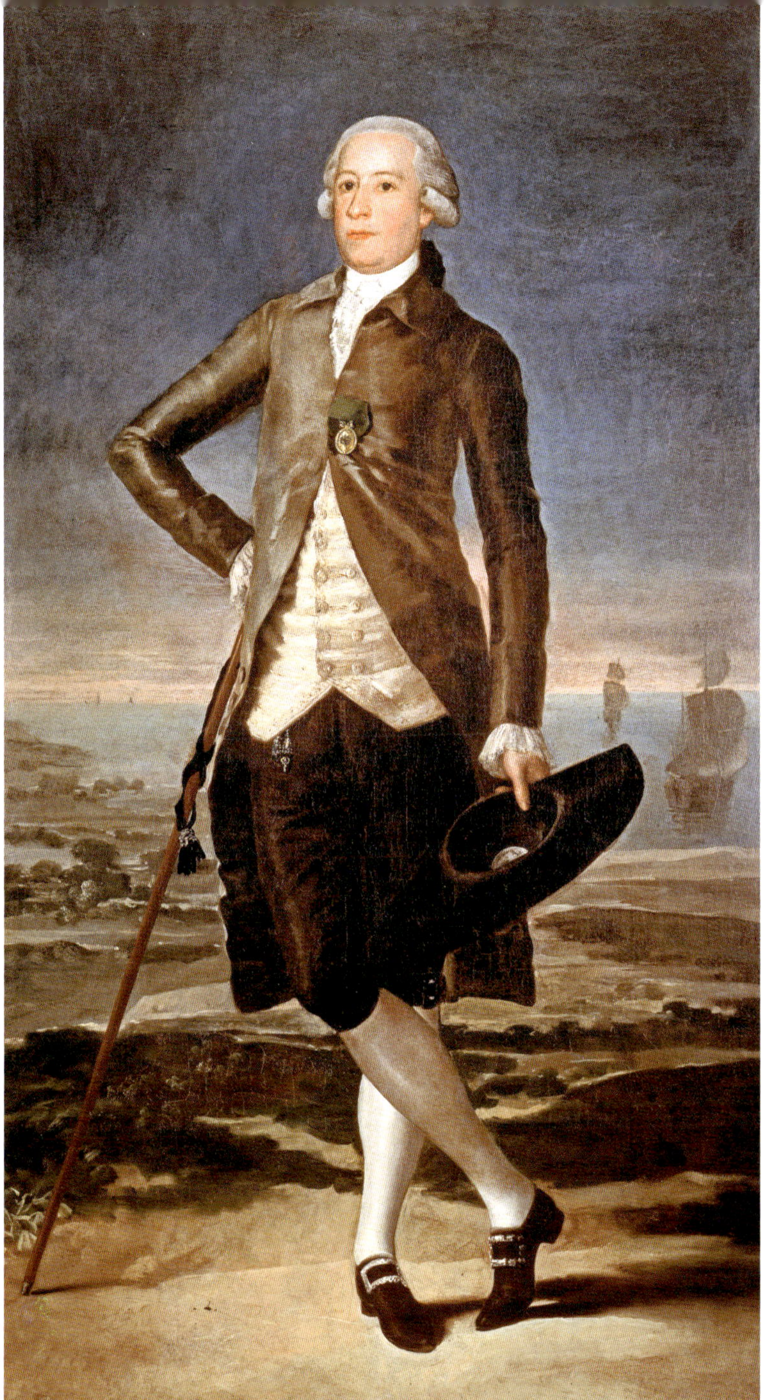

Gaspar Melchor de Jovellanos, c.1784–5, oil on canvas, Private Collection, 185 x 110cm (73 x 43in)

Jovellanos was a statesman, author, philosopher and a major figure of the Enlightenment in Spain. He became a criminal judge in 1767 and by 1780, he was an important figure in Spanish politics. At around this time, he befriended Goya, although later, from 1790 to 1797, he was banished from Madrid. This first portrait of him by Goya shows him as fashionable and hopeful for the future.

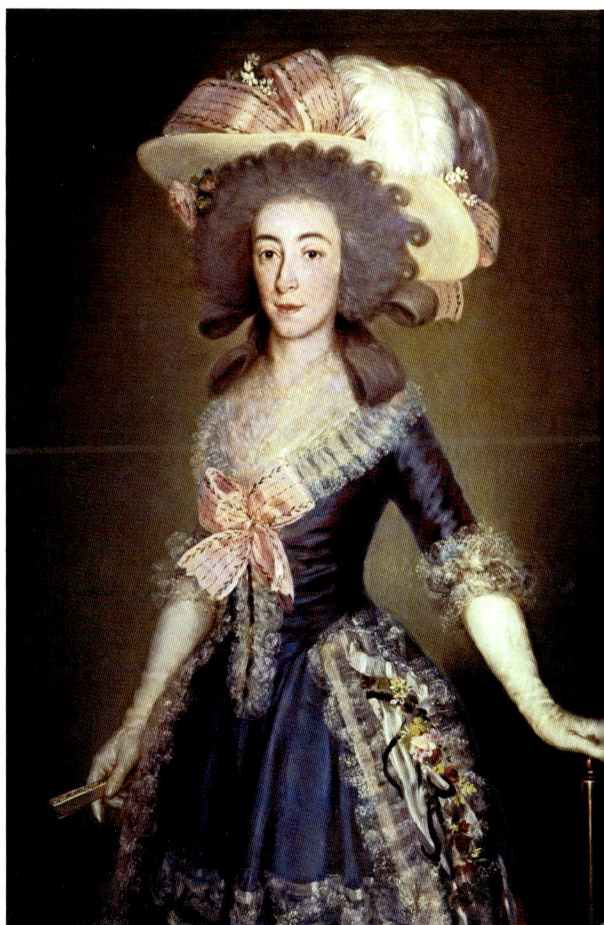

Condesa-Duquesa de Benavente, 1785, oil on canvas, Private Collection, 104 x 80cm (41 x 31½in)

Doña María Josefa Alonso-Pimentel y Téllez-Girón was the Duchess of Osuna, and the 12th Countess–Duchess of Benavente, the third most important woman in Spain. Renowned for her patronage of artists, writers and scientists, she was also a leader in fashions of the day. She and her husband befriended Goya when he first moved to Madrid and they became two of his most important patrons.

Francisco Javier de Larrumbe, 1787, oil on canvas, Banco de España, Madrid, Spain, 113 x 77cm (44½ x 30in)

Don Francisco Javier de Larrumbe turns to his left, displaying his expensive embroidered dress coat, with red embroidered undercoat and a frilled collar and lace cuffs. The Cross of the Order of Charles III hangs from his chest and he carries his tricorn hat under his left arm. His expression is almost contemptuous, unlike the other portraits in this series.

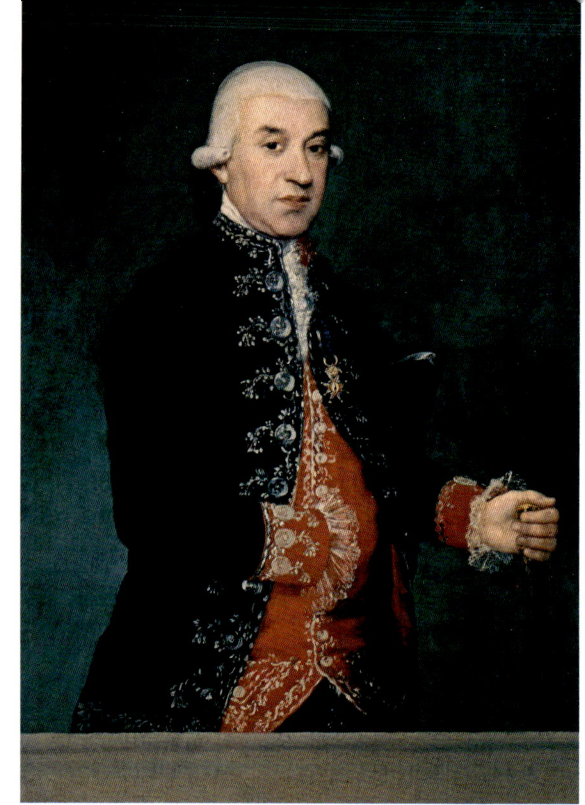

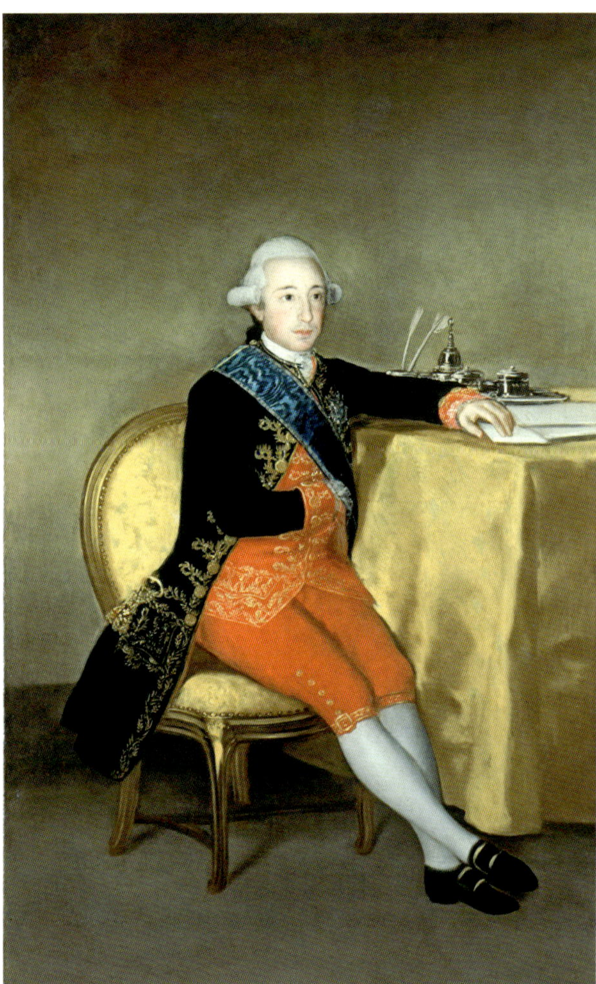

Conde de Altamira, 1787, oil on canvas, Banco de España, Madrid, Spain, 177 x 108cm (70 x 42½in)

The Count of Altamira, Isabel Vicente Ossorio, was one of the richest men of Spain and this portrait was the most important of Goya's official bank portraits in terms of the clever composition, and the self-confidence of the sitter. The count looks comfortable and relaxed with an air of nobility. He was very short and wanted that to be disguised, yet the large furniture seems to emphasize his diminutive size. Nevertheless, he was delighted with his portrait. It led directly to numerous further important commissions for Goya.

Marqués de Tolosa, 1787, oil on canvas, Banco de España, Madrid, Spain, 112 x 78cm (44 x 31in)

Another noble of the official bank of Spain, the Marquis of Tolosa stands proudly in a sideways position, looking at viewers. Although Goya's brushwork is sketchy and loose, he has rendered the elaborate embroidery of the man's clothing in great detail. The face is illuminated by a strong source of light, while the rich colours, medal and cane further highlight Tolosa's importance.

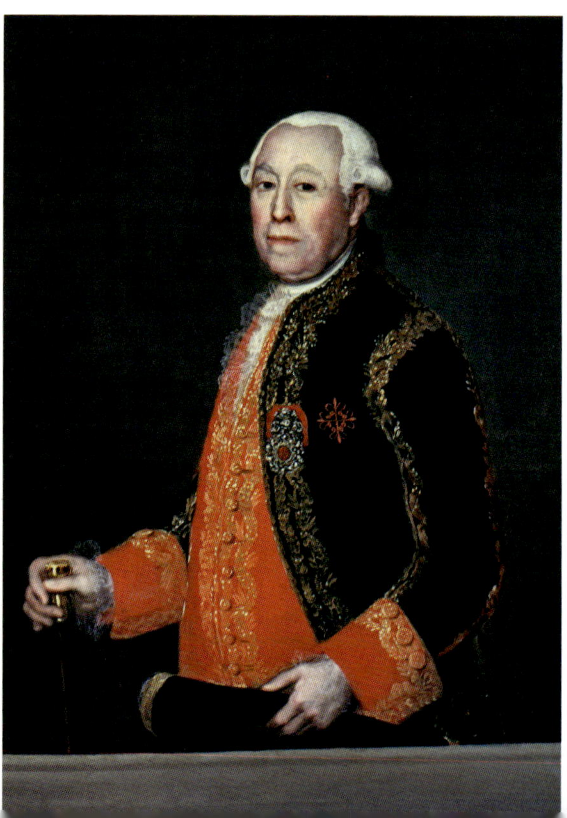

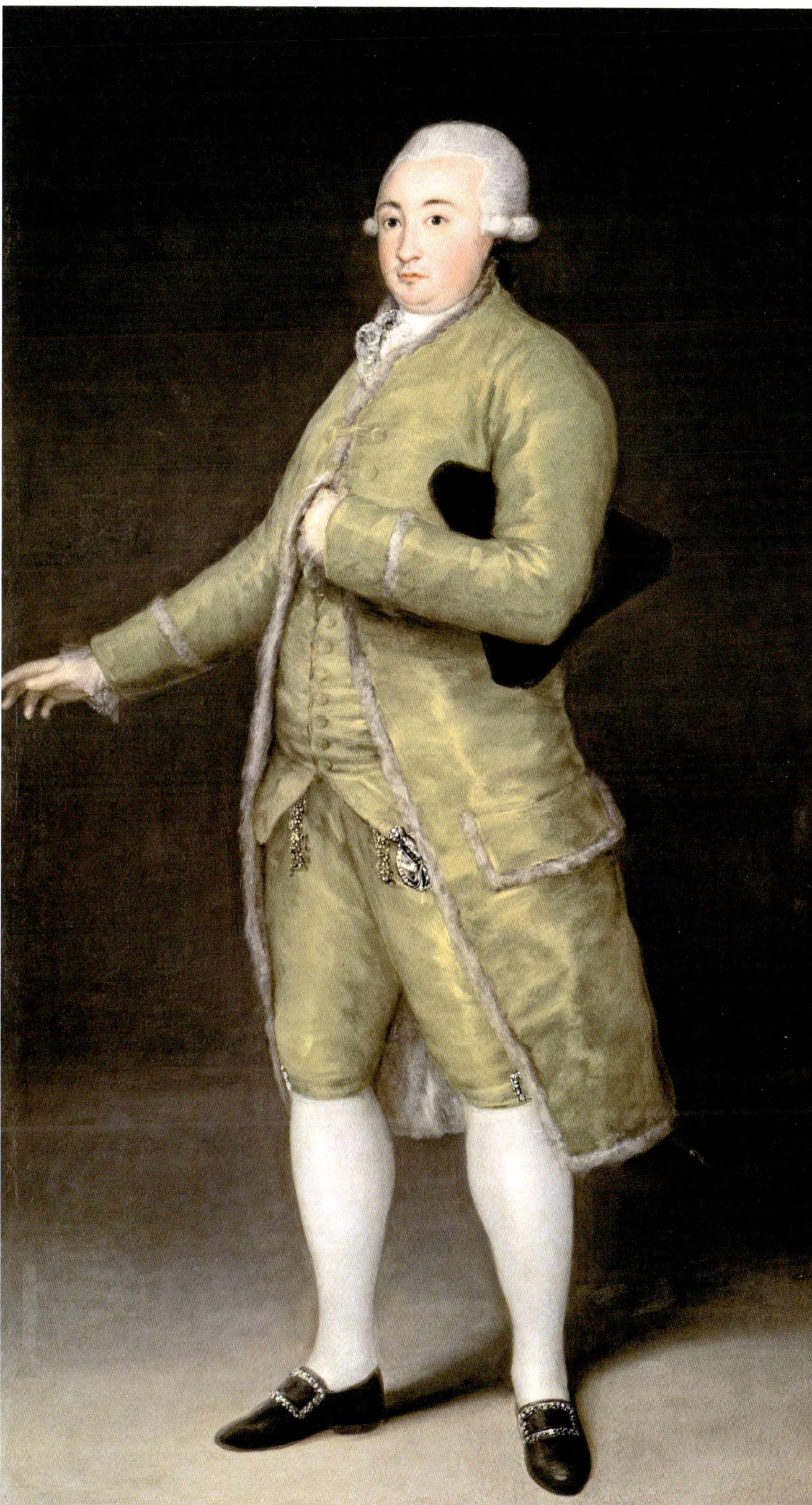

Conde de Cabarrús, 1788, oil on canvas, Banco de España, Madrid, Spain, 210 x 127cm (83 x 50in)

French-born Cabarrús settled in Madrid as a soap manufacturer, but soon became involved with a circle of enlightened reformers who advised the King. His ideas became an essential part of the creation of the first Spanish central bank in 1783, and he was made Conde de Cabarrús in 1789 by Charles IV. However in 1790 he was accused of embezzlement and imprisoned for two years.

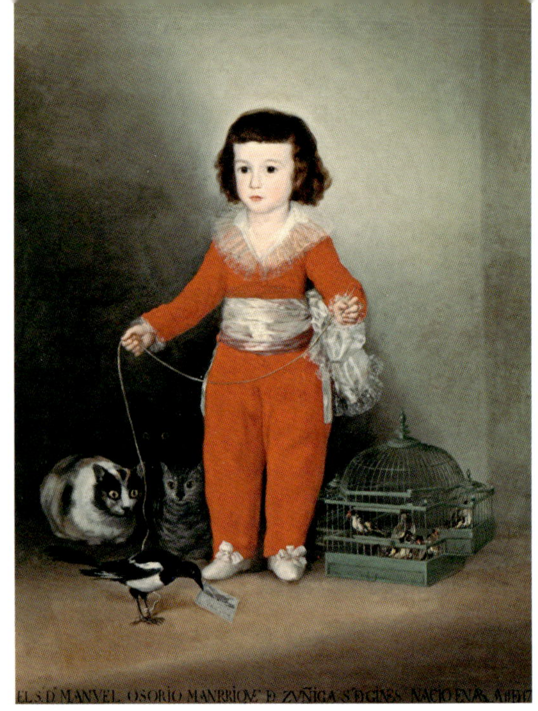

Manuel Osorio Manrique de Zuñiga, 1788, oil on canvas, The Metropolitan Museum of Art, New York, USA, 127 x 101cm (50 x 40in)

The son of the Count and Countess of Altamira plays with his pet magpie and is also surrounded by a cage of finches and three cats. In Baroque art, caged birds symbolized innocence. In January 1787, Goya was paid for his series of portraits for the Banco de San Carlos, and the success of these prompted the Count of Altamira to commission him to paint portraits of his family.

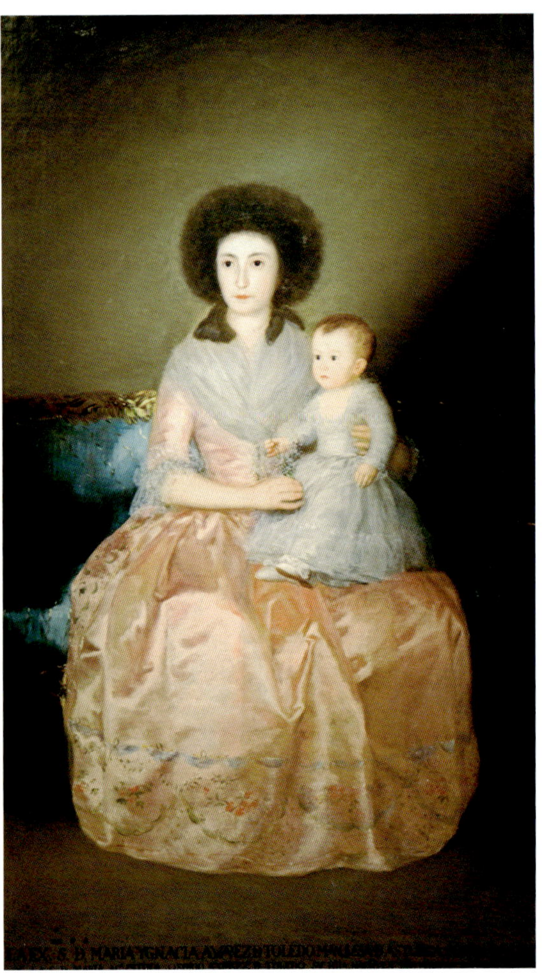

Condesa of Altamira and her Daughter, María Agustina, c.1787–8, oil on canvas, The Metropolitan Museum of Art, New York, USA, 195 x 115cm (76¾ x 45¼in)

One of four portraits by Goya of members of Count Altamira's family at this time, this sensitive, yet imposing portrait immediately helped to advance his career. Soon after this was completed, he was appointed Court Painter to Charles IV. As usual, he demonstrates his skills in depicting textures and drape of the clothing, and particularly in the shimmering dress and the softness of the shawl, although the overall image remains formal.

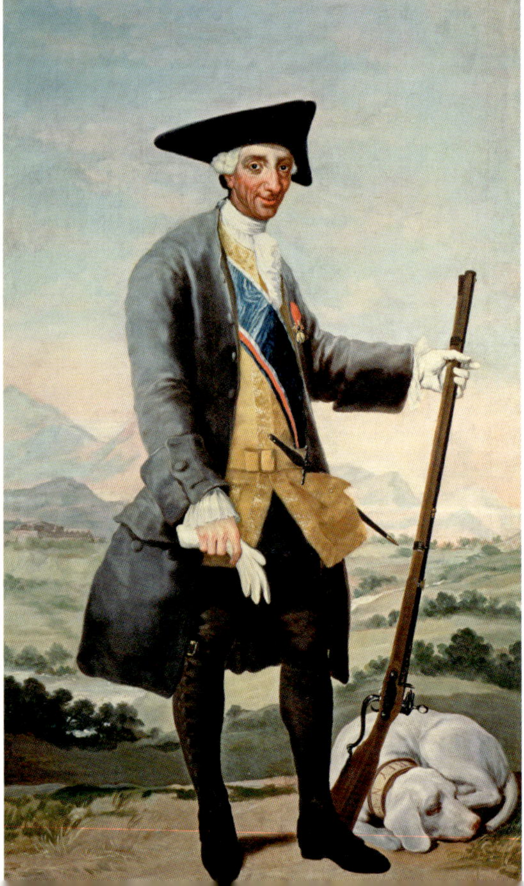

Charles III in Hunting Gear, c.1786–8, oil on canvas, Museo Nacional del Prado, Madrid, Spain, 207 x 126cm (81½ x 49½in)

King Charles III was favourable to reforms advocated by his circle of politicians, and through them, was helping to return Spain to the powerful position it had once held. Painted shortly before his death, this portrait shows him dressed for hunting in the mountains outside Madrid, and recalls various portraits by Velázquez. This is a copy by Goya of his original portrait of the King.

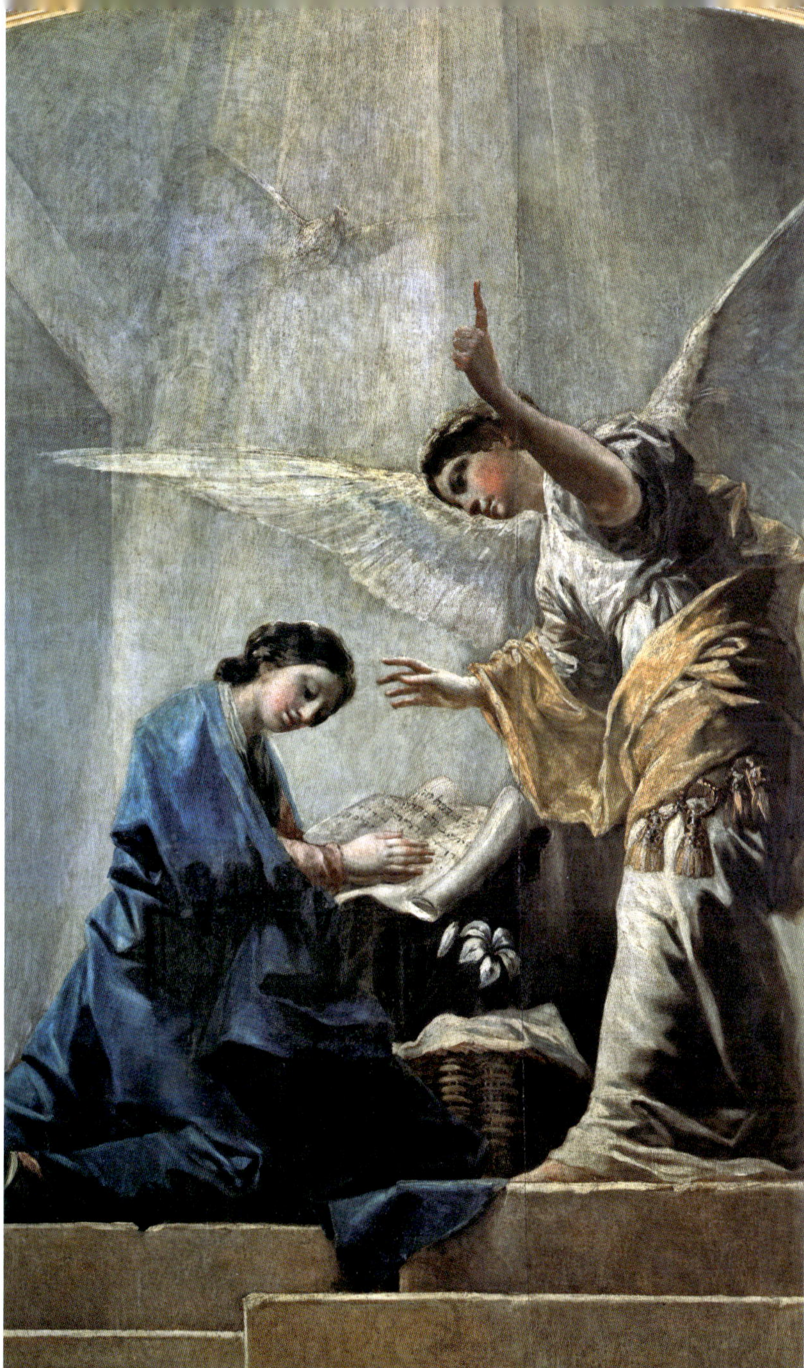

The Annunciation, 1785,
oil on canvas, Private
Collection, 280 x 117cm
(110 x 46in)

Another of Goya's
religious works that was
commissioned on the
strength of his rapidly
growing reputation. It is
painted in the Rococo style,
with pink-cheeked figures and
flowing drapery. This work
demonstrates that although
he was breaking new ground
in many of the methods he
was using in portraiture, for
some religious works, Goya
adhered to what he knew
would be generally admired.

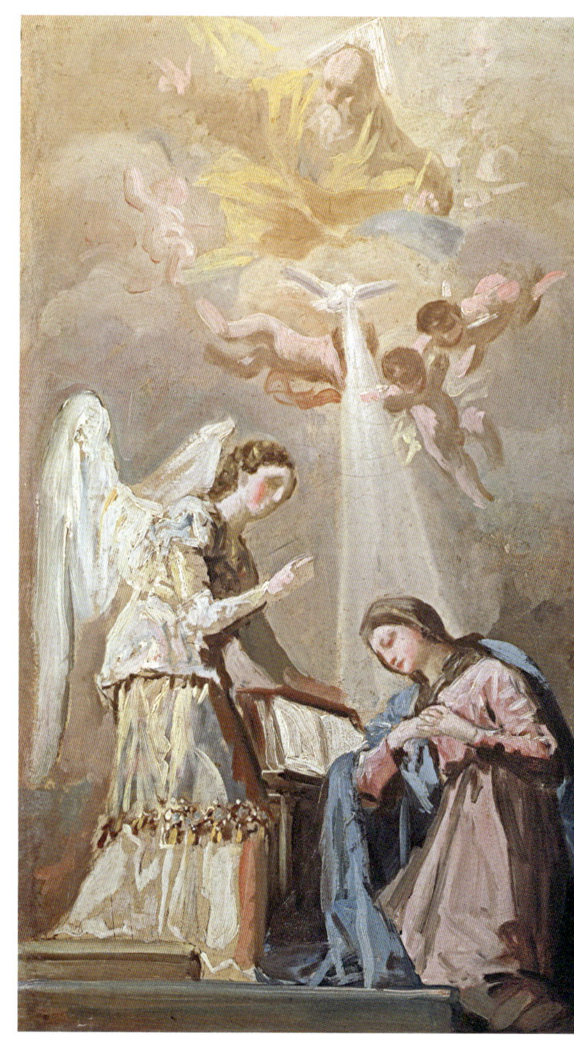

Sketch for previous painting,
oil on canvas, Private
Collection, 42 x 26cm
(16½ x 10in)

A small study for the
previous work, this
demonstrates Goya's
attention to detail and his
dramatic tonal contrasts. It
is a more powerful image
and less reverential to the
prevailing Rococo styles than
the finished painting. Goya
had been commissioned
to produce more religious
works after his recent
successful portraits, and since
his *Christ Crucified* (see page
132) had been displayed as
the altarpiece of the Church
of San Francisco el Grande.

The Death of Saint Joseph, 1787, oil on canvas, Church of the Convent of Saint Joachim and Saint Anne, Valladolid, Spain, 220 x 160cm (86½ x 63in)

In April 1787, Goya was commissioned by the King to paint three altarpieces for the Neoclassical style church designed by Francesco Sabatini (1722–97) for the convent of Saint Anne in Valladolid. By June, he had still not started the work, but by November, when the church was consecrated, he had painted all three works, of which this is one. To complement the architecture, he adhered to a Neoclassical style.

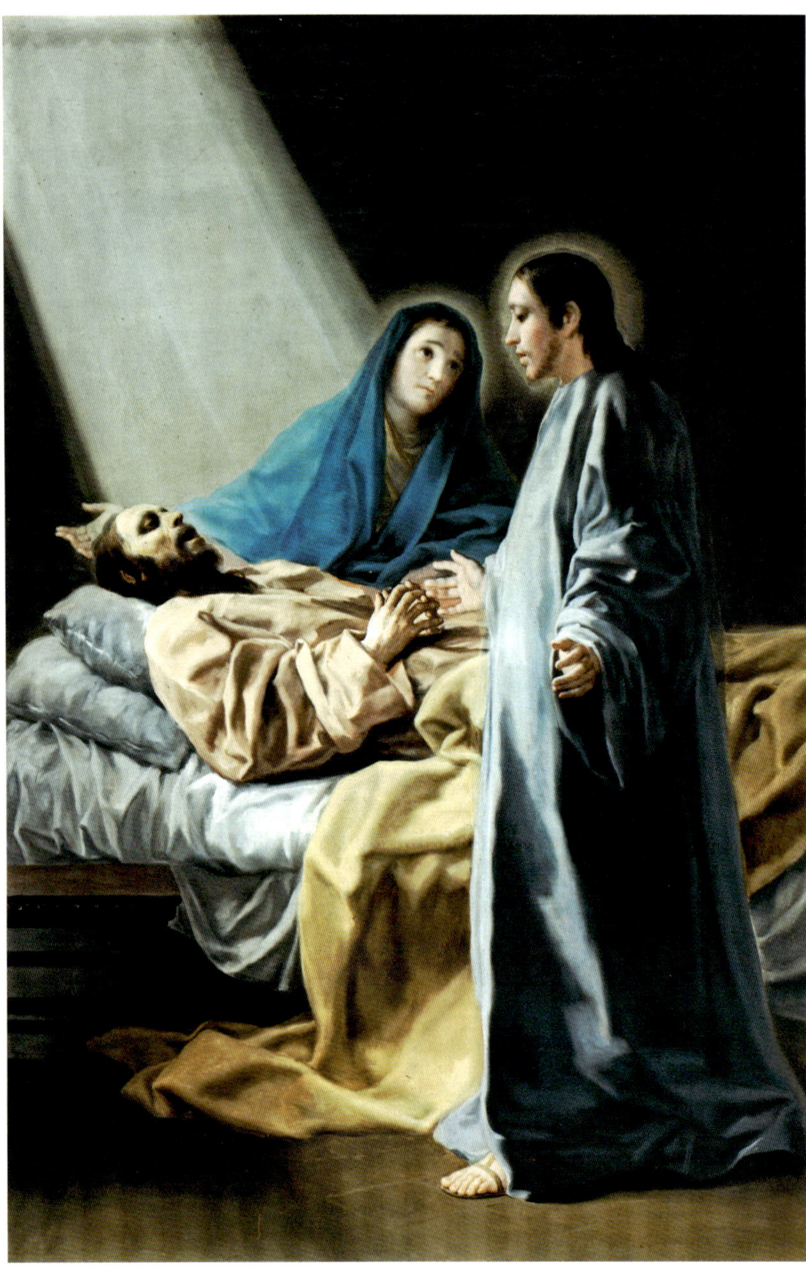

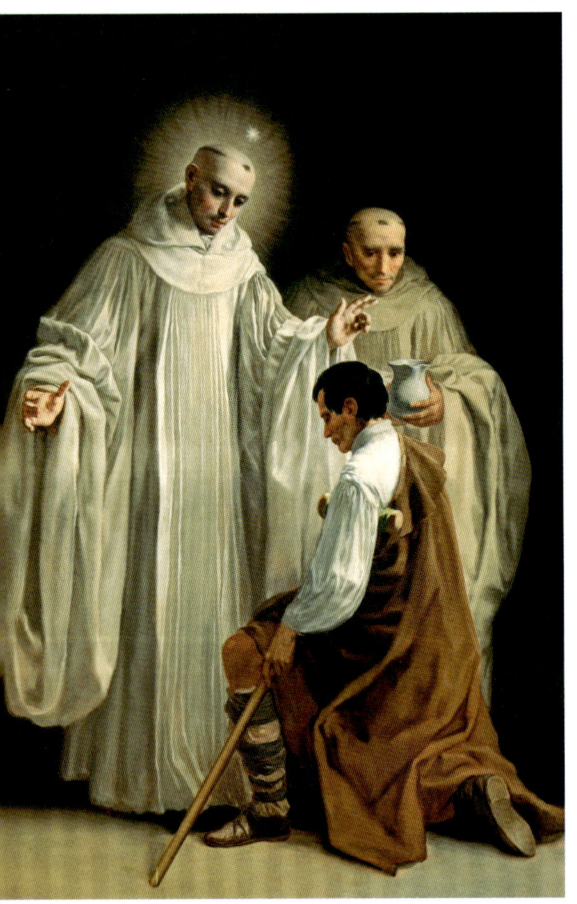

Saint Bernard and Saint Robert, 1787, oil on canvas, Church of the Convent of Saint Joachim and Saint Anne, Valladolid, Spain, 220 x 160cm (86½ x 63in)

This is another of the paintings Goya produced at great speed for the Order of Saint Joachim and Saint Anne (the Virgin Mary's parents). When unveiled, the paintings were highly admired, particularly as their proportions harmonized with the dimensions and elements of the interior of the church. Goya demonstrates his remarkable adaptability, creating strong chiaroscuro and emphasizing the cool contours of a style he did not admire.

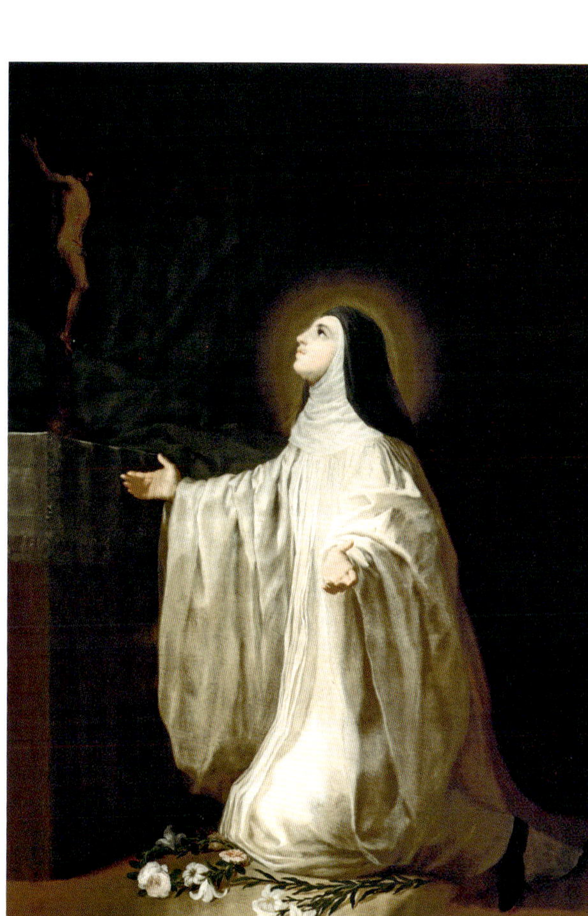

Saint Lutgarda, **1787**, oil on canvas, Church of the Convent of Saint Joachim and Saint Anne, Valladolid, Spain, 220 x 160cm (86½ x 63in)

Lutgarda was a Flemish saint who had many visions of Jesus throughout her life. Goya painted this pious work to help individuals focus on pure thoughts during prayer. Each image of his series is created with dramatic chiaroscuro and calm, column-like figures, with soft, supernatural light emanating from them. Unlike many of his other works, this painting is reverential in respect of its location.

Saint Francis Borgia Taking Leave of his Family, **1788**, oil on canvas, Chapel of Saint Francis Borgia, Valencia Cathedral, Valencia, Spain, 350 x 300cm (138 x 118in)

One of two paintings commissioned by the Duke and Duchess of Osuna for a new chapel in the Cathedral of Valencia, this represents the 16th-century Saint Francis Borgia, after whom the Osuna heir had been named. Goya was commissioned to produce these two paintings to hang on either side of the main altarpiece that was painted by one of his artistic rivals, Mariano Salvador Maella (1739–1819).

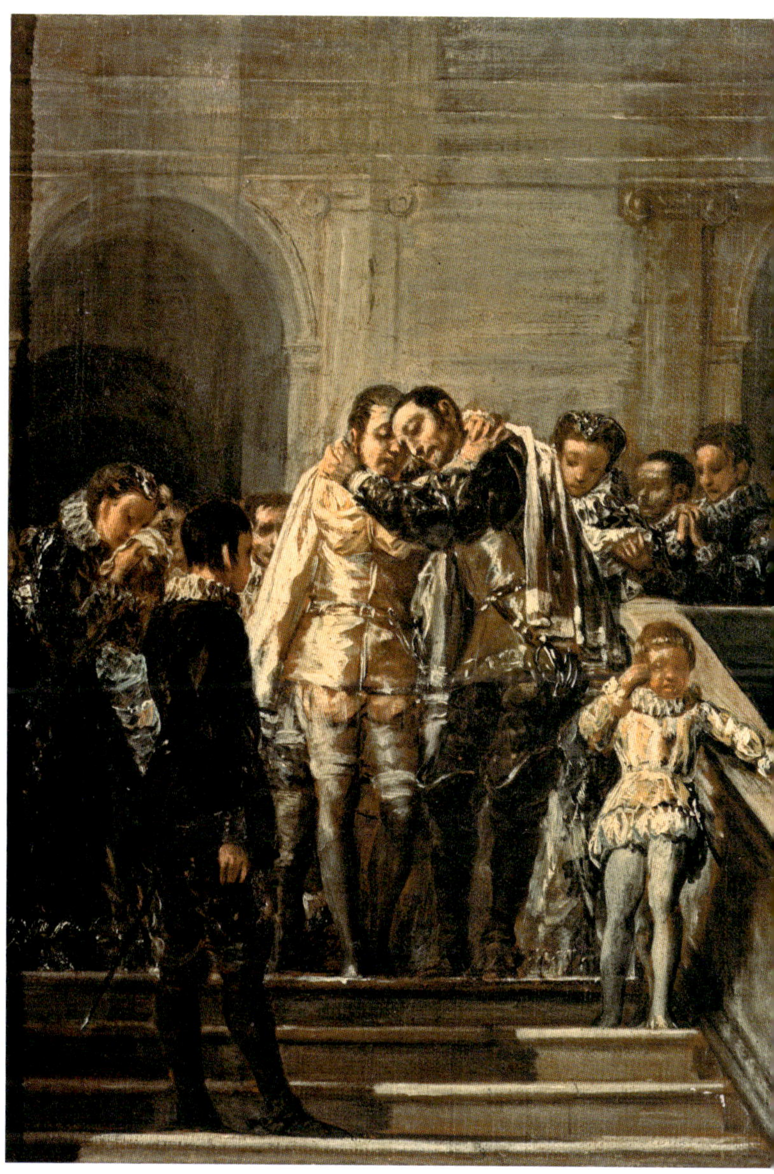

Highwaymen Attacking a Coach, 1787, oil on canvas, Private Collection, 169 x 127cm (66½ x 50in)

This is another of the country themes that Goya painted for the Duchess of Osuna, and delivered to her in spring 1787. The landscape is skilfully rendered, demonstrating his understanding of colour theory that was not widely explored at that time. Bold splashes of colour in the clothing has a brightening effect against the greenery, while the brilliant blue sky is a foil for the dark scene below.

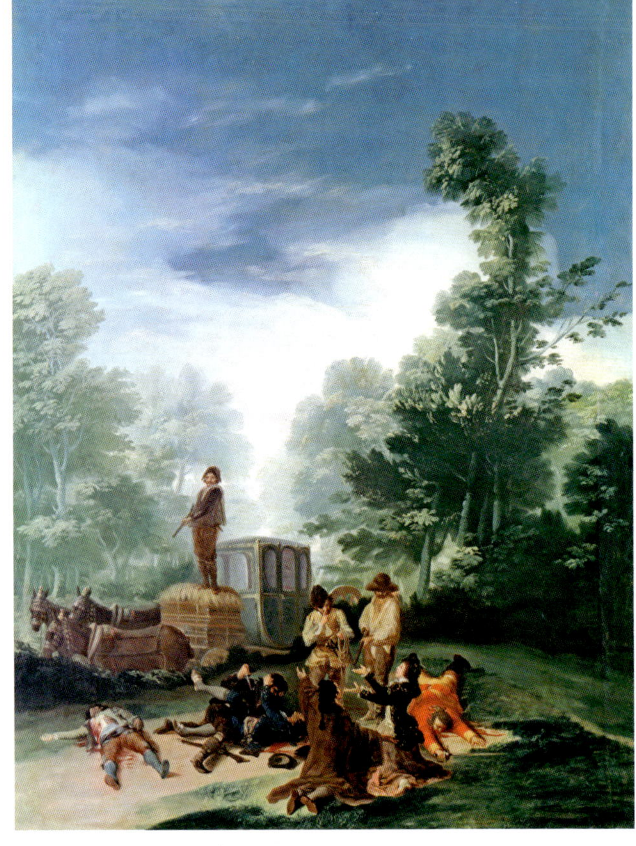

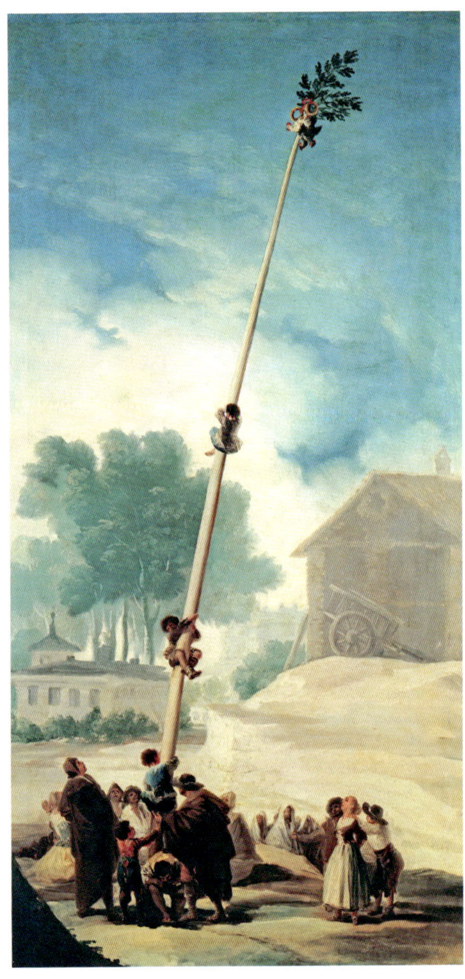

The Greasy Pole, 1786–7, oil on canvas, Private Collection, 169 x 88cm (66½ x 34½in)

Goya described this image (*La Cucana*) as 'a maypole on the village green, with boys climbing up it to win a prize of chickens and roscas (ring-shaped biscuits) in the form of crowns hanging from the top. People are watching them.' This was a traditional event at a fair; the pole was covered in grease, making an ascent by any participant almost impossible.

Saint Francis Borgia at the Deathbed of a Penitent (detail), 1788, oil on canvas, Chapel of Saint Francis Borgia, Valencia Cathedral, Valencia, Spain

This image of Saint Francis Borgia assisting a dying man presents a mysterious and dramatic event. Dressed in a simple priest's robe, the saint's head is encircled by a ring of divine light that follows the shape of the window behind him. In his hand, the carved image of the crucified Christ has brought about his revelation that the soul of the dying man cannot be saved.

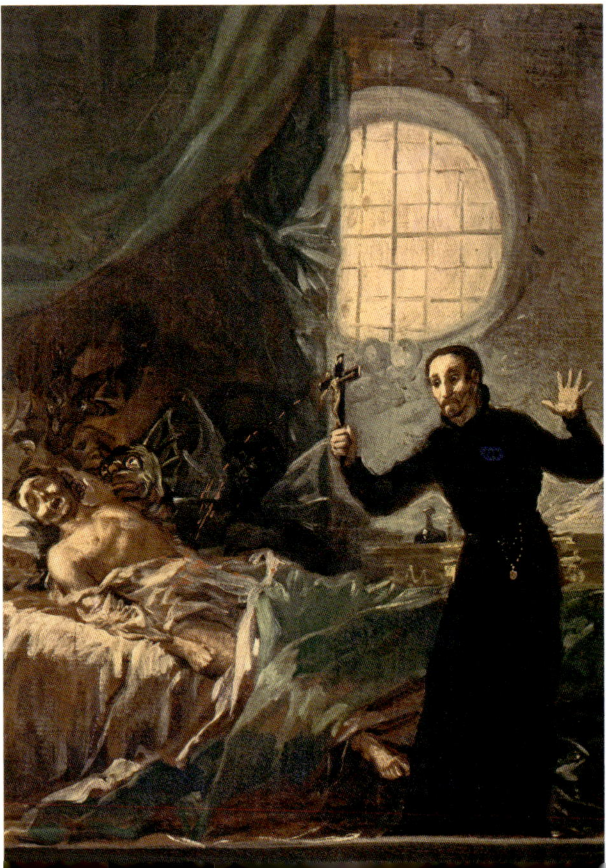

The Fall, 1786–7, oil on canvas, Private Collection, 169 x 100cm (66½ x 39in)

The Fall (*La Caída*) and *The Greasy Pole* (see opposite) belong to a series of seven country scenes that Goya made to decorate the large gallery in the Duchess of Osuna's apartment in the Alameda Palace. This was the Osuna country residence situated outside Madrid, also known as El Capricho. Goya described this as: 'an excursion in hilly country, with a woman in a faint after a fall from an ass.'

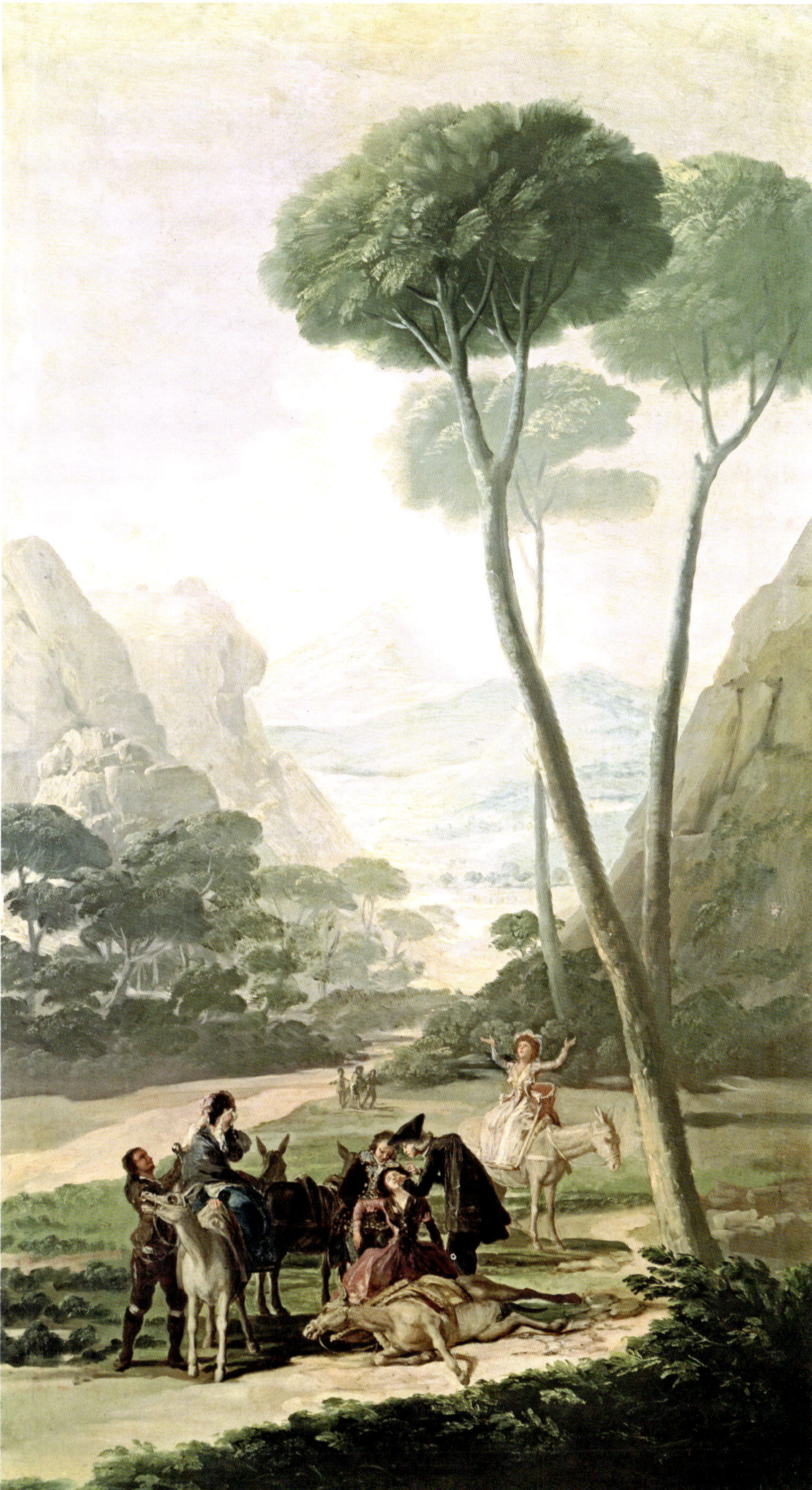

Spring or *The Flower Girls*, 1786, oil on canvas, Museo Nacional del Prado, Madrid, Spain, 277 x 192cm (109 x 75½in)

In an allegory to spring, in this tapestry cartoon, Goya rejects conventional representations of the goddess Flora and instead paints a young woman holding a little girl's hand, while receiving a rose from another young woman kneeling before her. A man standing behind them attempts to surprise the first woman with a baby rabbit. The two young women's poses echo figures painted by Velázquez in *Las Meninas* in 1656.

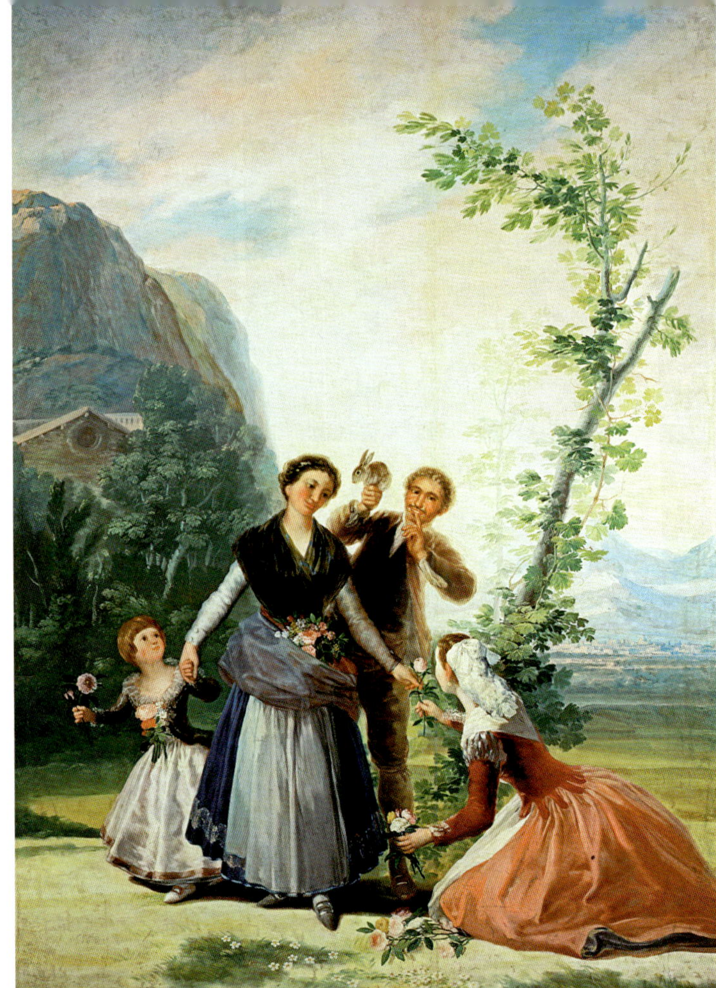

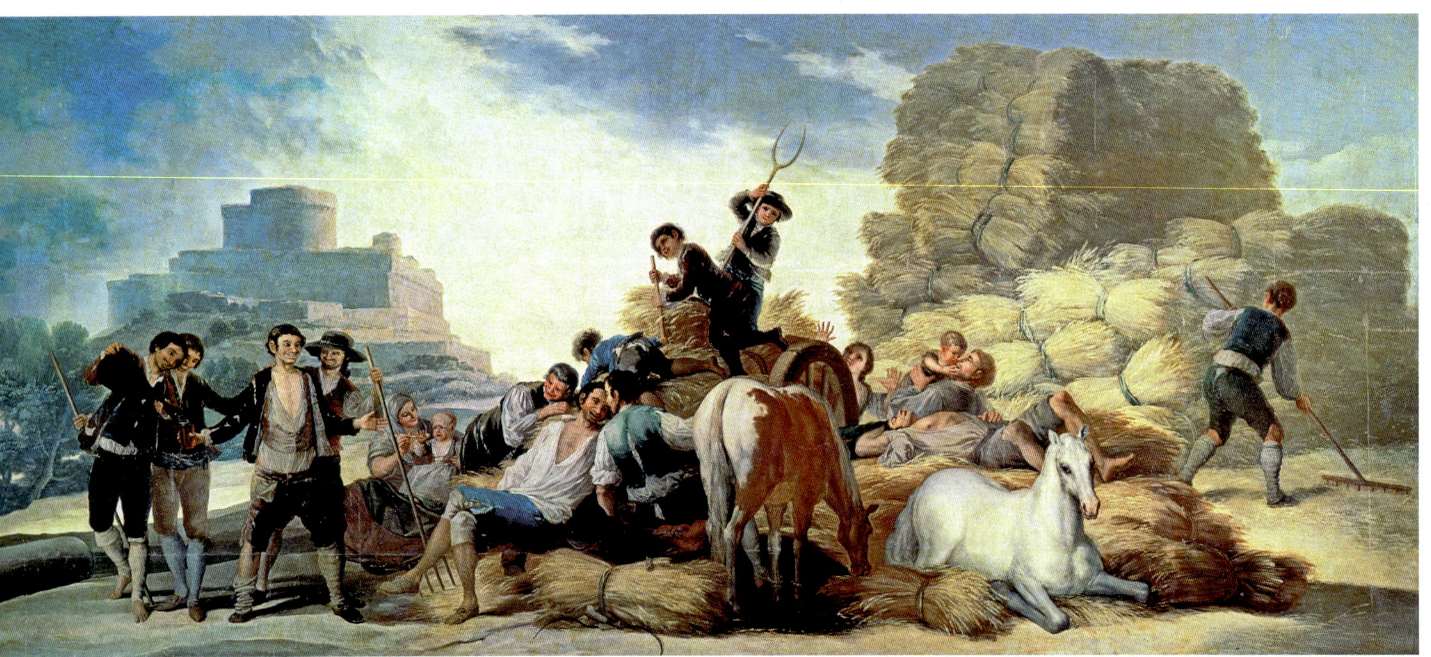

Summer or *The Harvest*, 1786, oil on canvas, Museo Nacional del Prado, Madrid, Spain, 276 x 641cm (109 x 252in)

Wars with England caused Spain financial problems, and in consequence, in 1780 the Royal Tapestry Factory closed. As soon as it opened again in 1786, Goya was commissioned to design more tapestries. This was one of his allegories of the four seasons he produced. Rather than depicting the traditional goddess Ceres, he painted a crowd of harvesters at different activities; some are working, some relaxing, and some are having a siesta.

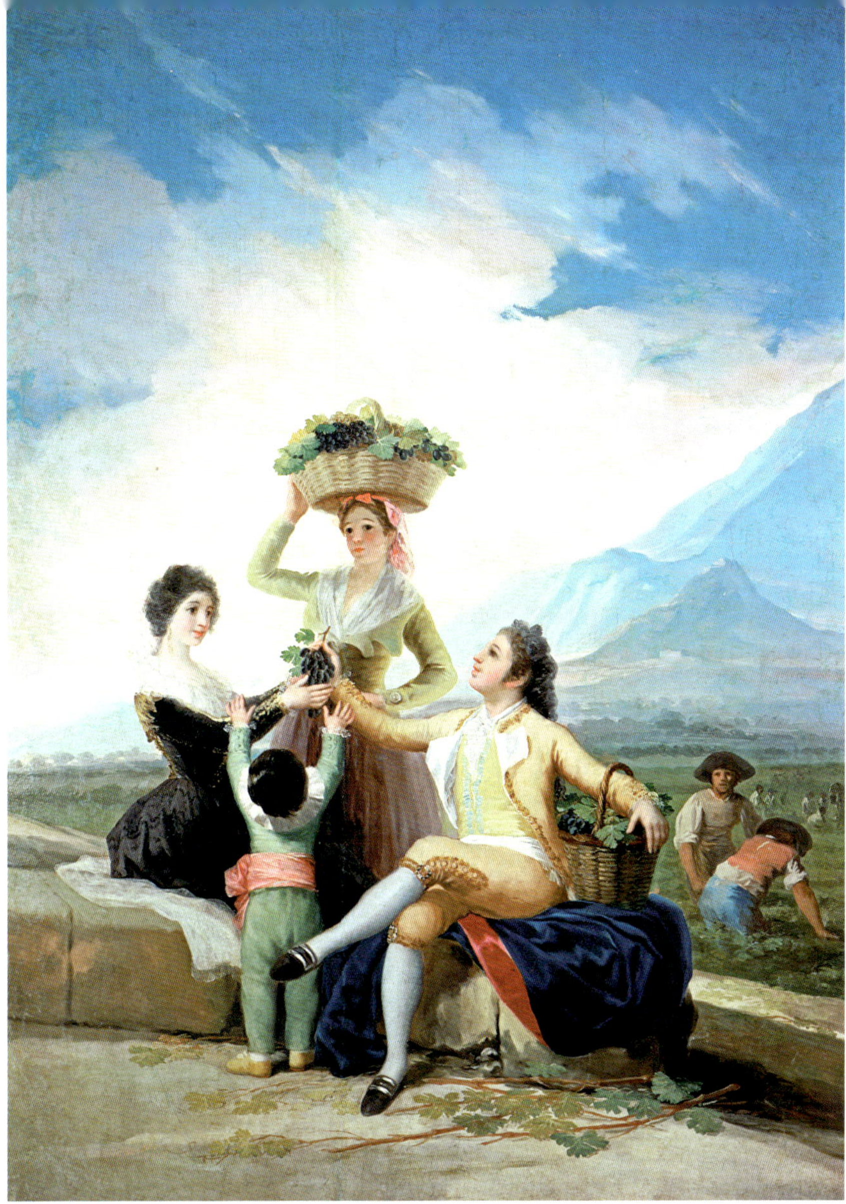

Autumn or *The Grape Harvest*, 1786, oil on canvas, Museo Nacional del Prado, Madrid, Spain, 267.5 x 190.5cm (105 x 75in)

Another of the four seasons tapestry cartoons that Goya made for the El Pardo Palace, here a young man in yellow sits on a stone and offers a cluster of black grapes to a lady. A boy tries to reach the grapes, while a woman stands next to them, holding a grape basket on her head. Behind are some grape harvesters. The grape harvest is Goya's allegory of autumn.

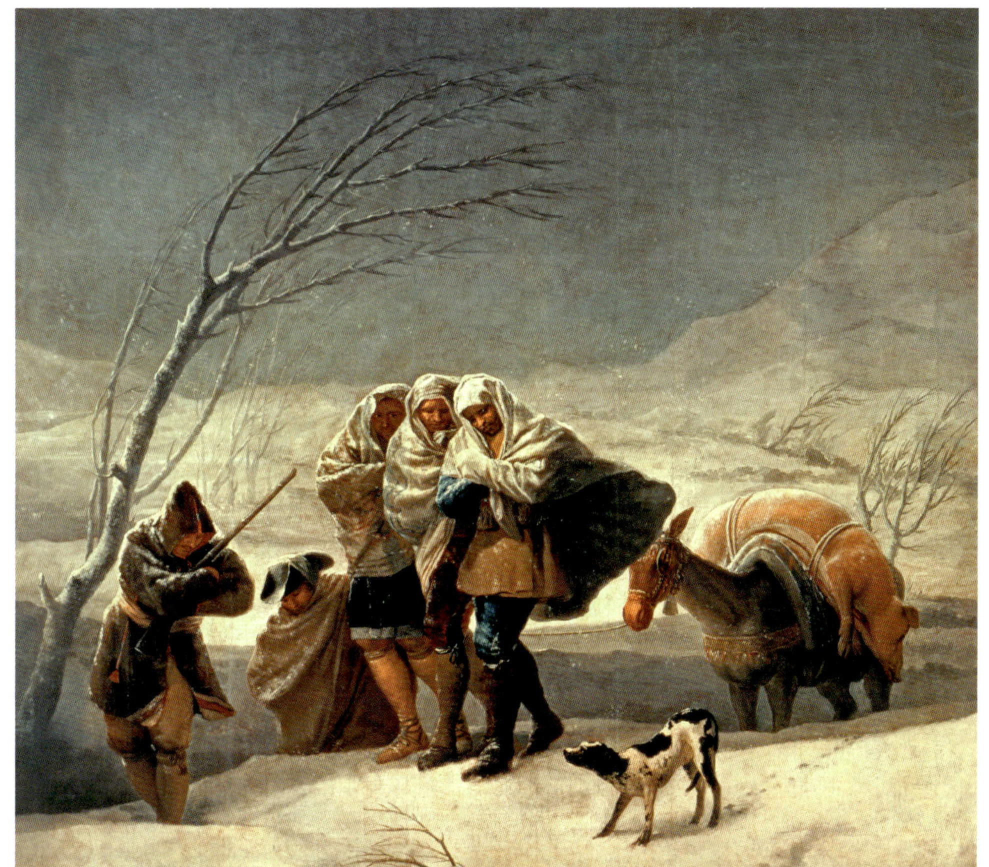

Winter or *The Snowstorm*, 1786–7, oil on canvas, Museo Nacional del Prado, Madrid, Spain, 275 x 293cm (108 x 115in)

Instead of showing the pleasures of the season, this unusual allegory for winter shows men enduring its hardships. Three cloaked peasants return home from the market. Near them are two wealthier-looking characters and behind, slung across a pony is a huge dead pig, probably belonging to the two richer men. The blizzard prevents the humans from seeing each other, but the dog – and viewers – can foresee an inevitable collision.

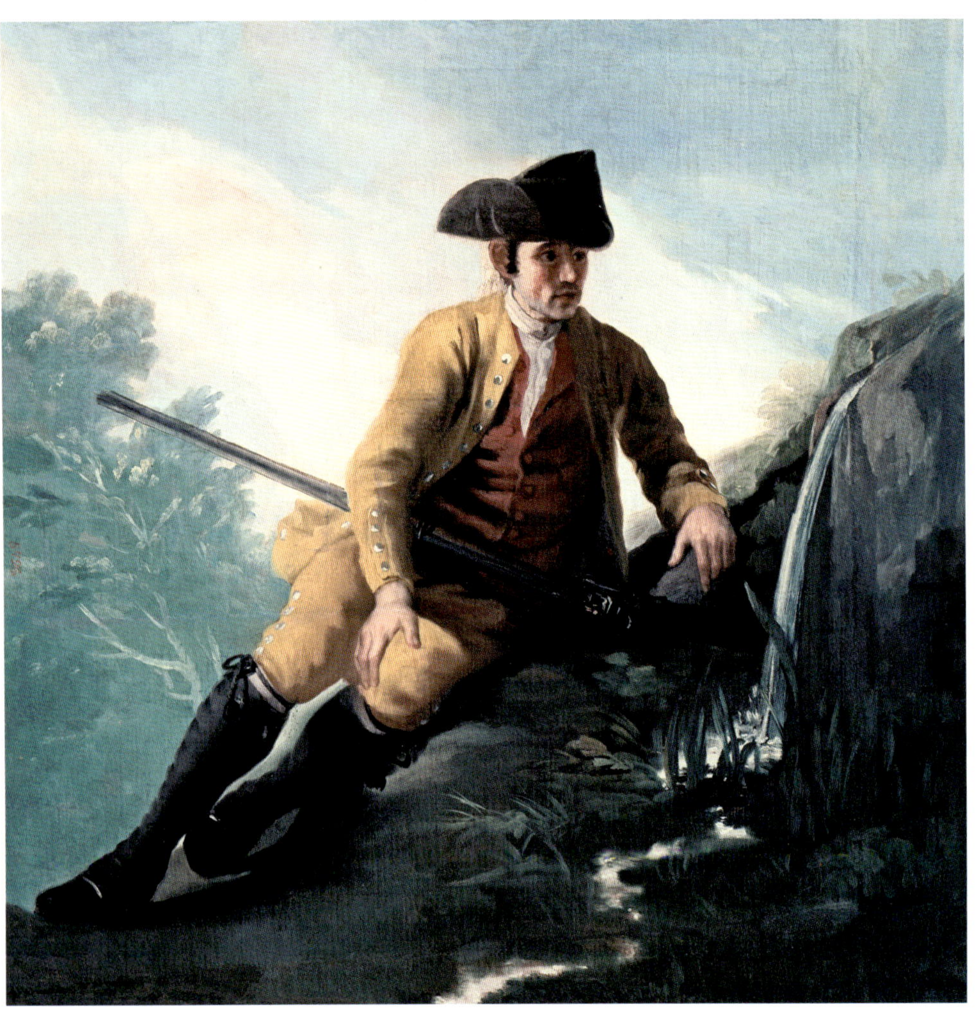

Hunter by a Spring, 1786–7, oil on canvas, Museo Nacional del Prado, Madrid, Spain, 130 x 131cm (51 x 51½in)

For the wall representing spring in the El Pardo Palace dining room, Goya designed this cartoon to accompany *Spring* or *The Flower Girls* (see page 150) and *Shepherd Playing a Dulzaina* (see page 36). A hunter rests beside a spring, his shotgun on his lap, his peaceful gaze emphasizing the tranquillity of life in the country. This was designed to hang above a window.

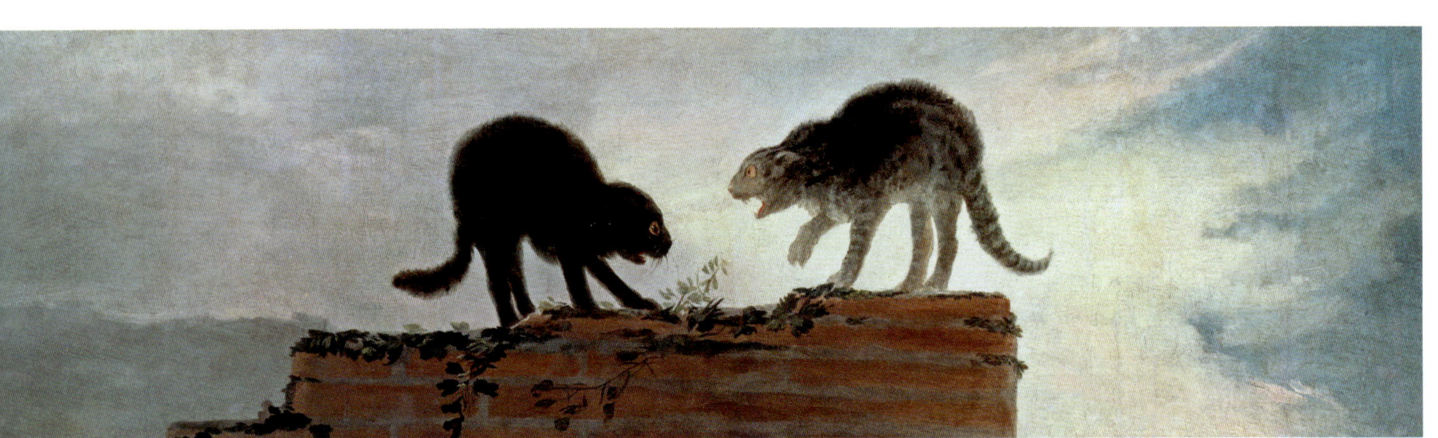

Cat Fight, 1786–7, oil on canvas, Museo Nacional del Prado, Madrid, Spain, 56.5 x 196.5cm (22 x 77in)

Backs arched, fur up, ears down, hissing; the unmistakable image of two cats fighting on a wall. Goya shows his sharp observations of animals' behaviour with this astutely rendered image. In a narrow format and painted as if viewed from below, this was another image that was designed to hang over a window; it was created to amuse the Prince and Princess of Asturias and their dinner guests.

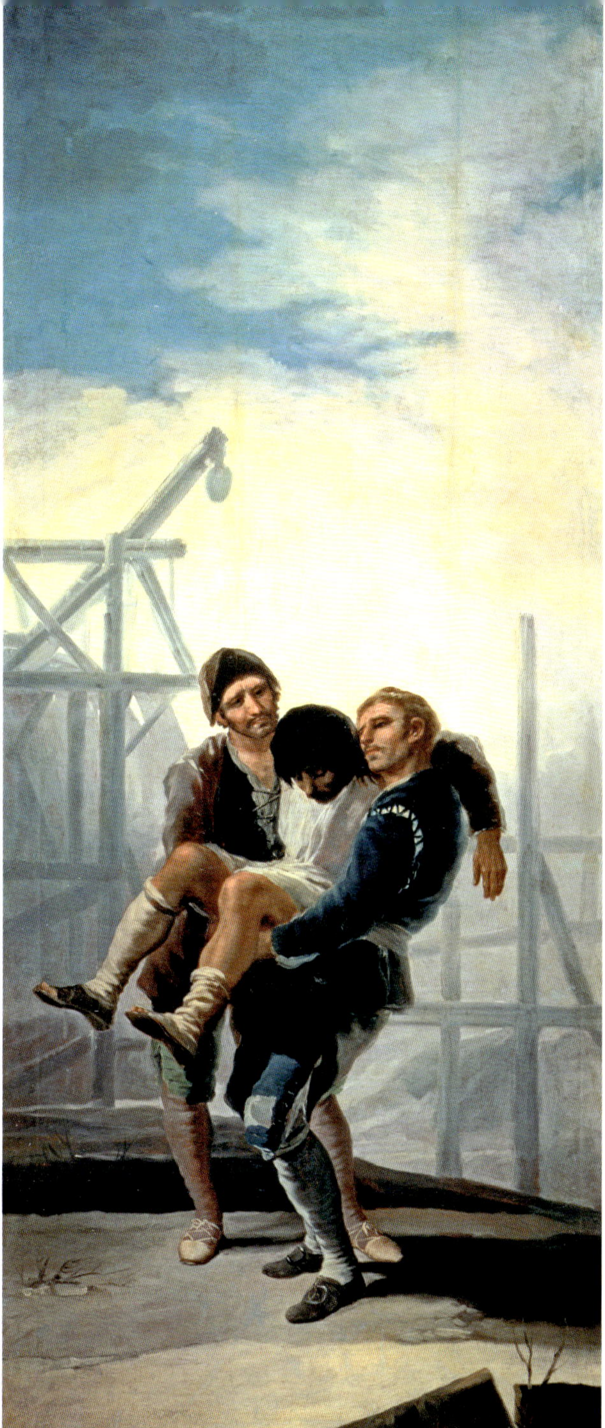

Poor People at a Fountain, 1786, oil on canvas, Museo Nacional del Prado, Madrid, Spain, 277 x 115cm (109 x 45in)

Each wall of the El Pardo Palace dining room was dedicated to a season. This is one of three cartoons Goya produced for the winter wall. All three depict figures in lively brushwork, with coldness expressed through colour. A woman and two boys have brought jugs to the fountain for water. Romantic critics gave this work its name, although the clothing indicates that the individuals are not particularly poor.

The Wounded Mason, 1786–7, oil on canvas, Museo Nacional del Prado, Madrid, Spain, 268 x 110cm (105½ x 43in)

This is another of the three winter-themed cartoons for the dining room of the El Pardo Palace. It is an unusual scene of two men carrying a wounded mason, with scaffolding visible behind them, and is related to a recent decree passed by Charles III, concerning building construction and specifically how scaffolding should be erected 'to avoid accidents and the death of workmen'.

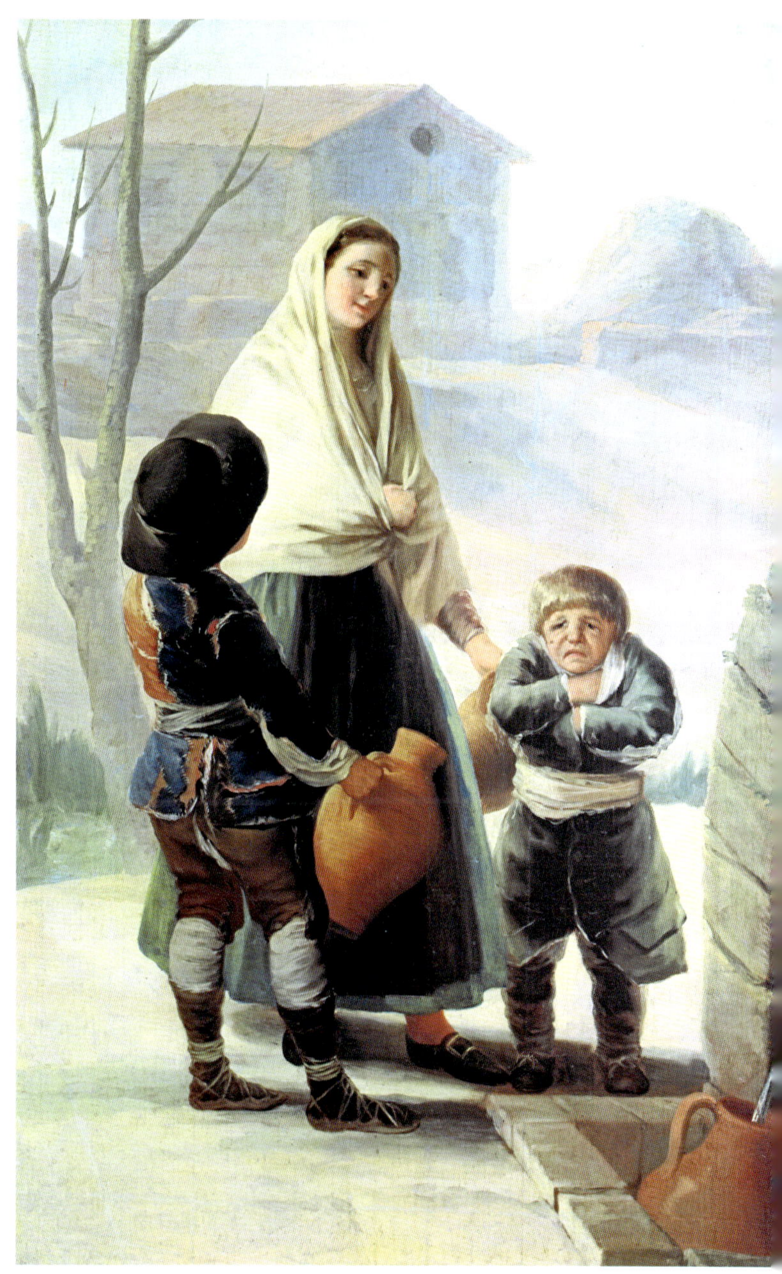

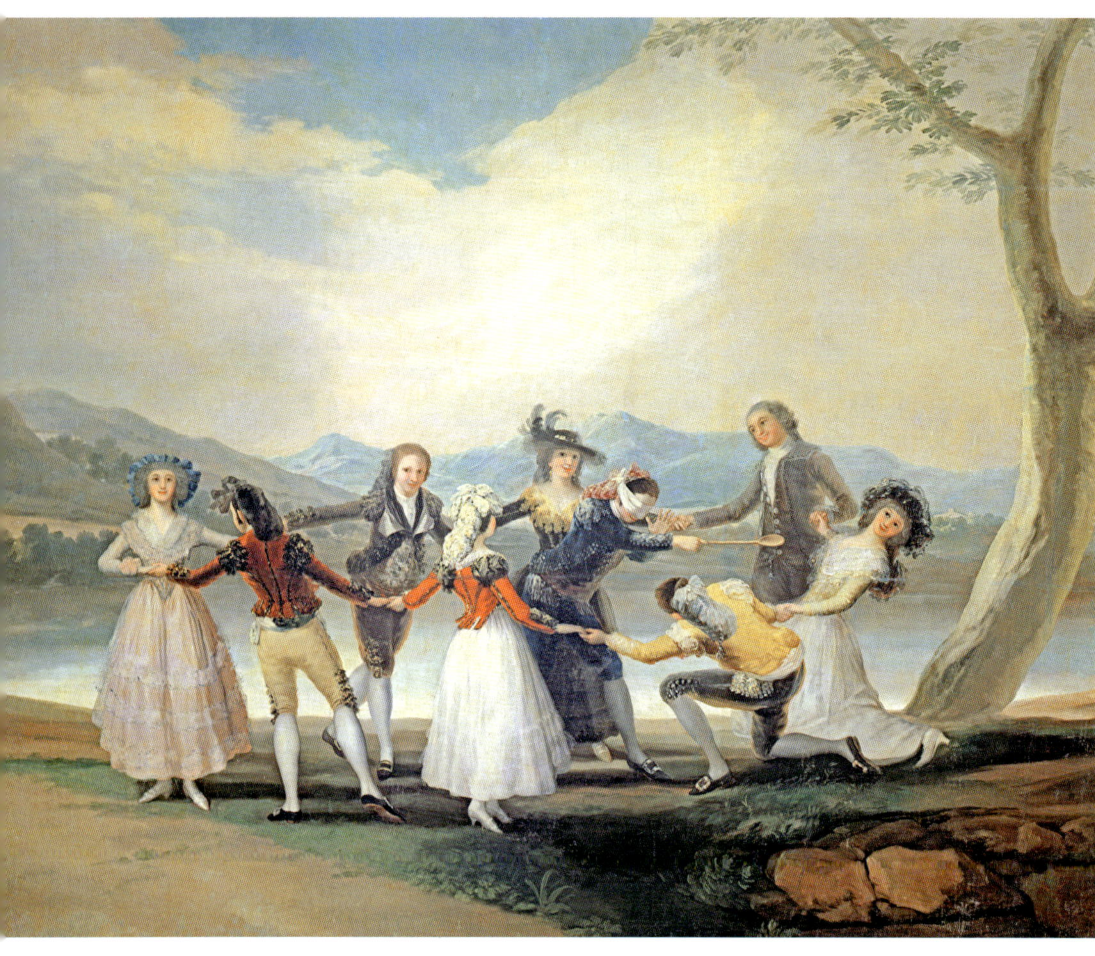

Blind Man's Buff, 1788–9, oil on canvas, Museo Nacional del Prado, Madrid, Spain, 269 x 350cm (106 x 138in)

Dressed as Spanish aristocrats, mainly as majas and majos, with two in the elegant French style, boys and girls play blind man's buff in the countryside. A boy is blindfolded and holding a large wooden spoon as he tries to catch someone in the circle around him. The liveliness of the content, soft colour scheme and luminous background scenery reminiscent of the Rococo, demonstrates Goya's adaptability.

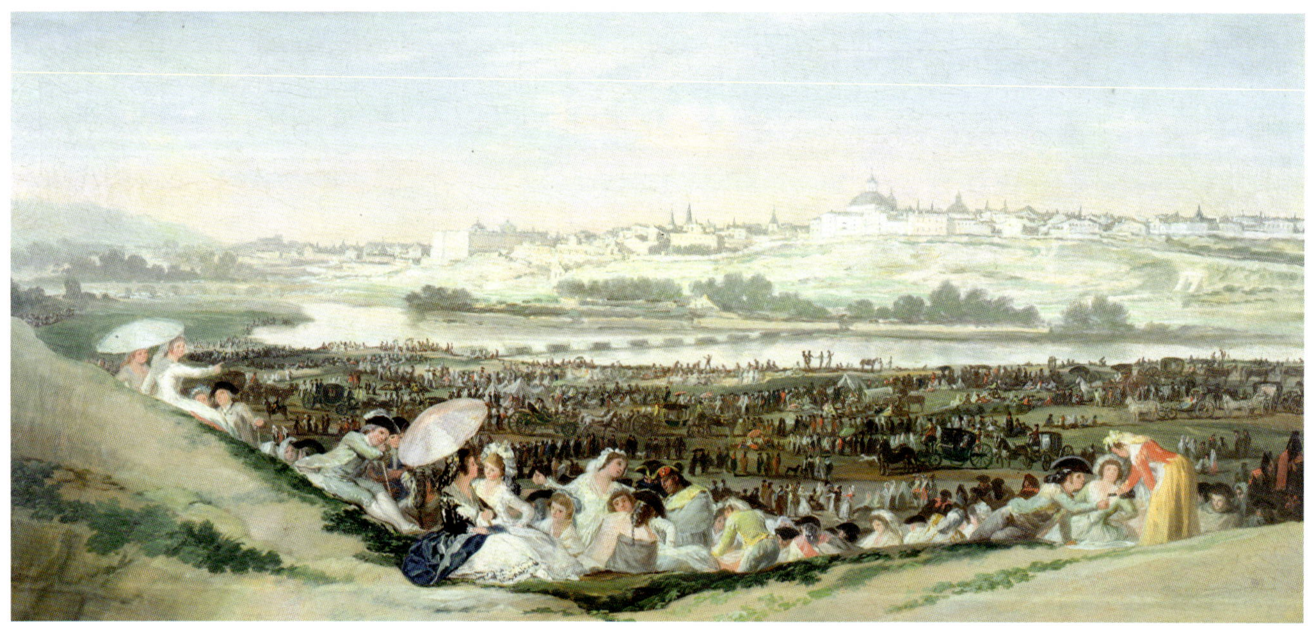

The Meadow of San Isidro on His Feast Day, 1788, oil on canvas, Museo Nacional del Prado, Madrid, Spain, 41.9 x 90.8cm (16½ x 36in)

Every year on 15 May, the people of Madrid celebrated the festival of their patron, San Isidro. They went in procession to the saint's hermitage on the bank of the Manzanares River, gave thanks and made vows, and then everyone congregated in the meadow nearby, and ate, drank and partied until late into the night. This panorama shows Goya's growing deftness in lively composition, energetic brushwork and subtle colour.

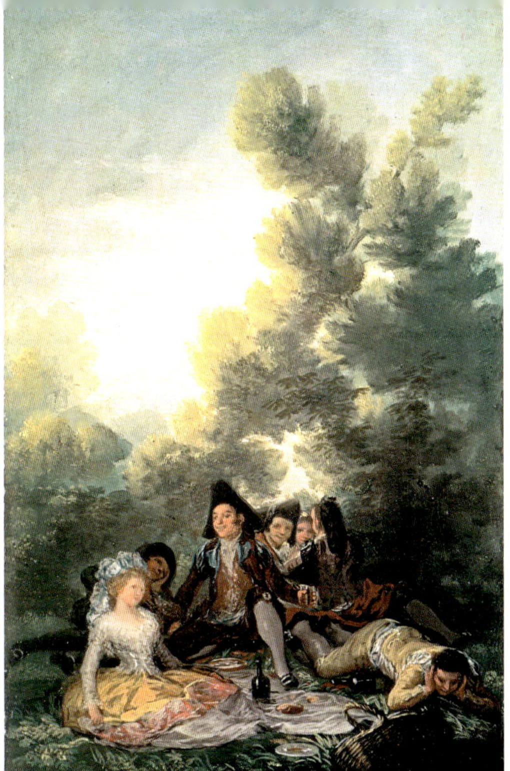

A Picnic, 1785–90, oil on canvas, The National Gallery, London, UK, 41.3 x 25.8cm (16 x 10in)

Believed to be a sketch made probably at the same time he painted *The Meadow of San Isidro* (see below), this little painting shows several well-dressed people from Madrid enjoying a picnic in the countryside. It was a theme that had been particularly exploited by artists such as Jean-Antoine Watteau (1684–1721) and later, notoriously by Manet in his painting *Le Déjeuner sur l'herbe* in 1862–3.

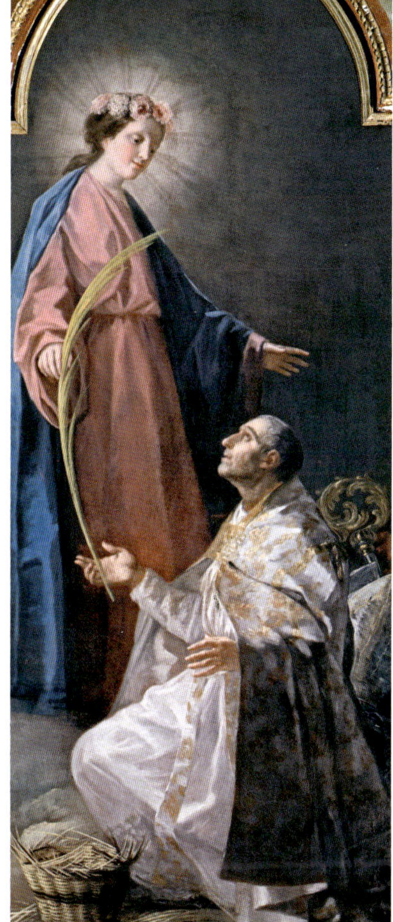

Apparition of the Virgin to Saint Julian, c. 1790, oil on canvas, Parish Church of Nuestra Señora de la Asunción, Valdemoro, Spain, 250 x 90cm (98½ x 35½in)

Clearly influenced by Mengs, Goya has used elements of Renaissance, Baroque, Rococo and Neoclassical painting styles in this religious work. His rich palette and chiaroscuro effects also show an influence of Mengs, but in addition, Goya expressed his individual approach. Saint Julian is placed as close to the viewer as possible, and both the holy figures have been imbued with 'real' personalities, connecting with each other through their eyes, expressions and hand gestures. Form is treated with great firmness, contour lines are drawn with clarity and tones lack the sfumato quality of many of his works.

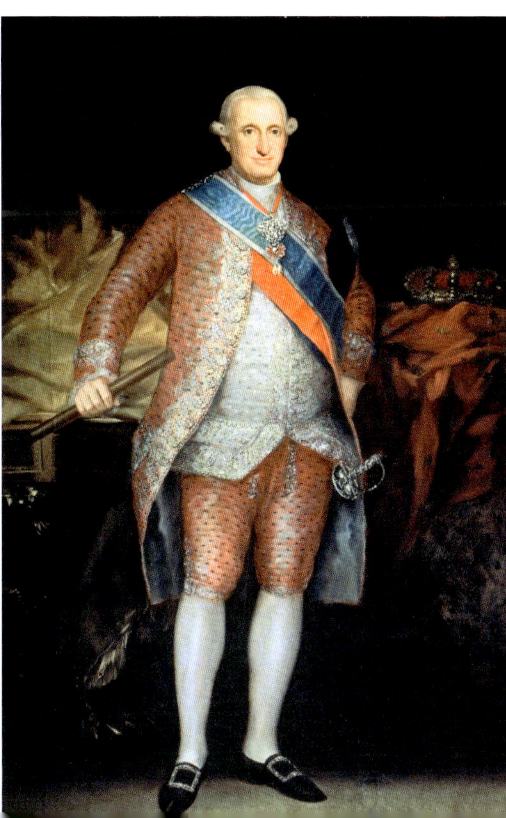

Charles IV, 1789, oil on canvas, Museo Nacional del Prado, Madrid, Spain, 203 x 137cm (80 x 54in)

This portrait of Charles IV was painted soon after Charles III had died and while the revolution in France was occurring. In an effort to portray royal control and continuity, Goya was commissioned to paint this with a companion portrait of María Luisa (see page 35). In a red frock coat adorned with various decorations, Charles carries his ruler's staff; his crown sits on an ermine-lined purple robe on a table.

The Straw Manikin, 1791–2,
oil on canvas, Museo
Nacional del Prado, Madrid,
Spain, 133 x 114.7cm
(52 x 45in)

Four young women laugh as
they toss a life-sized manikin
into the air. The work is an
allegory of men as playthings
of women; a reversal of the
usual domination of men
over women, which is why
the women are laughing.
This was extremely bold of
Goya, but it was a subject
he explored again later; an
interesting theme for the
King's office at El Escorial.

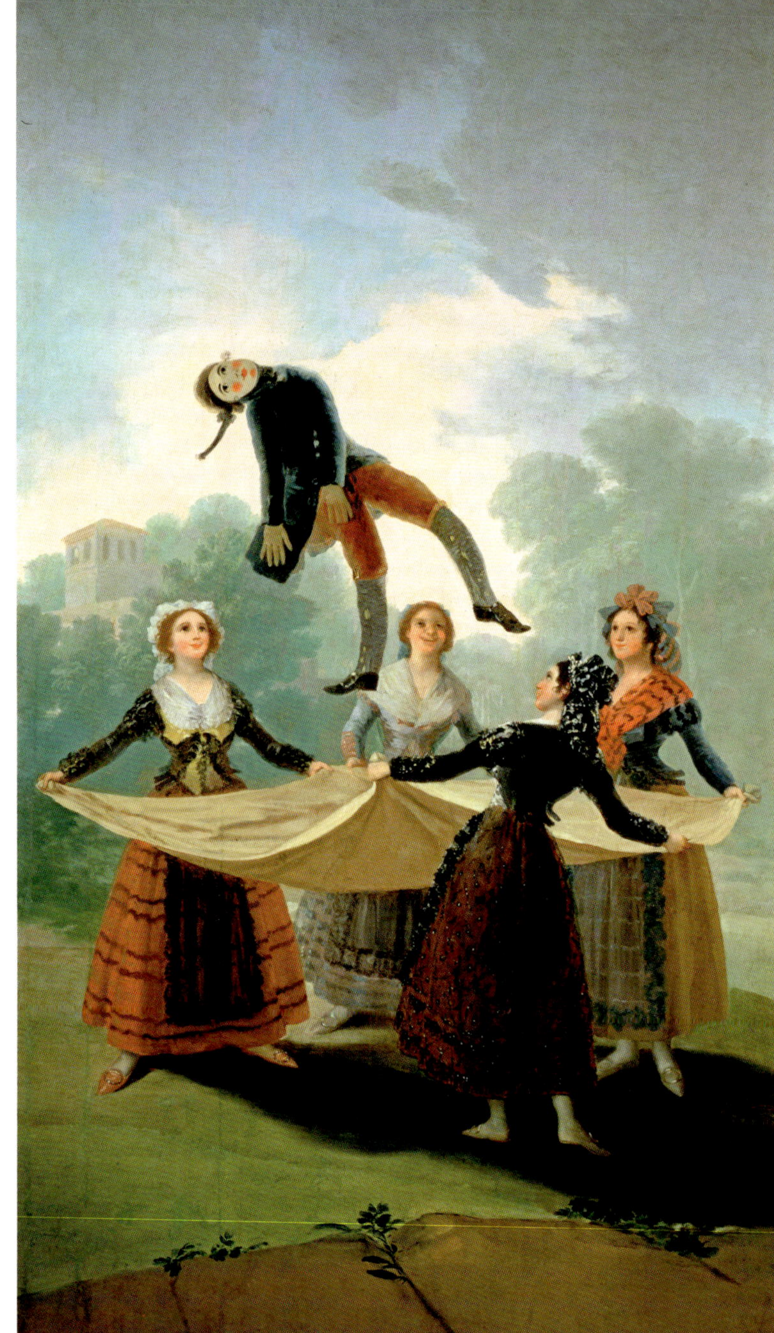

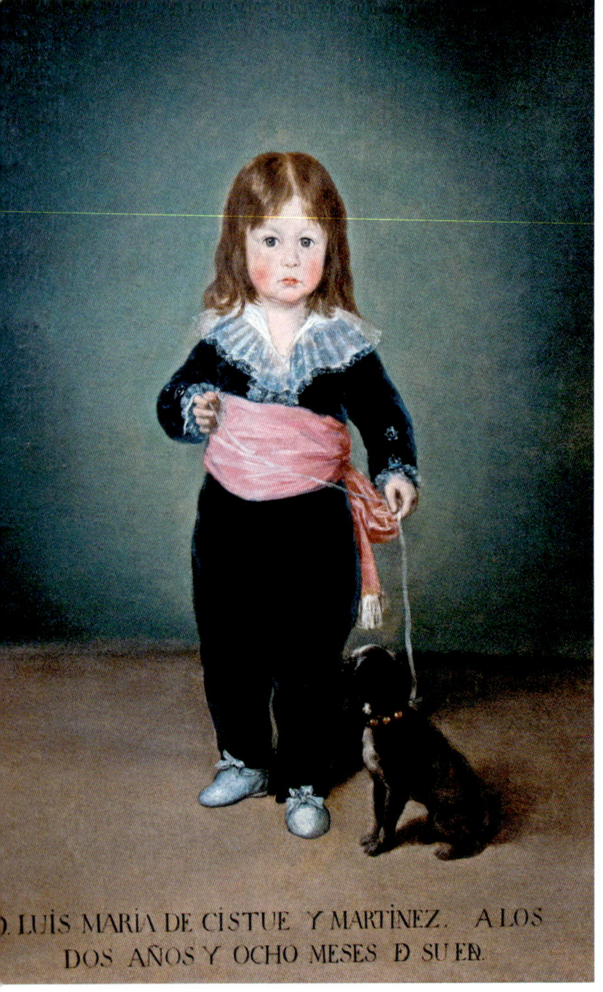

*Portrait of Luis Maria de
Cistué*, 1791, oil on canvas,
Musée du Louvre, Paris,
France, 133 x 114.7cm
(52 x 45in)

This is one of the few
children's portraits that
Goya executed, but as with
his other children's images,
he abandons all cynicism.

In a robe trimmed with green
velvet, lace and a
pink ribbon, the little boy
stands holding his pet.
An inscription gives his age
as two years and eight
months. The work shows
the influence of Velázquez,
and it later inspired Manet's
The Fife Player.

Charles IV, 1789, oil on canvas, Museo Lázaro Galdiano, Madrid, Spain, 220 x 140cm (86½ x 55in)

This is one of several portraits of Charles IV that Goya painted soon after his accession, to help establish his power and authority. Charles was 40 years old when he ascended the throne; a passionate huntsman, but unintelligent, and content to leave the affairs of state mainly to his wife. But he liked art and during his reign, he employed many artists to paint portraits and decorate his palaces.

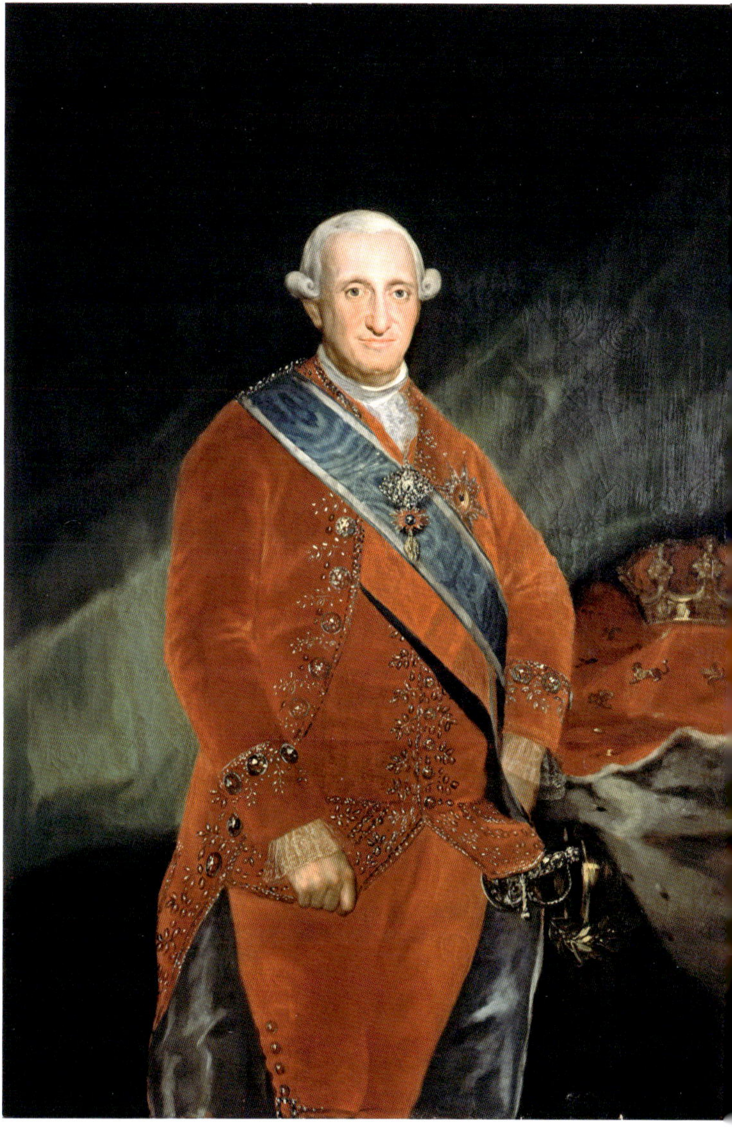

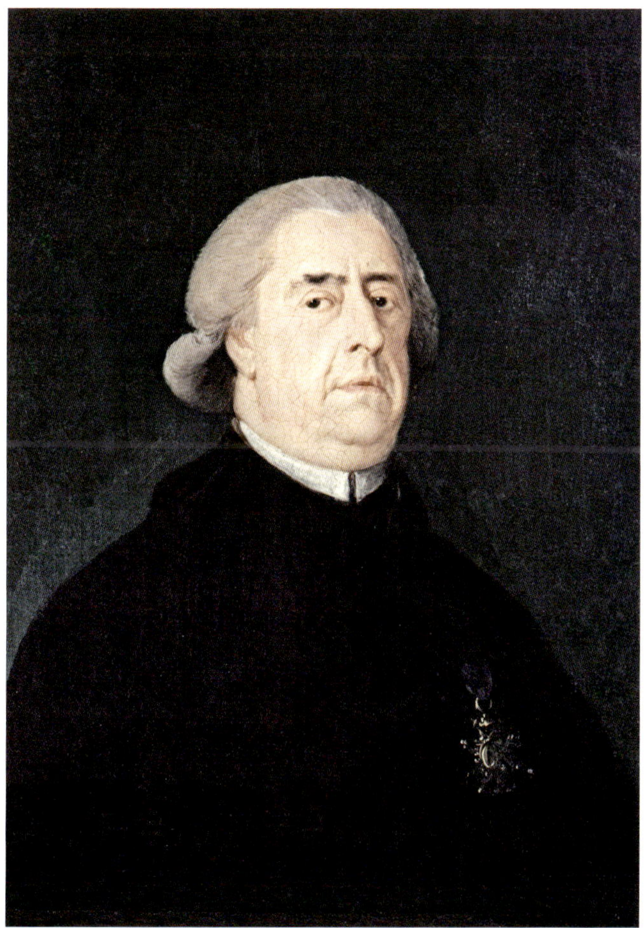

Study of Ramón de Pignatelli y Moncayo (1734–93), *c.*1790, oil on canvas, Private Collection, 79 x 62cm (31 x 24½in)

Don Ramón de Pignatelli (1734–93) was a cultured intellectual and a respected noble, clergyman and politician from Saragossa. He held various posts, including vice-rector of the University of Saragossa and the protectorate of the Imperial Canal of Aragon, for which this painting was commissioned. He was recognized for his work on a vital project that irrigated Aragon. This is the preliminary study for a full-length portrait.

Little Giants or *Chicken Fights*, 1791–2, oil on canvas, Museo Nacional del Prado, Madrid, Spain, 137 x 104cm (54 x 41in)

After Charles III died, the royal family moved from El Pardo. This is one of seven designs for the El Escorial Palace – one of Charles IV and María Luísa's favourite palaces. These cartoons all depict countryside scenes. Here, five boys ride on each other's shoulders playing a light-hearted game known as 'Chicken Fights' or 'Horse and Rider'.

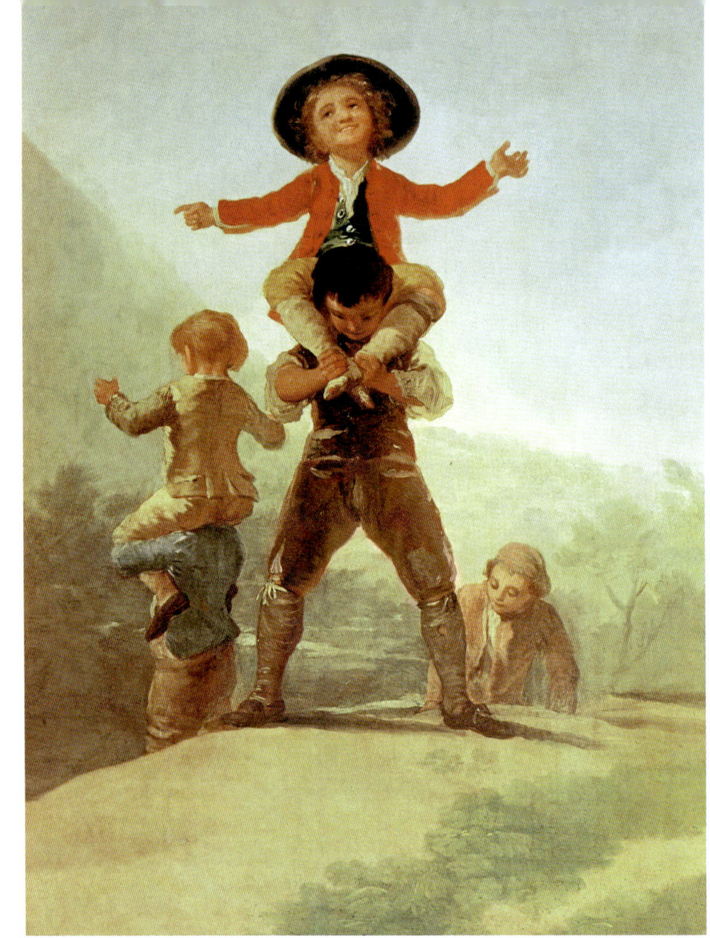

The Stilts, 1791–2, oil on canvas, Museo Nacional del Prado, Madrid, Spain, 268 x 320cm (105½ x 126in)

Two young men on stilts approach a window where a young woman leans out. They are accompanied by two other young men on foot, playing the dulzaina (an oboe-like instrument). Groups of figures watch the spectacle. As with all Goya's cartoons for Charles IV's office at El Escorial, this has an underlying meaning. It warns that Spain must step carefully in the current European troubles.

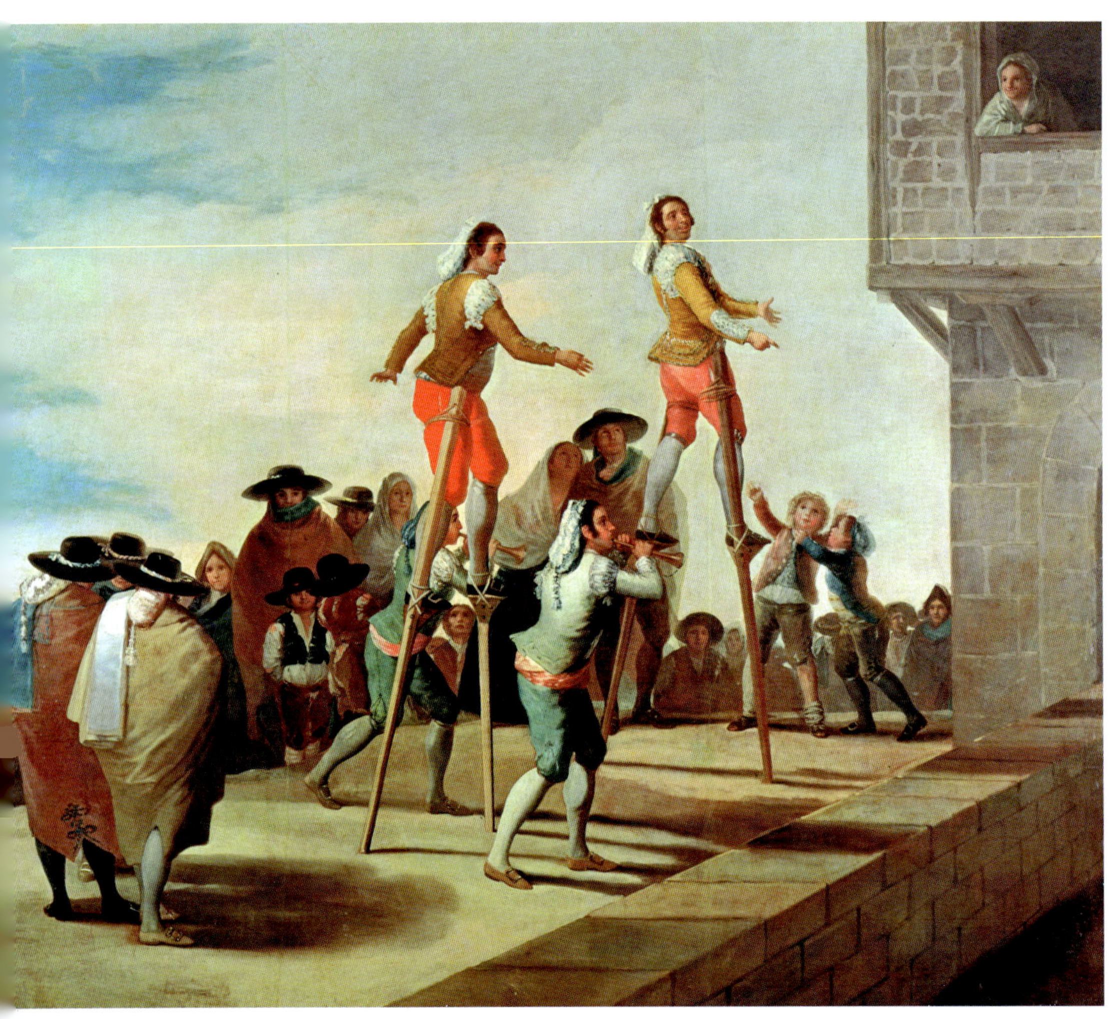

The Wedding, 1791–2, oil on canvas, Museo Nacional del Prado, Madrid, Spain, 269 x 396cm (106 x 156in)

Using an arch to frame the group, Goya introduces further satire about Spanish society. This depicts a wedding in which a beautiful young woman has just married a rich, but ageing and obese man. The shabbily dressed bride's father follows the procession. The story criticizes a common situation of the time: marriages of convenience in which a girl marries an old man for his money or title.

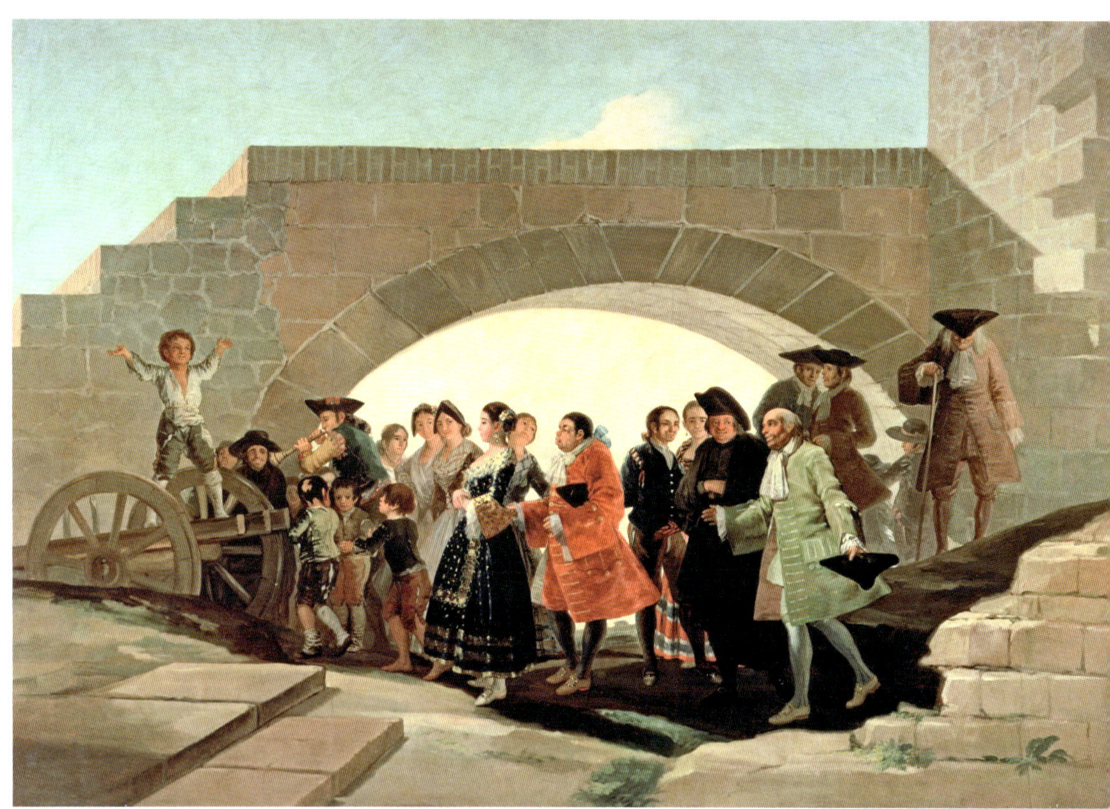

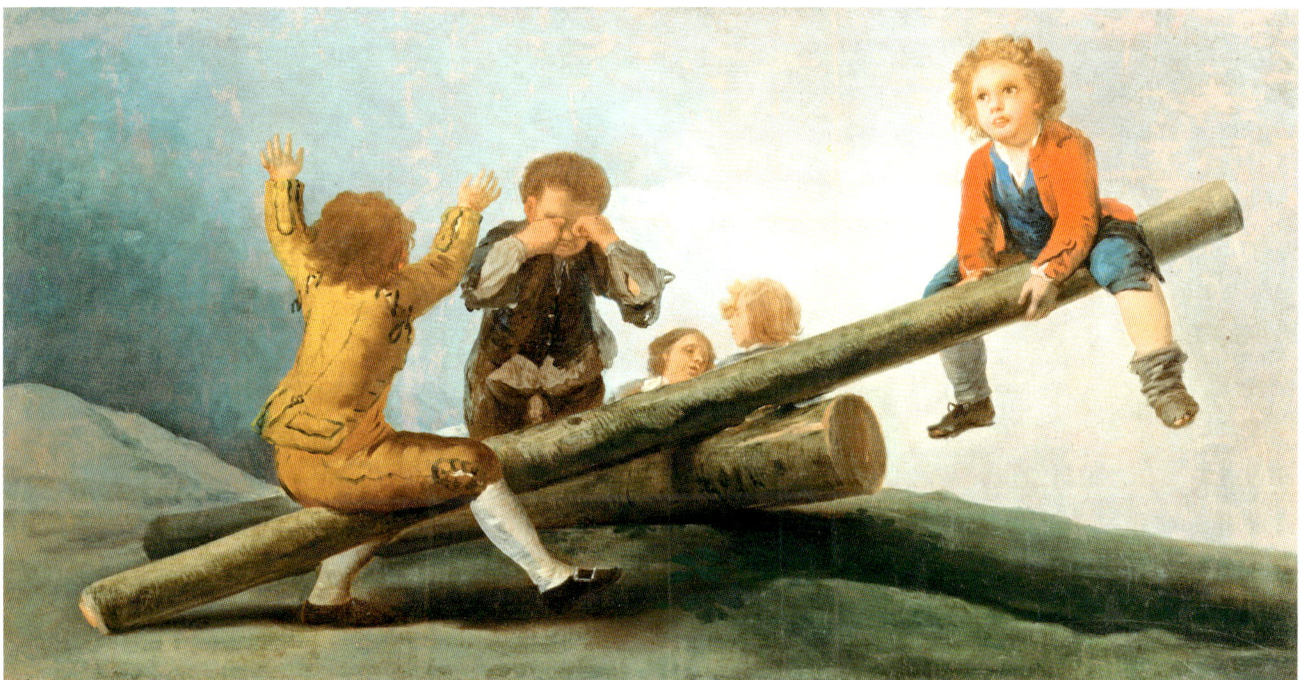

The See-saw, 1791–2, oil on canvas, The Philadelphia Museum of Art, Pennsylvania, USA, 82.4 x 163.2cm (32½ x 64in)

Over a decade after first illustrating a similar subject (see page 129), Goya once again portrays little boys playing on a see-saw. Designed to fit over a window, the small work expresses the empathy Goya felt for children, while he was amused at their mischievous behaviour. This work is often interpreted as a deliberate contrast of the innocence of childhood against the corruption of adults.

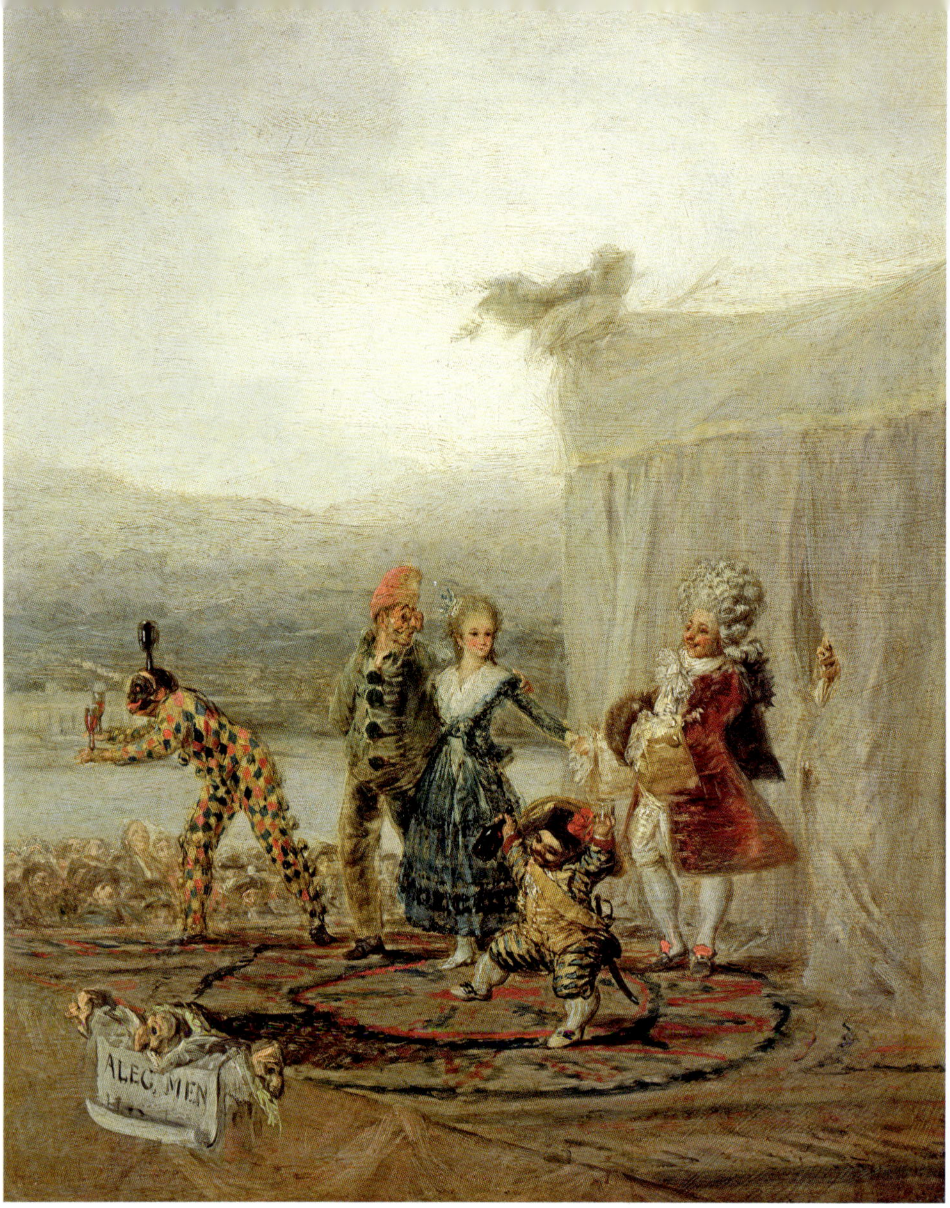

The Strolling Players, 1793, oil on canvas, Museo Nacional del Prado, Madrid, Spain, 43 x 32cm (17 x 12½in)

Featured in this tapestry cartoon are the familiar figures of the Commedia dell'Arte: Pierrot the juggling harlequin, the dancing dwarf and pretty Columbine, rehearsing on an improvized stage in front of a tent. A crowd gathers in the near distance. Written on a scroll hanging over the edge of the stage are the words: 'ALEG MEN' short for '*Alegoría Menandrea*' – the name of the play *Menandrean Allegory* was a moralizing comedy. Yet the enjoyment that should be conveyed appears to be missing here – a reflection of Goya's mind at this time, rather than the subject.

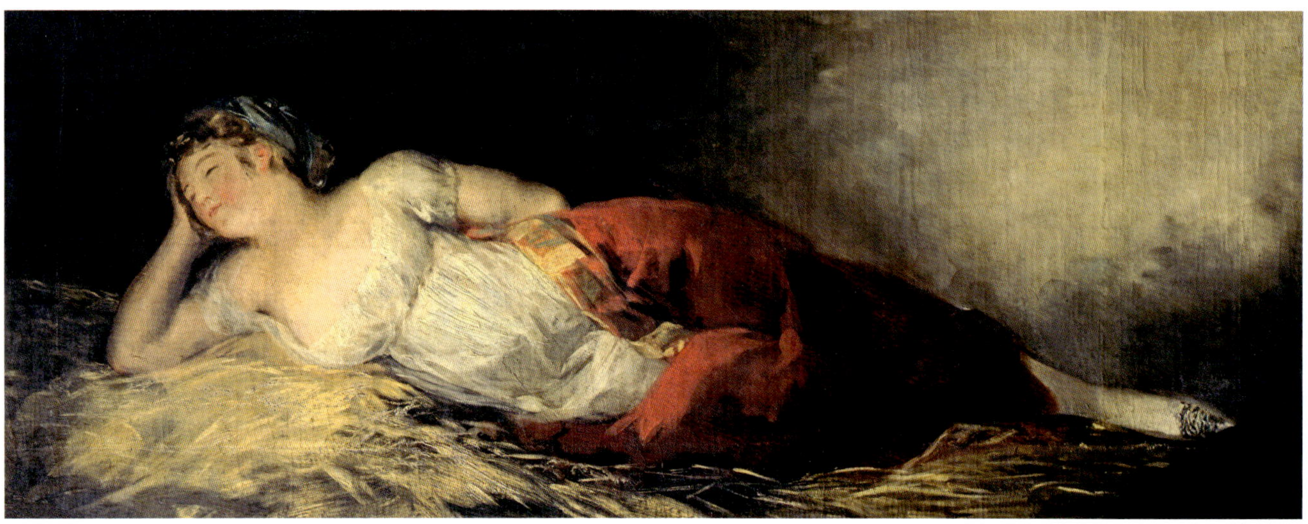

Young Woman Asleep, *c.*1792, oil on canvas, Private Collection, 59 x 145cm (23 x 57in)

This sensuous image of a woman asleep on a pile of straw, wearing a white dress, turban, slippers, and wrapped in a red and gold shawl is believed to have been one of three cartoons for tapestries that were never made. The other cartoons are *Gossiping Women* (Wadsworth Atheneum, Connecticut, USA) and *The Dream* (National Gallery of Ireland, Dublin, Ireland).

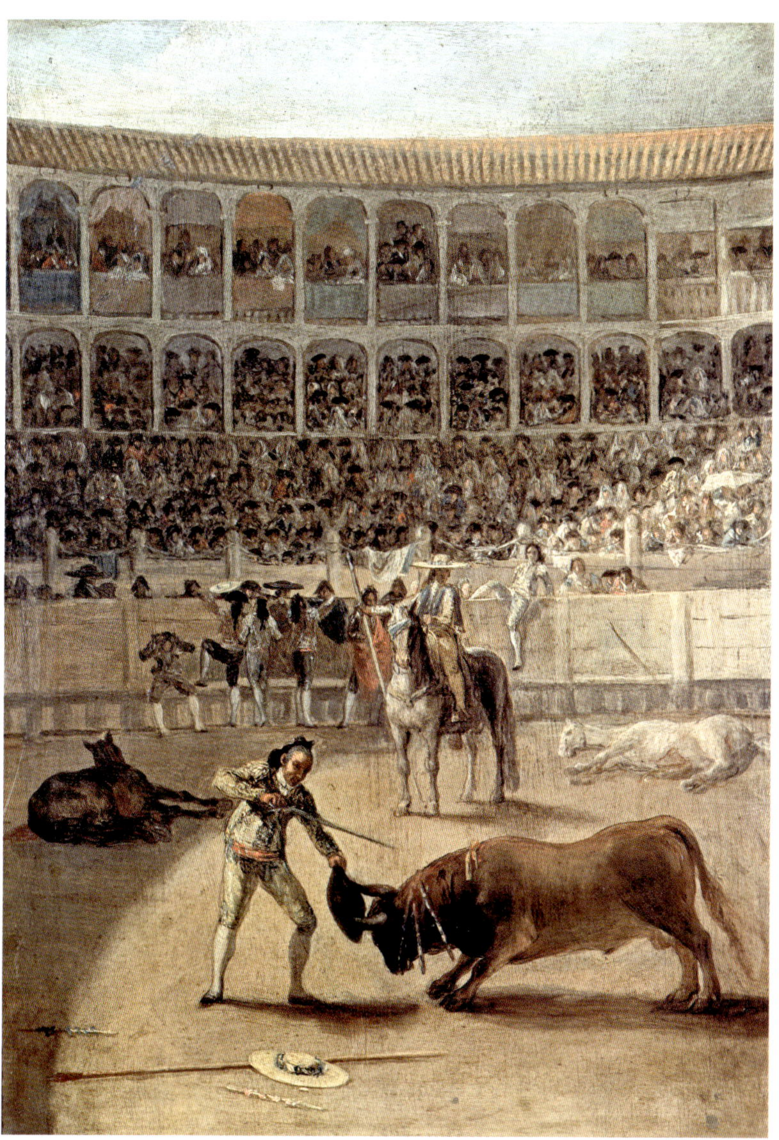

Matador Killing the Bull,
1793, oil on tinplate,
Casilda-Ghisla Guerrero
Burgos y Fernandez de
Cordoba Collection,
Madrid, Spain,
43 x 31.9cm (17 x 12½in)

Bullfighting in 18th-century
Spain was a symbol of
the struggle between the
matador, who represents
goodness and life, and the
bull, a symbol of evil and
death. The bull never wins.
Emphasizing the light and
shade – as seat price in the
shade was more expensive
than in the sun – this work
is ultimately a representation
of the contrast between
the rich and the poor.

Mules Dragging off the Bull,
1793, oil on tinplate,
The Medinaceli Collection,
Seville, Spain, 43 x 32cm
(17 x 12½in)

Spanish-style bullfighting is
called a 'corrida de toros' (a
'running of bulls'), or a 'fiesta
brava' ('brave festival'). After
the matador has killed the
bull, the body is dragged out
of the bullring by a team of
mules. At first glance, this
painting, like the others in this
series, appears sketchy, but
Goya planned it carefully for
dynamic effect, using light
and shadow to enhance
the drama.

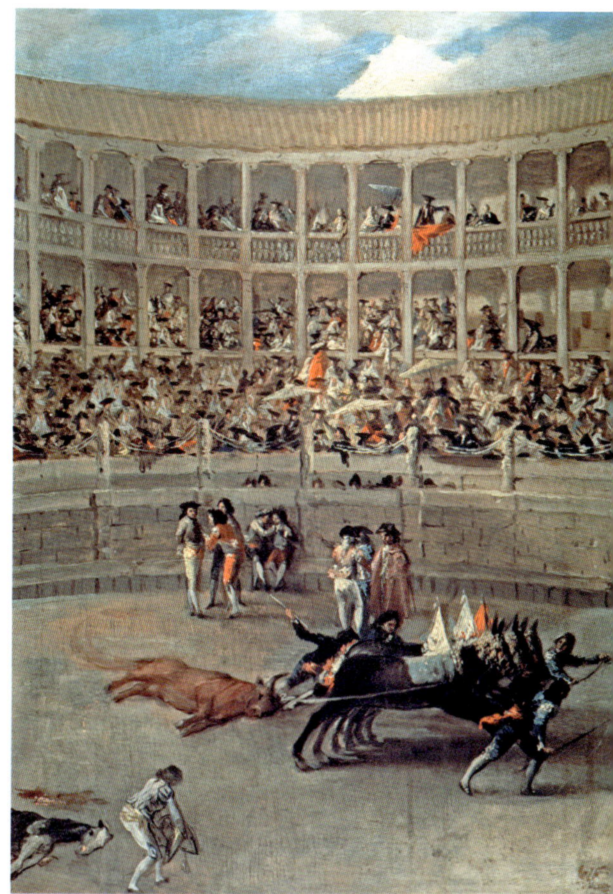

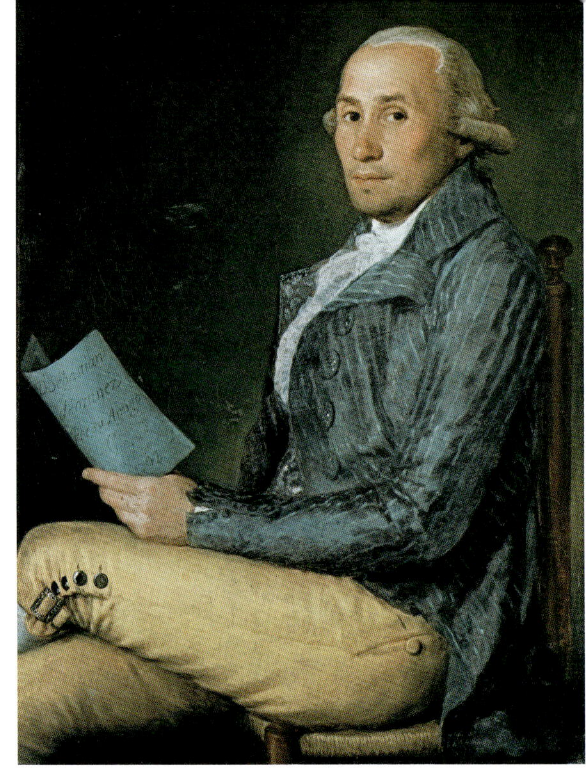

Portrait of Sebastian Martínez, 1792, oil on canvas, The Metropolitan Museum of Art, New York, USA, 92.9 x 67.6cm (36½ x 26½in)

A successful businessman and art collector, Martínez was the friend with whom Goya stayed during his lengthy illness in Cadiz.

Goya executed this before he became ill. Breaking with conventional portrait compositions of the time, in the image, Martínez appears as close to viewers as possible; the tones and colours are sharp, contours firm, brush marks are small and expressive, and the face and clothes are rendered with vibrancy.

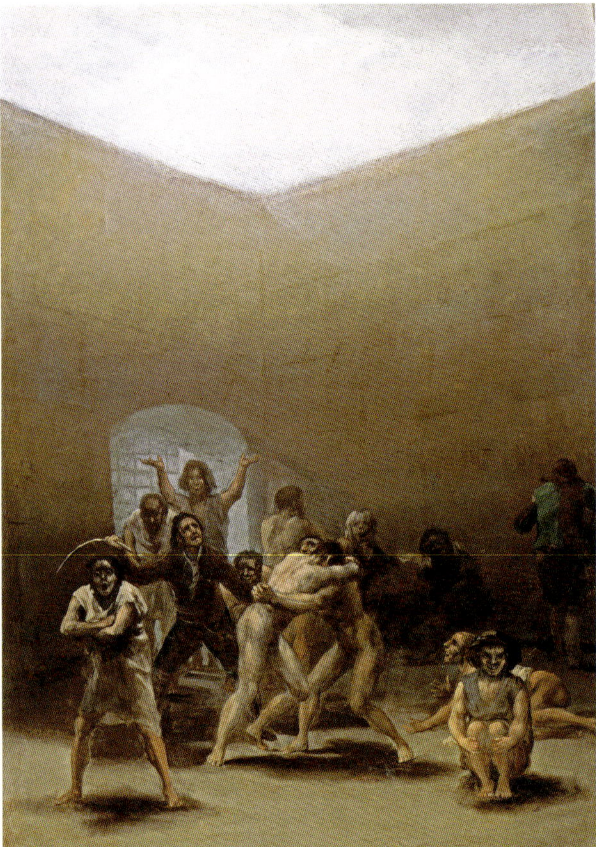

Yard with Lunatics, 1794, oil on tinplate, Meadows Museum, Dallas, USA, 32.7 x 43.8cm (13 x 17in)

Imagined rather than observed, Goya said that this painting was informed by institutions he had seen as a youth in Saragossa. Enclosed within high walls, semi-naked men grin, fight, or huddle together despairingly. At the time, Goya was weak from his illness; had discovered he was deaf and France had just declared war on Spain. No wonder he projected a horrifying vision of loneliness, fear and alienation.

Self-portrait in the Studio, c.1790–5, oil on canvas, Real Academia de Bellas Artes de San Fernando, Madrid, Spain, 42 x 28cm (16½ x 11in)

The loose style, delicate brushwork and distinctive colouring of this small portrait might have been made during Goya's convalescence, but his pose indicates a healthier man. With light pouring through from behind, it seems unlikely that he would have worked in such a fancy jacket, although he invented the hat with candle holders around the brim so he could paint at night, as Javier later verified.

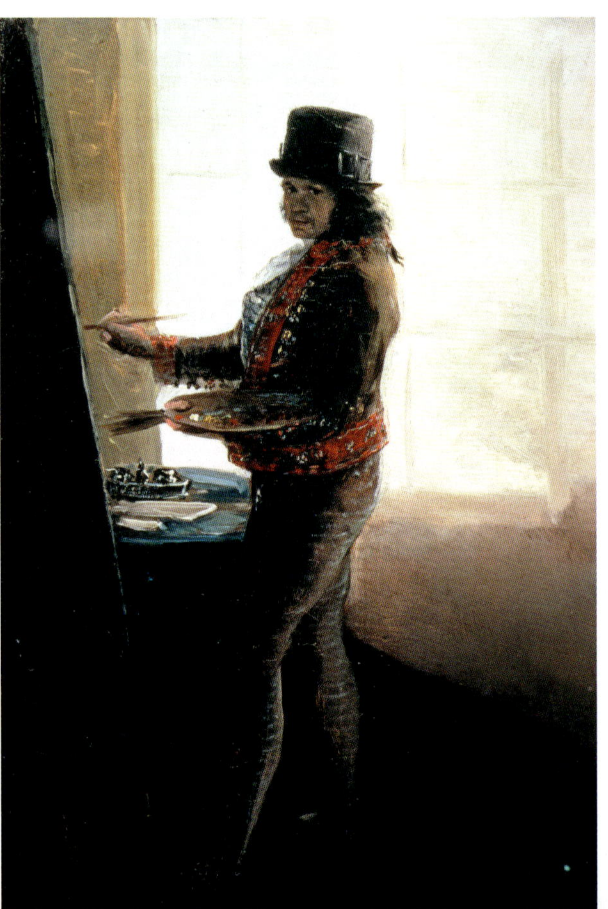

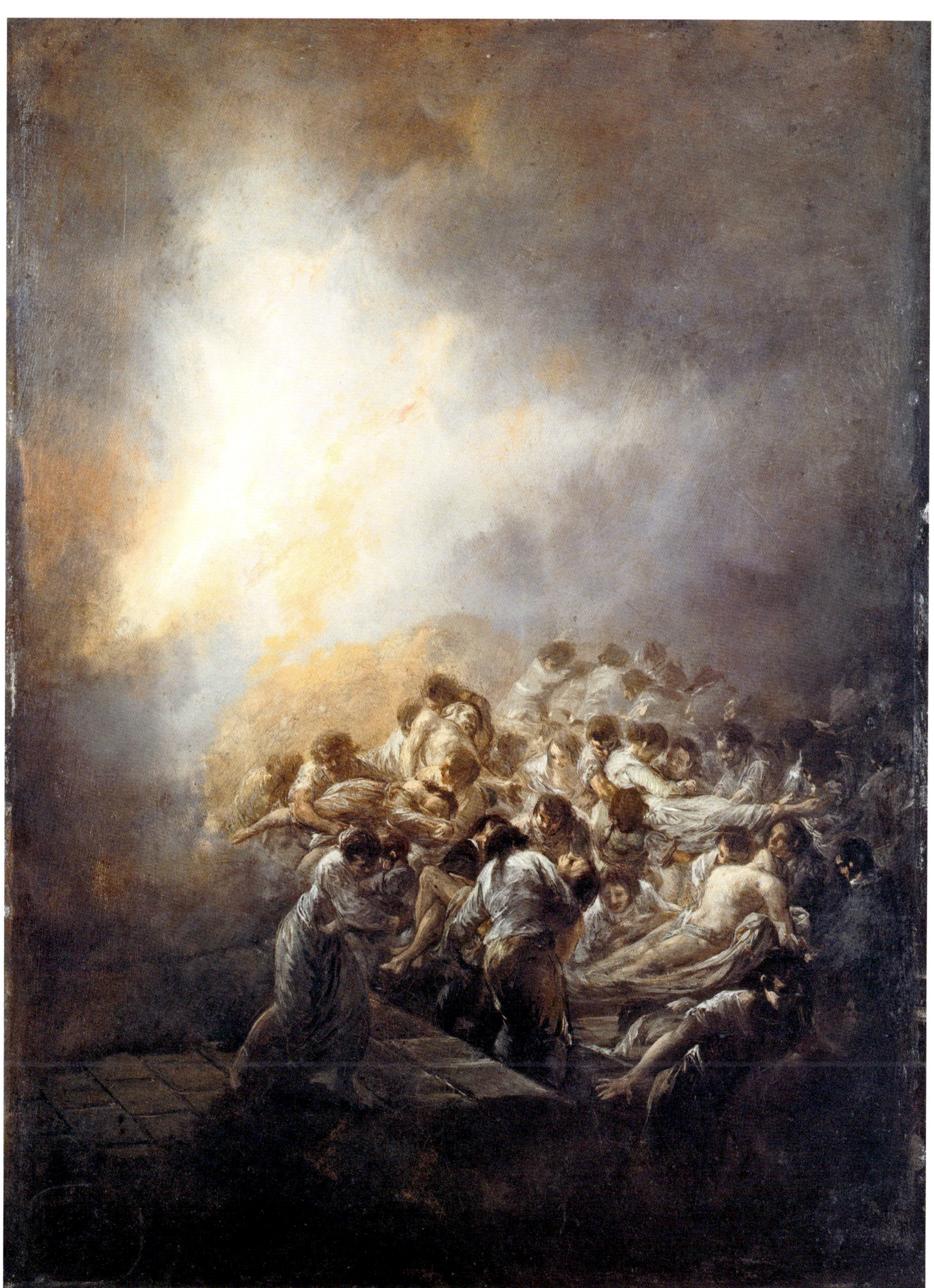

Fire at Night, 1793–4, oil on tinplate, Private Collection, 50 x 32cm (20 x 12½in)

In the autumn of 1792, Goya suffered the dreadful illness that changed his life. As he convalesced, he painted on small tin-coated iron sheets depicting scenes of his choice, including bullfights and other dramatic visions such as this fire, shipwrecks and robberies. He said that they 'represented observations for which there is usually no opportunity in commissioned works, which offer no scope for caprice and invention.'

Tadea Arias de Enríquez,
*c.*1793–4, oil on canvas,
Museo Nacional del Prado,
Madrid, Spain, 191 x 106cm
(75 x 42in)

Tadea Arias de Enríquez
(1770–1855) was the wife
of Captain Thomas de León
(who died in 1793). She
remarried the same year,
to Don Pedro Antonio
Enríquez Bravo. The crest
is of the Arias and León
families, and the work may
be a commemoration of her
first wedding in 1790. In a
white chiffon dress, standing
in a garden, Goya displays his
admiration of contemporary
English portraiture.

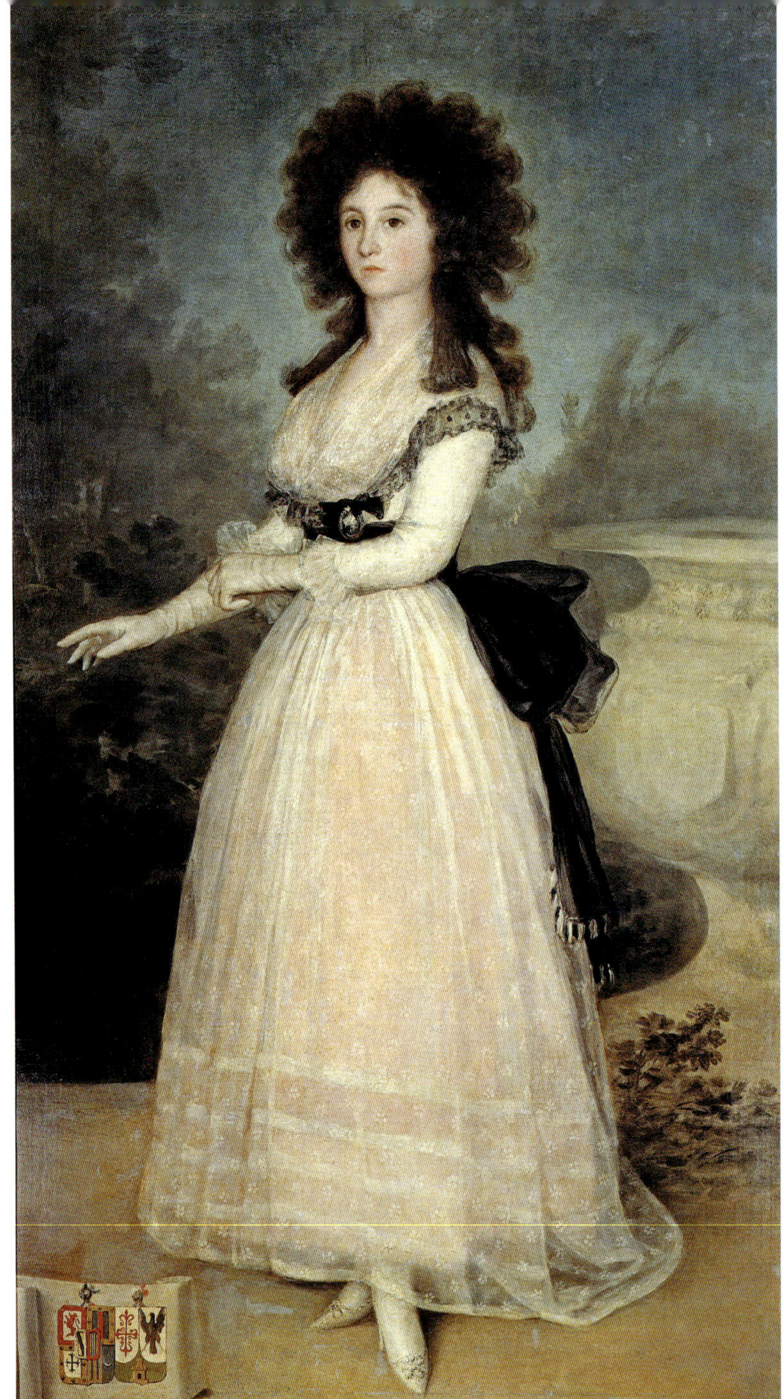

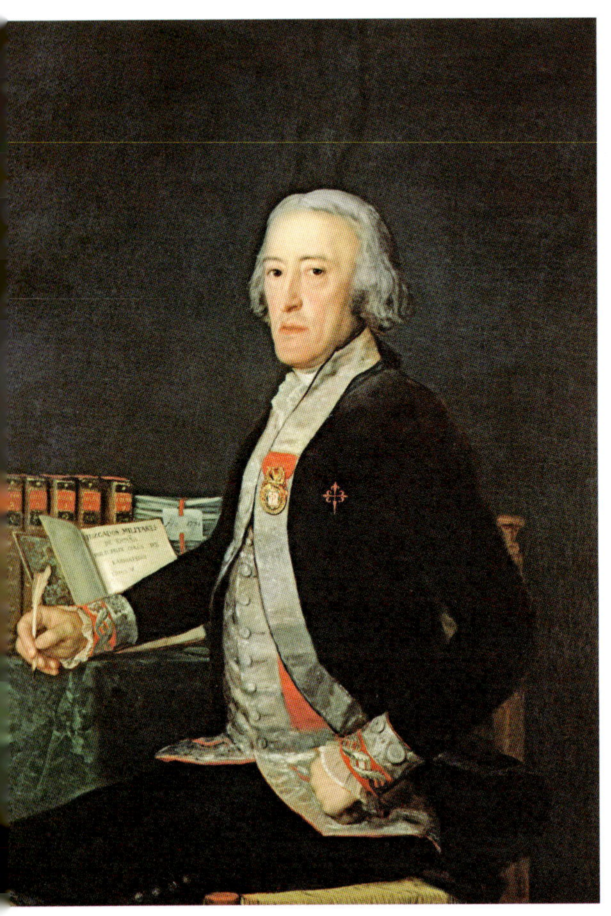

*Portrait of Félix Colón de
Larreátegui,* 1794, oil on
canvas, Indianapolis Museum
of Art, Indiana, USA,
111 x 84cm (44 x 33in)

Intent on capturing
something more than merely
an accurate portrayals of
each of his sitters, Goya
painted what he saw with
his sharp gaze. This was
particularly daring of him
as his subjects were paying
for likenesses, not for truth.
Yet his contemporaries
loved them. Colón was a
descendant of Christopher
Columbus, an officer and
the author of a treatise
on military justice.

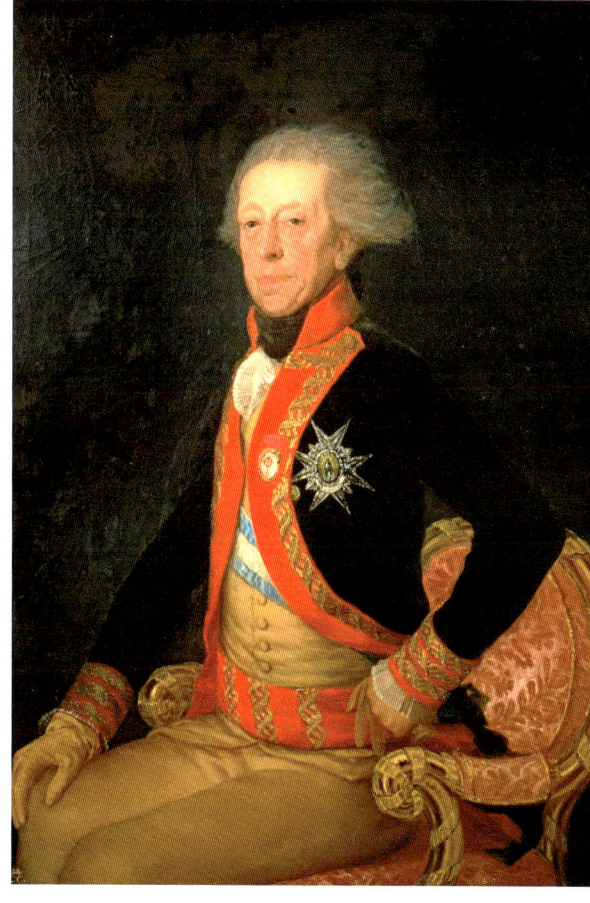

General Antonio Ricardos, 1793–4, oil on canvas, Museo Nacional del Prado, Madrid, Spain, 84 x 112cm (33 x 44in)

Antonio Ricardos Carrillo de Albornoz (1727–94) was a Spanish general who won several military feats. Sensitive and intelligent, he was also a poet and musician who embraced the ideas of the Enlightenment. This period has become known as the great age of portraiture. At the time, Goya studied his renowned English contemporaries Joshua Reynolds (1723–92), George Romney (1734–1802) and Gainsborough, and their influence is apparent in this work.

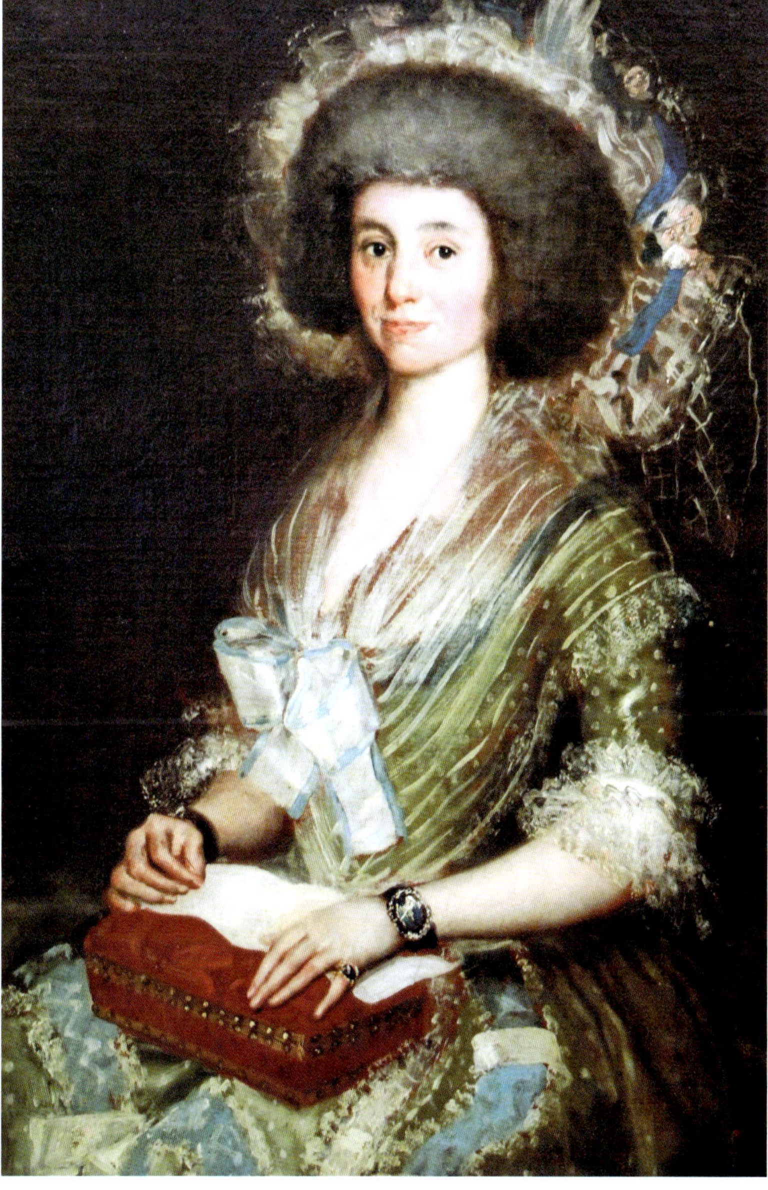

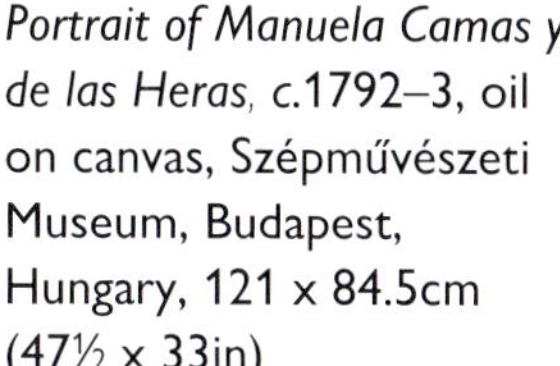

Portrait of Manuela Camas y de las Heras, c.1792–3, oil on canvas, Szépművészeti Museum, Budapest, Hungary, 121 x 84.5cm (47½ x 33in)

Before his illness, Goya travelled to Seville, where he painted portraits of his friend Juan Agustín Ceán Bermúdez (see page 44) and his wife. This is Bermúdez's wife in a pendant to her husband's portrait, one of two paintings conceived as a pair. Elegantly dressed in the fashion that was inspired by Queen Marie-Antoinette in France, Goya set her against a dark background and depicted a wide variety of textures through short, agitated brush marks.

*A Picador, c.*1795, oil on canvas, Museo Nacional del Prado, Madrid, Spain, 57 x 47cm (22½ x 18½in)

This portrait of a picador blends several of Goya's interests, including animals, bullfighting and portraiture. Mounted on a horse, the picador wears a traditional bullfighting outfit and carries a long pike. X-rays of this image show that it was painted over an earlier, unfinished equestrian portrait of Manuel Godoy wearing the sash of the Order of Charles III, which he received in 1791.

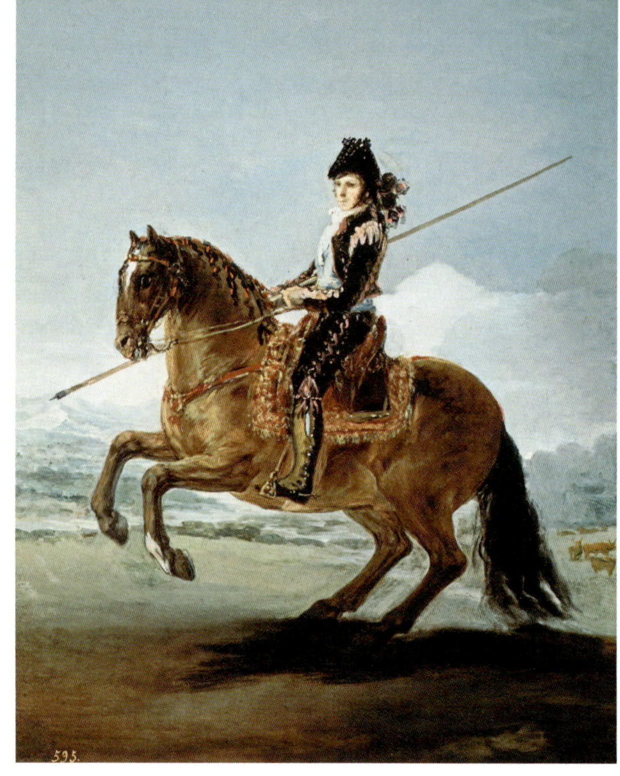

Francisco Bayeu y Subías, 1795, oil on canvas, Museo Nacional del Prado, Madrid, Spain, 112 x 84cm (44 x 33in)

Goya's portrait of his brother in-law, former teacher, and Director of painting at the Royal Academy of San Fernando, was probably painted after Bayeu's death in August 1795. It was based on a self-portrait by Bayeu, but Goya's skilful handling presents it as a fresh study from life. It was unfinished when it was exhibited in the Royal Academy of San Fernando in Madrid later in the same month.

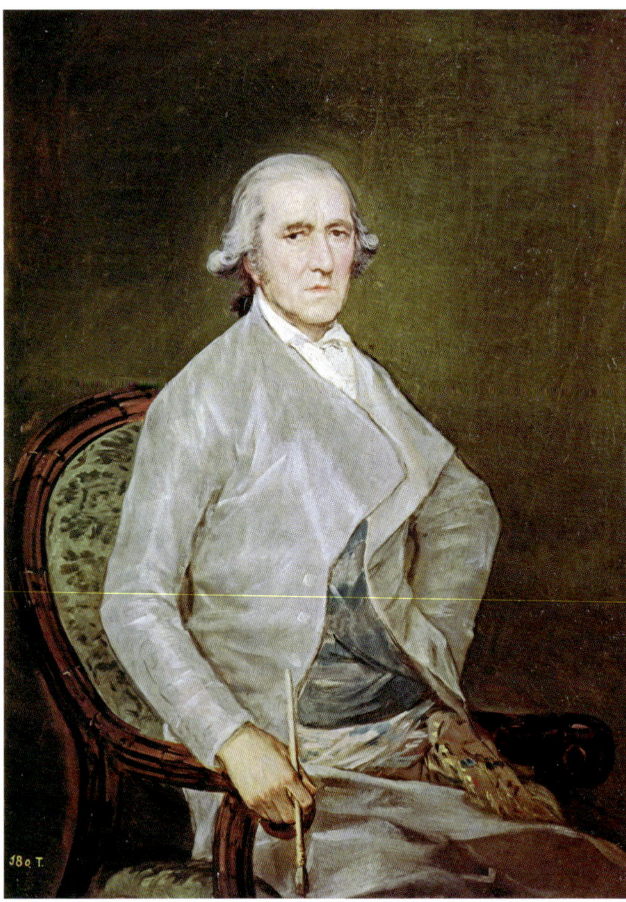

*The Countess of Carpio, Marquesa de la Solana, c.*1794–5, oil on canvas, Musée du Louvre, Paris, France, 181 x 122cm (71 x 48in)

The aristocrat and playwright María Rita Barrenechea (1757–95) wrote moralistic plays and was renowned for her charitable works. Married to the Count del Carpio, Marquis of Solana, she mixed in the same social and intellectual circles as Goya. At the time this work was painted, she was ill and facing an early death. Goya clearly felt empathy for her and captured her fragile health, but positive mentality.

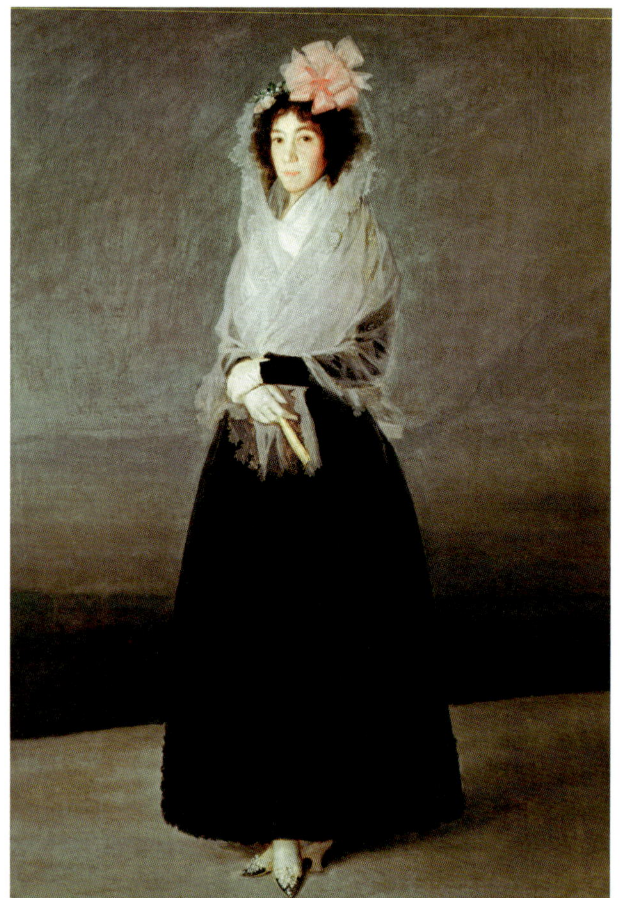

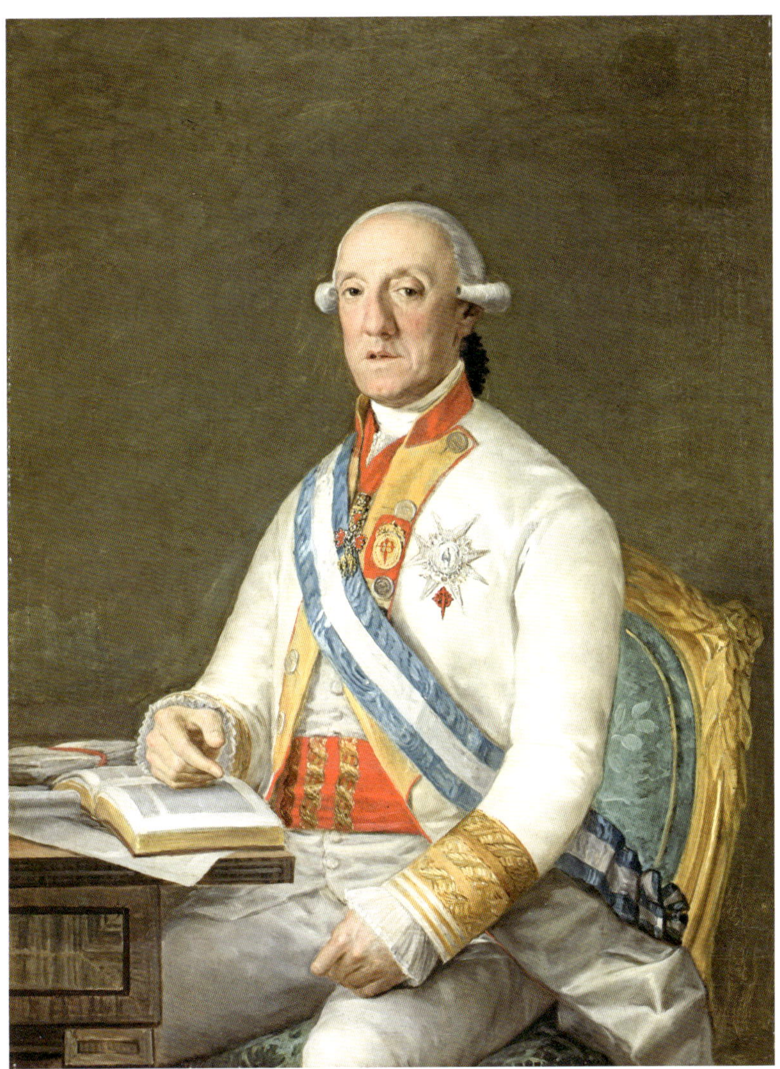

Portrait of the Marquis of Sofraga, c.1795, oil on canvas, San Diego Museum of Art, California, USA, 108.3 x 82.6cm (42½ x 32½in)

At this time, Don Vicente María de la Vera de Aragón y Ladrón de Guevara, Duke of la Roca and Marquis of Sofraga, was one of the most important men at the Spanish Court. Here, Sofraga, a politician, military man and enlightened thinker wears the sash and badge of the Order of Charles III, the scallop shell of the Order of Santiago and the Order of the Golden Fleece.

María del Rosario Fernández, 'La Tirana', 1794, oil on canvas, Private Collection, 112 x 79cm (44 x 31in)

A celebrated stage actress, María del Rosario (1755–1803) was known as 'La Tirana', (The Lady Tyrant) because her husband, also an actor, played villainous roles. However, her marriage was unsuccessful and she left, taking protection from the Duchess of Alba, which was how Goya came to know her. He also loved the theatre, and pictured María in elegant white lace at the peak of her career.

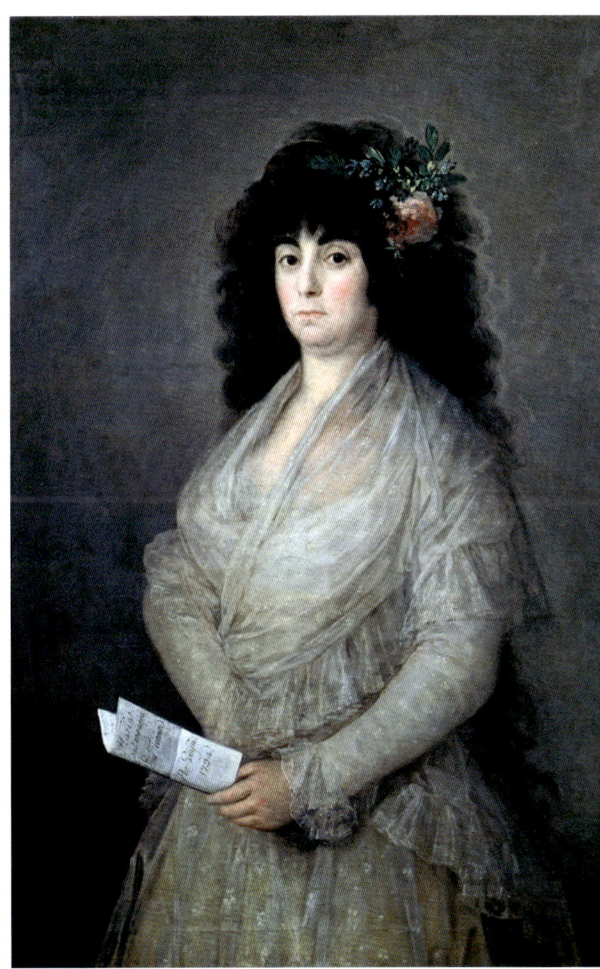

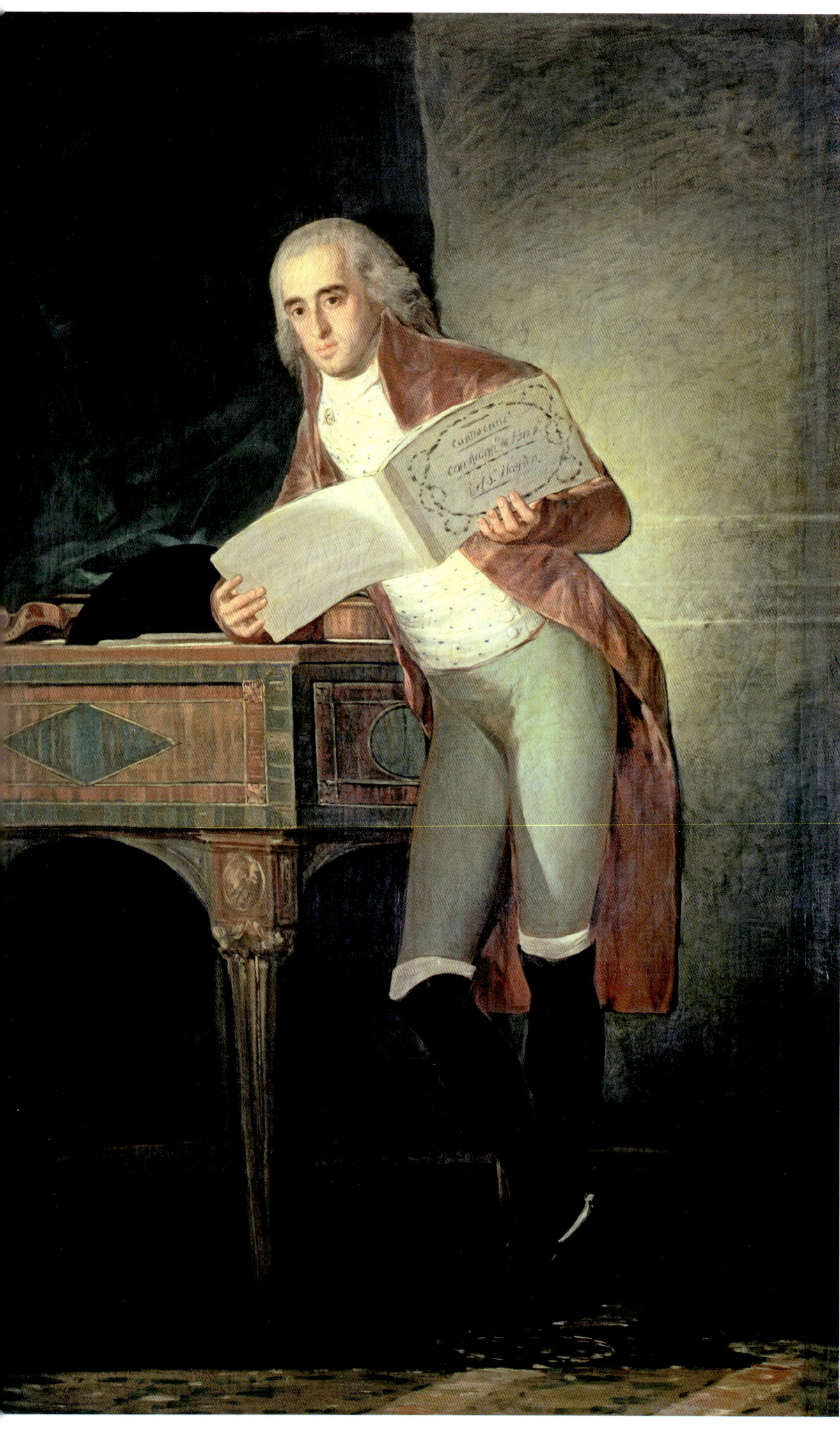

José Álvarez de Toledo, Marquis of Villafranca and Duke of Alba, c.1795, oil on canvas, Museo Nacional del Prado, Madrid, Spain, 195 x 126cm (77 x 49½in)

The son of María Antonia Gonzaga, Don José Alvarez de Toledo y Gonzaga, XIII Duke of Alba and XI Marquis of Villafranca was married to the Duchess of Alba. Goya presents him as an accomplished musician and horseman, fashionably dressed and leaning on a desk. On the desk are a violin and a black hat, and he holds a musical score by Franz Joseph Haydn (1732–1809).

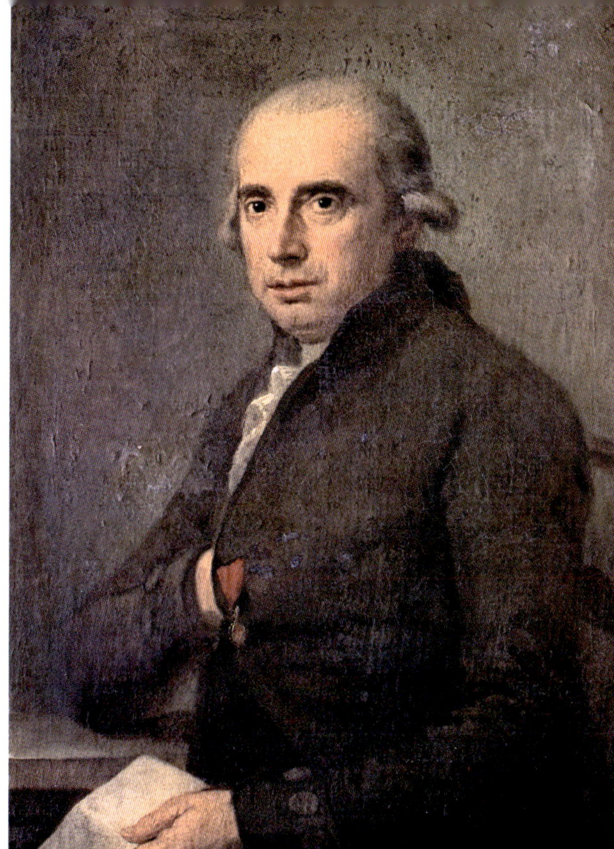

Portrait of Juan José Arias de Saavedra, c.1794–5, oil on canvas, Private Collection, 82 x 55cm (32 x 21½in)

By the time he painted this portrait of Juan José Arias de Saavedra (1737–1811), a friend of Jovellanos, Goya had perfected a personal style which brilliantly transposed and modernized his impression of Velázquez's style and blended this with the influence of the great English portraitists, particularly Gainsborough and Reynolds, through prints he had seen. This was still a conventionally accepted late 18th-century portrait, but it also accentuates Saavedra's humanity.

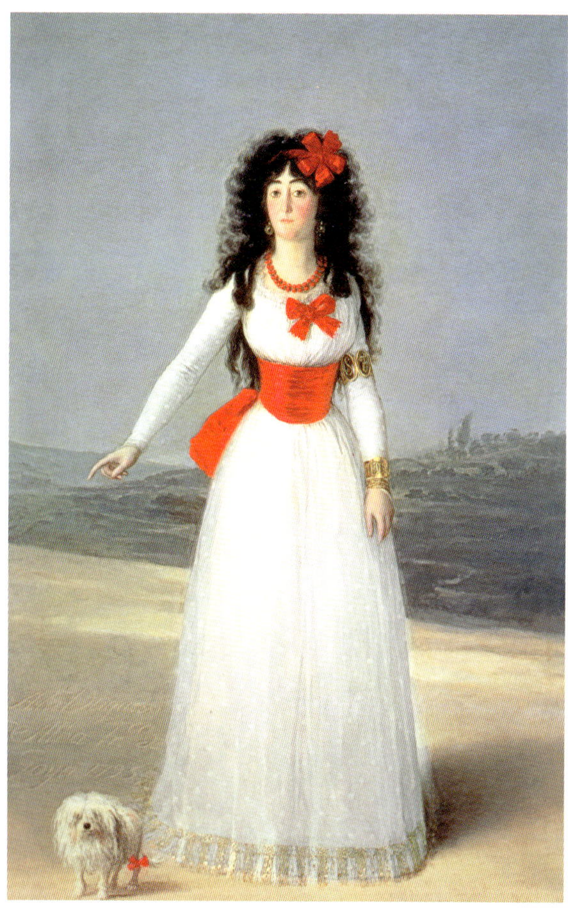

The Duchess of Alba, 1795, oil on canvas, The Alba Collection, Madrid, Spain, 194 x 130cm (76½ x 51in)

After his lengthy recuperation, Goya found a new and ardent patron in María Teresa de Silva, the Duchess of Alba. Whether he ever had a love affair with her is debatable, but he was clearly infatuated with her beauty and her flighty, exciting and eccentric personality. This is his first portrait of her. It exudes an imperious air, indicating her prominence within Spanish hierarchy.

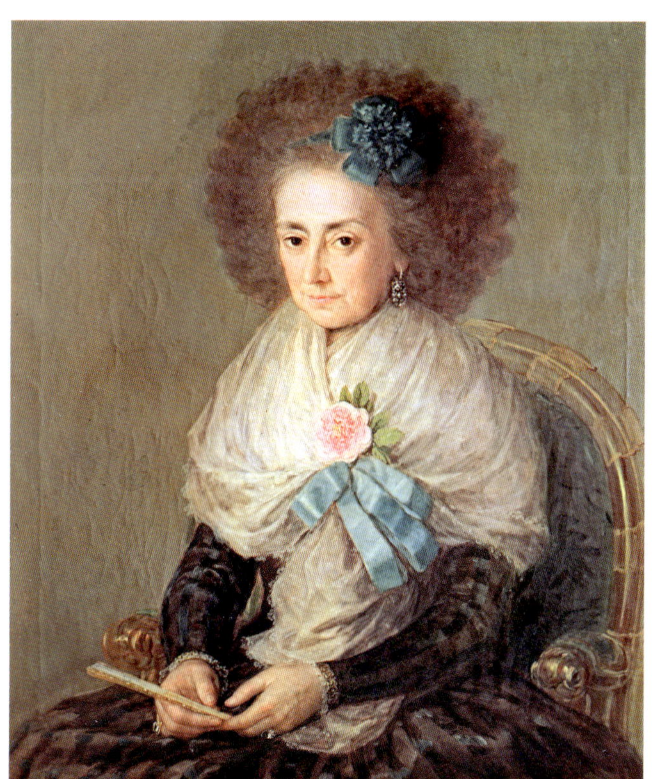

Marquesa Viuda de Villafranca, c.1795, oil on canvas, Museo Nacional del Prado, Madrid, Spain, 87 x 72cm (34 x 28in)

María Antonia Gonzaga (1735–1801), widow of Antonio Álvarez de Toledo, XI Marquise de Villafranca and mother-in-law of the Duchess of Alba, belonged to one of the most aristocratic families in Spain. Goya painted her in a dark dress, a large ribbon in her hair, and another large ribbon and rose pinned to her shawl. Despite her slight frame and 'little girl' accoutrements; her expression reveals a rather formidable character.

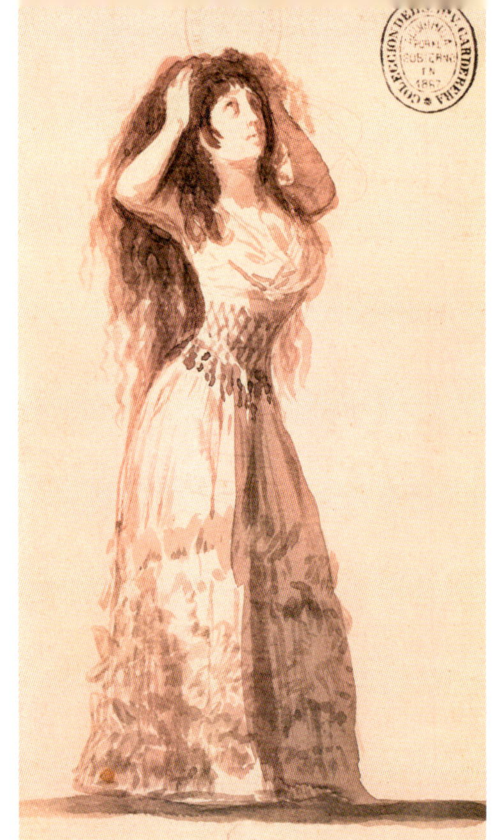

The Duchess of Alba Arranging Her Hair, 1796–7, Indian ink on paper, Biblioteca Nacional de Bellas Artes, Madrid, Spain, 24.5 x 18.3cm (9½ x 7in)

Goya had recently faced death. Now he was mixing with this aristocratic and whimsical young woman who was fun and unpredictable.

Although from one of the noblest families in Spain, she mixed happily with students, actors, commoners, bullfighters and peasants – as well as those of her own background. No contemporary or any other evidence tells of an affair between the artist and the Duchess, however.

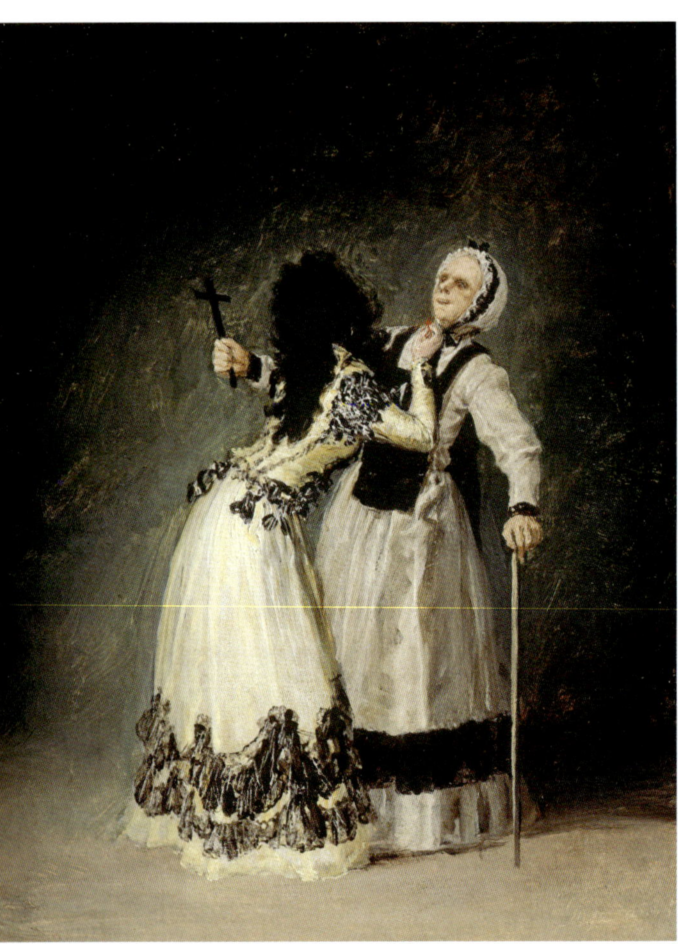

The Duchess of Alba and Her Duenna, 1795, oil on canvas, Museo Nacional del Prado, Madrid, Spain, 33 x 27.7cm (13 x 11in)

Thrusting a coral amulet (that was believed to protect against the evil eye) in her duenna's face, the Duchess of Alba is deliberately frightening the old woman. Panic-stricken, Rafaela Luisa Velázquez – known as La Beata – tries to defend herself with a cross. Although her back is turned to the viewer, the Duchess is recognizable by her abundant black curly hair, slender waist and expensive attire.

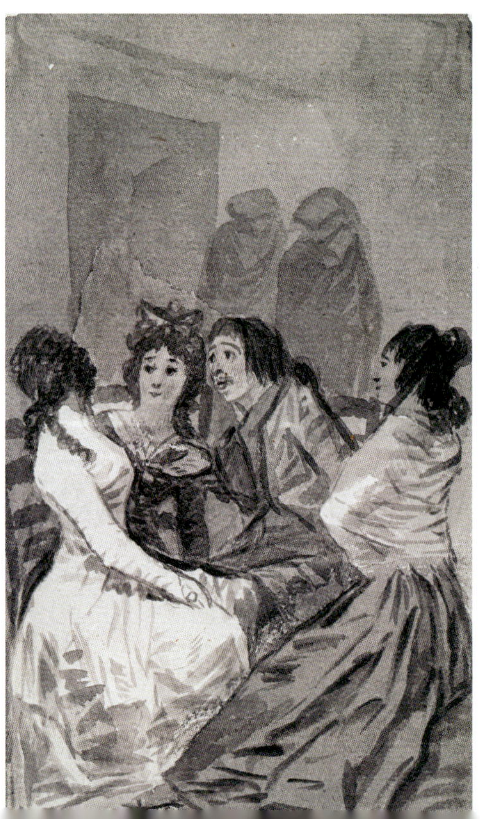

The Gathering (La Tertulia), c.1795, gouache and ink on paper, Museo Nacional del Prado, Madrid, Spain, 23.3 x 14.4cm (9 x 5½in)

After he befriended the Duchess of Alba, Goya often sketched her and her friends. This seemingly lighthearted gathering of four young women in conversation is somewhat overshadowed by two sinister, cloaked figures in the background. The menacing symbolism was deliberate: Goya drew this during the year in which Spain declared war on revolutionary France following the execution of Louis XVI.

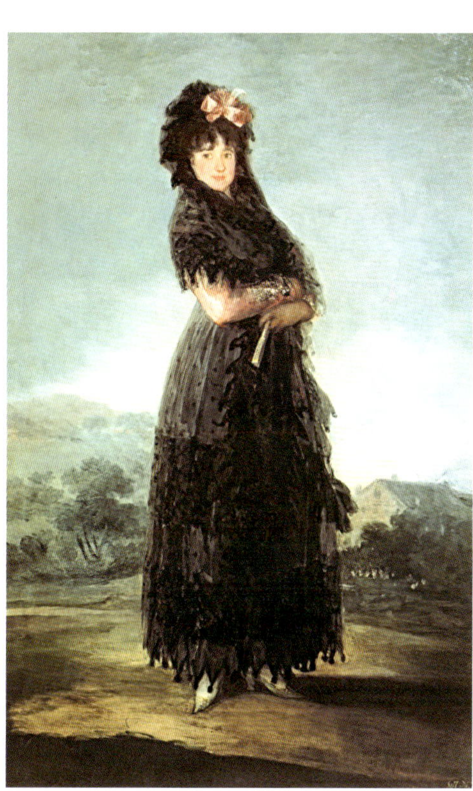

Mariana Waldstein, Ninth Marquesa of Santa Cruz, c.1797-8, oil on canvas, Musée du Louvre, Paris, France, 142 x 97cm (56 x 38in)

Mariana Waldstein (1763–1808) was Austrian-born and one of the most prominent women of late 18th-century Spain. By marriage, she became the Duchess of Alba's aunt and was friends with the Bonaparte brothers. She stands coquettishly in traditional Spanish dress with a large pink bow in her hair. Goya's background resembles the work of Gainsborough, while his light, sketchy brushwork anticipates the Impressionists of the next century.

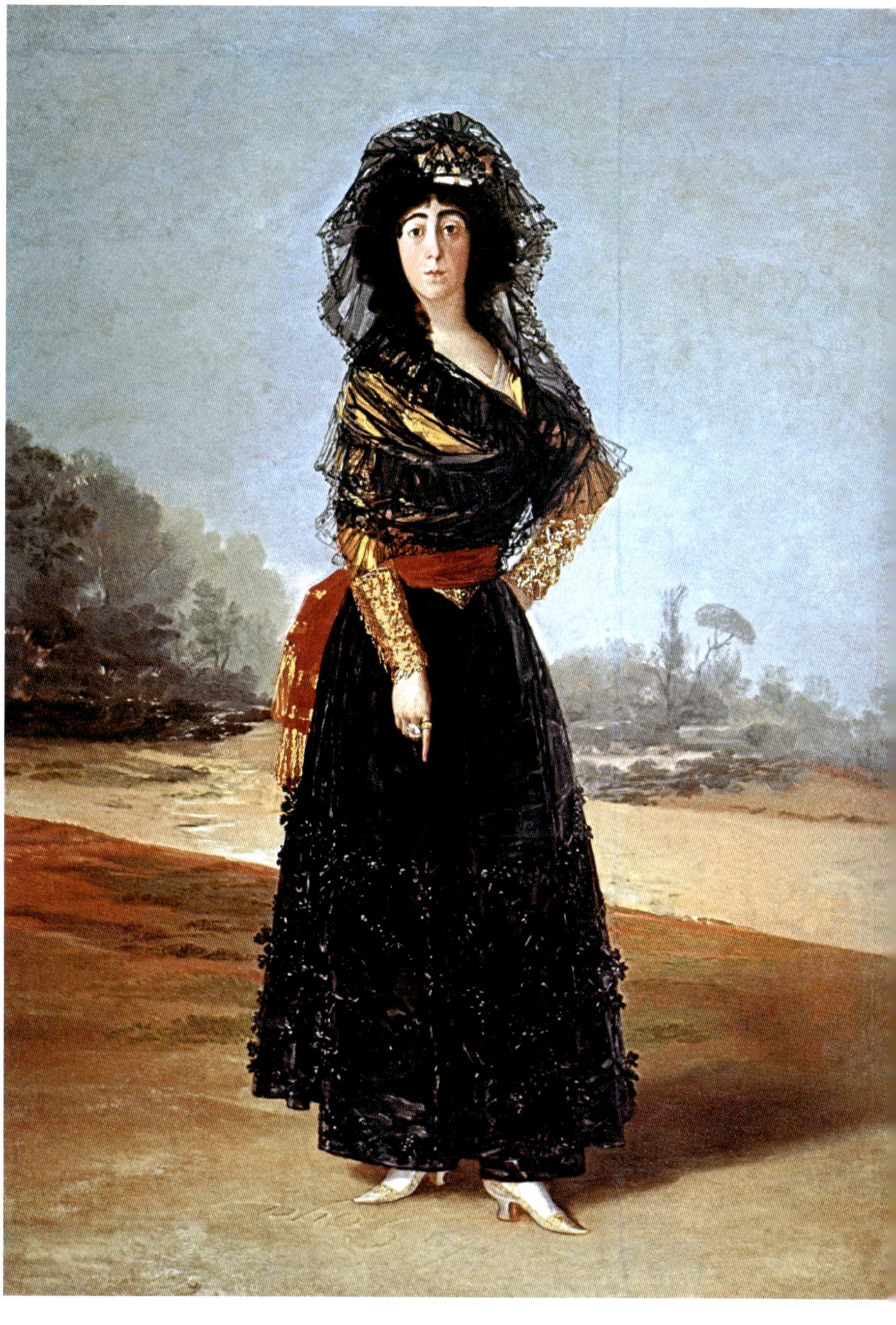

Portrait of the Duchess of Alba, 1797, oil on canvas, The Hispanic Society of America, New York, USA, 210 x 147cm (83 x 58in)

Dressed in mourning (albeit in majan style), the 35-year-old Duchess's proud pose evokes her personality. She points down to where, written in the soil, are the words: 'solo Goya' ('only Goya'). This had originally been covered, and as the painting stayed in Goya's possession until his death it is not known whether she ever knew about it. She also wears two rings inscribed with 'Alba' and 'Goya'.

The Siesta, 1796–7, gouache and ink on paper, Museo Nacional del Prado, Madrid, Spain, 17.2 x 9.7cm (7 x 4in)

An energetic sketch from life made by Goya in Andalucia, this is possibly the Duchess herself, taking the traditional Spanish siesta. While her mistress sleeps, the young maid tidies up. Using ink and watersoluble paint, Goya captured the two women at an intimate moment, rarely seen by others, 130 years after Jan Steen (1626–79) and 100 years before Edgar Degas (1834–1917) made similar observations.

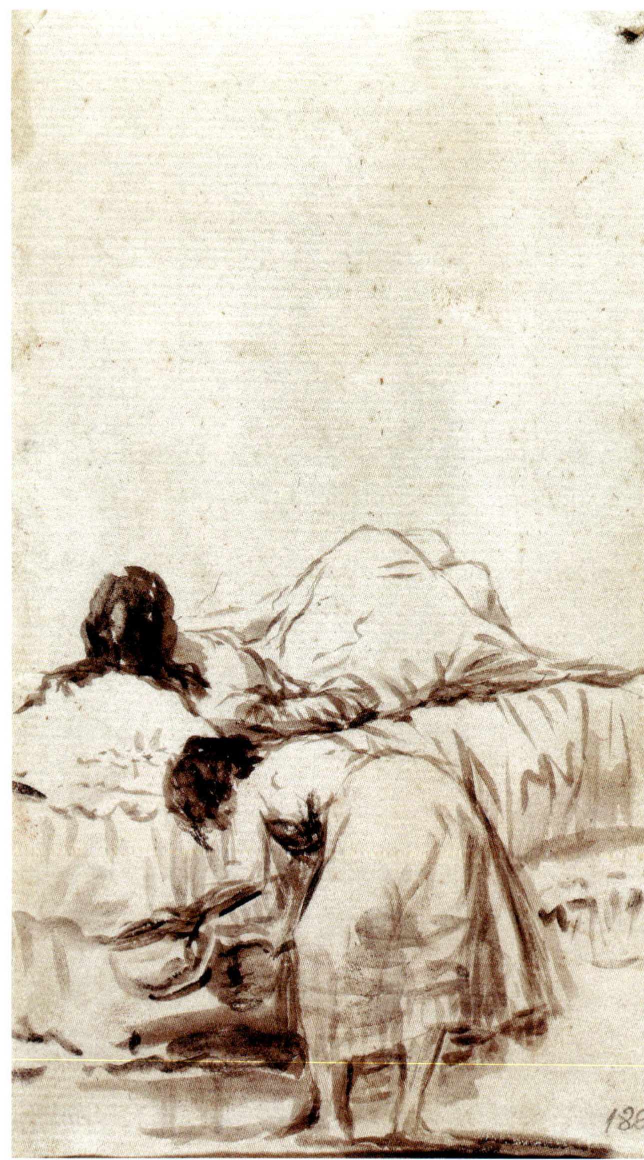

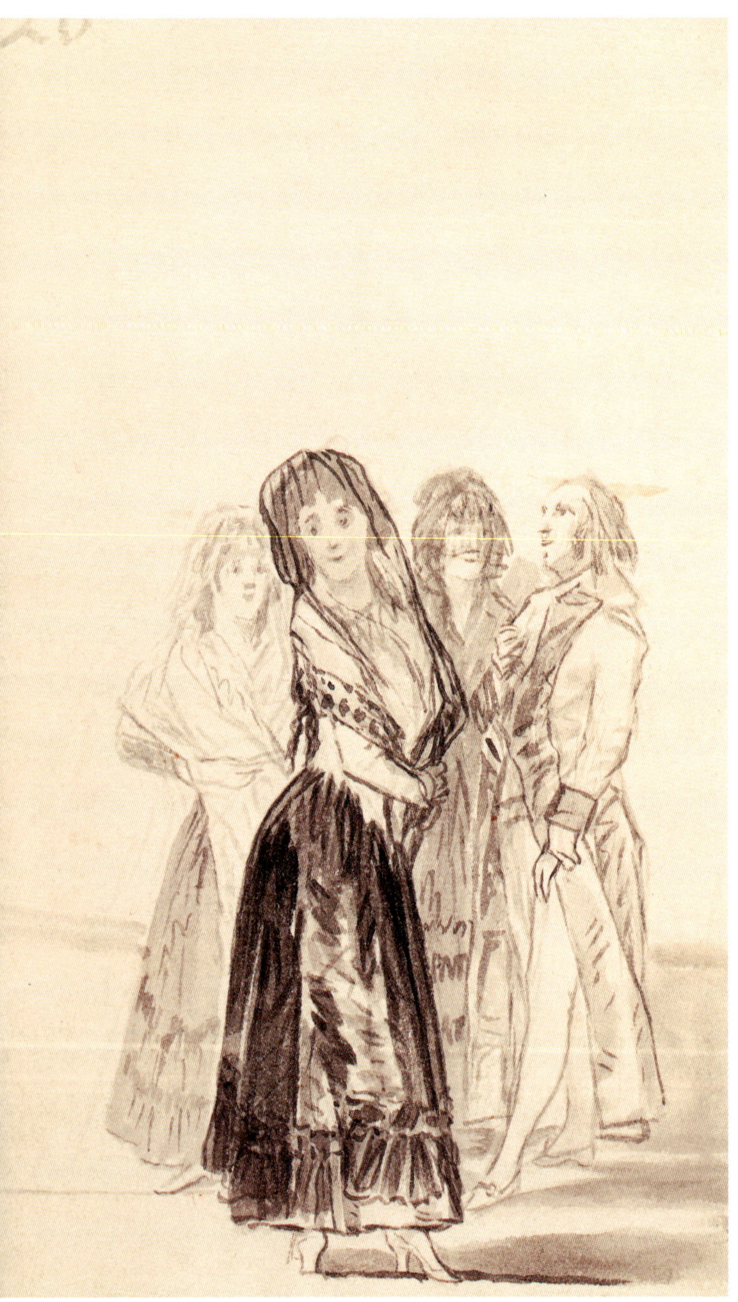

Maja Standing Before Three Companions, 1796–7, Indian ink on paper, Museo Nacional del Prado, Madrid, Spain, 21.9 x 13.5cm (8½ x 5in)

In another fleetingly observed moment in time, Goya has captured a flirtatious maja standing in front of two women and a man. This drawing was in a sketchbook full of these astute observances. Each page features a quick sketch, made with great economy of line to capture the essential characteristics of the figures. Here, the proud stance and traditional Spanish dress clearly portrays the lady's personality.

The Duchess Holding María de la Luz, 1796–7, Indian ink on paper, Biblioteca Nacional de Bellas Artes, Madrid, Spain, 10.5 x 9cm (4 x 3½in)

This affectionate sketch of the Duchess of Alba cradling a child belongs to Goya's first series of private drawings that he made while staying with her in Sanlúcar. This little girl, María de la Luz, was the daughter of an African slave. The Duchess virtually adopted her as she had no biological children of her own. She was besotted with the little girl.

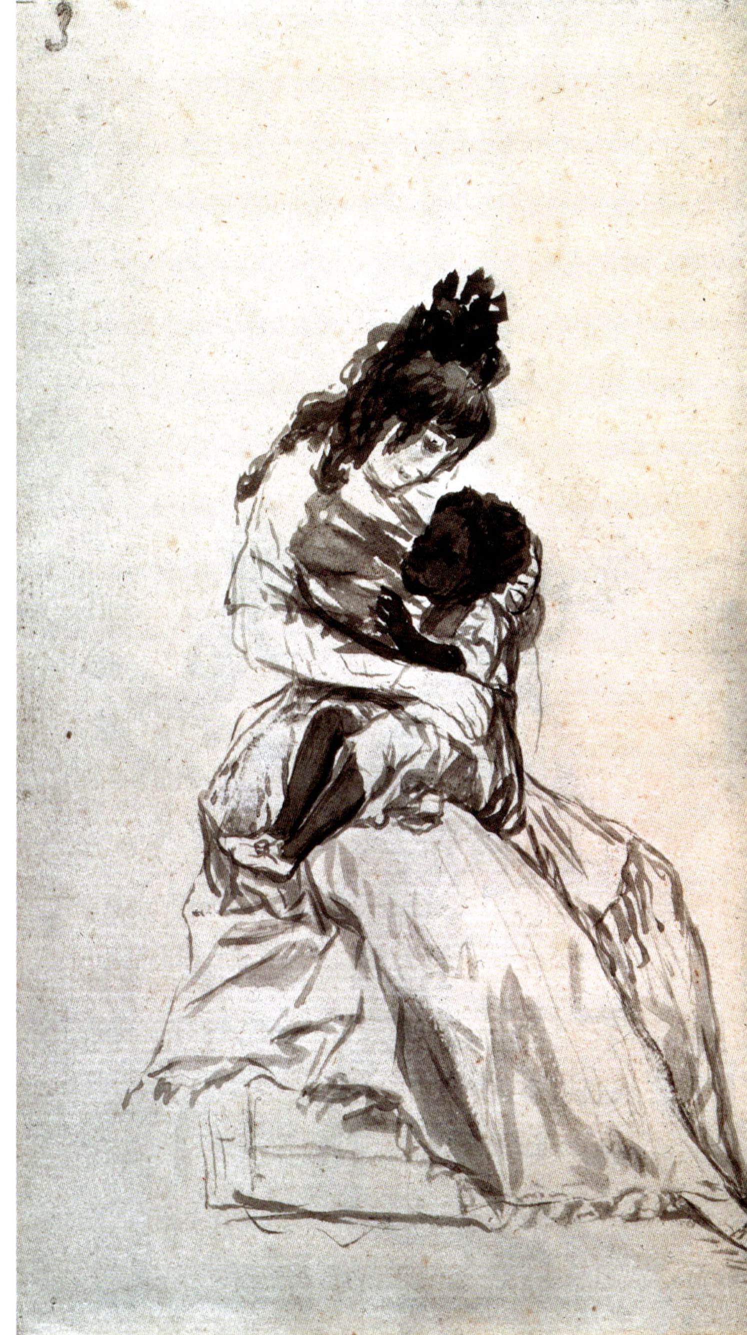

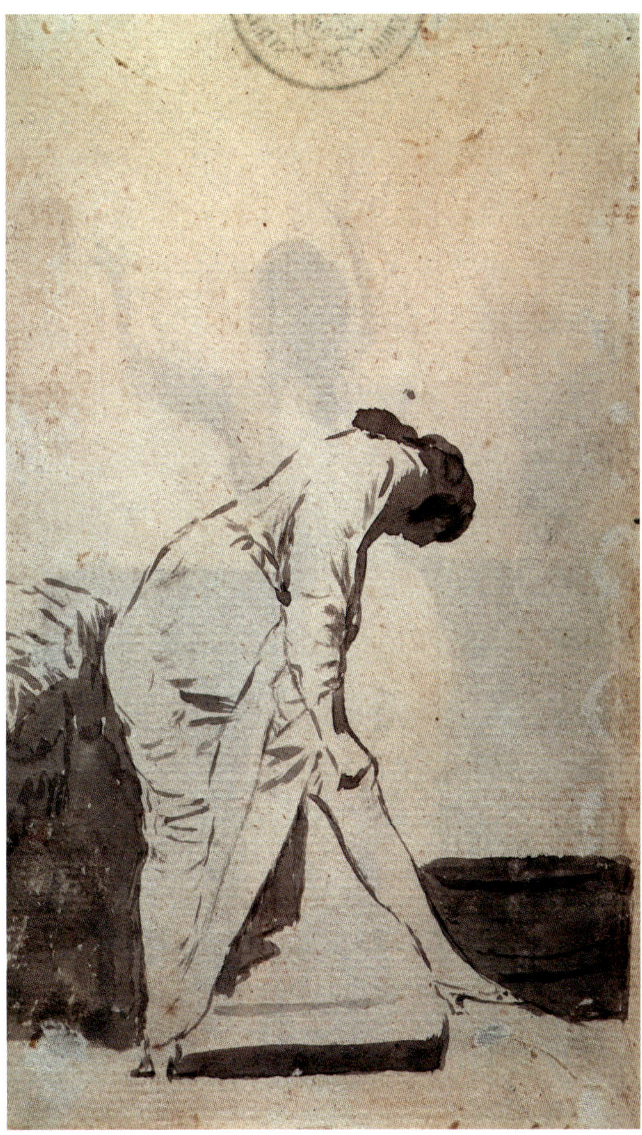

Young Woman Pulling up her Stockings, 1796–7, Indian ink on paper, Museo Nacional del Prado, Madrid, Spain, 17 x 10cm (7 x 4in)

A young woman is captured in a private moment, as she puts on her stockings. As it was considered too personal, unattractive and intimate for fine art, this was a rare theme for artists, but Goya was not attempting to make a beautiful or reverent image. This was part of his preparation for *Los Caprichos*, his first prints which commented satirically on contemporary Spanish society.

Concert at the Clavichord, 1796–7, Indian ink on paper, Museo Nacional del Prado, Madrid, Spain, 23.5 x 14.5cm (9 x 5½in)

The clavichord, a stringed keyboard instrument, was popular from the medieval period until the early 19th century. Goya enjoyed music, and in later life was described by a friend as playing the harpsichord, bending closely over the keys to try to hear. The Duchess of Alba was allegedly patient with him as he struggled to come to terms with his deafness, but she also often teased him.

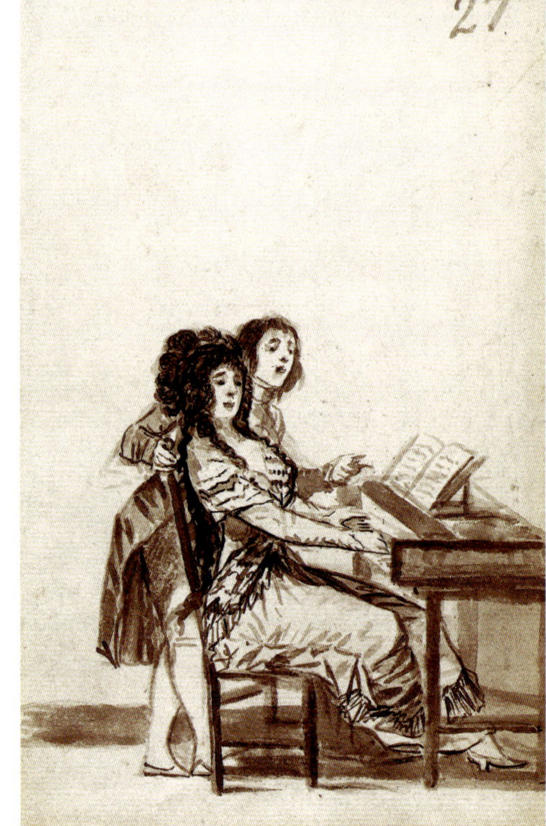

Couple with a Parasol, 1796–7, Indian ink on paper, Hamburger Kunsthalle, Hamburg, Germany, 22 x 13.4cm (9 x 5in)

For a long period, mainly from the influence of the Moors, Spanish women of the upper classes were made to live more cloistered lives than their counterparts elsewhere in Europe. By the end of the 18th century however, they were becoming more emancipated and Goya was quick to capture the novelty of women and men flirting on almost equal terms.

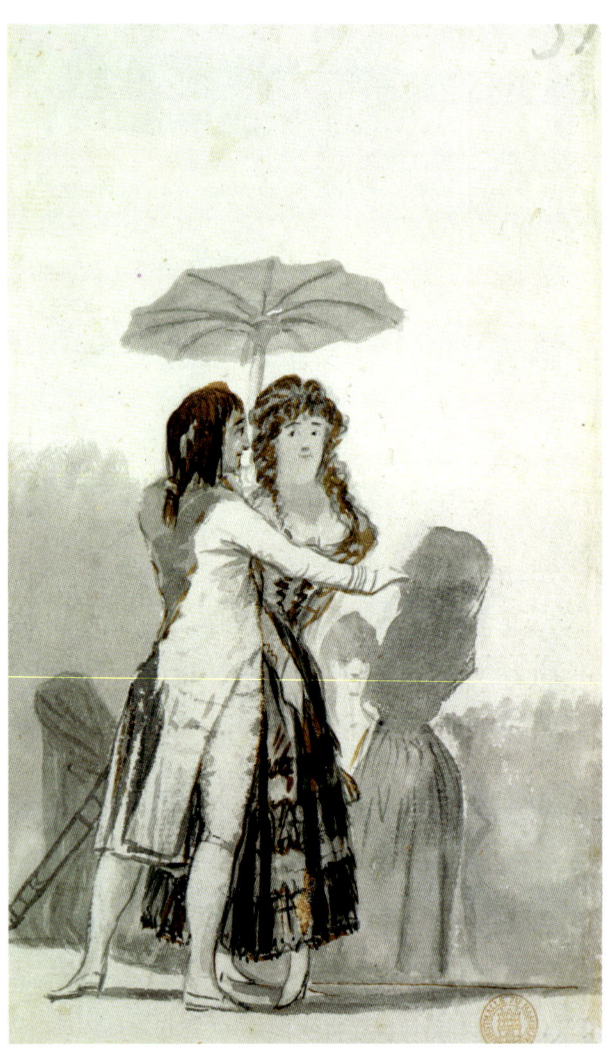

Encounter on the Paseo or *The Meeting*, 1796–7, Indian ink on paper, Museo Nacional del Prado, Madrid, Spain, 23.5 x 14.5cm (9 x 5½in)

Once again, this sketch was made by Goya from direct observation, and later used as a reference in a print. It seems to have been something Goya saw in passing: a casual encounter on the Paseo del Prado between a streetwalker and a possible client. He might have been struggling with his deafness, but nothing missed Goya's sharp notice. Everything useful to him was recorded for exploitation later.

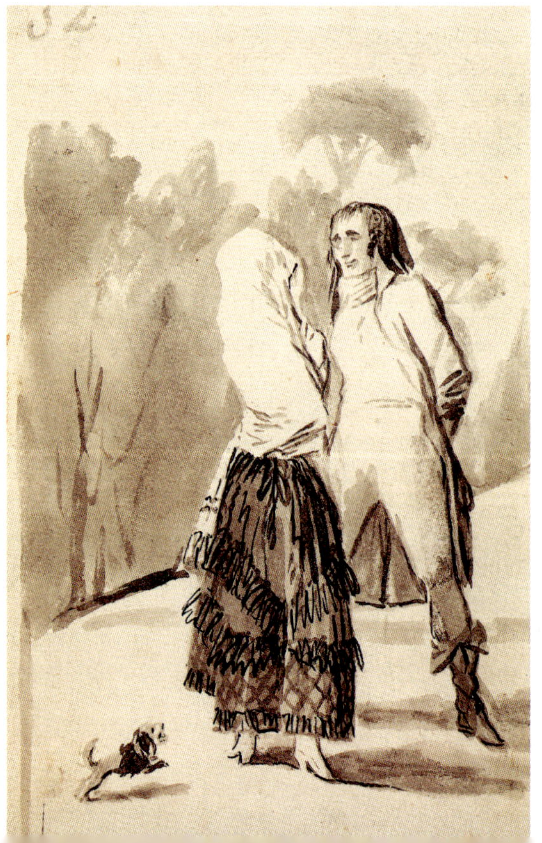

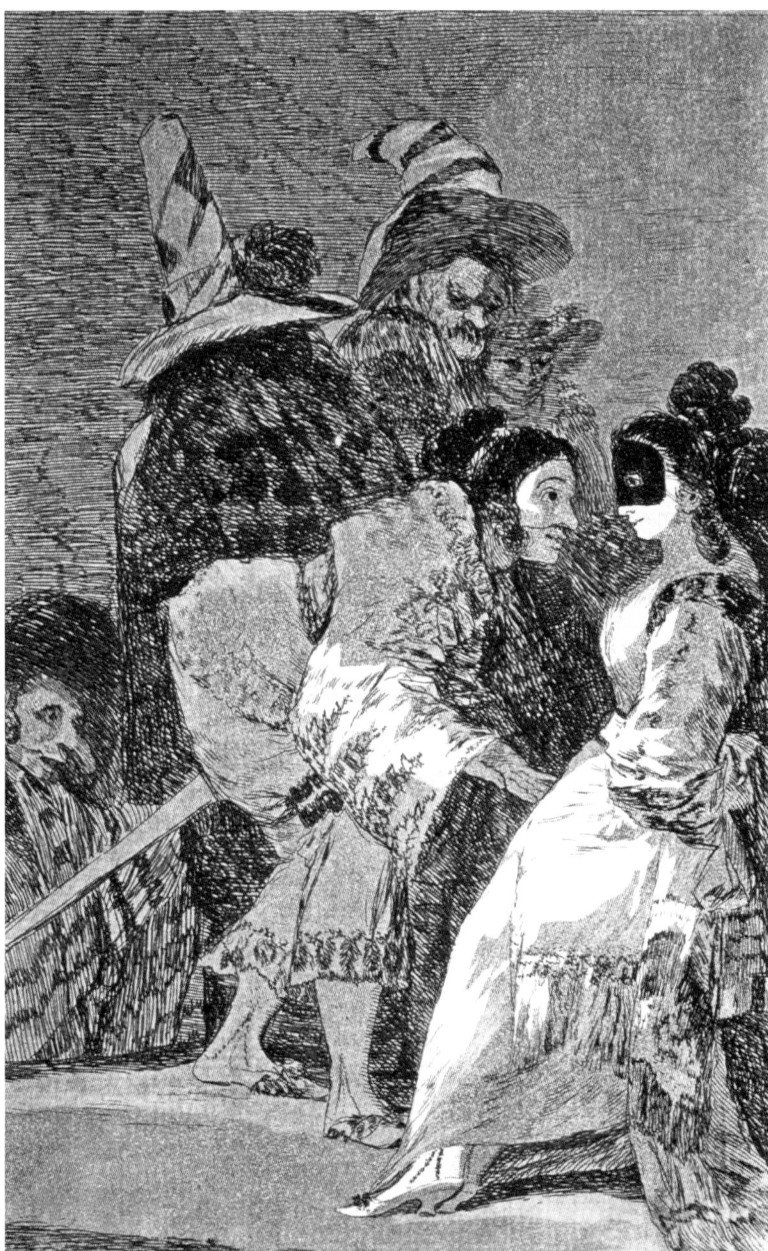

Nobody Knows Anybody,
1797–8, etching and
aquatint, Private Collection,
12.8 x 15.3cm (5 x 6in)

Just as Goya proved
himself to be a master of
the rapid sketch – with
speedily captured scenes
from everyday life – so he
became a master of etching.
He perfected a method that
included aquatint, which
made his prints superior to
previous methods used by
others. This is one of the 80
etchings he first published in
1799. They included scenes
of witchcraft and social satire.

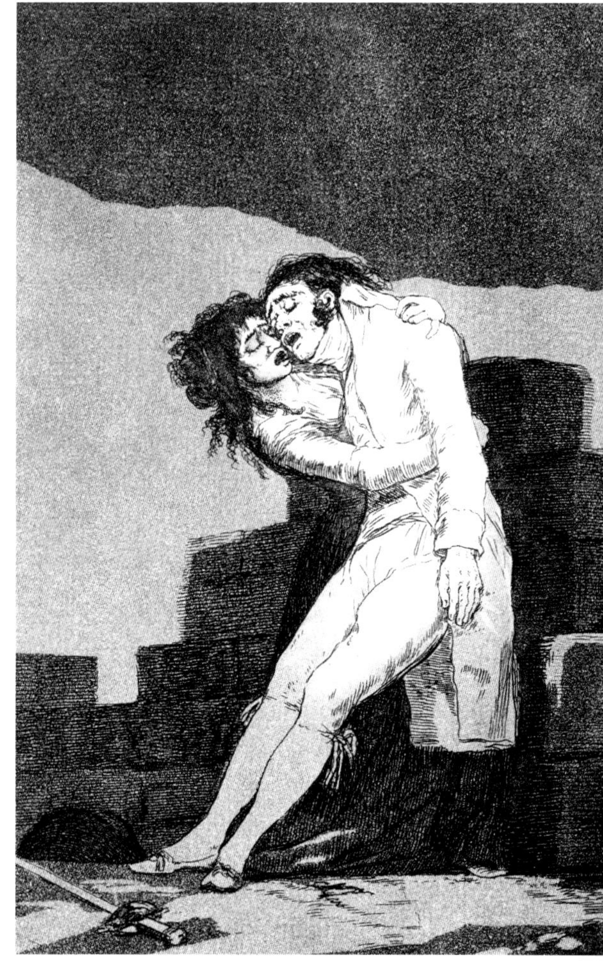

Love and Death, 1796–7,
etching and aquatint,
Metropolitan Museum
of Art, New York, USA,
21.5 x 15.5cm (8½ x 6in)

Goya's Caprichos series grew
out of the caricatures and
sketches that he drew while
regaining his strength after his
illness. Like the above work,
this was one of the 80 prints
he first published in 1799.
Many of the prints combine
ideas he had seen in etchings
by Giovanni Battista Tiepolo
(1696–1770) and Giovanni
Battista Piranesi (1720–78)
coupled with the humour
prevalent in contemporary
satirical prints.

Quien mas Rendido? (Who else Out?) 1797–8, etching and aquatint, Musée National Eugène Delacroix, Paris, France, 19.5 x 15cm (8 x 6in)

In another satirical image depicting the human condition, a fawning courtier bends over a haughty, beautiful woman.

Behind them stand a group of women who watch critically. Fascinated by Goya, Delacroix obtained this and other prints by him. Between 1820 and 1824, he produced numerous copies. In 1858, he was quoted as saying that Goya: 'is a great artist whose compositions and verve have often inspired me.'

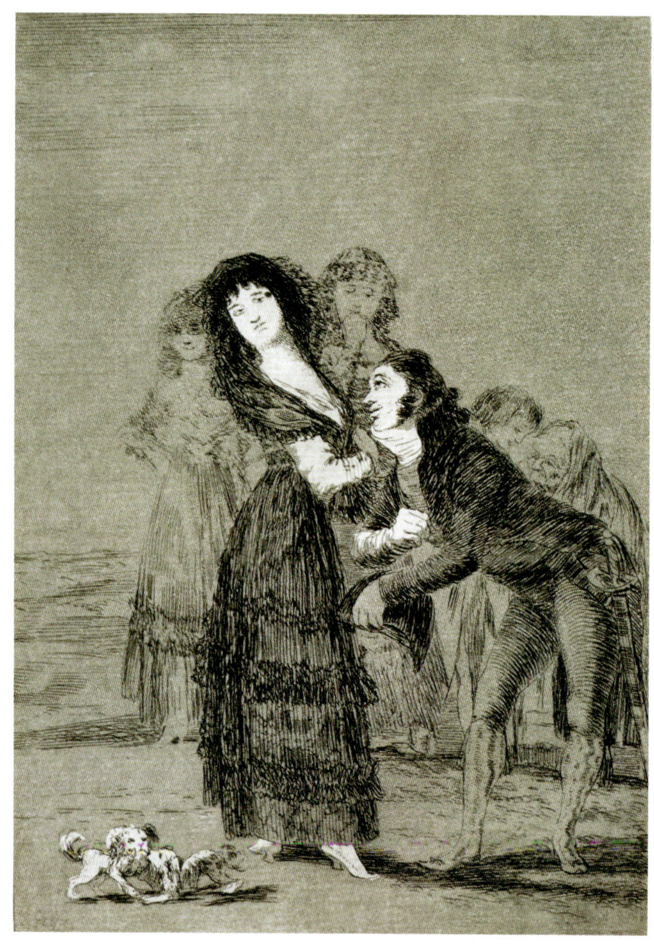

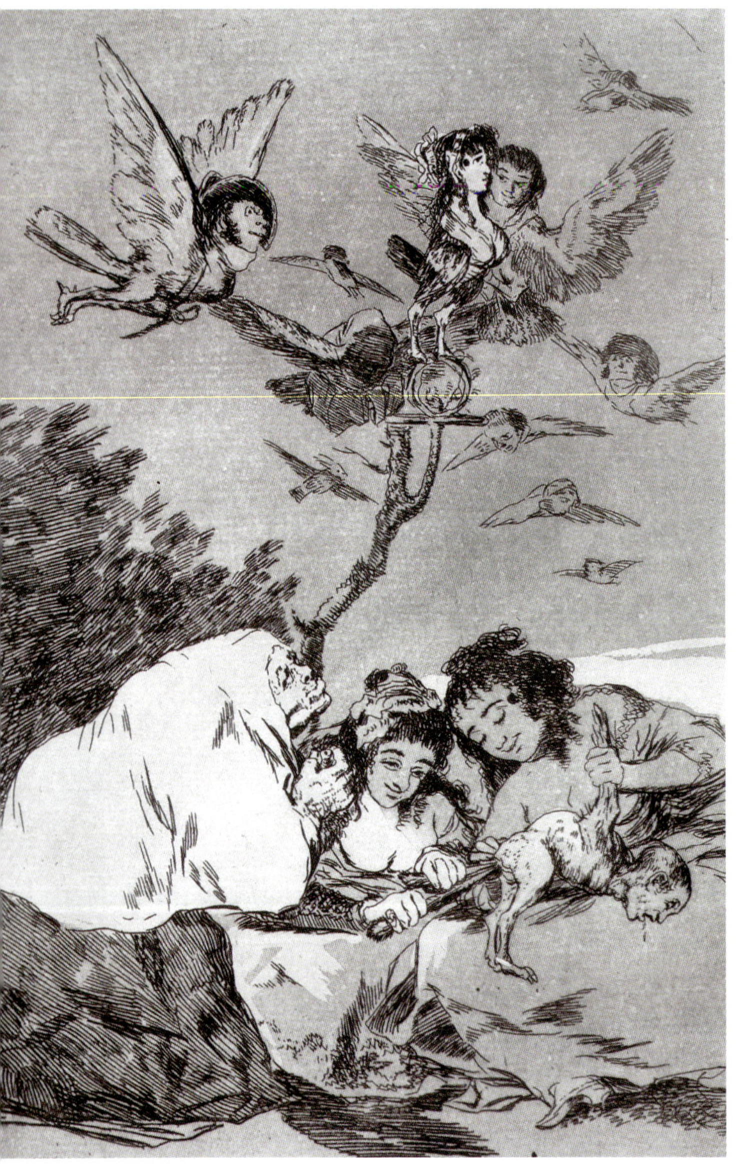

All Will Fall, 1797–8, etching and aquatint, Brooklyn Museum, New York, USA, 21.6 x 14.4cm (8½ x 5½in)

This is Plate 19 from *Los Caprichos*. Goya's intention was to warn men about their own weaknesses with prostitutes. An officer-bird, a monk-bird and other love-birds encircle a tempting woman-bird, while below, a fallen bird is plucked naked by two prostitutes. But the officer and monk ignore what is happening below. This is an allusion to the classical allegorical motif of Eros having his wings clipped.

Porque Esconderlos? (Why Hide Them?) 1797–8, etching and aquatint, Museum of Fine Arts, Boston, USA, 21.8 x 15.7cm (8½ x 6in)

This is a commentary on greed and indifference, and the widespread corruption of the clergy. A group of covetous young men stand behind an ageing clergyman who clutches two bulging sacks of money avariciously. He is trying to hide them from the men watching him, while they are working out how they can snatch the bags from him.

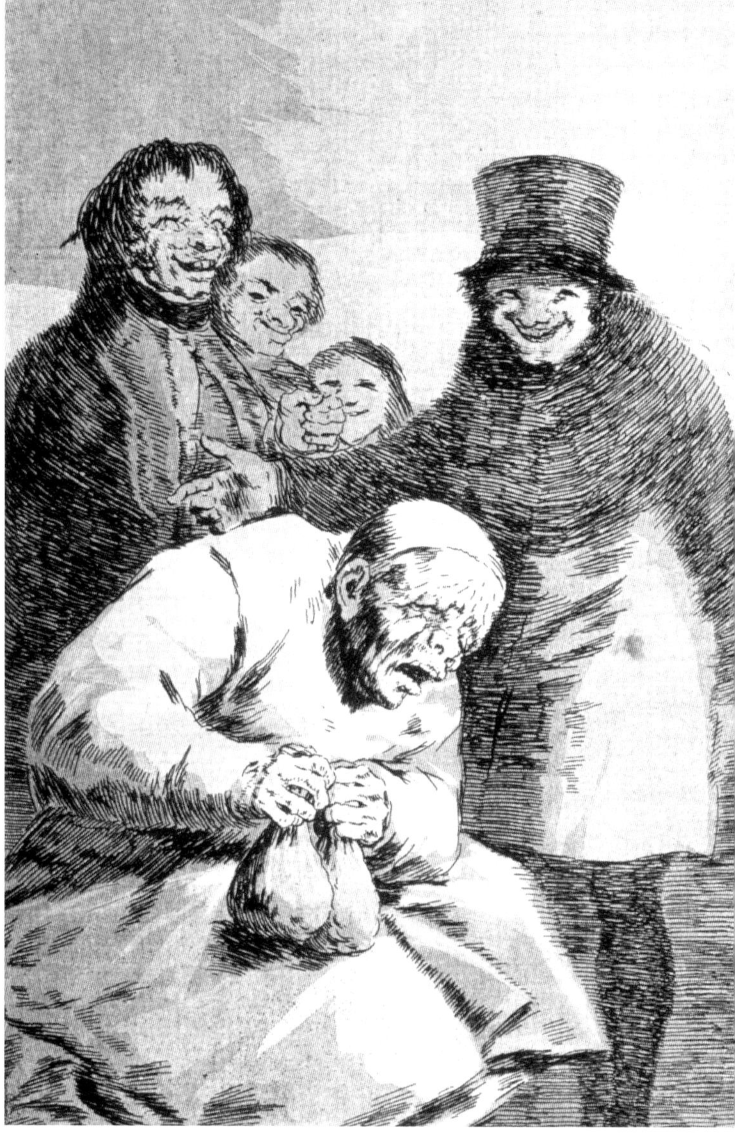

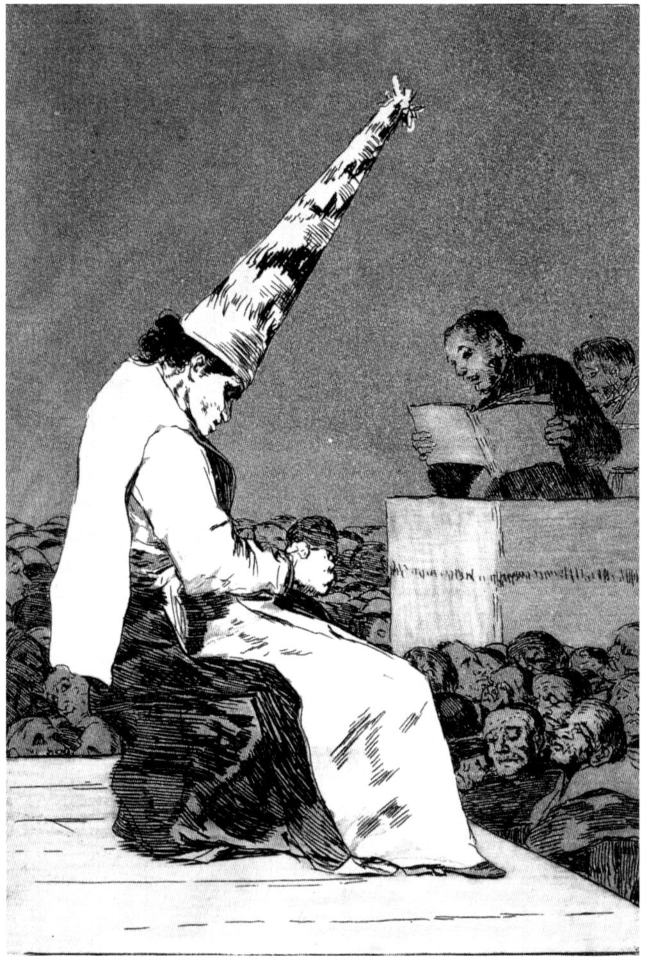

Those Specks of Dust, 1797–8, etching and aquatint, Private Collection, 21.5 x 15.5cm (8½ x 6in)

This is one of two prints from *Los Caprichos* that deal with the Inquisition. It portrays the trial of Perico; a disabled woman who was arrested for selling love potions. She sits hunched over, in front of Inquisitors robed in the penitential uniform known as 'San Benito'. Goya remarked about the actual incident: 'Badly done! To treat an honourable woman in this way...who for nothing served everyone so well.'

The Snitches (Soplones),
1797–8, etching and
aquatint, Bibliothèque
Nationale, Paris, France,
20.7 x15.1cm (8 x 6in)

A monstrous creature fills
priests' heads with filth
and obscenities. A robed
friar covers his ears to stop
himself from hearing the
words. This image is believed
to refer to the Inquisition,
as Goya frequently used a
grotesque winged creature
as an allegory for it. It is not
surprising therefore, that
within 15 days of printing
Los Caprichos the Inquisition
suppressed the public sale
of the prints.

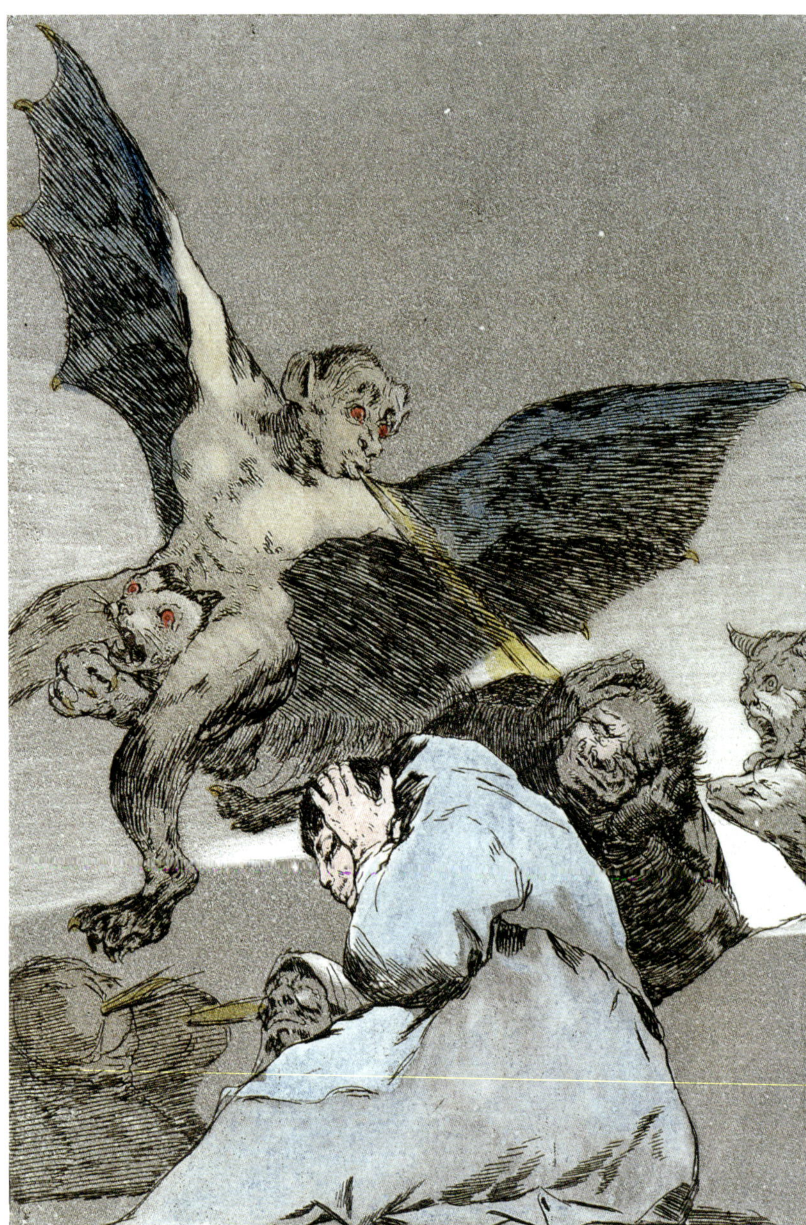

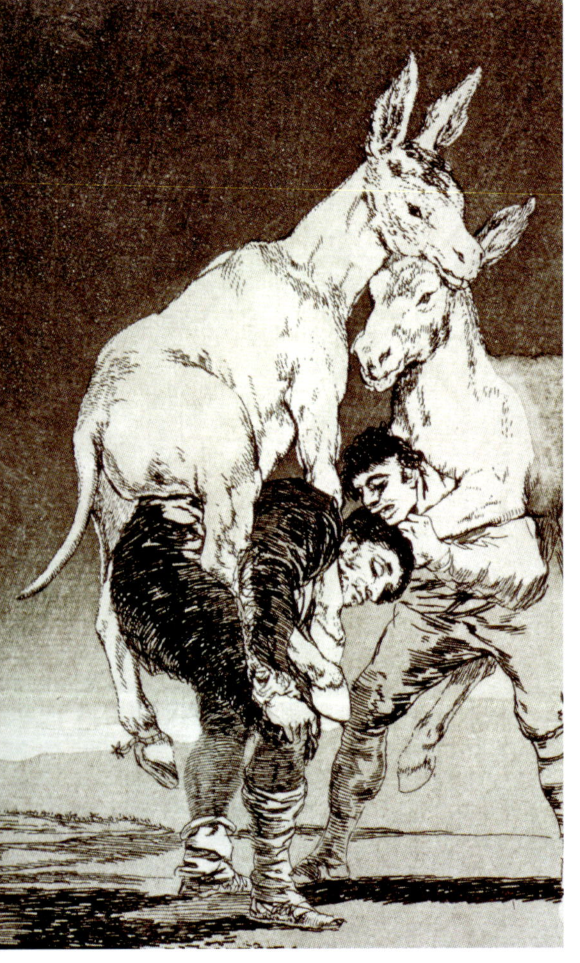

Thou Who Canst Not, 1797–
8, etching and aquatint, The
Metropolitan Museum of
Art, New York, USA,
21.7 x 15.1cm (8½ x 6in)

In an effort to highlight
repression of the working
classes, in *Los Caprichos*, Goya
portrayed the aristocracy
as stubborn, ignorant and
stupid. He often depicted
them literally as jackasses.
In this print, two peasants
are bent over carrying heavy
jackasses on their backs while
the jackasses appear perfectly
comfortable. The message
is that the working classes
maintained the ruling
classes in every way.

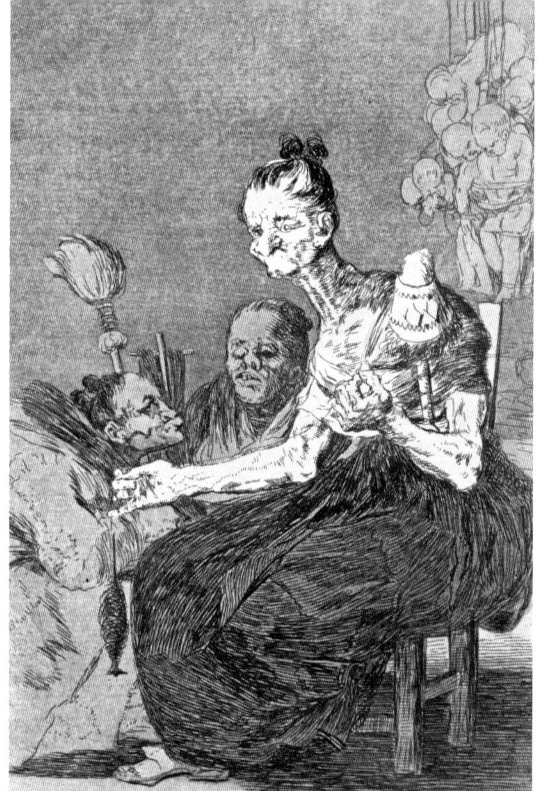

They Spin Finely, 1797–8, etching and aquatint, The National Museum of Western Art, Tokyo, Japan, 21.9 x 15.2cm (8½ x 6in)

The activities of three witches – or the Fates – are spinning problems for Spain. As he explained in the advertisement for *Los Caprichos*, Goya chose subjects 'from the multitude of follies and blunders common in every civil society, as well as from the vulgar prejudices and lies authorized by custom, ignorance or interest, those that he has thought most suitable matter for ridicule.'

The Sleep of Reason Produces Monsters (El sueño de la razón produce monstruos), 1797–8, etching and aquatint, The Metropolitan Museum of Art, New York, USA, 21.5 x 15cm (8½ x 6in)

Goya planned this as a frontispiece for a series within *Los Caprichos* about dreams. He portrays himself asleep at his drawing table, besieged by creatures from Spanish folk stories associated with mystery and evil, including owls symbolizing folly and bats signifying ignorance. On the front of the desk, the title proclaims the values of the Enlightenment: without Reason, evil and corruption prevail. References to the Spanish situation are evident.

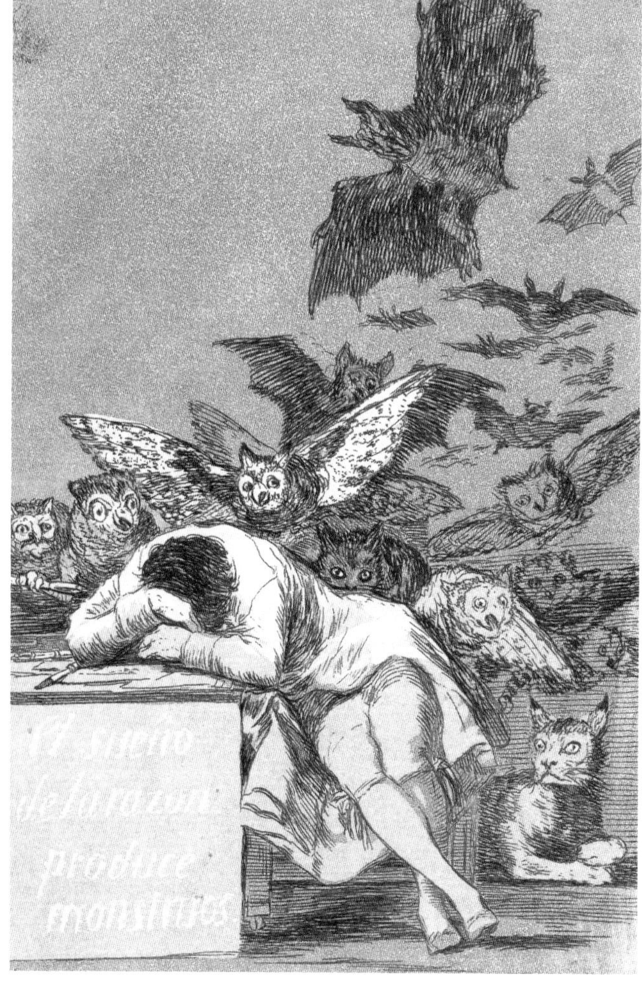

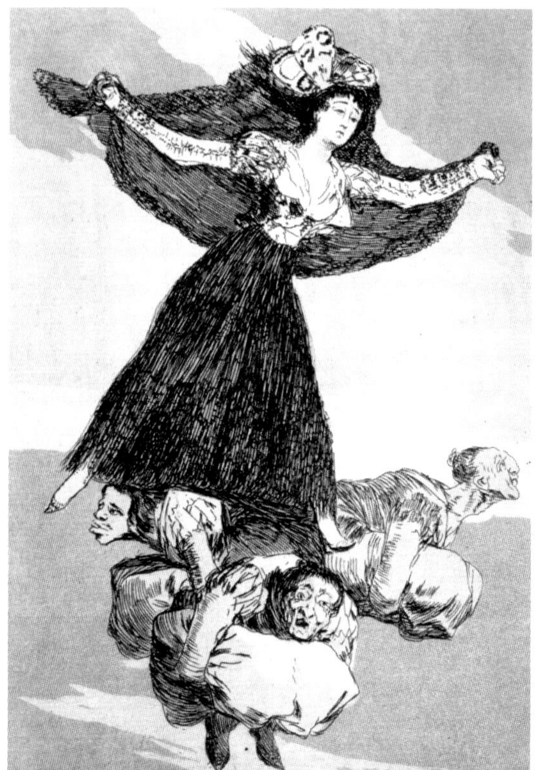

Gone for Good, 1797–8, etching and aquatint, Private Collection, 21.7 x 15.2cm (8½ x 6in)

The Duchess of Alba stands proudly with her arms outstretched, her shawl draping to each side, resembling wings. Beneath her feet, three witch-like figures carry her through the air. The heads of the figures are caricatures of famous bullfighters. The white, doll-like face of the Duchess appears disdainful and aloof, while in her hair she wears butterfly wings to symbolize her unpredictable flightiness.

The Witches' Sabbath, 1797–8, oil on canvas, Museo Lázaro Galdiano, Madrid, Spain, 43 x 30cm, (17 x 12in)

Goya depicted witches and witchcraft to deride the superstition, fear and irrationality that was commonly exploited for political gain. Here, beneath a crescent moon, the Devil is a male goat surrounded by a ring of witches, one holding a child for sacrifice. The goat extends his left hoof toward the child. The painting symbolizes the ignorance of the Church that denied scientific, religious and social progress.

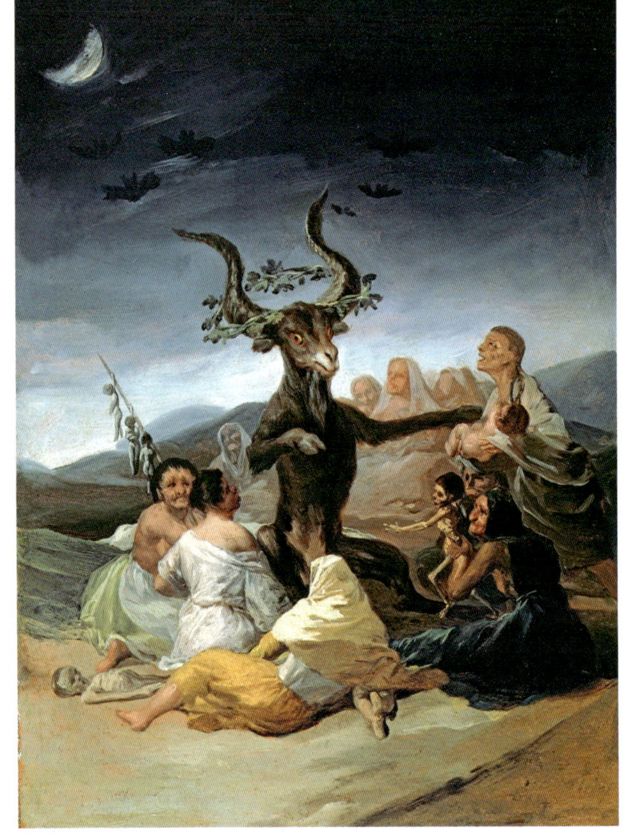

The Spell (El Conjuro o Las Brujas), 1797–8, oil on canvas, Museo Lázaro Galdiano, Madrid, Spain, 43 x 30cm (17 x 12in)

This and the previous two paintings were owned by the Duke and Duchess of Osuna. A coven of witches are practising magic at night. Nearby is a terrified man in a white shirt. One witch has a basket of stolen children, another sticks a pin in a wax effigy, another reads from a book of spells. Hovering overhead are bats, owls and a bizarre, human-like creature.

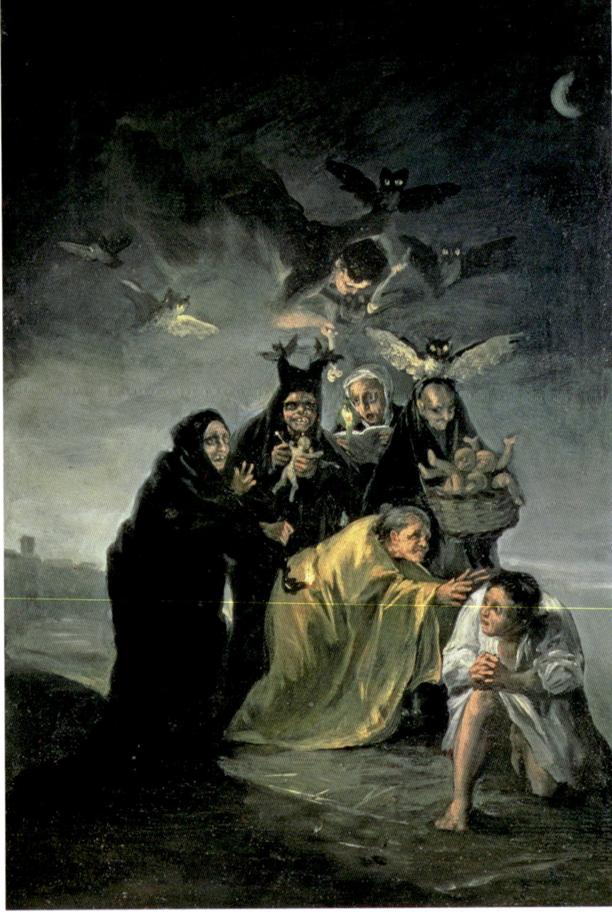

You Will Not Escape, 1797–8, etching and aquatint, Art Gallery of South Australia, Adelaide, Australia, 21.7 x 15.2cm (8½ x 6in)

Plate 72 of *Los Caprichos*, which were received by a somewhat depressed public. By the time Goya had published them, most of the original optimism of the Enlightenment had dimmed, but he maintained that Spain must must confront its social inadequacies and prejudices. This image of a young woman surrounded by winged demons, portrays the notion that Spain was full of hypocrisy and insincerity. The image expresses a collective lack of awareness in his country.

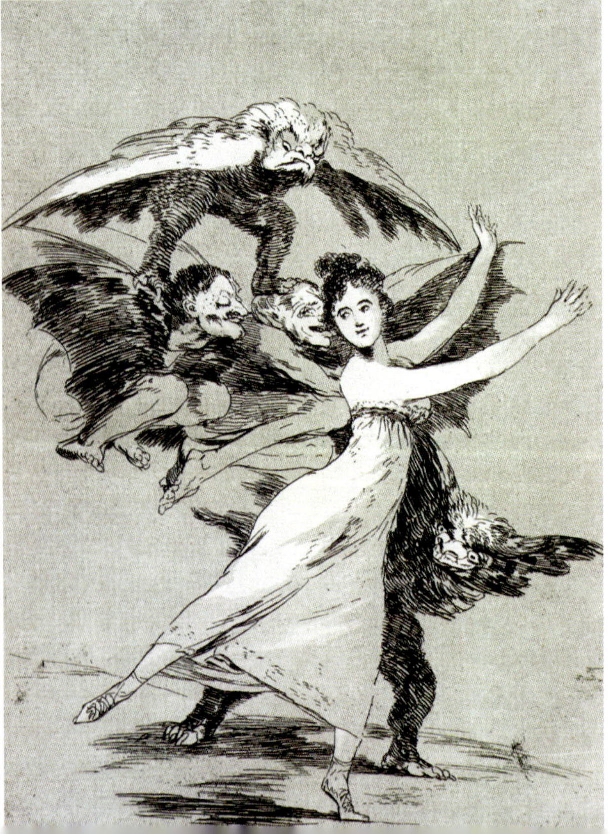

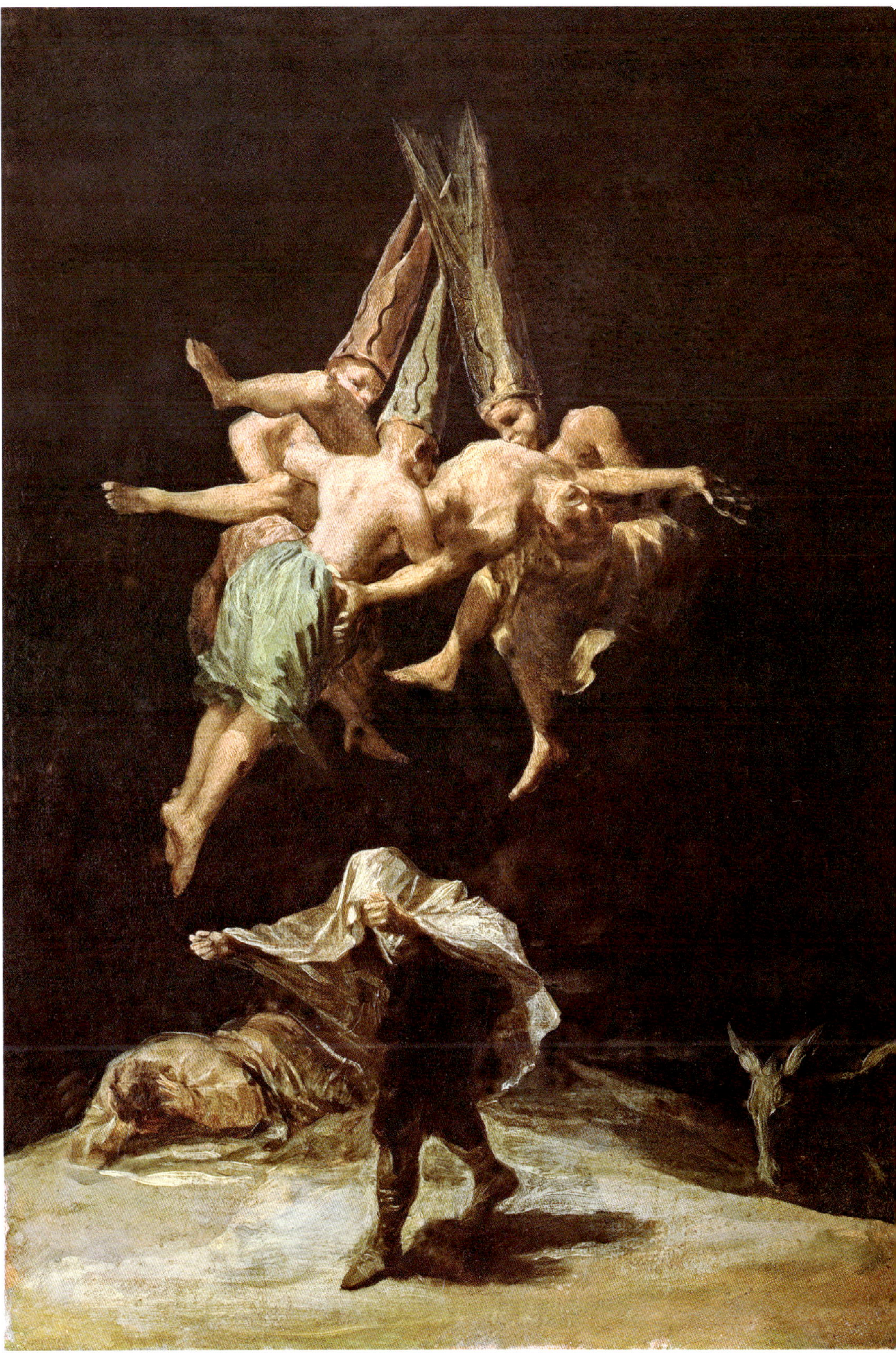

The Witches' Flight, 1797–8,
oil on canvas, Museo
Nacional del Prado, Madrid,
Spain, 43.5 x 30.5cm
(17 x 12in)

Witchcraft and superstition
helped to suppress the
Spanish population through
fear and ignorance. Here,
three bare-chested witches
wearing dunces' caps hold a
naked dead or dying figure
in the air and suck his blood,
while a clothed person lies on
the floor, covering his ears.
A sixth figure is escaping, his
head covered with a white
cloth. He makes a gesture
intended to protect him
from evil spirits.

Portrait of Bernardo de Iriarte, 1797, oil on canvas, Musée des Beaux-Arts, Strasbourg, Switzerland, 108 x 85cm (42½ x 33½in)

Don Bernardo de Iriarte (1735–1814), was Vice Protector of the Royal Academy and a prominent politician and diplomat, part of the circle of liberals who believed in redressing the balance between rich and poor. However, when Ferdinand VII regained the throne, he was classed as an afrancesado and took refuge in Bordeaux. An inscription on this states that Goya made the portrait as testimony of mutual esteem and affection.

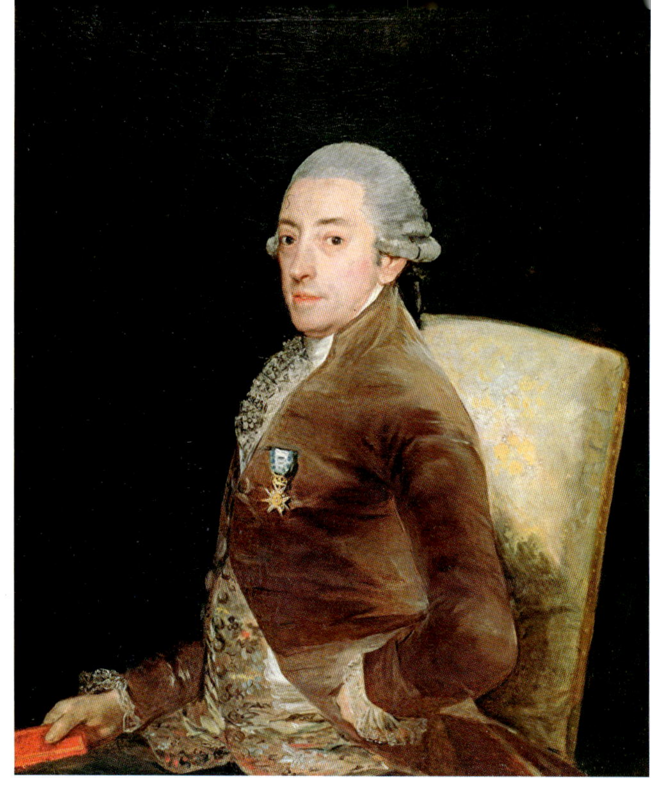

Don Andrés del Peral, c.1797–8, oil on canvas, The National Gallery, London, UK, 95 x 65.7cm (37½ x 26in)

Goya exhibited this at the Royal Academy of San Fernando in the summer of 1798. Andrés del Peral worked as a painter and gilder for the Spanish Court from the late 1770s to the early 1820s and had built up a large collection of small paintings by Goya, along with works by several other Spanish artists from previous centuries. Upright and stern-looking, Peral's image belies a sombre personality.

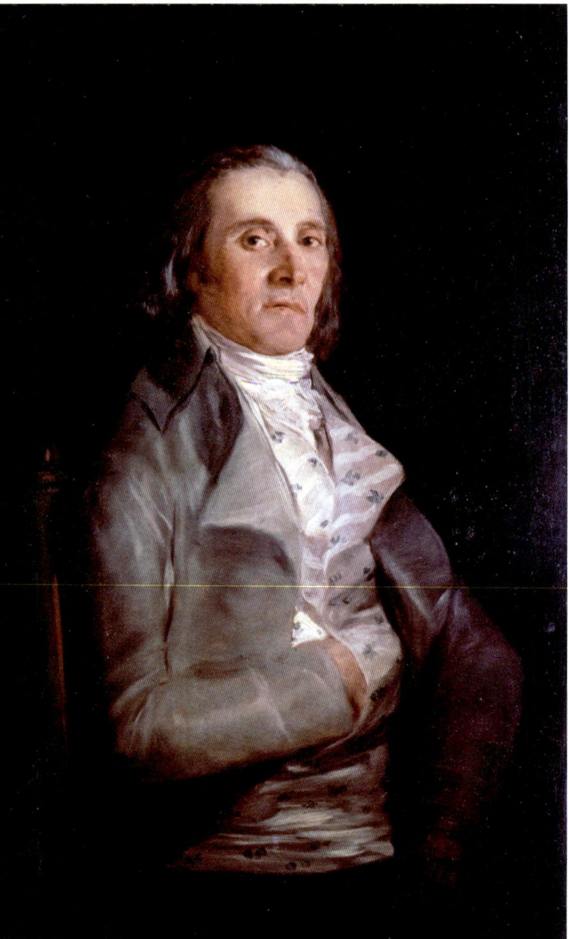

Self-portrait, c.1795–7, Indian ink on paper, Private Collection, 23.3 x 14.4cm (9 x 5½in)

Goya looks at viewers directly, a rather detached, preoccupied expression on his face. His untidy hair is parted in the middle and flops down into a short beard. It has never been recorded that he had a beard and in the previous self-portrait there is no evidence of one, so it is believed that this was his attempt at turning his face into a lion's for another painting.

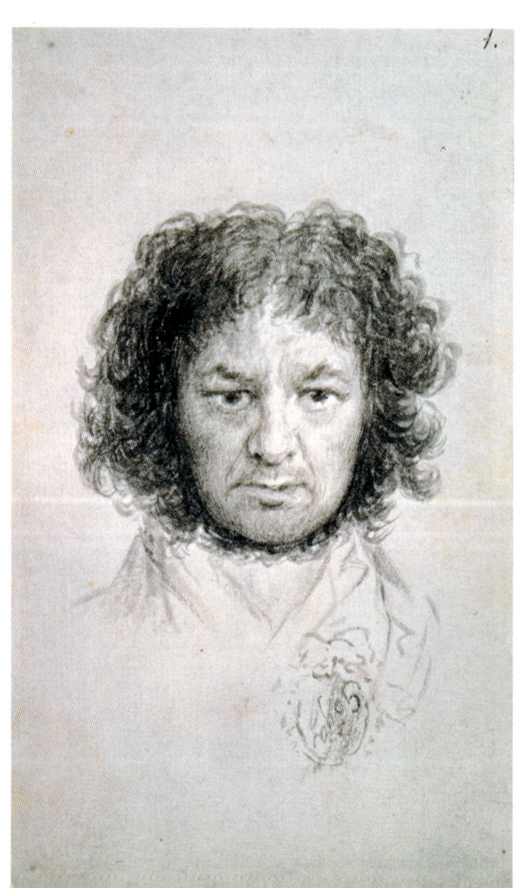

Portrait of the Matador Don Pedro Romero, 1795–8, oil on canvas, Kimbell Art Museum, Texas, USA, 84.1 x 65cm (33 x 25½in)

One of the most celebrated toreadors, Pedro Romero (1754–1839), was idolized for his courage and his handsome appearance.

He was the foremost exponent of the classical school of bullfighting that was established by his family, and was said to have killed over 5000 bulls. Here, at the age of 45, he is dressed characteristically flamboyantly, while the influence of Velázquez can be seen in the dexterous brushwork.

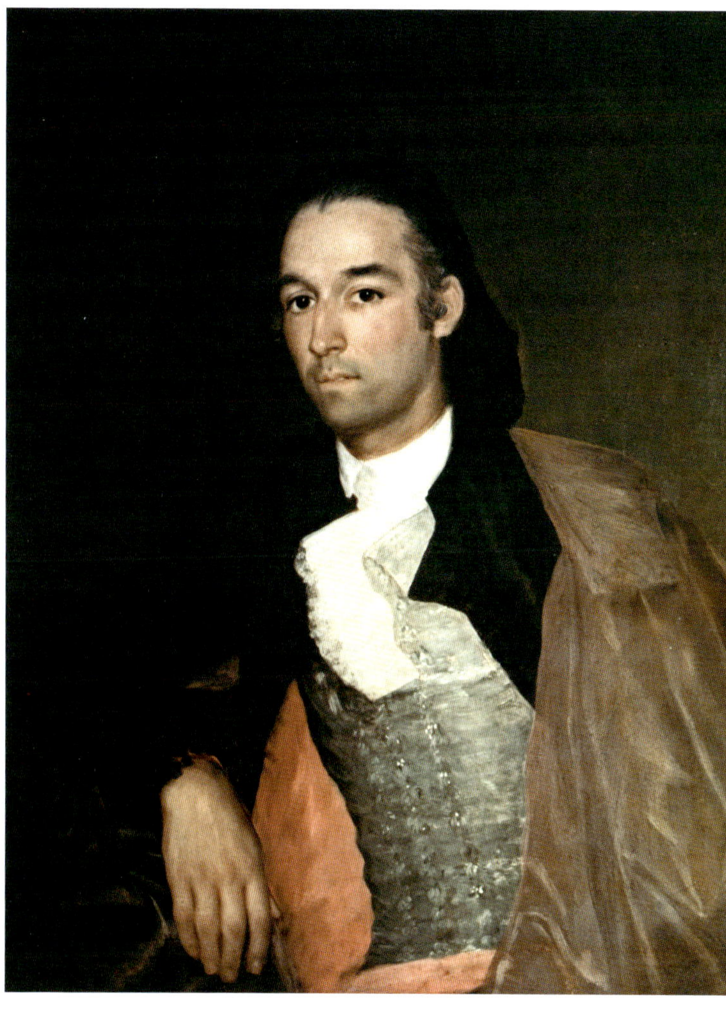

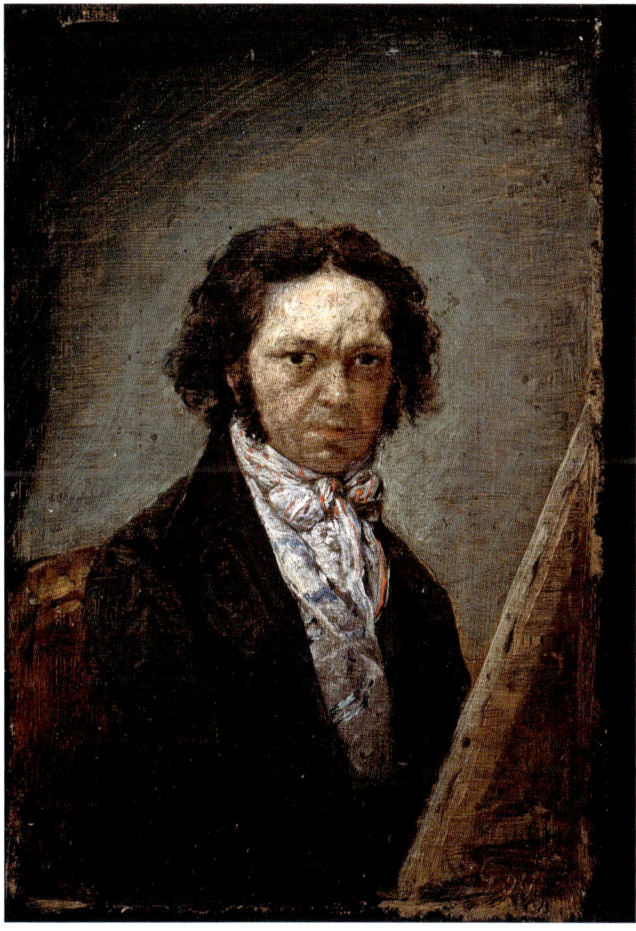

Self-portrait, c.1795–7, oil on canvas, Museo Nacional del Prado, Madrid, Spain, 18.2 x 12.2cm (7 x 5in)

In this self-portrait Goya stares at viewers, his long hair and sideburns reflecting the Romantic fashions of the day (and reminiscent of images of Beethoven at the time). Posing before a large canvas, his elegant frock coat, shirt and tie present him as a man of means. A small painting, it presents an intimate image, as he seems preoccupied with the work in hand.

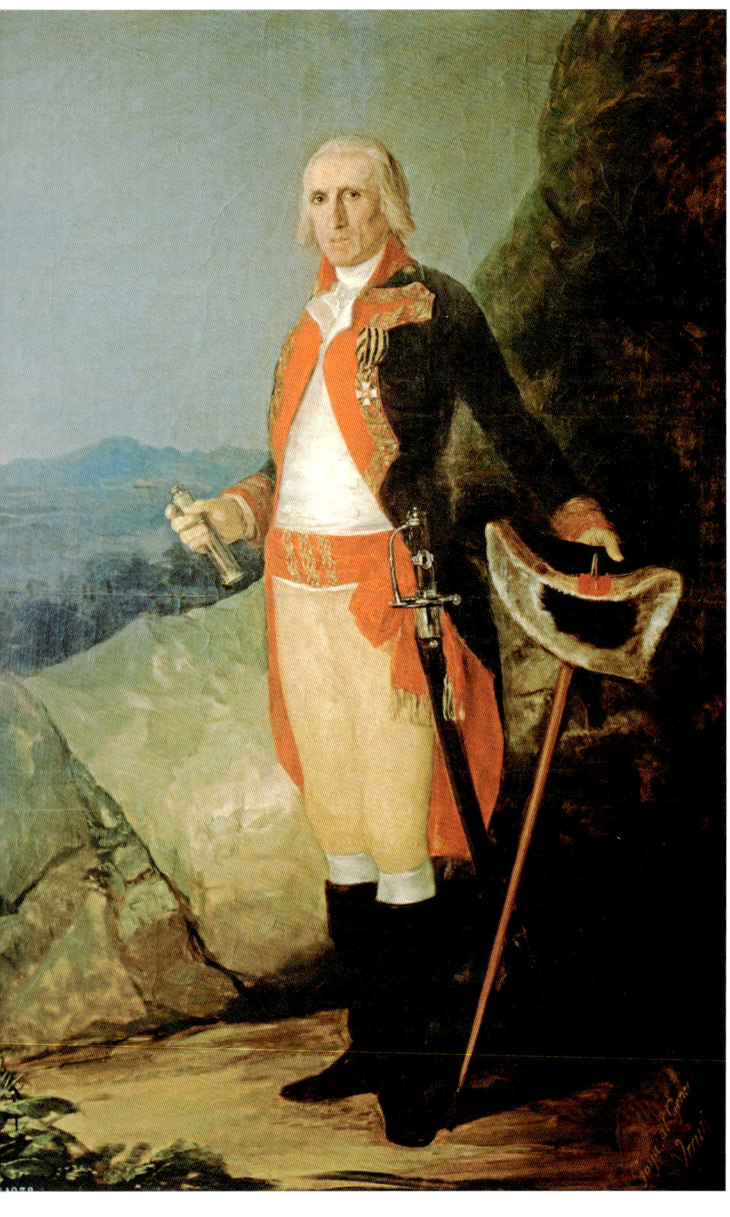

General José de Urrutia, c.1798, oil on canvas, Museo Nacional del Prado, Madrid, Spain, 199.5 x 134.5cm (78½ x 53in)

Like many of Goya's portraits, this recalls works by the English portraitists, particularly Gainsborough. Don José de Urrutia (1739-1803), was the only soldier of his day to reach the rank of Field Marshal without being a titled nobleman. He received the Cross of Saint George from Catherine the Great of Russia for his actions in the Crimean War, but in 1798, he was removed from all public office for disagreeing with Manuel Godoy.

Gaspar Melchor de Jovellanos, 1798, oil on canvas, Museo Nacional del Prado, Madrid, Spain, 205 x 133cm (81 x 52in)

At the time of his appointment as Minister of Grace and Justice, Goya painted this portrait of his friend and patron. Jovellanos was one of the most important thinkers of the Spanish Enlightenment, who fought for reforms and against ignorance, superstition and the Inquisition. Goya shows him leaning on a table covered with papers. A statue of Minerva, the goddess of wisdom and the arts, indicates his great learning.

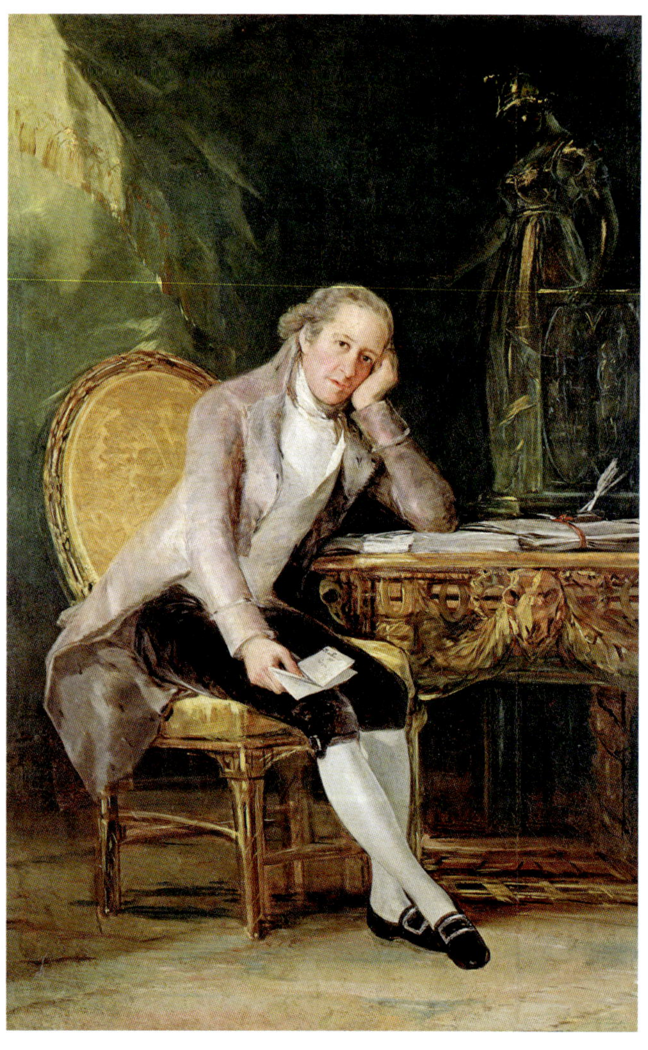

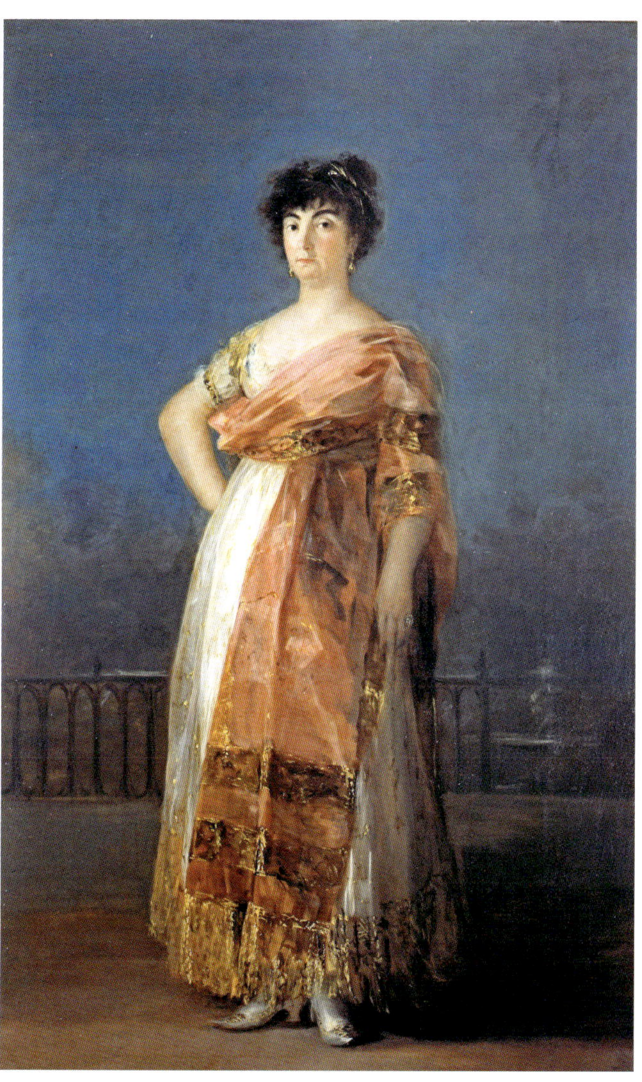

La Tirana, 1799, oil on canvas, Private Collection, 206 x 130cm (81 x 51in)

Five years after his first portrait of her (see page 167), Goya once again painted the actress María del Rosario Fernandez, this time full-length, in an outdoor space. In a white and gold chiffon dress, swathed with a bronze and gold shawl, she looks at viewers, a Neoclassical-style figure. Only one hand can be seen, possibly because Goya charged extra to paint hands. Touches of white draw viewers' eyes around the image.

Ferdinand Guillemardet, 1798, oil on canvas, Musée du Louvre, Paris, France, 185 x 125cm (73 x 49in)

A radiant and relaxed portrait of the self-assured and intelligent French ambassador to Spain from 1798 to 1800, featuring the colours of France on his sash and cocked hat. Goya was in a difficult position. Along with his friends including Jovellanos and Iriarte, he agreed with many of the reforms the French were making during their occupation of Spain, but he also remained loyal to his own royal family.

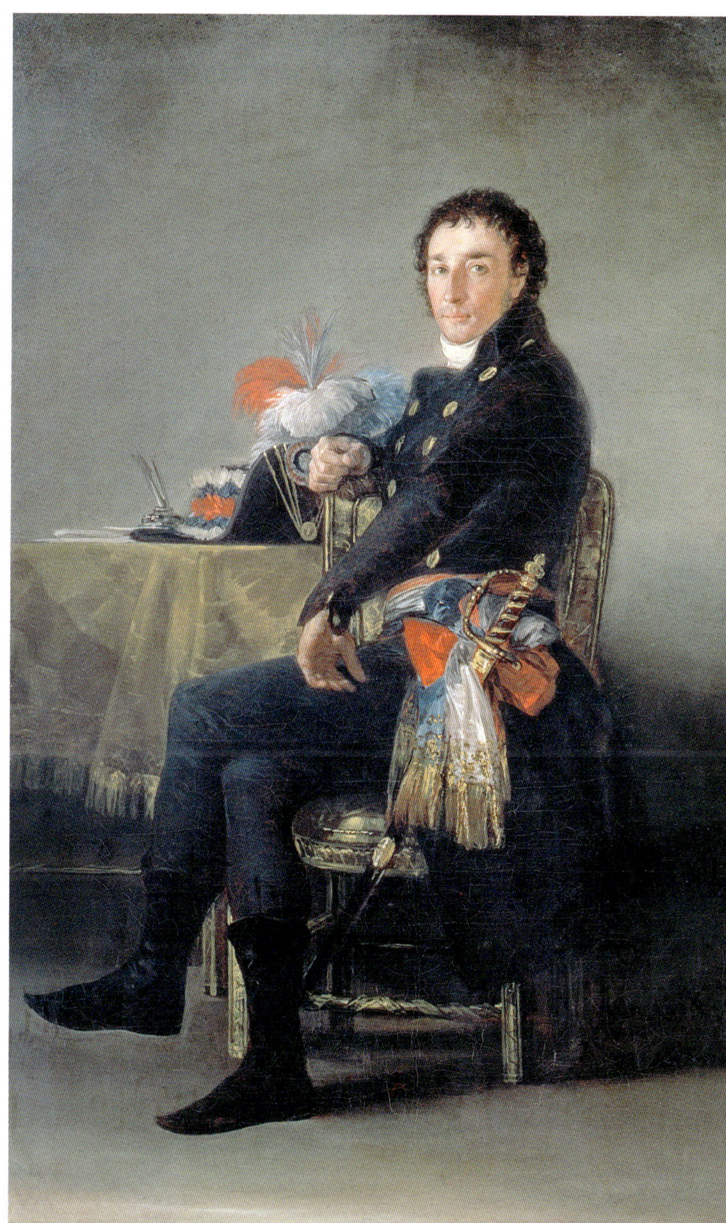

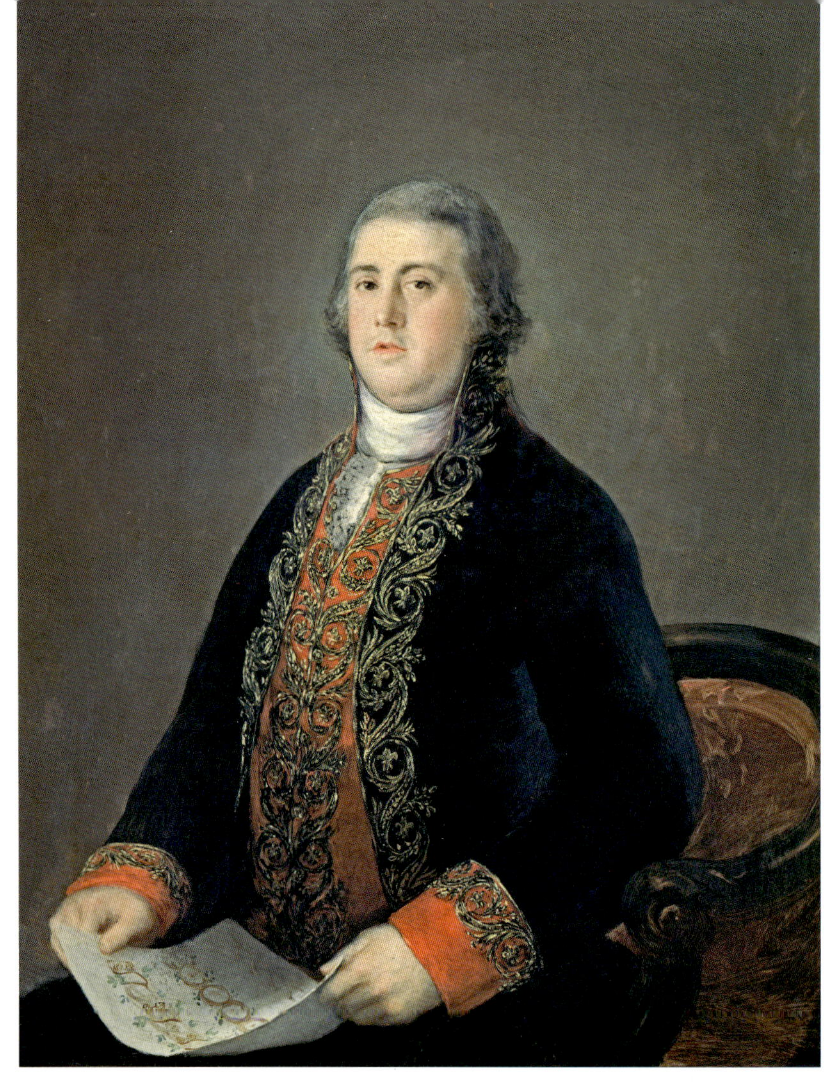

Juan López de Robredo,
c.1799, oil on canvas, Private
Collection, 107 x 81.5cm
(42 x 32in)

Don Juan López de
Robredo was Embroiderer
to King Charles IV, and
skilfully produced countless
hangings, upholsteries and
uniforms. He commissioned
this portrait when he had
– uniquely – been given
permission to wear this lavish
uniform. In commissioning
Goya, he confirmed his lofty
ambitions. Goya's depiction
of the gold embroidery on
the uniform is picked out in
impasto paint, recalling the
work of Rembrandt
and Velázquez.

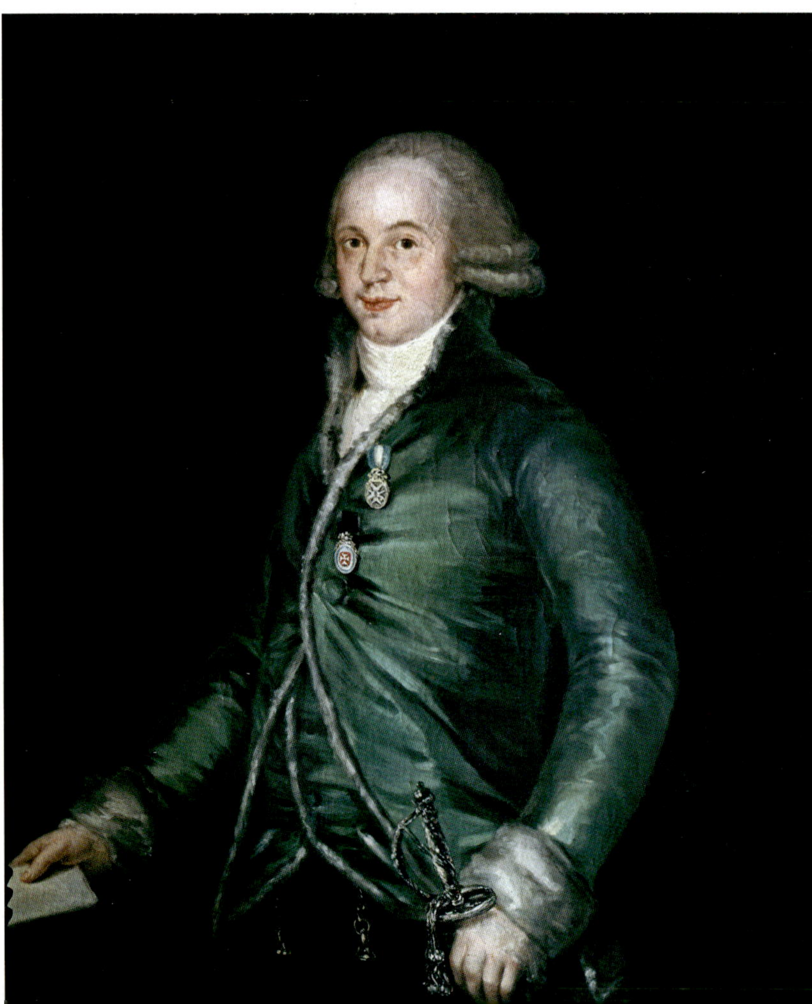

Mariano Luis of Urquijo,
c.1798–9, oil on canvas,
Academy of History,
Madrid, Spain, 128 x 97cm
(50 x 38in)

A powerful politician,
Mariano Luis de Urquijo
y Muga (1769–1817) was
Prime Minister of Spain from
12 February 1799 to 13
December 1799, and again
between 7 July 1808 and
27 June 1813, under Joseph
Bonaparte. While in office
the first time, he did all he
could to limit the power and
influence of the Inquisition.
He was particularly resented
by Godoy, who usurped him
while Charles IV reigned.

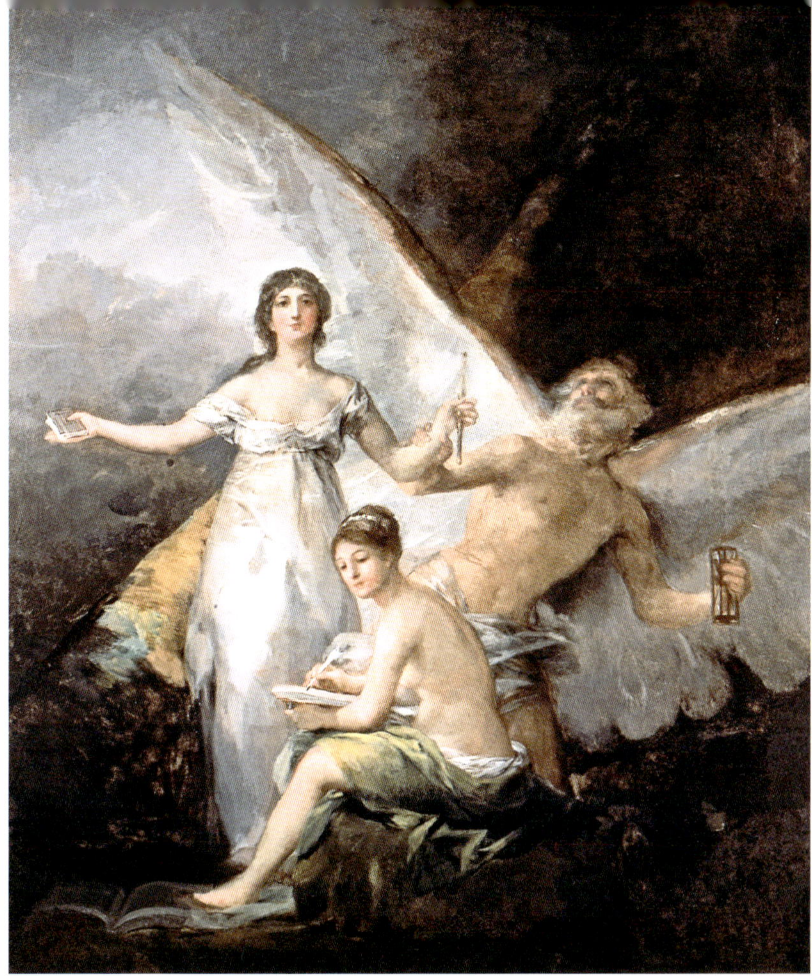

Truth Rescued by Time, Witnessed by History, 1800–1812, oil on canvas, Nationalmuseum, Stockholm, Sweden, 294 x 244cm (116 x 96in)

Commissioned by Godoy, this painting seems to be a work of propaganda, and part of Godoy's attempt to fashion his public self-image into that of an enlightened statesman. Dark-haired Truth is dressed in white, while History is naked. Time is represented as the traditional winged, elderly man. History sits by Truth while Time reads a book, her foot on an open copy of Goya's satirical etchings *The Disasters of War*.

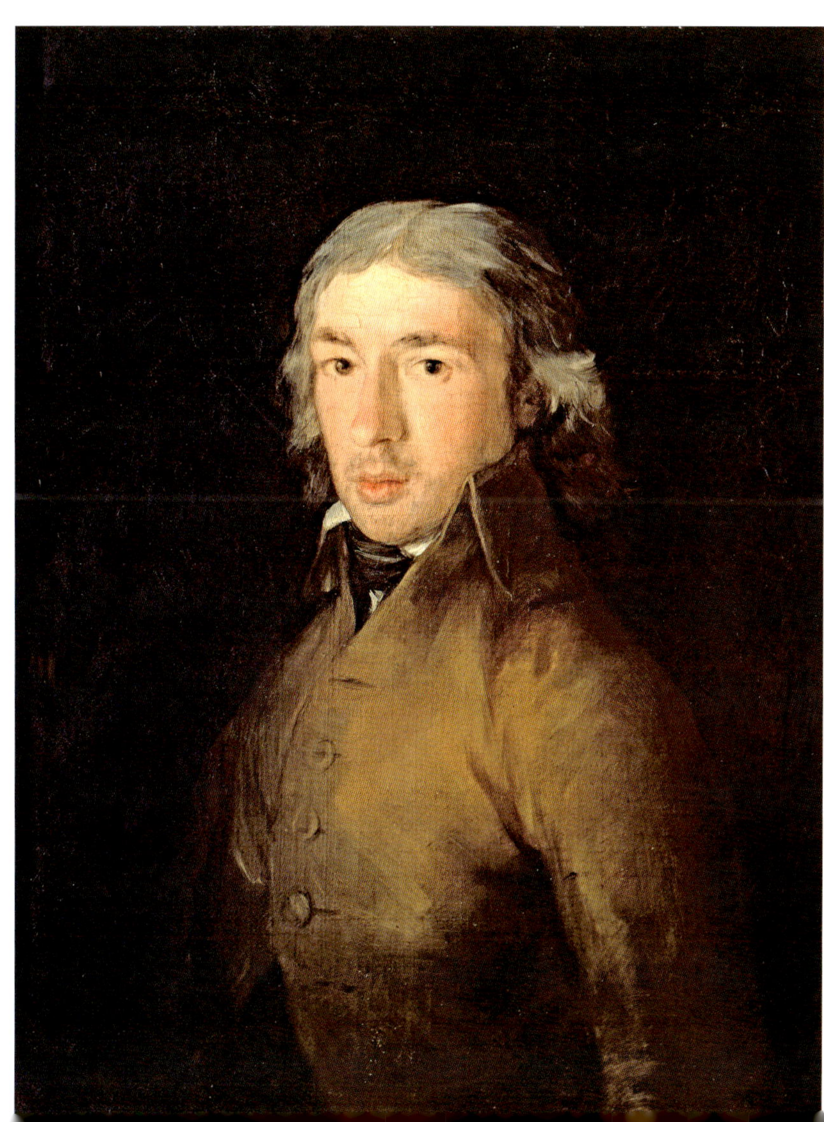

Leandro Fernández de Moratín, 1799, oil on canvas, Real Academia de Bellas Artes de San Fernando, Madrid, Spain, 56 x 73cm (22 x 29in)

A dramatist and poet, and one of the most influential literary figures of the Spanish Enlightenment, Moratín (1760–1828) was supported by Jovellanos, who arranged for him to study in Paris for a year. The Spanish government paid for his further education in England. During the French occupation, he was made royal librarian, but when Ferdinand VII regained the throne, he was forced into exile in France.

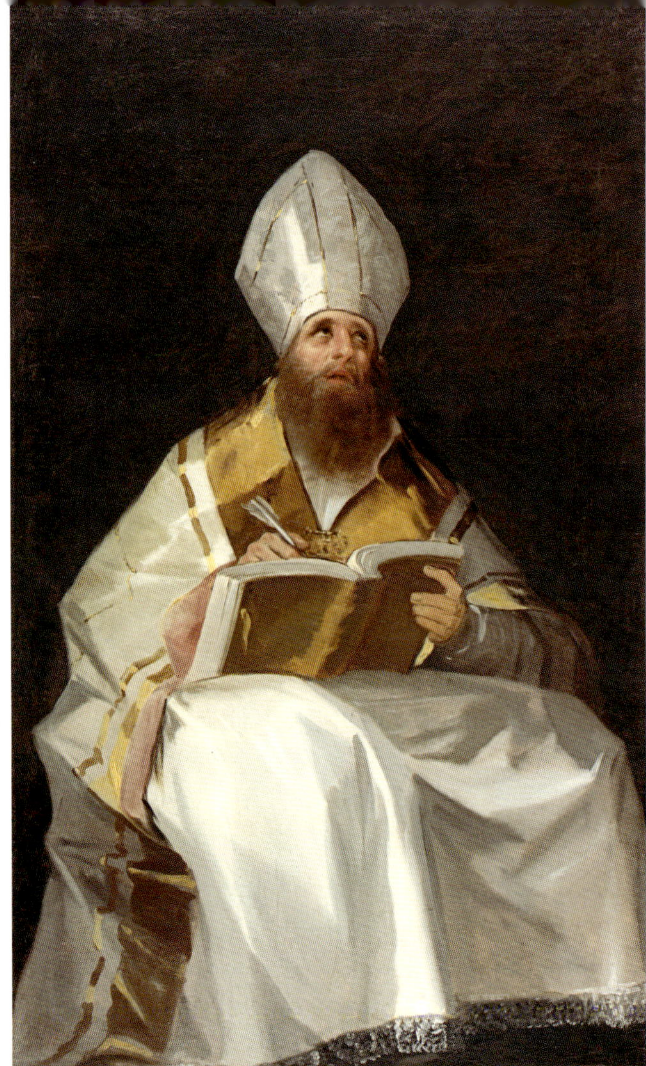

Saint Ambrose, c.1796–9,
oil on canvas, Cleveland
Museum of Art, Ohio, USA,
190 x 113cm (75 x 44½in)

Probably painted during or
after Goya's second visit to
Andalusia, this is one of four
works depicting the saints
Ambrose, Jerome, Augustine
and Gregory; all significant
figures of early Catholicism.
Ambrose (c.340–91), was
the bishop of Milan,
and resolved important
theological conflicts while
in office. The perspective
and large scale of the work
suggest that it was made to
hang high up, but this original
location remains unknown.

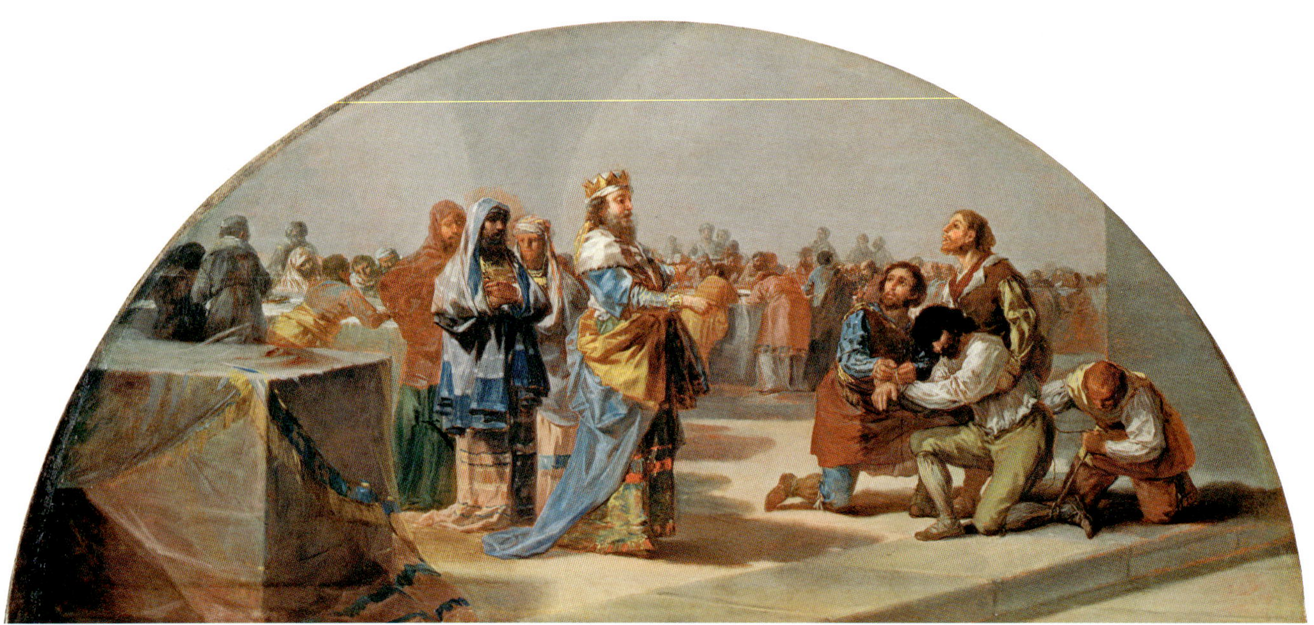

*Parable of the Guests at the
Wedding of the King's Son,*
c.1796–7, oil on canvas,
Museo Historico Municipal,
Cádiz, Spain, 146 x 340cm
(57½ x 134in)

It is likely that Goya's trip
to Cádiz in 1792 before his
illness was in connection
with this commission for
three large New Testament
scenes for the Oratory at
La Santa Cueva. His long
illness delayed the execution
of the works and he did
not deliver them until
approximately four years
later. They herald a period
that has become known as
his second great period of
religious painting.

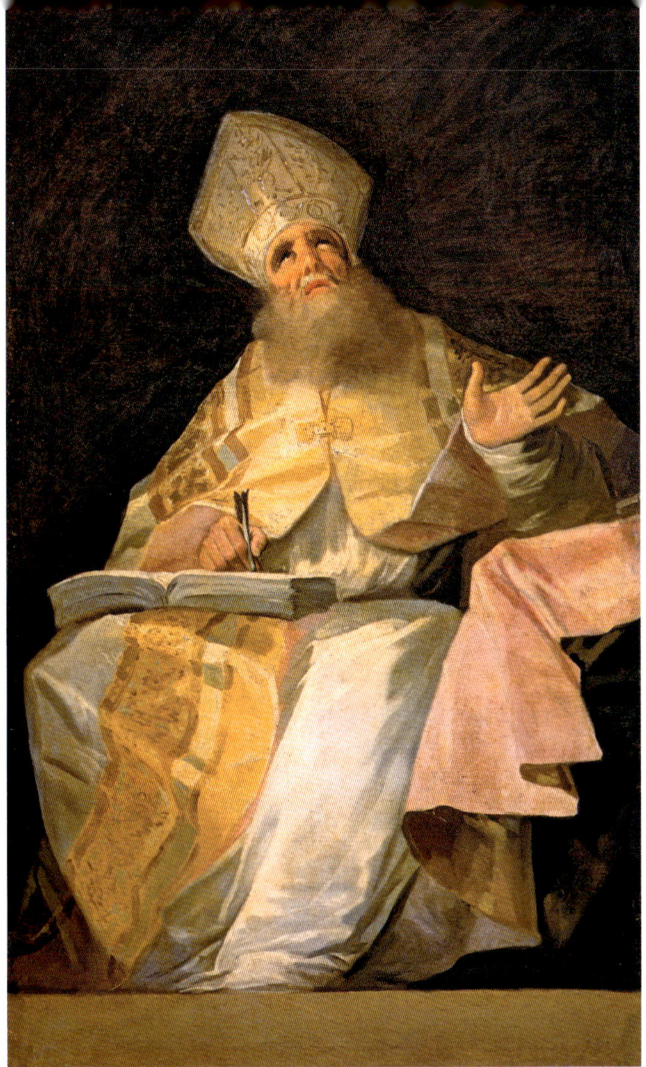

Saint Augustine, c.1796–9, oil on canvas, Private Collection, 190 x 115cm (75 x 45in)

In the late 1700s, Spain expelled its Jesuits which initiated huge changes within the Church. Many reformers looked back to early Church history for inspiration, and Saint Augustine, as one of the key figures of that time, became one of the focuses. Influences from the work of Murillo and Torrigiano can be seen here; Goya knew Murillo's work well and had recently seen a sculpture by Torrigiano in Andalusia.

Saint Gregory the Great, c.1796–9, oil on canvas, Museo Romántico, Madrid, Spain, 190 x 115cm (75 x 45in)

Another of the four Doctors of the Church, assumed to have been painted after Goya's visit to Andalusia in 1796 to 1797, because of their particular resemblance to Murillo's seated figures of Saint Isidore and Saint Leander he saw in Seville Cathedral. Sitting on a platform like Murillo's saints, Saint Gregory sits with a large book and his papal tiara identifying him as the particularly learned Pope.

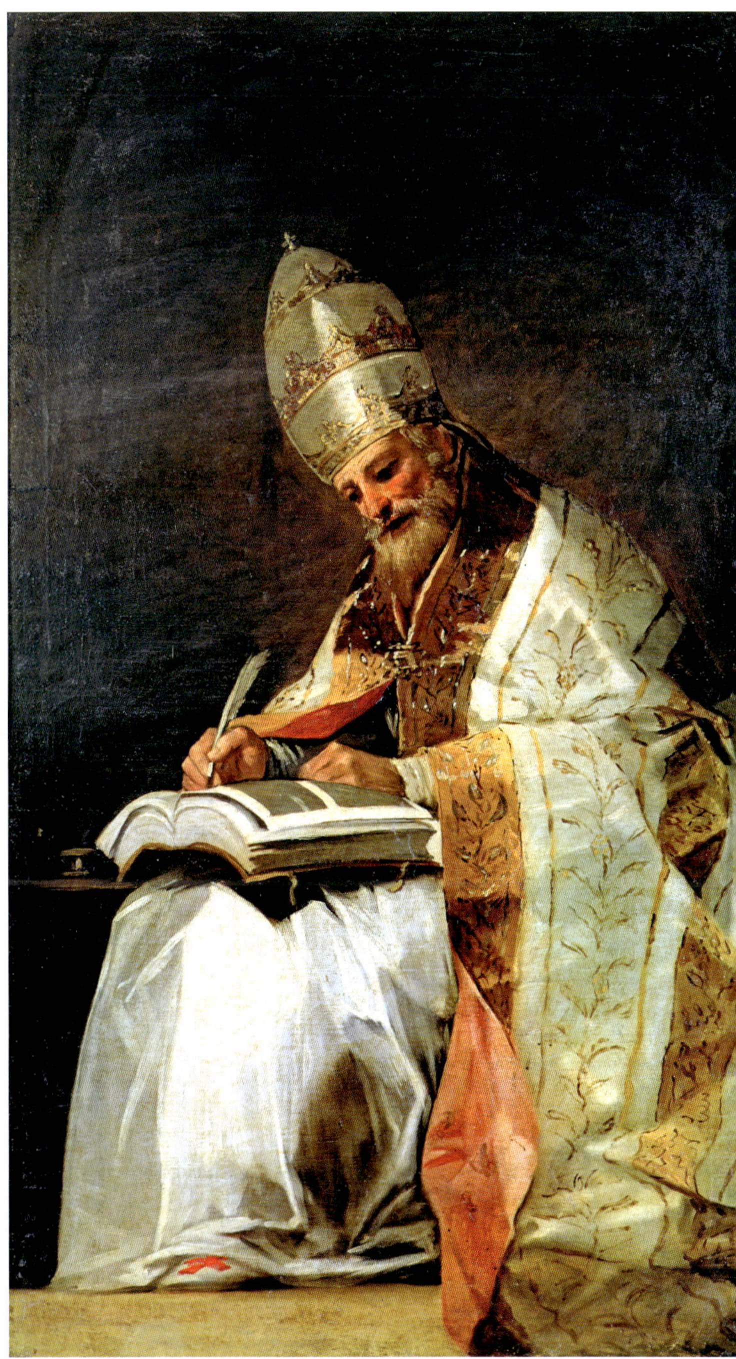

Detail from the fresco of
Miracle of Saint Anthony
of Padua (below)

In this detail, spectators
witness the miracle as it
occurs. The King and Queen
let Goya design his own
decorative scheme for this
chapel. Instead of filling the
ceiling with angels and other
holy figures, he represented
ordinary, happy human
beings. Not all of them are
watching the miracle – that is,
Saint Anthony bringing a dead
man back to life so that he
can reveal his murderer.

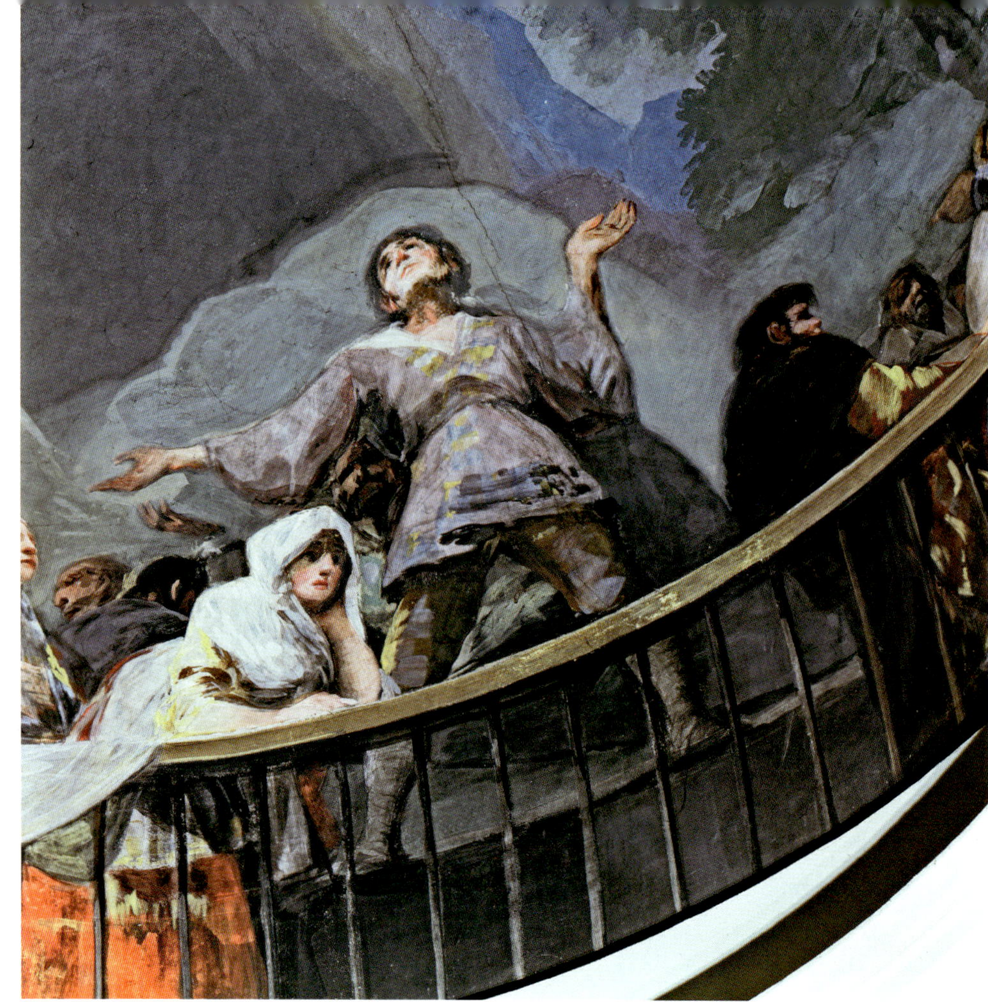

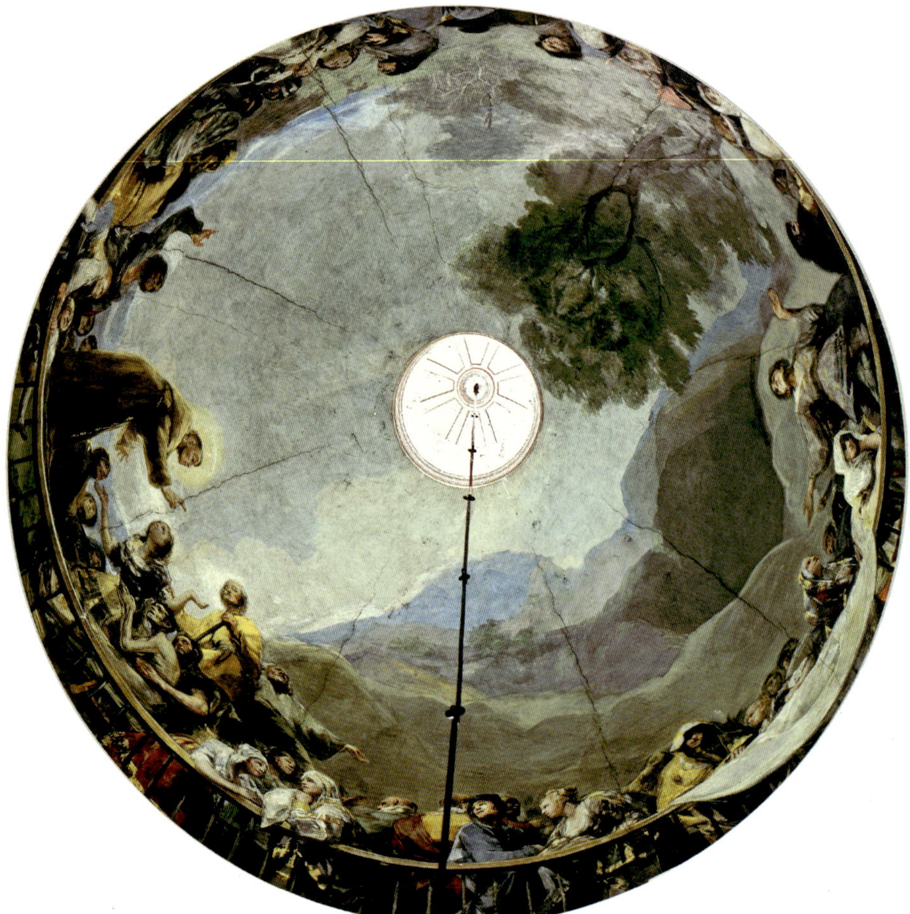

Miracle of Saint Anthony
of Padua, 1798, fresco,
San Antonio de la Florida,
Madrid, Spain, 550cm
diameter (216½in)

Goya's third and last great
fresco painting was this
commission for the newly
built hermitage, the chapel
of San Antonio de la Florida,
on the outskirts of Madrid.
In August 1798, he began
working on the project
and is said to have completed
the work in just 120 days.
As the church is dedicated
to Saint Anthony of Padua,
Goya painted one of his
miracles in the cupola.

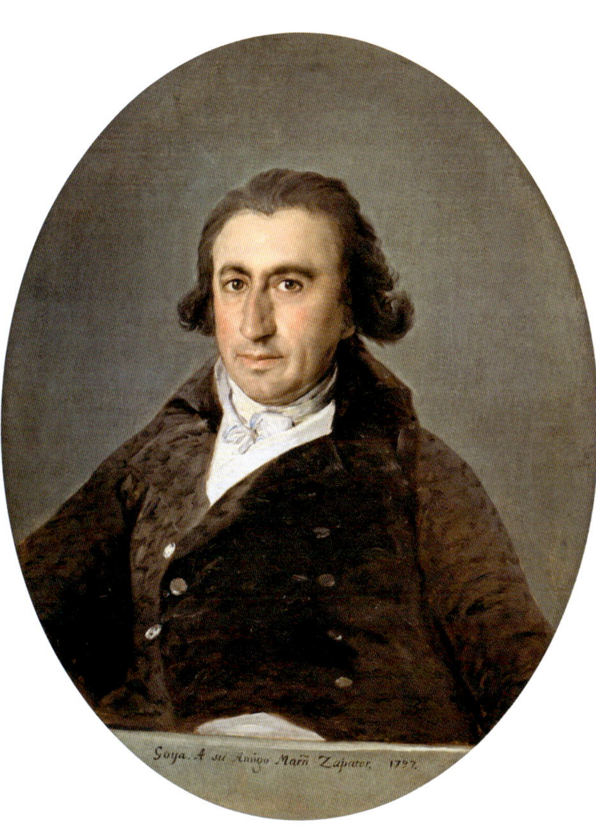

Portrait of Martin Zapater, 1797, oil on canvas, Bilbao Fine Arts Museum, Bilbao, Spain, 83 x 65cm (32½ x 25½in)

From his earliest school days, Goya had been friends with Martin Zapater. Throughout their lives, until Zapater died in 1803, the two men wrote to each other regularly, and much of what we know about Goya's thoughts and personality comes from this correspondence. Goya painted two portraits of Zapater who had become a wealthy corn-merchant, this and another, seven years previously.

Saint Jerome, 1798, oil on canvas, Norton Simon Museum, California, USA, 190.8 x 114.3cm (75 x 45in)

Another of Goya's Doctors of the Church; Saint Jerome translated the Bible from Hebrew to Latin, and lived in a desert cave for the last years of his life, studying and praying to eliminate worldly desire. Emaciated and scantily clad, he contemplates a crucifix. Around him lie his books and writing materials, as well as the scourge and skull (a symbol of death) that assisted his spiritual contemplation.

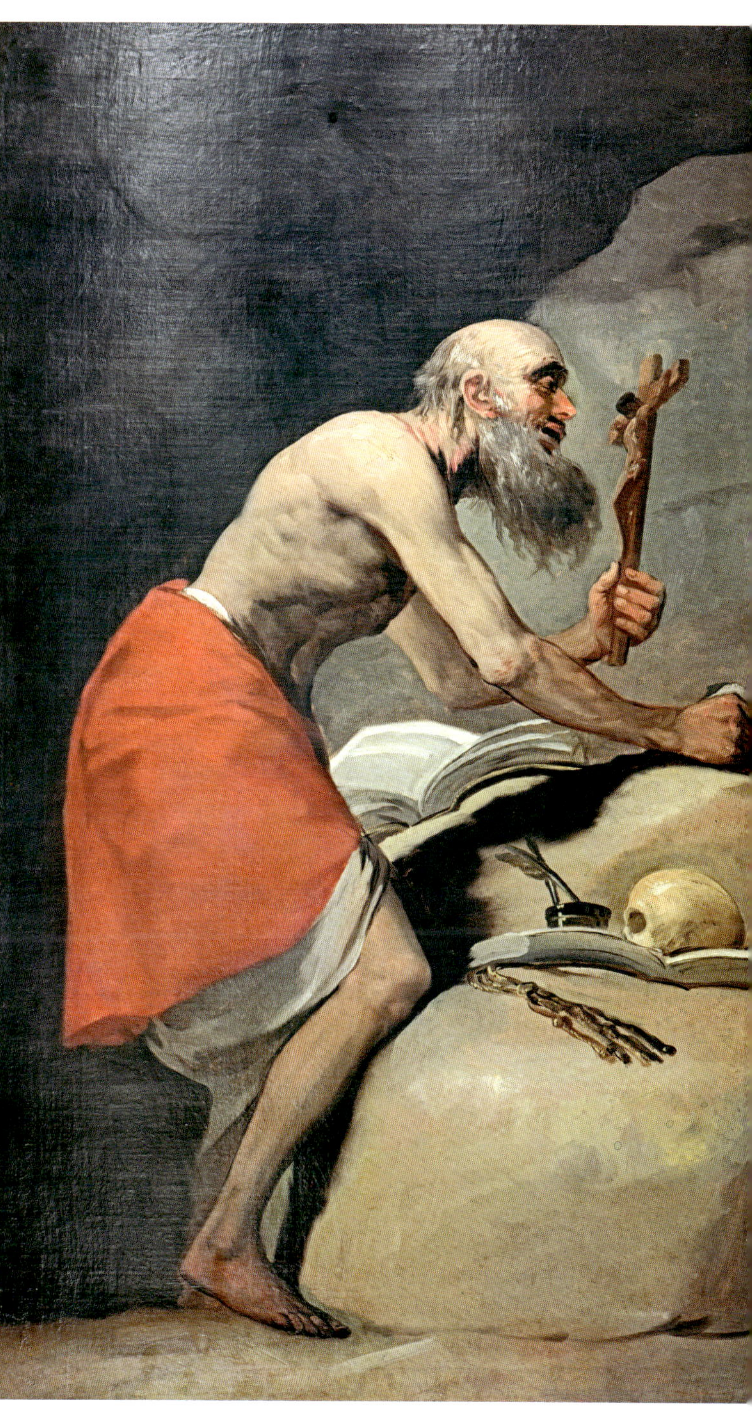

Sketch for the Taking of Christ, 1798, oil on canvas, Museo Nacional del Prado, Madrid, Spain, 40.2 x 23.1cm (16 x 9in)

This is the moment from the New Testament when Roman soldiers arrested Christ. It has always been a particularly emotive scene for Christians and Goya captures it with boldly applied paint. This is a small preparatory sketch for the painting that adorns one of the altars at the Sacristy of Toledo Cathedral. Rapid and energetic brushstrokes are used, colours have been jotted down, and the entire dramatic composition appears spontaneous and dynamic.

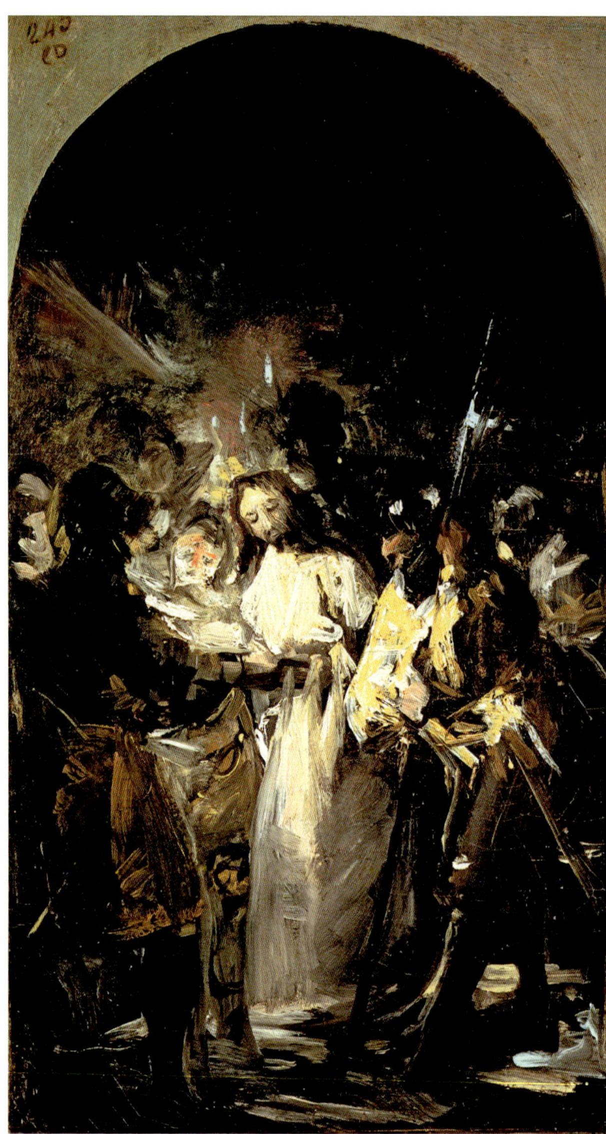

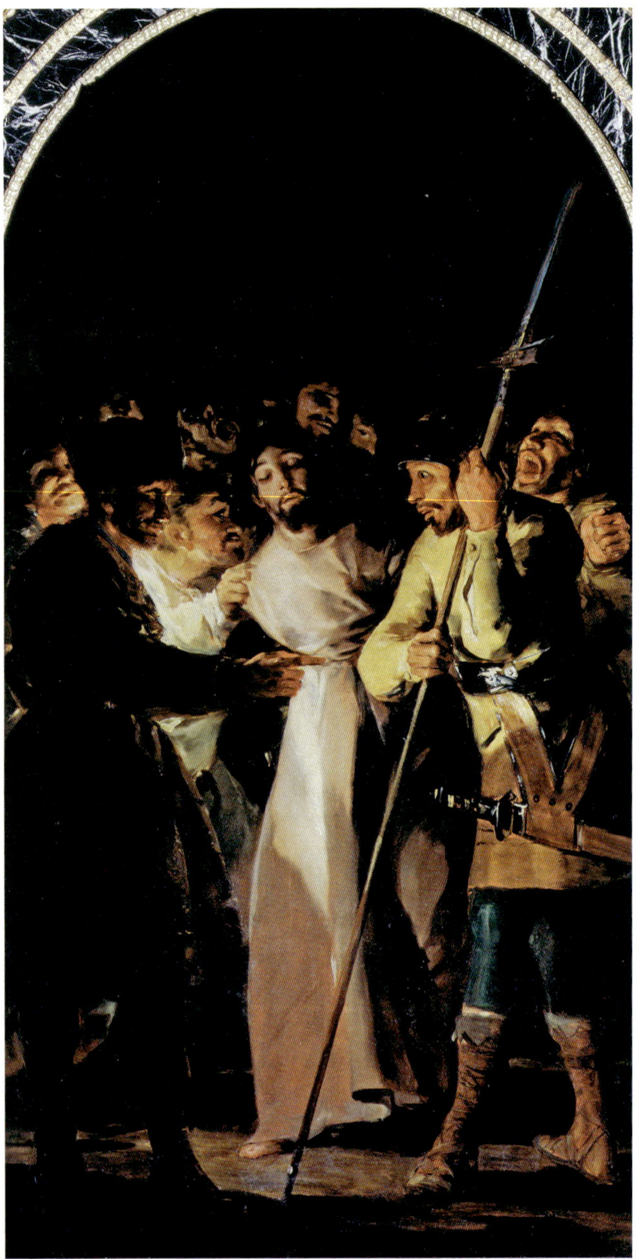

The Taking of Christ, 1798, oil on canvas, Cathedral of Toledo, Toledo, Spain, 300 x 200cm (118 x 79in)

Painted for the Archbishop of Toledo, this representation of the betrayal of Christ is believed to have possibly been commissioned ten years previously. Far less spontaneous than the sketch (above), this work nevertheless features dramatic lighting and a busy composition. Goya delivered it on 8 January 1799. Similar elements were featured in 1853–4 by William Holman Hunt (1827–1910) in *The Light of the World*.

Angels (from the vault),
1798, fresco, San Antonio
de la Florida, Madrid, Spain,
900 x 160cm (354 x 63in)

Using great economy of
line and minimal brushwork,
Goya also used a reduced
palette to create two angels,
dramatically angled and lit. He
gives them human qualities as
they too, are stunned at the
miracle being performed by
Saint Anthony. In defence
of his revolutionary methods,
he said: 'I see no lines or
details. There is no reason
why my brush should see
more than I do.'

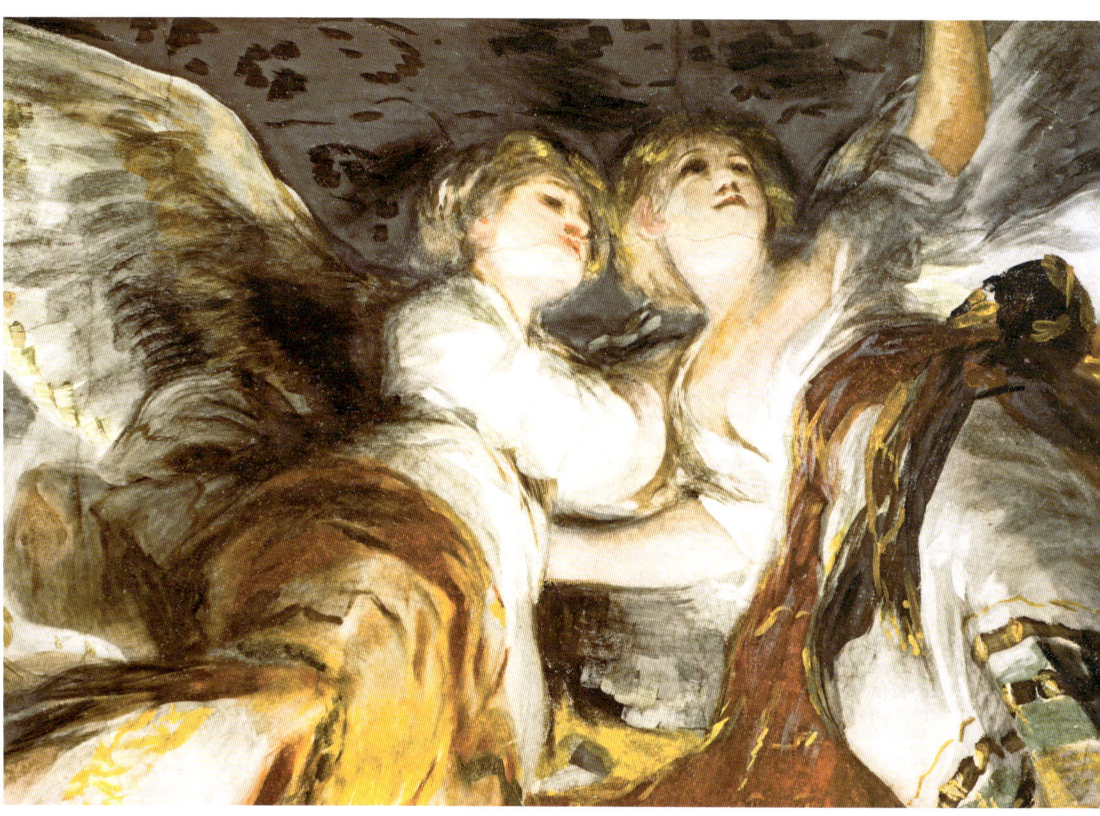

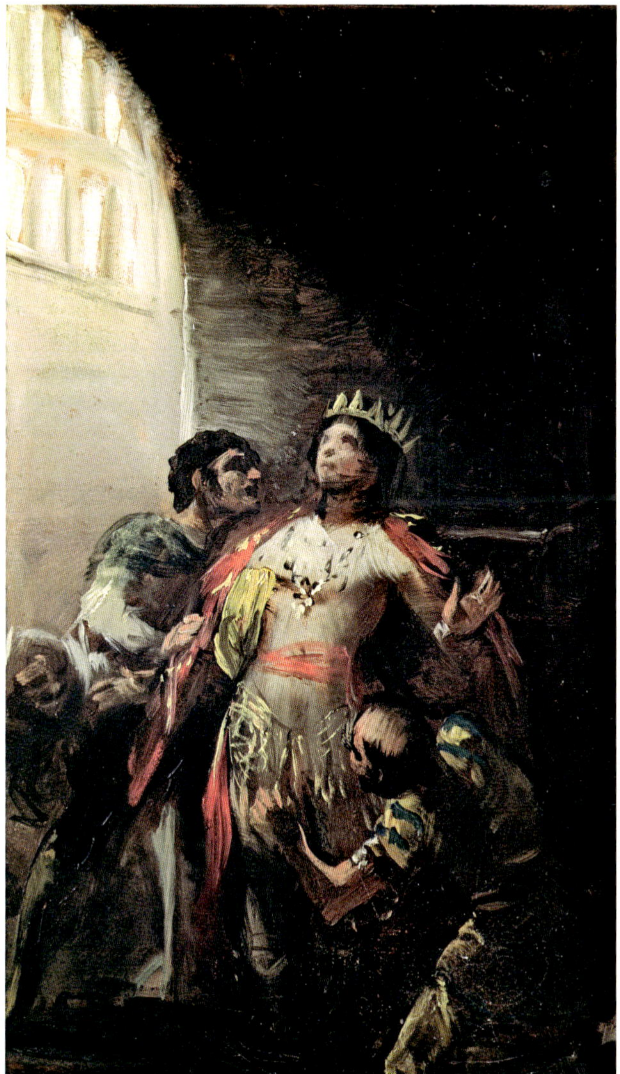

Saint Hermengild in Prison,
c.1798–1800, oil on canvas,
Museo Lázaro Galdiano,
Madrid, Spain, 33 x 23cm
(13 x 9in)

Inside a prison, Saint
Hermenegild stands between
two men. Light filters weakly
through a small window high
up. Hermengild was the son
of King Leovigild of Visigothic
Spain, but quarrelled with his
father in 579 and rebelled.
He converted from Arian
Christianity to Roman
Catholicism, and in 586 he
was beheaded by order
of his father. He became
worshipped as a martyr
by Roman Catholics.

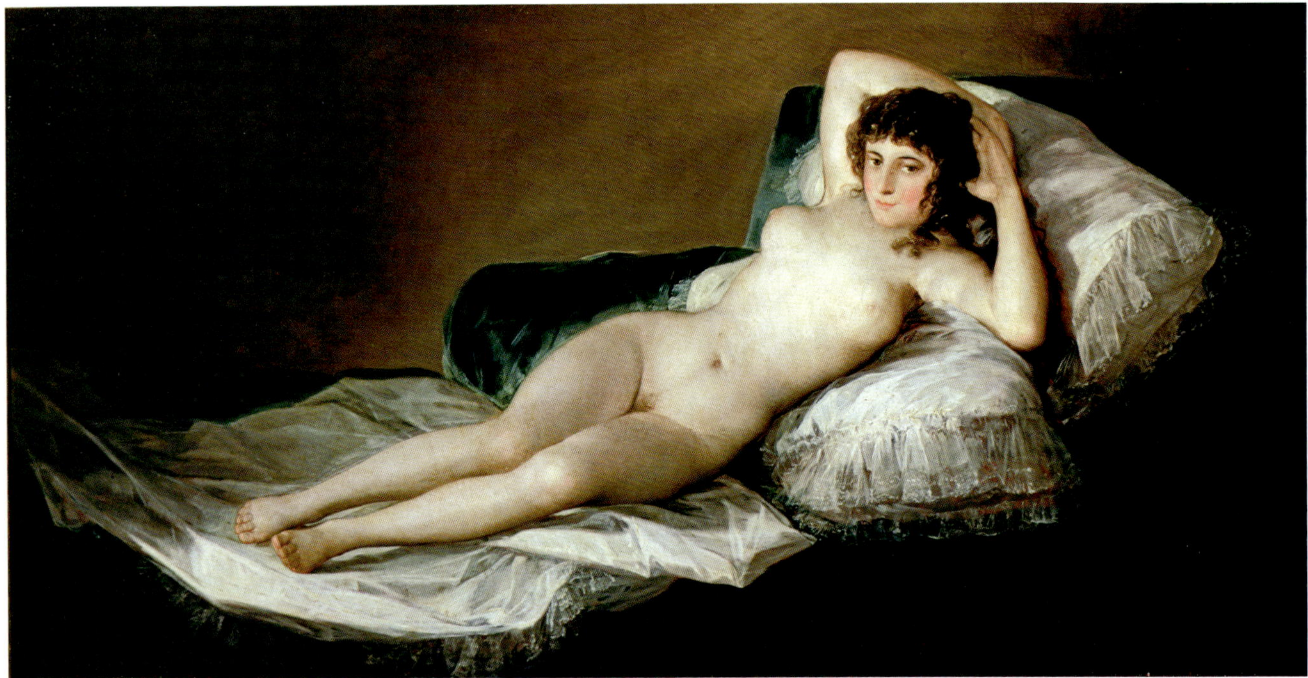

The Naked Maja or *La Maja Desnuda*, 1797–1800, oil on canvas, Museo Nacional del Prado, Madrid, Spain, 98 x 191cm (38½ x 75in)

The female nude is rare in Spanish art, yet Goya's presentation of the subject is uncompromising and provocative. The first painted image to include pubic hair, this is no Venus on a green velvet divan. The model remains unidentified and may be a composite of several women, or Godoy's mistress Pepita Tudó. In 1815, the Inquisition summoned Goya to reveal who commissioned this, but his response is unknown.

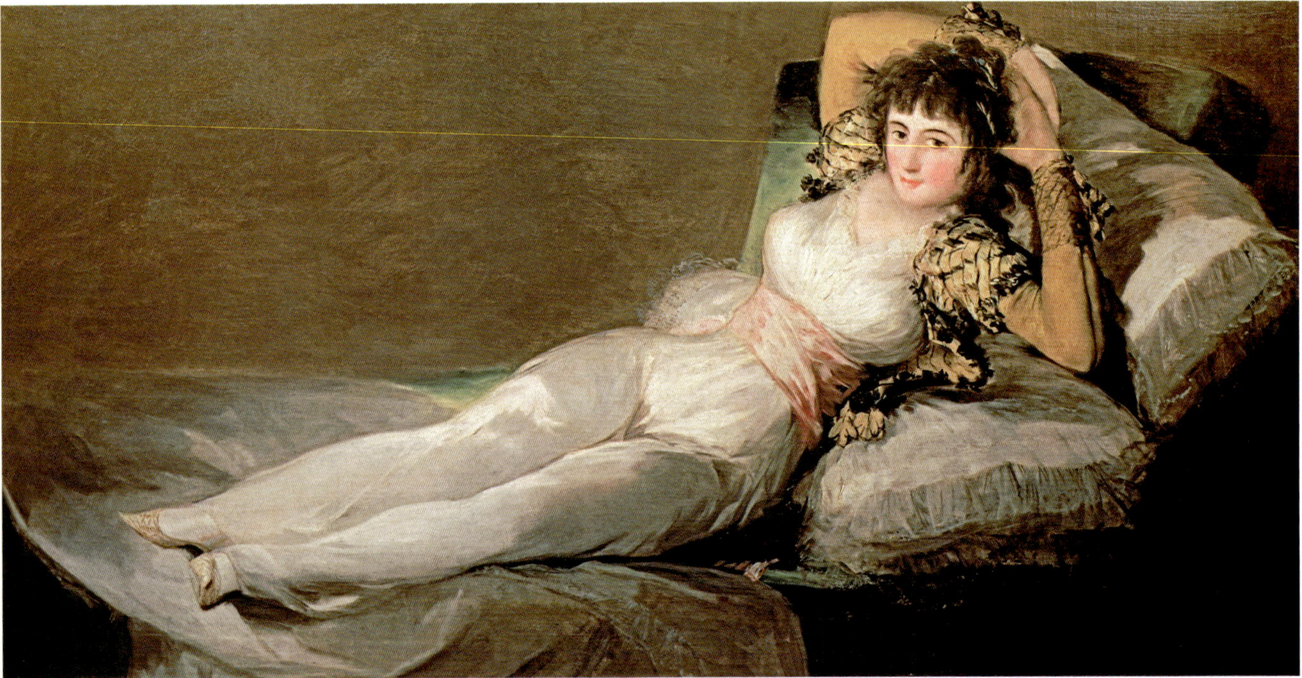

The Clothed Maja or *La Maja Vestida*, 1797–1800, oil on canvas, Museo Nacional del Prado, Madrid, Spain, 95 x 190cm (37½ x 75in)

Almost identical to *The Naked Maja*, except that she is clothed, the reason Goya painted these two images remains unknown. Both were first recorded as belonging to the collection of Prime Minister Godoy and when they were discovered, the ecclesiastical authorities were furious. Neither image even pretends to be a goddess, but a real woman, looking directly at viewers. Goya's originality here became highly influential to later artists.

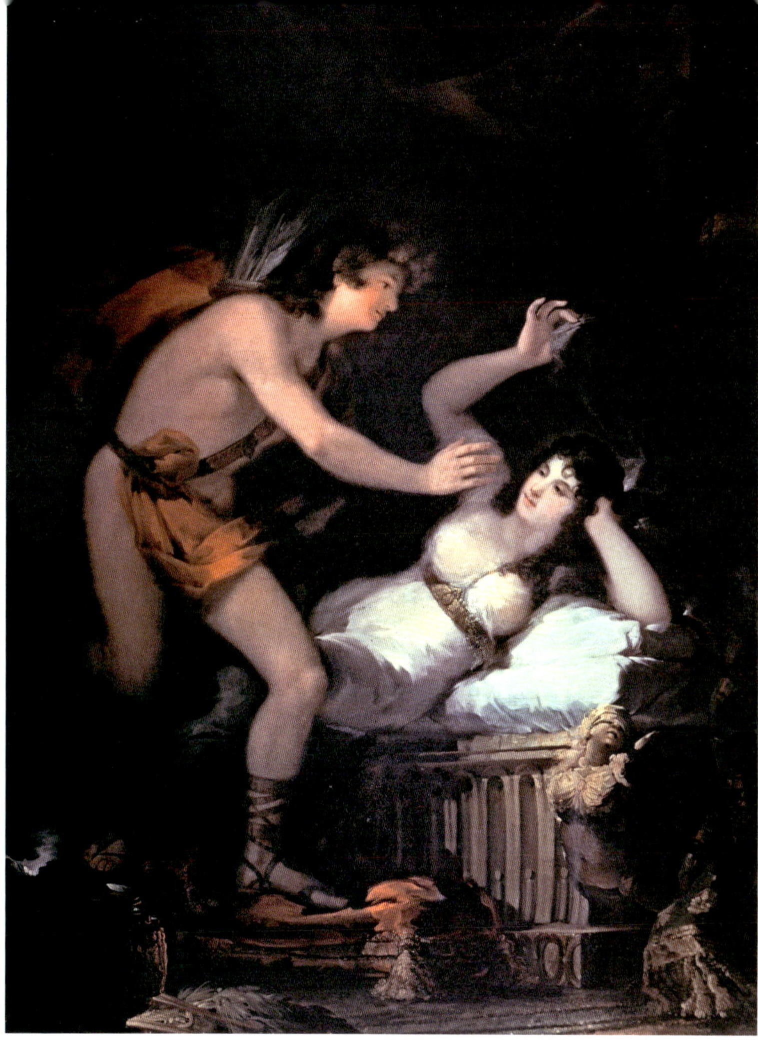

Cupid and Psyche, c.1798–1805, oil on canvas, Museu Nacional d'Art de Catalunya, Barcelona, Spain, 220.5 x 155.5cm (87 x 61in)

Goya painted extremely few mythological works. From the Latin novel *Metamorphoses*, written in the 2nd century CE by Lucius Apuleius (c.125–c.180CE), Cupid, the god of love falls in love with Psyche, a mortal. To conceal his identity, Cupid visits Psyche at night. Goya's composition recalls Titian's painting *Tarquin and Lucretia*, which he knew from the Spanish royal collection.

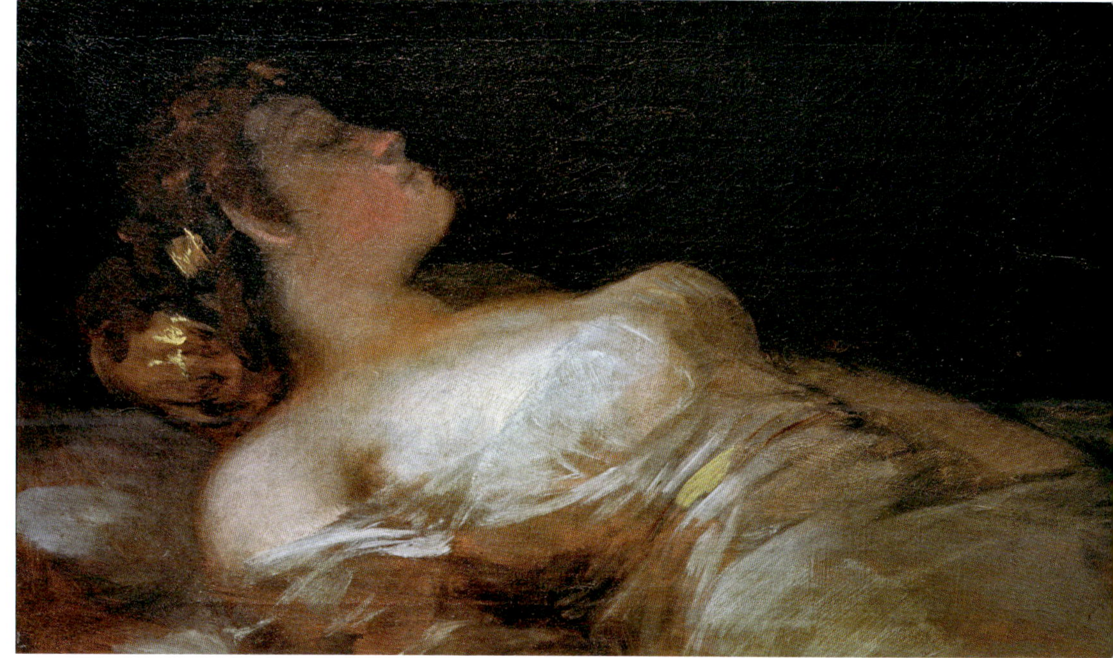

Sleeping Woman or *El Sueño*, c.1798–1808, oil on canvas, Dublin National Gallery, Dublin, Ireland, 44.5 x 76.5cm (17½ x 30in)

The dates and reasons for this painting are unknown, nor who commissioned it. The model is also unidentified. Dreams and sleep recur in Goya's work, but invariably, they are disturbing images. This however, is serene and calm. Goya built up the delicate work with thin-to-thick paint marks using a fairly restricted palette. The chiaroscuro creates a quiet, intimate atmosphere, as if viewers have intruded on the sleeping woman.

Portrait of María Teresa, Countess of Chinchón, c.1798, oil on canvas, Galleria degli Uffizi, Florence, Italy, 220 x 140cm (86½ x 55in)

Having painted the Countess as a child 1783 with her family, Goya felt particularly sympathetic to her. In 1785, at the death of her father, the Infante Don Luís, María Teresa de Borbón y Vallabriga was taken from her mother and sent to a convent where she remained for 12 years, until at 19 she was married to Godoy, who insisted on his mistress Pepita living with them.

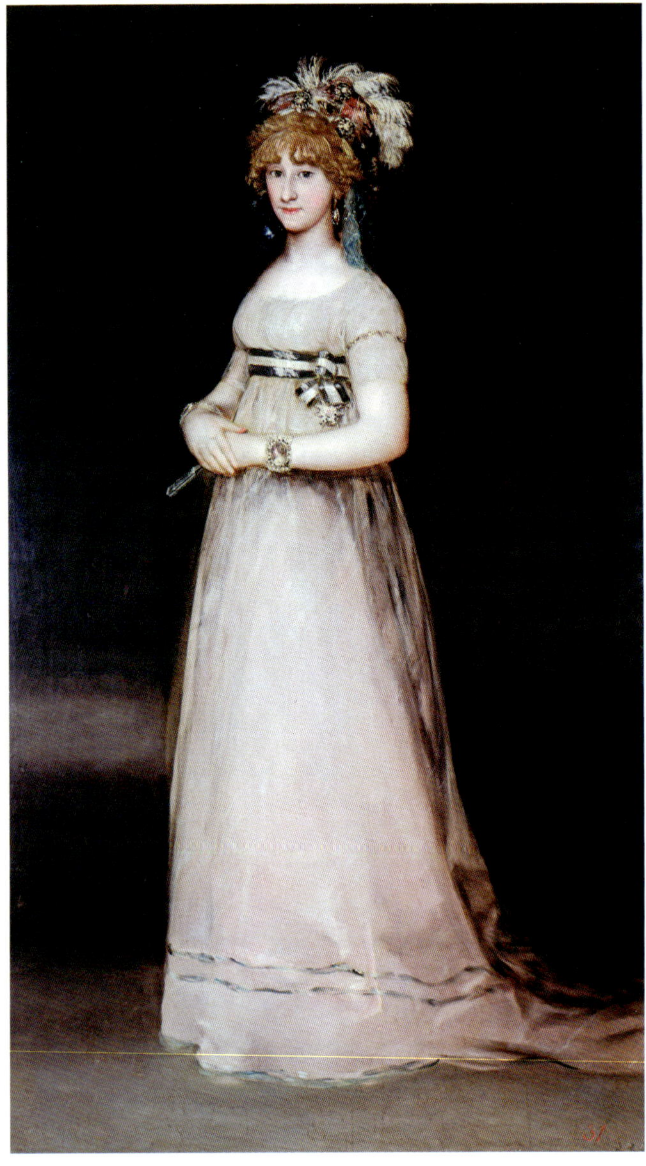

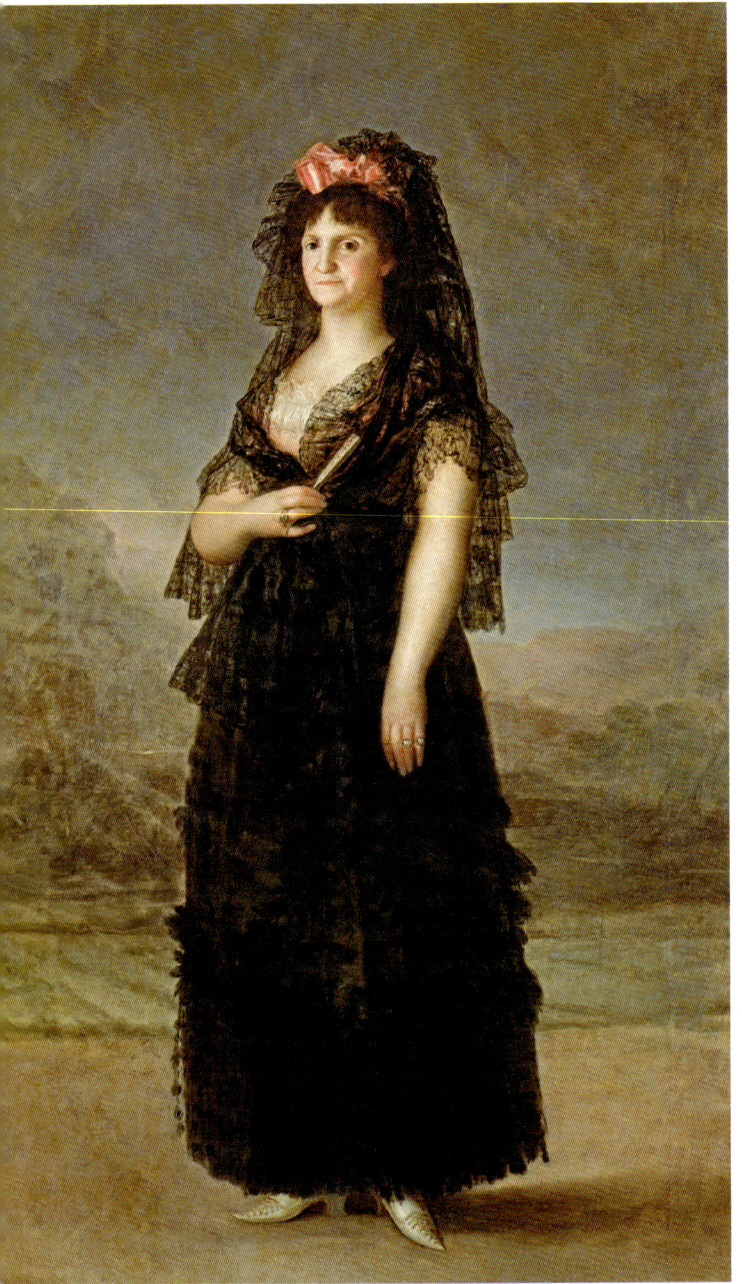

María Luísa of Bourbon-Parma, Queen of Spain, with a Mantilla, 1799–1800, oil on canvas, Museo Nacional del Prado, Madrid, Spain, 208 x 127cm (82 x 50in)

Supremely confident of his position as First Painter to the King, Goya boldly painted this portrait of the Queen with no attempt at flattery. With all his portraits, he attempted to bring out his sitter's personalities and he shows the Queen as complacent, lacking in self-awareness and rather foolish. Although the work appears detailed, Goya painted this loosely, making only essential marks to capture exactly what he saw.

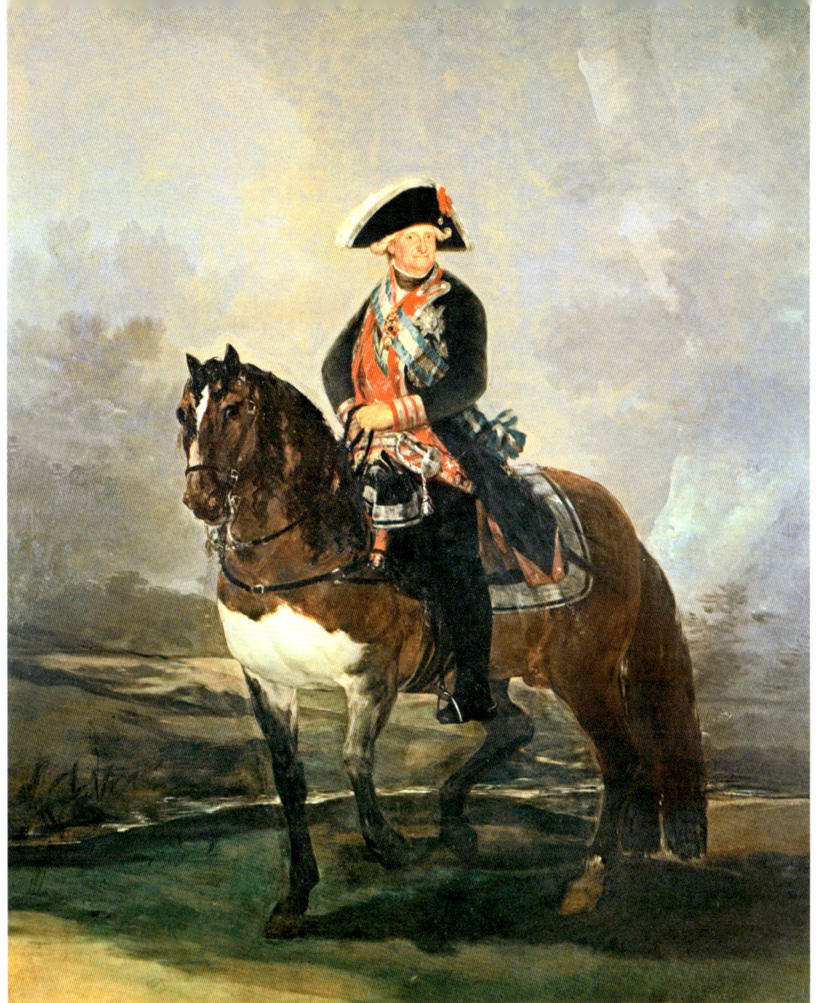

Equestrian Portrait of Charles IV, 1800–1, oil on canvas, Museo Nacional del Prado, Madrid, Spain, 336 x 282cm (132 x 111in)

Dressed in the uniform of a colonel of the Guardia de Corps, the King is also decorated with many honours. Along with its companion portrait of the Queen (see below), this was created to hang in a room with other equestrian portraits of previous Spanish kings and queens, including those by Velázquez. It was an attempt to strengthen the impression of continuity in the House of Bourbon at a difficult time.

Equestrian Portrait of María Luísa, 1799, oil on canvas, Museo Nacional del Prado, Madrid, Spain, 338 x 282cm (133 x 111in)

A companion painting to the equestrian portrait of the King (see above), the Queen like her husband, is depicted wearing the uniform of a colonel of the Guardia de Corps. She is mounted on Marcial, a horse given to her by Godoy. In the background can be seen the Monastery of El Escorial and the mountains of the Sierra Madrileña. Remarkably, Goya completed this portrait in three sittings.

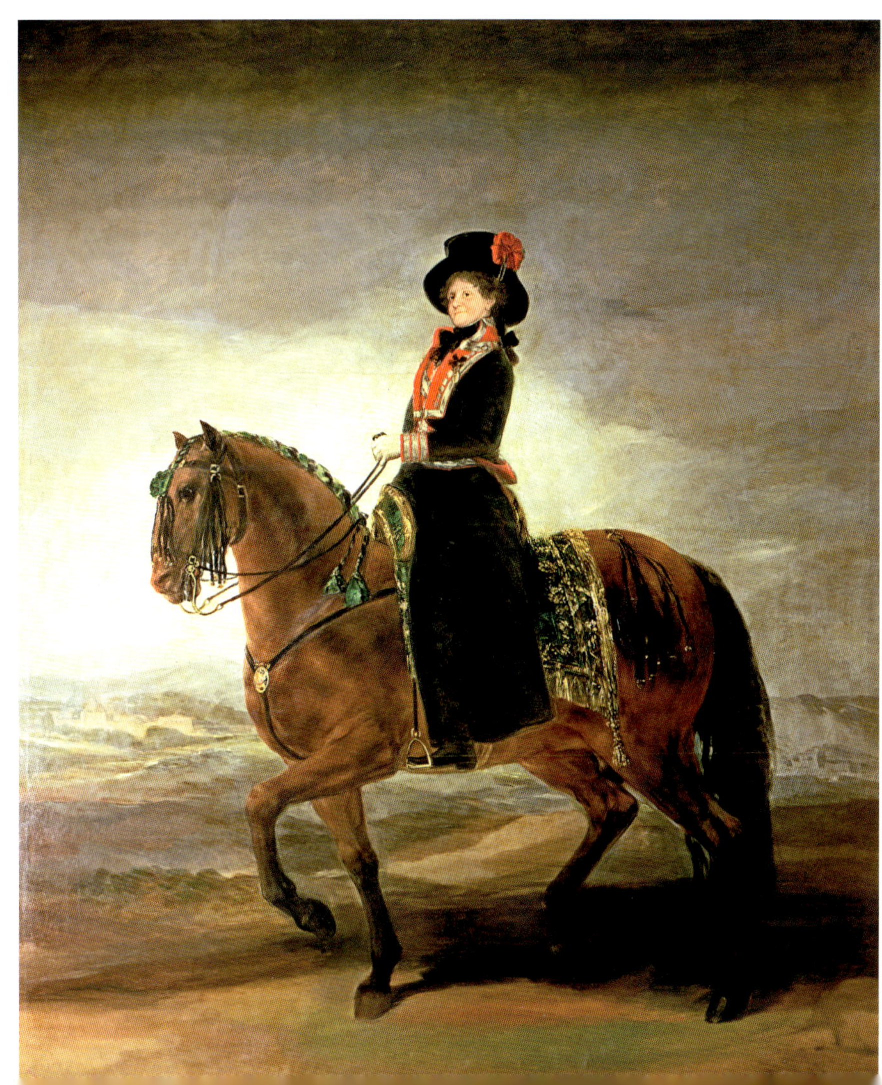

Queen María Luísa, 1799, oil on canvas, Private Collection, 63 x 52cm (25 x 20½in)

Despite the controversy over his *Caprichos*, Goya was still commissioned to paint portraits of the royals and nobles at Court. It was a great period of portraiture for him and his services were in great demand. Despite his free brushstrokes and vivacity, he always planned his work carefully. This was the sketch he made in preparation for the equestrian portrait of the Queen (see page 197).

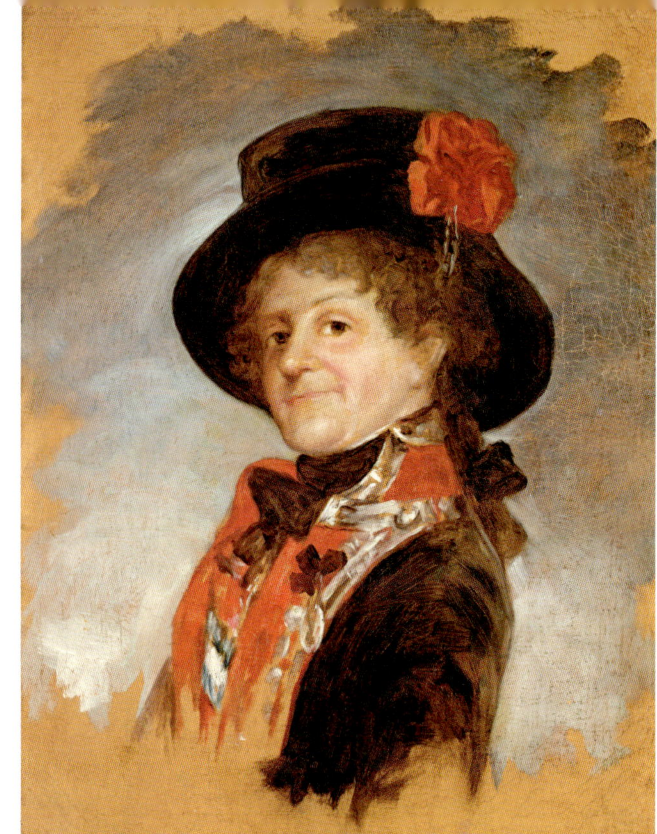

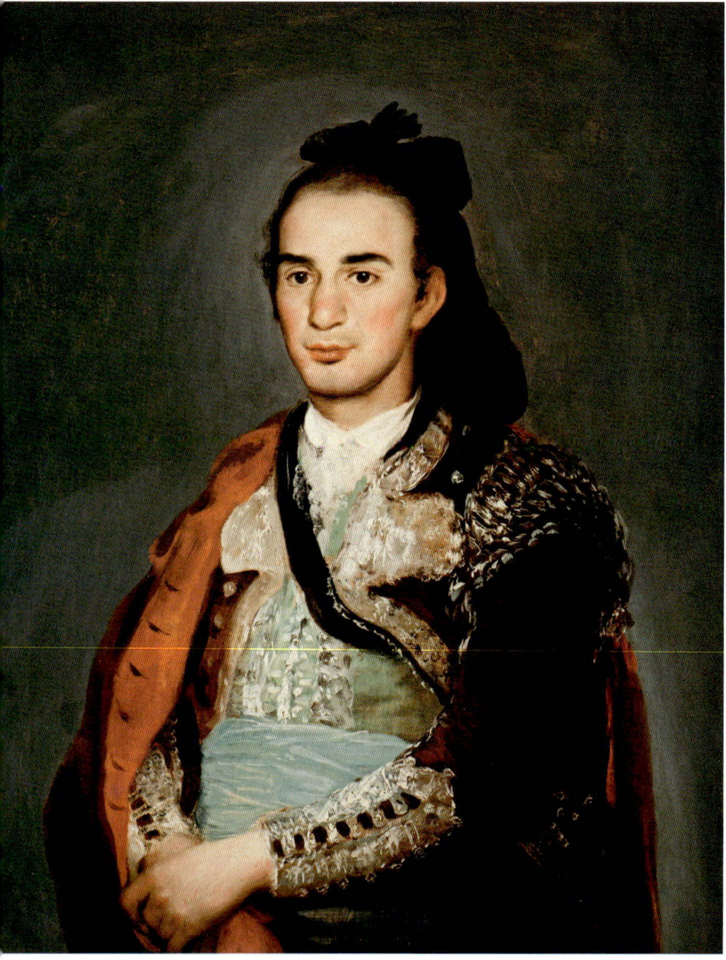

Portrait of the Toreador José Romero, c.1795, oil on canvas, Philadelphia Museum of Art, Pennsylvania, USA, 92.2 x 75.9cm (36½ x 30in)

An inscription on the back of this canvas explains that pieces of Romero's costume were given to him by admirers, including the Duchess of Alba. The inscription goes on to praise Romero's skill in killing bulls. While José – a toreador – was not as celebrated as his brother, the matador Pedro (see page 183), this remains a portrait of the bullfighter's character rather than simply his appearance.

Infanta María Josefa, 1800, oil on canvas, Museo Nacional del Prado, Madrid, Spain, 74 x 60cm (29 x 23½in)

This is María Josefa (1744–1801), the sister of Charles IV. Never married, she had lived at her father's Court and later with her brother Charles IV. Within the Spanish Court, she had assumed a role of minor importance, but she died shortly after this sketch and the family portrait were executed. Goya never flattered his subjects and with her bird-like features, large jewellery and feathered headdress, she appears slightly ridiculous.

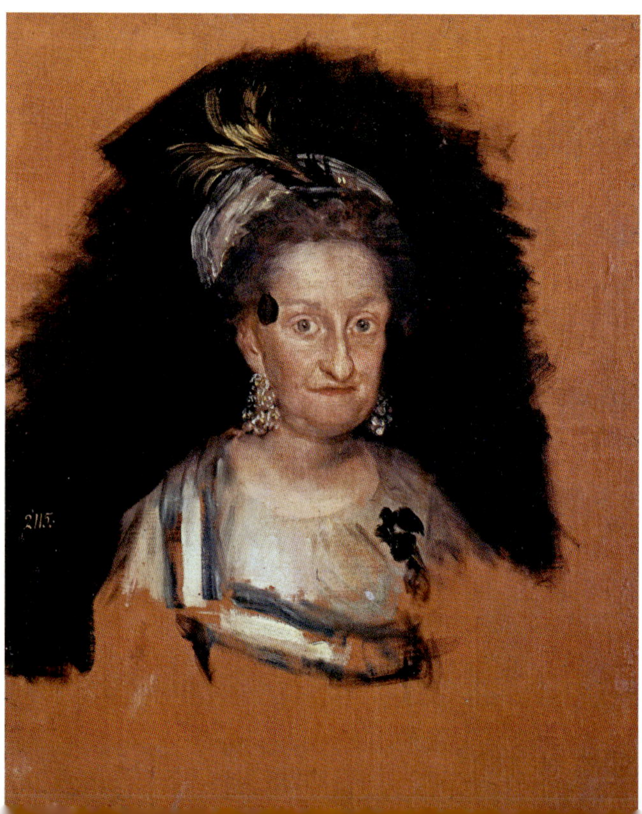

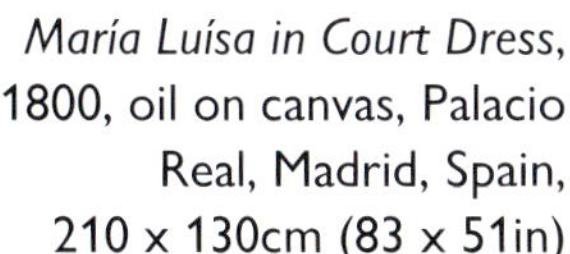

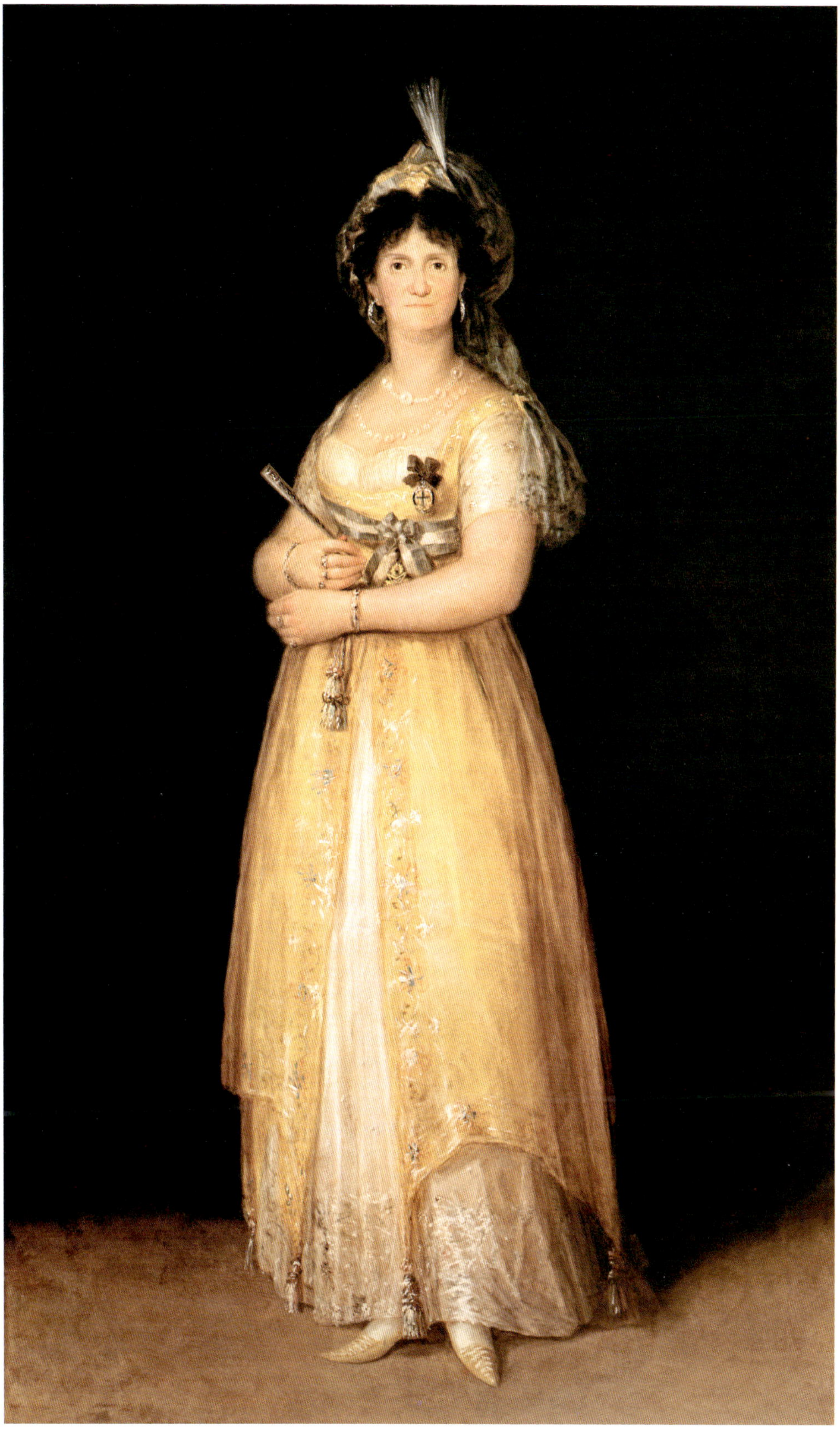

María Luísa in Court Dress, 1800, oil on canvas, Palacio Real, Madrid, Spain, 210 x 130cm (83 x 51in)

The high-waisted, embellished and gauzy silks worn by the Queen at Court followed French fashions closely, after Queen Marie Antoinette. Even María Luísa's ostentatious headdress in this portrait would have been either sent from France or made for her by a French milliner in Madrid. While French fashions were popular with Spanish ladies, Spanish dressmakers could not always interpret them, so French milliners and dressmakers were often employed.

Infante Carlos María Isidro, 1800, oil on canvas, Museo Nacional del Prado, Madrid, Spain, 74 x 60cm (29 x 23½in)

In preparation for the family portrait below, Goya made ten studies from life. Large areas of red underpainting are visible in each. This underpainting was usually concealed by further layers of paint in his finished works. Painted in May 1800, the Infante was then second in line to the throne. Thirty-three years later, on the death of his brother Ferdinand VII, he fought for the throne against his niece.

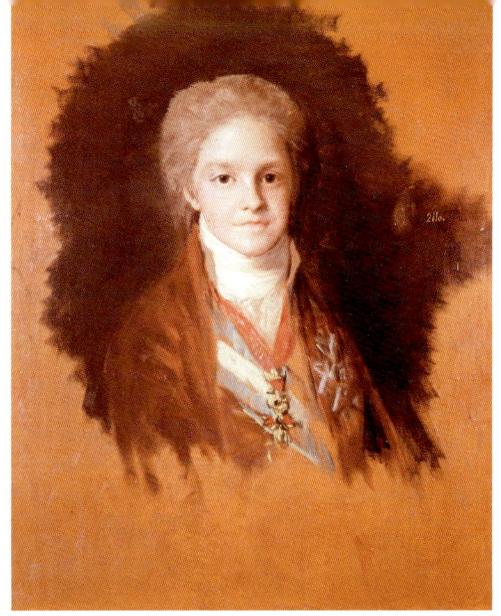

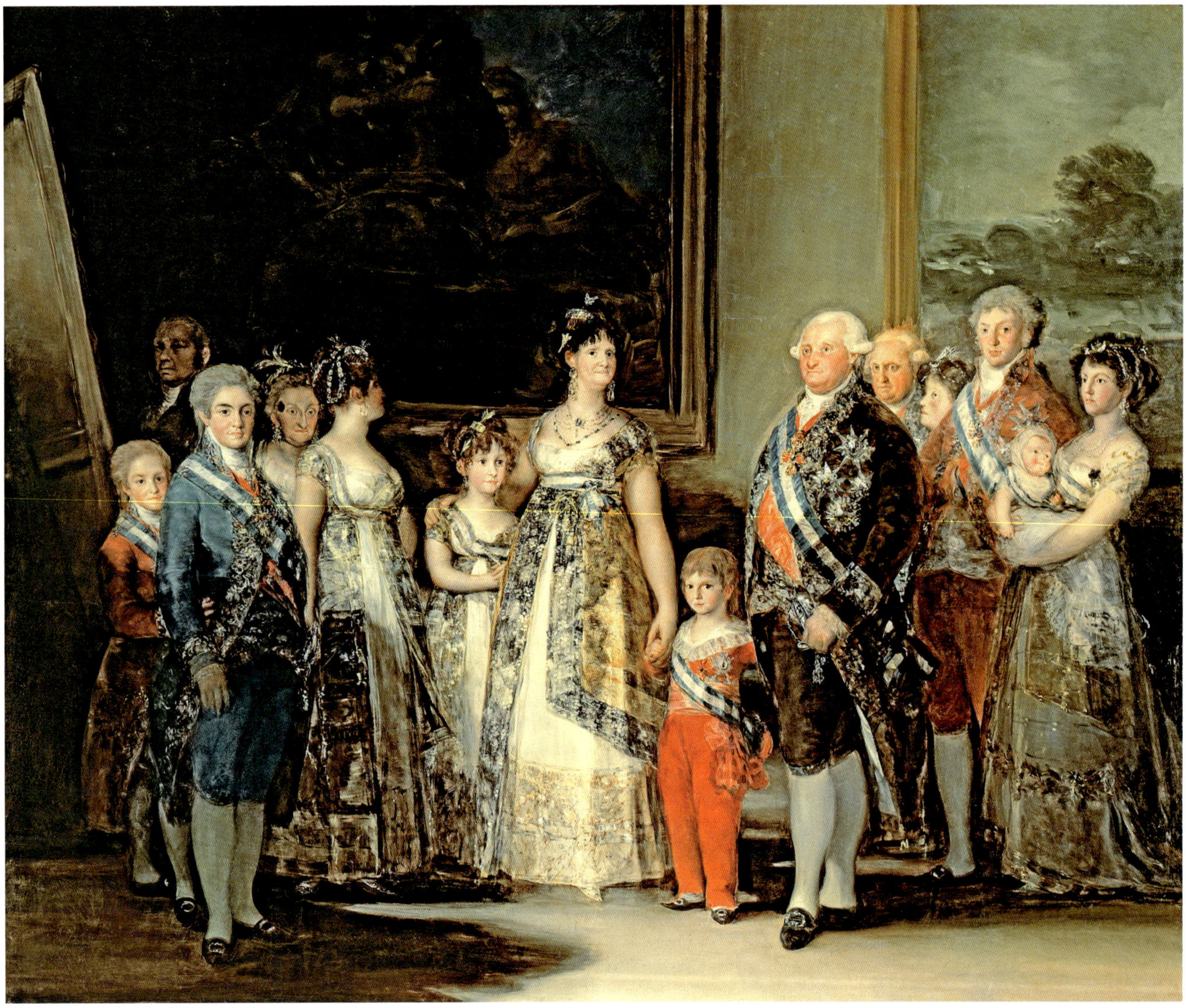

The Family of Charles IV, 1800–1, oil on canvas, Museo Nacional del Prado, Madrid, Spain, 280 x 336cm (110 x 132in)

A combination of yellow, grey and blue interspersed with touches of red, this was painted in Aranjuez and Madrid. Goya has individualized each character. The fussily-dressed Queen is in the centre, with the King standing, looking vacant, to her left. Their children surround them. The future Fernando VII is in shadow apart from his face. The adults appear superficial, detached, arrogant and materialistic.

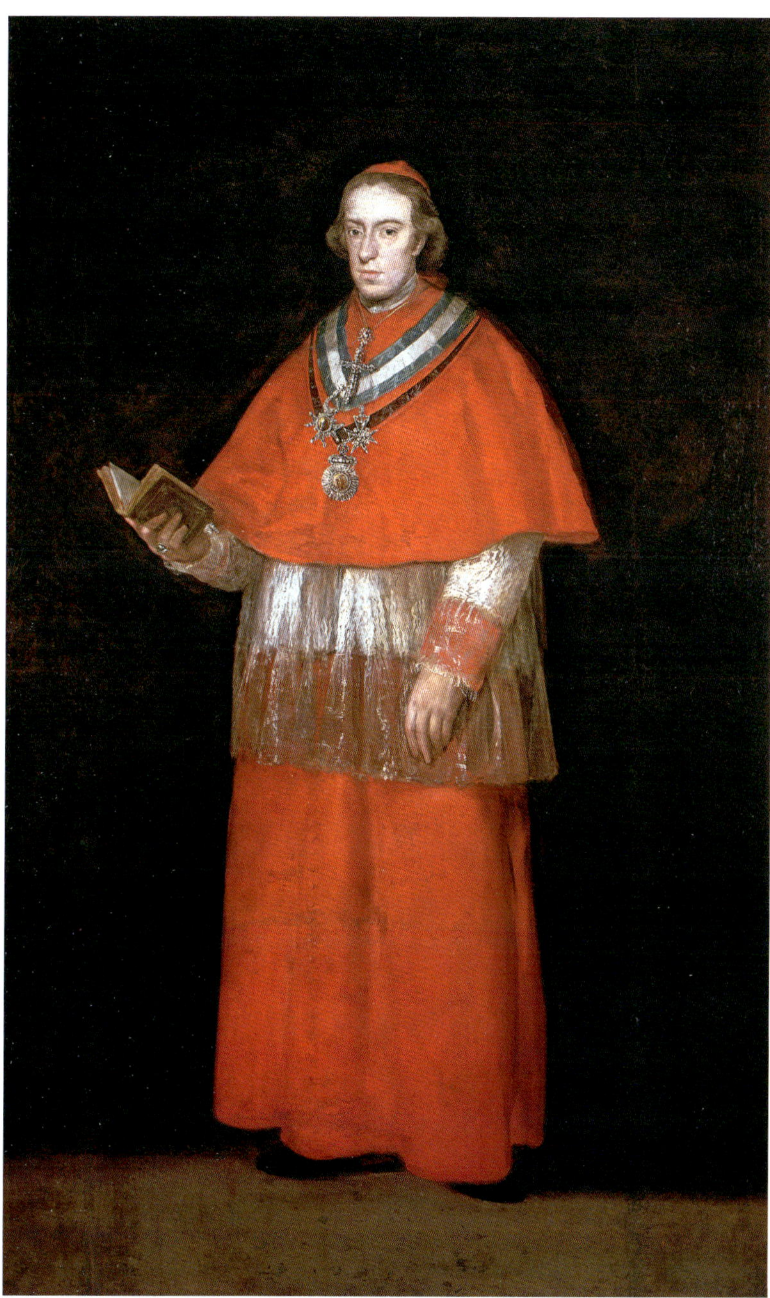

Cardinal Luís María de Borbón y Vallabriga, c.1800, oil on canvas, Museo Nacional del Prado, Madrid, Spain, 214 x 136cm (84 x 53½in)

The son of the Infante Don Luís, and elder brother of the Countess of Chinchón, Cardinal Luís had known Goya since he was a child. On the death of his father in 1785, as his mother was a commoner, he had gone into care with monks in Toledo. Through his sister's marriage to Godoy however, the family was able to use the surname Bourbon once again and they were awarded the status of grandees of Spain. Pictured here at the age of 23, Don Luís junior was both Cardinal and Archbishop of Toledo.

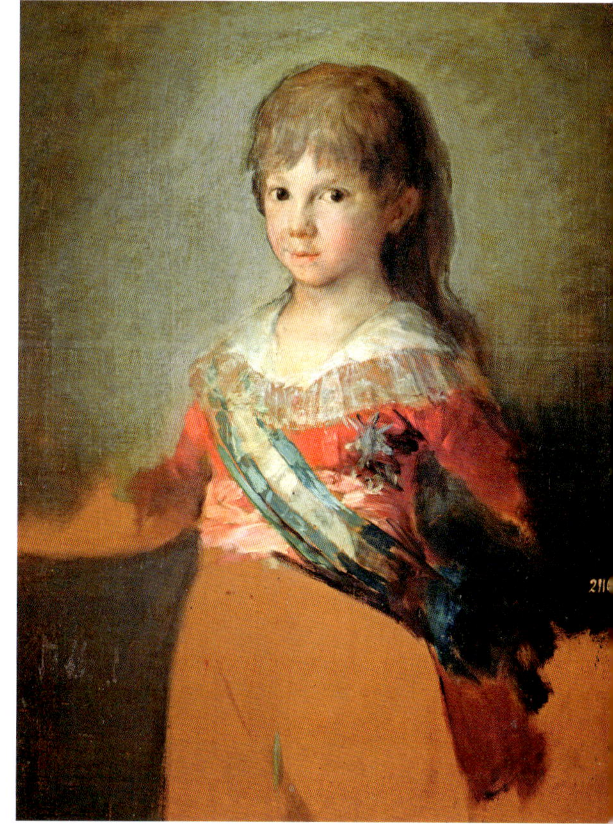

Infante Francisco de Paula Antonio, 1800, oil on canvas, Museo Nacional del Prado, Madrid, Spain, 74 x 60cm (29 x 23½in)

While Goya's image of the Infanta María Josefa shows her as a foolish, ignorant woman (see page 198). In contrast, this portrait sketch of her nephew, six-year-old Infante Don Francisco de Paula Antonio displays innocence and openness. This unfinished sketch shows Goya's method. He used the reddish paint in smooth, long strokes as a vibrant underpainting, building up small, looser brush marks to describe skin, hair and clothing.

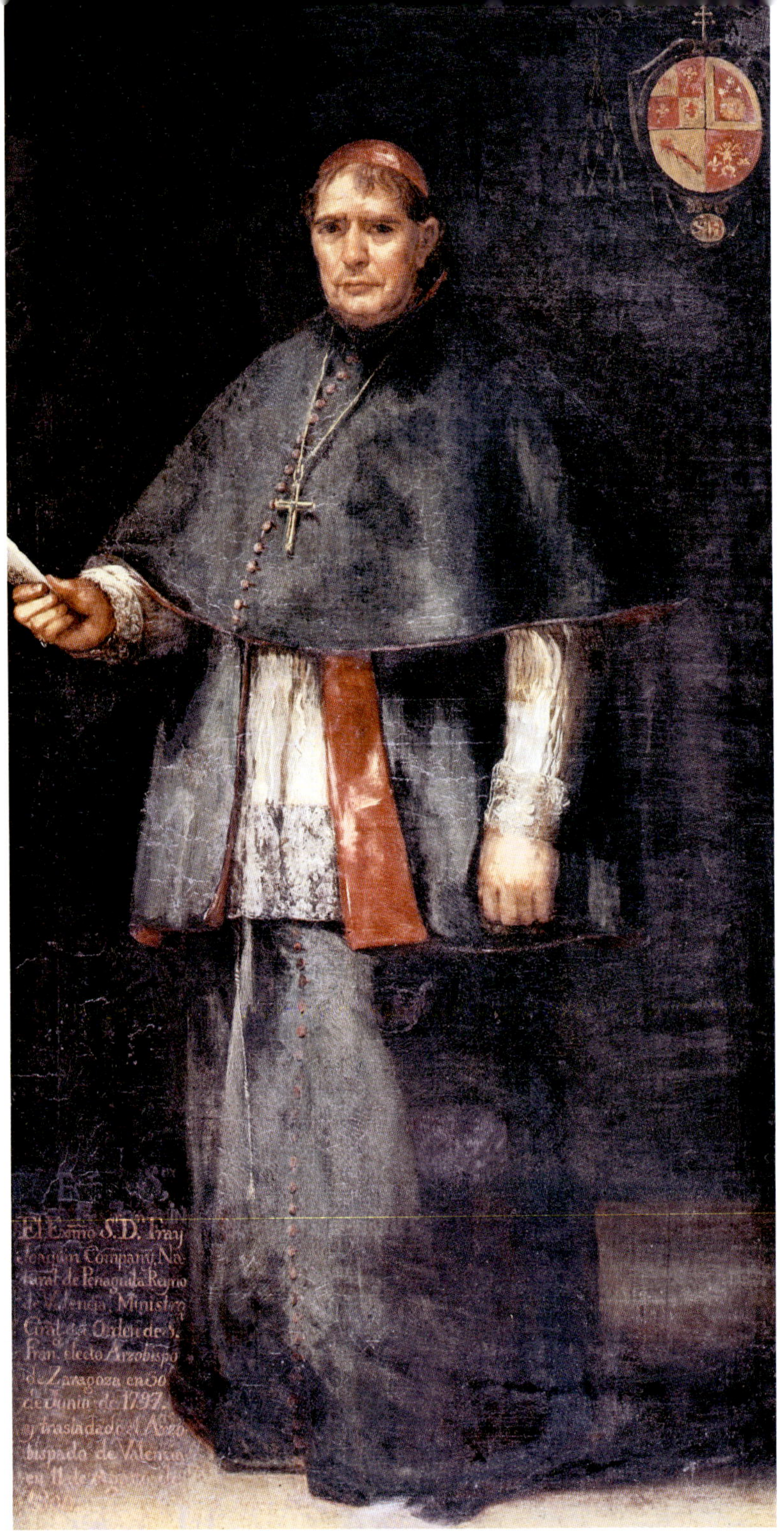

Archbishop Joaquín Company, 1800–1, oil on canvas, Palacio Arzobispal Saragossa, Saragossa, Spain, 199 x 102.5cm (78 x 40in)

A symphony in black and grey, Goya produced this portrait of Archbishop Joaquín Company (1732–1813), 70 years before *Whistler's Mother* was painted. This and another closer portrait (see below) were executed in celebration of the Archbishop moving to Valencia from Saragossa in 1800. Born in Saragossa, Joaquín was archbishop there from 1797 to 1800. His gentle and considerate character is made apparent in Goya's expressive work.

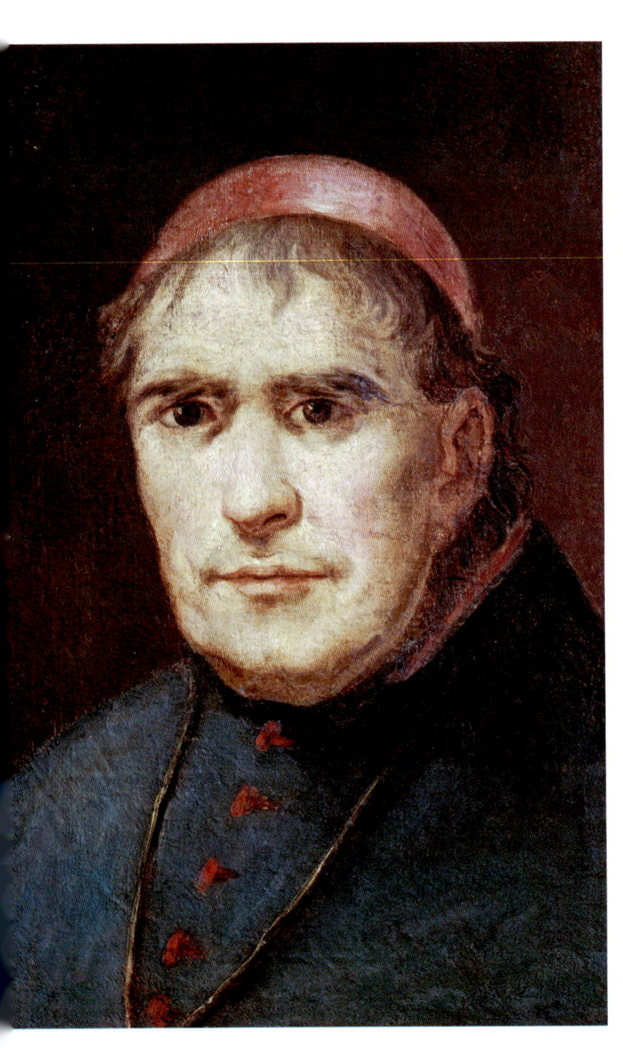

Archbishop Joaquín Company, c.1800, oil on canvas, Museo Nacional del Prado, Madrid, Spain, 44 x 31cm (17 x 12in)

In another portrait of Archbishop Joaquín Company from the same time as the above portrait, Goya's brushstrokes are even sketchier and looser. For this reason, it is believed that this was probably a preparatory sketch for one of the two official portraits Goya painted of the Archbishop.

In highlighting his sitter's face with a strong, clear light, Goya has projected an open and honest personality, with no underhanded traits.

Agriculture, 1804–6, tempera on canvas, Museo Nacional del Prado, Madrid, Spain, diameter: 227cm (89in)

Originally dated at 1797–1802, this allegory of Agriculture is now believed to have been executed between 1804 and 1806, as part of the decoration of the grand staircase of Godoy's palace, as documents have been discovered confirming that Goya undertook the restoration of the building between 1801 and 1805. He made three other companion circular works, or tondos (see page 204). Here, the goddess Ceres represents fertility and abundance.

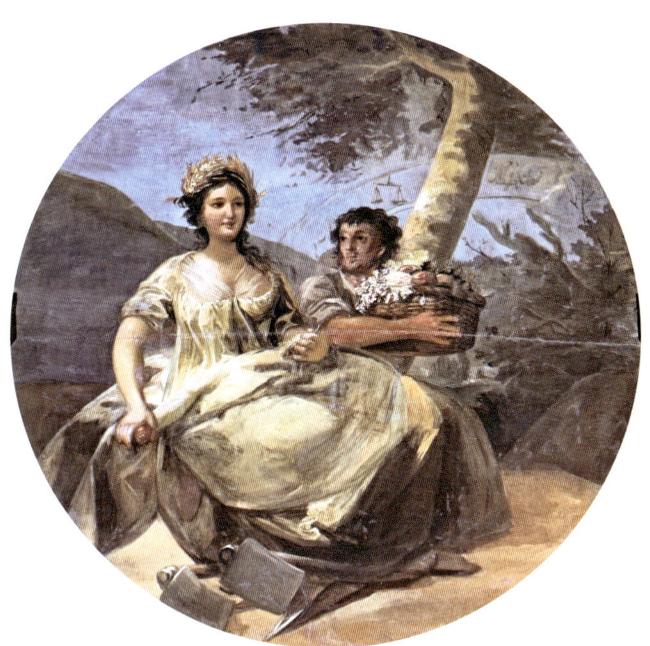

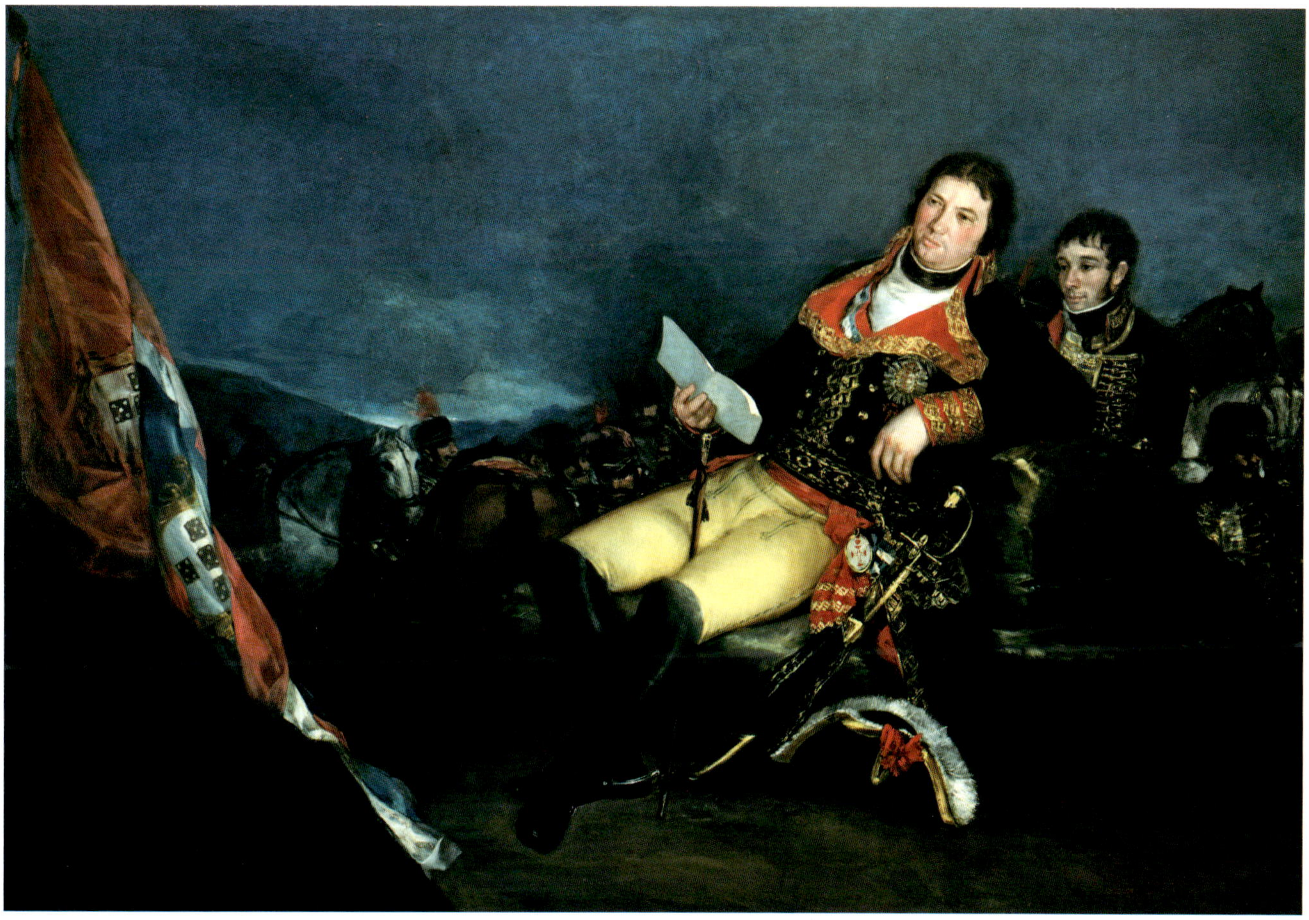

Portrait of Manuel Godoy, 1801, oil on canvas, Real Academia de Bellas Artes de San Fernando, Madrid, Spain, 180 x 267cm (71 x 105in)

Self-important and rather bloated, this was the most powerful man in Spain. Godoy's rapid rise to power, attributed to his liaison with the Queen, made him notorious and resented. This portrait was painted between July and October 1801 to commemorate his victory in Portugal with the 'War of the Oranges.' Goya has been rather disrespectful, and also targeted Godoy in several plates of *Los Caprichos*, yet this did not seem to harm their relationship.

Industry, 1804–6, tempera on canvas, Museo Nacional del Prado, Madrid, Spain, diameter: 227cm (89in)

A companion tondo to the allegories of Agriculture (see page 203), Commerce and Science, this represents Industry, and was part of the decoration of the grand staircase of Godoy's palace. Each of the four tondos were created to announce and promote Godoy's good work as Prime Minister. For this, Goya was inspired by Velázquez's painting *The Spinners* of *c*.1657. Two young women are spinning bathed in light; suggesting the light of progress.

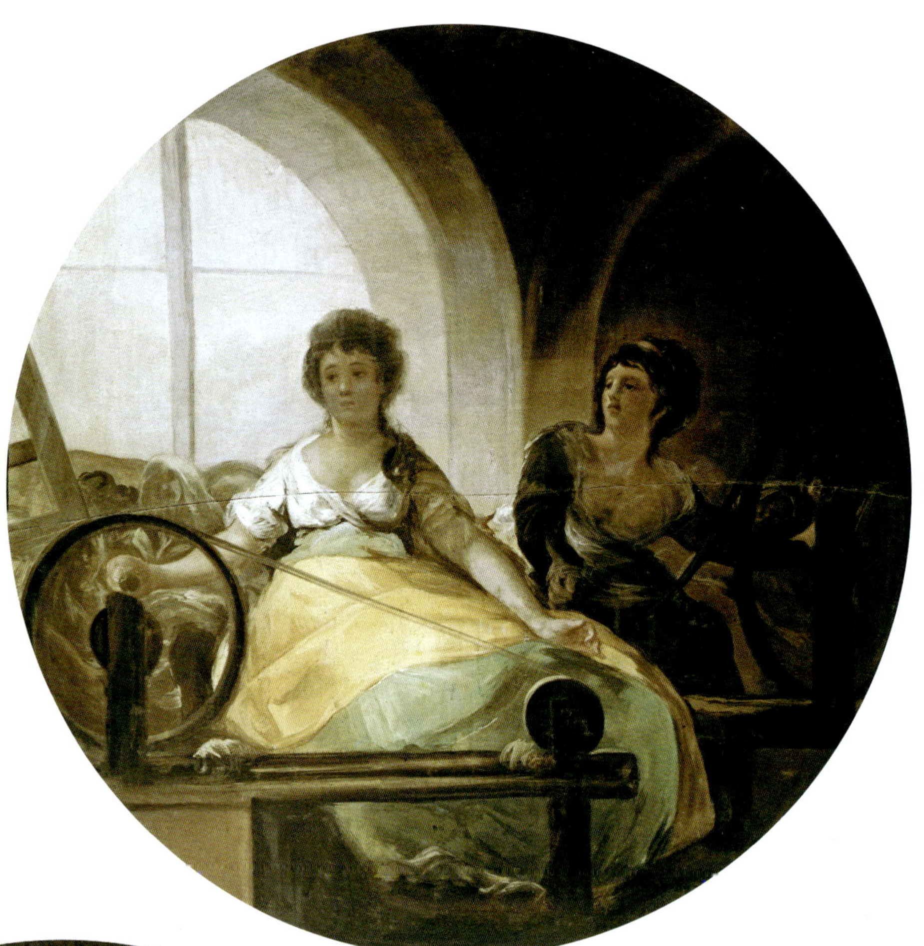

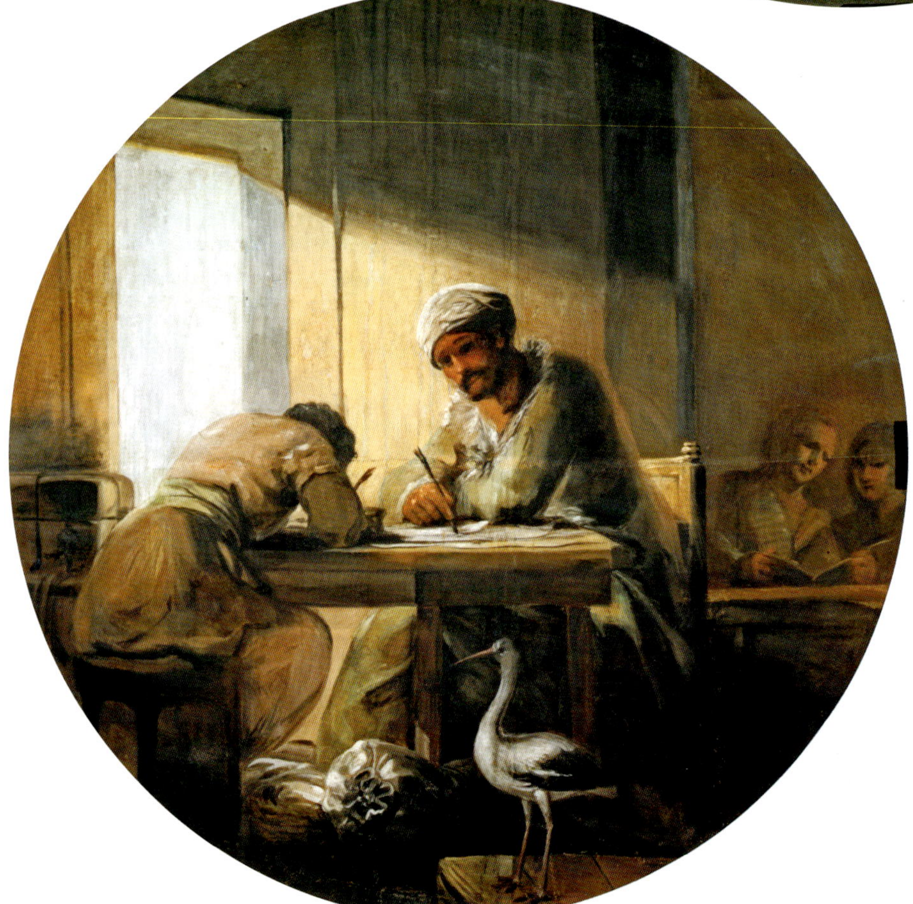

Commerce, 1804-6, tempera on canvas, Museo Nacional del Prado, Madrid, Spain, diameter: 227cm (89in)

This tondo represents Commerce and complemented the others. All four of the allegories symbolized some of the ideals of the Enlightenment. Here, trade is being undertaken with merchants from the East; an essential element of commerce and progress at that time. The stork in the foreground represents trust and loyalty. The whereabouts of the fourth composition of Science is currently unknown.

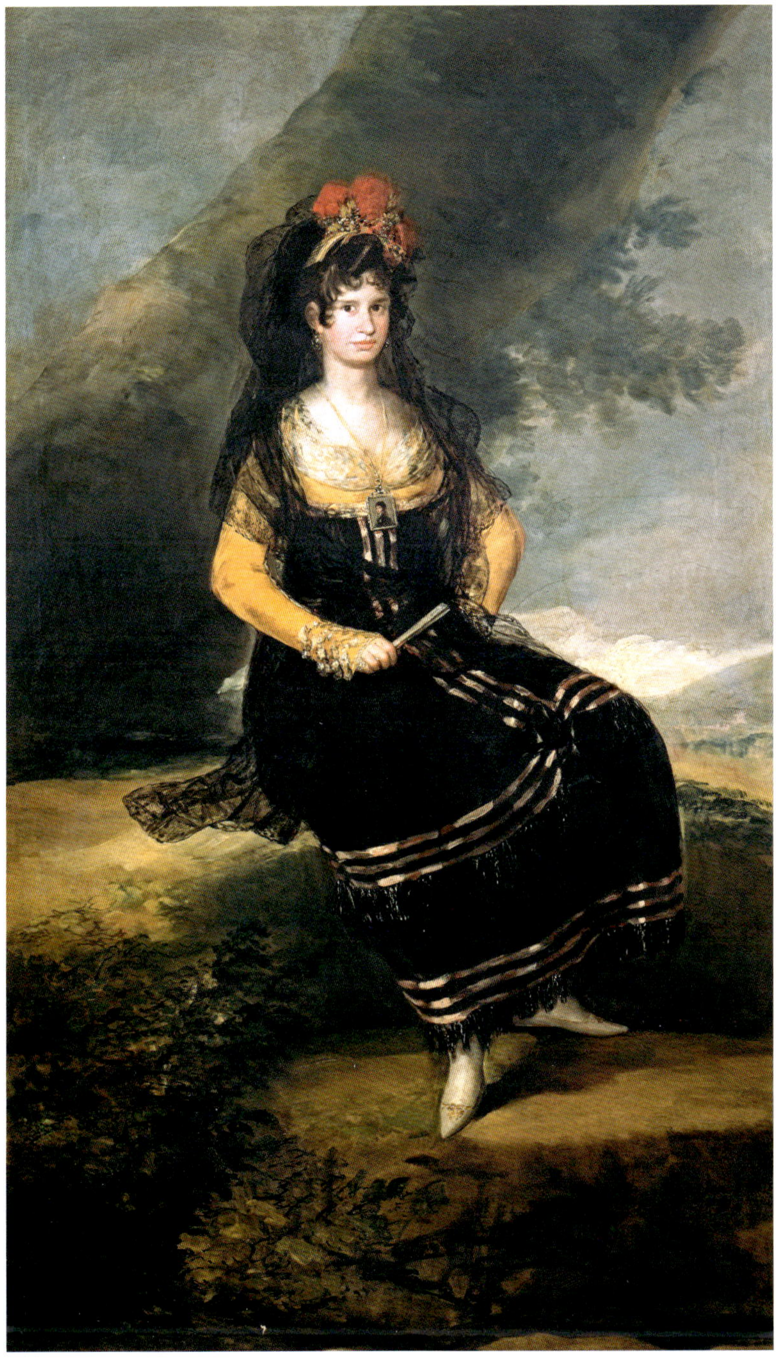

Countess of Nuñez, 1803, oil
on canvas, Private Collection,
211 x 137cm (83 x 54in)

Between 1800 and 1808
Goya produced many varied
portraits, all breaking with
stereotypical, contemporary
portrait styles, and creating
individual works for each of
his clients. Here, the 23-year-
old Countess of Fernán
Nuñez, María Vicenta Solís
Lasso de la Vega, sits on
a tree trunk in a highly
fashionable costume, including
a short jacket, mantilla, fichu
and large red ribbon, that
contrasted with the Queen's
French style.

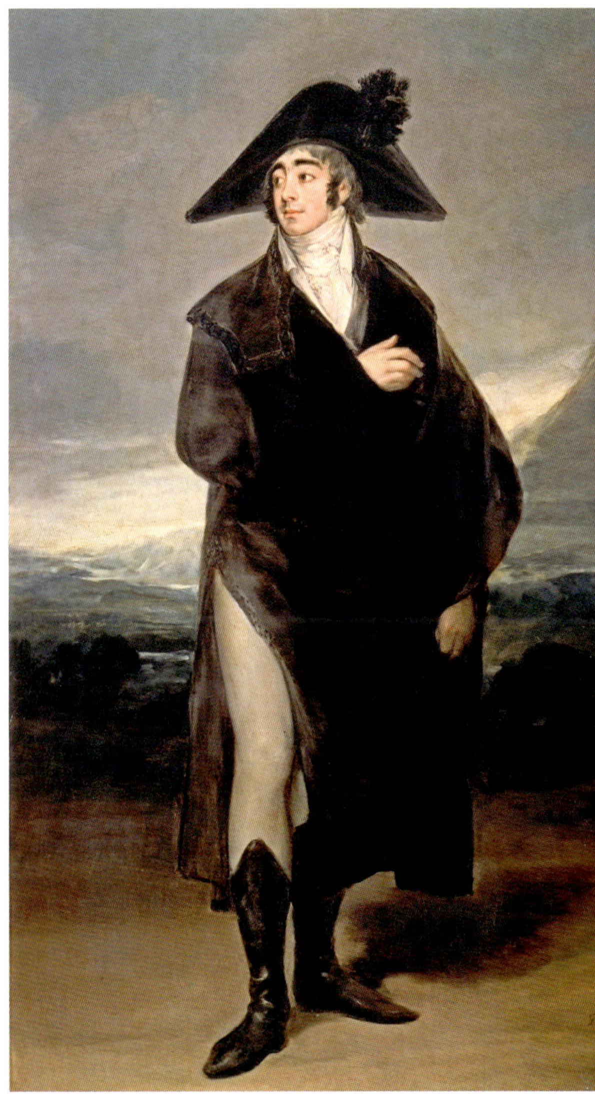

Count Fernán Nuñez, 1803,
oil on canvas, Private
Collection, 211 x 137cm
(83 x 54in)

Don Carlos Gutiérrez de los
Ríos y Sarmiento was the
seventh Count of Fernán
Núñez, later raised to
dukedom. His wife (above)
was born the Duchess of
Montellano and Arco, but the
marriage was simply a joining
of two noble Spanish houses
and an unhappy match.
Goya set the count against
a landscape, reminiscent of
both contemporary English
portraiture and the work of
Velázquez. Rapid brushwork
expresses texture
with vivacity.

Portrait of Joaquina Candado Ricarte, c.1802–4, oil on canvas, Museu de Belles Arts de Valencia, Valencia, Spain, 169 x 118.3cm (66½ x 46½in)

While this is usually identified as the noblewoman, Joaquina Candando Ricarte, this is not substantiated. The subject of the painting is elegant in a fashionable black chiffon Empire line dress, with a flowing black mantilla and fine suede long gloves, The dainty poodle – a symbol of her aristocracy – conveys her high social status. Sitting on a tree trunk in an open space, the young woman boldly watches the viewers.

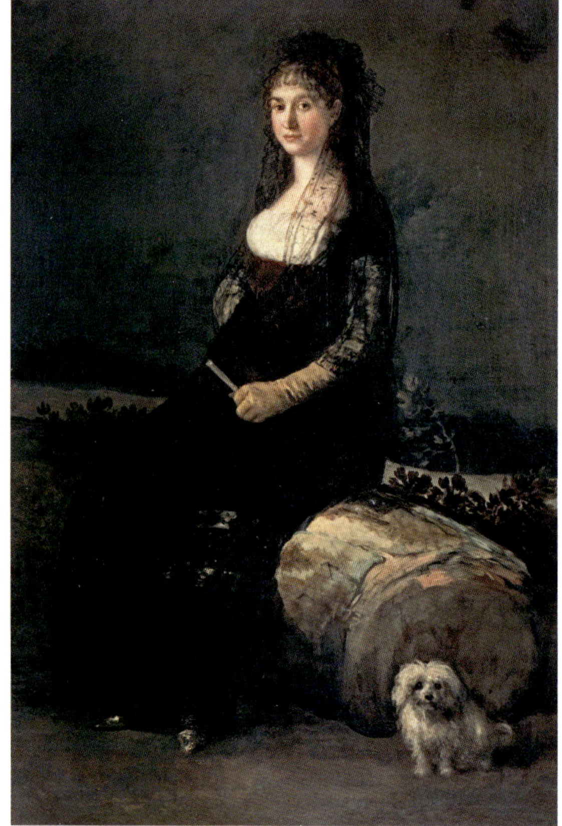

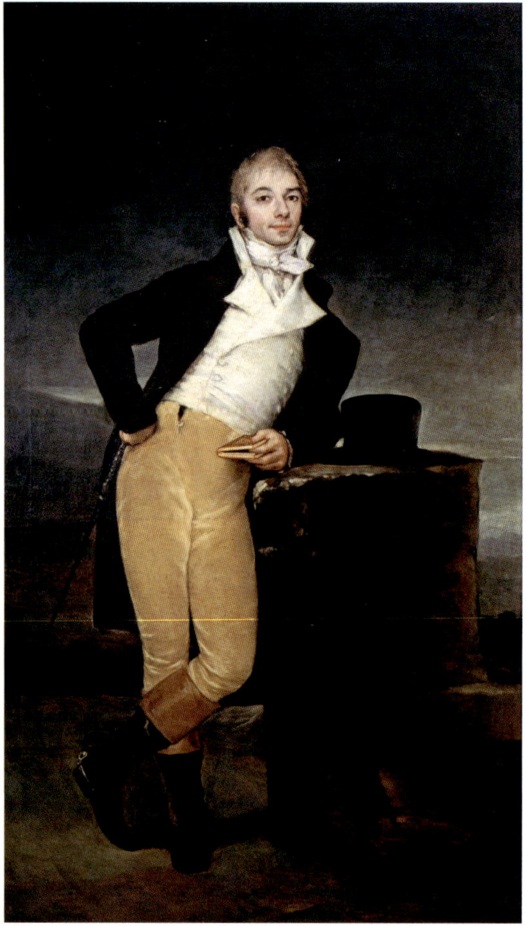

Marquis of San Adrian, 1804, oil on canvas, Museo de Navarra, Pamplona, Spain, 209 x 127cm (82 x 50in)

Despite suffering with ill-health and risking so much with the publication of his satirical prints, Goya's work had never been so much in demand. Following ideas of English Neoclassical portaitists, he placed Don José María Magallón y Armendáriz in the open air, leaning against two large blocks of stone. His bright dress shirt, waistcoat ochre breeches and riding boots with gold spurs lead viewers' eyes to his face.

Maria Tomasa Palafox y Portocarrero, Marchioness of Villafranca painting her husband, 1804, oil on canvas, Museo Nacional del Prado, Madrid, Spain, 195 x 126cm (77 x 49½in)

María Tomasa was the wife of the 11th Marquis of Villafranca. This is an unusual portrait by Goya. He depicts María, an amateur artist, sitting in a damask armchair at an easel, painting a portrait of her husband. Other accoutrements of painting are around her. The Marchioness was a lady of culture, a member of the Royal Academy of Fine Arts of San Fernando, and lover of the arts.

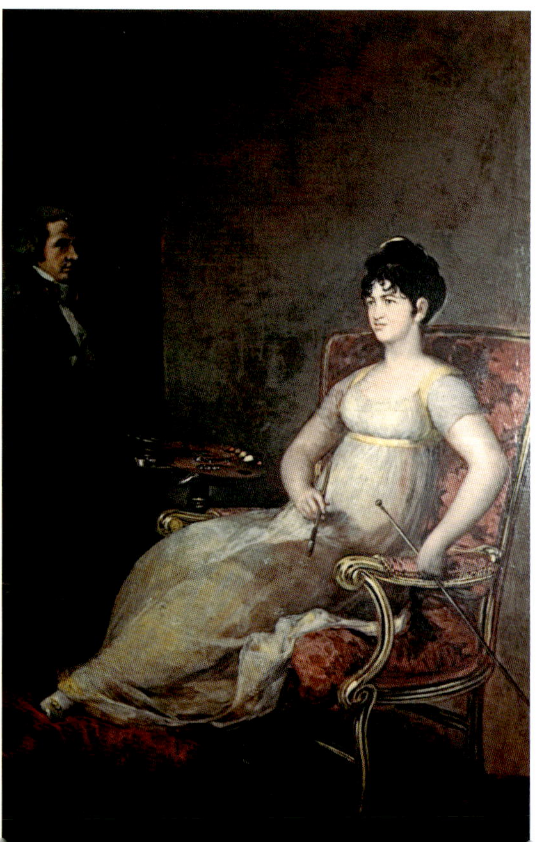

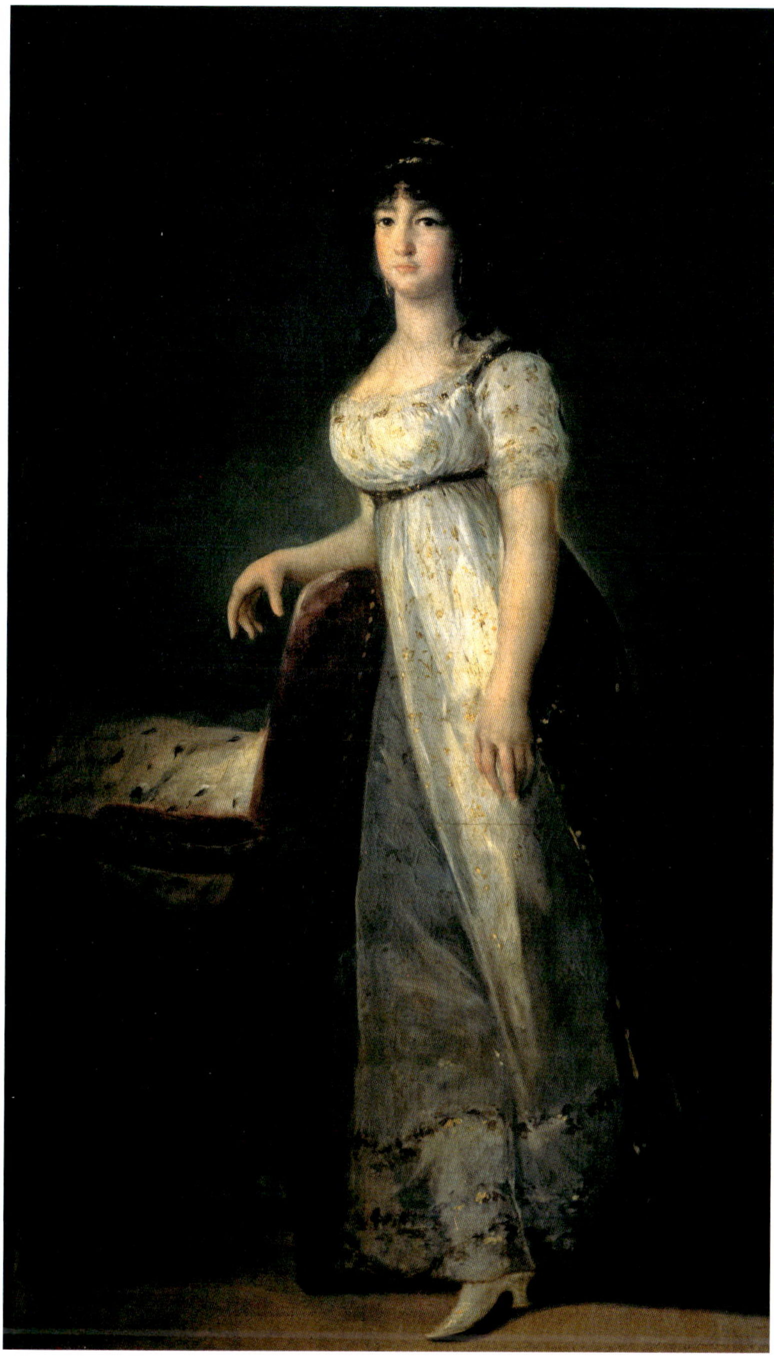

Bartolomé Sureda, c.1804–6, oil on canvas, National Gallery of Art, Washington DC, USA, 119.7 x 79.3cm (47 x 31in)

Bartolomé Sureda was a middle-class Spanish intellectual who studied cotton spinning in England and methods of porcelain manufacture in Sèvres, France, in order to introduce the progressive techniques to Spain. In 1802, he was made CEO of the Royal Porcelain Factory at Buen Retiro. Leaning nonchalantly on a pedestal, he appears as a refined young man, while the light illuminates his face and shoulders, suggesting his enlightened views.

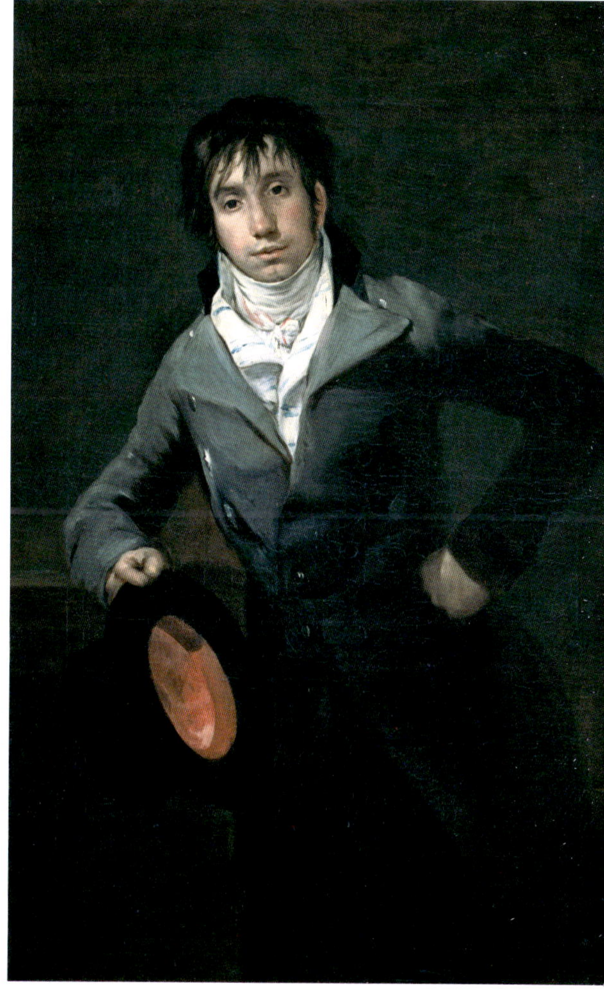

The Marchioness of Lazán, c.1804, oil on canvas, Private Collection, 193 x 115cm (76 x 45in)

Gabriela Maria Palafox y Portocarrero was the Marchioness of Lazán through marriage with her cousin, and a friend of the Prince of Asturias, the future Ferdinand VII. One of the most beautiful young ladies of the Spanish Court, she is shown here at about 25 years old, standing flirtatiously in an Empire style dress, bathed in clear, bright light. The dark background recalls portraits by Titian and Tintoretto.

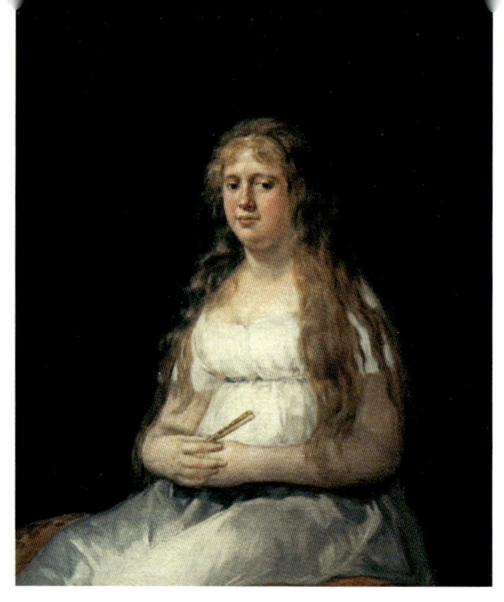

Josefa Castilla Portugal y van Asbrock de Garcini, 1804, oil on canvas, The Metropolitan Museum of Art, New York, USA, 104 x 82cm (41 x 32in)

When Goya painted Doña Garcini as a pendant (one of two paintings conceived as a pair) to the portrait of her husband, Ignacio Garcini y Queralt, she was 20 years old and evidently pregnant, which may account for the informality of her hair and dress. Her mother was of Flemish descent, which explains her voluptuous, blonde looks; a contrast with the dark Spanish beauties Goya usually painted. The influence of Rubens and Rembrandt are discernible.

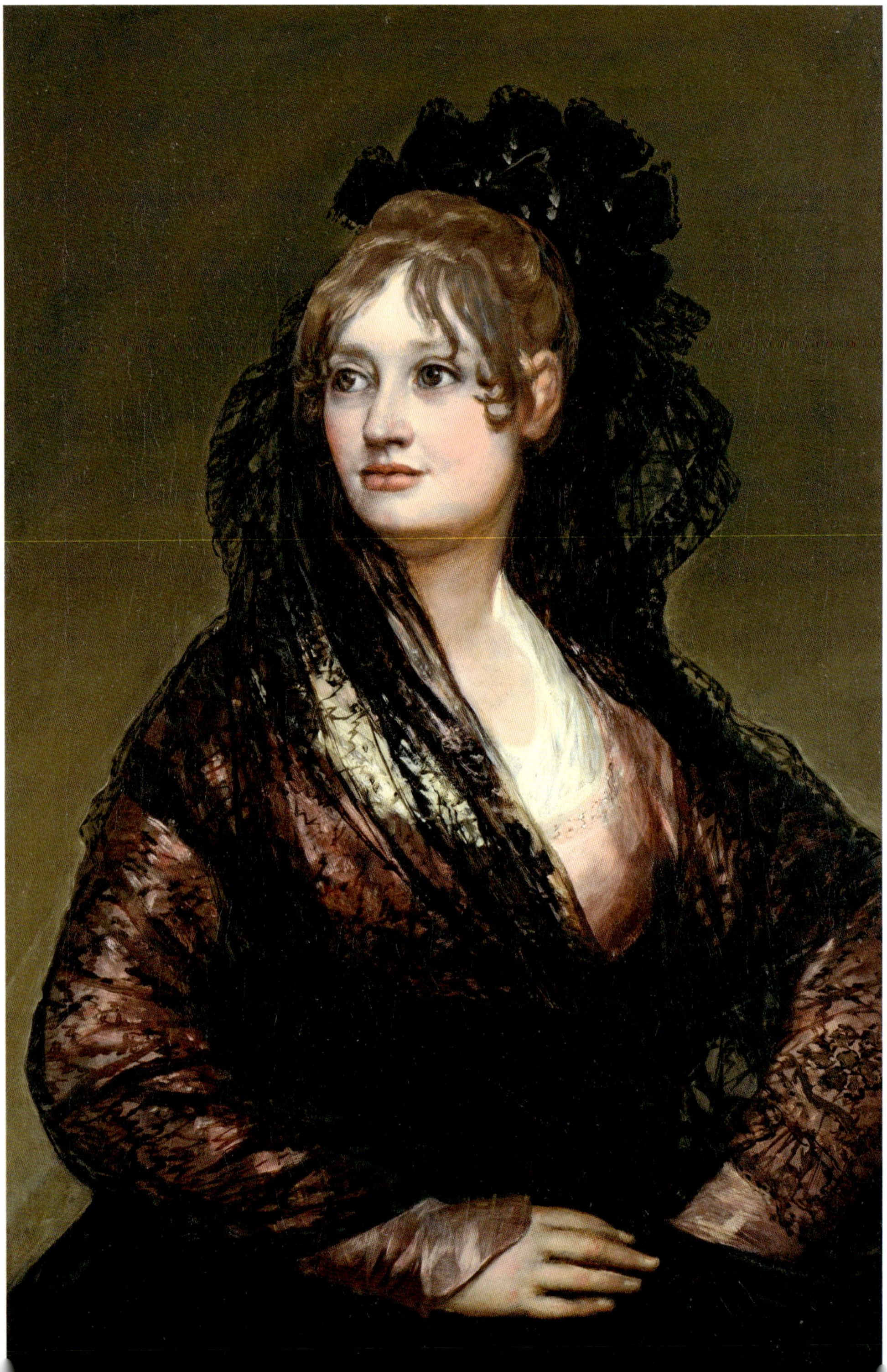

Doña Isabel de Porcel, 1804–5, oil on canvas, The National Gallery, London, UK, 82 x 55cm (32 x 21½in)

Dressed as a maja with the exotic, fashionable costume of Spain, Isabel Lobo Velasco de Porcel was the second wife of Antonio Porcel, a liberal and one of Godoy's associates. The painting was possibly a gift from Goya in return for the couple's hospitality to him. The dark lace mantilla sets off 25-year-old Isabel's pale skin, while her flamenco-style pose emphasizes her costume. The sideways glance was unusual in Goya's portraits.

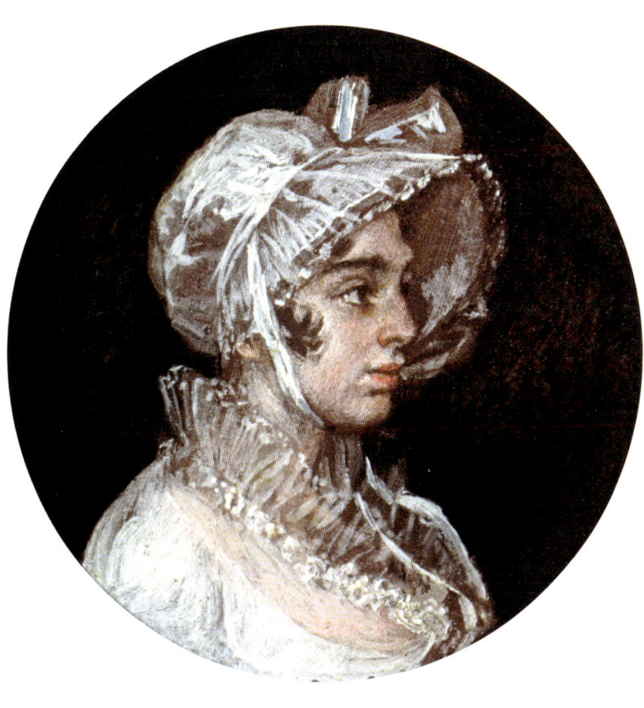

Manuela Goicoechea y Galarza, 1805–6, oil on copper, Museo Nacional del Prado, Madrid, Spain, diameter: 8cm (3in)

The elder sister of Goya's daughter-in-law Gumersinda, Manuela is represented here at the age of 20. The work forms part of a series of miniatures painted by Goya on copper to celebrate the marriage of his son Javier to Gumersinda. This for Goya, was an event of great happiness. He adored his son and was friends with Manuela and Gumersinda's parents, Juana Galarza and Martin Miguel de Goicoechea.

Joaquina Téllez-Girón and Pimentel, Marchioness of Santa Cruz, 1805, oil on canvas, Museo Nacional del Prado, Madrid, Spain, 124.7 x 207.7cm (49 x 82in)

The daughter of the ninth Duke of Osuna, Doña Joaquina Téllez-Girón and Pimentel was one of the most admired ladies at Court, representing the ideal of the cultivated aristocrat; a modern, educated young woman with an understanding of the Enlightenment. Portrayed here in her 20s, the unusual portrait follows a Neoclassical style, as she reclines in an elegant white chiffon dress, holding a lyre-shaped guitar.

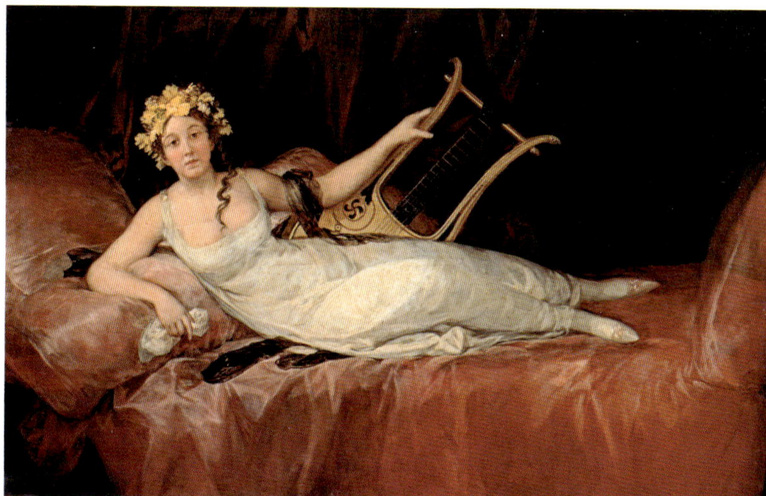

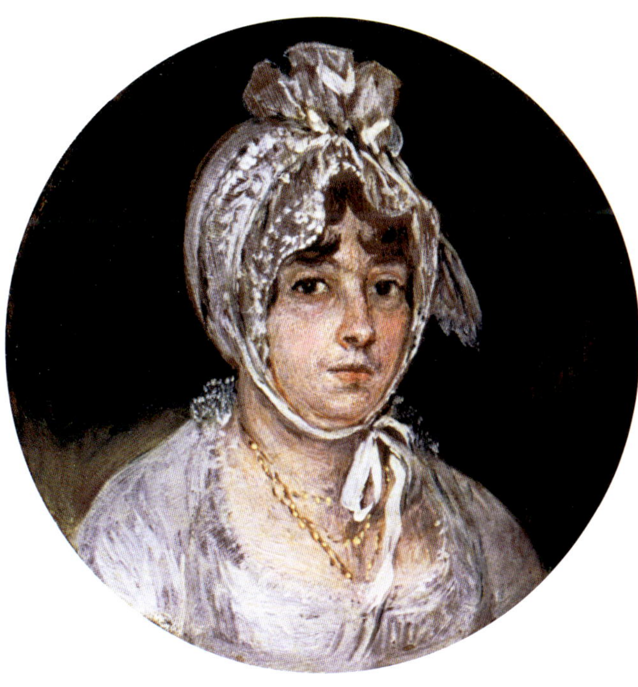

Juana Goicoechea, 1805–6, oil on copper, Museo Nacional del Prado, Madrid, Spain, diameter 8cm (3in)

Doña Juana Galarza de Goicoechea was Javier's new mother-in-law. In 1775, she had married the merchant Don Martín Miguel de Goicoechea. His successful business involved the sale of fabrics, lace and jewellery, but when Ferdinand VII regained the throne, they escaped to Bordeaux to avoid persecution for their liberal inclinations. All these small works show Goya's freedom of touch and unusual approach with miniatures.

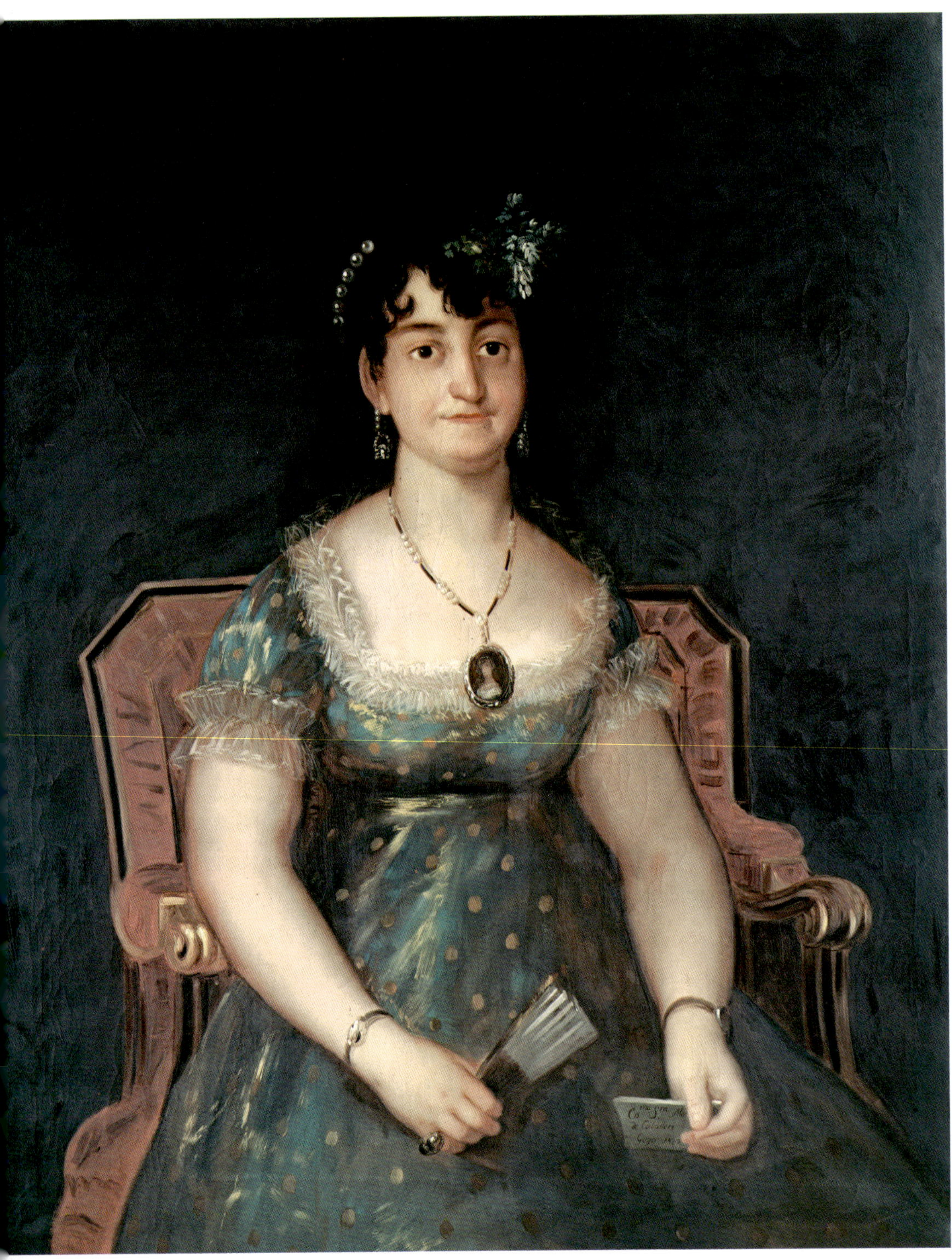

The Marchioness of Caballero, 1807, oil on canvas, Neue Pinakothek, Munich, Germany, 104.7 x 83.7cm (41 x 33in)

Maid of Honour to Queen María Luísa, the Marchioness Doña María Soledad Rocha Fernández de la Peña sits in a red velvet armchair, in a shimmering blue-green and gold Empire-line dress. Fussy jewellery, plus the unflattering portrayal of her facial features, suggest that Goya did not admire the Marchioness. Yet she must have been pleased with the painting, as she paid Goya to make two copies.

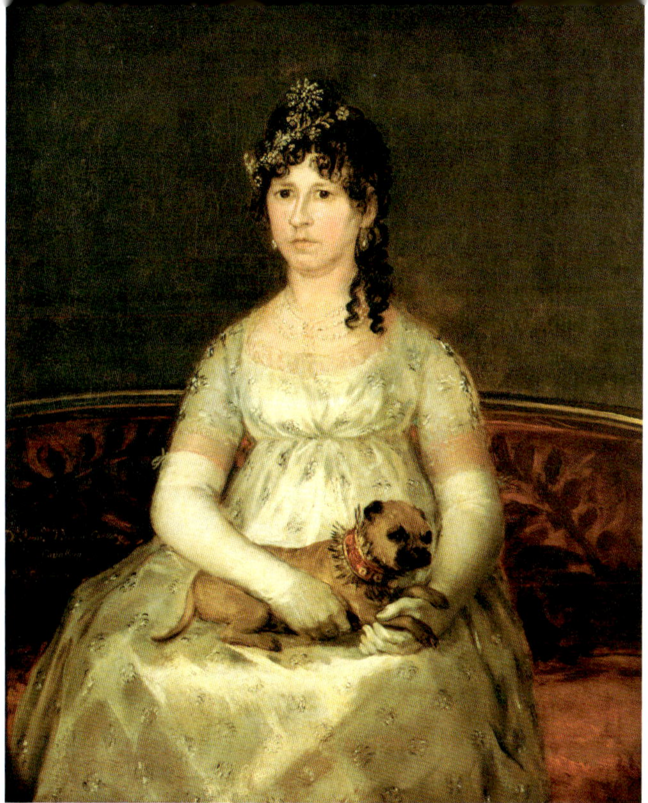

Doña Francisca Vicenta Chollet y Caballero, 1806, oil on canvas, Norton Simon Museum, California, USA, 102.9 x 80.9cm (40½ x 32in)

In elegant long white gloves, with a small pug dog on her lap, Doña Francisca sits in a satin evening gown and looks directly at viewers. Goya creates an impression of realism through this straightforward, simple composition, free and perceptible brushwork, a strong sense of colour and delicately rendered details, including the embroidery of the dress, the jewellery and the dog's collar.

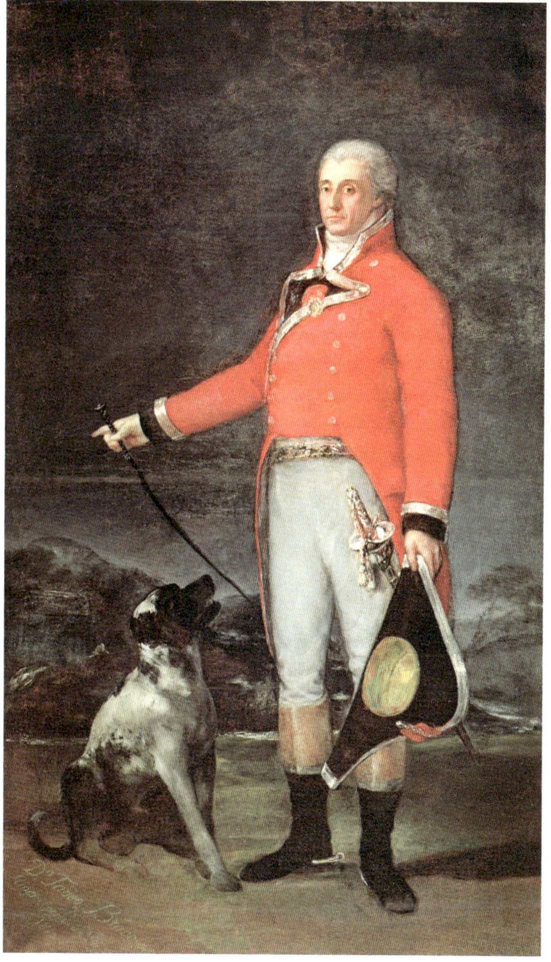

Portrait of Don Tadeo Bravo de Rivero, 1806, oil on canvas, Brooklyn Museum of Art, New York, USA, 207 x 116cm (81½ x 46in)

In the scarlet uniform of a cavalry officer, Tadeo Bravo de Rivero stands next to his dog (a symbol of fidelity, suggesting Tadeo's loyalty to the King). As always, Goya has rendered the textures masterfully, including the gold and silver braid (and medal of the Order of Santiago), boots, spurs, ceremonial sword and tri-cornered hat. The dark sky appears to be closing in, implying an ensuing battle.

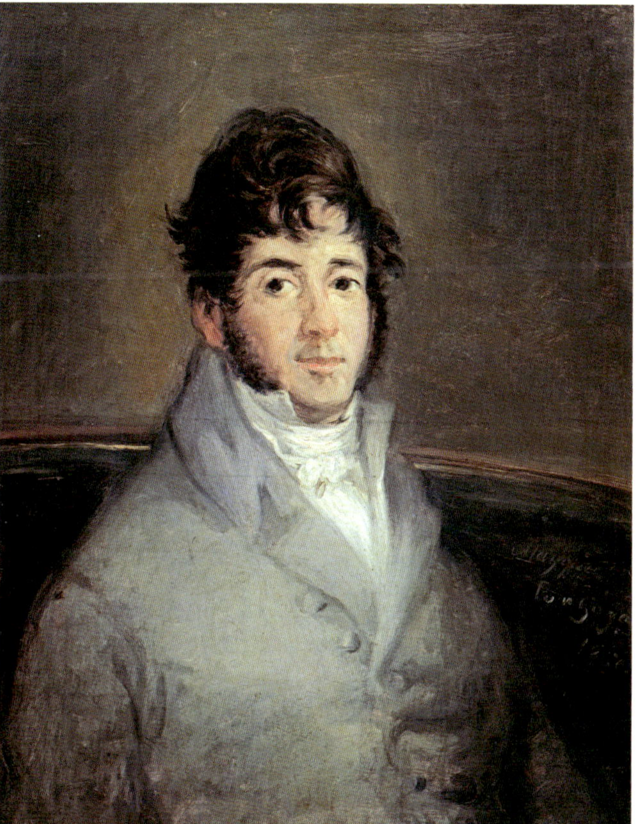

Portrait of Isidro Máiquez, 1807, oil on canvas, The Art Institute of Chicago, Illinois, USA, 82.3 x 63.3cm (32 x 25in)

Isidro Máiquez (1768–1820) was a celebrated Spanish actor who had made his first appearance on stage in 1791. At the outbreak of the Revolutionary War, he took part in the Second of May uprisings and was sent to France as a prisoner of state, but Joseph Bonaparte revoked the command and recalled him to Spain. Once Ferdinand VII resumed his crown however, Isidro was persecuted for his liberal ideas.

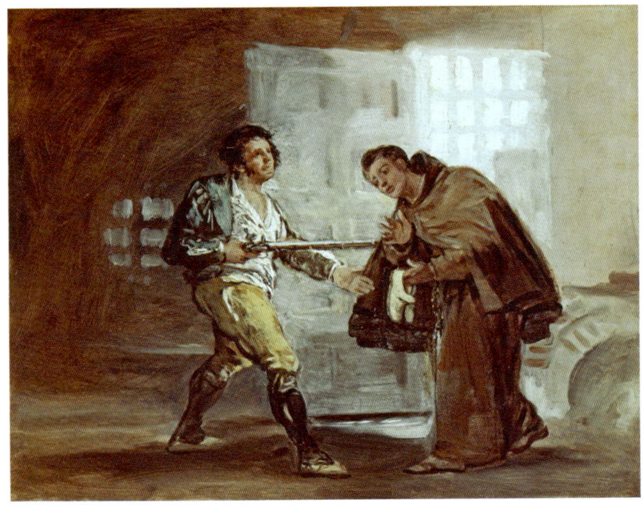

Friar Pedro Offers Shoes to El Maragato and Prepares to Push Aside his Gun, c.1806, oil on panel, The Art Institute of Chicago, Illinois, USA, 29.2 x 38.5cm (11½ x 15½in)

The true story of the capture of the notorious Spanish bandit El Maragato in 1806 by a monk, Pedro de Zaldivia, captured the Spanish people's imagination.

Ballads were sung about the occurrence, accounts were written in newspapers and pamphlets, and Goya made a series of six panels to illustrate the events. However, he did not illustrate the final event of this story that was the public hanging, drawing and quartering of El Maragato in Madrid.

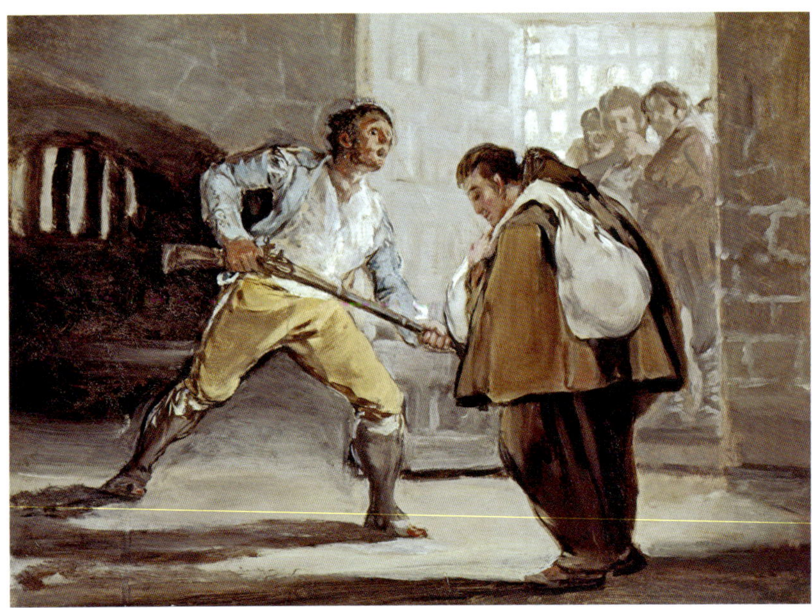

El Maragato Frightens Friar Pedro de Zaldivia with his Gun, c.1806, oil on panel, The Art Institute of Chicago, Illinois, USA, 29.2 x 38.5cm (11½ x 15½in)

Repaying the humble Friar's kindness with violence, the bandit El Maragato pulls out his gun and frightens the gentle man. At this point, the monk bows his head as if he will simply submit to the other man's intimidation. A small crowd of onlookers gathers nearby.

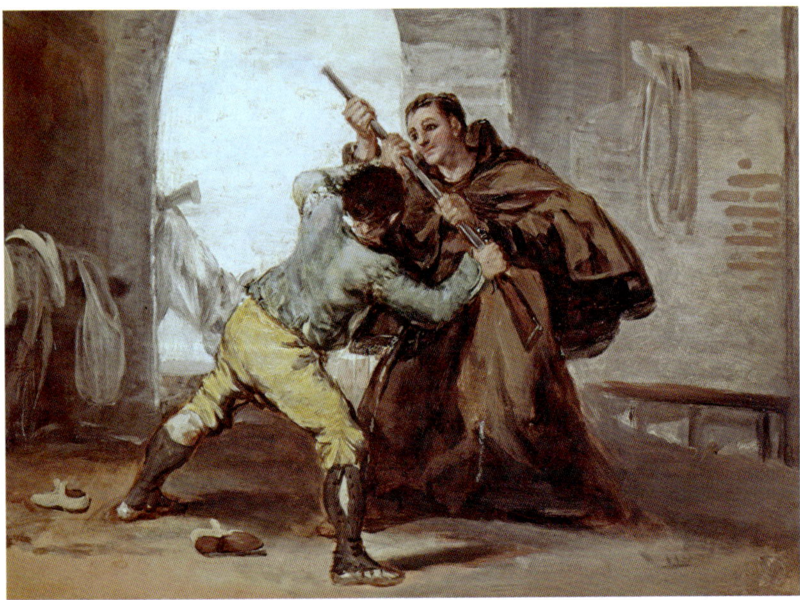

Friar Pedro Wrests the Gun from El Maragato, c.1806, oil on panel, The Art Institute of Chicago, Illinois, USA, 29.2 x 38.5cm (11½ x 15½in)

Suddenly, Friar Pedro does not look so frail. He springs into action and wrestles with the bandit for his weapon. The onlookers seem to have vanished, leaving the monk to manage alone. The only colour in this image is in the figures, the background blurs in a monochromatic, distant haze.

Friar Pedro Clubs El Maragato with the Butt of the Gun, *c.*1806, oil on panel, The Art Institute of Chicago, Illinois, USA, 29.2 x 38.5cm (11½ x 15½in)

In the fourth panel of the events, looking somewhat apologetic, Friar Pedro stands above El Maragato poised and about to hit the rather startled bandit who had terrorized everyone for so long. Goya's broad marks and quick brushwork express the drama and activities as they unfold. The image appears as if it is a sketch from life, resembling a direct, impactful newspaper report.

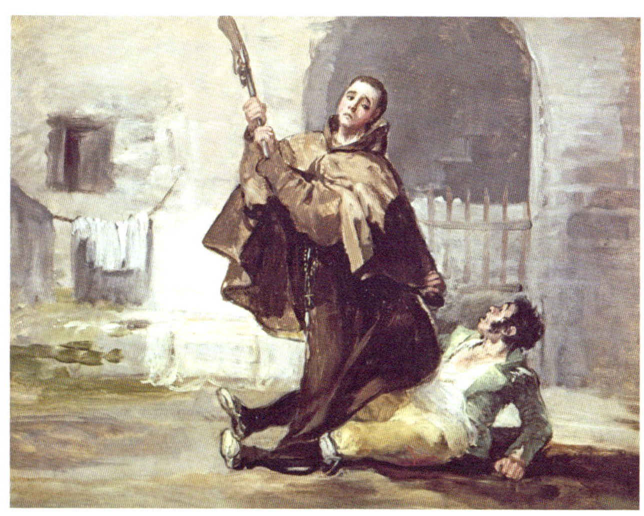

Friar Pedro Shoots El Maragato as his Horse Runs Off, *c.*1806, oil on panel, The Art Institute of Chicago, Illinois, USA, 29.2 x 38.5cm (11½ x 15½in)

The fifth image in Goya's series, this shows Pedro shooting El Maragato in the buttocks to prevent him from escaping. Goya's short, dynamic paint marks emphasize the action and humour of the story with the minimum of fuss.

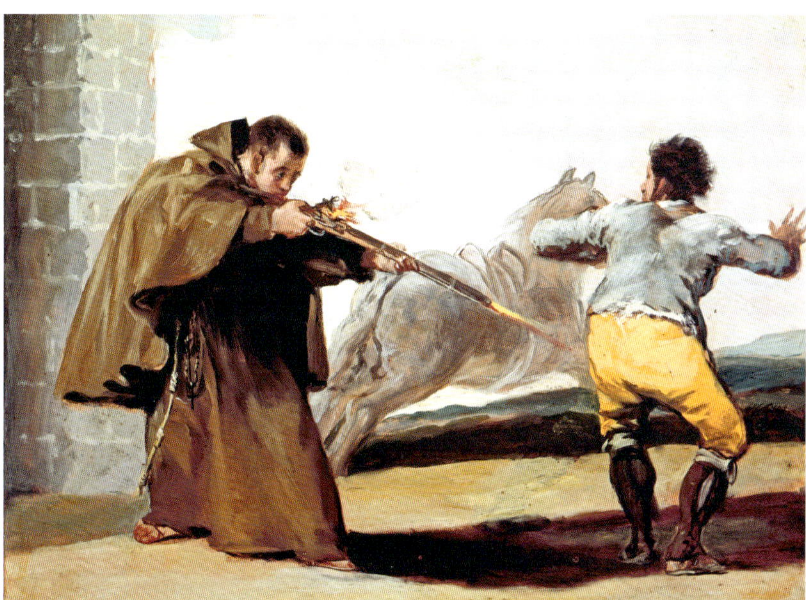

Friar Pedro Binds El Maragato with a Rope, *c.*1806, oil on panel, The Art Institute of Chicago, Illinois, USA, 29.2 x 38.5cm (11½ x 15½in)

In this painting, as Friar Pedro's involvement comes to an end, the fierce bandit seems to have been tamed. The friar ties him up ready for his arrest. The onlookers have reappeared and now El Maragato is safely secured, they run forward to help.

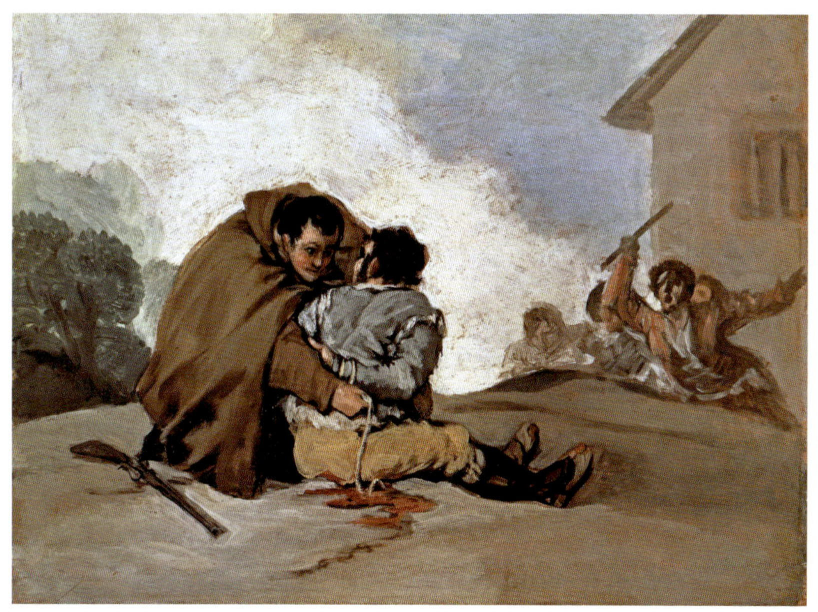

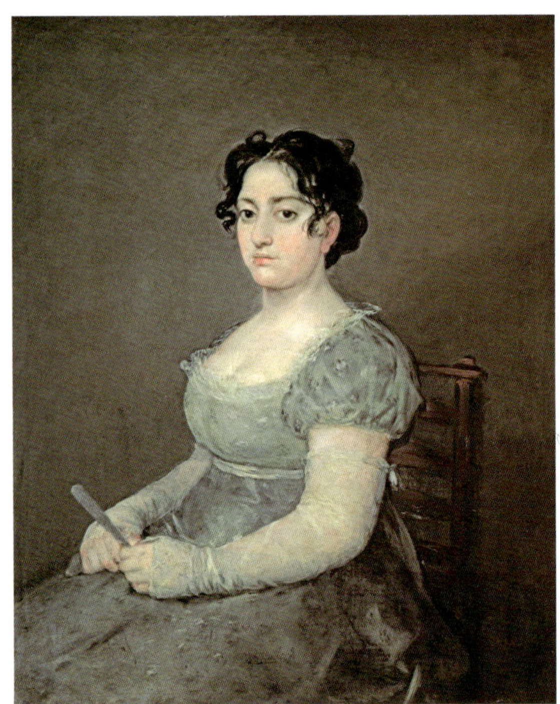

Portrait of a Lady with a Fan, Young Woman with a Fan, c.1805–10, oil on canvas, Musée du Louvre, Paris, France, 84 x 103cm (33 x 40½in)

This painting was in Javier Goya's collection, and it has been suggested that the plump young woman is his wife, Gumersinda

Goicoechea, with the portrait painted soon after the birth of their son Mariano. However, it is difficult to compare the resemblance of Gumersinda to Goya's other portraits of her, which include a profile drawing, a miniature and a full-length portrait of a slimmer figure with a different hairstyle.

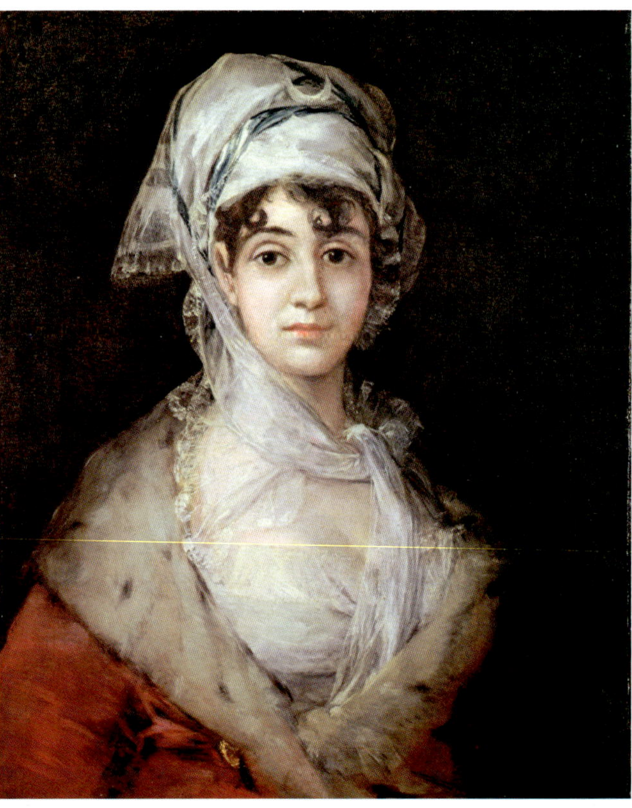

Portrait of the Actress Antonia Zárate, c.1810–1, oil on canvas, The State Hermitage Museum, St Petersburg, Russia, 71 x 58cm (28 x 23in)

Antonia Zárate was a leading actress and this was probably completed in the year of her early death when she was 36. Goya painted another portrait of her about five years previously. His lively brushwork and dark background was typical of his style at that time, while the subject's mesmerizing eyes and curly dark hair gives the impression of an alluring young woman who fascinated the artist.

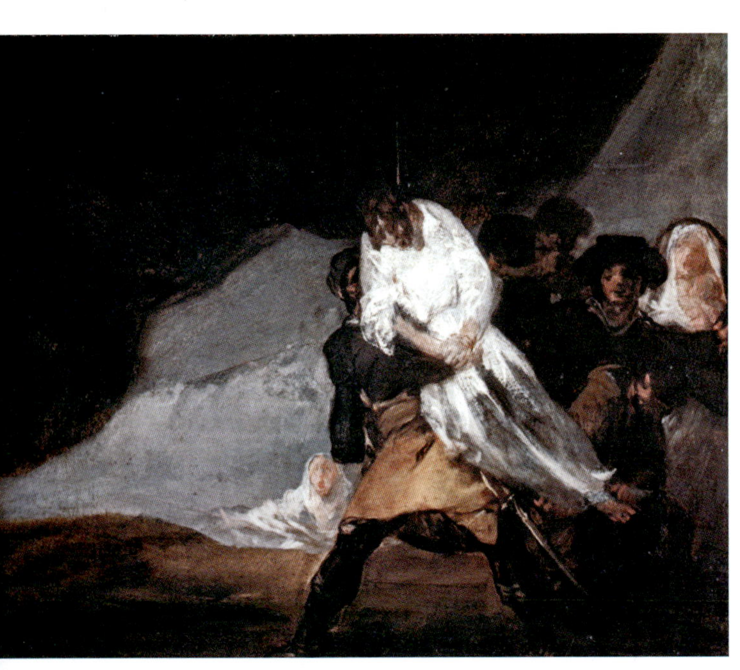

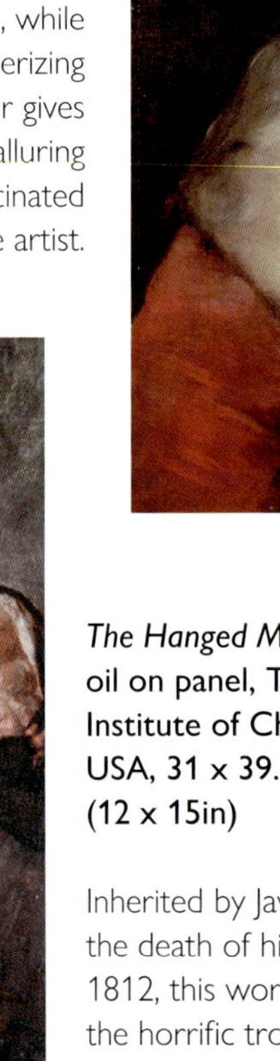

The Hanged Monk, c.1810, oil on panel, The Art Institute of Chicago, Illinois, USA, 31 x 39.2cm (12 x 15in)

Inherited by Javier after the death of his mother in 1812, this work expresses the horrific troubles that were devastating Spain.

Goya painted it soon after Napoleon had suggested that the number of monks in Madrid should be limited, to prevent any overly-large groups from becoming corrupt. The sketchiness of his application anticipates Impressionism and the emotion conveyed is a forerunner to Expressionism.

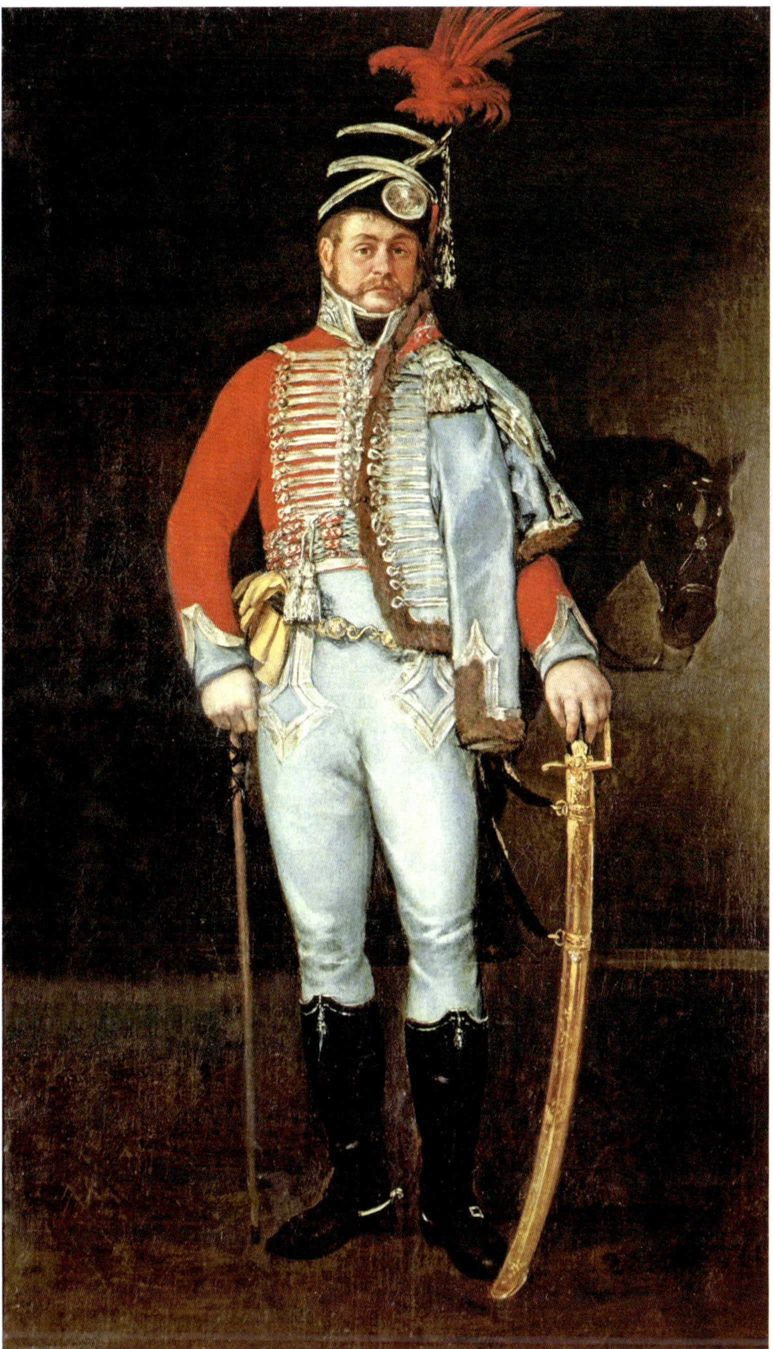

Juana Galarza de Goicoechea,
1810, oil on canvas, Private
Collection, 82 x 59cm
(32 x 23in)

Goya had already depicted
the wife of his friend Martín
Miguel de Goicoechea twice
before when he painted this.
Also his son's mother-in-law,

Juana sits in a grey dress,
her ample figure set against
a dark background. Despite
her smile, her eyes are rather
melancholy; at the time, Spain
was embroiled in the War of
Independence. Rapid, thick
brushwork suggests
the intricate delicacy
of the lace collar.

Pantaleón Pérez de Nenín,
1808, oil on canvas, Banco
Exterior de España, Madrid,
Spain, 206 x 125cm
(81 x 49in)

Don Pantaleón came from
a wealthy merchant family
in Bilbao and had a dazzling
military career. By 16 he
was First Lieutenant and in
1808, he was made Captain
Adjutant. Goya painted this
in January 1808, showing him
wearing the winter uniform
of the Hussars of María Luísa.
The brushwork is fairly tight,
emphasizing the fine details
of the uniform. The stance is
confident, but the face is not.

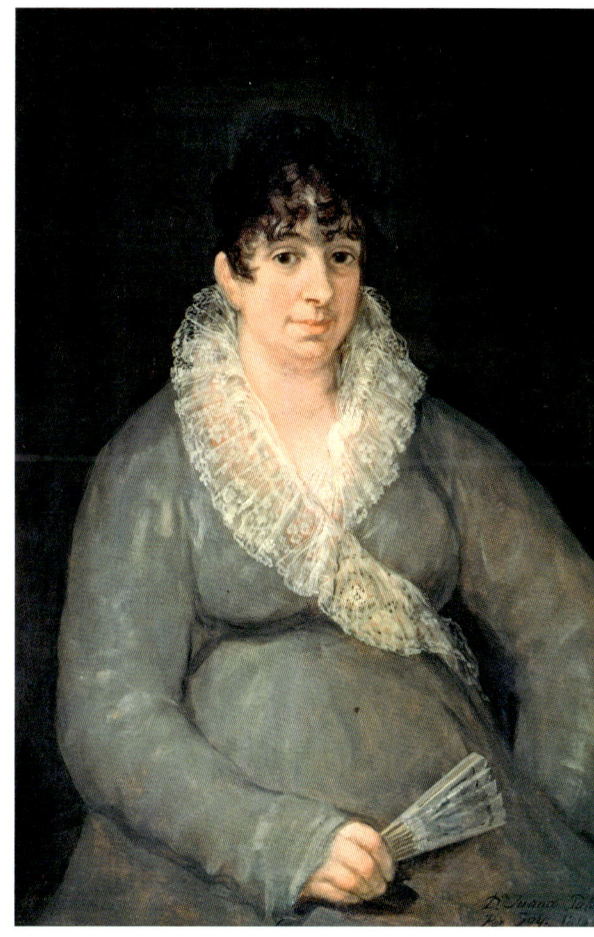

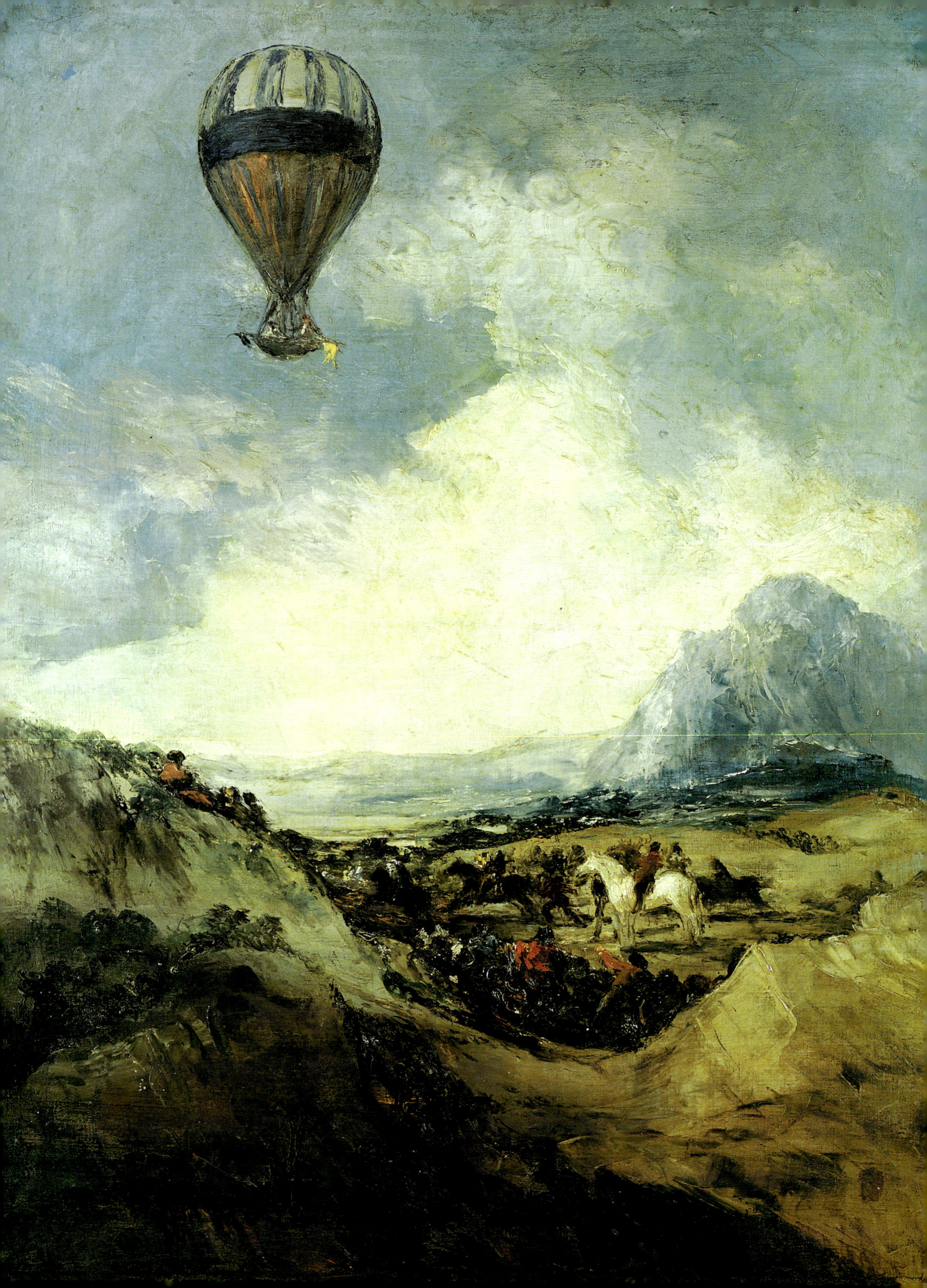

WEAKENING SIGHT, GROWING VISION

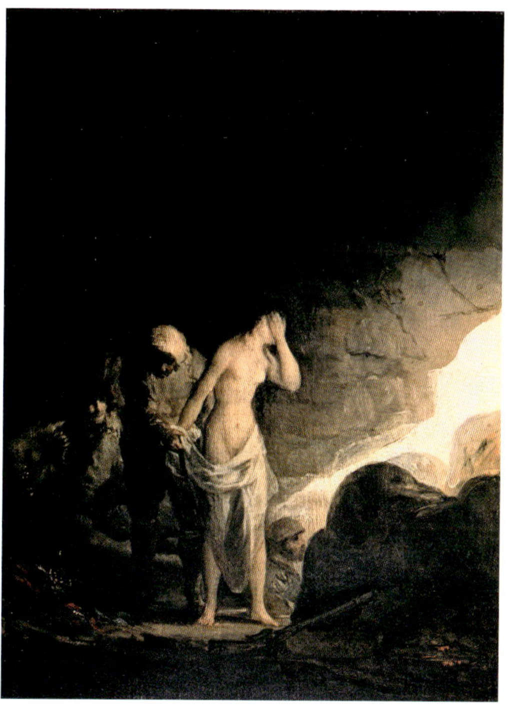

The shocking events that had initially rumbled far away in other parts of Europe eventually gripped Spain with devastating intensity. From his studio, Goya saw only the brutality and pointlessness of it all. Before him, artists often showed war as a heroic, ennobling act. But Goya revealed the atrocities in brutal honesty. With failing sight added to his deafness, Goya retreated from Court. After another serious illness in 1819, he expressed his feelings privately on the walls of Quinta del Sordo. In 1824, he left for France. Despite his age and infirmities, his creative energy never diminished.

Above: Brigand Stripping a Woman, c.1808–12, oil on canvas, 41.5 x 31.8cm (16 x 12½in), Private Collection. In a dark cave, a woman endures a horrific attack by brigands. The strong chiaroscuro reflects the dark and fearful atmosphere.

Left: The Balloon or The Ascent of the Montgolfier, 1812–16, oil on canvas, 103 x 83cm (40½ x 33in), Musée des Beaux-Arts, Agen, France. Goya's hot air balloon hangs threateningly over a mountainous landscape. Below, people are dispersing in panic.

Arthur Wellesley, the Duke of Wellington, 1812–14, oil on mahogany, The National Gallery, London, UK, 64.3 x 52.4cm (25 x 20½in)

The first Duke of Wellington entered Madrid in August 1812 and finally defeated the French forces soon after. Goya's admiration of him is apparent from the liveliness and sympathy of this portrait. It was first painted in 1812, and modified two years later after Wellington had been awarded Spain's highest honour, the Order of the Golden Fleece. Goya changed the picture to show him in full dress uniform with decorations.

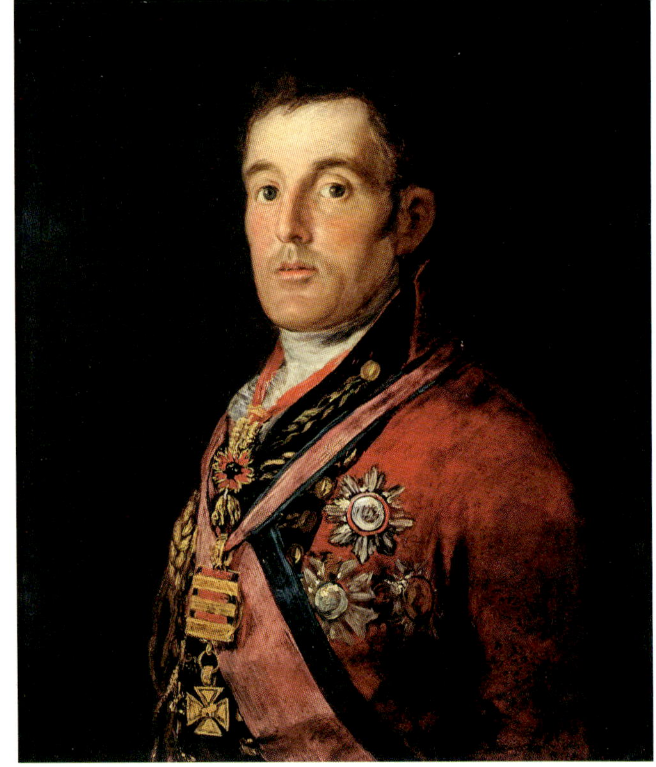

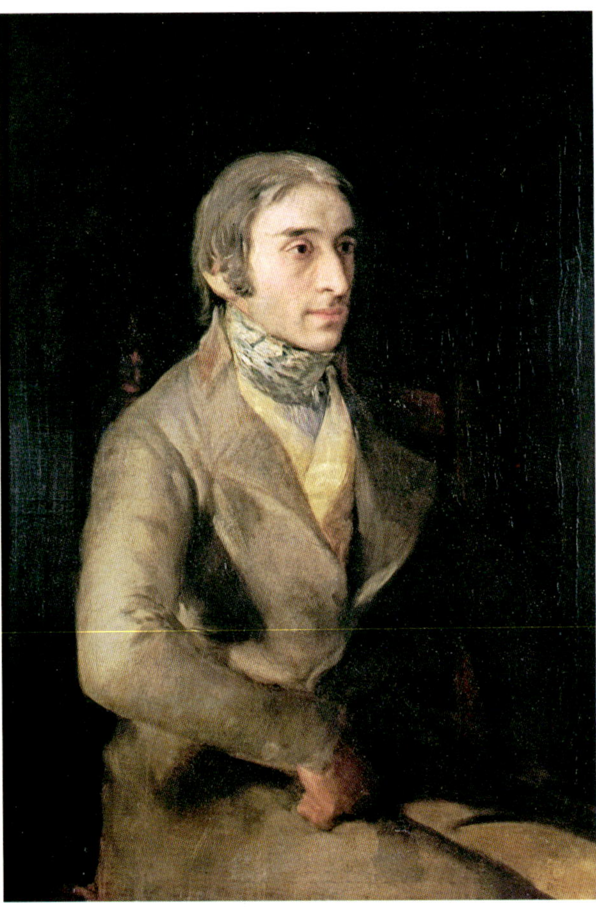

Don Manuel Silvela, 1810–13, oil on canvas, Museo Nacional del Prado, Madrid, Spain, 95 x 68cm (37 x 27in)

Don Manuel Silvela (1781–1832), was a writer, lawyer and magistrate. He moved from Valladolid to Madrid during the French occupation, and as he was fluent in French and Spanish, he worked as an intermediary within Joseph Bonaparte's government. Although he worked to help the Spanish during that time, like so many, he was persecuted once Ferdinand VII had returned, and fled to France.

Portrait of a Woman, (formerly thought to be Josefa Bayeu), *c*.1814, Museo Nacional del Prado, Madrid, Spain, 82.5 x 58.2cm (32½ x 23in)

Traditionally identified as Josefa Bayeu, this is now thought to be either Leocadia Weiss or more probably, another woman. The original date of the work was believed to be 1798, when Josefa was 50 and this is a much younger woman. The current date of the work, suggested by the clothing style and lighting, was two years after Josefa's death. Goya could have painted it posthumously, but this seems unlikely.

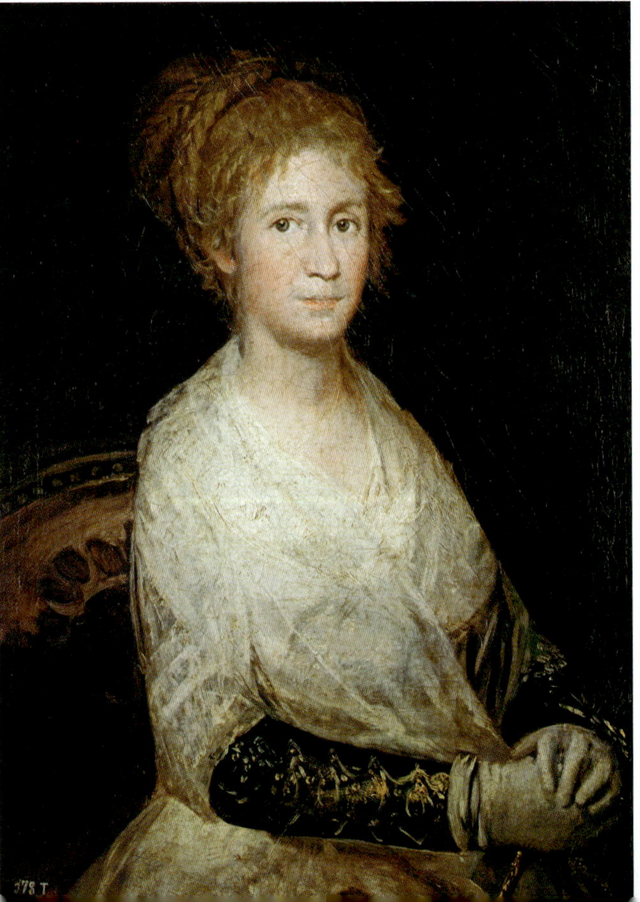

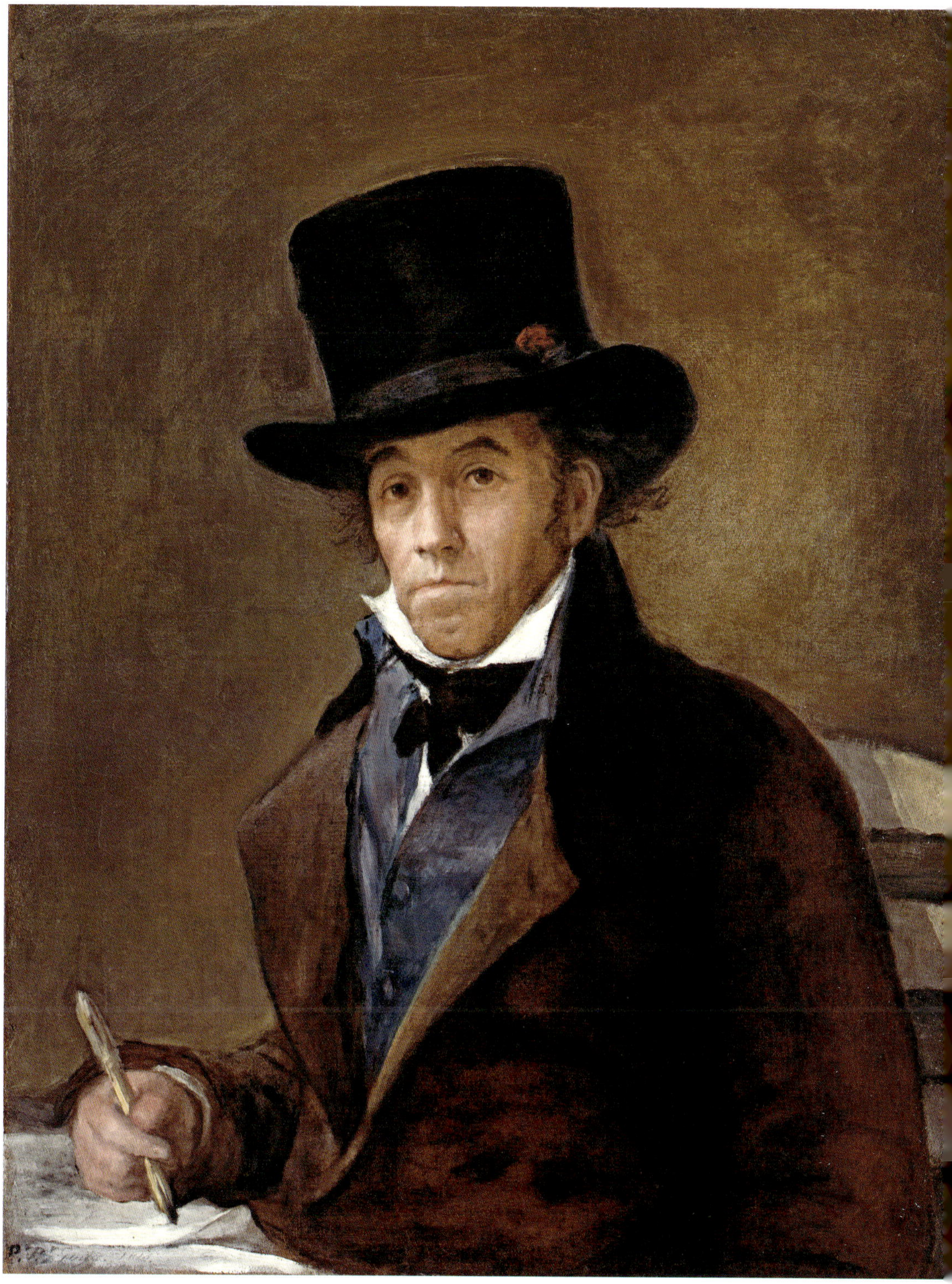

Asensio Julià, 1814, oil on canvas, Sterling and Francine Clark Institute, Massachusetts, USA, 73.2 x 57.7cm (29 x 23in)

Asensio Julià i Alvarracín (1760–1832) was a Spanish painter and engraver. He was one of the few of Goya's students whose name has come down to us. In 2008, *The Colossus* (see page 223), for so long attributed to Goya, was re-attributed to Juliá by specialists at the Museo del Prado. The attribution of this portrait, relaxed, charismatic and compelling, is generally but not universally, accepted.

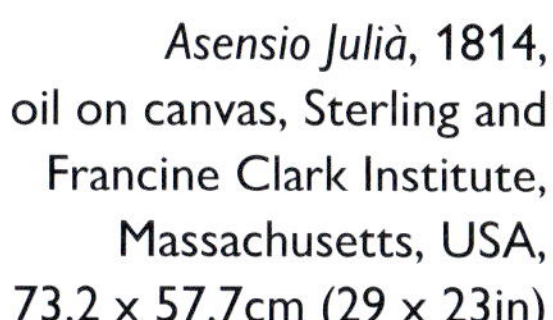

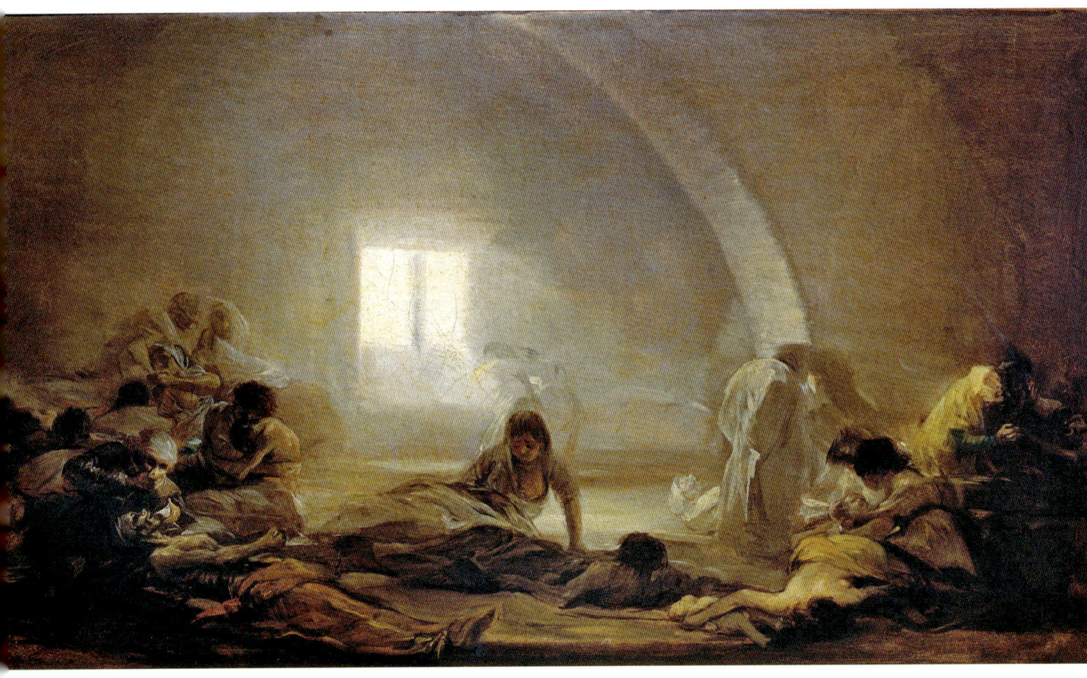

*Plague Hospital, c.*1808–12, oil on canvas, Private Collection, 32.5 x 57.3cm (13 x 22½in)

This is a cellar hospital to which the sick had been condemned. During that time in Spain, hospitals and prisons had great similarities; both involved the loss of liberty and misery. On the straw-covered floor lie the sick and dying, left to fend for themselves. A friend of Goya's was trying to introduce reforms to hospitals, to secularize them, but the Church opposed him. This is Goya's protest.

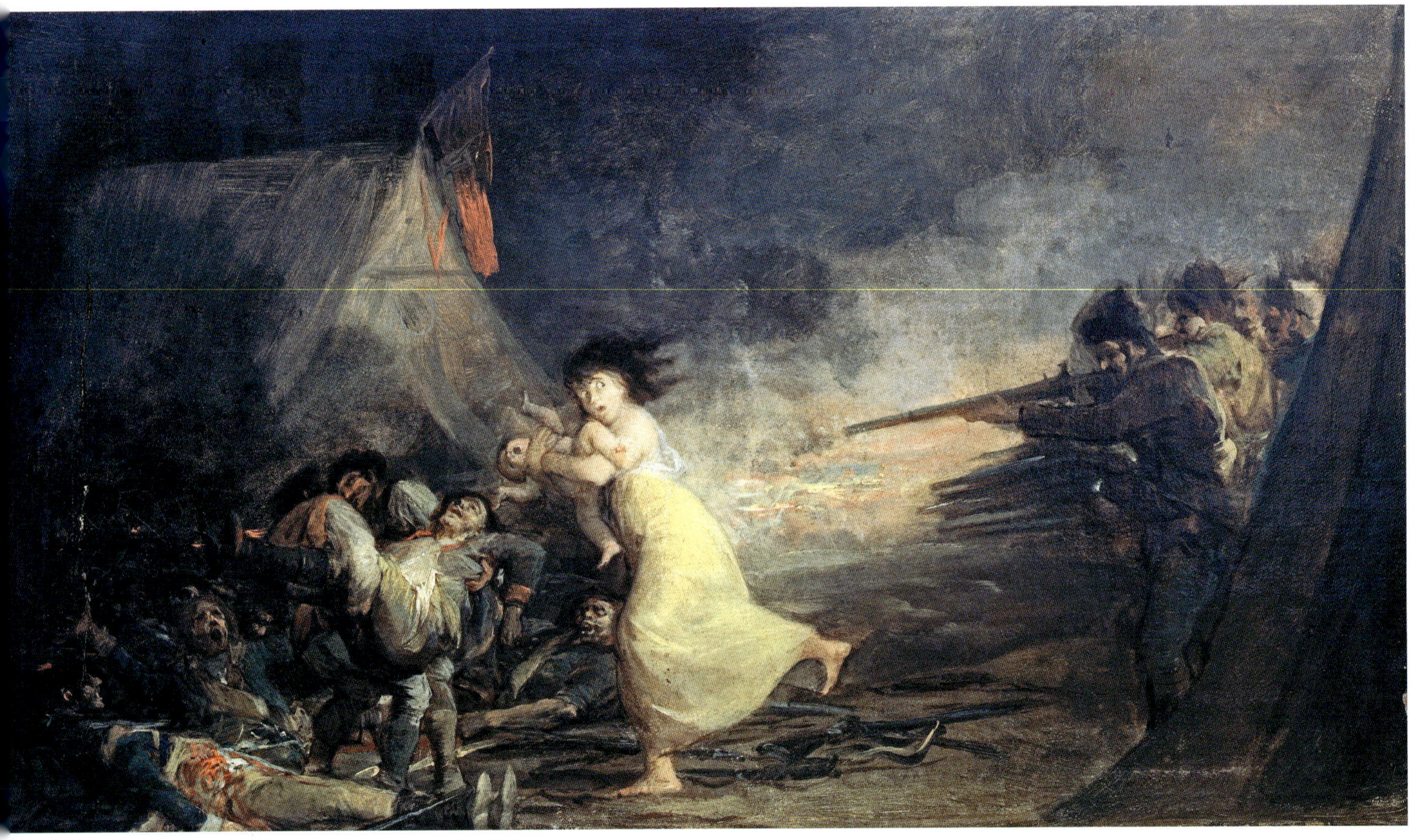

Shooting in a Military Camp, *c.*1808–12, oil on canvas, Private Collection, 32.6 x 57cm (13 x 22½in)

This distressing image shows French soldiers shooting at close range at a military camp and specifically, at a fleeing woman with a baby in her arms. The soldiers block the side of the canvas, creating a feeling of no escape. The young mother's innocence is emphasized through her pale dress and youthful glow. She is probably a young soldier's wife. Strong chiaroscuro emphasizes the main area of action of the painting.

Martyrdom or *Cannibals Preparing Their Victims*, c.1800–12, oil on panel, Musée des Beaux-Arts et d'Archéologie, Besançon, France, 32.8 x 46.9cm (13 x 18½in)

One of two paintings symbolizing the martyrdom of two French missionaries by Iroquois – a powerful Native American alliance of indigenous people. Sainte-Marie among the Hurons was a French Jesuit settlement in Ontario from 1639–49. In 1649, eight Jesuit missionaries there were attacked and captured by the Iroquois. This depicts two of them; Brébeuf and Lallemont, being skinned by the cannibalistic Iroquois.

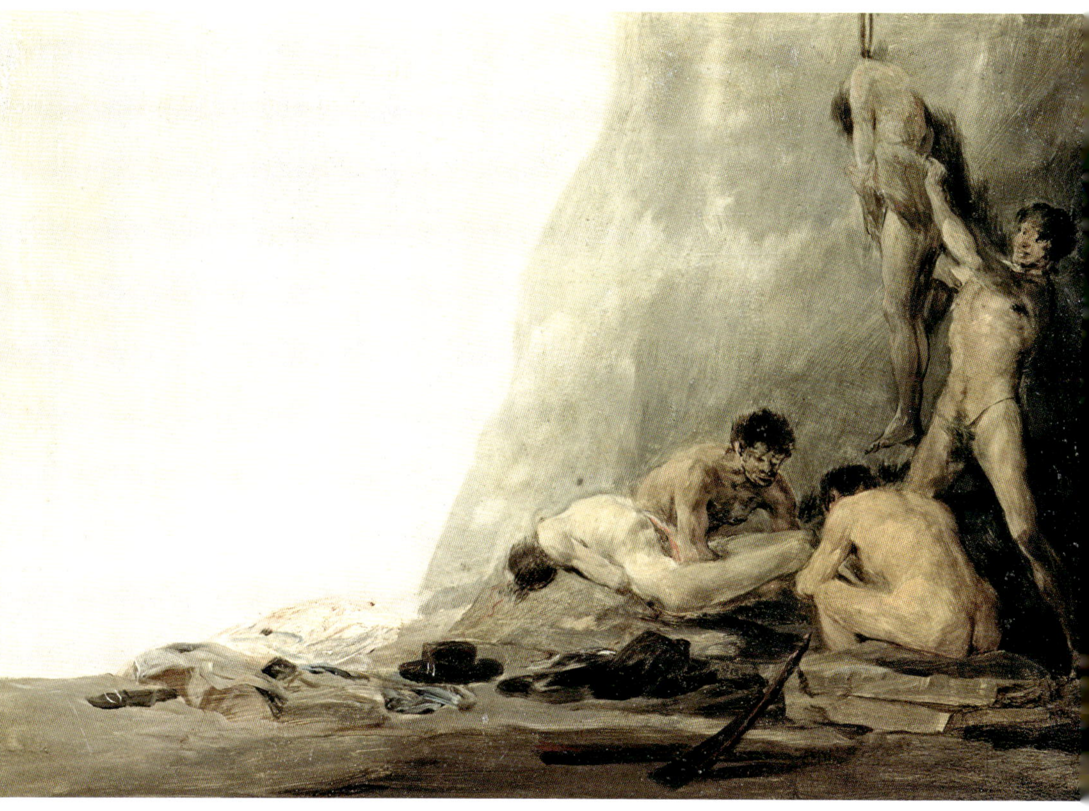

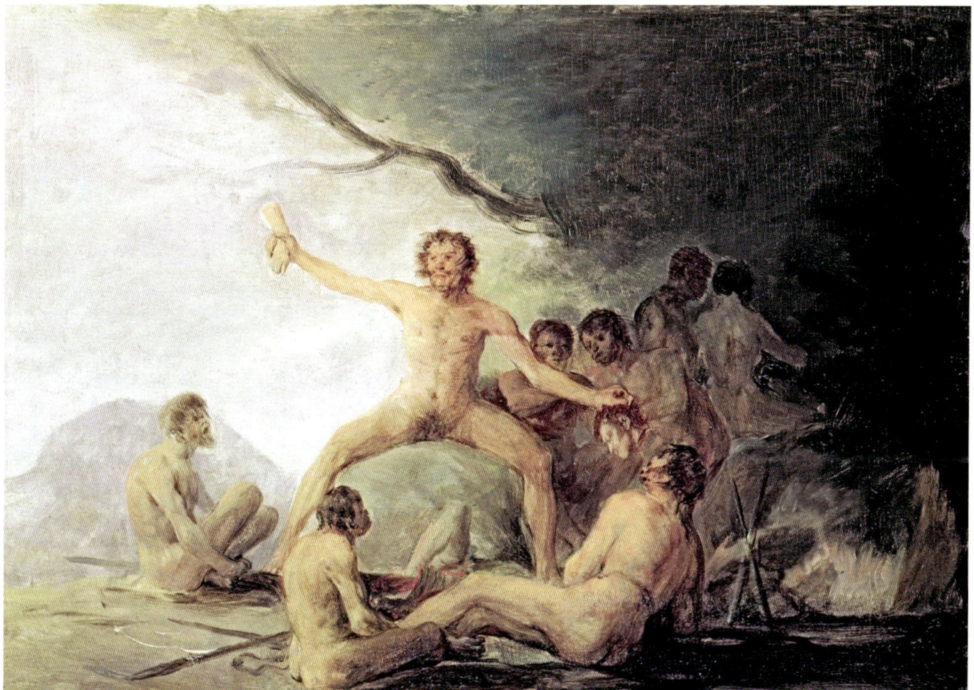

Martyrdom or *Cannibals Beholding Human Remains*, c.1800–12, oil on panel, Musée des Beaux-Arts et d'Archéologie, Besançon, France, 32.7 x 47.2cm (13 x 18½in)

The second of the small paintings depicting cannibals and their victims. Goya treats these repulsive visions almost with humour. The central figure is straddled across a rock, triumphant at catching and killing his victims. In his right hand he waves a severed hand, in his left, a head. No one had ever painted such scenes before. They portray Goya's comparison of the brutality of the European wars with cannibalism.

Confessions in Jail, 1812, oil on canvas, Royal Monastery of Santa Maria de Guadalupe, Cáceres, Spain, 31.5 x 40cm (12½ x 16in)

With the promise of the Enlightenment long gone, during 1812, Goya produced a series of six small paintings of fairly distressing scenes, such as women being attacked by soldiers, rape, murder and this somewhat depressing image of a prison. Three prisoners huddle in the gloom, one sleeps on the floor, one confesses to a priest in the background shadows, while another stands in front of them all, staring out, wrapped in a blanket.

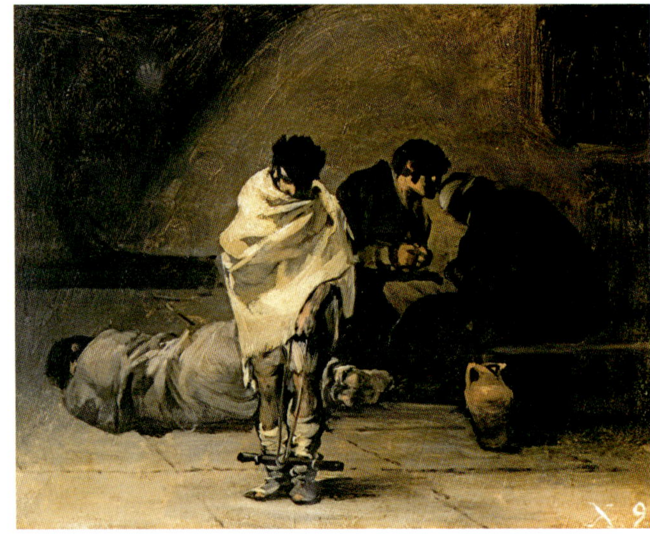

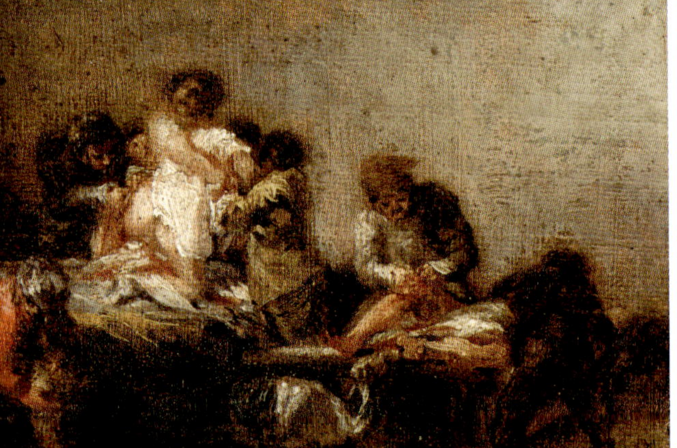

Wounded in a Hospital, c.1808–12, oil on canvas, Private Collection, 31 x 41cm (12 x 16in)

This is one of a group of paintings that Goya produced before he made the series of etchings he called *The Disasters of War*. This was not the first time he had depicted the horrors of contemporary hospitals; at that time they were dirty and squalid. Goya and his friends knew they needed urgent improvement, but the King's absolutist government did nothing to help.

The Maypole (La Cucaña), c.1810–12, oil on canvas, Staatliche Museen Berlin, Berlin, Germany, 82.7 x 103.5cm (32½ x 41in)

Another uncommissioned small painting by Goya, using a greater range of colours than he had of late, this depicts a group of people looking up at a maypole, watching three figures climbing it. The light is quite eerie; the foreground is predominantly in shadow, while in the distance, a glowing light reflects on the mountainous background in variegated colours, and bright white on a large building.

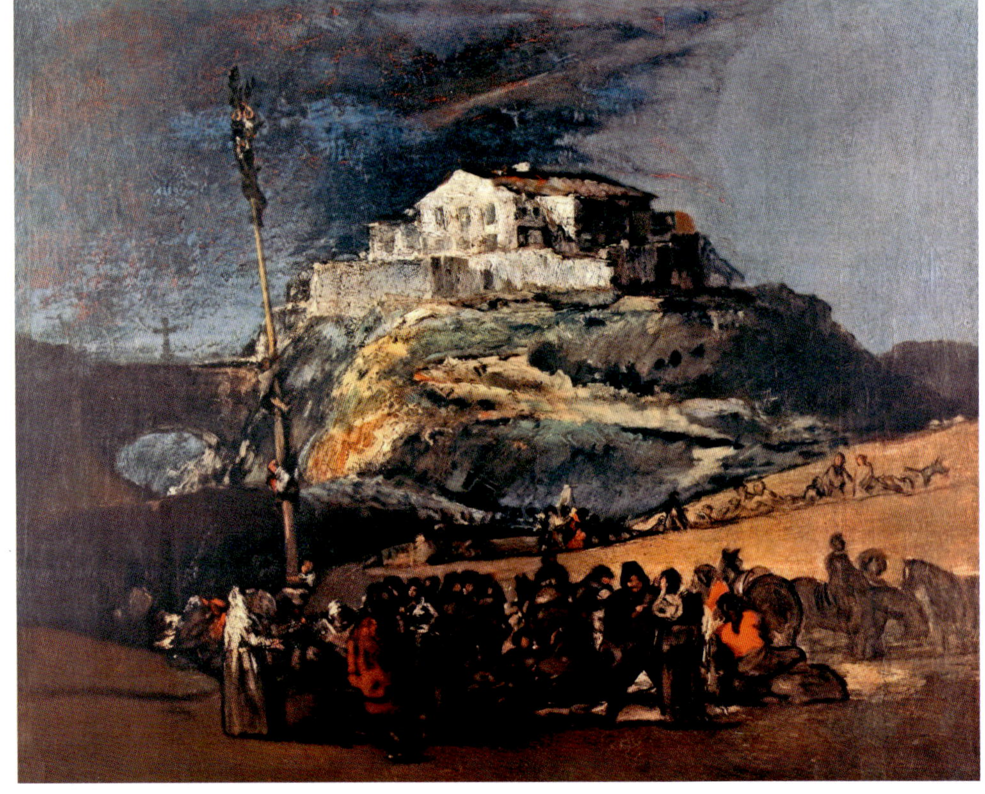

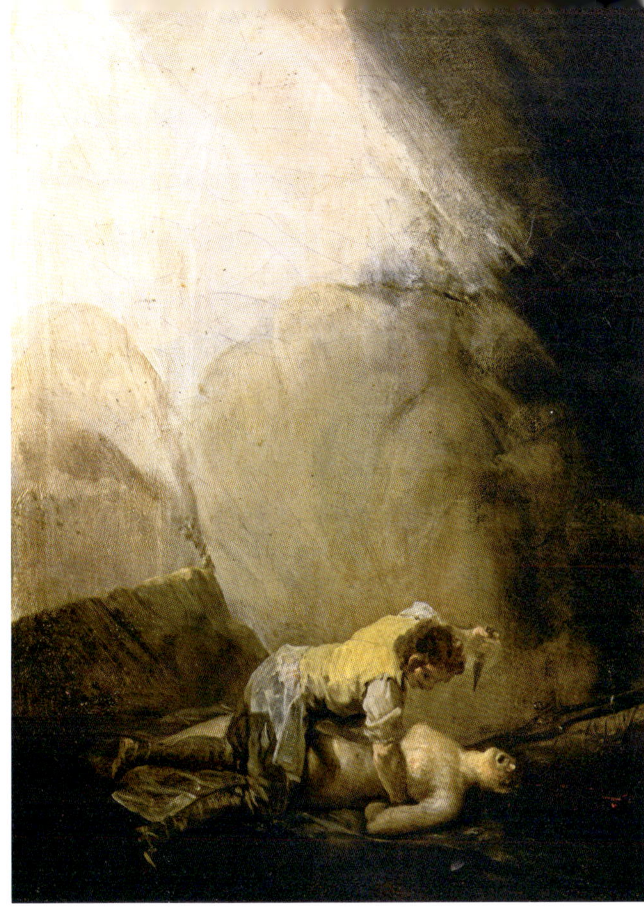

Brigand Murdering a Woman, c.1808–12, oil on canvas, Private Collection, 105.4 x 80.7cm (41½ x 32in)

Rape and pillage were just two of the horrendous consequences of the war in Spain. Goya created several small paintings showing secular violence involved. This is the murder of a woman by a brigand. He has dragged her from the cave; a streak of crimson blood trickles from her mouth. Despite the small formats of these works, the quality of the light and shade imbue them with immediacy.

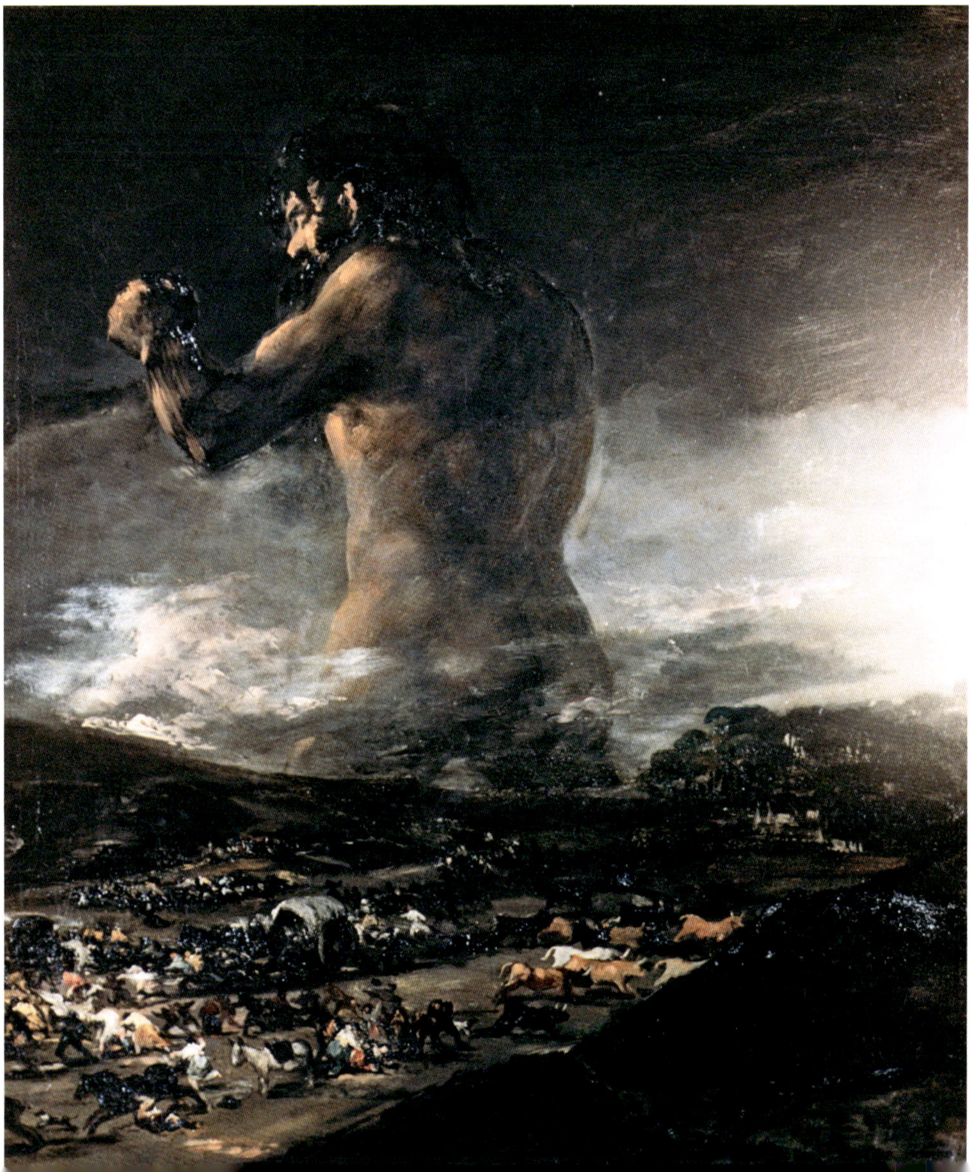

The Colossus, 1808–12, oil on canvas, Museo Nacional del Prado, Madrid, Spain, 116 x 105cm (46 x 41in)

This painting has been the subject of huge debate. Experts are still divided over its attribution. Some are convinced that it was painted by Asensio Juliá (see page 219), others insist it is definitely by Goya. Either way, the giant has been interpreted as an allegory of Napoleon's armies invading Spain, or the 'spirit of the Pyrenees' rising up to destroy the French troops, from a patriotic poem of 1808 by Juan Bautista Arriaza (1770–1837).

El Lazarillo de Tormes, 1808, oil on canvas, Private Collection, 80 x 65cm (31½ x 25½in)

This is Goya's depiction of an episode in the 16th-century novel *El Lazarillo de Tormes*. The subject could have made uncomfortable viewing, but Goya shows his humorous side. The blind old man is trying to smell whether his supper has been eaten by Lazarillo. He forces open the young boy's mouth and pushes his long thin nose close to it to sniff.

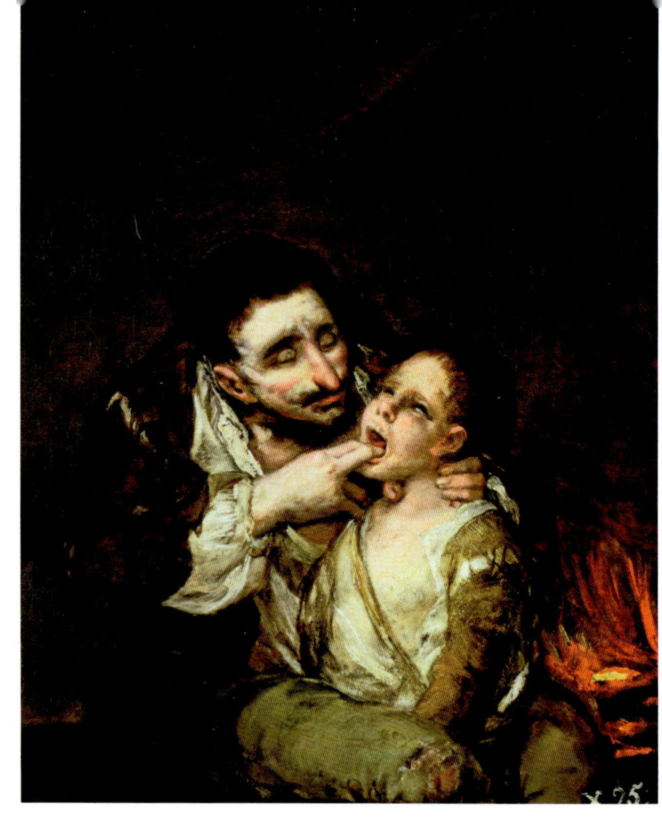

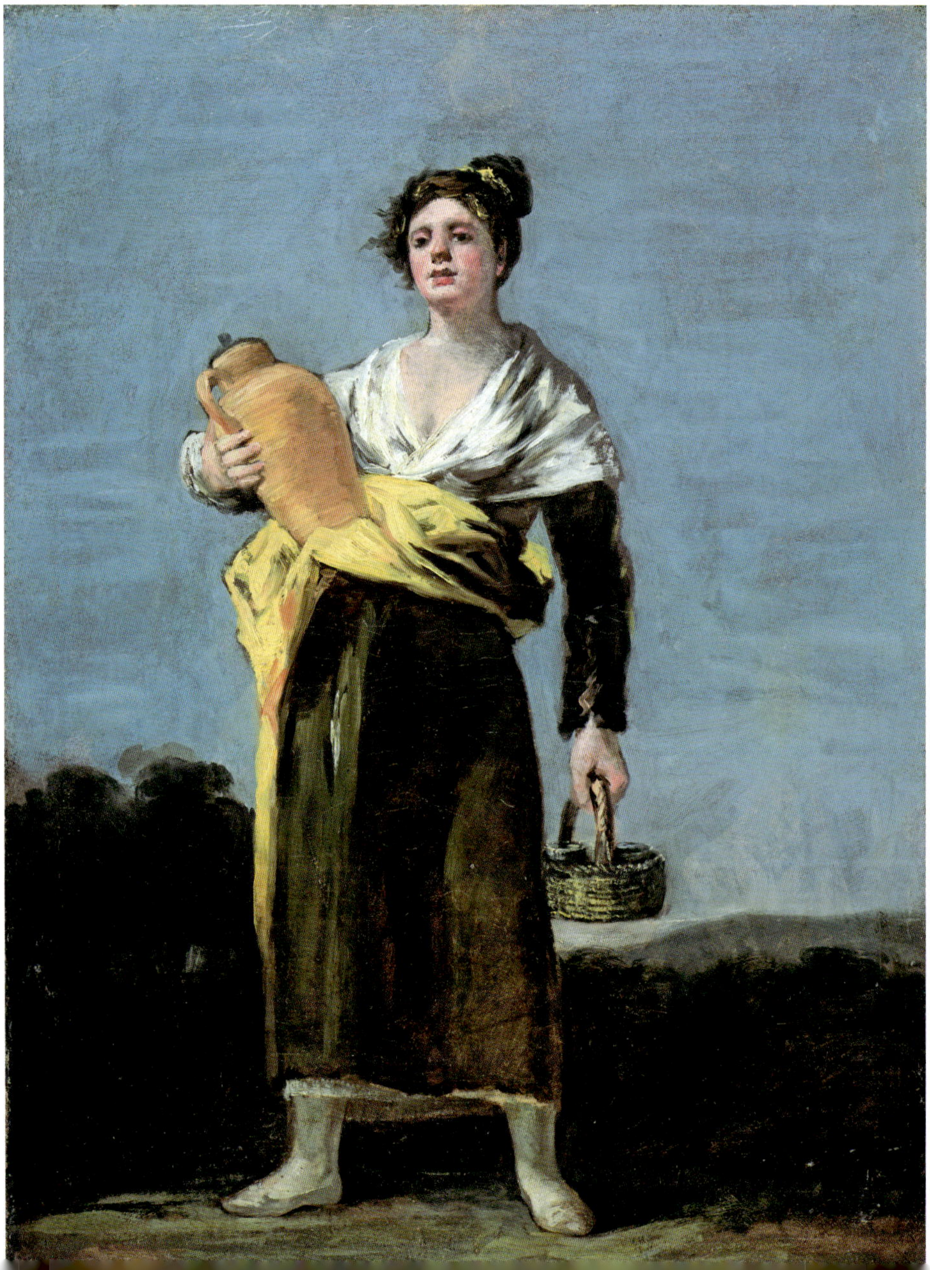

The Water Carrier, 1810–12, oil on canvas, Szépmıvészeti Múzeum, Budapest, Hungary, 68 x 52cm (27 x 20½in)

At first glance, this appears to be a simple image of a peasant girl, perhaps even a revisiting of Goya's earlier tapestry cartoons. But his ideals and hopes had changed by this time. While he painted this, war was ravaging his country, and on closer inspection, a sense of foreboding can be discerned behind the girl, although she seems to represent the strength of the ordinary Spanish people.

The Celestina and her Daughter on a Balcony or *Young Woman at the Balcony*, c.1808–12, oil on canvas, Private Collection, 166 x 118cm (65 x 46½in)

The depiction of beautiful young Spanish majas and allegories were two themes that Goya particularly enjoyed. This is one of the works listed in an inventory of his possessions drawn up in 1812 on the death of Josefa. Time is the theme here, and the work is an allegory of the vanity of worldly things, and the transitory nature of youth and beauty.

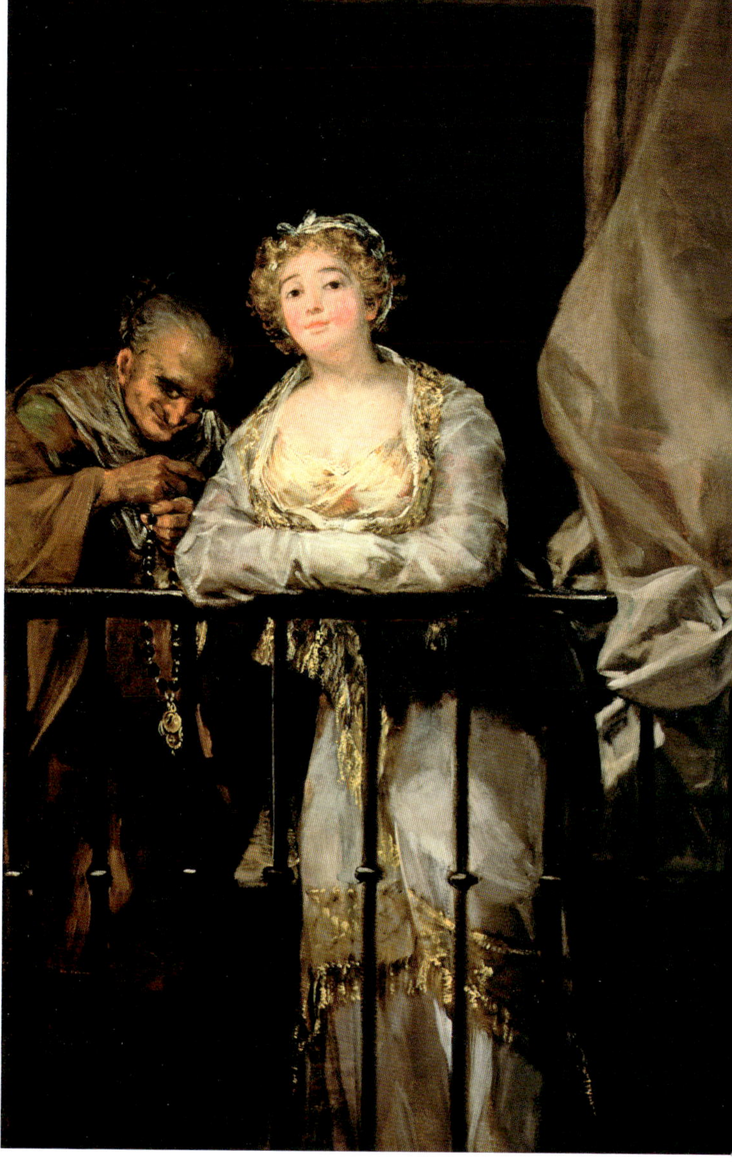

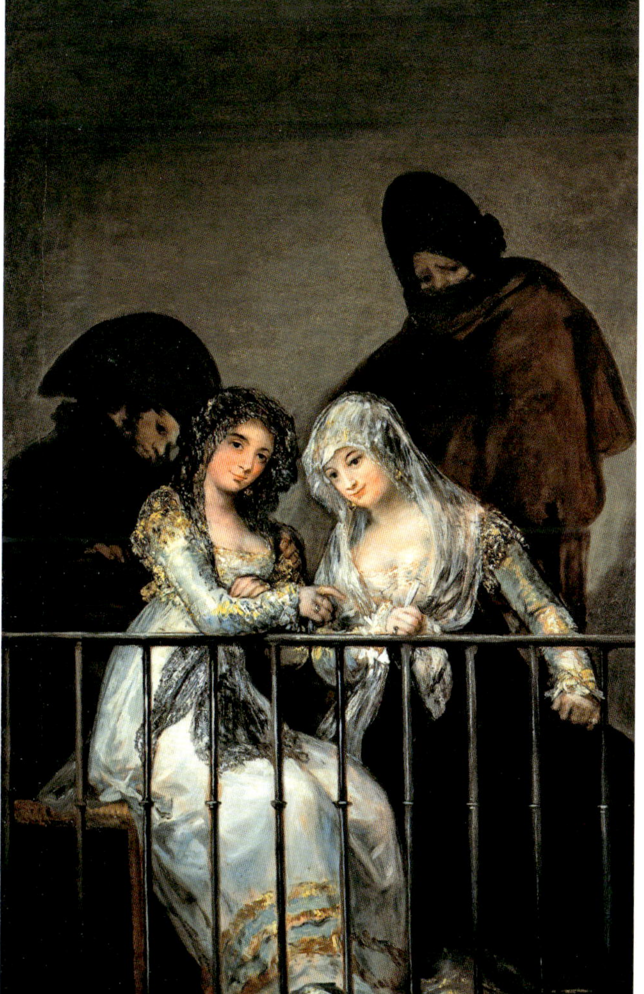

Majas on a Balcony, c.1808–12, oil on canvas, The Metropolitan Museum of Art, New York, USA, 194 x 125cm (76 x 49in)

Goya painted two versions of this. In the other work, the two dark figures are closer to the young women, and their faces look more sinister. Two young women sit on a balcony in expensive lace mantillas. Behind them, two dark figures are obscured in capes and hats. Their dark looming shapes contrast with the pure and gentle elegance of the two females, conveying a menacing air of foreboding.

*Time and the Old Women,
The Old Girls (Las Viejas) or
Que Tal? (How Are You?),*
1810–12, oil on canvas,
Palais des Beaux-Arts, Lille,
France, 181 x 125cm
(71 x 49in)

Interpretations for this work
vary widely. The two ugly old
crones are dressed in overly
adorned finery. They have
not noticed Time hovering
behind them, while they
peer into what appears to
be a small compact mirror.
The old woman in white is
wearing a diamond arrow
also seen in the hair of
Queen María Luísa in the
portrait of *The Family
of Charles IV* (see page 200).

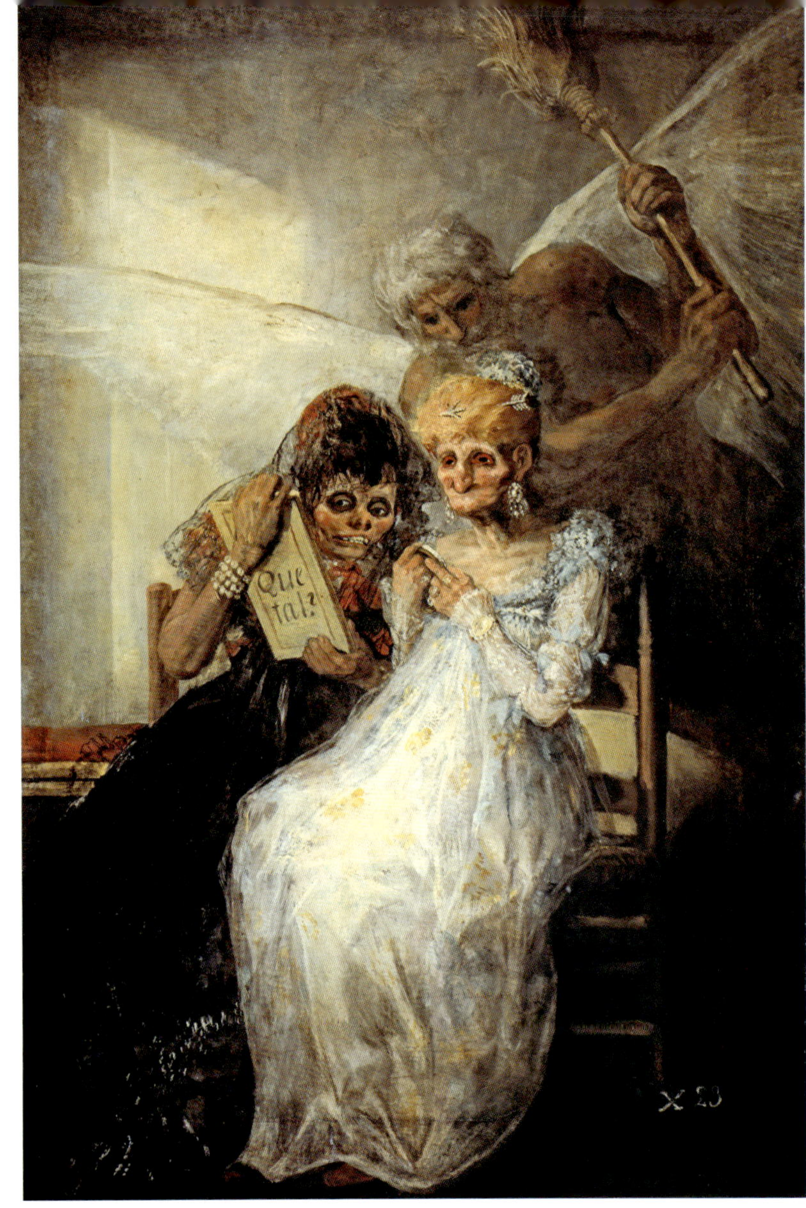

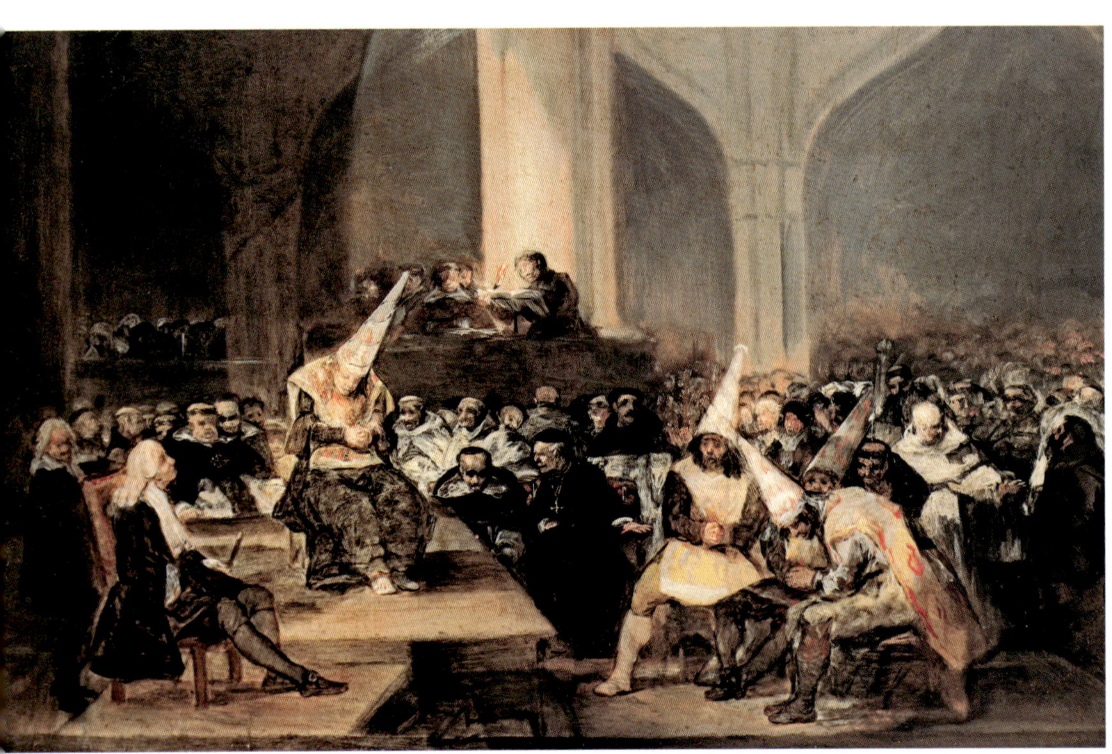

*Inquisition Scene, c.*1812–19,
oil on panel, Real Academia
de Bellas Artes de San
Fernando, Madrid, Spain,
46 x 73cm (18 x 29in)

This is an 'Auto de Fe', or
an accusation of heretics by
the tribunal of the Spanish
Inquisition. The accused sit
in chains and pointed hats in
front of an audience and their
accusers. This was probably
based on descriptions of the
famous witch trials of the
auto de fe in 1610. Goya is
comparing the cruel practices
of the past with events in his
own present-day Spain.

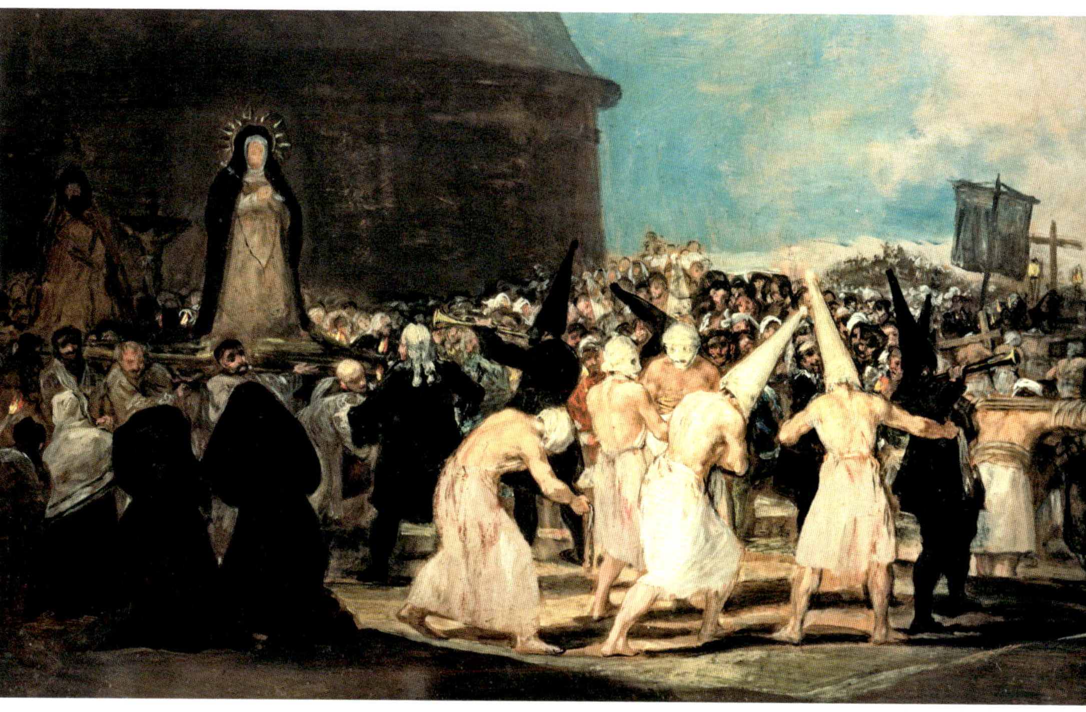

Procession of the Flagellants, c.1812–19, oil on panel, Real Academia de Bellas Artes de San Fernando, Madrid, Spain, 46 x 73cm (18 x 28½in)

Satirizing the horrors of penitential rituals, Goya shows flagellants stripped to the waist and bleeding, made to wear the tall, pointed hats of accused heretics and forced to parade in the streets on Good Friday. This belongs to a series of paintings illustrating aspects of Spanish life that the liberals had tried to reform, but which were retained by Ferdinand VII. His restoration of the Inquisition created widespread fear.

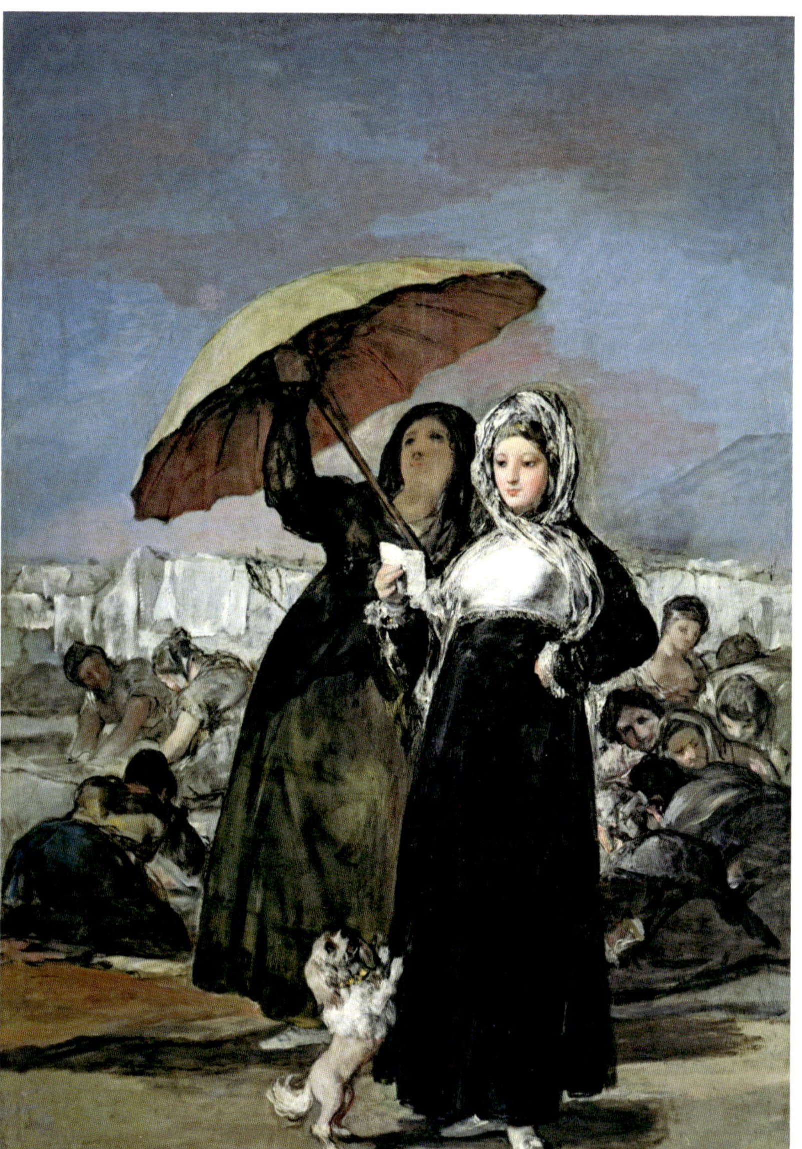

Young Women or *The Letter,* c.1814–19, oil on canvas, Palais des Beaux Arts, Lille, France, 181 x 125cm (71 x 49in)

A fashionable, wealthy young woman stands under a parasol held by her maid. She reads a love letter as her little dog jumps up at her. In contrast, behind her is a crowd of common people. This painting symbolizes the futility of idleness – and of lust. Some of Goya's reddish underpainting can be seen, while black dominates the palette, and brushstrokes are loose and confident. The style was later emulated by Manet.

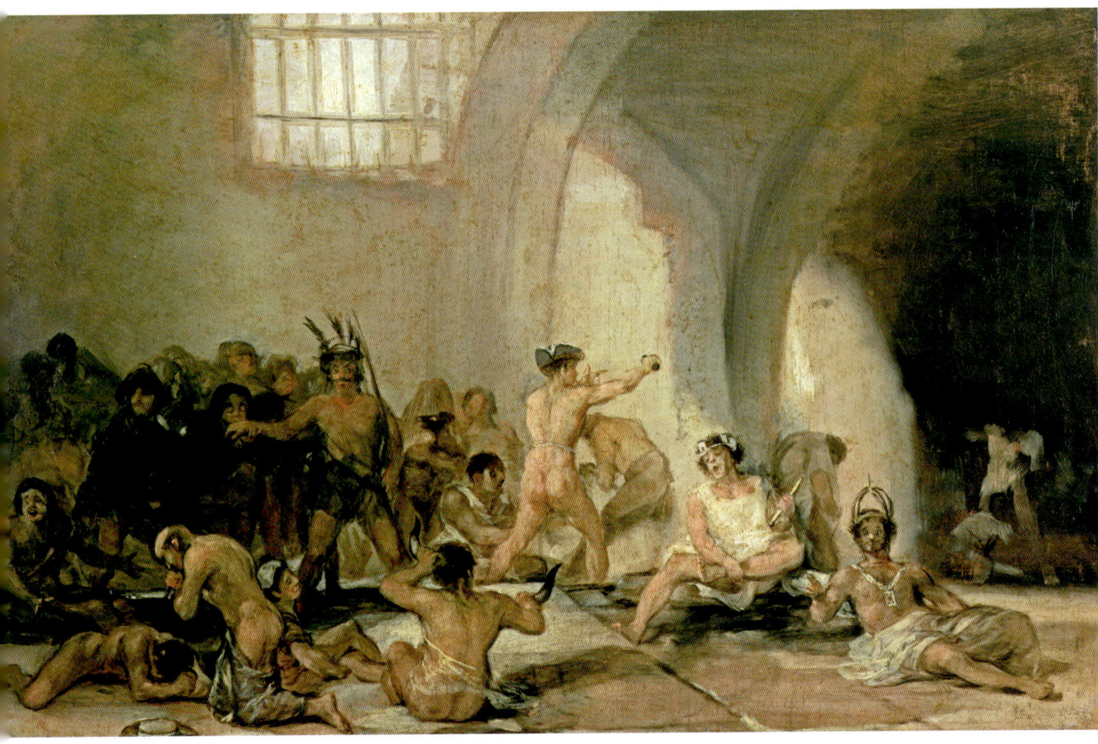

The Madhouse, c.1812–19, oil on panel, Real Academia de Bellas Artes de San Fernando, Madrid, Spain, 45 x 72cm (18 x 28in)

With a juxtaposition of the joviality of the madmen and the harsh reality of their condition, Goya creates this scene with shadows; figures can be discerned indistinctly. One wears a crown, another wears a feathered headdress and one holds tarot cards. Although unaware of their plight, their postures and gestures indicate the pitiful situation. Goya was concerned about the treatment of the insane, physically sick and prisoners.

The Burial of the Sardine, c.1812–19, oil on panel, Real Academia de Bellas Artes de San Fernando, Madrid, Spain, 82.5 x 62cm (32.5 x 24in)

This was a three-day carnival celebrated in Madrid leading up to Ash Wednesday, marking the beginning of Lent. Most of the revellers dressed in grotesque masks and disguises and the celebrations ended with a procession to the banks of the Manzanares where they buried a ceremonial papier-mâché 'sardine'. Goya does not illustrate the sardine however, but a banner featuring a grinning fool; suggestive of the Bourbon monarchy.

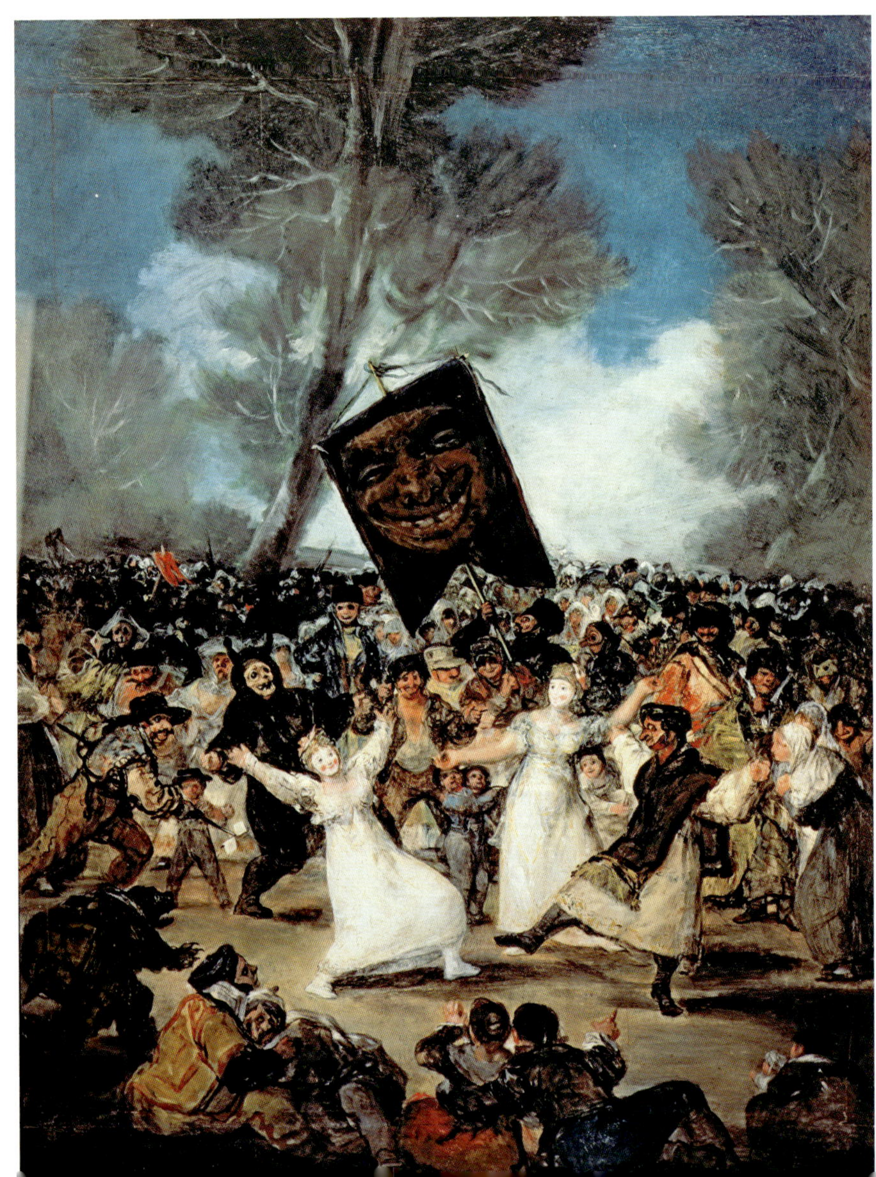

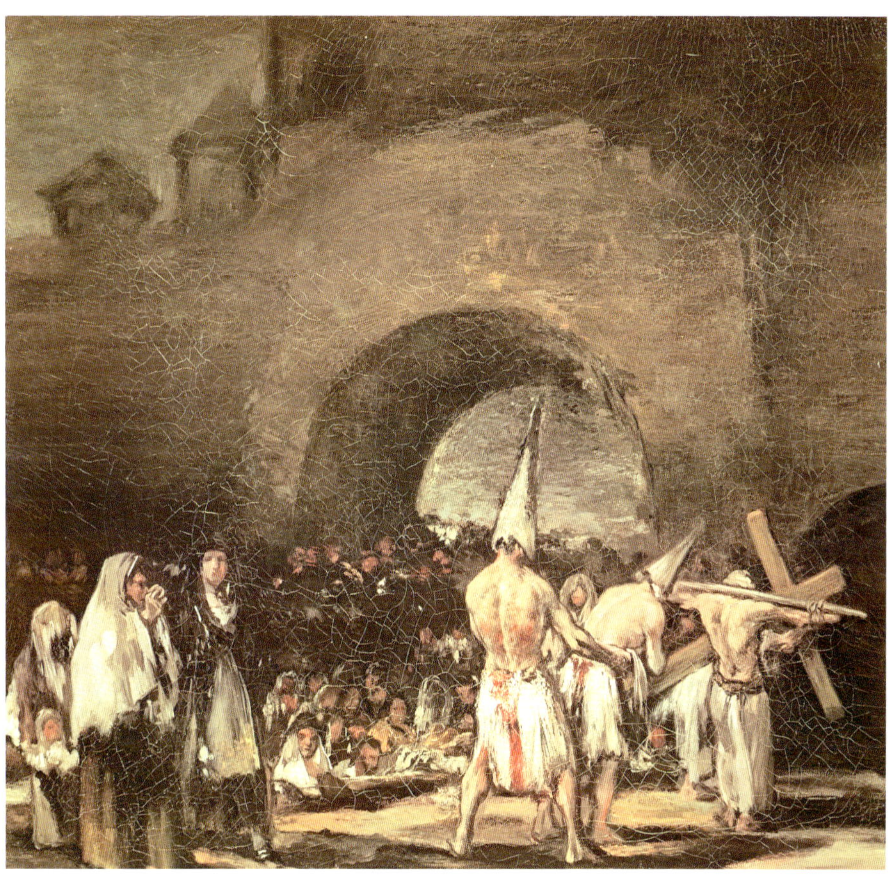

Flagellants Near an Arch, c.1812–20, oil on canvas, Museo Nacional de Belles Artes, Buenos Aires, Argentina, 72 x 100cm (28 x 39in)

Flaunting the barbaric practice of parading flagellants in the streets, Goya explicitly conveys their misery and humiliation. As in the painting on page 227, the flagellants are stripped to the waist and bleeding, wearing the tall, conical hats of accused heretics. Some are made to carry heavy crosses to emulate Jesus on his way to the Crucifixion. The spectators appear to be watching in horrified silence.

The Mass at Parida, c.1812–20, oil on canvas, Museo Lázaro Galdiano, Madrid, Spain, 36 x 46cm (14 x 18in)

In Christian tradition, the churching of women is a blessing given to new mothers after childbirth and the baptism, when they gave thanks to God for the birth and received the graces necessary to raise their children in a manner pleasing to God. This church scene features a kneeling mother with her baby in her arms, being blessed by a priest in front of a congregation.

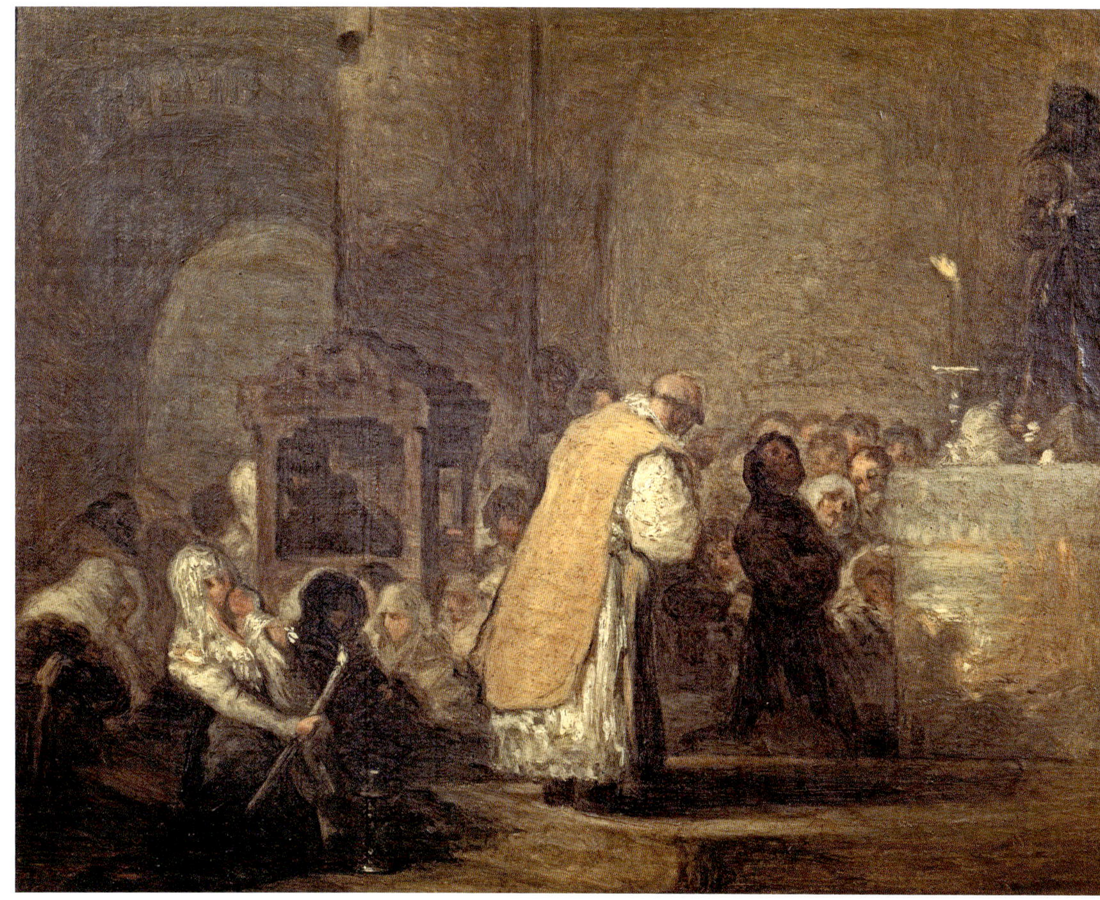

Still Life with Three Salmon Steaks, c.1808–12, oil on canvas, Oskar Reinhart Collection, Winterthur, Switzerland, 44 x 62cm (17 x 24½in)

Although Goya painted prolifically and was one of the earliest artists to spend much of his time painting for his own pleasure, rather than purely relying on commissions, few of these were still lifes. This demonstrates his ability to paint exactly what he saw in front of him. A pile of salmon steaks are reproduced with utmost clarity in dramatic lighting. The subject is modest, but the treatment is noble.

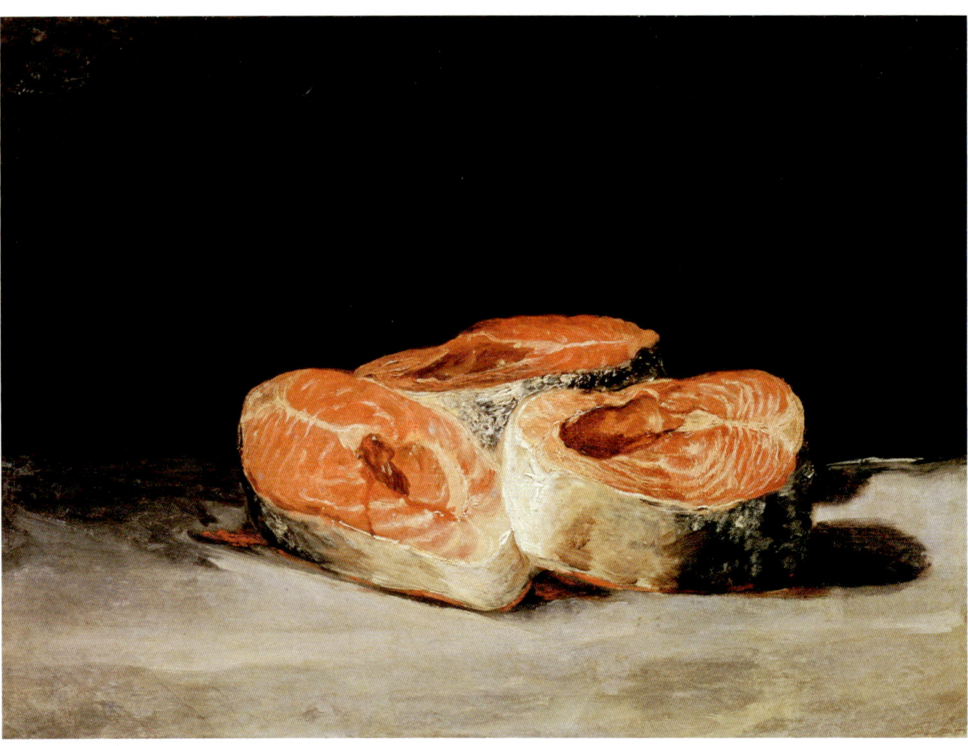

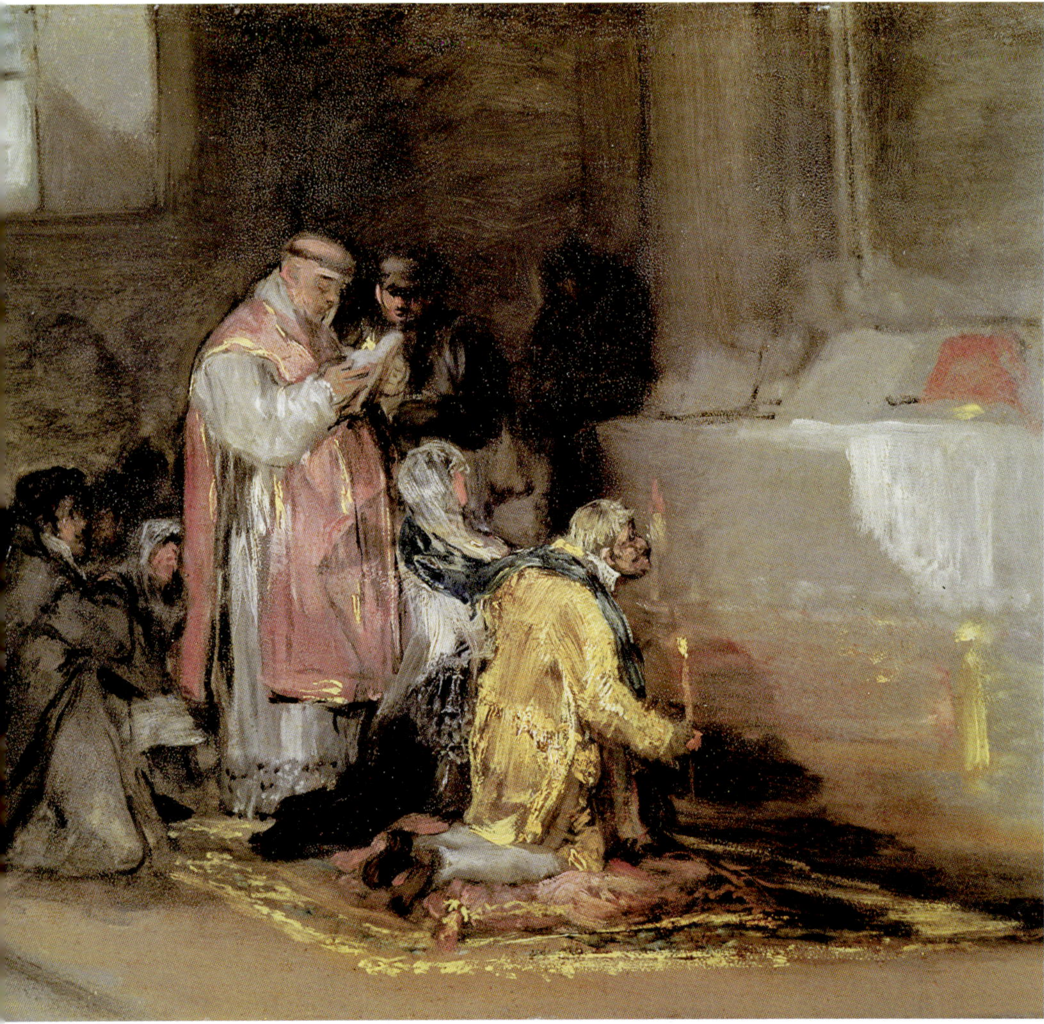

The Unequal Wedding or *Wedding of the Ill-Assorted Couple*, c.1819, oil on tin plate, Museo Lázaro Galdiano, Madrid, Spain, 32 x 41.5cm (12½ x 16in)

This is a theme that Goya had represented previously in 1791–2 in a tapestry cartoon. Here, in a vibrant, sketchy and expressive technique, using his predominantly black and gold palette of that time, a bent old man in a gaudy gold coat kneels next to an upright, youthful young woman in a veil. A plump priest in pink and gold vestments stands over them to bless their union.

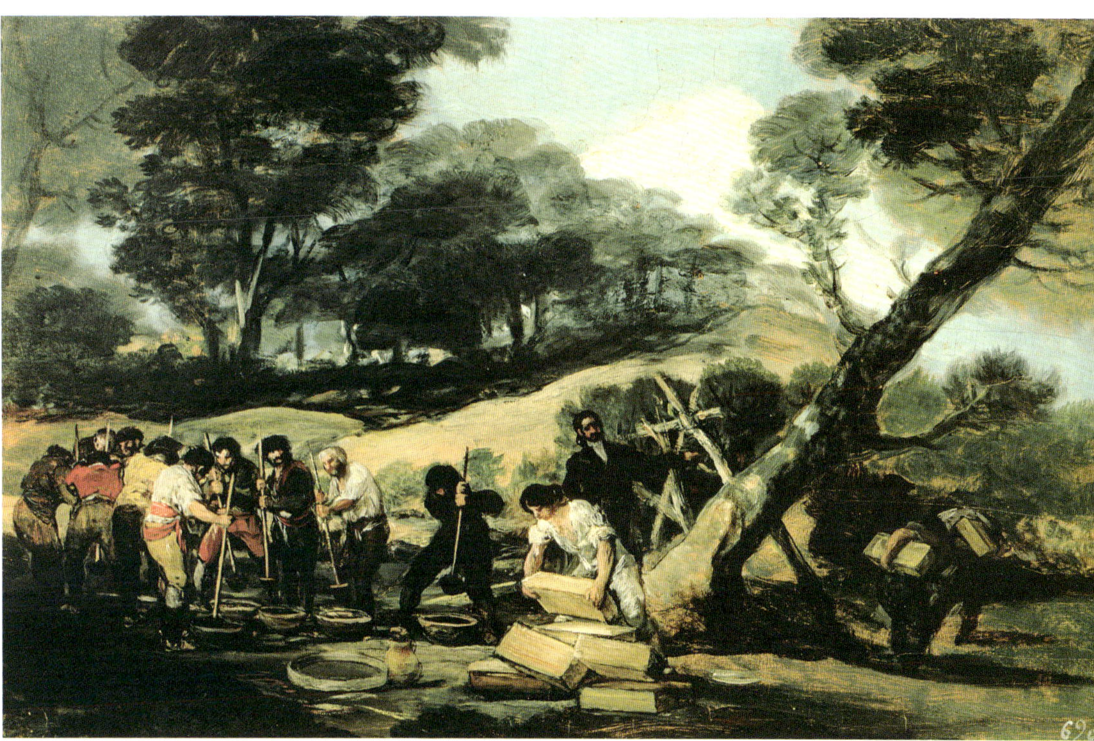

Making Gunpowder in the Sierra, c.1810–14, oil on panel, Palacio Real, Madrid, Spain, 33 x 52cm (13 x 20½in)

This is one of two small paintings showing the clandestine making of powder and shot in Aragon during the war years. They were precursors to Goya's two huge masterpieces of the events of May 1808 (see pages 70–1 and 233). Although his palette here is still not as bright as his earlier work, this is nonetheless brighter than many of his more recent works. He once again creates a dynamic composition using unexpected arrangements.

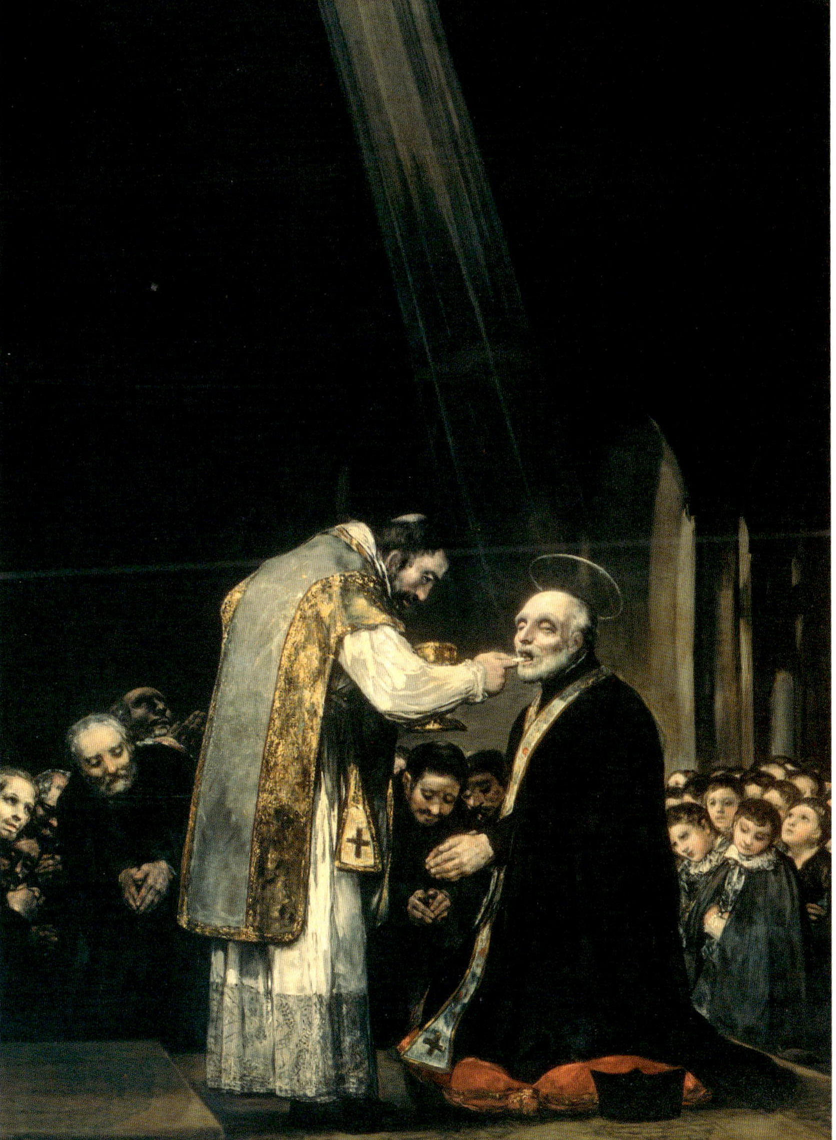

The Last Communion of San José de Calasanz, 1819, oil on canvas, Escuelas Pías de San Antón, Madrid, Spain, 250 x 180cm (99 x 71in)

Fatally ill, Saint José had risen from his bed to receive his last holy communion. Here, he kneels before an administering priest. Both figures are almost in profile, while his students and monks of the church of San Pantaleon in Rome can be seen behind them. José's gentle face and lowered eyelids depict a divine man who served others throughout his life.

Detail from *The Second of May, 1808* (opposite)

This figure is stabbing one of the Mamluks' horses. With loose and gestural brushstrokes and blocks of colour, Goya has captured the Spaniard's facial expression. The red blood pouring on the white horse is in stark contrast, while legs, bodies, heads and arms all combine to convey an impression of confusion, action and noise. Goya used a brighter palette than he had been working with in recent works.

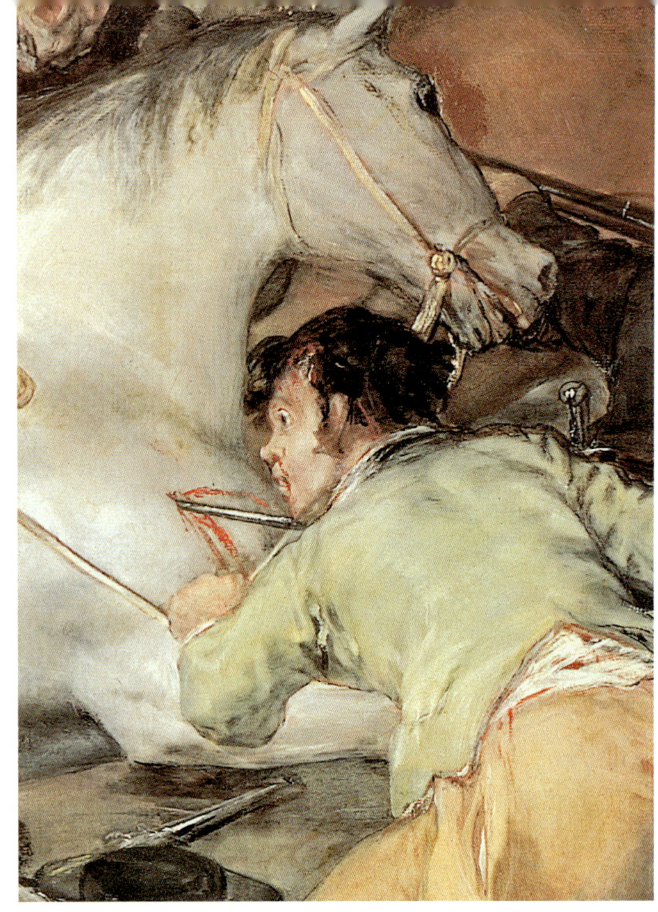

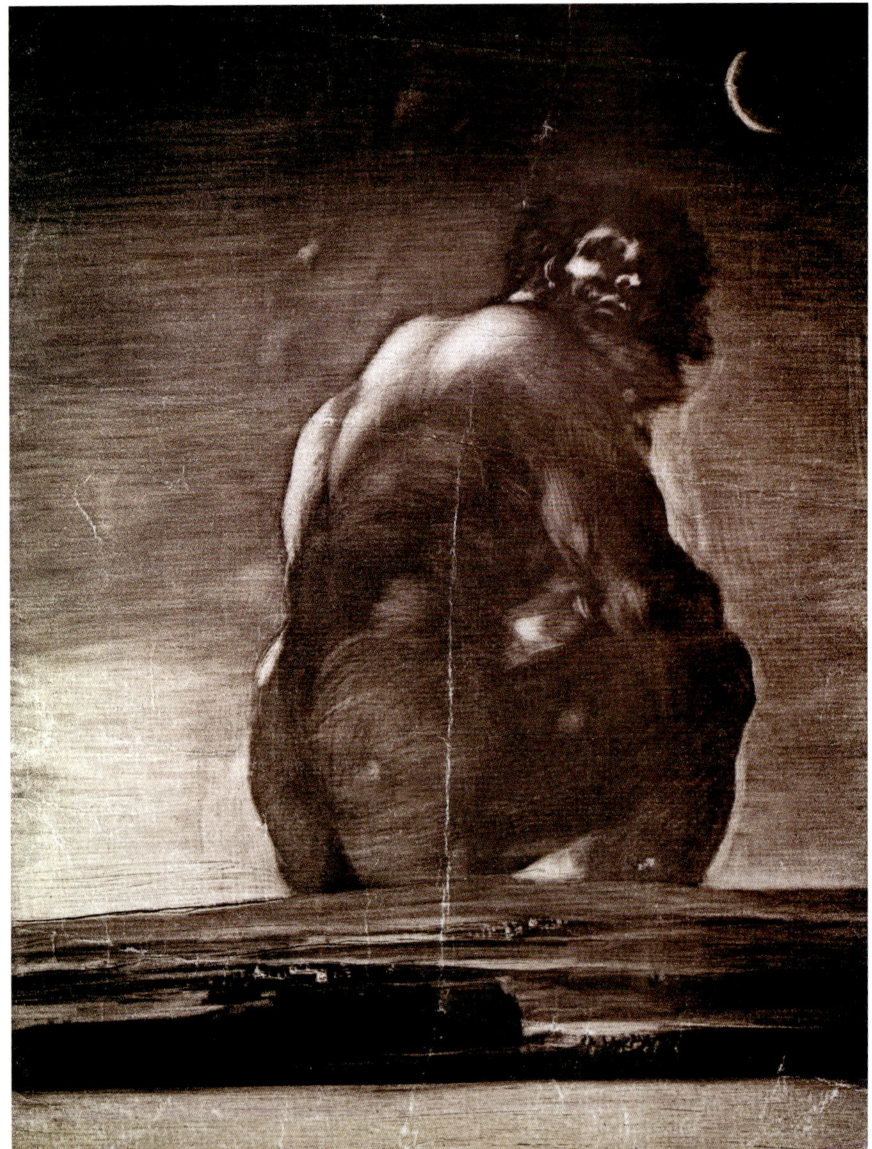

The Colossus, c.1810–18, mezzotint, Biblioteca Nacional de Bellas Artes, Madrid, Spain, 28.5 x 21cm (11 x 8in)

Evoking the anxiety created by the confrontation of an overwhelming power, Goya's Giant sits with his back to viewers, a menacing presence in the landscape. This is the only mezzotint etching that Goya made, but like all his prints, it is exceptionally accomplished and subtle. The procedure requires specialist skill, but Goya took to it with alacrity. Interpretations of this image remain enigmatic and mysterious.

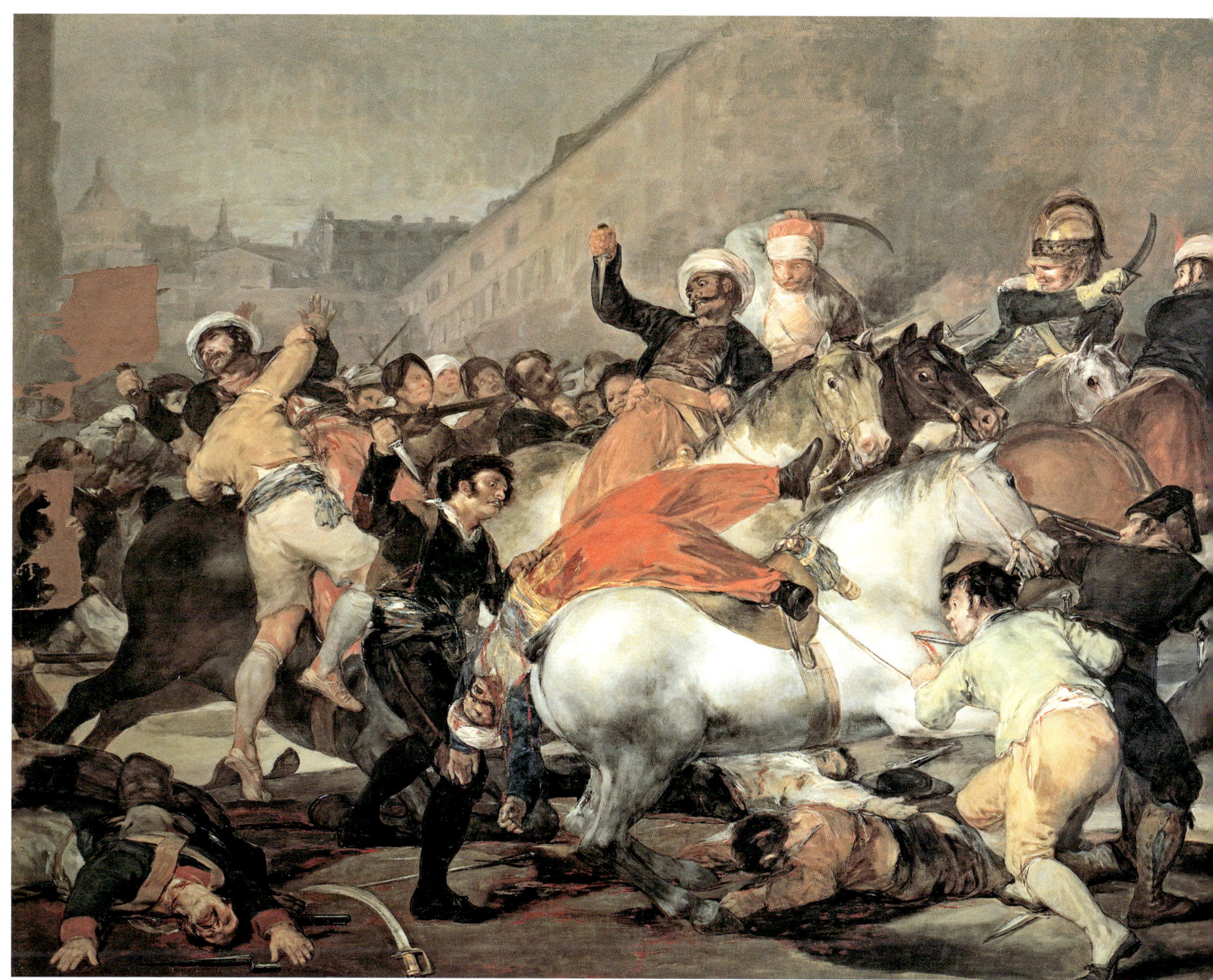

The Second of May, 1808, 1814, oil on canvas, Museo Nacional del Prado, Madrid, Spain, 268.5 x 347.5cm (106 x 137in)

Representing the spontaneous uprising of Madrid's population against the Mamluks of the Napoleonic cavalry on 2 May 1808, this records acts of heroism in the face of overpowering strength. In the riotous scene, the people of Madrid, armed with knives and rough weapons attack the mounted Egyptian soldiers and a cuirassier of the Imperial army. With no focal point, the colourful confusion is created with dense impasto paint.

Detail from *The Third of May, 1808* (below)

The head of one of the dead rebels, shot for his involvement on 2 May in the uprising against the Mamluks at the Puerta del Sol, is meant to shock. Soaked in blood, this exemplifies the horrific murder of defenceless individuals. The loose brush marks, composition, colouring and lurid elements are all original to Goya. His complete break with the painting traditions of the past are consolidated.

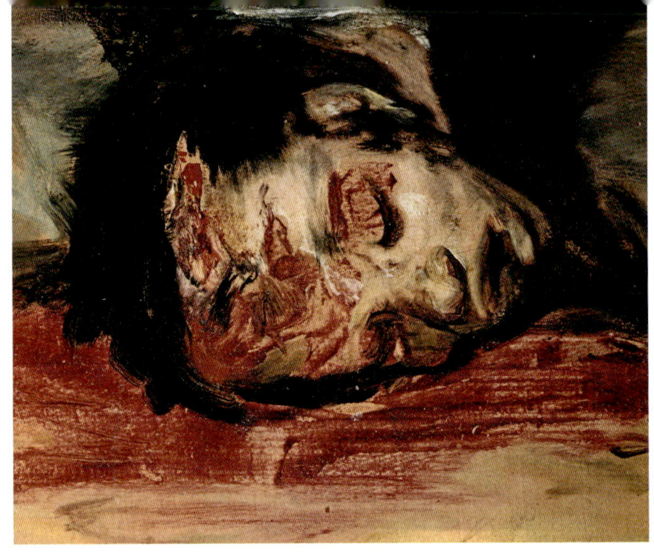

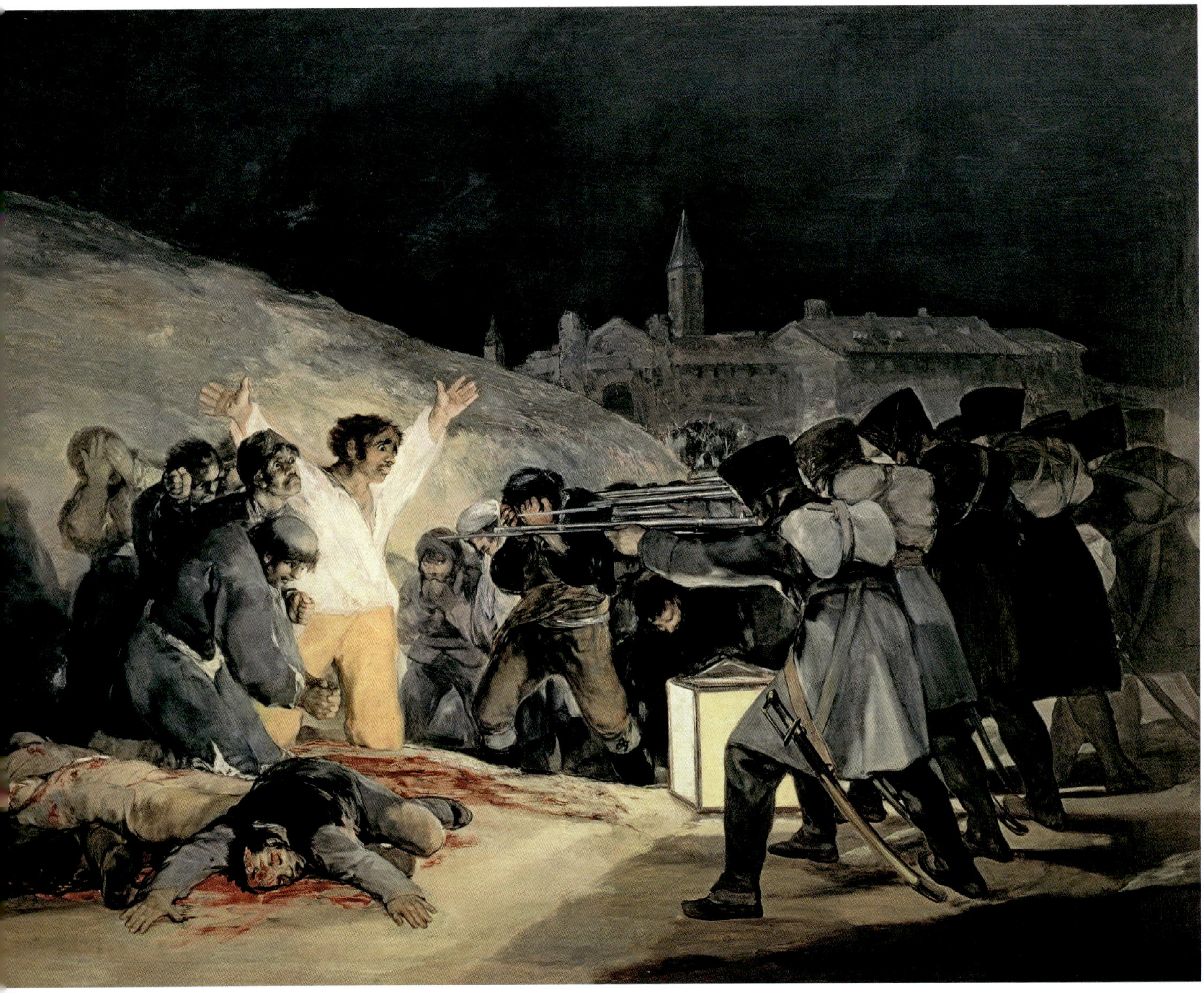

The Third of May, 1808, 1814, oil on canvas, Museo Nacional del Prado, Madrid, Spain, 266 x 345cm (105 x 136in)

While *The Second of May* depicts the bloody battle between rebels and Mamluks as a frenzied affray, this shows the executions of the following day. Under a dark sky, French soldiers shoot citizens taken from the streets of Madrid at close range. The lantern, the only source of light, heightens the impact of the scene, highlighting dead bodies soaked in blood and dazzlingly illuminates the central figure; a poor man, sacrificing himself for his country. See also pages 70–1.

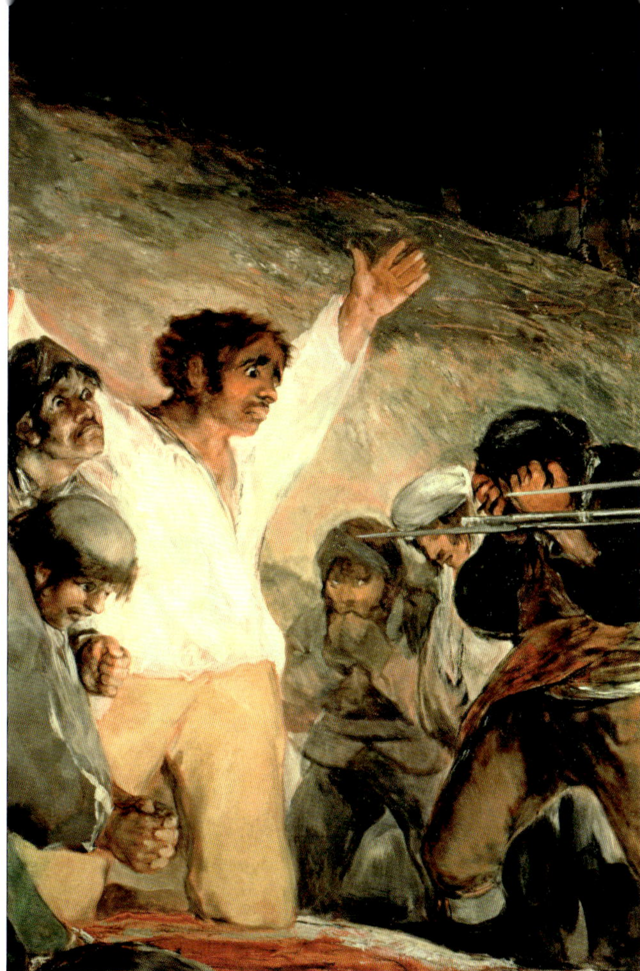

Detail from *The Third of May, 1808* (opposite below)

The central figure, being shot at point blank range, is reminiscent of Christ on the Cross. His white shirt illuminated by the lantern, is the brightest element in the painting, and a symbol of purity and innocence. These are ordinary Spanish men with no military experience. Dignified and terrified, this man is a hopeless victim in a doomed situation, Goya's reference to Christ is a deliberate comparison.

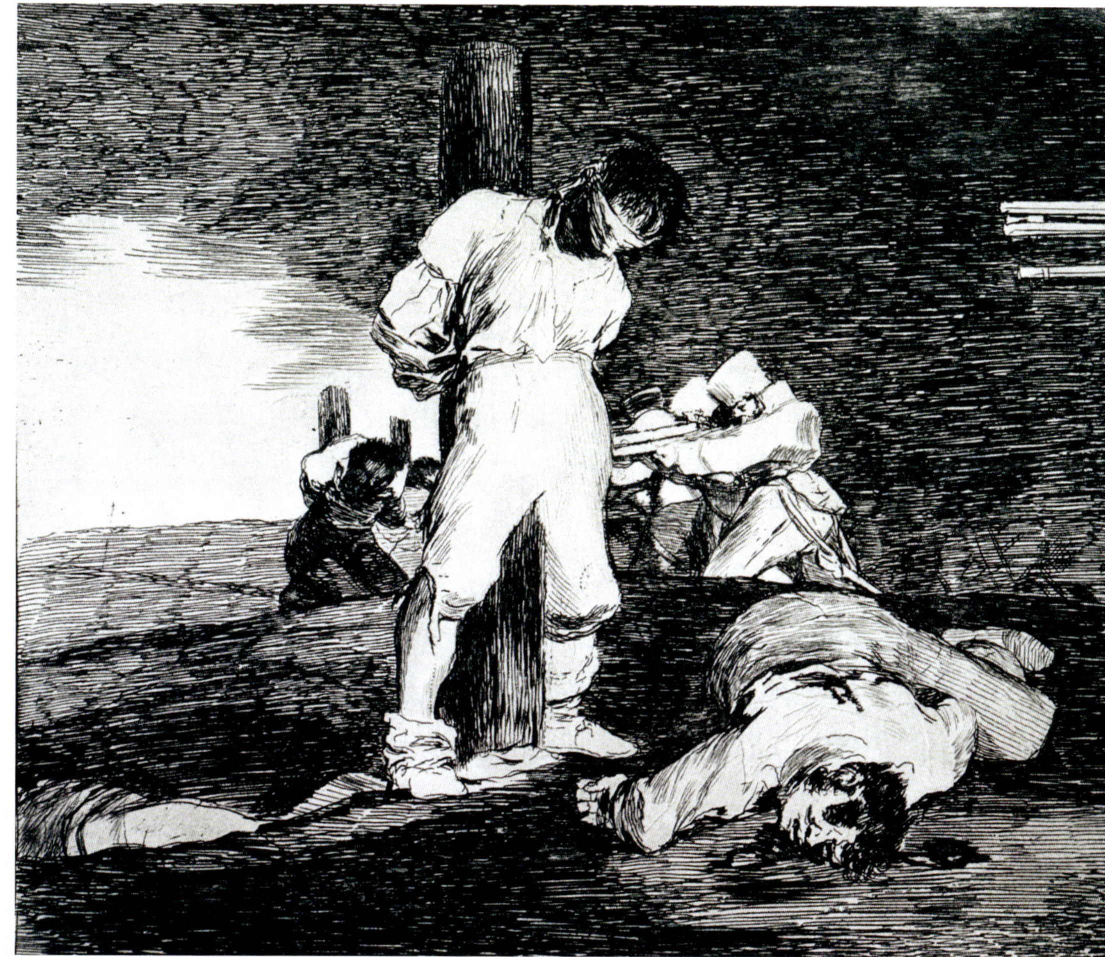

And It Can't Be Helped, c.1810–11, etching, Private Collection, 14.1 x 16.8cm (5½ x 6½in)

French soldiers often executed rebellious peasants, and this etching, which form part of Goya's series, *The Disasters of War*, prefigures elements of *The Third of May, 1808*. The radical composition shows only the barrels of the soldiers' guns to the right, while the defenceless, condemned man is tied to a post in the centre. In this way, Goya emphasizes the lack of emotion and immorality of the war.

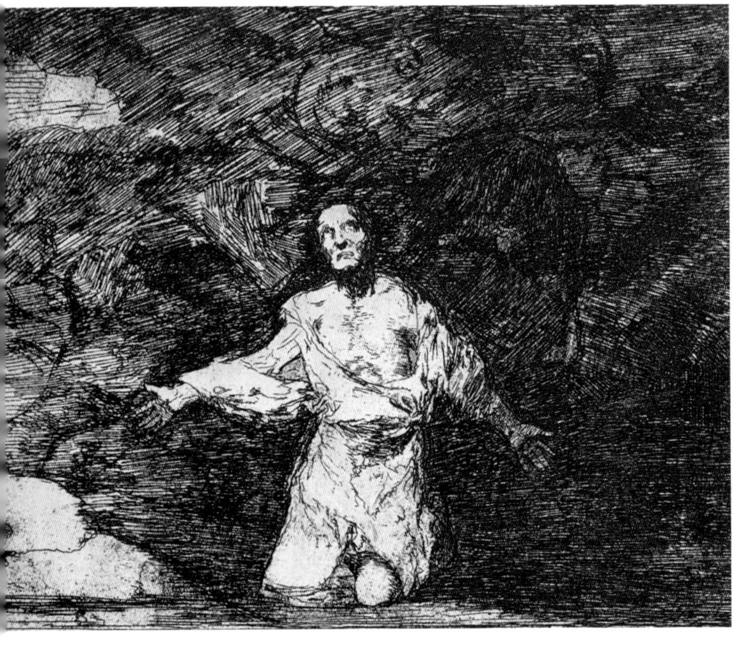

*Sad Forebodings of What is Going to Happen, c.*1810, drypoint and etching, Private Collection, 17.8 x 22cm (7 x 8½in)

A kneeling man in torn clothing, his eyes looking up, was the first of Goya's *The Disasters of War*. The series was executed over several years and included three main groups; war scenes, scenes of famine and anticlerical images. The provocative plates were stored away when Goya left Spain and were not printed in his lifetime. The first edition was made in Madrid in 1863.

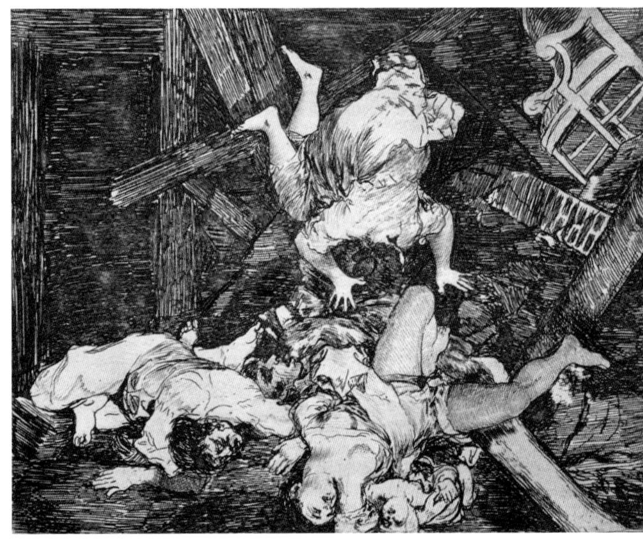

*Ravages of War, c.*1810–11, etching, The Metropolitan Museum of Art, New York, USA, 14.1 x 17cm (5½ x 7in)

With a dramatic inverted triangle-shaped composition, this etching shows a family annihilated by war. Their house destroyed, the people have been killed and tossed aside; their lives are deemed unimportant by the French soldiers. This image emphasizes the hopelessness, desolation and senseless killing of war. From 1810 to 1820, Goya produced 82 prints in this series and 73 preparatory drawings, all promoting an unreserved, powerful anti-war message.

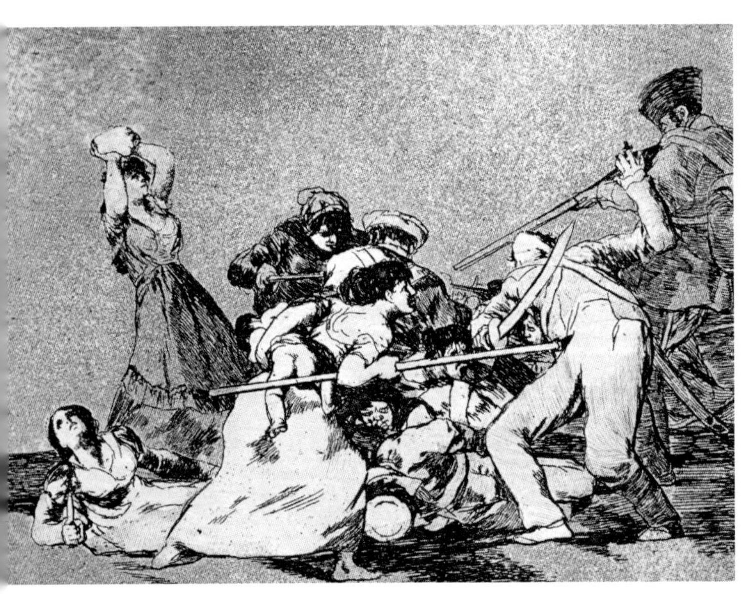

*And They Are Like Wild Beasts, c.*1812–15, etching and aquatint, Norton Simon Museum, California, USA, 15.5 x 21cm (6 x 8in)

Goya's *Disasters of War* depict the brutality and senselessness of war. In the images, his interpretations of the horrific events reached an unprecedented level of violence and modern compositions. Even more graphic than *Los Caprichos*, they include depictions of torture, rape, mutilation and execution – an entire gamut of human suffering. No other artist before him had portrayed such negative representations of war.

Neither Do These, c.1810–15, etching, drypoint, aquatint and burin, Museum of Fine Arts, Boston, USA, 15 x 21.6cm (6 x 8½in)

After the horrific images of war, Goya created three prints showing the violent and shocking elements of rape. Set in shadows under an archway, a helpless baby lies at the feet of a young woman dressed in pure white, being man-handled. In the background is a church; close, but not close enough. Despite the time that has passed since Goya created these, the images remain distressing.

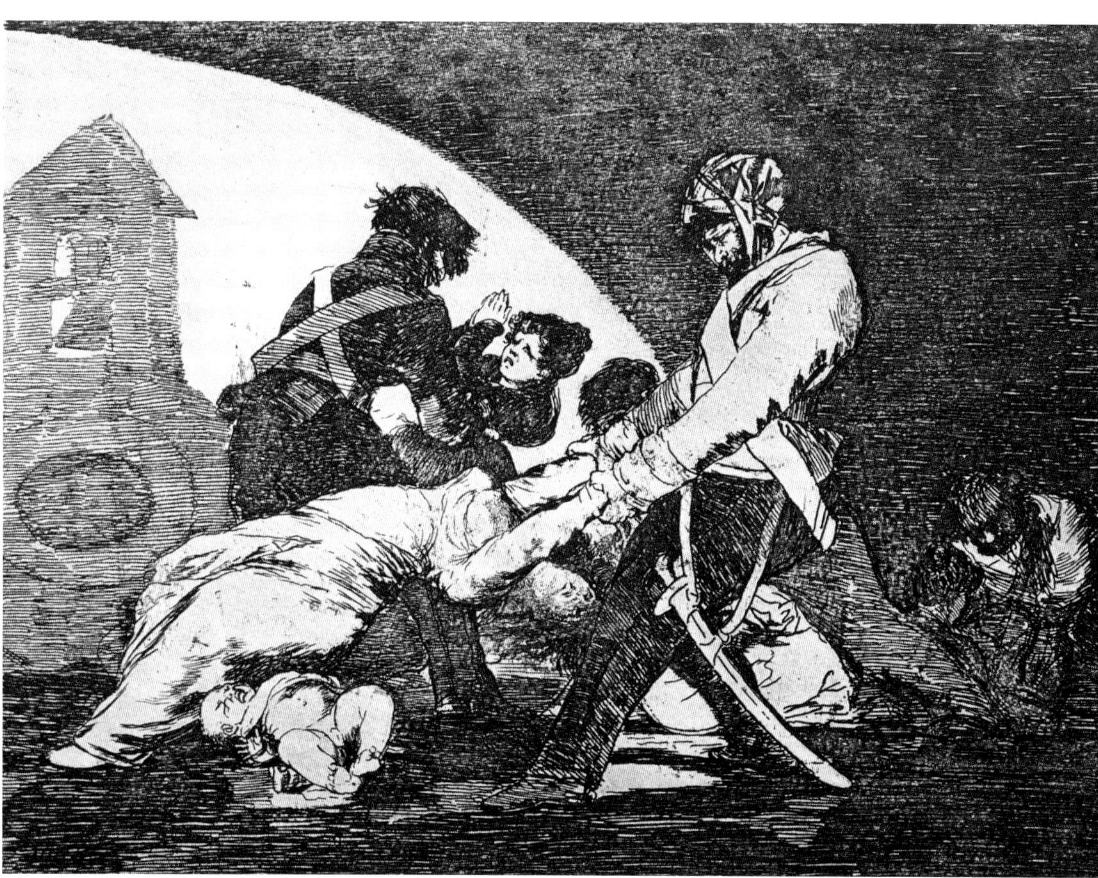

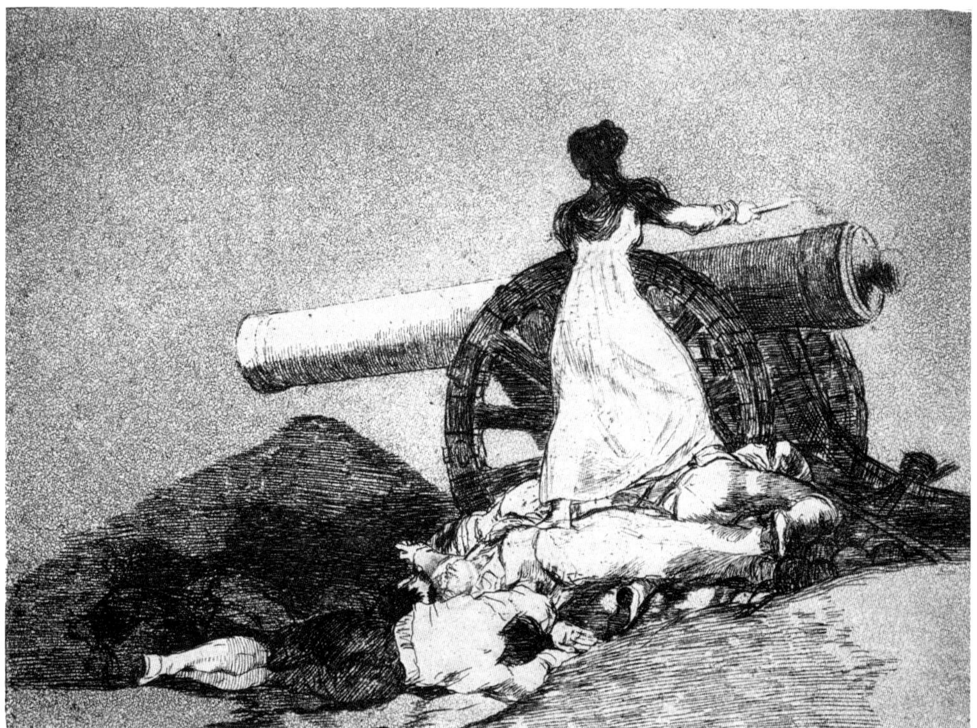

*What Courage! (Que Valor!) c.*1810–15, etching, aquatint, drypoint, burin and burnisher on paper, National Galleries of Scotland, Edinburgh, UK, 15.5 x 21cm (6 x 8in)

This is one of the few of Goya's *Disasters of War* to depict a well-known event. It shows 22-year-old Augustina Zaragoza (also known as Agustina de Aragon) during the 1807 Napoleonic siege of Saragossa. She stands on the bodies of fallen Spanish artillerymen as she fires a canon at the French army, her white dress contrasting dramatically with the dark canon and dead soldiers.

Barbarians, c.1812–15,
etching, burnished aquatint,
burin and burnisher,
Museum of Fine Arts,
Boston, USA, 15.5 x 20.6cm
(6 x 8in)

Similar to *The Third of May,
1808* (see pages 70–1), in
this print, French soldiers
fire at a helpless man from
a point-blank range. In this
image, however, the man's
face cannot be seen as he is
tied firmly to a tree. Goya's
shocking, immediate and
impactful compositions had
no precedent and influenced
generations of subsequent
artists. By this time, every
image Goya produced he
was completely unique
and innovative.

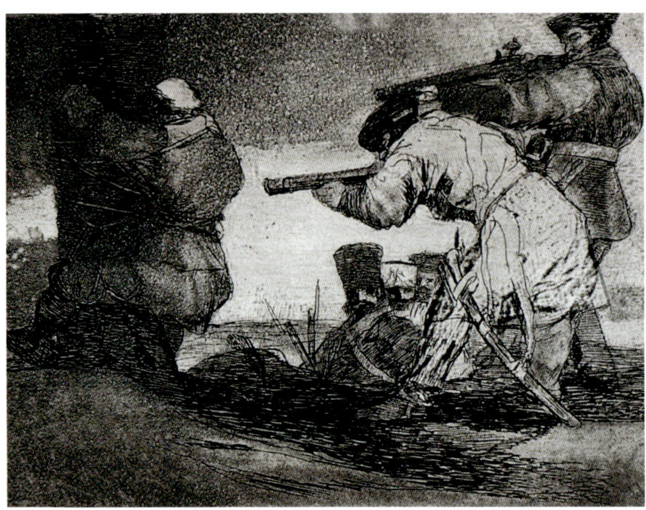

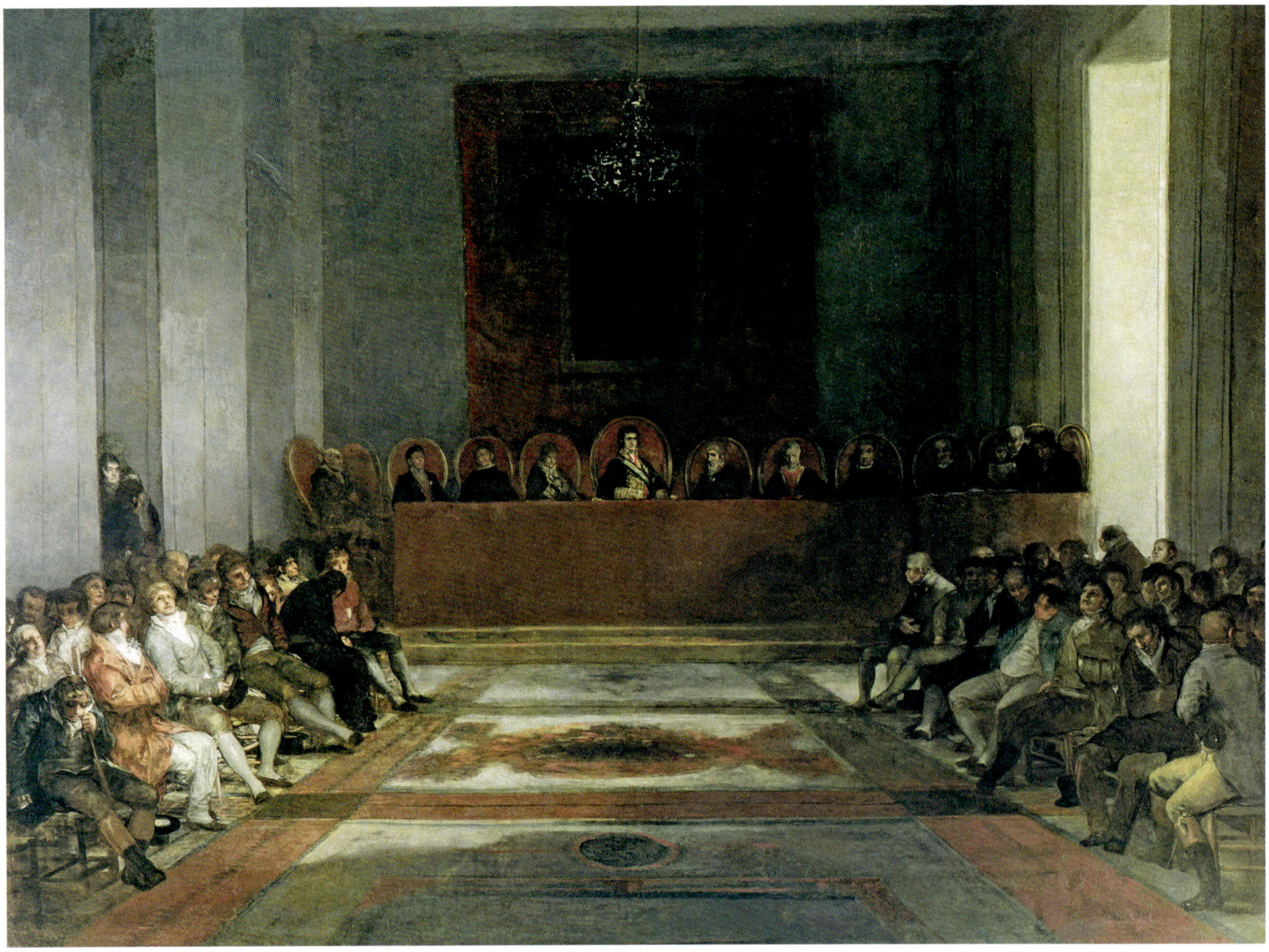

The Junta of the Philippines,
1815, oil on canvas, Musée
Goya, Castres, France,
327 x 447cm (129 x 176in)

In April 1815, Goya was
commissioned to paint this
to record the annual general
meeting of the publicly-held
trading company, the Royal
Company of the Philippines.
On 30th March 1815,
Ferdinand VII attended the
meeting for the first time.
Two groups of bored-looking
men face each other across
a wide room. It is the largest
canvas Goya painted, created
to hang in the hall itself.

Ferdinand VII, 1814, oil on canvas, Museo de Bellas Artes, Santander, Spain, 225.5 x 124.5cm (89 x 49in)

With the King's restoration, Goya turned again to portraiture. From the end of 1814 and throughout 1815 he produced a remarkable series of masterpieces including this portrait of the King himself, which was one of six he executed during that time commissioned by ministers and others. This was painted at the end of 1814 from the preparatory sketches he had made of Ferdinand before the war.

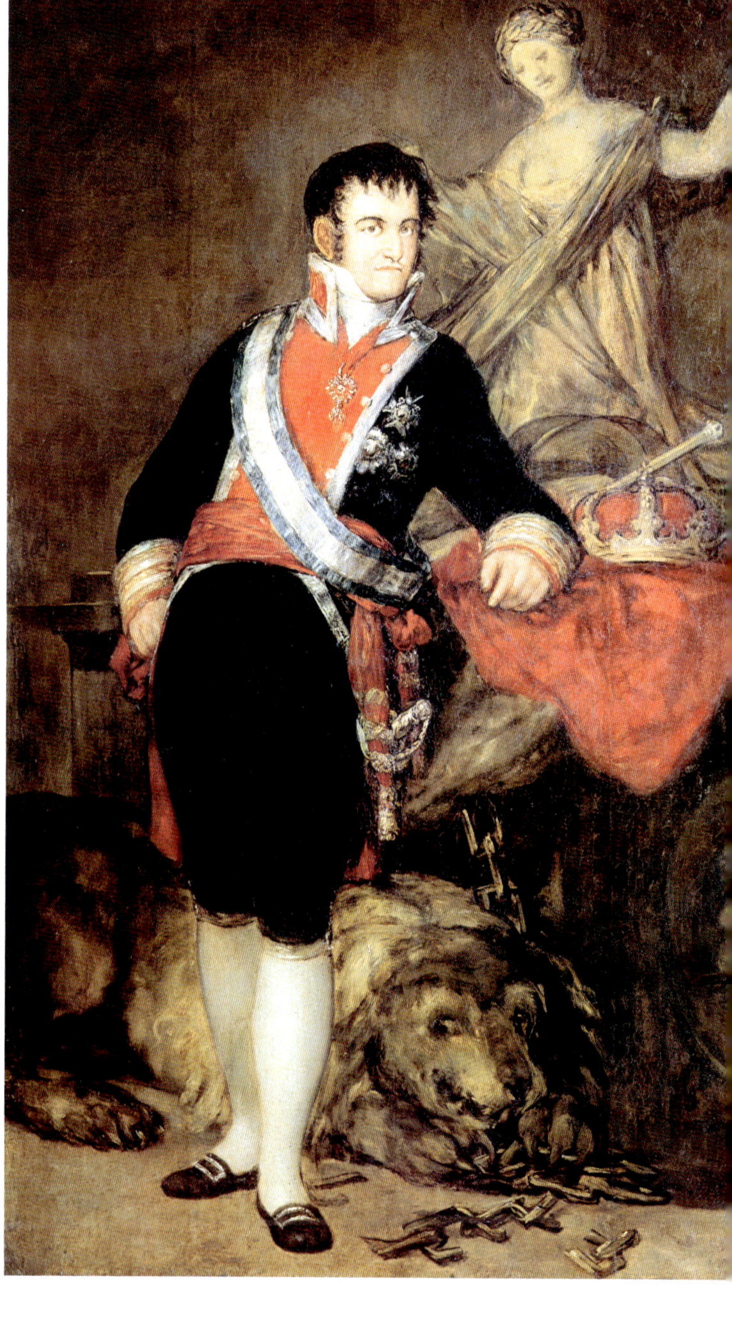

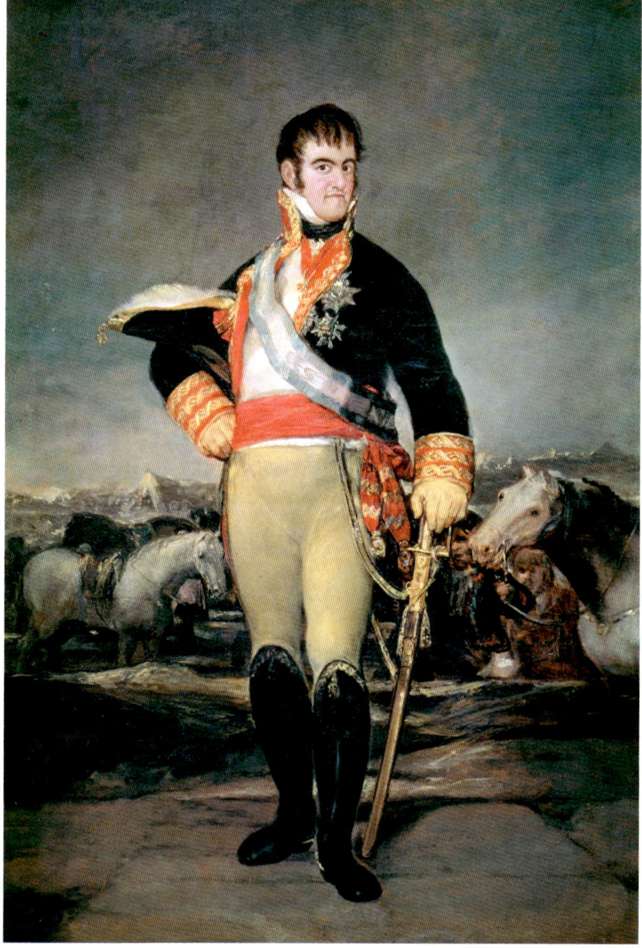

Ferdinand VII in an Encampment, 1814, oil on canvas, Museo Nacional del Prado, Madrid, Spain, 207 x 140cm (81½ x 55in)

In the dress uniform of a Captain General and sporting numerous honours, including the Grand Cross of the Order of Charles III, the cross of the Order of Saint Januarius Naples and the Golden Fleece hanging from a red ribbon around his neck. Horses stand behind him as he stands holding his hat in the crook of his arm, his left hand resting on the hilt of his ornamental sword.

The Duke of San Carlos, 1815, oil on canvas, Musée des Beaux-Arts, Saragossa, Spain, 280 x 125cm (110 x 49in)

In 1815, Goya was commissioned by the Council in charge of the Imperial Canal of Aragon to paint portraits of Ferdinand VII and the Duke of San Carlos, the King's closest adviser. The Duke, Don José Miguel de Carvajal Vargas y Manrique, had supported Ferdinand VII since before the war and remained with him in France. He convinced Ferdinand to keep Goya as his First Court Painter. Yet he was ugly and short-sighted, and the King later dismissed him using this as a pretext.

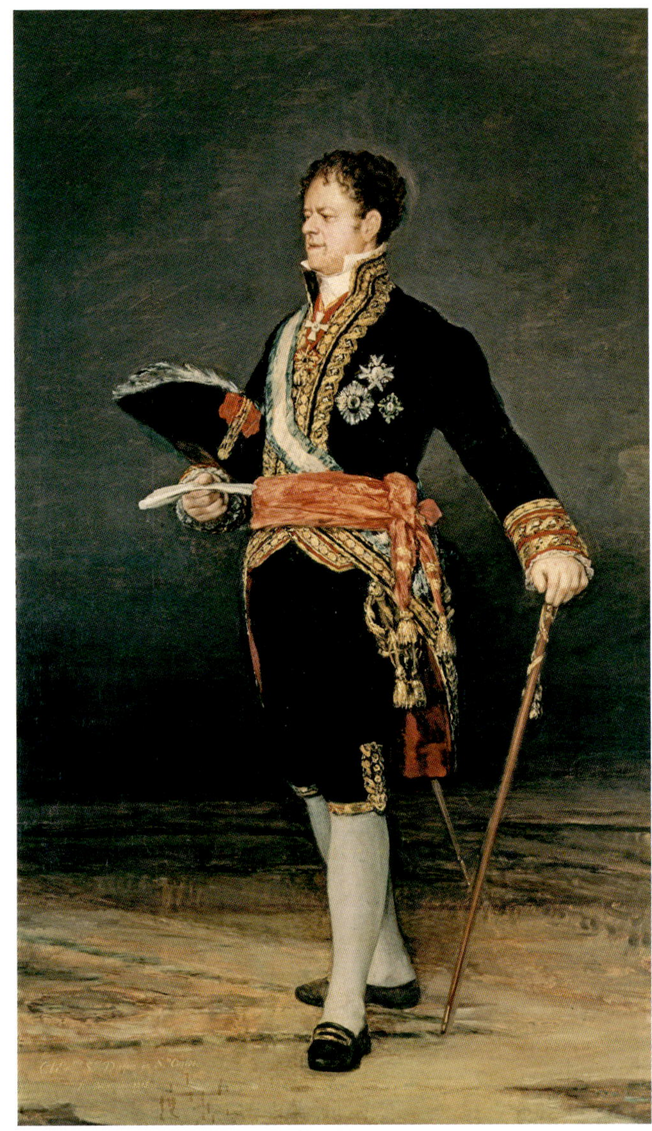

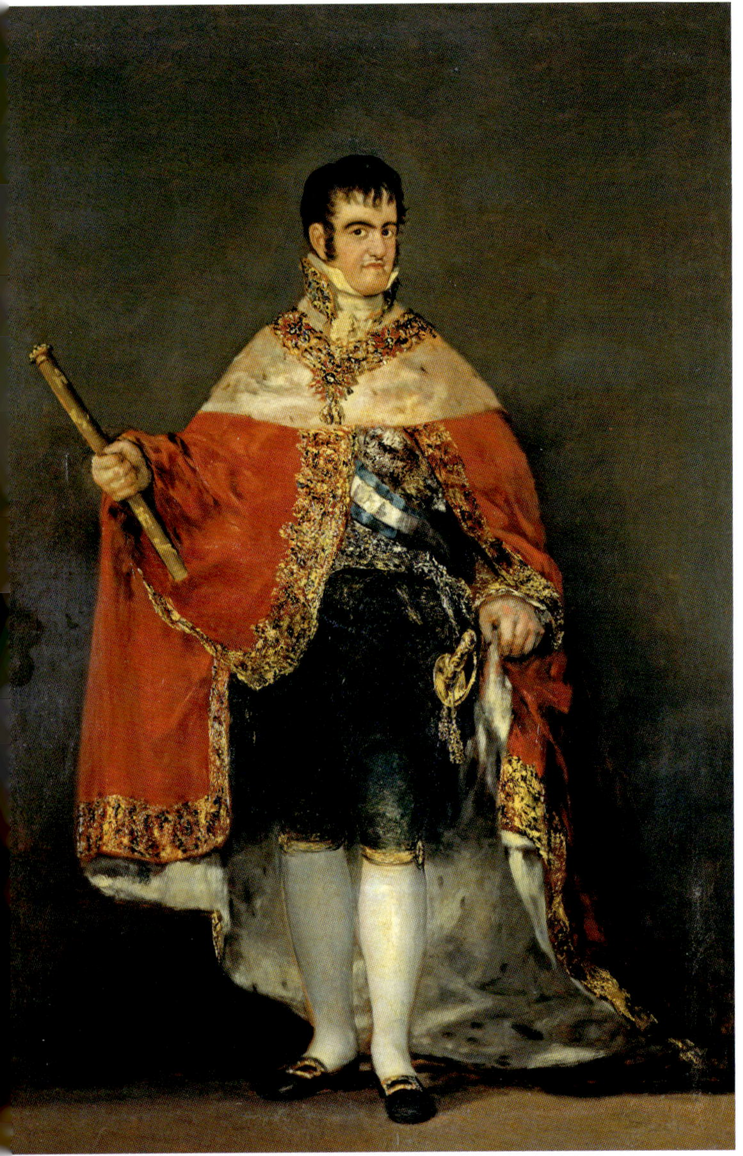

Ferdinand VII with a Royal Robe, 1814-15, oil on canvas, Museo Nacional del Prado, Madrid, Spain, 208 x 142.5cm (82 x 56in)

The portraits of the King painted at this time were commissioned by various societies and organizations. As he could not obtain sittings from Ferdinand, he only had his original sketches from before the war to rely on. So he struggled to make each look different. Unlike his previous intrepid royal portraits, they appear a little stiff and lack the vivacity and personal insights of the artist.

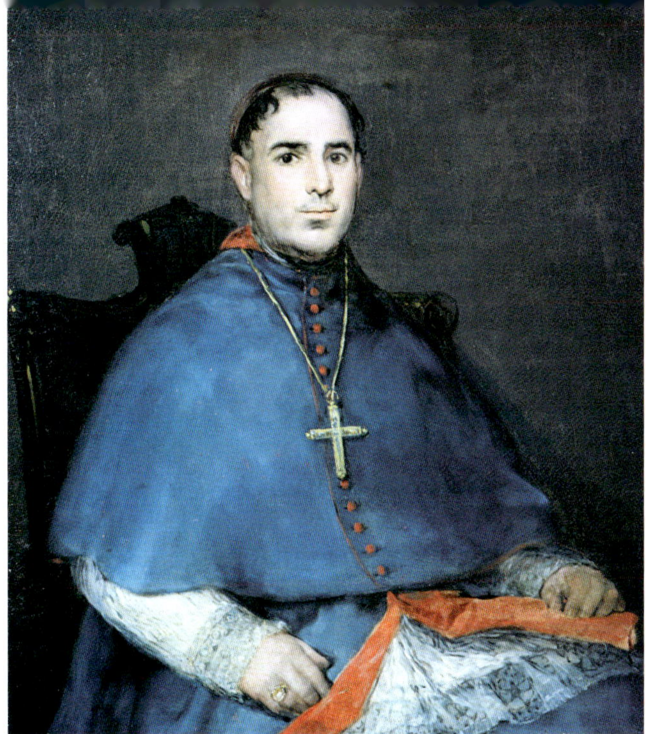

Bishop Don Fray Miguel Fernández, 1815, oil on canvas, Worcester Art Museum, Massachusetts, USA, 100 x 84cm (39 x 33in)

Painted in the year that Bishop Fernández was appointed to the diocese of Quito in Ecuador, this work is inscribed with: 'The most illustrious Señor Don Fr Miguel Fernández, Bishop of Marcopolis, Apostolic Administrator of Quito.' However, Fernández never did assume his position, as he became Archbishop of Seville instead. Despite the brilliant colours in this portrait, unusually, Goya has revealed little about the underlying personality of the sitter.

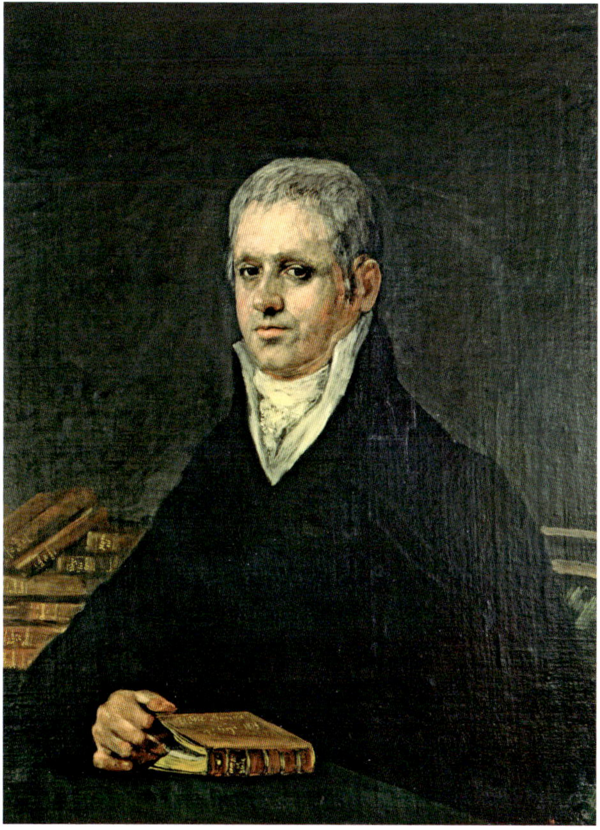

José Luis Munárriz, 1815, oil on canvas, Real Academia de Bellas Artes de San Fernando, Madrid, Spain, 85 x 64cm (33½ x 25in)

A writer, translator and literary critic, in the year of this portrait, José Luis Munárriz (1752–1830) was made secretary and director of the Company of the Philippines, and was also an honorary member of the Royal Academy of Fine Arts of San Fernando. When the French invaded Spain, he emigrated to Galicia, south of Portugal, and returned to Madrid in 1813.

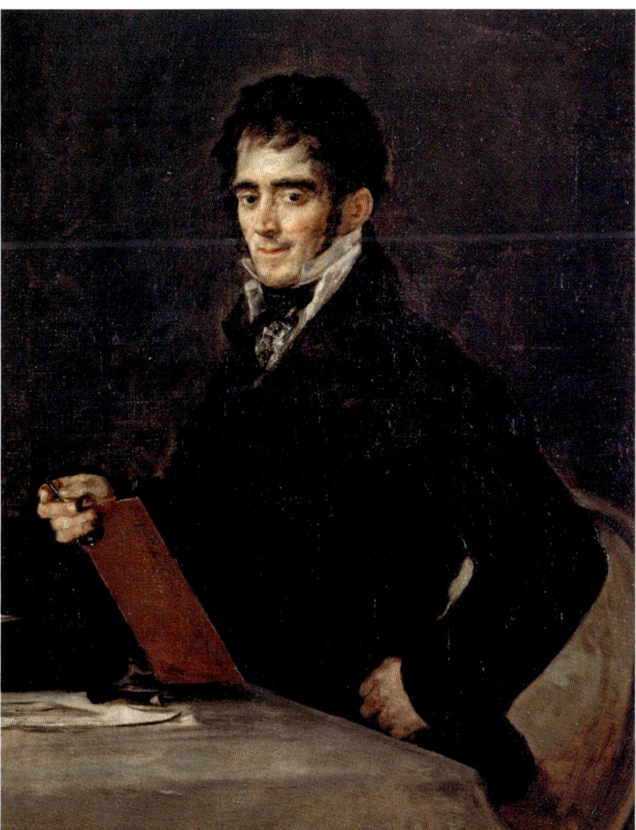

Rafael Esteve, 1815, oil on canvas, Museum of Fine Arts, Valencia, Spain, 100.6 x 79.5cm (39½ x 31in)

Etching is a skilled and intuitive process and the use of aquatint in etching was little used. Goya experimented and perfected the process, but he also worked with others to develop ideas, including Rafael Esteve y Vilella (1772–1847). Although their methods were different, Goya and Esteve shared a passion for their printing and they had a long friendship. This portrays Esteve at the height of his successful career.

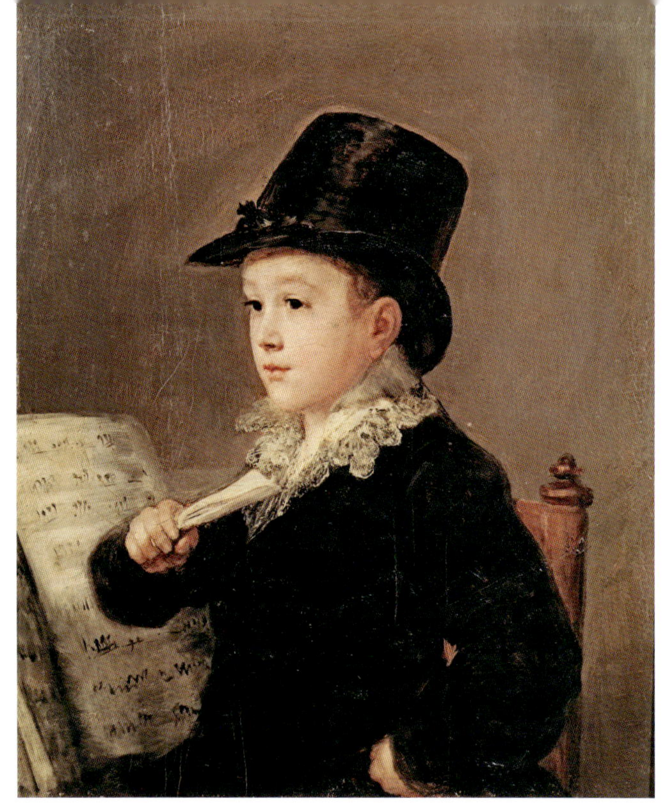

Portrait of Mariano Goya, c.1813–15, oil on panel, Private Collection, 59 x 47cm (23 x 18½in)

Born on 11 July 1806, Mariano was Goya's only grandchild. This shows him at the age of about eight, sitting beside a large musical score beating time with a roll of paper. The informal pose and thoughtful look on the child's face reflects the great affection that Goya felt for him. The painting is signed on the back of the panel: 'Goya, a su nieto' (Goya, to his grandson).

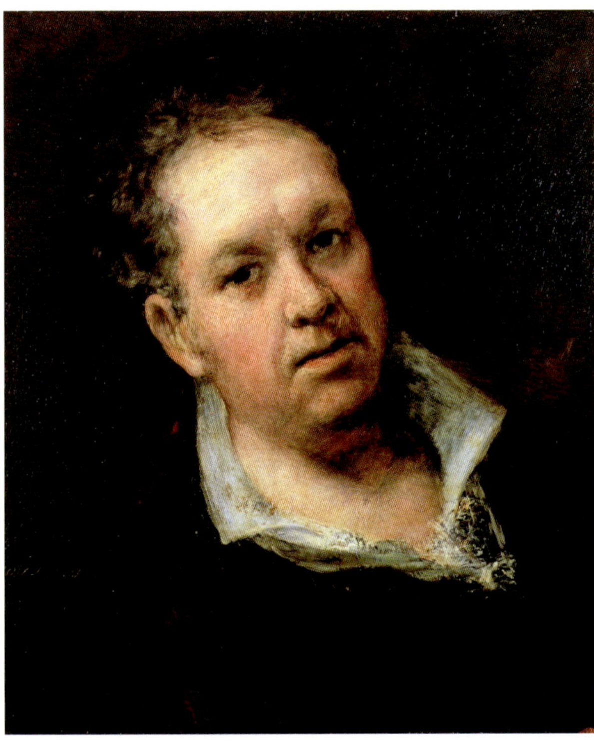

Self-portrait, 1815, oil on panel, Real Academia de Bellas Artes de San Fernando, Madrid, Spain, 51 x 46cm (20 x 18in)

Goya painted this self-portrait after Ferdinand's monarchy had been re-established. The tilt of his head and concentrated gaze give the impression of an ordinary working artist, not a Court Painter. At 69 years old, this is one of his last and most intimate self-portraits. A similar portrait from the same time is in the Prado. Both reflect a gentle, resigned expression, with none of the arrogance of his predecessors.

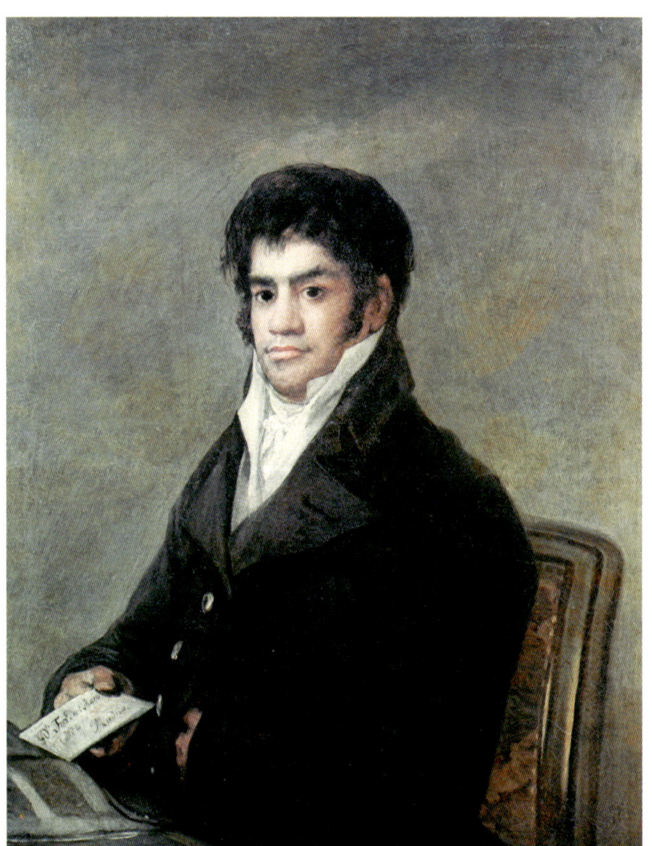

Portrait of Don Francisco del Mazo, c.1815, oil on canvas, Musée Goya, Castres, France, 90 x 71cm (35½ x 28in)

After Ferdinand's period of removing all those from Court he believed to have been traitorous during the French occupation, with the help of the Duke of San Carlos, Goya retained his official post. He remained in demand as all the important nobles wanted their portraits painted by him. Francisco del Mazo was a confident, proud and stubborn man and Goya has depicted him without any flattery.

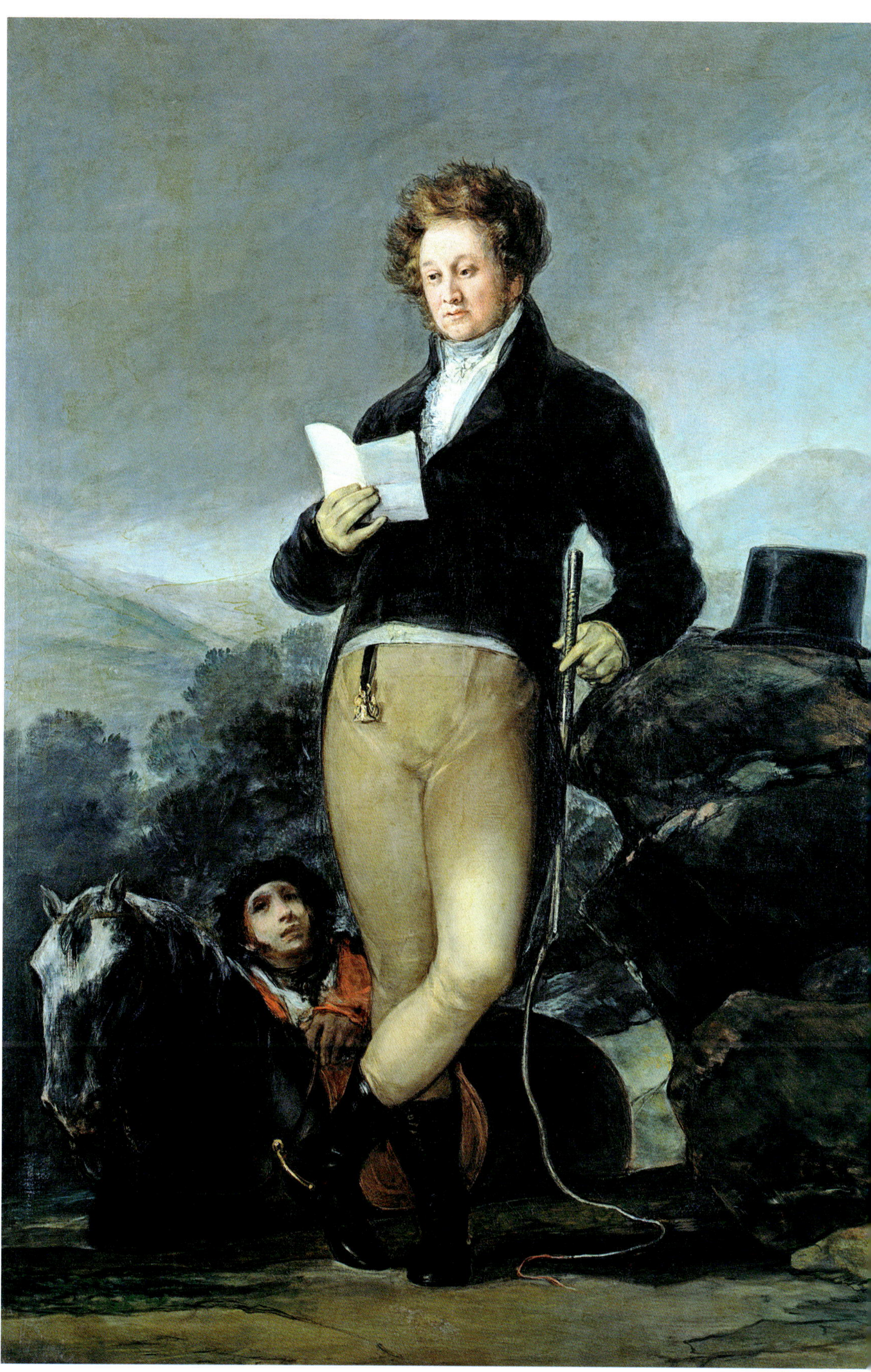

Portrait of Don Francisco de Borja Tellez Giron, 1816, oil on canvas, Musée Bonnat, Bayonne, France, 202 x 140cm (79½ x 55in)

The tenth Duke of Osuna, Don Francisco (1786–1851) had inherited his title in 1807. His father had been Goya's great friend and patron. As one of the highest-ranking nobles in Spain, Don Francisco was particularly close to the King and had accompanied him and Godoy to the Bayonne interview with Napoleon before the war. Setting him in the open air, Goya depicts him relaxed, but with a palpably aristocratic air.

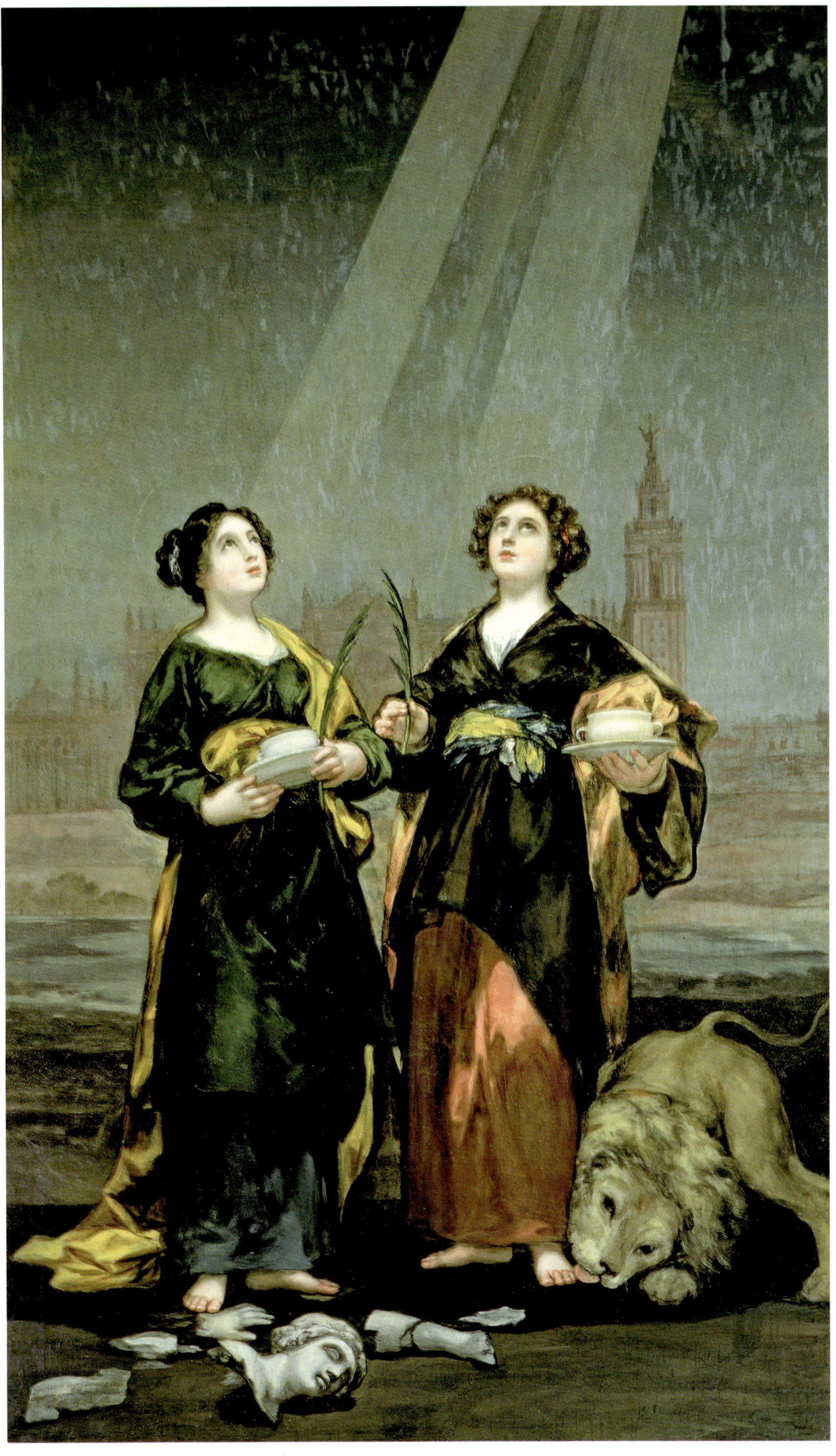

Saint Justa and Saint Rufina, 1817, oil on canvas, Cathedral of Saint Maria of the Assumption, Seville, Spain, 309 x 177cm (121½ x 70in)

Justa and Rufina were Christian potters from Seville who were martyred for refusing to worship an image of the goddess Venus. Goya portrayed them with their clay pots and the palms of martyrdom, while a lion licks Saint Rufina's foot. In the background, the Giralda tower of Seville Cathedral can be seen, as after an earthquake in 1504, the tower remained standing, apparently thanks to the saints' miraculous intervention.

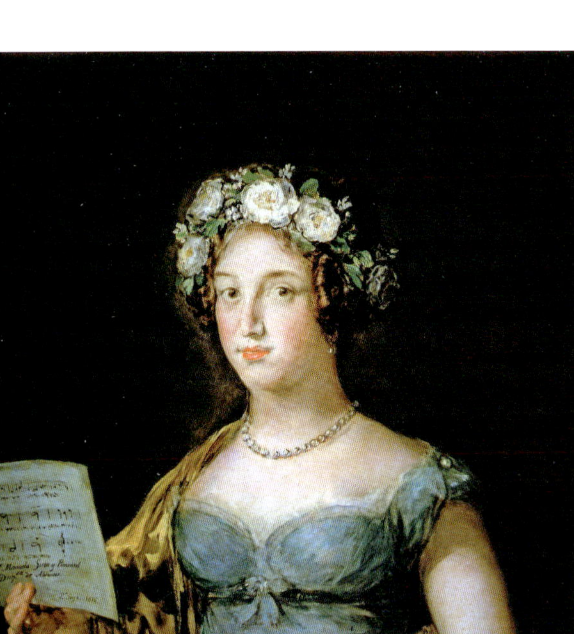

The Duchess of Abrantes, 1816, oil on canvas, Museo Nacional del Prado, Madrid, Spain, 92 x 70cm (36 x 27½in)

Laure Junot, Duchess of Abrantès (1784–1838) was the wife of the French general Jean-Andoche Junot and was noted for her beauty, caustic wit and extravagance. Goya has depicted her dressed in the French fashion, with a floral diadem on her head, and a piece of music in her hands, alluding to her love of music and singing. The brushwork is rapid and loose, and the colours are vibrant, reflecting her vivacious personality.

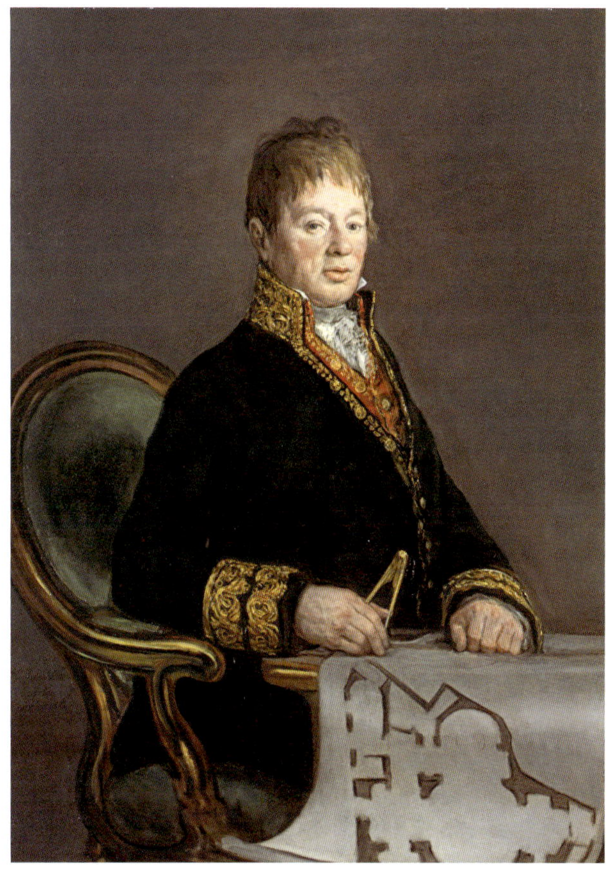

Juan Antonio Cuervo, 1819, oil on canvas, Cleveland Museum of Art, Ohio, USA, 120 x 87cm (42 x 34in)

Juan Antonio Cuervo (1757–1834) was an architect who was appointed Director of the Royal Academy of San Fernando in August 1815.

Wearing the uniform of his office, he holds dividers to indicate his profession. The architectural plan on the table beside him is probably for the church of Santiago in Madrid on which he had worked in 1811 and which made his reputation.

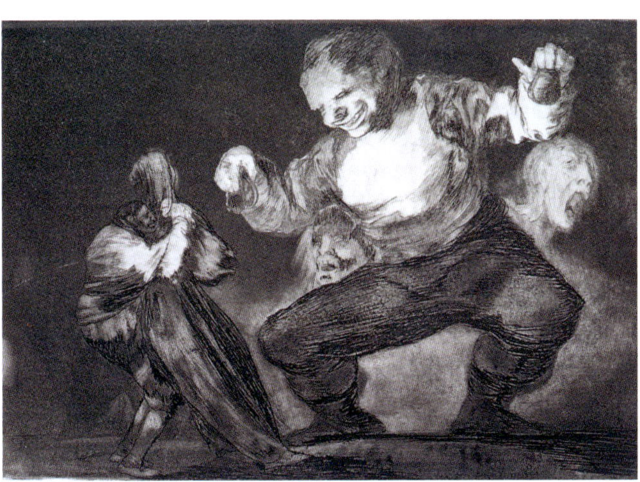

Blockhead Folly (Disparate de Bobo) or *The Dancing Giant (Bobalicón),* c.1816–23, etching, burnished aquatint, burin, and drypoint, The Metropolitan Museum, New York, USA, 24.5 x 35cm (9½ x 14in)

From *Los Disparates* (Follies) or *Los Proverbios,* the last series of etchings Goya produced, this criticizes the Church. The laughing giant – Bobalicón or 'Big Booby', a traditional Spanish clown – clicks his castanets and looms menacingly over a man clinging in vain for protection to the image of the Virgin Mary. The implication is that superstition and religious belief are both absurd.

*Flying Folly, c.*1816–23, etching and aquatint, Metropolitan Museum, New York, USA, 24.5 x 35cm (9½ x 14in)

Los Disparates depict monsters and mysterious creatures. Several relate to known Spanish proverbs, while others are allegories. The series was published after Goya's death in 1864 (see page 86). A monster comprising the body of a horse and the head and talons of a bird of prey carries a man and a woman through the air. The image is believed to be a criticism of marriages of convenience.

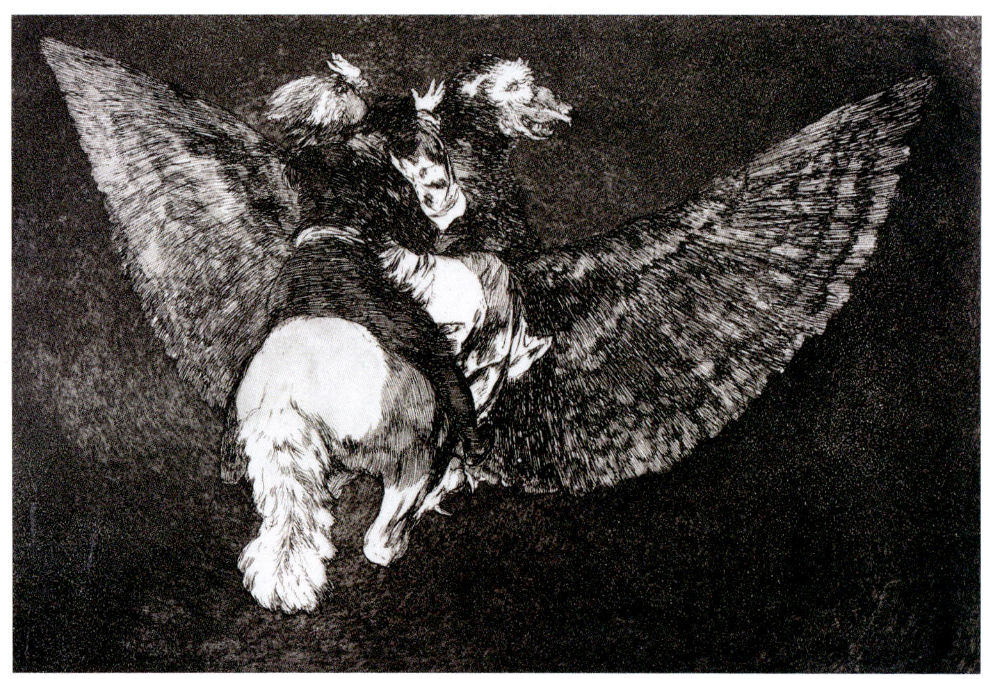

Men Reading, The Reading or *Politicians*, 1820–23, oil on gesso, Museo Nacional del Prado, Madrid, Spain, 126 x 266cm (49½ x 105in)

Another of Goya's 14 Black Paintings, this is difficult to interpret, due to lack of details in the painting and the poor state of conservation, as it lost part of its original paint when transferred from the wall to canvas. A group of men read a book, newspaper or magazine. It is thought that they are politicians and they are reading about themselves.

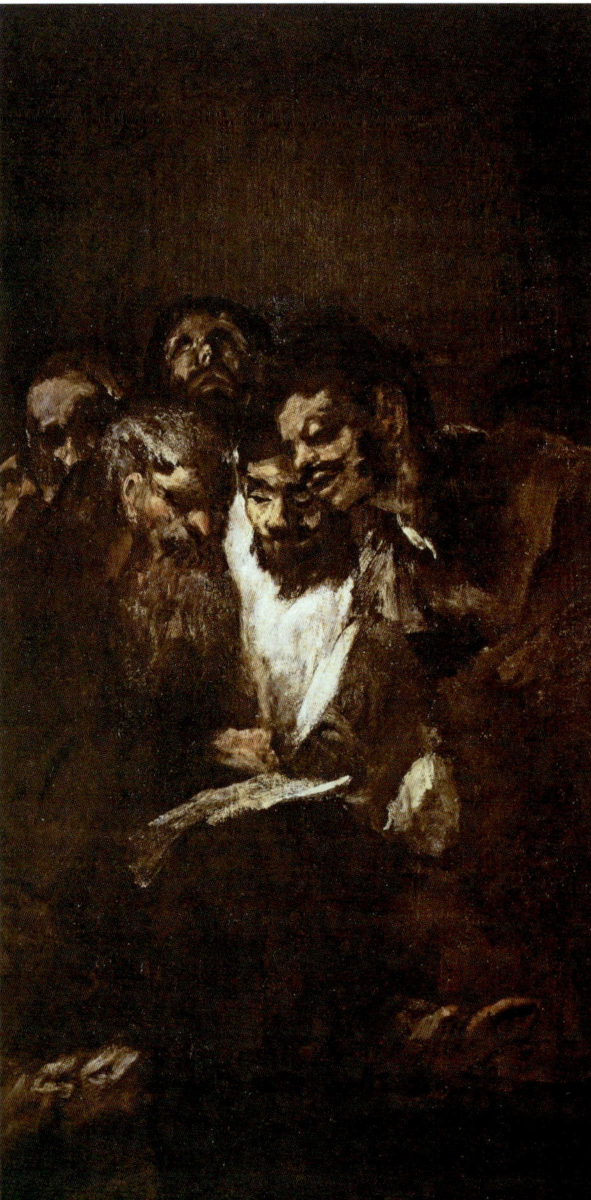

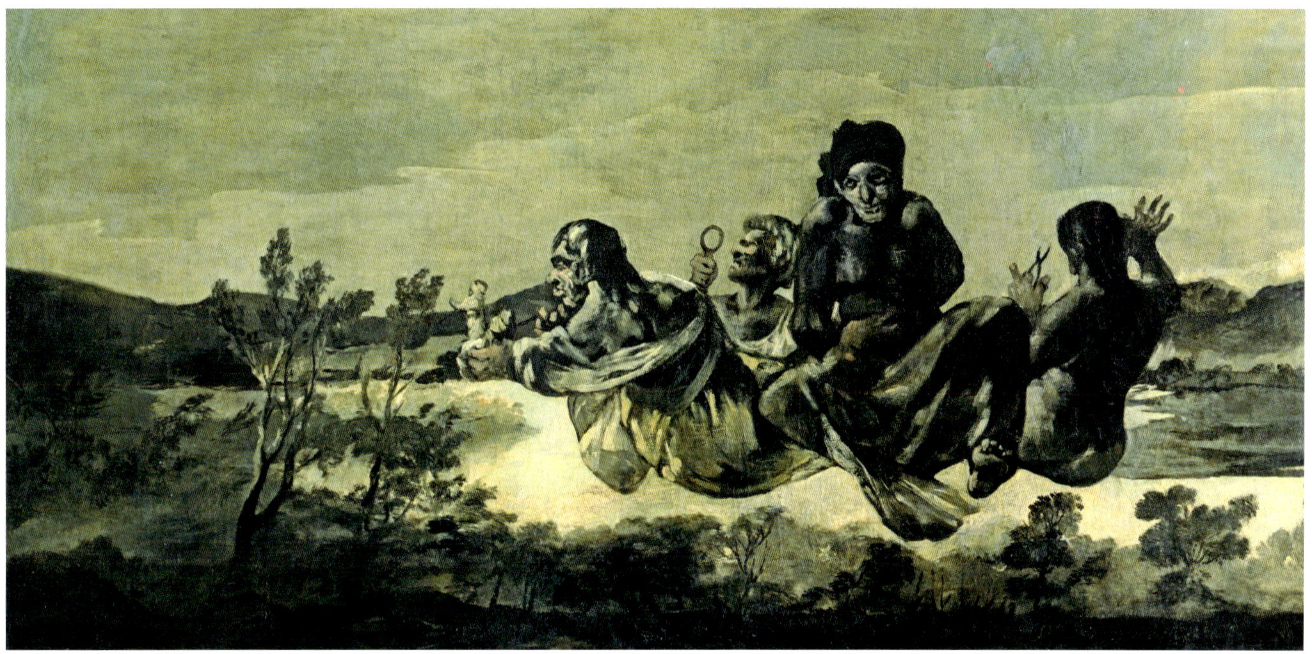

The Fates, 1821–23, oil on plaster mounted on canvas, Museo Nacional del Prado, Madrid, Spain, 123 x 266cm (48½ x 105in)

The murals Goya painted in La Quinta del Sordo, the house he bought in 1819 were little known for 50 years. After 1874, they became called the Black Paintings (see pages 78–9) because so many dark pigments were used in them, and because of their sombre subject matter.

In mythology, the Fates control human destiny. For instance, the figure on the right holding scissors is ready to cut the thread of life.

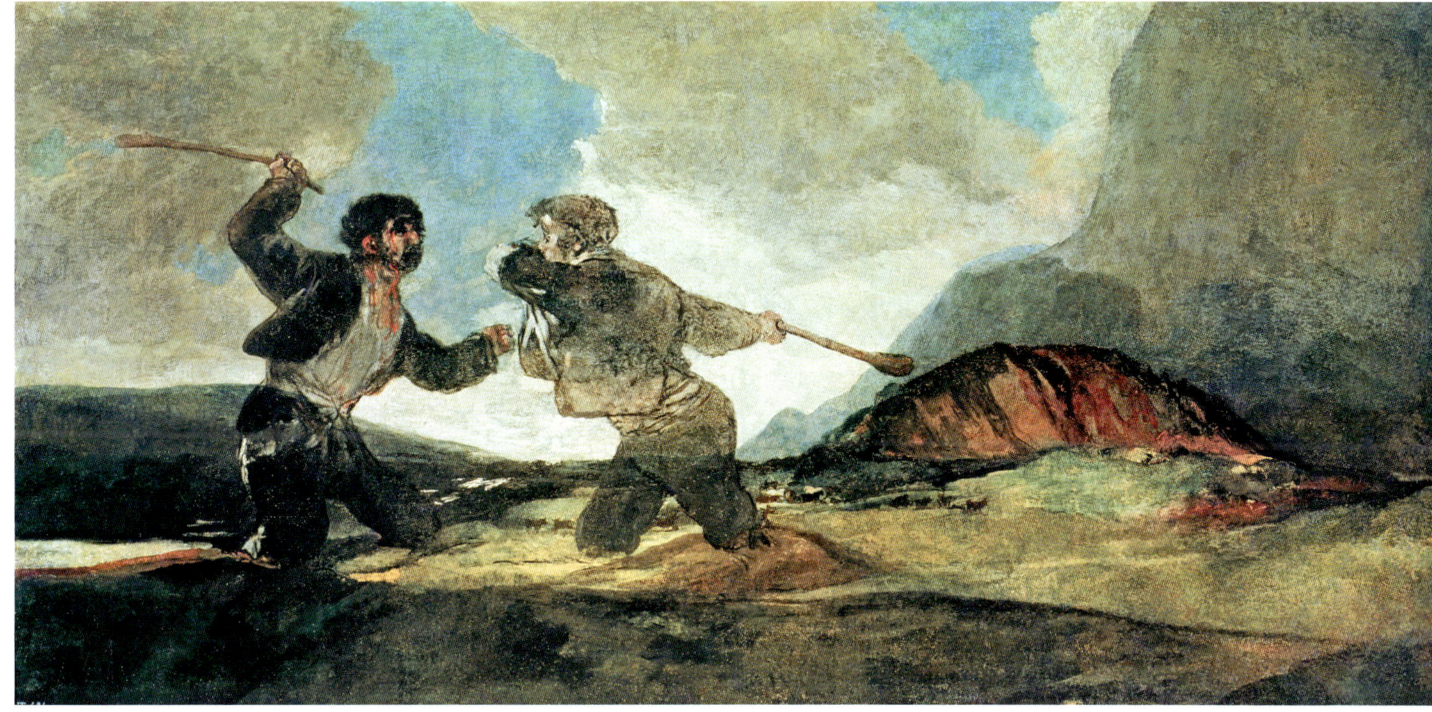

Duel with Cudgels, 1820–23, oil on canvas, Museo Nacional del Prado, Madrid, Spain, 123 x 266cm (48½ x 105in)

Two men – possibly brothers – are fighting with cudgels. Both are up to their knees in sand, so neither can run away. At this time, there were many bitter clashes between monarchists and liberals in Spain, and so Goya may have intended this to be an allegory of civil war. All his paintings from the walls of La Quinta del Sordo were meant to be private, so he freely expressed his personal feelings. In 1873, the Baron Émile d'Erlanger acquired Goya's house, and had the paintings transferred to canvas.

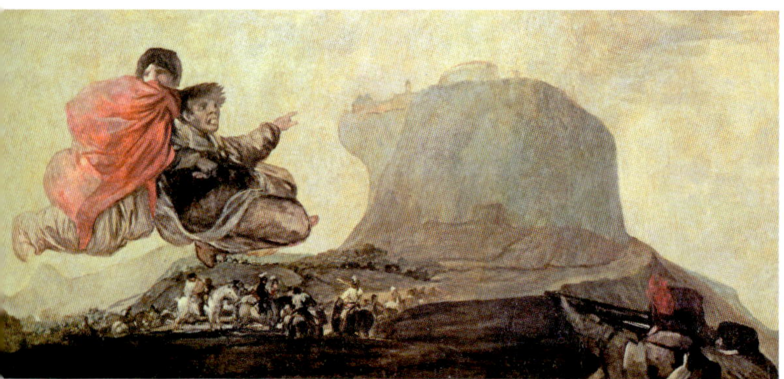

Asmodea or *Fantastic Vision (Vision Fantástica)*, 1820–23, oil on gesso, transferred to linen, Museo Nacional del Prado, Madrid, Spain, 127 x 263cm (50 x 103½in)

Two figures fly over a landscape dominated by a large, flat mountain in the distance. One seems to be carrying the other. In the foreground, French soldiers aim at a group of people. The title *Asmodea* was given to this work later by Goya's friend, the painter Antonio Brugada (1804–63). Asmodeus was a demon king in a religious text and Aesma Daeva was an angry genie in Persian folklore.

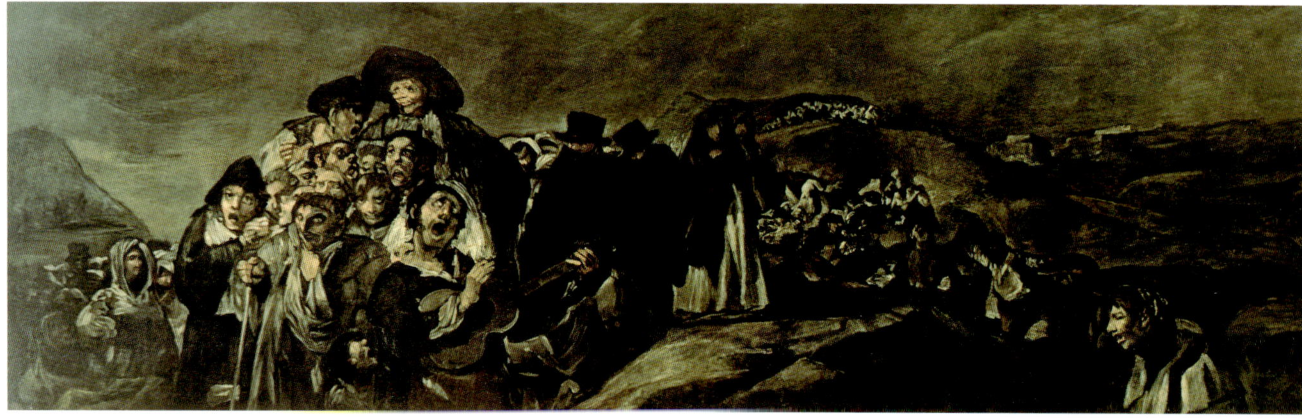

Pilgrimage to San Isidro's Fountain, 1820–23, oil on plaster mounted on canvas, Museo Nacional del Prado, Madrid, Spain, 140 x 438cm (55 x 172½in)

In contrast with the lighthearted painting *The Meadow of San Isidro* (see page 154) that Goya painted in 1788, this seems to express his contempt of the superstition and ignorance that surrounded him. La Quinta del Sordo was close to this location and familiar to Goya. This was on a wall opposite *The Witches' Sabbath* (below). The jumbled confusion of people with distorted, drunken faces (see page 78) are on an annual pilgrimage to the shrine of Saint Isidro; they embody folly and fanaticism.

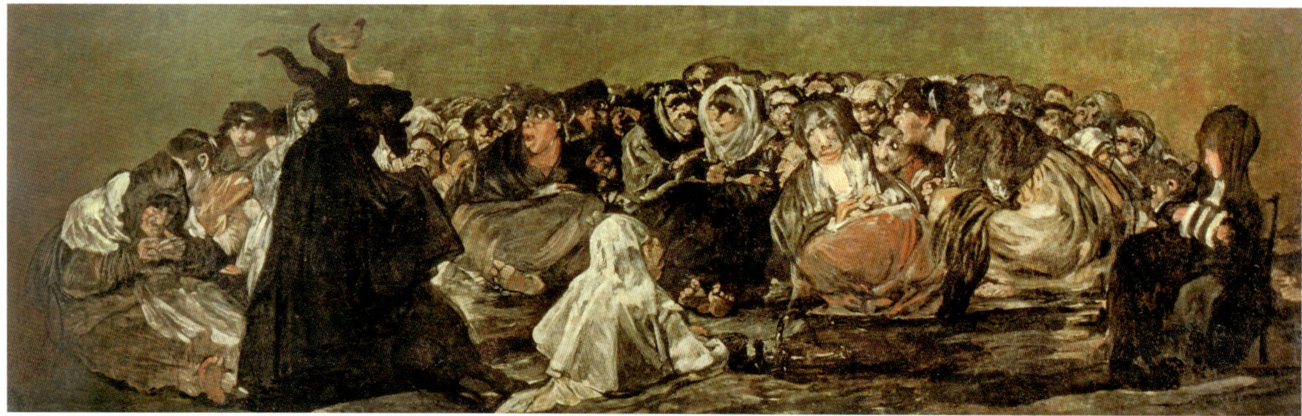

Aquelarre, The Witches' Sabbath or *The Great He-Goat*, 1821–23, oil on canvas, Museo Nacional del Prado, Madrid, Spain, 140.5 x 435.7cm (55⅓ x 171½in)

In this huge painting that was never meant to be seen by the public, a coven of ugly, disfigured witches gather in the moonlight. A young woman is either about to be initiated into their rites, or she is a victim. A silhouetted goat in a monk's cloak represents Satan (see page 79). The painting is considered to be a satire on blind trust, a condemnation of prevalent superstitions in society and the terrible witch trials of the Inquisition. The painting was originally much wider, but was reduced when it was taken from the wall of Goya's house, 50 years later.

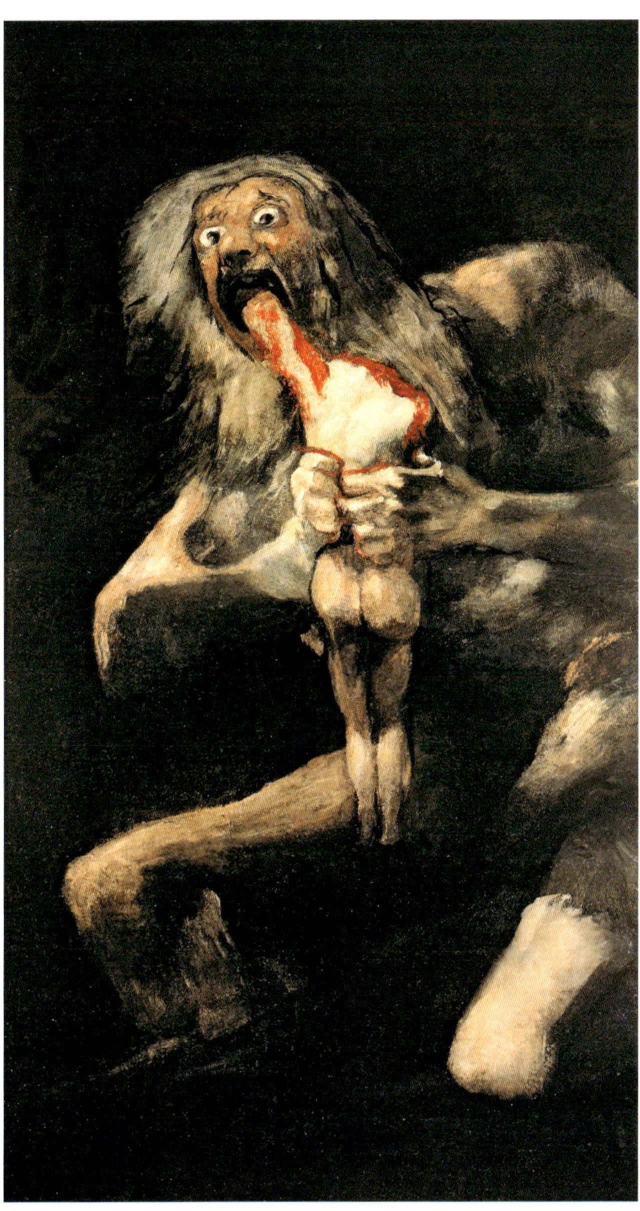

Saturn Devouring One of his Children, 1821–23, plaster mounted on canvas, Museo Nacional del Prado, Madrid, Spain, 143.5 x 81.4cm (56½ x 32in)

Disturbing and menacing, this is the darkest of Goya's Black Paintings (see pages 78–9. Probably a symbol of melancholy, it is also an allegory for Spain's helplessness through wars, revolutions and persecution. From despotic rulers, to the Inquisition, to French invaders, ordinary Spanish people were powerless to stop the overwhelming forces against them. Goya painted this in his dining room, possibly as a macabre joke.

Leocadia Zorilla or *La Leocadia*, 1820–23, oil on canvas, Museo Nacional del Prado, Madrid, Spain, 145.7 x 129.4cm (57 x 51in)

Also known as *Una Manola* meaning an elegant woman of Madrid, this is Goya's housekeeper, Leocadia Zorilla de Weiss. A relative of Gumersinda, Leocadia's relationship with Goya caused trouble between him and Javier. Here, she leans on a wall or burial mound. Her veil implies mourning, and this work could be an introduction to the other Black Paintings (see pages 78–9) that all seem to be based on the theme of death.

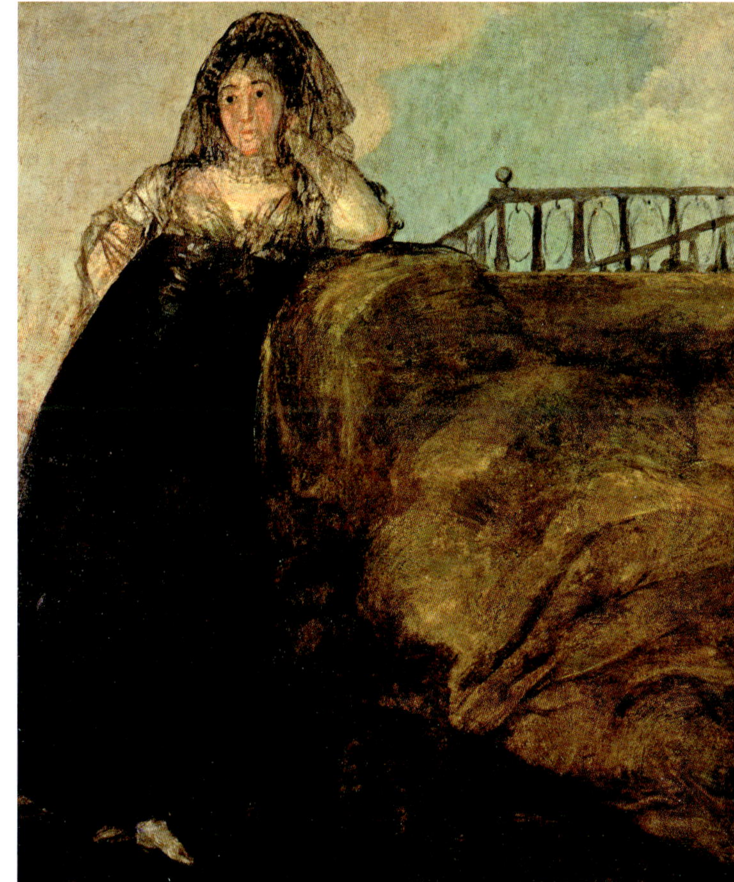

Tio Paquete, c.1820–23, oil on canvas, Museo Thyssen-Bornemisza, Madrid, Spain, 39 x 31cm (15 x 12in)

The sitter was a well-known beggar in Madrid, who was invited to play his guitar and sing to members of the Royal Court. His blind eyes and toothless, jovial expression are reminiscent of Velázquez's pictures of Court dwarfs, but also follow the style of Goya's Black Paintings (see pages 78–9). Emerging from the dark background, the face occupies almost all the space. Tilted to one side, it is painted with heavy impasto and loose brushstrokes, a sketchy style that inspired later artists.

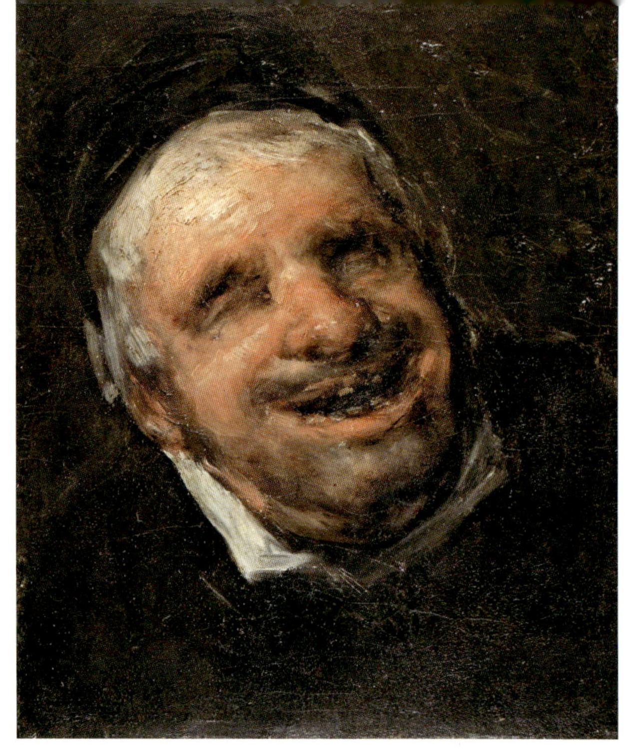

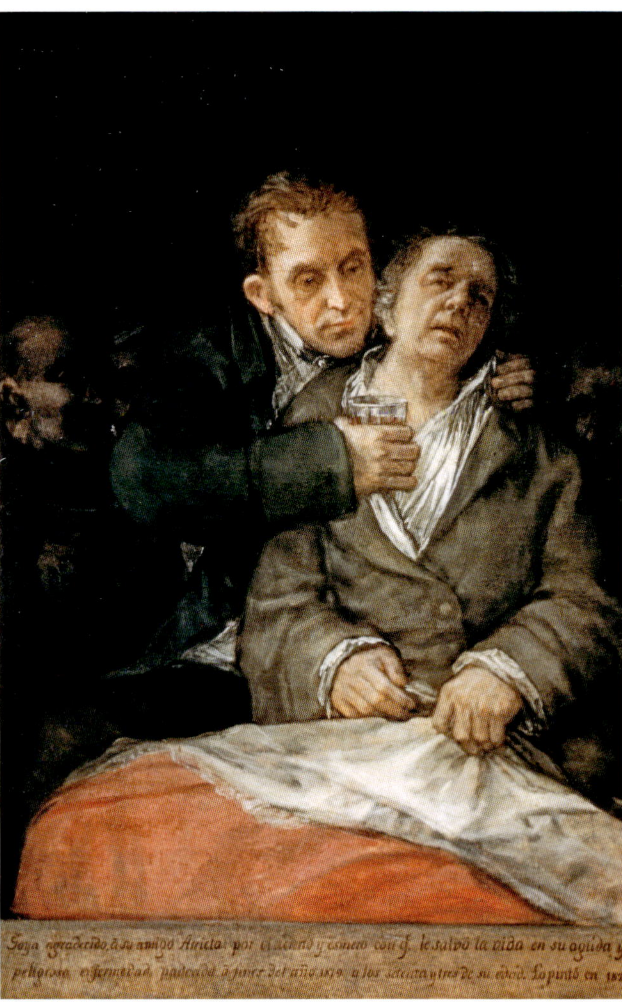

Self-portrait with Dr Arrieta, 1820, oil on canvas, oil on canvas, The Minneapolis Institute of Art, Minnesota, USA, 117 x 79cm (46 x 31in)

In Goya's last self-portrait, Goya's doctor, Eugenio García Arrieta is portrayed supporting him during his illness of 1819. After recovering, Goya presented Arrieta with the work, featuring the inscription (see page 81): 'Goya gives thanks to his friend Arrieta for the expert care with which he saved his life from an acute and dangerous illness, which he suffered at the close of the year 1819 when he was 73 years old.'

Portrait of Don Ramón Satué, 1820–23, oil on canvas, Rijksmuseum, Amsterdam, The Netherlands, 107 x 83.5cm (42 x 33in)

A judge in the Supreme Court in Madrid, Don Ramón Satué was a friend of Goya's, which is why this portrait appears informal rather than official. In casual clothing with his hands in his pockets, Satué appears as a more modern portrait than it is. X-ray images show this was painted over a portrait of a high-ranking member of the French military, possibly Joseph Bonaparte himself.

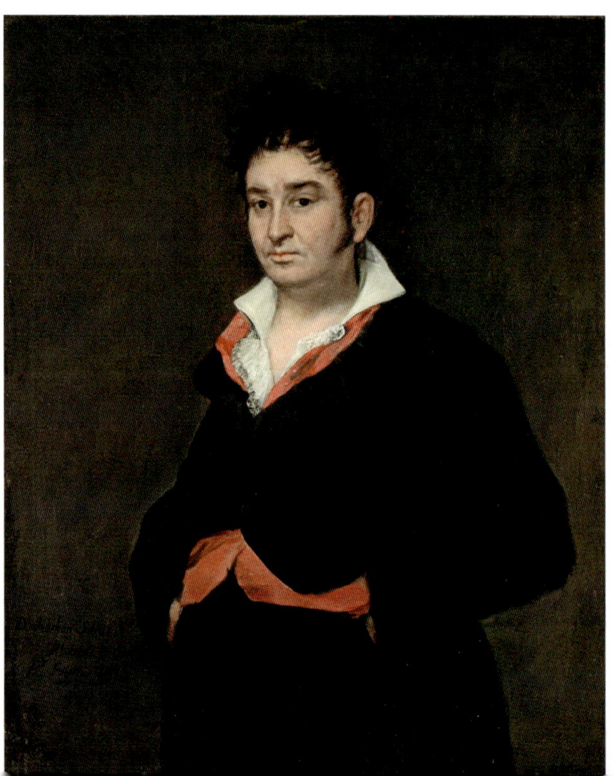

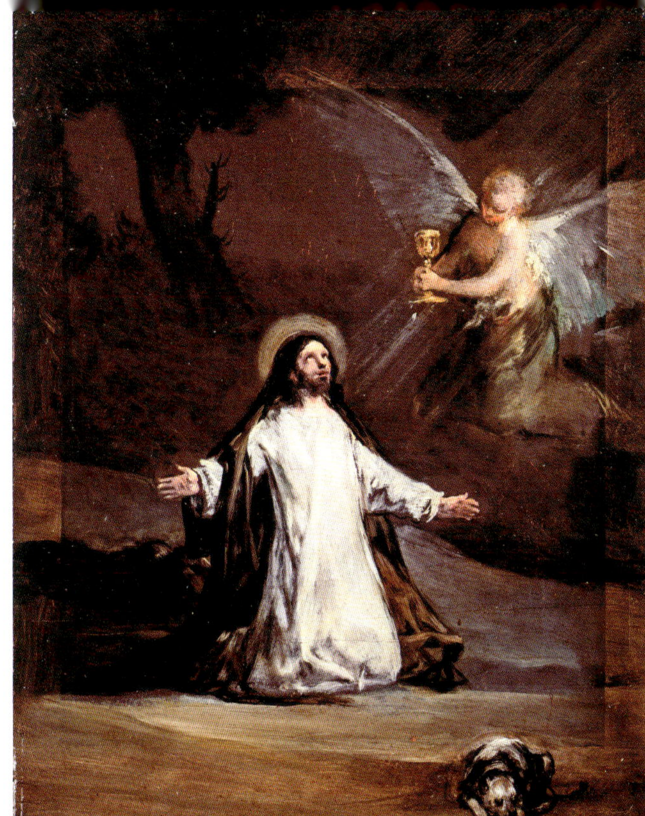

Christz on the Mount of Olives, 1819, oil on panel, Colegio Escolapios de San Antón, Madrid, Spain, 47 x 35cm (18½ x 14in)

Depicting the moment before Christ was arrested, he is alone and desperate. Goya's rapid brushwork and impasto paint portrays the urgency and desperation of the moment. The scene is from the Gospel of Luke: '[Christ] knelt down and prayed, "Father, if you are willing, take this cup from me; yet not my will, but yours be done". An angel from heaven appeared to him and strengthened him.'

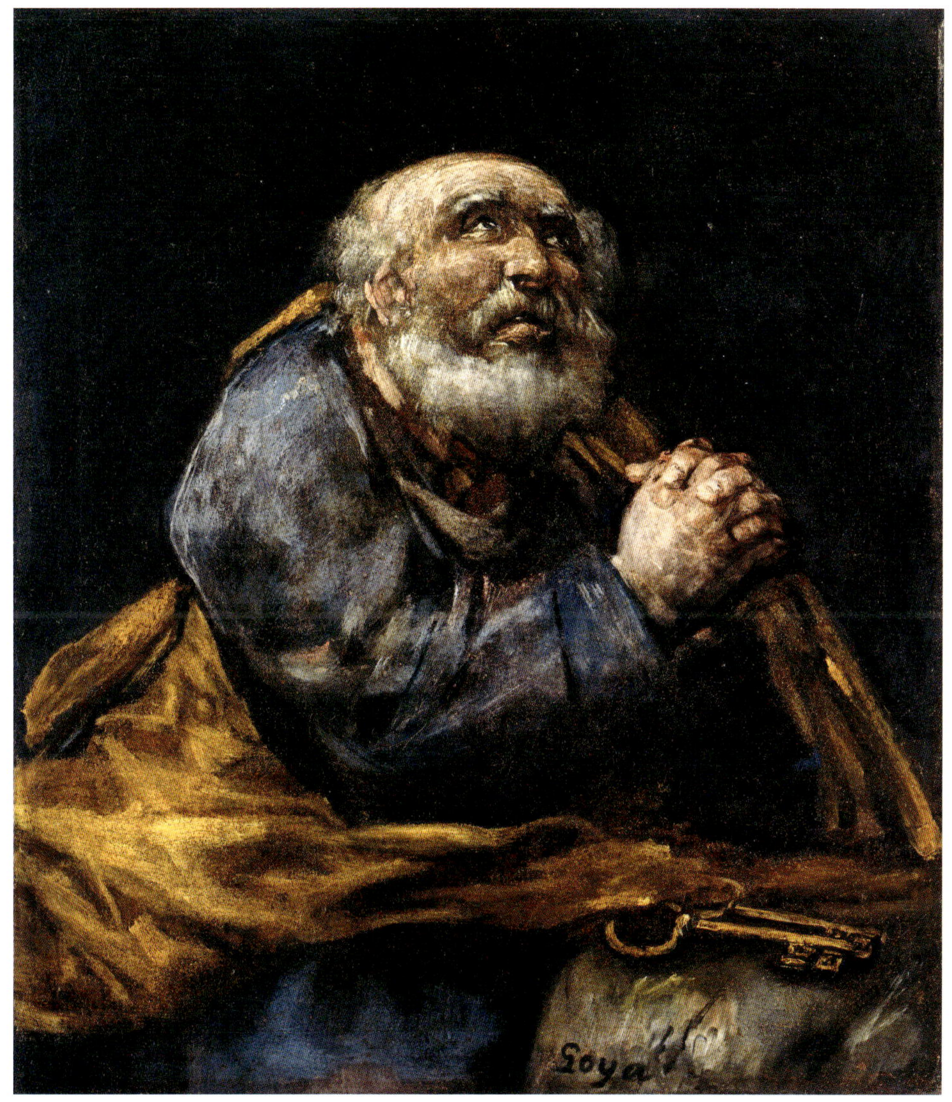

The Repentant Saint Peter, c.1820–24, oil on canvas, The Phillips Collection, Washington DC, USA, 73 x 64cm (29 x 25in)

Probably painted shortly before Goya's departure for France, it is not known whether this painting was commissioned or not. It is believed to be a pair with a painting of Saint Paul. Both works display an emotional intensity and are among Goya's last devotional subjects. This portrayal of an old man praying is particularly expressive, created with his powerful later palette, giving the impression of monumentality.

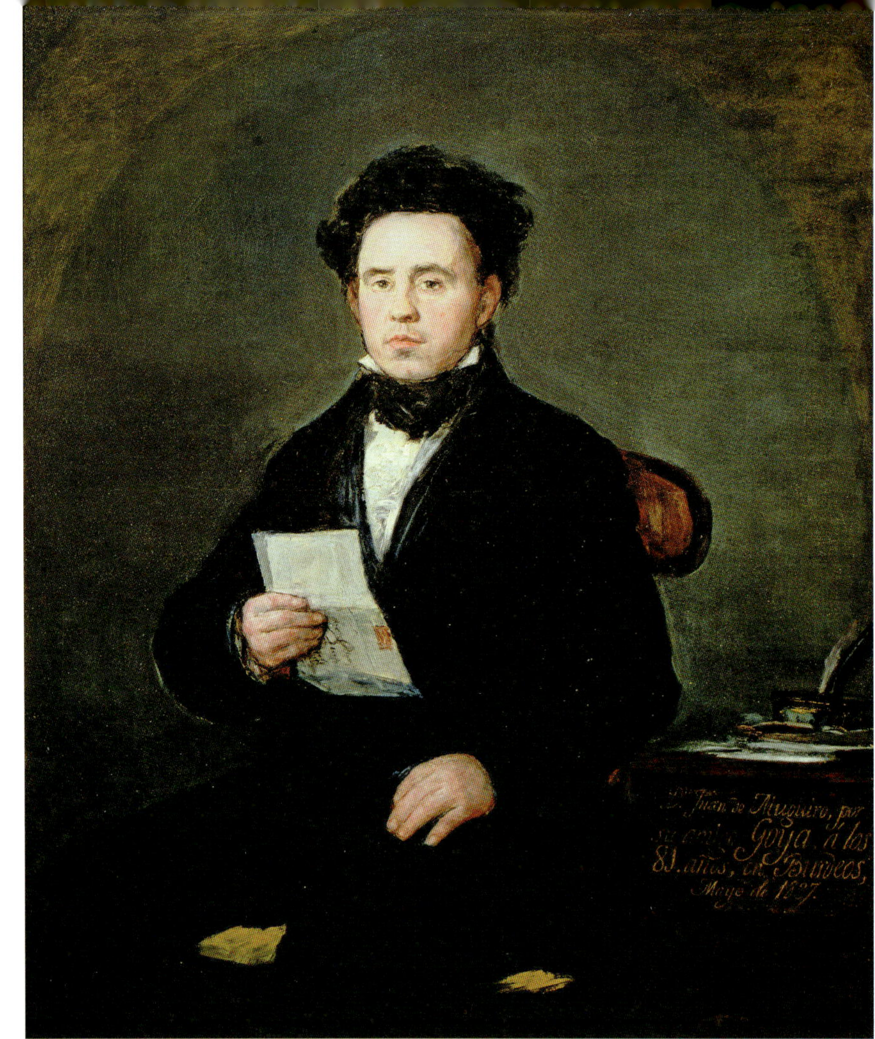

Juan Bautista de Muguiro, 1827, oil on canvas, Museo Nacional del Prado, Madrid, Spain, 103 x 85cm (40½ x 33½in)

With a letter in his hand, the banker Juan Bautista de Muguiro sits beside his desk. An inscription explains that the painting was made by Goya in May 1827 in Bordeaux, when he was 81, 11 months before his death. Some of the brushstrokes appear somewhat trembly, but in certain areas his application remains detailed and the rich application of paint shows his advanced thinking, even in his old age.

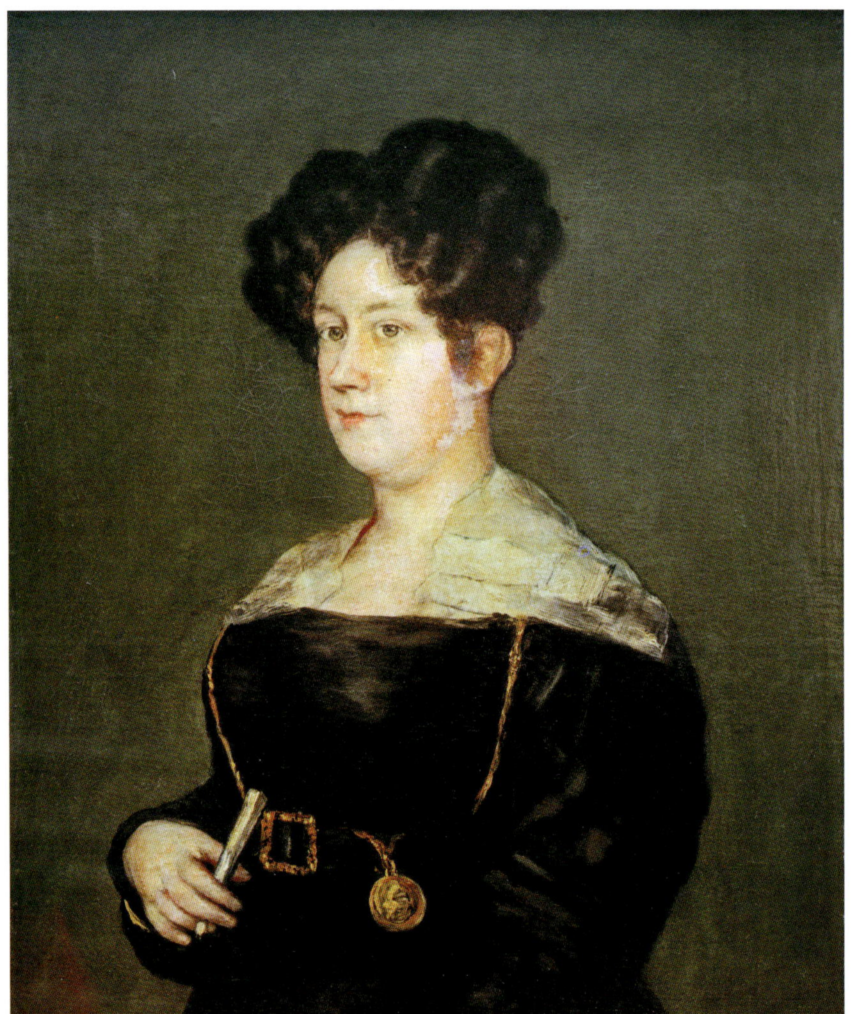

Manuela Alvarez Coiñas y Ferrer, 1824, oil on canvas, Private Collection, 73 x 60cm (29 x 23½in)

Despite his age and infirmities, once in Bordeaux, Goya continued to work with his firm hand and sharp eye. With his eyesight continuing to weaken, although his work was even less finished and detailed than in previous years, his broad handling and restricted palette create an intensity of expression and vivacity, even though his sitter is dressed in a more restricted and sombre fashion than many of his previous female sitters.

The Milkmaid of Bordeaux,
1825–27, oil on canvas,
Museo Nacional del Prado,
Madrid, Spain, 74 x 68cm
(29 x 27in)

Possibly Goya's last great
painting created in Bordeaux,
a young milkmaid wearing
an apron, shawl and a
scarf in her hair reflects a
lighter palette that seems to
rise above the gloom and
despondency of the Black
Paintings (see pages 78–9).
Mixing oil paint with fine sand
and starch, lighter colours
and an unambiguous subject
matter, even near the end of
his life, Goya proves himself
to be an innovator
and pioneer.

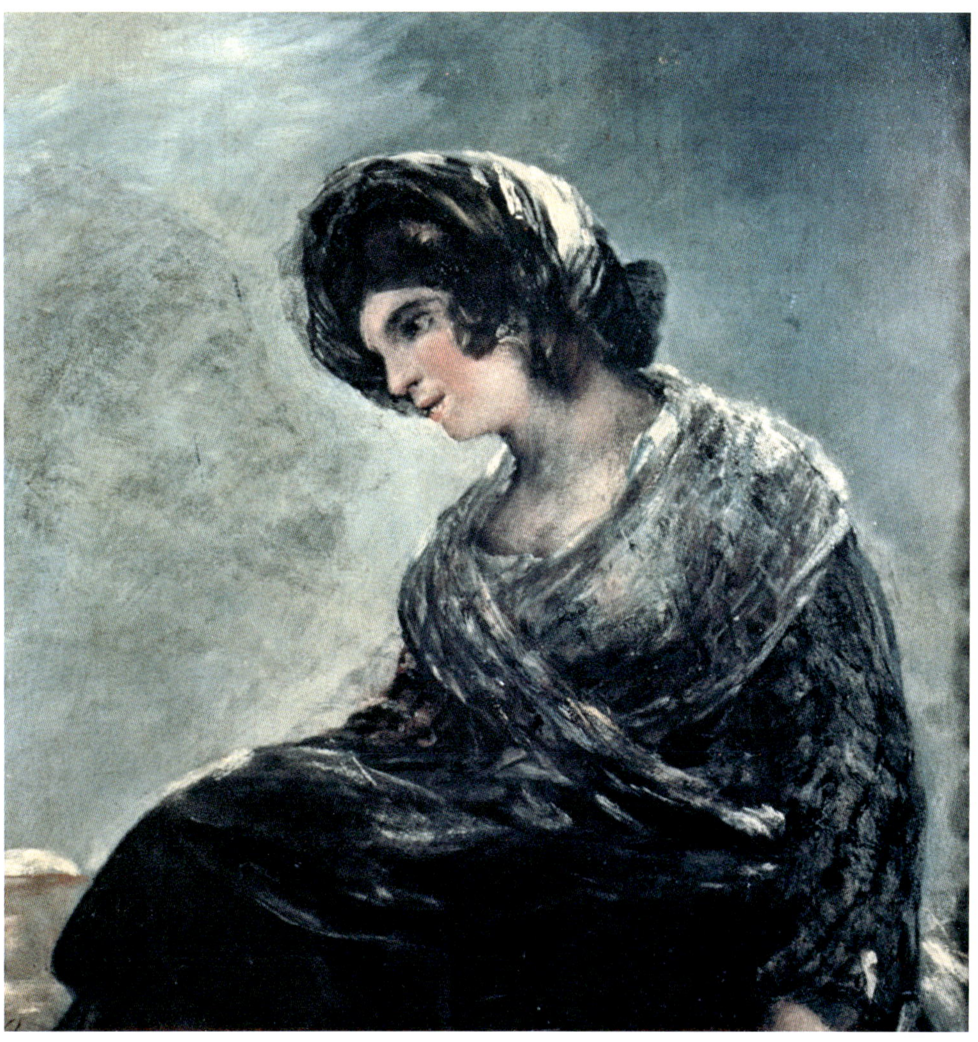

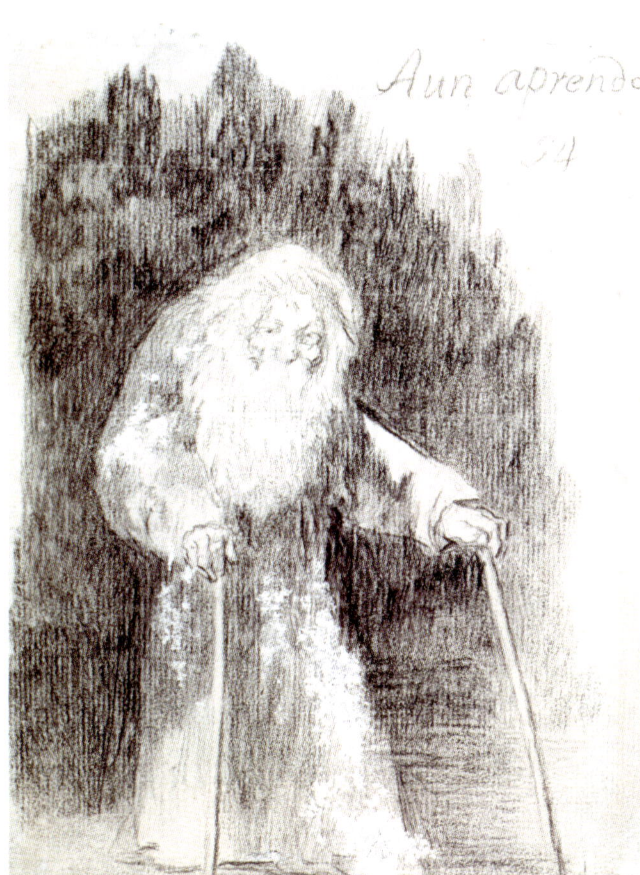

I Am Still Learning, 1824–28,
charcoal on paper, Museo
Nacional del Prado, Madrid,
Spain, 19.5 x 15cm (8 x 6in)

From 1824 until his death,
Goya filled two albums
with over 100 drawings and
sketches from his time in
Bordeaux. Many are satirical,
several are amusing and some
are poignant. They represent
what he saw on the streets
of Bordeaux – and his
memories. This old man with
his long white beard, hobbling
forward on two sticks bears
Goya's inscription: 'Aun
aprendo' – 'I am still learning.'
And even at the end, Goya
still was.

INDEX

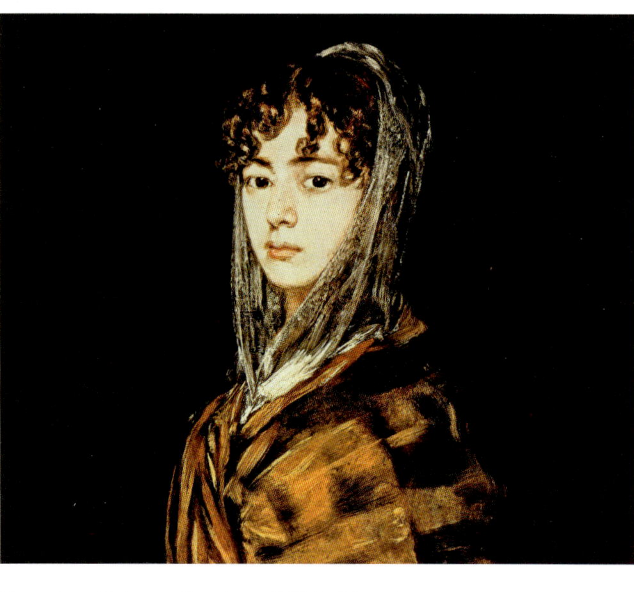

Francisca Sabasa Garcia, c.1806–11, oil on canvas.

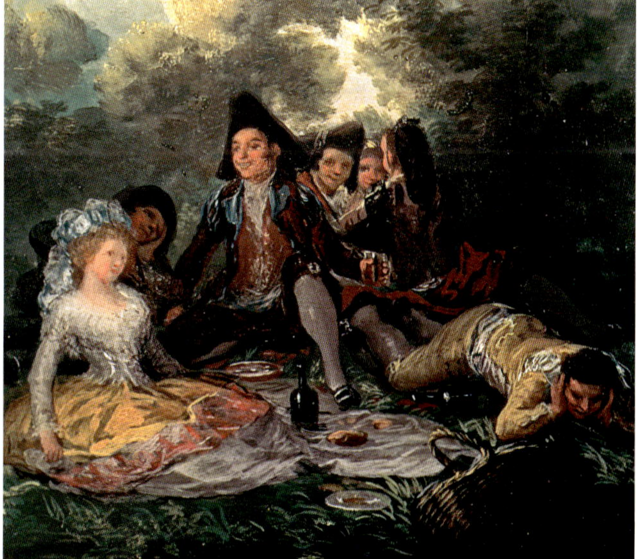

A Picnic (detail), 1785–90, oil on canvas.

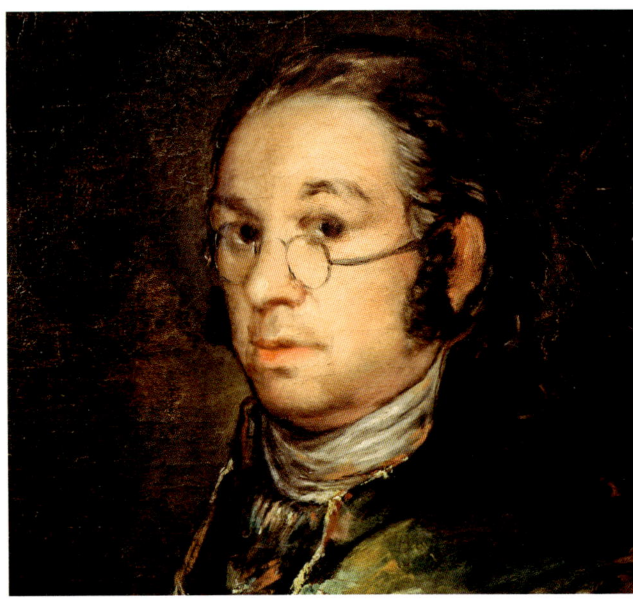

Self-portrait in Glasses (detail), c.1797–1800, oil on canvas.

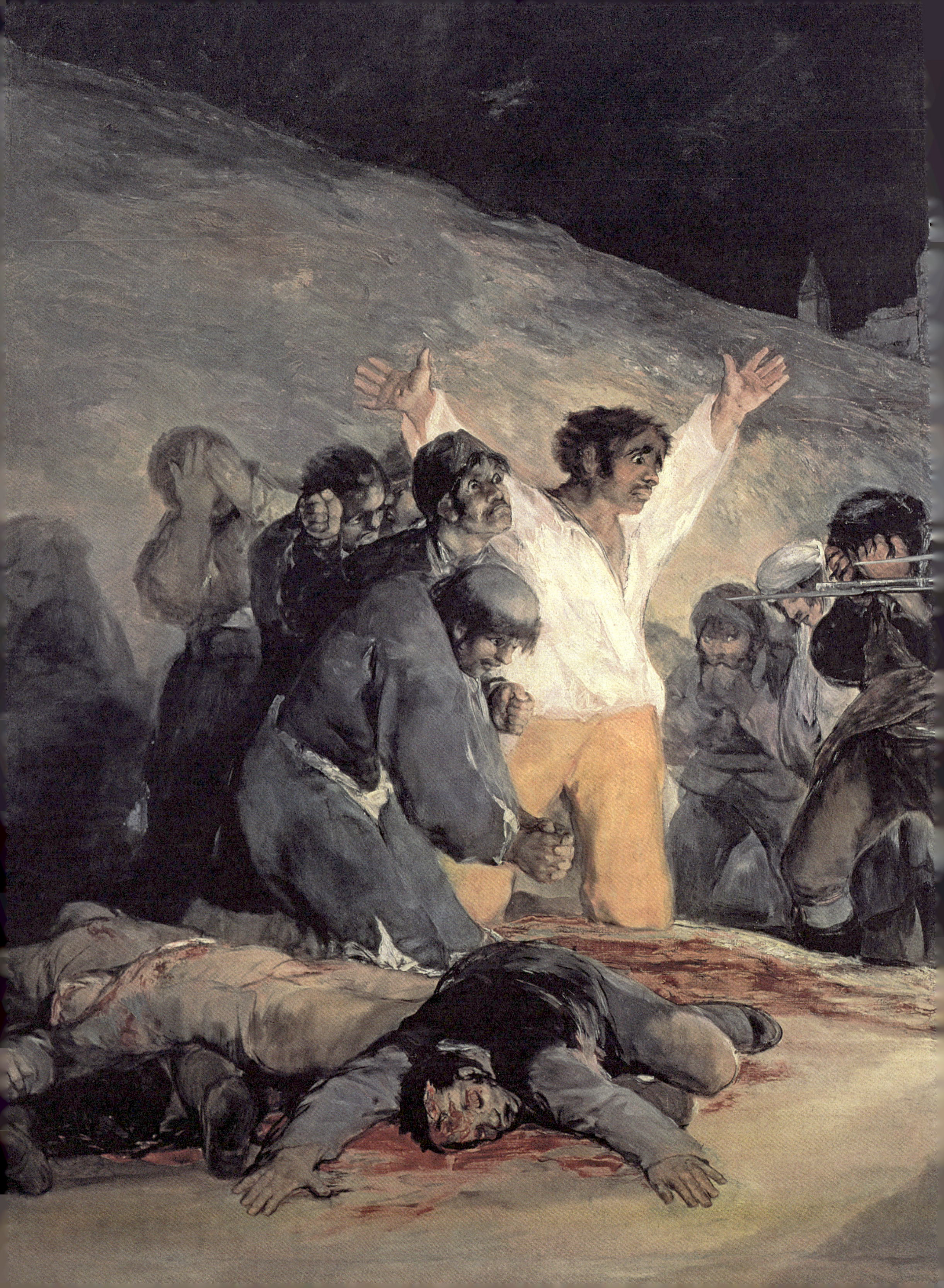